HALF THE HUMAN EXPERIENCE

Half the Human Experience

The Psychology of Women

SIXTH EDITION

Janet Shibley Hyde
University of Wisconsin–Madison

Houghton Mifflin Company
Boston New York

To Margaret and Luke
the two best kids a
professor/author/mom
could ever have

Publisher: Charles Hartford
Senior sponsoring editor: Kerry Baruth
Senior development editor: Sharon Geary
Senior project editor: Carol Newman
Editorial assistants: Kendra Johnson, Marlowe Shaeffer
Production/design assistant: Bethany Schlegel
Senior manufacturing coordinator: Marie Barnes
Senior marketing manager: Katherine Greig

About the Cover

" . . . I pondered, if I surrendered all notions of God as an elderly
Michelangelo male and reinvented a figurative image of a creator, what would
it look like? I thought it would be young because the creative force is
all-powerful and life giving. Perhaps feminine—just past puberty, because the force
would be fully formed and desire to re-create itself. The creator would
have large hands—in palmistry, large hands belong to those who can handle
small details and are very capable. And it would be hidden, veiled from our
eyes—not able to be fully known. The cosmic curtain, slightly
transparent, forces us to imagine what is not known and what we do perceive
is just illusion, self-reference and interpretation, but even this game of
mystery was created by the creator's hand."

> *Life Is but a Dream*
> 2002 oil on canvas, from *Behind the Curtain* series
> artist Pamela Grau Twena

Text and photo credits begin on page 556.

Printed in the U.S.A.

Library of Congress Catalog Card Number: 2002109481

ISBN: 0-618-30632-3

1 2 3 4 5 6 7 8 9–DOC–07 06 05 04 03

Contents

v

Preface

My basic goal in preparing this new, sixth edition of *Half the Human Experience* is to provide a text on the psychology of women written in a way so that it is accessible to undergraduates who have little background in psychology—perhaps only an introductory course—yet also challenging and thought provoking for senior psychology majors.

Although the book is designed as a core text for psychology of women courses, it may also serve appropriately as one of several texts in a women's studies course or as a supplementary text in a variety of psychology courses.

Three characteristics of this book—its readability, comprehensiveness, and scholarship—have been well received in previous editions, and I have worked to retain and improve those features. I have come to believe that the readability of texts is a feminist principle. One of the goals of feminists has been to demystify science, and as part of that effort we must demystify psychology, including the psychology of women. My goal therefore has been to provide a text with solid, cutting-edge scholarship, clearly explained so that students can grasp it—indeed, be captivated by it.

What's new in this edition?

Gender and Emotion

The Cognitive Revolution has dominated psychology since the 1960s and has resulted in some important contributions to the psychology of women, such as gender schema theory. Lost in the Cognitive Revolution was emotion, but emotion research has seen a resurgence in the last decade. And what could be more relevant to the psychology of women and gender than emotion? Although many gender stereotypes have been challenged in contemporary society—such as the stereotype that girls can't do sports or that girls can't do math—emotion stereotypes remain unchallenged and function powerfully but nonconsciously in everyday interactions. Much evidence has accumulated on the gendered socialization of emotions in childhood. Other evidence indicates that the same facial expression of emotion is interpreted differently depending on whether it is a man's face or a woman's face. Believing that emotion is crucial to understanding women and gender issues today, I have added a completely new chapter on gender and emotion (Chapter 6).

Women of Color

As in previous editions, I have placed a high priority on integrating the new scholarship on women of color into the book. That scholarship is flourishing now, and it is not difficult to find numerous excellent studies on any topic.

With material on women of color, the author and the instructor must face an important question: separation or integration? That is, should there be a separate chapter focusing on and highlighting research on women of color? Or should this material be integrated throughout the book? I see no reason why these strategies must be mutually exclusive, and so I chose a "both/and" strategy. An entire chapter is devoted to women of color (Chapter 4); it provides information on the historical and cultural heritages of African American, Asian American, Latino, and Native American women, setting the stage for material in other chapters. I worry that, without a separate chapter devoted to women of color, the discussion descends to difference, that is, to research on ethnic-group differences. The real issue is cultural heritage and how it shapes women of all ethnic groups. Chapter 4 is the forum for discussion of these heritages. I have also integrated research on women of color throughout all other chapters. I have placed the chapter on women of color early in the book, immediately following the chapter on gender stereotypes, to make it clear that both gender and ethnicity require attention.

Rebuilding the House from the Basement Up

It has been a long time since I revised this book; the fifth edition appeared in 1996. Although I regret the factors that kept me from revising it sooner (such as serving as chair of my department), at the same time I was glad for the longer interval. An enormous amount of truly superb research appeared during that time. It was a pleasure to read it and recognize how far our field has come. The longer interval and greater amount of research also forced me to rethink more of the conceptualizations in the book. More than most revised editions, then, this book is truly a house that has been rebuilt from the basement up.

As some indication of the extent of revision, 95 new references were added to Chapter 7, "Development Across the Lifespan," and 107 references were added to Chapter 11, "Psychology and Women's Health Issues." A total of 807 new references were added to the book.

In preparing this edition, I realized that I was revising it approximately 28 years after I did the intensive research and writing on the first edition. Psychology of women as an academic field has changed a great deal in those 28 years. As an author, I found that I faced different problems in 2002 from those I faced in 1974. Then, the problem was that the field was too new and the research therefore too thin. Often I would come to a major point that needed to be addressed and find little data, perhaps not even a single study. In 2002 the problem was the opposite:

There was almost too much research—not that there can ever be too much research, but rather that there is more than one can possibly include in a single undergraduate text. Our field is filling the pages of three major journals—*Psychology of Women Quarterly, Sex Roles,* and *Feminism and Psychology*—at impressive rates, and other major psychology journals regularly feature articles on gender or the psychology of women. This abundance of research is a marvelous state for our field to be in, but it also means that I had to pick and choose and could not include all studies. I feel that one of my most important responsibilities as an author is to make careful decisions about which research is best and to include and highlight it.

New Features

A new end-of-chapter feature, *Women and the Web,* lists reliable web sites providing information relevant to that chapter. Coordinated with this, I have included a web-site exercise in the Instructor's Manual, which I have pretested with my own students.

Learning Aids

A number of learning aids for students are included in the text. Each chapter begins with an outline, providing students with the structure of the chapter, to help in their cognitive processing of it.

Each chapter has a boxed insert at the end, *Experience the Research,* designed to give students active experience with research in the psychology of women. Each one includes exercises such as collecting a small amount of data from friends to replicate a study in the text, or analyzing the gendered content of computer games at a local store. Although each individual student may collect only a small amount of data, if data are pooled across all students in the class, a data set large enough for statistical analysis can be produced. I hope that students will benefit from these experiences and that faculty will find them useful to assign.

A margin glossary is provided, with terms defined clearly when they are first mentioned, and a comprehensive glossary can be found at the end of the book. These features should help students learn the meaning of important terms in our field.

Ancillaries

The ***Instructor's Resource Manual/Testbank*** contains several useful resources for instructors. This ancillary begins with an opening classroom activity to introduce students to the many different roles women play in today's society. Each chapter of the IRM/TB provides test questions (including multiple-choice, matching, true/false, short-answer, and fill-in-the-blank) along with essay questions and research example questions. In addition, the Class Projects and Media Resources sections in each chapter allow instructors to supplement their course with interesting and relevant materials and web exercises related to the psychology of women.

The *Instructor/Student Web Site* offers links to the web sites highlighted at the end of each text chapter, providing students and instructors with additional resources for conducting research or further exploration of key topics. In addition, interactive activities related to the psychology of women are available to enrich the text's experience.

Acknowledgments

I feel deep gratitude to many people who contributed to the quality of this book although errors, of course, remain my responsibility. Many reviewers were helpful with their critical comments and suggestions:

Chieh-Chen Bowen, Cleveland State University
Jane P.S. Boyd, San Jose State University
Frances K. Grossman, Boston University
Deborah Harris O'Brien, Trinity College
Rosemary Krawczyk, Minnesota State University
Karen M. McCord, Solano College
Gloria Mitchell, De Anza College
Janice M. Steil, Derner Institute, Adelphia University

I remain indebted to reviewers of earlier editions, because their input continues to be felt.

Many close colleagues in women's studies at the University of Wisconsin have helped me to enrich my understanding of feminist theory and feminist psychology. My colleagues in the psychology department provide an intellectual environment that is nothing short of thrilling, and I always feel them encouraging and prodding me on to do ever better work. I especially thank Lyn Abramson, for helping me understand depression better; Trish Devine, for her contributions to my understanding of prejudice and social psychology more broadly; and Richie Davidson, for exposing me to the world of emotion research.

Many good friends in the Society for the Psychology of Women (APA Division 35) have stimulated my thinking about the psychology of women. I am not able to list all of them here because the list would be too long; I also fear that I would leave someone important off the list. You know who you are, and I thank you.

HALF THE HUMAN EXPERIENCE

Introduction

1

> *The first thing that strikes the careless observer is that women are unlike men. They are "the opposite sex"—(though why "opposite" I do not know; what is the "neighboring sex"?). But the fundamental thing is that women are more like men than anything else in the world.*
>
> — DOROTHY SAYERS, UNPOPULAR OPINIONS

One day when my daughter Margaret was four and a half (the half was very important to her), she told me about the games she had been playing at her preschool. She played with her boyfriend, Dimitrios. He said he'd marry her when they grew up. They played "Superfriends." She told me that Dimitrios chose a character he wanted to be, such as Superman, and then she played the female counterpart, Supergirl. I had to sit down for a minute while processing the significance of all she was saying. She hadn't even started kindergarten yet, and her femaleness and its requirements were so clear to her. She understood that the male chooses what he wants to be and then she follows, picking up the female counterpart role. She had learned that he is Super*man* while she is Super*girl*. I tried to talk her out of it. I said if he is Superman, she could be Super*woman*. She said there is no Superwoman. I asked her why Dimitrios always got to choose what they played. Why couldn't she pick Wonderwoman and he could be Wonderman? or Wonderboy? She said it couldn't be played that way. I asked why. She said it just couldn't. After a while I gave up (partly for theoretical reasons that will be discussed in Chapter 2). But the point of the story is that gender, and specifically femaleness, is such an important quality in our society. Even preschoolers understand the social significance of these attributes. Margaret and her friends had already learned (and believe me, I didn't tell her all this) that males choose and lead and females follow. They already understood heterosexuality and marriage as important parts of their role requirements.

This book is about being female, what it means in our society, what it means biologically, and how all of this is incorporated into the behavior, thoughts, and feelings of girls and women.

Why Study the Psychology of Women?

Most textbooks include an introductory section on why people should study that particular topic. Such a section does not seem quite so necessary in a book on the psychology of women. The main reason for studying it is obvious: It is interesting. The questions raised in a psychology of women course are fascinating. Why do women and men interact the way they do? How are women doing in their efforts to combine work and family? Why are more women than men depressed? Is adolescence really as awful a time for girls as we hear in the popular media? Many women take this course because they want to understand themselves better, a goal they may feel was not met by their other psychology courses. Men may take this course wanting to understand women better; certainly it is of interest and practical value to understand one's spouse, girlfriend, daughter, boss, or co-worker better. Many good, practical reasons exist for wanting to study the psychology of women.

There are also some good academic reasons for studying the psychology of women. Many traditional psychological theories have literally been theories about men. They have treated women, at best, as a variation from the norm. Perhaps the best example is psychoanalytic theory, to be discussed in Chapter 2. Similarly, sex bias has existed in many aspects of psychological research, a point to be discussed later in this chapter. As a result, traditional psychology has often been about men, and it has often operated from very traditional assumptions about gender roles. One way to correct these biases is to recognize a psychology of women. The psychology of women thus provides information about a group that has often been overlooked in research and theory, and it opens up new perspectives on gender roles and ways they might be changed.

Finally, one other reason for studying the psychology of women is that the female experience differs *qualitatively* from the male experience in some ways. Only women experience menstruation, pregnancy, childbirth, and breastfeeding.

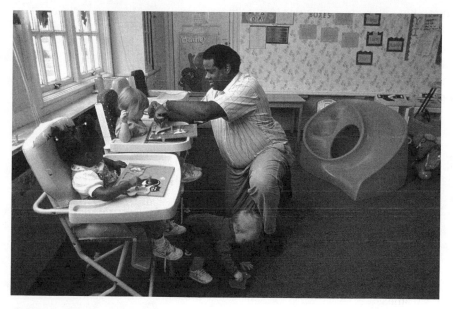

The questioning of traditional gender roles in recent years has made us wonder whether men could take on traditional female roles such as caregiver at a daycare center.

In addition to these biologically produced experiences, there are culturally produced uniquenesses to women's experience produced by the gender roles in our culture. For example, in U.S. culture, walking down the street and being whistled at is an experience nearly unique to women. One of the points of the feminist movement is that women need to communicate more with one another about these female experiences. Therefore, a course that provides information on these topics is worthwhile, and also gives people a chance to express their feelings about their experiences. Such communication should help women survive and thrive in the female experience, or change the aspects of it that need to be changed.

Sex, Gender, and Sexism

Before proceeding, some terms need to be defined. First, it is worth noting that in our language the term *sex* is sometimes used ambiguously. That is, sometimes it is used to refer to sexual behaviors such as sexual intercourse, whereas at other times it is used to refer to males and females. Usually, of course, the meaning is clear from the context. For example, if an employment application says "Sex: __," you don't write, "As often as possible." In that context the question clearly is about whether you are a female or a male. On the other hand, what is the topic of a book entitled *Sex and Temperament in Three Primitive Societies*? Is it about female roles and male roles in those societies, or is it about the sexual behavior of primitive people?

To reduce this ambiguity, I am going to use the term *sex* to refer to sexual behaviors and the term **gender** to refer to males and females (Hyde, 1979). *Gender differences,* then, refers to differences between females and males. Other scholars have adopted other conventions. For example, some scholars prefer to use the term *sex differences* to refer to innate or biologically produced differences between females and males, and *gender differences* to refer to male-female differences that result from learning and the social roles of females and males (e.g., Unger, 1979). The problem with this terminology is that studies often document a female-male difference without providing any evidence as to what causes it—biology, society, or both. Furthermore, the sharp distinction between biological causes and cultural causes fails to recognize that biology and culture may interact. Therefore, I am simply going to use the term *gender differences* for male-female differences, and leave their causation as a separate question.

> **Gender:** The state of being male or female.

Sexism is another term that will be relevant in this book. Sexism can be defined as discrimination or bias against people based on their gender. Some people use the term *reverse sexism* for discrimination against males, although it is preferable to use the term *sexism* for discrimination against either females or males on the basis of their gender. (Actually, within my terminology, the term should probably be *genderism,* but it will not be used, because *sexism* and *sex bias* are the standard terms.) Here we will be concerned with sexism as discrimination against women. Some people feel

> **Sexism:** Discrimination or bias against people based on their gender. Sex bias.

uncomfortable using the term *sexism,* because they think of it as a nasty label to hurl at someone or something. Actually, however, it is a good, legitimate term that describes a particular phenomenon—namely, discrimination on the basis of gender, particularly discrimination against women. It will be used in that spirit in this book, not as a form of name-calling. It is also important to recognize that not only men, but women as well, can be sexist.

One final term that needs to be defined in this context is **feminist.** A feminist is a person who favors political, economic, and social equality of women and men, and therefore favors the legal and social changes that will be necessary to achieve that equality. Feminists generally consider this term preferable to others, such as *women's libber,* which is often used in a derogatory manner. A wide spectrum of feminist beliefs exists, ranging from those of women in an organization who want to improve it to those of radical feminists. These different varieties are discussed in Chapter 2.

> **Feminist:** A person who favors political, economic, and social equality of women and men, and therefore favors the legal and social changes necessary to achieve that equality.

Let us turn now to the topic at hand.

Is There a Psychology of Women?

Depending on the inflection, the above question has different meanings, and therefore requires different answers. Is there a *psychology* of women? Stated in that manner, the question refers to whether a psychological approach to understanding women, as compared with, say, a political or historical one, is valuable. I will leave this question unanswered for the present, but I hope to demonstrate in the course of this book that the psychological approach is both interesting and important, and that attempts to remedy women's political status, by themselves, may leave a host of psychological ills still present and in need of attention.

Is there a psychology of women? The second variation of inflection raises the issue of whether the psychology of women actually exists, whether it is a legitimate

area of specialization within the field of psychology. Does the area contain sufficient content, research, and theory to be considered a subdiscipline of psychology? Or is it just a fad, another kind of "pop psych" that will produce a flurry of
paperbacks and then be forgotten, a field with which no "respectable" psychologist would want to be associated?

In fact, the psychology of women has quite respectable ancestry in a traditional field of psychology known as *differential psychology*. That people differ one
from another in their behavior has probably been obvious ever since humans became self-aware. For the past century these individual differences in behavior
have been the subject of scientific study. One particular dimension of individual
differences is the differences between males and females, and these have received
their due—perhaps more than their due—attention, both in research and in theories. Theorists, from Freud to the modern cognitive theorists, have given considerable attention to gender differences in behavior. Generally traditional psychological theories have had the problem (to which we will return later) of viewing
the male as normative and the female as a deviation from this norm.

In the past 30 years, the psychology of women has emerged as a distinct area,
which already has to its credit the discovery of many phenomena—including the
psychological effects of sexist language, the psychological responses of rape victims, and a better understanding of female sexuality. There is no doubt, then, that
there *is* a psychology of women, with a long history of theory and research and
with a current life of new and important discoveries. Acknowledging this, there is
a recognized group (Division 35, The Society for the Psychology of Women) in
the American Psychological Association on the psychology of women.

Finally: Is there a psychology of *women*? This inflection raises the question of
whether women have a special psychology different from that of men. Certainly
there are abundant stereotypes implying that women differ psychologically from
men—they are reputed to be less logical and more emotional, and to have different attitudes toward and motivations for sex. (Author John Gray has sold millions
of copies of *Men Are from Mars, Women Are from Venus,* which trades on gender
stereotypes.) Psychological research indicates that some of these stereotypes have a
basis in reality, and that many simply do not. It is this research—showing when
men and women differ psychologically and when they don't, and what this tells us
about women's psychology—that is one of the topics of this book.

There is a paradox inherent in trying to understand the psychology of
women, a paradox that is captured in the quotation at the beginning of this chapter. Women and men are at once different and similar. Although gender differences are important in defining women's psychology, gender similarities are
equally important. Both scientific and nonscientific views of women have concentrated on how they differ from men; this leads to a distorted
understanding unless there is equal emphasis on similarities.
This paradoxical tension between *gender differences* and **gender
similarities** will be a continuing theme throughout the book.

Gender similarities: Ways
in which males and fe-
males are similar rather
than different.

Sources of Sex Bias in Psychological Research

Research in the psychology of women is progressing at a rapid pace. Certainly I will be able to provide you with much important information about the psychology of women in this book, but there are still more questions yet to be answered than have already been answered. With research on the psychology of women expanding so rapidly, many important discoveries will be made in the next 10 or 20 years. Therefore, someone who takes a course on the psychology of women should do more than just learn what is currently known about women. It is even more profitable to gain the skills to become a "sophisticated consumer" of psychological research. That is, it is very important that you be able to read intelligently and to evaluate future studies of women that you may find in newspapers, magazines, or scholarly journals. To do this, you need to develop at least three skills: (1) Know how psychologists go about doing research, (2) be aware of ways in which sex bias may affect research, and (3) be aware of problems that may exist in research on gender roles or the psychology of women. In general, one of the most valuable things you can get from a college education is the development of *critical thinking skills*. The feminist perspective encourages critical thinking about psychological research and theory. The following discussion is designed to help you develop these skills.

How Psychologists Do Research   Figure 1.1 is a diagram of the process that psychologists go through in doing research, shown in rectangles. The diagram also indicates some of the points at which sex bias may enter, shown in ovals.

The process, in brief, is generally this: The scientist starts with some theoretical model, whether a formal model, such as social learning theory, or merely a set of personal assumptions. Based on the model or assumptions, the scientist then formulates a question. The purpose of the research is to answer that question. Next, she or he designs the research, which involves several substeps: A behavior must be selected; a way to measure the behavior must be devised; a group of appropriate participants must be chosen; and a research design must be developed. One of these substeps—finding a way to *measure* the behavior—is probably the most fundamental aspect of psychological research. Two interesting examples of measuring behavior relevant to the psychology of women are the tests that measure attitudes toward women (on a scale from traditional to egalitarian) and those that assess attitudes toward rape (Chapter 14).

The next step is for the scientist to collect the data. The data are then analyzed statistically and the results are interpreted. Next, the scientist publishes the results, which are read by other scientists and incorporated into the body of scientific knowledge (and also are put into textbooks). Finally, the system comes full

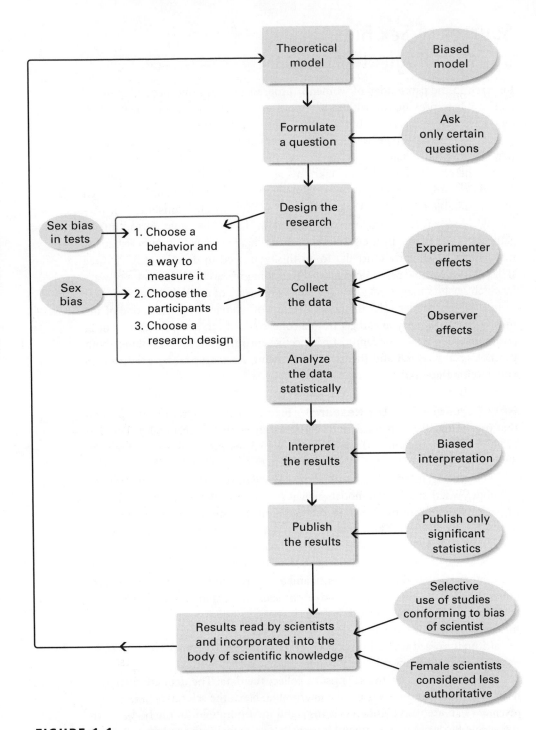

FIGURE 1.1
The process of psychological research (rectangles) and ways in which sex bias may enter (ovals).

circle, because the results are fed into the theoretical models that other scientists will use in formulating new research.

Now let us consider some of the ways in which sex bias—bias that may affect our understanding of the psychology of women or of gender roles—may enter into this process (Caplan & Caplan, 1994; Denmark et al., 1988; McHugh et al., 1986).

Biased Theoretical Model   The theoretical model or set of assumptions the scientist begins with has a profound effect on the outcome of the research. Sex bias may enter if the scientist begins with a biased theoretical model. Perhaps the best example of a biased theoretical model is psychoanalytic theory as formulated by Freud (see Chapter 2). A person with a psychoanalytic orientation might design research to document the presence of penis envy, or masochism, or immature superego in women; someone with a different theoretical orientation wouldn't even think to ask such questions. You need to become sensitive to the theoretical orientation of a scientist reporting a piece of research—and sometimes the theoretical orientation isn't stated, it has to be ferreted out—because that orientation affects the rest of the research and the conclusions that are drawn.

What Questions Are Asked   The questions a scientist asks are shaped not only by a theoretical model but also by gender-role stereotypes. Bias may enter when only certain questions are asked and others ignored, partly as a result of stereotypes. For example, there are many studies of fluctuations in women's moods over monthly cycles. However, until recently no one had thought to ask whether men also might experience monthly mood fluctuations (see, for example, Kimura & Hampson, 1994). Reading the research, one might get the impression that women are moody and men are not; but the research appears to indicate this only because no one has investigated men's mood shifts. Stereotypes about women and men have thus influenced the kinds of questions that have been investigated scientifically.

Feminist scholars advocate an important method for overcoming the problems of biased theoretical models and stereotyped research questions: go to the community of people to be studied and ask them about their lives and what the significant questions are. For example, research on lesbians may be limited if it is conducted by heterosexual women working from theories developed by heterosexual men. It is better scientific practice to begin by asking lesbians for input on the research design. Theories can be built at a later stage, once a firm foundation has been laid beginning from the women's own experience and perspectives.

Sex Bias in Psychological Tests   As shown in Figure 1.1, the next step in psychological research is designing the research, which in turn involves three steps: choosing a behavior or psychological trait and a way to measure it; choosing the participants; and choosing a research design. Let's first consider the step that involves choosing a behavior or trait and a way to measure it.[1]

Psychological measurement may take many forms. If the researcher wants to measure aggressive behavior in preschool children, the measurement technique may involve having trained observers sit unobtrusively in a preschool classroom and make check marks on a research form every time a child engages

Psychological measurement: The process of assigning numbers to characteristics of people, such as aggressiveness or intelligence.	

in an aggressive act. Here, however, we will concentrate on psychological tests, some of which have been the objects of sharp criticism for problems of sex bias.

Let's consider as an example the mathematics portion of the Scholastic Aptitude Test (SAT-Math), which is taken widely by high school seniors who are planning to attend college. The SAT-Math has been criticized a great deal on the grounds that it is biased against women. In 2001, for example, women taking it scored an average of 498, compared with an average of 533 for men (College Board, 2001). How could such a test be biased against women? One major issue is the content and wording of questions. If the content of an item involves situations that men experience more frequently, or requires knowledge to which men have more access, then the item is sex biased. As an example, consider the following item, which actually appeared on the SAT in 1986:

> A high school basketball team has won 40 percent of its first 15 games. Beginning with the sixteenth game, how many games in a row does the team now have to win in order to have a 55 percent winning record?
>
> (a) 3
> (b) 5
> (c) 6
> (d) 11
> (e) 15

Males, who have more experience with team sports and computing win-loss records, have an advantage. There is a direct algebraic solution, which a female could do if she had mastered algebra, but it is time consuming, and the test is timed. A male might say, "I know that 11 out of 20 is a 55 percent record. Will that work? Yes. The answer is 5."

If females score lower than males on a particular psychological test, then, there often are two possible interpretations: (1) Females are not as skilled at the ability being measured; or (2) the gender difference simply indicates that the test itself contained biased items.

---

[1]When psychologists measure a trait, they are creating an *operational definition*, which refers to defining some trait by how it is measured, for example, defining intelligence as those abilities that are measured by IQ tests.

Sex Bias in Choice of Sample   There is good evidence that bias exists in choosing participants for psychological research. In particular, males are used more frequently as participants than females are. For example, in 1970 in the journal *Psychophysiology,* 38 percent of the articles reported on male-only studies, and in 1990 the percentage was still 35 percent (Gannon et al., 1992).

Some entire areas of research have had this problem. A good example is the classic research on achievement motivation, which was based on males only (McClelland et al., 1953). Milgram's (1965, 1974) classic study of obedience to authority—in which people were willing to deliver extraordinarily high levels of shock to another person simply because the experimenter told them to do so—was based on an all-male sample. Such practices can create whole areas of research that have little or no relevance to women's lives. Researchers can make a second error that compounds the use of an all-male sample: the error of **overgeneralization.** That is, having used a single-gender (usually all-male) sample, the researchers then discuss and interpret the results as if they were true of all people, male and female.

> **Overgeneralization:** A research error in which the results are said to apply to a broader group than the one sampled; for example, saying that results from an all-male sample are true for all people.

The choice of research participants is probably influenced in part by the kind of behavior the psychologist is studying, as well as by gender-role stereotypes. For example, in social psychologists' research on aggression—a "masculine" behavior—nearly 50 percent of the studies were done using males only, as compared with about 10 percent using females only and 40 percent using both genders. This 50 percent was higher than the percentage of male-only research in psychology in general at the time (McKenna & Kessler, 1977). Therefore, it seems that when psychologists study a stereotyped "masculine" behavior—aggression—they are not likely to include females.

Feminist psychologists raised a ruckus about these all-male designs. So did other feminist scientists, and they joined with women in Congress to bring about change. One result was the Women's Health Equity Act of 1990 (Blumenthal & Wood, 1997), which mandated, among other things, that women must be included in clinical research trials, such as trials on the effectiveness of drugs. Before that, for example, the research conducted to determine whether small daily doses of aspirin would ward off heart attacks was based on an all-male sample. What was a woman to do if she wanted to reduce *her* risk of heart attack?

The problem with this kind of bias is that it creates not a psychology of human behavior, but rather a psychology of male behavior. Yet the problem is even worse because psychologists have been guilty of an overreliance on college-student samples. Such samples are typically homogeneous in several ways, including age (most participants are between 18 and 22), ethnicity (mostly White), and social class (mostly middle class). Feminist psychologists argue for the importance of recognizing the diversity of human experience.

Your family's ethnic group and social class influenced the environment in which you grew up and therefore influenced your behavior. Feminist psychologists urge researchers to use samples that will allow an exploration of ethnic and social class diversity.

Sex Bias in Choice of Research Design   Research methods in psychology can be roughly classified into two categories: laboratory experiments and naturalistic observations. In the laboratory experiment, the research participant is brought into the psychologist's laboratory and his or her behavior is manipulated in some way in order to study the phenomenon in question. In contrast, with naturalistic observations, researchers observe people's behavior as it occurs in natural settings and do not attempt to manipulate the behavior. In practice, the distinction between these categories is sometimes muddied; for example, it is possible to conduct an experiment in a naturalistic setting. Nonetheless, the distinction between the two basic categories is useful.

Some scholars argue that laboratory experiments are inherently sex biased, although this point is controversial (Peplau & Conrad, 1989). This question will be considered in greater detail later in the chapter.

It is also possible to talk about **quasi-experimental designs** (*quasi* meaning "not quite"). This term refers to designs in which there may be two (or possibly more) groups, so that the design looks like an experiment, but the experimenter did not manipulate which group each person was assigned to, so that there is no true experiment. A good example is studies of gender differences: There are two groups, males and females, but certainly the researcher did not randomly assign people to be in one or another group at the beginning of the research session. Studies of gender differences are not true experiments, but rather quasi-experiments.

> **Quasi-experimental design:** A research design that uses two or more groups, but participants are not randomly assigned to groups so it is not a true experiment. An example is two-group designs comparing males and females.

Experimenter Effects   In the step of research in which the data are collected, two important kinds of bias may enter: experimenter effects and observer effects.

Experimenter effects occur when some characteristic of the experimenter affects the way respondents behave, and thus affects the outcome of the experiment. For example, in one experiment, questionnaires about sexuality were administered to college students by either a psychologist, a rabbi, or a priest (Winer et al., 1988). Students tested by clergy omitted responses to sensitive items to a greater extent than did students tested by the psychologist. In particular, the gender of the experimenter may affect respondents' behavior. The evidence indicates that children cooperate better with female experimenters, whereas adults cooperate better with male experimenters (Rumenick et al., 1977; see also Harris, 1971).

> **Experimenter effects:** When some characteristics of the experimenter affect the way participants behave and therefore affect the research outcome.

It is rather disturbing to realize that an experiment might have different outcomes, depending on whether the experimenter was a man or a woman.

The problem of experimenter effects is not unsolvable. The situation can be handled by having several experimenters—half of them female, half of them male—collect the data. This should balance out any effects due to the gender of the experimenter, and demonstrate whether the gender of the experimenter did have an effect on the participants' behavior. Unfortunately, this procedure is seldom used, mostly because it is rather complicated.

Observer Effects   Another important bias that may enter at the stage of data collection is observer effects.

Observer effects occur when the researcher's expectations for the outcome of the research influence his or her observations and recording of the data (Hoyt & Kerns, 1999; Rosenthal, 1966). For example, in one study, observers (really the research participants) were to count the number of turning movements by planaria (flatworms); half the observers had been led to expect a great deal of turning, the other half very little. The observers who expected a great deal of turning reported twice as many turns as the observers who expected little (Cordaro & Ison, 1963). In psychology as in many other areas of life, what you expect is what you get.

> **Observer effects:** When the researcher's expectations affect his or her observations and recording of the data.

Observer effects may be a source of bias in gender-role research and psychology of women research. In particular, scientists are no more immune than laypeople are to having stereotyped expectations for the behavior of females and males. These stereotyped expectations might lead scientists to find stereotyped gender differences in behavior where there are none. As an example, consider research on gender differences in aggression among preschool children. If observers expect more aggression from boys, that may be just what they get, even though the boys and the girls behaved identically. This is analogous to the observers who expected more turns from the planaria and found just that.

The technical procedure that is generally used to guard against observer effects is the "blind" study. It simply means that observers are kept unaware of (blind to) which experimental group participants are in, so that the observers' expectations cannot affect the outcome. Unfortunately, the blind method is virtually impossible in gender-differences research, as the gender of a person is almost always obvious from appearance, and therefore the observer cannot be "blind" to it or unaware of it.

One exception is infants and small children, whose gender is notoriously difficult to determine, at least when clothed. This fact was used in a clever study that provides some information on whether observer effects do influence gender-role research. The study is discussed in detail in Chapter 6, but in brief, adults rated the behavior of an infant on a videotape (Condry & Condry, 1976). Half the observers were told the infant was a male, and half were told it was a female. When the infant showed a negative emotional response, those who thought the infant was a male tended to rate the emotion as anger, whereas those observing a "female" rated "her" as showing fear. The observers rated behavior differently depending on whether they thought they were observing a male or a female.

Bias in Interpretations   Once the scientist has collected the data and analyzed them statistically, the results must be interpreted. Sometimes the interpretation a scientist makes is at best a large leap of faith away from the results. Therefore this is also a stage at which bias may enter.

As an example, let us consider a fairly well documented phenomenon of psychological gender differences. A class of students takes its first exam in Introductory Psychology. Immediately after taking the exam, but before getting the results back, the students are asked to estimate how many points (out of a possible 100) they got on the exam. On average, males will estimate that they got higher scores than females will estimate they got (see Chapter 3). At this point, the data have been collected and analyzed statistically. It can be stated (neutrally) that there are statistically significant gender differences, with men estimating more points than women. The next question is, How do we interpret that result? The standard interpretation is that it indicates that women lack self-confidence or have low confidence in their abilities. The interpretation that is not made, although it is just as logical, is that men have unrealistically high expectations for their own performance.

The point is that, given a statistically significant gender difference, such a result can often be interpreted in two opposite ways, one of which is favorable to men, one of which is favorable to women.

A persistent tendency has existed in psychology to make interpretations that are favorable to men; these interpretations are essentially based on a **female deficit model.** Sometimes there is no way of verifying which interpretation is right. As it happens in the example above, there is a way, because we can find out how the students actually did on the exam. Those results indicate that women underestimate their scores by about as much as men overestimate theirs (Mednick & Thomas, 1993). Thus the second interpretation is as accurate as the first. In one study, women estimated the same number of points as men did, but then the women actually scored better than the men (Beyer, 1999). The men were therefore decidedly overconfident.

Female deficit model: A theory or interpretation of research in which women's behavior is seen as deficient.

Becoming sensitive to the point at which scientists go beyond their data to interpret them, and becoming aware of when those interpretations may be biased, is extremely important. Another example of bias in interpretations occurs in research on gender differences in language (Chapter 5).

Publishing Significant Results Only   Once the data have been analyzed and interpreted, the next step is to publish the results. There is a strong tendency in psychological research to publish "significant" results only. This does not necessarily mean significant in the sense of "important"; it means significant in the sense of being the result of a statistical test that reaches the .05 level of significance.[2]

What are the implications of this tendency for our understanding of gender roles and the psychology of women? It means that there is a tendency to report statistically significant gender differences and to omit mention of nonsignificant gender differences. That is, we tend to hear about it when males and females differ, but we tend not to hear about it when males and females are the same. Thus there would be a bias toward emphasizing gender differences, and ignoring *gender similarities.*

This bias may also enter into psychology of women research such as menstrual-cycle studies (a point to be discussed in detail in Chapter 11).

Other Biases   The final two biases shown in Figure 1.1 are fairly self-explanatory and require little discussion here. If there is a tendency for reports by female scientists to be considered less authoritative than reports by male scientists, this would introduce bias, particularly when combined with bias due to experimenter effects as discussed previously. Research on whether this is really a problem has produced mixed results (Goldberg, 1968; Swim et al., 1989), and so these concerns are somewhat speculative. Also, another kind of bias is introduced if scientists have a tendency to remember and use in their work those studies that conform to their own biases or ideas, and to ignore those that do not.

Conclusion   I have discussed a number of problems with psychological research that may affect our understanding of women—and men. Of course, these problems are not present in every study in the area, and certainly I don't mean to suggest that all psychological research is worthless. The point is to learn to think critically about biases that may—or may not—be present when you are reading reports of research. Thinking critically about the theoretical orientation of a writer and about biased interpretations of results is important.

A more general point emerges from this whole discussion of sex bias in research methods in psychology. Traditional psychology has historically viewed itself as an objective and value-free science. Today, many psychologists, feminist psychologists among them, question whether psychological research is objective and value free (Peplau & Conrad, 1989). They point out that psychological research might more appropriately be viewed as an interaction between researcher and research participant that occurs in a particular context. To that interaction the researcher brings certain values that may influence its outcome—in short, the results cannot be totally objective.

---

[2]For those who have not studied statistics, "significant at the .05 level" means roughly that the results that were obtained would have happened by chance only 5 times out of 100.

Psychology, of course, is not the only science that has claimed to be objective and value free when it isn't. Another example is physics and its groundbreaking discoveries of ways to generate nuclear power. These discoveries can be used to manufacture weapons capable of annihilating thousands, or they can be used to generate electricity for cities. Values are closely connected with science.

Feminist Alternatives   All the preceding criticisms are important and you should be aware of them, but we need to go beyond those criticisms to offer some constructive alternatives. In doing so, we can think about *gender-fair research* and *feminist research.*

Gender-fair research is research that is not guilty of any of the biases discussed in the previous sections (Denmark et al., 1988; McHugh et al., 1986). Some characteristics of gender-fair research are as follows: (1) Single-gender research is never, or almost never, done. Even in situations where a single-gender design might seem to be justified—for example, examining women's fluctuations in mood over the menstrual cycle—the demand for gender fairness and inclusion of the other gender might lead to better understandings—for example, a discovery of fluctuations in men's moods. (2) Theoretical models, underlying assumptions, and the kinds of questions asked should always be examined for gender fairness. For example, the minute someone proposes to do research on the effects of mothers' depression on their children, it should be asked whether fathers' depression also has an effect on children. Otherwise, we assume that only mothers influence children and that fathers have no influence, which is fair to neither mothers nor fathers. (3) Both male and female researchers should collect data in order to avoid experimenter effects. (4) Interpretations of data should always be examined carefully for gender fairness, and possibly several interpretations should be offered. For example, if there is a significant gender difference in the number of points students estimate they will get on an exam, two interpretations should be offered: that women underestimate and lack self-confidence, and that men overestimate and have inflated expectations for their performance. In a sense, then, gender-fair research proposes that we continue to play the research game by the same set of rules it has always had—tight controls, careful interpretations, and so on—but that we improve things so that the rules are observed fairly.

> **Gender-fair research:** Research that is free of gender bias.

Feminist researchers might argue that we need to go even further in reforming psychological research. There really is no single, comprehensive, definitive statement of the principles of **feminist research,** but many scholars have made contributions (e.g., Kimmel & Crawford, 2001; Crawford & Kimmel, 1999; Parlee, 1981; Rabinowitz & Sechzer, 1993; Reinharz, 1992; Wallston, 1981; Wittig, 1985) and I will present some of those ideas here.

> **Feminist research:** Research growing out of feminist theory, which seeks radical reform of traditional research methods.

Feminist researchers might argue that the classic form of psychological research—the tightly controlled laboratory experiment—needs to be revised. It is manipulative, intended to determine how manipulations of the independent variable cause changes in the dependent variable. It objectifies and dehumanizes the people it studies, calling them "subjects." It strips away the context of behavior, taking people out of their natural environments in order to control all those things the experimenter considers irrelevant. In all these senses—the manipulativeness, the objectification, the context stripping—traditional psychological experimentation might be accused of being masculine or patriarchal.

The feminist alternatives are several:

1. Do not manipulate people, but rather observe them in their natural environment and try to determine how they experience their natural lives and worlds, thus emphasizing relatedness rather than differentiation.

2. Do not call the people who are studied "subjects," but rather "participants."

3. Do not think in simple terms of variable A causing effects on variable B, but rather in terms of complex, interactive relationships in which A and B mutually influence each other. Again, relatedness is emphasized.

4. Devote specific research attention to the special concerns of women.

5. Conduct research that will empower women and eliminate inequities.

6. Do not assume that scientific research and political activism are contradictory activities (Wittig, 1984). Good research—by documenting current conditions—can facilitate social change. And the psychologist who has political activism and social change as goals can still do good research; such researchers are obligated to articulate their values, but that is a good rule for all scientists.

7. Consider innovative methods for studying human behavior (Crawford & Kimmel, 1999; Kimmel & Crawford, 2001).

In regard to innovative methods, one example is focus groups (which are scarcely that innovative, being in widespread use in business research), in which women gather as a group to discuss a particular focused topic (Wilkinson, 1999). They create the social context in which women often make meaning of their experiences, and the discussion itself becomes the data. A second example is the use of qualitative methods or the combination of qualitative and quantitative methods (Denzin & Lincoln, 1994; Tolman & Szalacha, 1999). Traditional psychological research has relied on quantitative methods, that is, behavior is studied by converting it to numbers, whether IQ scores or individuals' ratings of their attitude toward legal abortion on a scale from 1 (*strongly disapprove*) to 7 (*strongly approve*). With qualitative methods, in contrast, the data are often text or talk. For example, an interviewer may pose open-ended questions, tape-record and transcribe the respondent's answers, and then analyze the answers for themes. In one such study, Deborah Tolman and Laura Szalacha (1999) interviewed teenage girls about their experiences of sexual desire and then analyzed the themes that emerged from the

FOCUS 1.1

FACTS ABOUT AMERICAN WOMEN TODAY

- The American population, according to the 2000 census, numbers 281.4 million. Women constitute 143.4 million, or 50.9 percent of that number.

- Of those women, 107.7 million (75 percent) are White, 18.2 million (12.6 percent) are Black, 17.1 million (12 percent) are Latina, 5.3 million (3.7 percent) are Asian American, and 1.2 million (1 percent) are Native American. (These numbers add up to somewhat more than 100 percent because Latinas can be White.)

- In the 106th Congress, the last of the twentieth century, women were 9 of 100 senators and 56 of 235 members of the House.

Over the past 30 years, American women have made substantial gains in both business and politics: (a) Carly Fiorina, CEO of Hewlett-Packard; (b) Rosa de Lauro (D-CA), flanked by other Congresswomen, speaks at a meeting of the Democratic National Committee.

girls' responses. (See Chapter 12 for a discussion of the intriguing findings.) All these principles of feminist methods open up new vistas for researchers and you.

Personally, I think we ought to integrate and respect both approaches, gender fair and feminist. The traditional psychological experiment needs reform, but I would hate to throw it out entirely. It functions best when combined with natu-

- Of the 100 largest cities in the United States, 16 had women mayors in 1999, including San Diego (Susan Golding) and Minneapolis (Sharon Sayles Belton).

- Women make up 40 percent of executives, administrators, and managers in American business. Among Fortune 500 companies, women constitute 11 percent of the directors but fewer than 1 percent of CEOs (4 of the 500 CEOs are women).

- Whereas in 1978 women between the ages of 25 and 34 earned 66.2 cents for every dollar earned by men, in 1998 women in that same age range earned 82.9 cents for every dollar earned by men.

- Following Operation Desert Storm in the early 1990s, Congress repealed all its restrictions on women in the armed services, although Department of Defense restrictions remain. Whereas women made up 1.6 percent of the military in 1973, that figure was 14 percent by 1999, and in 1998 women accounted for 27 percent of new Air Force recruits.

- Among babies born in 2001, the average projected life expectancy is 79.8 years for women and 73.1 years for men. Among Whites, the expectancy is 80.6 years for women and 74.4 for men, compared with 74.5 years for Black women and 64.2 years for Black men, 82.9 years for Hispanic women and 75.2 years for Hispanic men, 80.7 years for American Indian women and 72.2 years for American Indian men, and 85.2 years for Asian/Pacific Islander women and 79.8 years for Asian/Pacific Islander men.

- Today, women are equaling or surpassing men in education. In 1998, among people between the ages of 25 and 34, 28.7 percent of women had a college degree or higher, compared with 26.2 percent of men.

Sources: Costello & Stone (2001); U.S. Bureau of the Census (2000).

ralistic research looking at complex mutual influences. Gender-fair research and feminist research might diverge on some issues, though. For example, feminist researchers would value the investigation of battered wives as an issue of special concern to women. Gender-fair researchers would point out that there are some battered husbands and that they should be researched as well. Feminist researchers might reply that there are far more battered wives than battered husbands and that feminist research need not necessarily concern itself with battered husbands. I cannot easily resolve this issue, and so I encourage you to think about it yourself.

Are We Making Progress?   Feminist psychologists began to publish their critiques of traditional research methods over 30 years ago. Has there been any progress? Have psychologists changed their methods to respond to these criticisms?

An analysis of articles published in the most important psychology journals from 1970 to 1990 indicates that there has been some progress, but that some areas still need improvement (Gannon et al., 1992). One issue is the use of all-male samples. In 1970, 42 percent of the articles in the prestigious *Journal of Abnormal Psychology* were based on all-male samples; by 1990 the use of all-male samples had declined to 20 percent. That represents progress, but still, one article in five was based on males only, even in 1990.

The representation of women as researchers in psychology has seen great progress. For example, in 1970, only 27 percent of the articles in *Developmental Psychology* had a woman as first author; by 1990 that number had risen to 53 percent (Gannon et al., 1992). Similar trends were present for other journals. In 1970 only 6 percent of the articles in *Journal of Personality and Social Psychology* had women as first authors, compared with 30 percent by 1990.

A striking change is the trend toward using nonsexist language (see Chapter 5). In 1970, 29 percent of the articles in *Journal of Personality and Social Psychology* used nonsexist language, compared with 99 percent by 1990 (Gannon et al., 1992). This cannot be attributed entirely to the spontaneous goodwill of psychologists, though. Beginning in 1983, the American Psychological Association's official *Publication Manual* required the use of nonsexist language in all APA journal articles. Institutional norms can definitely have an effect on the behavior of scientists.

In conclusion, then, substantial shifts have been made toward nonsexist methods in psychological research. There are more women researchers and fewer all-male samples, and research is more likely to be reported using nonsexist language. Nonetheless, substantial numbers of studies are still based on all-male samples, and continued monitoring of methods is important.

Looking Ahead

A number of themes will recur in this book. Some of them have appeared repeatedly in history and then crop up in the United States today and are even found in modern psychology. Other themes are derived from current scientific psychological research on women.

The male as normative is a theme throughout history. An example is the Adam and Eve story, in which Adam is created first and Eve is later made from his rib.

Recurring Themes Rooted in History One historical theme is the **male as normative.** Throughout mythology the male is seen as normative, the female as a variant or deviation. That is, the male is the important one, the major representative of the species, the "normal" one, and the female is a variation on him. As Simone de Beauvoir (1952) expressed it, woman is the Other.

In the biblical creation story (Genesis 2), Adam, the man, is created first; Eve, the woman, is later fashioned out of his rib, almost as an afterthought. In this and many other creation myths, man is created first; he is the major, important part of the species. Woman comes second and is only a variant on the man, the normative. There are even myths in which a woman is created by castrating a man.

Male as normative: A model in which the male is seen as the norm for all humans, and the female is seen as a deviation from the norm.

Perhaps the best example of the male-as-normative theme is in our language. The word *man* is used to refer not only to a male, but to people in general. When the gender of a person is unknown, the pronoun *he* is used to refer to "him." (Would we dare have said "to refer to her"?) The species as a whole is man; woman is merely a subset. This topic will be discussed in detail in Chapter 5.

To explain the concept of "normativeness," an analogy can be made to handedness. In our society, right-handedness is normative, and left-handedness is considered unusual or deviant. The world is basically set up for right-handed people, and lefties have difficulty adjusting in everything from finding scissors that fit them to finding a satisfactory place at the dinner table. Just as left-handed people live in a world made for the right-handed, so women live in a world made for men, in which the male is normative.

A closely related concept is **androcentrism** (Bem, 1993). It means, literally, male centeredness, or the belief that males are the standard or norm.

> **Androcentrism:** Male centered; the belief that the male is the norm.

Throughout mythology and history, then, a dominant theme is that the male is normative. He is the chief member of the species and woman is a variation or deviation. It seems likely that psychological effects result from this view, particularly as it is expressed in language. This concept of the male as normative crops up in a number of places in modern psychology, including some of the theories discussed in Chapter 2.

A second recurring theme rooted in history is **feminine evil.** One of the clearest images of women in mythology is their portrayal as the source of evil (Hays, 1964). In the Judeo-Christian tradition, Eve disobeyed God's orders and ate from the fruit of the tree of knowledge. As a result, Adam and Eve were forced to

> **Feminine evil:** The belief that women are the source of evil or immorality in the world, as in the Adam and Eve story.

leave the Garden of Eden, and Eve, the woman, became the source of original sin, responsible for the fall of humanity. In a more ancient myth, the Greek god Zeus ordered Vulcan to create the lovely maiden Pandora to bring misery to earth in revenge for the theft of fire by Prometheus. Pandora was given a box or jar containing all the evils of the world, which she was told not to open. But Pandora opened the box, and thus all the evils it contained spread over the world. In Chinese mythology the two forces yin and yang correspond to feminine and masculine, and yin, the feminine, is seen as the dark, or evil, side of nature.

Historically, perhaps the most frightening manifestation of the belief in feminine evil was the persecution of witches beginning in the Middle Ages and persisting into Puritan America. Guided by the Catholic Church in a papal bull of 1484, the Malleus Maleficarum, the Inquisition tortured or put to death unknown numbers of witches. The objective fact appears to be that the vast majority of those accused and tried were women (Hays, 1964). Thus, it is woman who is seen as being in collaboration with the devil, visiting evil upon humans.

Recurring Themes Rooted in Modern Science   Other repeated themes in this book are derived from current scientific research on the psychology of women. One important theme is *gender similarities,* the phenomenon that females and males are psychologically more similar than they are different. Another is the difference between *theory* and *empirical evidence.* Many theories of women's behavior have been proposed. Some have solid data (empirical evidence) backing them, whereas others do not. Not every theory is true, nor is every one a good description or explanation of behavior. Just because Freud said something does not make it true (or false). Readers need to become critical thinkers about the difference between statements based on theory and statements based on empirical evidence.

Another important distinction is **traits** versus *situational determinants* of behavior. A continuing controversy in psychology is whether behavior is determined more by a person's enduring traits (such as a personality trait), or whether behavior is determined more by the particular situation the person is in. Advocates of the latter position point out how inconsistent people's behavior can be from one situation to another—for example, a man may be aggressive toward a business competitor, but passive or nurturant toward his wife. This suggests that his behavior is not determined by an enduring personality trait (aggressiveness), but rather by the particular situation he is in. Later in the book we will also refer to this issue as a distinction between intrapsychic or internal factors (traits) and external (situational) factors. Applied to the psychology of women, the question becomes whether women are more influenced by personality traits that distinguish them from men, or whether their behavior is more determined by the situations they find themselves in. For example, is the lack of professional accomplishments by women due to some trait, such as the motive to avoid success (Chapter 6), or to situational factors, such as job discrimination? This distinction also has practical implications. In trying to improve women's lives, if we decide that the problem is personality traits, then we would try to change the early experiences or childrearing practices that create those personality traits. If we decide, on the other hand, that situational factors are more important, we would want to change the situations women are in, such as ending job discrimination.

> **Trait:** An enduring characteristic of a person, such as extraversion.

Another recurring theme is the pervasiveness of *female deficit models* in psychology. In the nineteenth century, scientists found women had slightly smaller brains than men and interpreted this as a sure reason why women were not as intelligent as men (Shields, 1975). Today some researchers argue that girls are not as good at math as boys are. No matter the century, researchers always seem to try to find female deficits.

Finally, one other recurring theme is the importance of *values* in a scientific understanding of women. Values affect the scientific theories that are proposed and the way research is done (Rabinowitz & Sechzer, 1993). In particular, they

FOCUS 1.2

PSYCHOLOGY'S FOREMOTHERS

One emphasis of the feminist movement has been recognizing and valuing the accomplishments of women. In part, that involves rediscovering some important contributions women have made. Here is a short self-quiz about some significant achievements made by eminent psychologists. Take the quiz before turning to the answers on the next page.

Q1. Who did the research on Black children that was critical in the U.S. Supreme Court decision to desegregate the nation's schools (*Brown* v. *Board of Education*)?

Q2. Who established that babies can swim?

Q3. Who conducted the famous social psychology study "The Robbers' Cave Experiment"?

Q4. Who authored the famous study "Albert and the White Rat"?

Q5. Who produced the widely used Stanford-Binet IQ Test?

Q6. Who developed the Cattell Infant Intelligence Test Scale?

Q7. What do the following books have in common: *The Growth of Logical Thinking of the Child, The Child's Conception of Space, The Child's Conception of Geometry,* and *The Early Growth of Logic in the Child*?

Q8. Who did the landmark research on the authoritarian personality?

Q9. Who wrote "Learning to Love," the classic report of research on the development of bonds of affection in monkeys?

affect the way research is interpreted, a point discussed earlier in the chapter. Readers need to become sensitive to the values expressed by a particular scientific position.

Chapter Previews   In the next chapter we will look at the contributions to the understanding of female development that have been made by some of the major theoretical systems of psychology—psychoanalytic theory, social learning theory, and cognitive-developmental theory. A controversial theory, sociobiology, is examined, as is gender schema theory and feminist theory.

Here are the answers to the questions on the previous page:

A1. Kenneth Clark and *Mamie Phipps Clark.*

A2. *Myrtle McGraw.*

A3. Muzafer Sherif, O. J. Harvey, W. E. Hood, and *Carolyn Sherif.*

A4. John B. Watson and *Rosalie Raynor.*

A5. Lewis Terman and *Maud Merrill.*

A6. *Psyche Cattell.*

A7. You are partially correct if you said that they were all authored by the famous male psychologist Jean Piaget; but they were all coauthored by his longtime female collaborator, *Bärbel Inhelder.*

A8. *Else Frenkel-Brunswick.*

A9. Harry Harlow and *Margaret Harlow.*

Sources: Lal (2002); Russo & O'Connell (1980).

Following these theoretical views, later chapters will focus on research about what women are actually like psychologically. Chapter 3 reviews evidence on gender stereotypes and gender differences, to see the ways in which women and men differ and the ways in which they are similar. Chapter 4 examines the new scholarship in psychology concerning women of color. Because feminist scholars have emphasized the importance of language, Chapter 5 is about women and language—whether there are gender differences in language use, how the structure of the English language treats women, and how women and men communicate nonverbally. Chapter 6 presents the important new research on gender and emo-

Dr. Mamie Phipps Clark, who, with her husband, Dr. Kenneth Clark, did the research on Black children that was critical in the 1954 Supreme Court decision to desegregate the nation's schools.

tion. In Chapter 7 we discuss female experiences, adjustment, and roles across the lifespan from birth to old age. We look at women and achievement in Chapter 8, by considering research on gender differences in intellectual abilities, research on achievement in women, and several psychological factors (achievement motivation, the motive to avoid success, and attribution patterns) that may contribute to women's success or lack of it. Chapter 9 is about women and work, and issues involved in women balancing work and family.

Chapters 10 through 12 are about women in relation to their bodies. Chapter 10 considers the evidence on whether there are biological influences—such as hormone effects—on gender differences and female behaviors. Chapter 11 discusses psychological research on several women's health issues, including menstruation, menopause, pregnancy and childbirth, abortion, breast cancer, and AIDS. Chapter 12 explores female sexuality, including research on the physiology of the female sexual response, research on the psychology of female sexuality, and sexual dysfunction and therapy for women. Chapter 13 is about lesbian and bisexual women. Chapter 14 centers on the victimization of women as seen in rape, battering, sexual harassment, and child sexual abuse. Chapter 15 considers various problems that may occur in female adjustment, what happens to women

EXPERIENCE THE RESEARCH

**UNDERSTANDING SEX BIAS
IN PSYCHOLOGICAL RESEARCH**

Design an experiment to determine whether adults are more likely to help a 4-year-old child who is crying and apparently lost, depending on whether the adult is alone and there are no other adults close by (no bystander condition) or there are other adults present (bystander condition). Design two versions of the experiment. First, create the experiment as a traditional, pre-feminist psychologist might have done. Then, using Figure 1.1, make a list of all the examples of sex bias in the research. Finally, re-create the experiment to correct all the elements of sex bias, so that it will meet the standards for gender-fair research.

when they seek psychotherapy for their problems, and what new feminist therapies are being developed for women.

In Chapter 16 we examine the "new research," done from a feminist perspective, on the psychology of men and the male role. The final chapter summarizes some of the major themes of the book and suggests important questions for the future.

Suggestions for Further Reading

Caplan, Paula J., & Caplan, Jeremy B. (1994). *Thinking critically about research on sex and gender.* New York: HarperCollins. This brief book includes a feminist critique of several major areas of psychological research on women and provides helpful guides for critical thinking about research.

Crawford, Mary, & Kimmel, Ellen. (1999). Promoting methodological diversity in feminist research. *Psychology of Women Quarterly, 23,* 1–6. This is the introduction to an entire special issue of articles on new methods in feminist psychological research.

Lewin, Miriam, & Wild, Cheryl L. (1991). The impact of the feminist critique on tests, assessment, and methodology. *Psychology of Women Quarterly, 15,* 581–596. Provides a fascinating look at the way in which feminists have changed psychological testing practices.

Peplau, L. Anne, & Conrad, Eva. (1989). Beyond nonsexist research: The perils of feminist methods in psychology. *Psychology of Women Quarterly, 13,* 381–402. These authors argue that no research method (laboratory experimentation or naturalistic observation) is inherently subject to sex bias and that all research methods can be used in feminist ways in psychology—points that are controversial among feminist scientists.

Women and the Web

Society for the Psychology of Women. This is the website for Division 35 of the American Psychological Association.

 www.apa.org/divisions/div35

ivillage. This commercial website offers information and chat rooms on a wide variety of topics that are important to women, ranging from babies, health, and sexuality to money.

 www.ivillage.com

Women's Studies Librarian of the University of Wisconsin System. This website includes links to a wealth of resources, including women's organizations, bibliographies, and journals.

 www.library.wisc.edu/libraries/WomensStudies/

Theoretical Perspectives

2

[Girls] notice the penis of a brother or playmate, strikingly visible and of large proportions, at once recognize it as the superior counterpart of their own small and inconspicuous organ, and from that time forward fall a victim to envy for the penis.

— SIGMUND FREUD, COLLECTED PAPERS

Understanding the nature of the differences between males and females has fascinated people probably since the dawn of the human species. In the past century, science has come to dominate intellectual thought. And so it is not surprising that men and women have attempted scientific understandings of women. In this chapter we will examine some major psychological theories that have been formulated to explain women and the differences between women and men. The theories are presented in roughly chronological order, beginning with the earliest and most traditional theories and progressing to more modern ones.

Psychoanalytic Theory

Psychoanalytic theory was formulated by Sigmund Freud. Despite the advent of new models of human psychological development, few can doubt the influence of psychoanalytic theory in psychology, not to mention its penetration into the language and thinking of most laypeople. Psychoanalytic theory not only describes human behavior but also has acted to shape human behavior. For example, Freud's theory of female sexuality (see Chapter 12) held that women could have two kinds of orgasm—vaginal or clitoral—and that the vaginal orgasm was the more "mature," that is, the better, of the two. Some women have spent hours trying to achieve the elusive vaginal orgasm and have sought psychotherapy when they were unable to attain it, all as a result of Freud's theory.

> **Psychoanalytic theory:** A psychological theory originated by Freud; its basic assumption is that part of the human psyche is unconscious.

Freud viewed humans as being dominated by two basic instincts: *libido* (the sex drive or life force) and *thanatos* (the death force, which causes phenomena such as warfare). The libido is focused on various areas of the body known as the **erogenous zones.** Each zone is a part of the skin or mucous membrane highly endowed with blood supply and nerve endings that are very sensitive to stimulation. The lips and mouth constitute one such region, the anal region another, and the genitals a third. Thus Freud noted that sucking produces pleasure, as do elimination and stroking the genitals.

> **Erogenous zones:** Areas of the body that are particularly sensitive to sexual stimulation.

Stages of Development   One of Freud's greatest contributions was to promote the view of human personality as being the result of *development*. That is, he saw the personality of an adult as the result of previous experiences, and he believed that early childhood experiences were most critical. He proposed a stage theory of psychosexual development, each stage being characterized by a focus on one of the erogenous zones. According to his view, all humans pass through the stages in a fixed, chronological sequence—first the oral, then the anal, and then the phallic stage—during the first five or six years of life. During the first stage, the oral, the infant derives pleasure from sucking and eating and experiences the world mainly through the mouth. Following this is the anal stage, in which pleasure is focused on defecating.

In attempting to explain the development of gender identity and differences between males and females, Freud postulated that boys and girls pass through the first two stages of psychosexual development, the oral and the anal, in a similar manner. For both genders at this time, the mother is the chief object of love. It is during the **phallic stage,** around the ages of 3 to 6, that the development of boys and girls diverges. As one might suspect from the name for this stage, females will be at somewhat of a disadvantage in passing through it.

Phallic stage: The third stage of development in psychoanalytic theory, around 3 to 6 years of age, during which the pleasure zone is the genitals and sexual feelings arise toward the parent of the other gender.

During the phallic stage, the boy becomes fascinated with his own penis. It is a rich source of pleasure and interest for him. A critical occurrence during the phallic stage is the formation of the **Oedipal complex,** named for the Greek myth of Oedipus, who unknowingly killed his father and married his mother. In the Oedipal complex, the boy sexually desires his mother. His attachment to her is strong and intense. He also wishes to rid himself of the father, who is a rival for the mother's affection. But the father is too powerful an opponent, and the boy fears that the father will retaliate. He fears that the father will do him bodily harm, particularly to his beloved penis, so that the boy comes to feel *castration anxiety.* The anxiety becomes so great that the boy seeks to resolve the problem. He represses his libidinal impulses toward the mother, and makes the critical shift to identifying with the father. In the process of *identification* with the father, the boy introjects (takes into himself as his own) the values and ethics of society as represented by the father and thus comes to have a conscience or **superego.** But more important for our purposes is that in identifying with the father, he comes to acquire his gender identity, taking on the qualities the father supposedly possesses—strength, power, and so on.

Oedipal complex: In psychoanalytic theory, a boy's sexual attraction to and intense love for his mother, and his desire to do away with his father.

Superego: Freud's term for the part of the personality that contains the person's ideals and conscience.

The sequence of events in the phallic stage is considerably different, more complex, and more difficult for the girl. According to Freud, the first critical event is the girl's stark realization that she has no penis. Presumably she recognizes that

FOCUS 2.1

A CASE HISTORY ILLUSTRATING PENIS ENVY

The following is an example of a case history that a psychoanalyst would see as demonstrating penis envy.

An unsuccessful artist who had always resented being a woman came to treatment very depressed and anxious at having allowed herself to become pregnant. Her husband had recently become extremely successful, and her envy of and competition with him were enormous, especially since she was blocked in her own professional development. She felt that the best way to "show up" her husband was to do the one thing he could not do—bear a child.

She expressed only hatred and contempt for her mother, who had been a dependent, ineffectual housebound woman. This resentment seemed to have started at the birth of her sister, three years younger, at which time the patient hid herself and refused to talk for days. The mother was hospitalized for depression when the patient was twelve. The father was an unsuccessful artist, an exciting, talented person whom the patient adored. She turned away from her mother and spent the next ten years of her life trying to be her father's son. He encouraged her painting and took her to exhibitions. However, he was very inconsistent and bitter, given to terrifying rages; he would alternate between leading her on and slapping her down. Her fantasy of being like a boy was brutally crushed at a time when she was preparing for a bas mitzvah; she thought she would be allowed to have one "as good as a boy's" but was suddenly humiliated publicly at puberty and sent home from the synagogue on the Sabbath because it was decided that she was now a woman and could no longer stay and compete with the men and boys. Menarche intensified her resentment of female functions, but she compensated with fantasies of having a son and traveling around the world with him—self-sufficient, no longer needing her family or her father. While in

Europe on a scholarship, she fell in love and, while petting with the boy, had the only orgasm she has ever experienced. She feared his increasing power over her, experienced a resurgence of dependency needs and fled home. She felt she had spent her life trying to win her father's approval. But when she finally had a solo exhibit of her art, he taunted her, "Why not give it up, go home, and make babies?"

After his death and her professional failure, she became increasingly depressed. At the age of thirty, she decided to get pregnant—after having been married four years. (She had previously been phobic about pregnancy and remained a virgin until her marriage.) She felt that her baby was conceived out of emptiness, not fullness, and then feared that the child would take her life from her. Having a baby trapped her, she felt; she could no longer try to be like a man. It was as though she had had a fantasy penis which she finally had to relinquish.

There was plenty of evidence of typical penis envy in this case. As a girl, the patient even tried to compete with boys in urinary contests, and was furious because she always lost. She first associated her bedwetting with rage at not having a penis, but finally viewed it as a way to punish [her] mother for turning to [the] sister, and as an effort to recover the maternal solicitude she had lost. She envied, and was attracted to, men who had powerful drives for achievement and were free to pursue them. The penis was for her a symbol of such drives; to possess it would also save her from being like her mother. In one sense, she wanted a baby as a substitute for not having a penis; but she also had a burning wish to be a good mother—to prove her own validity as well as to "undo" her past. Her difficulty in achieving this wish forced her to work through her relationship with her mother, which she had contemptuously shelved, finding competition with men more exciting and less anxiety-provoking.

SOURCE: Abridged from Moulton (1970).

the penis is superior to her clitoris. She feels cheated and envious of males, and thus comes to feel *penis envy* (see Focus 2.1). She also feels mutilated, believing that at one time she possessed a penis, but that it had been cut off—indeed Freud believed that the fires of the boy's castration anxiety are fed by the boy's observation of the girl's anatomy, which he sees as living proof of the reality of castration. Her desire for a penis, her penis envy, can never be satisfied directly, and instead becomes transformed into a desire to be impregnated by her father. Holding her mother responsible for her lack of a penis, she renounces her love for her mother and becomes intensely attracted to her father, thus forming her own version of the Oedipal complex, called the **Electra complex.** The desire to be impregnated by the father is a strong one, and persists in the more general form of maternal urges, according to Freud.

| **Electra complex:** In psychoanalytic theory, a girl's sexual attraction to and intense love for her father. |

Passivity, Masochism, and Narcissism   Freud believed that there are three key female personality traits: passivity, masochism, and narcissism. Here I will focus on passivity and masochism.

In the outcomes of the Electra complex Freud saw the origins of the two well-known—at least to Victorians—feminine qualities of *passivity* and **masochism.** In choosing the strategy for obtaining the desired penis by being impregnated by the father, the girl adopts a passive approach—to be impregnated, to be done to, not to do—and this passive strategy persists throughout life. The desire to be impregnated is also masochistic, in that intercourse (in which, in Freudian terminology, the woman is "penetrated") and childbirth are painful. The female, therefore, in desiring to be impregnated seeks to bring pain to herself.

| **Masochism:** The desire to experience pain. |

Lest the foregoing strains your credulity, perhaps some quotations from Marie Bonaparte, a follower of Freud, will indicate the strength of these convictions.

> Throughout the whole range of living creatures, animal or vegetable, passivity is characteristic of the female cell, the ovum whose mission is to *await* the male cell, the active mobile spermatozoan to come and *penetrate* it. Such penetration, however, implies infraction of its tissue, but infraction of a living creature's tissue may entail destruction: death as much as life. Thus, the fecundation of the female cell is initiated by a kind of wound; in its way, the female cell is primordially "masochistic." (1953, p. 79)

> Vaginal sensitivity in coitus for the adult female, in my opinion, is thus largely based on the existence, and more or less unconscious, acceptation of the child's immense masochistic beating fantasies. In coitus, the woman, in effect, is subjected to a sort of beating by the man's penis. She receives its blows and often, even, loves their violence. (1953, p. 87)

As we saw, the resolution of the Oedipal complex is critical for the boy's development, being necessary for the formation of his gender identity and superego. Unfortunately, for the girl the resolution of the Electra complex is not as complete.

She was led to the Electra complex by her desire for a penis, a desire that can never truly be satisfied. More importantly, the prime motivation in the boy's resolving his Oedipal complex was his overpowering fear of castration. For the girl, castration is an already accomplished fact, and thus her motivation for resolution of the Electra complex is not so strong, being motivated only by the comparatively abstract realization that her desires for her father cannot be gratified.

Immature Superego   For girls, according to the theory, the Electra complex is never as fully resolved as it is for boys. According to Freud, this leads the girl to lifelong feelings of inferiority, to a predisposition to jealousy, and to intense maternal desires. Furthermore, it leads females to be characterized by an *immature superego*. For the boy, one of the positive outcomes of resolving the Oedipal complex is the internalization, or introjection, of society's standards, thereby forming a superego. But the girl's attachment to the parents is never "smashed" as is the boy's, and she continues to be dependent on the parents for her values. She never internalizes her own values as completely as does the boy; continuing to rely on others, she is thus characterized by a less mature sense of morality, or an immature superego. In Freud's own words,

> Their [girls'] superego is never so inexorable, so impersonal, so independent of its emotional origins as we require it to be in men. . . . That they show less sense of justice than men, that they are less ready to submit to the great necessities of life, that they are more often influenced in their judgments by feelings of affection or hostility—all these would be amply accounted for by the modification in the formation of their superego which we have already inferred. (1948, pp. 196–197)

> Girls remain in it [the Electra conflict] for an indeterminate length of time; they demolish it last, and even so incompletely. In these circumstances the formation of the superego must suffer; it cannot attain the strength and independence which give it its cultural significance. (1933, p. 129)

In summary, Freud postulated a basic model for the acquisition of gender identity in the male, with a parallel model for the female. A primary assumption is the importance and superiority of the male phallus. It is so important to the boy that, in the throes of love for his mother, he fears that his father will harm the penis and he thus gives up his love for his mother and comes to identify with his father, thereby acquiring his own gender identity and introjecting the values of society. For the girl, in contrast, penis envy—an instant recognition of the superiority of the penis and a sense of envy over not having one—is primary. She turns her love away from her mother and toward her father in an attempt to regain the penis, but is unsuccessful. Her Electra complex is never completely resolved, and as a result her moral development is less adequate.

Criticisms of Psychoanalytic Theory   Numerous general criticisms and feminist criticisms of Freudian theory have been made.

From a scientific point of view, a major problem with psychoanalytic theory is that most of its concepts cannot be evaluated scientifically to see whether they are accurate. Freud believed that many of the most important forces in human behavior are unconscious, and thus they cannot be studied by any of the usual scientific techniques.

Another criticism that is often raised is that Freud derived his ideas almost exclusively from work with patients who sought therapy. Thus his theory may describe not so much human behavior as disturbed human behavior. In particular, his views on women may contain some truth about women who have problems of adjustment, but may have little to do with women who function well psychologically.

Many modern psychologists feel that Freud overemphasized biological determinants of human behavior and did not give sufficient attention to the influences of society and learning in shaping behavior. In particular, his views on the origin of differences between males and females, and on the nature of female personality, are heavily biological, relying mostly on anatomical differences—as the famous phrase has it, "Anatomy is destiny." In relying on anatomy as an explanation, Freud ignored the enormous forces of culture acting to create differences between females and males.

Feminists have raised numerous criticisms of Freudian theory, including those noted above (e.g., Lerman, 1986; Sherman, 1971; Weisstein, 1971). They are particularly critical of Freud's assumption that the clitoris and vagina are inferior to the penis. Freud's views have been termed **phallocentric**. The superiority of the penis may have seemed a reasonable concept in the Victorian era in which Freud wrote, but it is difficult to believe today, and certainly has no scientific documentation backing it.

Phallocentric: Male centered, or, specifically, penis centered.

A related question is whether little girls would, in fact, instantly recognize the superiority of the penis. Although psychoanalysts can provide case histories to document the existence of penis envy among women seeking therapy (see Focus 2.1), it remains to be demonstrated that penis envy is common among women, or that it has a large impact on their development. Indeed, empirical research indicates that in psychiatric studies the penis-envy theme is not nearly so common among women as is castration anxiety among men (Bosselman, 1960). This suggests that Freud, in writing from his own male point of view, accurately observed the castration anxiety of the male,[1] but was less accurate when constructing a parallel—penis envy—for the female.

---

[1]The 1994 case of Lorena Bobbitt and John Wayne Bobbitt speaks volumes on this issue. Lorena Bobbitt cut off her husband's penis with a knife, apparently following years of being beaten by him (surgeons were able to reattach the penis successfully). The story generated enormous publicity and a whole set of "Bobbitt jokes." Why? The case simultaneously touched on and allowed men to express their deep-seated castration anxieties. The publicity was particularly ironic because thousands of women each year have their genitals damaged in sexual assaults and female circumcision rituals. These cases receive little or no publicity.

Feminists also note the similarities between psychoanalytic theory and some of the myths about women discussed in Chapter 1. In this context, Freud seems simply to be articulating age-old myths and images about women in "scientific" language. The image of women as sinful and the source of evil is translated into the scientific-sounding "immature superego." Certainly Freud's phallocentrism is a good example of a male-as-normative or *androcentric* model. Basically, for Freud, a female is a castrated male. His model of development describes male development, female development being an inadequate variation on it.

Nonetheless, it is important to acknowledge Freud's contributions in his recognition of the importance of development in shaping human behavior and personality, and particularly in shaping gender identity.

Variations on a Freudian Theme

Various attempts have been made within the psychoanalytic school to reform Freud's theory. Here we will look briefly at some of the proposed variations that are relevant to women.

Karen Horney (1885–1952)   Several of the most prominent psychoanalytic theorists were women, and not surprisingly, they made some modifications on Freud's theory. Karen Horney's theoretical papers show an evolution over time in her own thinking. Originally Horney (pronounced Horn´-eye) accepted Freud's ideas wholeheartedly; in a 1924 paper she eagerly documented the origins of penis envy and of the castration complex in women. However, she soon became critical of these notions, and in a 1926 paper she pointed out that Freudian notions really articulate the childish views boys have of girls (much as I have pointed out that they represent age-old myths), and that Freud's psychological theory of women was phallocentric.

Her chief disagreement with Freud was over his notion that penis envy was the critical factor in female development. Horney used the master's tricks against him and postulated that the critical factor was male envy of the female, particularly of her reproductive potential (**womb envy**), and suggested that male achievement really represents an overcompensation for feelings of anatomical inferiority (a femininity complex). Bettelheim (1962) elaborated on this notion with observations on puberty rites of preliterate tribes, from which he concluded that womb envy is a strong force.

Womb envy: In Horney's analytic theory, the male's envy of woman's uterus and reproductive capacity.

This early work redefining psychoanalytic theory was done while Horney was in her native country, Germany. In 1932 she immigrated to the United States. There she continued her reformulations and articulated a personality theory that—in contrast to Freud's emphasis on biological and intrapsychic forces—emphasized cultural and social influences and human growth (O'Connell, 1990).

Three women who made substantial contributions to psychoanalytic theory: (Left) Helene Deutsch. (Center) Anna Freud. (Right) Karen Horney.

Indeed, she has the distinction of being the only woman whose theory is included in personality textbooks.

Helene Deutsch (1884–1982)   In 1944, Helene Deutsch published a weighty two-volume work entitled *The Psychology of Women,* the major attempt within the psychoanalytic school for a complete understanding of the psychological dynamics of women. Deutsch's major contribution was to extend Freud's analysis of female development, which essentially ended with the phallic stage and Electra complex, to later stages of development. She began in the prepuberty period because she saw the critical processes in woman's psychological development revolving around the transition from being a girl to being a woman. She then continued to describe female development and personality in adolescence and adulthood.

Deutsch largely retained a Freudian orthodoxy in her thinking. For example, she believed that to be a woman one must develop a "feminine core" in the personality, including the traits of narcissism, masochism, and passivity. She also held that instinct and intuition were very important to feminine personality.

Deutsch coined the term *masculinity complex* to refer to certain instances of women's failure to adjust. Such women are characterized by a predominance of masculine active and aggressive tendencies, which brings them into conflict with both their surrounding environment and their own feminine tendencies.

Deutsch viewed motherhood as the most critical feature in woman's psychological development. Indeed, the whole second volume of *The Psychology of*

Women was devoted exclusively to this topic, and she saw prepuberty and adolescence as mainly an anticipation of motherhood.

> Thus woman acquires a tendency to passivity that intensifies the passive nature inherent in her biology and anatomy. She passively awaits fecundation: her life is fully active and rooted in reality only when she becomes a mother. Until then everything that is feminine in the woman, physiology and psychology, is passive, receptive. (1944, Vol. I, p. 140)

Deutsch's view of the psychology of women is at once insightful and laden with the confusion of cultural and biological forces typical of psychoanalytic theory. For example, she believed that female passivity is a result of anatomy and biological functioning and failed to recognize that it is a culturally assigned part of the female role.

Anna Freud (1895–1982)   Although she did not focus specifically on the psychology of women, Anna Freud deserves mention here because she was one of the most—perhaps the most—outstanding contributor to psychoanalytic theory after Sigmund Freud (Fine, 1990). Most importantly, she was the founder of child psychoanalysis.

The youngest of the six children born to Sigmund and Martha Freud, she was the only one to take an interest in her father's work. She was also stimulated by the writings of Maria Montessori, and she originally trained to be an elementary school teacher.

The first major milestone in her career was the publication of her book *Introduction to the Technique of Child Analysis* in 1926. Her important work on ego psychology, *The Ego and the Mechanisms of Defense*, was published in 1936.

By 1938, Nazis had invaded Vienna. After a day of Gestapo interrogation, Anna Freud was convinced that she and her parents must flee to England. There she founded a school for children made homeless by the war. Her observations of these children and their disturbances led to a number of books, including *War and Children* (1943). Many of the major European psychoanalysts were murdered by Nazis, but Anna Freud lived to rebuild the movement following World War II.

Anna Freud's contributions to psychoanalysis were enormous. She founded child psychoanalysis and pioneered such techniques as play therapy for children.

Nancy Chodorow   Nancy Chodorow's book *The Reproduction of Mothering* (1978) is a more recent addition to the psychoanalytic literature. In her book Chodorow fuses psychoanalytic theory, sociological theory, and the feminist perspective (strange alliances, indeed!) in an attempt to answer the question, Why do women mother? That is, why is it that in all cultures it is the women who do almost all of the care of children? Her thesis, in brief, is that childcare done by women produces vastly different experiences for daughters than for sons.

Childcare done by mothers produces daughters who want to mother, and thus mothering reproduces itself. Women's mothering also produces sons who dominate and devalue women.

Infants start life in a state of total dependency, and given the current division of labor in most families, those dependency needs are satisfied almost exclusively by the mother. In addition, infants are narcissistic, or self-centered, and have trouble distinguishing between the primary caretaker—the mother—and themselves. Because mothers do such a good job of meeting their every need, infants blissfully assume that mothers have no interests besides themselves. As babies grow, perhaps as younger siblings are born, unpleasant reality eventually becomes clear as they come to understand that mothers do have other interests.

Chodorow contends that the early, intensely close relationship with the mother affects the sense of self and attitudes toward women, for both boys and girls. Both males and females continue to expect women to be caring and sacrificing, and that forever shapes their attitudes toward women. The girl's sense of self is profoundly influenced because her intense relationship to her mother is never entirely broken. Therefore, girls never see themselves as separate in the way boys do, and girls and women continue to define themselves more in *relational* terms.

Boys, in contrast, begin with the same intense attachment to the mother. But in order to develop a masculine identity, they must smash or repress the relationship to the mother. Thus masculinity comes to be defined negatively, as nonfemininity. Masculinity involves denying feminine maternal attachment. And thus all

Chodorow argues that mothering (most childcare being done by women) produces vastly different experiences for boys and girls, resulting in girls who want to mother and boys who dominate and devalue women.

women come to be devalued as part of the male's need to separate himself from his mother (and all women) and define a masculine identity for himself. Fathers in most families are essentially absent, and therefore their masculine qualities become idealized, and the notion of masculine superiority emerges. Simultaneously, men's capacity for parenting is reduced by their denial of relatedness.

In adulthood, men's relational needs are less than women's, and men's needs are satisfied by a relationship with a woman, in which they recapture the warmth of the infant relationship with their mother. Adult women have greater relational needs that cannot entirely be satisfied by a man. So women have babies, their relational needs are satisfied, and the cycle repeats itself.

According to Chodorow's analysis, her question, "Why do women mother?" is not so small as it might appear. Women's mothering perpetuates the whole division of labor by gender, for once women are committed to be the exclusive childrearers, men must do the other jobs necessary for society to continue. Furthermore, women's mothering creates the devaluation of women. Thus exclusive childrearing by women is a central issue.

How can Chodorow claim to have integrated feminism into her theory when her ideas so clearly smack of psychoanalytic theory? First, Chodorow engages in feminist reconstruction of some of Freud's ideas. For example, she argues that girls' penis envy results not from a girl's recognition of the inherent superiority of the penis (as Freud said), but rather from the fact that the penis symbolizes the power men have in our society. Second, Chodorow does not stop with her analysis of the family dynamics that produce the whole situation. She gives a prescription for social change to eliminate inequities for women. She says that the only way for the cycle to be broken is for men to begin participating equally in childcare. She believes that unless men do so, women will perpetually be devalued. As she concludes,

> Any strategy for change whose goal includes liberation from the constraints of an unequal social organization of gender must take account of the need for a fundamental reorganization of parenting, so that primary parenting is shared between men and women. (Chodorow, 1978, p. 215)

A few researchers have tested parts of Chodorow's theory. In one study, 4- and 5-year-olds were videotaped while playing with their mothers (Benenson, 1998). The results indicated that mother-daughter pairs were indeed closer to each other than mother-son pairs. This was true both physically   girls were physically closer to their mothers—and psychologically—mother-daughter pairs expressed more mutual enjoyment. These findings support Chodorow's assertion that girls are closer to their mothers and that boys separate themselves from their mothers.

Criticisms of Chodorow's theory have been raised as well (e.g., Lorber et al., 1981). First, the theory has a heterosexist bias. It explains in detail why children grow up heterosexual and seems to assume that all of them would, while making no attempt to understand lesbian development (Rich, 1980). Second, from the viewpoint of feminist theory, Chodorow's theory has been criticized for focusing exclusively on the impact of gender in people's lives, while ignoring the powerful influences of race and social class (Spelman, 1988). Third, most of the evidence Chodorow cites in her book is clinical—that is, it comes from individual histories of people seeking psychotherapy. As such, Chodorow's theory is open to the same criticism that was made of Freud's, namely, that it is based on disturbed personality and experience. On occasion, Chodorow does mention more solid scientific findings, but then proceeds to ignore them. For example, she mentions an important finding that parents tend to treat children quite similarly, regardless of gender, but that finding is not consistent with her theory, and so she dismisses it (Chodorow, 1978, p. 98). Finally, she advocates social change by having fathers participate equally in childcare, but her theory indicates that present-day fathers, who are the products of the last generation of mothering, should be incapable of childrearing. How can change ever be made, then? (Personally, I think that men right now are perfectly capable of being good childrearers, but that idea does not follow logically from her theory.) Nonetheless, many feminists agree that men must participate more equally in childcare.

Sociobiology and Evolutionary Psychology

Sociobiology is a controversial theory initially proposed by Harvard biologist E. O. Wilson in his book *Sociobiology: The New Synthesis* (1975), a massive, 700-page work filled with countless examples from insect life. He followed this with a popularized version, *On Human Nature* (1978).

> **Sociobiology:** The application of evolutionary theory to explaining the social behavior of animals, including people.

Wilson originally defined *sociobiology* as "the systematic study of the biological basis of all social behavior" (1975, p. 4). But I think a better definition is provided by David Barash (1982): "Sociobiology is the application of evolutionary theory to understanding the social behavior of animals, including humans." That is, sociobiologists are specifically concerned with understanding how social behaviors—such as aggression or caring for the young—are the product of evolution. In fact, a better term for this theory would probably be *socioevolution,* but I will stick to *sociobiology* because it is the standard term.

To understand what sociobiology has to say about women and gender roles, we must first discuss evolutionary theory. Evolution, as modern biologists understand it, is a product of **natural selection,** a mechanism first proposed by Charles Darwin. His basic observation was that living things overreproduce—that is, they produce far more young than would be needed simply to replace themselves. Yet population sizes remain relatively constant. Therefore, many individuals must not survive. There must be differential survival, with the fittest organisms surviving and others not. In popular concep-

> **Natural selection:** According to Darwin, the process by which the fittest animals survive, reproduce, and pass their genes on to the next generation, whereas animals that are less fit do not reproduce and therefore do not pass on their genes.

tions the "fittest" animal is the most aggressive, but evolutionary theory defines fitness differently. **Fitness** is defined in this theory as the relative number of genes an animal contributes to the next generation. The bottom line is producing lots of offspring, specifically healthy, viable offspring. Thus a man who jogs 10 miles a day,

Fitness: In evolutionary theory, an animal's relative contribution of genes to the next generation.

lifts weights, and has a 50-inch chest but whose sperm count is zero would be considered to have zero fitness according to sociobiologists. Over generations, there is differential reproduction, the fittest individuals producing the most offspring. Genes that produce fitness characteristics become more frequent, and fitness characteristics ("adaptive" characteristics) become more frequent; genes and associated characteristics that produce poor fitness become less frequent.

The basic idea of the sociobiologists is that the evolutionary theory of natural selection can be applied to social behaviors. That is, a particular form of social behavior—let's say, caring for one's young—would be adaptive, in the sense of increasing one's reproductive fitness. Other social behaviors—for example, female infanticide—would be maladaptive, decreasing one's reproductive fitness. Over the many generations of natural selection that have occurred, the maladaptive behaviors should have been weeded out, and we should be left with social behaviors that are adaptive because they are the product of evolutionary selection. From this logic flows the *central theorem of sociobiology:* When a social behavior is genetically influenced, the animal should behave so as to maximize fitness (Barash, 1982).

With this as background, let us now consider some specific arguments of sociobiologists that are of special relevance to women.

Parental Investment   One of the things sociobiologists have attempted to explain is why it is typically the female of the species that does most of the care of offspring. Remember that this phenomenon was also central to Chodorow's theory, but the sociobiologist offers a very different explanation for it. The sociobiologist's explanation rests on the concept of **parental investment,** which refers to behaviors or other investments of the parent with respect to the offspring that increase the offspring's chance of survival, but that also cost the parent something (Trivers, 1972). This all becomes relevant to gender because females generally have a much larger parental investment in their offspring than

Parental investment: In sociobiology, behaviors or other investments in the offspring by the parent that increase the offspring's chance of survival.

males do. At the moment of conception, the female has the greater parental investment—she has just contributed one of her precious eggs. The male has contributed merely a sperm. Eggs are precious because they are large cells, and the female produces only one per month (at least in humans, and perhaps only one or several per year in other species of mammals). Sperm are "cheap" because they are small cells and are produced in enormous numbers. For example, there are 300 million sperm in the average human male ejaculate, and a man can produce that number again in 24 to 48 hours. So at the moment of conception the female has invested much with her precious egg, but the male has invested little with a single sperm. In mammals, the female then proceeds to gestate the young (for a period of nine months in humans). Here again she makes an enormous investment of her body's resources, which otherwise could have been invested in doing something else. Then the offspring are born, and the female, at least among mammals, nurses them, once again investing time and energy.

The next step in the logic is this: It is most adaptive for whichever parent has the greater parental investment to continue to care for the offspring. Here we have the female, who has invested her precious egg, her gestation, and her nursing; it would be evolutionary insanity for her to abandon the offspring when they still need more care in order to survive. In contrast, the male has invested relatively little and his best reproductive strategy is to "sleep around" and impregnate as many females as possible, producing more offspring carrying his genes. This works particularly well if he can count on the female to take care of the offspring so that they survive.

In short, the sociobiologist says that women are the ones who do the childcare for two reasons. The first is that the female has a greater parental investment and therefore it is adaptive for her to continue to care for her offspring. The second reason arises from a basic fact: Maternity is always certain, whereas paternity is not. The female is sure that the offspring are hers. The sociobiologist would say that she knows that those young carry her genes. The male cannot be sure that they are his offspring, carrying his genes. It is thus adaptive for the female—it increases her fitness—to care for the offspring to make sure that they, and her genes, survive. It does not increase the male's fitness to care for offspring that may not carry his genes. Therefore, females do the childcare.

There are exceptions to this pattern, and they are worth considering. One is songbirds, who are notable because the male and female participate quite equally and cooperatively in care of their young (Barash, 1982). But sociobiologists believe that their theory can explain the exception as well as the general rule. Songbirds have a monogamous mating system that makes paternity a near certainty. Thus it is adaptive for the male to care for the young because he can be sure that they carry his genes. In addition, young birds require an enormous amount of food per day. It is doubtful that they could survive on the amount of food brought to them by a single parent. Thus it is highly adaptive for both parents to participate in care of the offspring, and would be highly maladaptive for fathers or mothers to neglect them.

Sociobiologists extend the logic of evolution to explain why female orgasm evolved in humans. The background is that female orgasm is thought to exist in few, if any, other species. Why, then, does it exist in humans?

Sociobiologists say that human female orgasm has evolved because human babies are born particularly helpless, dependent, and in need of parental care (Barash, 1982). Essentially, they need two parents in order to survive. A monogamous mating system, with permanent pairing of mother and father, would be adaptive and favored in evolution. The female orgasm (and the human female's continuous interest in sex at all phases of the menstrual cycle) thus evolved in order to hold together that permanent pair.

Sociobiologists also extend their theorizing to explain the **double standard**—that is, that among humans the male is allowed, even encouraged, to be promiscuous, whereas the female is punished for engaging in promiscuous sex and instead is very careful and selective about whom she has sex with (Barash, 1982). The explanation has to do with that precious egg and those cheap sperm. It is adaptive for her to be careful of what happens to the egg, whereas it is adaptive for him to distribute sperm to as many females as possible. Anticipating her greater parental investment, the female must also be careful about whose genes she mixes with her own.

> **Double standard:** Tolerance of male promiscuity and disapproval of female promiscuity.

Sexual Selection   Sexual selection is an evolutionary mechanism originally proposed by Darwin to act in parallel to natural selection and to produce gender differences. Essentially, sexual selection means that different selection pressures act on males and females, and thus males and females become different. **Sexual selection** consists of two processes: (1) Members of one gender (usually males) compete among themselves to gain mating privileges with members of the other gender (usually females); and (2) members of the other gender (usually females) have preferences for certain members of the first gender (usually males) and decide which of them they are willing to mate with. In short, males fight and females choose. Process (1) neatly explains why the males of most species are larger and more aggressive than the females—aggression is adaptive for males in competition, and they are the product of sexual selection. Sexual selection explains, for example, why among many species of birds it is the male that has the gorgeous plumage while the female is dowdy. Plumage is a way that males compete among themselves, and females are attracted to the most gorgeous males. Females, on the other hand, in their roles as choosers, need not be gorgeous and have not been selected to be so. Perhaps they have been selected for wisdom. (I said that, not a sociobiologist!)

> **Sexual selection:** According to Darwin, the processes by which members of one gender (usually males) compete with each other for mating privileges with members of the other gender (usually females), and members of the other gender (females) choose to mate only with certain preferred members of the first gender (males).

Sexual selection, then, is a mechanism that is used to explain gender differences. It is particularly useful in explaining the greater size, strength, and aggressiveness of males.

Many more examples could be given, but you have seen the main ones dealing with women's issues. The thrust of the argument is clear: The sociobiologist argues that the social behaviors we see in animals and humans today evolved because these behaviors were adaptive, and they continue to be biologically programmed.

Sociobiologists argue that gender differences in aggression in humans and other species are a result of sexual selection in evolution. Here two males fight while the female looks on.

Evolutionary Psychology   Evolutionary psychology is an updated and more elaborate version of sociobiology, proposed by psychologist David Buss (1995; Buss & Schmitt, 1993; see also Tooby & Cosmides, 1992). The basic idea is that humans' complex psychological mechanisms are the result of evolution based on natural selection. These evolved psychological mechanisms exist because, over thousands of years, they solved problems of survival or reproduction. For example, according to evolutionary psychology, fear of snakes is common precisely because it helped people avoid being bitten and poisoned by snakes.

Buss proposed *sexual strategies theory* as a way of articulating the evolved psychological mechanisms that are related to sexuality and, according to the theory, explain certain psychological gender differences (Buss & Schmitt, 1993). This theory distinguishes between short-term mating strategies (e.g., a one-night stand) and long-term mating strategies (e.g., married with children), and it proposes that women and men had different problems to solve in short-term as well as long-term mating. Because it is to men's evolutionary advantage to inseminate many females, men put more of their energy into short-term mating. Women, having the greater parental investment, are more interested in ensuring that their offspring survive and therefore put more of their energy into long-term mating strategies that will ensure the long-term commitment of a man who will provide resources for them and their children. Men's evolutionary problems centered on identifying fertile females and removing the uncertainty of paternity. Women, in contrast, had to identify men willing to make a long-term commitment, who were also willing and able to provide resources. Thus men have evolved psychological mechanisms that lead them to prefer as sexual partners women who are in their 20s—even if the men are in their 60s—because women are at their peak fertility in their 20s. Men are notoriously jealous about their mates' sexual infidelity because of the problem of paternity certainty. Women have evolved psychological mechanisms that lead them to prefer long-term mates who possess resources such as wealth, or qualities such as ambition or a law degree, that should indicate good capacity to provide resources in the future. Buss (1989) provided data supporting his theory from a study in which he collected data on mate preferences in 37 distinct cultures around the world and found results generally consistent with his predictions.

Feminist Criticism   Feminists are not exactly delighted with sociobiology and evolutionary psychology (for feminist critiques, see Hrdy, 1981; Janson-Smith, 1980; Weisstein, 1982). Three basic criticisms have been raised. First, many feminists are wary of biological explanations of anything. The reason is that biology always seems to end up being a convenient rationalization for perpetuating the status quo. For example, the sociobiologist's belief is that the greater aggression and dominance of males are a result of sexual selection and are controlled by genes. Therefore, men are genetically dominant, and women are genetically subordinate, and the subordinate status of women will have to continue because it is genetic. That kind of logic is a red flag to a feminist. Sociobiologists are not so naive that they ignore environmental influences entirely, and so the argument becomes a question of emphasis, sociobiologists emphasizing biology and feminists emphasizing environment.

Second, feminists object that sociobiologists do a highly selective reading of both data and theories. Sociobiologists tend to view data from an *androcentric* (male-centered) perspective and to talk selectively about those studies that confirm their androcentric theory, ignoring those studies that contradict it. For example, the female chimpanzee—the chimpanzee is our nearest evolutionary relative—is notoriously promiscuous (Janson-Smith, 1980). When she is in estrus ("heat"), she mates indiscriminately with many males. That does not fit into sociobiology, which says that she should be choosy about the male with whom she mates and that the most aggressive, dominant male should be the only one to have the privilege of inseminating her. The sociobiologists tend to ignore chimpanzees.

As another instance of androcentric bias, consider the case of a famous young female macaque (monkey) named Imo, living with her troop on an island off Japan.

> Scientists provisioned the troop there with sweet potatoes. Imo discovered that washing sweet potatoes got the sand off. Her discovery quickly spread among the other juniors in the troop, who then taught their mothers, who

in turn, taught their infants. Adult males never learned it. Next, scientists flung grains of wheat in the sand to see what the troop would do. Rather than laboriously picking the wheat out of the sand grain by grain, Imo discovered how to separate the wheat from the sand in one operation. Again this spread from Imo's peers to mothers and infants, and, again, adult males never learned it. The fact that these Japanese macaques had a rudimentary culture has been widely heralded. (Weisstein, 1982, p. 46)

Had the genders been reversed, with Imo being a male and the females being unable to learn, one can imagine the attention these facts would have been given by sociobiologists. They would have made much of the genius of the male and the lack of intelligence of females. As it is, Imo's gender is not discussed, and the learning failure of the males is similarly ignored.[2] Sociobiologists, then, seem to ignore many animal examples that contradict human stereotypes.

From a feminist perspective, even the sociobiologists' attention to theory is selective and androcentric. For example, sexual selection, as noted above, contains two parts. The part that produces competition and aggression in males has received much attention from sociobiologists. But they have ignored the second part, in which females make choices among males. The second part could be used as an explanation for human females' being more intelligent, more perceptive, or more powerful and controlling than human males, but that avenue of thought is never explored by sociobiologists.

Sociobiologists also rely heavily on data from nonindustrial societies, specifically hunter-gatherer societies that are supposed to be like those that existed at the dawn of the human species, millions of years ago. Once again, the emphasis is androcentrically selective. The sociobiologist emphasizes "man the hunter" and how he evolved to be aggressive and have great physical prowess. In discussing this, Wilson (1978, p. 127) makes much of how natural selection for these traits is reflected in men's current superiority in Olympic track events. Later on the same page, he mentions that women are superior in precision archery and small-bore rifle shooting in the Olympics, but does not seem to see this as inconsistent with the evolution of only man as the hunter. "Woman the gatherer" is ignored, although she may have formed the foundation for early human social organization (Janson-Smith, 1980).

Third, sociobiology has been criticized for resting on an outmoded version of evolutionary theory that modern biologists consider naive (Gould, 1987). For example, sociobiology has focused mainly on the individual's struggle for survival, whereas modern biologists focus on more complex issues such as the survival of the group and the species, and the evolution of a successful adaptation between the species and its environment.

---

[2]In case you are not sufficiently impressed with Imo, have you figured out a good way to separate the wheat from the sand? Imo did it by throwing both into the water, where the wheat floated and the sand sank to the bottom.

The feminist criticisms, then, are that sociobiology can rationalize and perpetuate the subordination of women; that its evidence rests on a selective, androcentric citing of the data, ignoring many contradictions; and that it relies on an outdated and oversimplified view of evolution.

I can't resist pointing out one other criticism, which is of a general scientific nature rather than specifically feminist. Sociobiologists fail to specify the biological mechanisms from evolution to behavior. Their basic arguments are that evolution occurred over millions of years and, voilà, we have a certain pattern of gender differences in the 21st century. But evolution can act only through genes, and genes influence behavior because they direct the synthesis of certain proteins and not others, leading to differing levels of biochemicals such as neurotransmitters or hormones. This is the era of the Human Genome Project, in which specific genes that create specific medical conditions and behaviors are being identified. Sociobiology has failed to incorporate this work, and fails to specify which genes and biochemicals are responsible for the patterns of gender differences that they claim have evolved.

Social psychologists Alice Eagly and Wendy Wood (1999) have provided a probing critique of Buss's evolutionary psychology and its explanations for psychological gender differences. They have also articulated an alternative, social-structural explanation for Buss's findings that explains gender differences as resulting from women's and men's different positions in the social structure.

Eagly and Wood's alternative explanation, **social-structural theory**, emphasizes not cross-cultural universals, but rather the variability across cultures in patterns of gender differences. According to this view, a society's division of labor by gender drives all other gender differences in behavior. Psychological gender differences result from individuals' accommodations or adaptations to the particular restrictions on or opportunities for their gender in their society. Social structuralists acknowledge biological differences between women and men, such as differences in size and strength and women's capacity to bear and nurse children, but emphasize that these physical differences are important mainly because they are amplified by cultural beliefs. Men's greater size and strength have led them to pursue activities such as warfare that in turn gave them greater status, wealth, and power than women. Once men were in these roles of greater status and power, their behavior became more dominant and, similarly, women's behavior accommodated and became more subordinate. The gendered division of labor, in which women were responsible for home and family, led women to acquire role-related skills such as cooking and caring for children. In this way, women acquired nurturing behaviors and a facility for relationships. Men, specializing in paid employment in male-dominated occupations, adapted with assertive and independent behaviors.

> **Social-structural theory:** A theory of the origin of psychological gender differences that focuses on the social structure, particularly the division of labor between men and women.

Eagly and Wood (1999) reanalyzed Buss's 37-cultures data to test the predictions of social-structural theory. Their basic hypothesis was that the greater the gender differences in status in a culture, the greater would be the psychological gender differences; societies characterized by gender equality would show far less psychological gender differentiation. Conveniently, the United Nations maintains a database that indexes gender equality in all nations. Correlations were high between societies' gender inequality and the magnitude of the difference between women and men in that society on psychological measures of mate preferences. If mate preferences were determined by evolution thousands of years ago, they should not vary across cultures and they definitely should not correlate with a society's gender equality or lack thereof. These findings provide powerful evidence in support of social-structural theory.

Feminist Sociobiology?   Primatologist Sarah Blaffer Hrdy considers herself to be a feminist sociobiologist. Impossible, you say? In a wonderful book, *Mother Nature: Maternal Instincts and How They Shape the Human Species* (1999), Hrdy assembled the evidence on evolutionary forces on mothering behaviors in humans and other species, while at the same time taking a decidedly feminist approach. Moreover, she has the biological sophistication and complex knowledge of primate behavior that many sociobiologists and evolutionary psychologists lack.

Hrdy's basic argument is that women have evolved to care for their children and ensure their survival, but in reality these evolved tendencies are miles away from romanticized Victorian notions of all-loving, self-sacrificing motherhood. Hrdy notes, for example, that female primates of all species combine work and family—that is, they must be ambitious, successful foragers or their babies will starve. Males are not the only ones who have status hierarchies; a female chimp's status within her group has a powerful influence on whether her offspring survive and what the status of those offspring will be when they reach adulthood. In contrast to other sociobiologists' views of females as being highly selective about whom they mate with, Hrdy notes that female primates of many species will mate promiscuously with males invading their troop, even if they are already pregnant. Essentially, the females seem to be trying to create some confusion about paternity, because males happily commit infanticide against infants that are not theirs but generally work to protect infants they have sired. Under these circumstances the best thing a pregnant female can do for her unborn infant is to have sex with strangers! Hrdy's arguments subvert many ideas about traditional gender roles in humans and whether these roles have an evolutionary basis.

Social Learning Theory

A popular explanation for gender differences in behavior is "conditioning." That is, boys and girls act appropriately for their gender because they have been rewarded for doing some things and punished for doing others. The notion is that principles of operant conditioning explain the acquisition of gender roles. Thus, for girls, some behaviors are rewarded (positively reinforced), whereas others either are not rewarded or are even punished, so that the girl comes to perform the rewarded behaviors more frequently and the unrewarded ones less frequently or not at all. For example, little girls are rewarded for being quiet and obedient, whereas little boys are rewarded for athletics and achievement. Consequently, children acquire gender-typed behaviors because they are rewarded or approved.

Social learning theory is a major theoretical system in psychology, designed to describe the process involved in human development (see Bandura & Walters, 1963). In particular, it has been used to explain the development of gender differences (Lott & Maluso, 1993; Mischel, 1966). In explaining the shaping of children's behavior, social learning theory uses the notion of **reinforcement** described above—that is, the idea that rewards and punishments are given differentially to boys and girls for gender-typed behaviors, and that children therefore come to perform the rewarded, gender-appropriate behaviors more frequently and the punished, gender-inappropriate behaviors less frequently. But social learning theory also emphasizes the importance of two additional processes: **imitation** and **observational learning.** Imitation means simply that children do what they see others doing. Observational learning refers to situations in which children learn by observing the behavior of others, even though they may not actually perform the behavior at the time, perhaps not using the information until months or years later. These three mechanisms, then—reinforcement, imitation, and observational learning—are thought to underlie the process of gender typing, that is, the acquisition of gender-typed behaviors, according to social learning theory.

> **Reinforcement:** In operant conditioning, something that occurs after a behavior and makes the behavior more likely to occur in the future.

> **Imitation:** When people do what they see others doing.

> **Observational learning:** When a person observes someone doing something, and then does it at a later time.

Children's imitation is motivated partly by the power of authority figures, so they are particularly likely to imitate parents or other adults. With regard to gender-role learning, the theory assumes that children tend to imitate the same-gender parent and other same-gender adults more than opposite-gender adults. That is, the little girl imitates her mother and other women more than she does men. This mechanism of imitation helps to explain the acquisition of the complex and subtle aspects of gender roles that probably have not been the object of reinforcements. Furthermore, imitation and reinforcement may interact. For example, the girl may imitate a behavior of her mother's and then be rewarded for it, once again furthering the process of gender typing.

The child does not actually have to perform a behavior in order to learn it. A behavior may become part of the child's repertoire through observational learning. Such information may be stored up for use perhaps 10 or 15 years later, when a situation in adolescence or adulthood calls for a knowledge of gender appropriate behaviors. For example, a young girl may observe her mother caring for an infant brother or sister. Although the little girl may not perform any infant-care behaviors at the time, much less be rewarded for them, she nonetheless

Children learn gender roles in part by imitation of adults.

may store up the information about infant care for use when she herself is a mother. Once again, gender typing occurs through mechanisms other than reinforcement.

In more advanced learning, children learn to anticipate the consequences of their actions. Here also, an action need not be performed for the child to understand the reinforcements or punishments that will result. The little girl knows in advance that her attempts to join Little League will be met with opposition, and perhaps even with punishments.

According to social learning theory, then, gender typing results from differential rewards and punishments, as well as learning in the absence of reinforcement: by imitation of same-gender models and by observational learning.

Evidence for Social Learning Theory   Social learning theory has stimulated a great deal of research aimed at documenting the existence—or nonexistence—of the mechanisms it proposes. This research makes it possible to assess the adequacy of the social learning model for the development of gender differences.

There have been numerous demonstrations of the effectiveness of imitation and reinforcements in shaping children's behavior, in particular gender-typed behaviors such as aggression. A good example is a classic study by the psychologist Albert Bandura (1965). In the first phase of this experiment, children were randomly assigned to one of three groups and shown one of three films. In all the films, an adult model was performing aggressive behavior, but in one film the model was rewarded; in another, punished; and in the third, left alone without consequences. The children's aggressive behavior was then observed. As the social learning approach would predict, children who had viewed the model being punished performed the least aggressive behavior. Furthermore, and consistent with the findings of many other investigators (see Chapter 3), boys performed more aggressive behavior than girls. In the second phase of the experiment, the children were offered attractive reinforcements (pretty sticker pictures and juice treats) for performing as many of the model's aggressive responses as they could remember. Gender differences nearly disappeared in this phase, and girls performed nearly as many aggressive behaviors as boys.

This experiment illustrates several important points. The first phase demonstrated that children do imitate, and that they do so differentially depending on the perceived consequences of the behavior. Notice that in this phase the children themselves were not actually reinforced, but simply observed the model being reinforced. The second phase illustrated how gender differences in aggressive behavior can be influenced by reinforcements. When girls were given equal reinforcement for aggression, they were nearly as aggressive as boys. Certainly the experiment is evidence of the power of imitation and reinforcement in shaping children's behavior.

There is evidence that parents treat boys and girls differently, and that they differentially reward some—though certainly not all—behaviors in boys and girls (Block, 1978; Sherman, 1978). In one study, based on a review of 172 studies of parents' socialization practices, the authors concluded that there was a significant tendency for parents to encourage gender-typed activities in their children, especially in areas such as play and household chores (Lytton & Romney, 1991). Interestingly, in some areas where one might expect differential socialization of boys and girls, no differences were found. For example, boys and girls were equally encouraged to achieve.

Of course, there is plenty of evidence of gender stereotyped role models in the media. The findings are discussed in Chapter 7.

Cognitive Social Learning Theory   Cognitive approaches have become popular in psychology in the last several decades. (We will consider cognitive theories of gender development in later sections.) Not to be outdone, social learning theorists have incorporated cognitive approaches into their theories, which are now called cognitive social learning theory or social cognitive theory (Bandura, 1986; Bussey & Bandura, 1999). The emphasis on reinforcements, punishments, and modeling remains, but to those are added cognitive processes such as attention, self-regulation, and self-efficacy.

Every day, children observe thousands of behaviors in the complex environment surrounding them, yet they imitate or model only a few of them. *Attention* is the cognitive process that weeds out most of the behaviors that are irrelevant to the child and focuses on the few that are most relevant. Gender makes some behaviors relevant and others not. Once children can differentiate males and females, they pay more attention to same-gender than to other-gender models (Bussey & Bandura, 1992). And children model the behaviors that they attend to, ignoring all the others.

According to cognitive social learning theory, as children develop, regulation of their behavior shifts from externally imposed rewards and punishments to internalized standards and self-sanctions. As children learn to regulate themselves, they guide their own behavior, a process known as *self-regulation;* and as they learn the significance of gender, they monitor and regulate their own behavior according to internalized gender norms. Children are more likely to monitor their behavior for gender-appropriateness when they are in mixed-gender groups than when they are in single-gender groups (Bussey & Bandura, 1999).

Self-efficacy is an important concept in social cognitive theory. Self-efficacy should not be confused with self-esteem, which refers to our global sense of how good we feel about ourselves. Rather, self-efficacy refers to our beliefs about our

> **Self-efficacy:** A person's belief in her or his ability to accomplish a particular task.

ability to accomplish something, to produce a particular level of attainment. Self-efficacy involves our beliefs about how well we can perform in a given situation. People can have a global sense of self-efficacy, but efficacy beliefs also tend to vary depending on the area or task. You may feel certain that you can earn an A in a psychology course but have no confidence that you can pass a Spanish class.

Efficacy beliefs are extremely important in individuals' lives. They affect the goals we set for ourselves, how much time and effort we put into attaining the goal, and whether we persist in the face of difficulties. People with strong efficacy beliefs redouble their efforts in the face of challenges, whereas those with a low sense of efficacy give up.

Efficacy beliefs, for example, play a large role in career choice and pursuing a career, perhaps over many years of necessary education (Bandura et al., 2001). Occupations are highly gendered (see Chapter 9). As girls observe teachers and see many women successfully doing the job, their sense of self-efficacy at being a teacher increases. But when they observe few or perhaps no women among airline pilots, their sense of efficacy at being a pilot declines and they don't even consider becoming one. Too bad. Pilots make more than $100,000 a year. Teachers don't.

Overall, though, cognitive social learning theory is an optimistic theory for those who want to see social change in gender roles. It says that children can and will learn a very different set of gender roles if powerful others—for example, parents and the media—change the behaviors they reinforce and model.

Cognitive-Developmental Theory

In terms of impact, perhaps the closest equivalent in the second half of the 20th century to Freud's work in the first half was the developmental theory founded by Jean Piaget, together with his colleague Bärbel Inhelder. Lawrence Kohlberg (1966) then extended Piaget and Inhelder's cognitive principles to the realm of gender roles.

Much of Piaget and Inhelder's thinking arose from their observations of the errors children made in answering questions such as those asked on intelligence tests. They concluded that these errors did not indicate that the children were stupid or ignorant, but rather that they had a different worldview, or *cognitive organization,* from that of adults. Piaget and Inhelder discovered that the cognitive organizations of children change systematically over time, and they constructed a stage theory of cognitive (intellectual) development to describe the progression of these changes. Interestingly, concepts of gender and gender identity undergo developmental changes parallel to the development of other concepts.

Gender Identity   Around the age of 18 months to 2 years, children form a concept of **gender identity;** that is, they know whether they are boys or girls. Soon after this, they learn to identify the gender of their mother and father, and then other people around them generally. However, at this stage they do not realize that gender is a permanent characteristic. That is, a girl may think that when she grows up she can be a boy if she wants to (Kohlberg, 1966).

> **Gender identity:** In cognitive developmental theory, the individual's knowledge that she or he is a female or male.

Gender Roles and Gender Constancy   If you ask a 3-year-old girl whether she is a boy or a girl, she will answer correctly that she is a girl. But if you ask her whether she can grow up to be a daddy, she will incorrectly answer yes. A 6- or 7-year-old girl will not make this error. The 3-year-old understands the concept of gender, but does not yet have the concept of **gender constancy**—the knowledge that gender is a permanent part of the self or identity. The development of these concepts was amusingly illustrated by Kohlberg (1966, p. 95):

> **Gender constancy:** According to cognitive-developmental theory, a child's understanding that gender is a permanent, unchanging characteristic of the self.

> (Jimmy has just turned four, his friend Johnny is four and a half)

JOHNNY: I'm going to be an airplane builder when I grow up.

JIMMY: When I grow up, I'll be a mommy.

JOHNNY: No, you can't be a mommy. You have to be a daddy.

JIMMY: No, I'm going to be a mommy.

JOHNNY: No, you're not a girl, you can't be a mommy.

JIMMY: Yes, I can.

Apparently Johnny has acquired the concept of gender constancy, whereas Jimmy hasn't.

According to Kohlberg, the acquisition of this basic concept of gender constancy (around the ages of 4 to 6) is the crucial basis for the acquisition of gender roles. Once the little girl knows she is a girl and will always be female, this gender identity becomes an important part of personal identity. Gender identity then determines basic valuations (whether a person or behavior is believed to be "good" or "bad"). Motivated to have a positive sense of self, the girl comes to see femaleness as good. She then associates this valuation with cultural stereotypes, so that the female role becomes attractive to her. And finally she identifies with her mother, who is a readily available example of the female role the girl wishes to acquire. Thus children are motivated to adopt gender roles as part of their attempt to understand reality and to develop a stable and positive self-concept.

Cognitive-developmental theory essentially views gender-role learning as one aspect of cognitive development. The child learns a set of rules regarding what males do and what females do, and behaves accordingly. In this theory, gender-role learning is not externally imposed, but rather is largely self-motivated. The child essentially engages in self-socialization and self-selects the behaviors to be learned and performed on the basis of rules regarding the gender appropriateness of the behavior.

Criticisms of Cognitive-Developmental Theory   Kohlberg's basic argument is that the acquisition of the concept of gender constancy is the crucial step in gender typing. Once these concepts have been formed, say, at around 5 to 7 years of age, the child essentially "self-socializes." What evidence is there supporting these ideas?

First, a concept of gender constancy clearly develops in children around the ages of 5 to 7. Evidence comes from children's comments such as those quoted earlier in this chapter and from their responses to direct questioning by psychologists (e.g., Marcus & Overton, 1978). There is also some evidence that kindergartners who have acquired gender constancy prefer to observe same-gender models, as compared with opposite-gender models, whereas children who do not yet have a concept of gender constancy display no such preference (Slaby, 1974, cited in Maccoby & Jacklin, 1974, p. 365). Preschoolers who have acquired gender constancy are more stereotyped in their views of adult occupations than are preschoolers who do not have gender constancy (O'Keefe & Hyde, 1983).

However, children's gender-typed interests appear when they are far too young to have acquired the concept of gender constancy (Maccoby & Jacklin, 1974; O'Keefe & Hyde, 1983). That is, gender-typed toy and game preferences appear when children are 2 or 3, yet children do not develop gender constancy until they are between the ages of 5 and 7. This is inconsistent with Kohlberg's theory, which would say that gender-typed interests should not appear until after gender constancy develops.

It seems reasonable to conclude that Kohlberg's notion of gender constancy and "self-socialization" explains some aspects of gender-role development, but that other mechanisms—such as those specified by social learning theory—are also functioning.

According to the theory, one of the child's main motives for adopting a gender role is the power and value the child sees in that role; yet the female role has less power and value. Is the girl therefore less motivated to adopt her role than the boy is? Kohlberg (1966, pp. 121–122) attempted to avoid this problem by saying that girls are motivated by the competency and "niceness" they perceive the female role to represent, but the real status issues remain unresolved.

Kohlberg on Moral Development   Kohlberg's other major contribution to psychology was his analysis of moral development, that is, children's changing cognitions or understandings about morality (Kohlberg, 1969; Colby et al., 1983). First, you need to know how Kohlberg studied moral development and how he determined that there are stages in the development of moral reasoning.

Kohlberg studied moral thought by presenting children or adults with a moral dilemma, of which the following is an example:

> In Europe, a woman was near death from a special kind of cancer. There was one drug that the doctors thought might save her. It was a form of radium that a druggist in the same town had recently discovered. The drug was expensive to make, but the druggist was charging 10 times what the drug cost him to make. He paid $200 for the radium and charged $2,000 for a small dose of the drug. The sick woman's husband, Heinz, went to everyone he knew to borrow the money, but he could only get together about $1,000, which is half of what it cost. He told the druggist that his wife was dying and asked him to sell it cheaper or let him pay later. But the druggist said, "No, I discovered the drug and I'm going to make money from it." So Heinz gets desperate and considers breaking into the man's store to steal the drug for his wife.

Following presentation of the dilemma, the participant is asked a number of questions, such as whether Heinz should steal the drug and why. The important part is not whether the person says Heinz should or should not steal, but rather the person's answer to the question, Why?—which reflects the stage of development of moral reasoning.

Based on his research, Kohlberg concluded that people go through a series of three levels in their moral reasoning as they mature, and that each level is divided into two stages, for a total of six stages. These stages are defined on the left side of Table 2.1. In Level I, **preconventional morality,** children (usually preschoolers) have little sense of rules and obey simply to avoid punishments or to obtain rewards. For example, Heinz should not steal because he

Preconventional morality: In Kohlberg's theory, the earliest stage of moral reasoning, in which children do the right thing simply to gain rewards or avoid punishments.

TABLE 2.1
Kohlberg's and Gilligan's Understanding of Moral Development

Kohlberg's Levels and Stages	Kohlberg's Definition	Gilligan's Levels
Level I. Preconventional morality		
Stage 1. Punishment orientation	Obey rules to avoid punishment	Concern for the self and survival
Stage 2. Naive reward orientation	Obey rules to get rewards, share in order to get returns	
Level II. Conventional morality		
Stage 3. Good-boy/ good-girl orientation	Conform to rules that are defined by others' approval/disapproval	Concern for being responsible, caring for others
Stage 4. Authority orientation	Rigid conformity to society's rules, law-and-order mentality, avoid censure for rule breaking	
Level III. Postconventional morality		
Stage 5. Social-contract orientation	More flexible understanding that we obey rules because they are necessary for social order, but the rules could be changed if there were better alternatives	Concern for self and others as interdependent
Stage 6. Morality of individual principles and conscience	Behavior conforms to internal principles (justice, equality) to avoid self-condemnation, and sometimes may violate society's rules	

might get caught and put in jail. In Level II, **conventional morality,** children (usually beginning in elementary school) are well aware of society's rules and laws and conform to them rigidly; there is a law-and-order mentality and a desire to look good in front of others. For example, Heinz should not steal be-

Conventional morality:
In Kohlberg's theory, an intermediate level of moral reasoning, in which children and adults understand rules and obey them rigidly.

cause stealing is against the law. Finally, in Level III, **postconventional morality,** a person transcends the rules and laws of society and instead behaves in accordance with an internal, self-defined set of ethical principles. For example, it is acceptable for Heinz to steal because human life is more important than property. In Level III, it might be judged acceptable to violate laws in some instances in which they were unjust. The perfect example of Level III morality is the life of Mahatma Gandhi, as shown so clearly in the movie *Gandhi.* For him, equality and freedom were self-accepted, internalized values that allowed him to violate the laws of his country, and he persisted in following his own principles despite the disapproval of authorities, which was so severe that he was beaten.

> **Postconventional morality:** In Kohlberg's theory, the most mature level of moral reasoning, in which the person understands that rules are not absolute, but rather are part of a social contract; the person behaves from internalized ethical principles.

According to Kohlberg's research, most adults never reach Level III, and instead persist in Stages 3 and 4 of Level II, stoutly believing in law and order and conforming to rules in order to avoid the disapproval of their neighbors.

Kohlberg also found evidence of gender differences in moral development, and here the interest for the psychology of women begins. Kohlberg found that most males eventually reach Stage 4, whereas most females reach only Stage 3. From this it might be concluded that females have a less well developed sense of morality. Freud's immature superego returns dressed up in a modern, scientific costume.

In evaluating Kohlberg's theory, the evidence indicates that children pass through the early stages he specified, in the order in which he specified them (e.g., Kuhn, 1976). On the other hand, certain value judgments are involved in setting up the hierarchy of stages in the way he did; in particular, it seems odd to have a Level III that few adults ever reach (someone once joked that the only people who reached Level III were Kohlberg and his graduate students). One of the most influential critiques of Kohlberg's ideas is the feminist analysis by Gilligan (1982).

Gilligan: A Different Perspective on Moral Development   Psychologist Carol Gilligan provided a feminist critique of Kohlberg's work on moral development in her influential book *In a Different Voice* (1982). She also provided a reformulation of moral development from a woman's point of view.

Several of Gilligan's criticisms parallel our earlier discussion of sex bias in research. The main character of Kohlberg's dilemma is Heinz, a man. Perhaps girls and women have trouble identifying with him. Some of the other moral dilemmas Kohlberg used are more gender-neutral, but one is about the captain of a company of marines. Once again, women may find this a bit hard to relate to. Gilligan also pointed out that the people who formed the basis for Kohlberg's theorizing were a group of 84 *males,* whom he followed for 20 years, beginning in their childhood. When a theory is based on evidence from males, it is not surprising that it does not apply well to females. Finally, Gilligan identified a bias in

Kohlberg's interpretation: The phenomenon that women reach only Stage 3 is interpreted as a deficiency in female development, whereas it might just as easily be interpreted as being a deficiency in Kohlberg's theory, which may not adequately describe female development.

Gilligan did not stop with a critique of Kohlberg. She extended her analysis to provide a feminist reformulation of moral development. Her reformulation is based on the belief that women reason differently about the moral dilemmas— that is, they are speaking in a different voice (hence the title of her book)—and that their voices had not been listened to. To understand her ideas, listen to the voices of 11-year-old Jake and 11-year-old Amy responding to the Heinz dilemma. First Jake:

> For one thing, human life is worth more than money, and if the druggist only makes $1,000, he is still going to live, but if Heinz doesn't steal the drug, his wife is going to die. (*Why is life worth more than money?*) Because the druggist can get a thousand dollars later from rich people with cancer, but Heinz can't get his wife again. (Gilligan, 1982, p. 26)

Now Amy, asked if Heinz should steal the drug:

> Well, I don't think so. I think there might be other ways besides stealing it, like if he could borrow the money or make a loan or something, but he really shouldn't steal the drug—but his wife shouldn't die either. (*Why shouldn't he steal the drug?*) If he stole the drug, he might save his wife then, but if he did, he might have to go to jail, and then his wife might get sicker again, and he couldn't get more of the drug, and it might not be good. So, they should really just talk it out and find some other way to make the money. (Gilligan, 1982, p. 28)

Jake would be scored as showing a mixture of Stages 3 and 4, but also as reaching some elements of mature Level III morality (Gilligan, 1982, p. 27). Amy, in contrast, just doesn't fit very well into the scoring system. Jake, like Kohlberg, sees the issue as one of rules and balancing the rights of individuals: the right of the druggist to profit, and the right of Heinz's wife (who remains nameless) to life. In contrast, Amy sees the issue as one of relationships: the problem that the druggist fails to live up to a relationship to the dying woman, the need to preserve the relationship between Heinz and his wife, and the need to avoid a bad relationship between Heinz and the druggist. Amy's solution does not involve rules, but rather relationships—they should "talk it out" and mend the relationships.

Gilligan contrasts these two approaches to moral reasoning in several ways. The **justice perspective** views people as differentiated and standing alone and focuses on the rights of the individual; the **care perspective** emphasizes relatedness between

Justice perspective: According to Gilligan, an approach to moral reasoning that emphasizes fairness and the rights of the individual.

Care perspective: According to Gilligan, an approach to moral reasoning that emphasizes relationships between people and caring for others and the self.

people and communication. According to Gilligan, males tend to stress justice; females tend to stress caring. Males focus on contracts between people; females focus on attachments between people. In essence, women tend to think differently about moral questions. Kohlberg devised his stages of moral reasoning with the male as norm; thus women's answers appear immature, when in fact they are simply based on different concerns.

What evidence is there for Gilligan's theorizing? Gilligan herself also presented several studies in support of her views. Here I will consider one of these, the abortion decision study. She interviewed 29 women between the ages of 15 and 33, all of whom were in the first trimester of pregnancy and were considering abortion. They were interviewed a second time one year later. Notice how she shifted the moral dilemma from a male stranger named Heinz to an issue that is far more central to women. Just as Kohlberg saw three major levels of moral reasoning, so Gilligan found three levels among these women, but the focus for the levels was different (see the right-hand side of Table 2.1). In Level I, preconventional morality, the woman making the abortion decision is concerned only for herself and her survival. An example is Susan, an 18-year-old, who was asked what she thought when she found out that she was pregnant:

> I really didn't think anything except that I didn't want it. (*Why was that?*) I didn't want it, I wasn't ready for it, and next year will be my last year and I want to go to school. (Gilligan, 1982, p. 75)

Women who have reached Level II have shifted their focus to being responsible and to caring for others, specifically for a potential child. Women in Level II see their previous, less mature Level I responses as selfish. These themes are articulated by Josie, a 17-year-old, in discussing her reaction to being pregnant:

> I started feeling really good about being pregnant instead of feeling really bad, because I wasn't looking at the situation realistically. I was looking at it from my own sort of selfish needs, because I was lonely. Things weren't really going good for me, so I was looking at it that I could have a baby that I could take care of or something that was part of me, and that made me feel good. But I wasn't looking at the realistic side, at the responsibility I would have to take on. I came to this decision that I was going to have an abortion because I realized how much responsibility goes with having a child. . . . And I decided that I have to take on responsibility for myself and I have to work out a lot of things. (Gilligan, 1982, p. 77)

Typical of Level II thinking, Josie sees Level I thinking as selfish, and shifts her concern to being responsible to the child. Notice that deciding to have an abortion or not to have an abortion is not what differentiates Level I from Level II. Either decision can be reached at either level. For example, in Level I the concern for self and survival can lead to having an abortion so that a baby does not interfere with one's life. However, the Level I concern for self and survival can also lead one not to have an abortion in order to have a baby for the anticipated fun of giving and receiving love.

Finally, in Level III moral reasoning, the self and others are seen as interdependent, and there is a focus on balancing caring for others (the fetus, the father, parents) with caring for oneself. A woman must have reasonably high self-esteem to reach this level, for without it the "caring for self" aspect looks like a return to the selfishness of earlier levels, rather than a complex balancing of care extended to all, including herself. In this stage, caring is not the crude product of female socialization, but rather is a universal ethical principle that all should follow. A recapitulation of her earlier moral reasoning and her current balancing of caring is articulated by Sarah, who is faced with a second abortion:

> Well, the pros for having the baby are all the admiration that you would get from being a single woman, alone, martyr, struggling, having the adoring love of this beautiful Gerber baby. Just more of a home life than I have had in a long time, and that basically was it, which is pretty fantasyland. . . . Cons against having the baby: it was going to hasten what is looking to be the inevitable end of the relationship with the man I am presently with. I was going to have to go on welfare. My parents were going to hate me for the rest of my life. I was going to lose a really good job that I have. I would lose a lot of independence. Solitude. . . . Con against having the abortion is having to face up to the guilt. And pros for having the abortion are I would be able to handle my deteriorating relation with [the father] with a lot more capability and a lot more responsibility for myself. I would not have to go through the realization that for the next twenty-five years of my life I would be punishing myself for being foolish enough to get pregnant again and forcing myself to bring up a kid just because I did this. Having to face the guilt of a second abortion seemed like not exactly—well, exactly the lesser of two evils, but also the one that would pay off for me personally in the long run because, by looking at why I am pregnant again and subsequently have decided to have a second abortion, I have to face up to some things about myself. (Gilligan, 1982, p. 92)

Gilligan summarized the differences between men's and women's moral reasoning as follows:

> The moral imperative that emerges repeatedly in interviews with women is an injunction to care, a responsibility to discern and alleviate the "real and recognizable trouble" of this world. For men, the moral imperative appears rather as an injunction to respect the rights of others and thus to protect from interference the rights to life and self-fulfillment. . . . Development for both sexes would therefore seem to entail an integration of rights and responsibilities through the discovery of the complementarity of these disparate views. (Gilligan, 1982, p. 100)

How good is Gilligan's theory? First, it is an example of many of the qualities of the "new feminist scholarship." She detected the male centeredness of Kohlberg's analysis of moral reasoning. She then reconstructed the theory after listening to what females said and shaped a developmental model from it. My reservation about it comes from my own firm belief in gender similarities. Much of Gilligan's writing sounds as though men display one kind of moral thinking and women display a totally different kind. I am certain that there are some men who show "female" moral reasoning of the kind quoted earlier and some women who display "male" moral reasoning.

By now, several important studies have tested various aspects of Gilligan's theory. One was a major meta-analysis (for an explanation of meta-analysis, see Chapter 3) of studies that had examined gender differences in responses to Kohlberg's moral dilemmas; the conclusion from this review was that there were no gender differences (Walker, 1984; see also Mednick, 1989). That is, there is no evidence to support Gilligan's basic accusation that Kohlberg's scales shortchange women and cause them to score as less morally mature. Females score at the same moral level, on average, as males.

In another meta-analysis, Sara Jaffee and I (2000) examined studies that had tested the use of justice reasoning versus care reasoning, to test Gilligan's assertion that girls and women preferentially use care reasoning and boys and men use justice reasoning. Averaged over all studies, the gender difference in care orientation did favor females but was small: $d = -0.28$. (The d statistic is explained in Chapter 3.) The average gender difference in justice orientation favored males, but also was small: $d = 0.19$. In short, although females have a tendency to emphasize care reasoning and males have a tendency to emphasize justice reasoning, the differences are small, and most people use mixtures of justice and care in their thinking about moral issues. It simply would not be accurate to say that girls and women speak in one moral voice and boys and men in another.

In conclusion, Gilligan's main contribution was to articulate a different side of moral reasoning, one based on relationship and caring. Gender differences in the use of either the justice or the caring perspective are small; both males and females use both (Friedman et al., 1987; Jadack et al., 1995; Jaffee & Hyde, 2000).

Gender Schema Theory

This brainteaser has been popular for the past few years:

> A father and his son were involved in a car accident in which the father was killed and the son was seriously injured. The father was pronounced dead at the scene of the accident and his body was taken to a local mortuary. The son was taken by ambulance to a hospital and was immediately wheeled into an operating room. A surgeon was called.

Upon seeing the patient, the attending surgeon exclaimed, "Oh my God, it's my son!"

Can you explain this? (Keep in mind that the father who was killed in the accident is not a stepfather, nor is the attending physician the boy's stepfather.)

If you have not heard this before, give yourself some time to solve it before reading the next paragraph, which contains the solution.

The solution is that the surgeon is the boy's *mother*. But why is it so difficult for most people to think of this solution? It is exactly this sort of question that is addressed by psychologist Sandra Bem's gender schema theory (1981).

First, you need to understand what a schema is. Schema is a concept from cognitive psychology, the branch of psychology that investigates how we think, perceive, process, and remember information (for a good summary of schema theory, not applied to gender, see Alba & Hasher, 1983). A **schema** is a general knowledge framework that a person has about a particular topic. A schema organizes and guides perception. To gain a more specific understanding of what a schema is, read the following description carefully and then, without looking back at it, answer the questions that follow.

Schema: In cognitive psychology, a general knowledge framework that a person has about a particular topic; the schema then processes and organizes new information on that topic.

> You decide to go to your favorite restaurant for dinner. You enter the restaurant and are seated at a table with a white tablecloth. You study the menu. You tell the waiter that you want potato skins for an appetizer, then fettuccine alfredo with shrimp, and a salad with blue-cheese dressing on it. You also order red wine. A few minutes later the waiter returns with your appetizer. Later he brings the rest of the meal, all of which you enjoy, except that there weren't as many shrimp as you expected.

Now answer the following questions:

1. What kind of salad dressing did you order?

2. Was the tablecloth red-checked?

3. What did you order to drink?

4. Did the waiter give you a menu?

You probably found the questions easy to answer. The important point is, what was your answer for question 4? The correct answer is "no," because there is no mention in the story of the waiter handing you a menu. Many people incorrectly answer "yes" to this question. The reason is that most of us have a restaurant schema in our stored knowledge. This schema contains certain characteristics that are common to most restaurants, as well as events that generally occur in them. A schema typically helps us process and remember information, and your restaurant schema helped you answer questions 1, 2, and 3. But schemas also act to *filter and interpret* information, and they can therefore cause errors in memory. A common part of a restaurant schema is that a waiter hands you a menu. Therefore, your restaurant schema probably filled in this piece of information that really was not described in the story and thereby caused you to make an error. An individual's perception and memory of information, then, are a result of the interaction of the incoming information with the individual's preexisting schema.

Psychologist Sandra Bem (1981) applied schema theory to understanding the gender-typing process in her gender schema theory (see also Martin & Dinella, 2001; Martin & Halverson, 1983). Her proposal is that each one of us has as part of our knowledge structure a **gender schema,** a set of gender-linked associations. Furthermore, the gender schema represents a basic predisposition to process information on the basis of gender. That is, it represents our tendency to see many things as gender-related and to want to dichotomize things on the basis of gender. The gender schema processes new, incoming information, filtering and interpreting it. Thus gender schema

Gender schema: A person's general knowledge framework about gender; it processes and organizes information on the basis of gender-linked associations.

theory provides a ready answer for why the brainteaser at the beginning of this section is so difficult. Most of us have a gender schema that contains a link between man and surgeon. Therefore, making an association from surgeon to woman or mother is difficult, if not impossible.

Bem says that the developmental process of gender typing or gender-role acquisition in children is a result of the child's gradual learning of the content of society's gender schema. The gender-linked associations that form the schema are many: Girls wear dresses and boys don't; boys are strong and tough, girls are pretty (perhaps learned simply from the adjectives adults apply to children, rarely or never calling boys *pretty,* rarely or never calling girls *tough*); girls grow up to be mommies, boys don't.

Our gender schemas make us assume that the head of the household is male, and we are amused when it's not.

In a further process, the gender schema becomes closely linked to the self-concept. Thus five-year-old Maria knows she is a girl and also has a girl schema that she attaches to her own sense of girlhood. Maria's self-esteem then begins to be dependent on how well she measures up to her girl schema. At that point, she becomes internally motivated to conform to society's female gender role (a point much like Kohlberg's). Society does not have to force her into the role. She gladly does it herself and feels good about herself in the process. Finally, Bem postulates that different individuals have, to some extent, different gender schemas. The content of the schema varies from one person to the next, perhaps as a result of the kinds of gender information to which one is exposed in one's family throughout childhood. And the gender schema is more central to self-concept for some people—those who are highly gender typed (traditionally masculine males and feminine females).

Evidence for Gender Schema Theory   Let us look at three studies that illustrate how the theory can be tested, all of which support the theory.

In one study, Bem (1981) gave a list of 61 words, in random order, to respondents who were college students. Some of the words were proper names, some referred to animals, some to verbs, and some to articles of clothing. Half the names were masculine and half were feminine. One-third of the animal words were masculine (*gorilla*), one-third were feminine (*butterfly*), and one-third were neutral (*ant*). Similarly, one-third of the verbs and the articles of clothing were each masculine, feminine, and neutral. The participants' task was to recall as many of the 61 words as they could, in any order. It is known from many previous studies that in memory tasks such as these, people tend to cluster words into categories based on similar meaning; this is indicated by the order in which they recall the words. For example, if the person organized the words according to gender, the recall order might be *gorilla, bull, trousers;* but if the organization was according to animals, the recall order might be *gorilla, butterfly, ant.* If gender-typed people (masculine males and feminine females, as measured by the Bem Sex Role Inventory, a test to be discussed in Chapter 3) do possess a gender schema that they use to organize information, then they should cluster their recalled words into gender groupings. That is exactly what occurred. Gender-typed persons tended to cluster words according to gender, a result that supports gender schema theory.

In another experiment, 5- and 6-year-old children were shown pictures of males and females performing stereotype-consistent activities (such as a boy playing with a train) and stereotype-inconsistent activities (such as a girl sawing wood) (see Figure 2.1) (Martin & Halverson, 1983). One week later the children were tested for their recall of the pictures. The results indicated that the children distorted information by changing the gender of the people in the stereotype-inconsistent pictures, while not making such changes for the stereotype-consistent pictures. That is, children tended to remember the picture of the girl sawing wood as having been a picture of a boy sawing wood. That result is just what would be pre-

FIGURE 2.1

Pictures used in the Martin and Halverson research on gender schemas and children's memory. (Left) A girl engaged in a stereotype-consistent activity. (Right) Girls engaged in a stereotype-inconsistent activity. In a test of recall a week later, children tended to distort the stereotype-inconsistent pictures to make them stereotype-consistent; for example, they remembered that they had seen boys boxing. (SOURCE: National Institute of Mental Health.)

dicted by gender schema theory: Incoming information that is inconsistent with the gender schema is *filtered out* and *reinterpreted* to be consistent with the gender schema. This study also indicates that the gender schema is present even in 5-year-olds. (For other evidence of gender schemas in children, see Levy, 1994.)

In a third study, Bem (1981) measured the reaction times of college students to gender-linked adjectives, such as *independent, feminine, competitive,* and *loves children.* The words were projected, one at a time, on a screen. The participant's task was to press one of two buttons, "me" or "not me," according to whether the adjective was characteristic of him or her. The reaction time is the amount of time from presentation of the word until the person presses either button. If there is a gender schema that processes incoming information, then information that is consistent with one's gender schema, particularly as it relates to the self, should be processed faster than information that is not consistent with the gender self-schema. As an example, if I asked you "Is a robin a bird?" you would probably respond quickly. If I asked you "Is a penguin a bird?" you would respond more slowly. Robins fit your bird schema, and so you can process that question quickly. Penguins do not fit your bird schema as well, and so that question is processed more slowly—essentially you have to think about it longer. The results were that gender-typed participants did indeed make schema-consistent judgments faster than they made schema-inconsistent judgments, a result that supports gender schema theory.

Feminist Theories

Many people view the feminist movement as a political group with a particular set of goals to work for, a lobbying group trying to serve its own ends, as the National Rifle Association does. What is less recognized is that feminism has a rich, articulated theoretical basis. This viewpoint spans many areas besides psychology, but it certainly fits well in any psychological approach to understanding women.

Feminist theories were created by no single person. Instead, numerous writers have contributed their ideas, consistent with the desire of feminists to avoid power hierarchies and not to have a single person become the authority. But it also means that the feminist perspective as I have crystallized it here has been drawn from many sources. For that reason, I have titled this section "Feminist Theories," rather than "Feminist Theory." Some of the central concepts and issues of feminist theories follow.

Gender as Status and Power   Feminists view gender as similar to a *class* variable in our society. That is, males and females are unequal just as the lower class, the working class, the middle class, and the upper class are unequal. Men and women are of unequal *status,* women having the lower status.

After reviewing studies of people's interactions in small groups, two sociologists concluded that the best explanation for the results was the gender-as-a-status-variable hypothesis proposed by feminists (Meeker & Weitzel-O'Neill, 1977). When a small group of people are brought together to work on a task, sharp gender differences sometimes emerge: The men are highly task-oriented, making lots of comments to "get things done," whereas the women are more ori-

A key point of feminist theory is that women have less power than men do, yet feminist theory also challenges us to wonder what the world might be like if women held the power.

ented toward the relationships among the group members. Yet other studies do not find this pattern of gender differences. The authors concluded that these contradictory results can best be explained by the hypothesis that men have higher status than women. Thus in small-group interactions men are expected to be more competent than women, and competitive and dominating behavior is therefore seen as legitimate for men but not for women. However, in certain special circumstances these effects can be reversed, and assertive, competitive behavior becomes legitimate for women; examples of such situations are (1) when a woman has been appointed to be the leader of the group by an authoritative outsider such as the experimenter, and (2) when the content of the task is seen as an area of competence for women rather than for men, such as evaluating the quality of daycare centers. Thus these authors concluded that the evidence—at least from studies of small-group interactions—supports the hypothesis that gender is a basic status variable.

From the observation of the lesser status of women comes another basic feminist argument, that *sexism is pervasive.* Women are discriminated against in diverse ways, from the failure of the passage of the Equal Rights Amendment (which means that it is still legal to discriminate on the basis of gender) to the male centeredness of psychological theories, from the different pay scales for women and men to the boss propositioning his secretary. Thus sexism exists in many spheres: political, academic, economic, and interpersonal.

A closely related concept is the *inequality of power* between men and women, men having greater power (Brace & Davidson, 2000). Male dominance is therefore paired with female subordination. One of the classic works of the feminist movement is Kate Millett's *Sexual Politics* (1969); she defined "politics" as the study of power, and thus in analyzing sexual politics she focused on power relationships between women and men. The areas of male power and dominance are diverse and occur at many levels, from institutions to marital interactions. Most political leaders are men, and men therefore have the power to pass laws that have a profound effect on women's lives. Feminist analysis has extended the power principle to many other areas, for example, to viewing rape not as a sexual act but as an expression of men's power over women (e.g., Brownmiller, 1975). The concept of power is key to feminist analysis (Yoder & Kahn, 1992).

One saying of the feminist movement has been "the personal is political" (MacKinnon, 1982). Once again, "political" refers to expressions of power. Feminists have reconceptualized many acts that were traditionally viewed as personal, as simple interactions between individuals, into acts that are seen as political, or expressions of power. As examples, Mr. Executive pats the fanny of Miss Secretary, or John rapes Mary. Traditionally, these were thought of as personal, individual acts. They were understood to be the product of an obnoxious individual such as Mr. Executive, or of a rare, disturbed individual such as John, or of the inappropriately seductive behavior of Miss Secretary or Mary. The feminist recasts these, not as personal acts, but as political expressions of men's power over women. The greater status of men gives them a sense of entitlement to engage in such acts. At the same time, by these acts men exert power and control over women.

Sexuality   One of the central issues for feminists is sexuality (MacKinnon, 1982). There have been many specific feminist issues: rape, incest, abortion, birth control, sexual harassment on the job, pornography. Although these issues are diverse, note that all have the common link of sexuality. Female sexuality has been repressed and depressed, but rarely expressed. The problem, according to feminist analysis, is that women's sexuality is controlled by men. The issue, again, is power: Men have the power to control and exploit women's sexuality, for example, the power to deny abortion. As law professor Catharine MacKinnon put it, "Sexuality is to feminism what work is to marxism: that which is most one's own, yet most taken away" (1982, p. 1). We will explore women's sexuality in detail in Chapter 12.

Two other central issues in the feminist perspective are *the family* and *work.* Space does not permit a discussion of those issues here, but Chapter 9 is devoted to women and work, and Chapter 7 discusses women in relation to the family.

Gender Roles and Socialization   Feminists have highlighted the importance of gender roles and socialization in our culture. American society has well-defined roles for males and for females. From their earliest years, children are socialized to conform to these roles. In this regard, the feminist perspective is in close agreement with social learning theory. The feminist sees these roles as constricting to individuals. Essentially, gender roles tell children that there are certain things they may not do, whether telling a girl that she cannot be a physicist or a boy that he cannot be a nurse. Because gender roles shut off individual potentials and aspirations, feminists believe that we would be better off without such roles, or at least that they need to be radically revised.

Cross-cultural evidence indicates that American society is not unique in its emphasis on gender roles and socialization. Anthropologists such as Margaret Mead (1935, 1949) have discovered that other cultures have gender roles considerably different from our own; for example, in some other cultures men are reputed to be the gossips, and women are thought to be the appropriate ones to carry heavy loads. But despite all the cross-cultural diversity in gender roles, one universal principle seems to hold: Every known society recognizes and elaborates gender differences (Rosaldo, 1974), a point that is consistent with feminists' emphasis on the power and pervasiveness of gender roles.

Beyond this recognition of the universality of gender roles, there is disagreement among feminist anthropologists. Some argue that the male role, whatever it is, is always valued more (Mead, 1935; Rosaldo, 1974). For example, in some parts of New Guinea the women grow sweet potatoes and the men grow yams; but yams are the prestige food, the food used in important ceremonies. Even in this case where the labor of females and males is virtually identical, what the male does is valued more. This finding is consistent with the feminist concept of gender as a class or status variable. Other anthropologists argue that there are exceptions to the rule that the male role is always valued more. They point to societies in which there is gender equality or in which the female role is valued more (Lepowsky, 1993; Sanday, 1988). For example, the Minangkabau of West Sumatra are proud of being described as a matriarchate (a society in which many important activities are matricentered, or female centered, and women are more important than men) (Sanday, 1988). Members of that society say that men are dominant in matters related to traditions and customs, but that women are dominant in matters related to property. Such discussions often end in laughter as everyone agrees that the sexes are equal. I cannot resolve this debate here, except to note that patriarchal societies are by far in the majority, and egalitarian or matriarchal societies, if they exist, constitute a small minority.

External Versus Internal Attributions of Problems   Latoya was raped; Suzanne is depressed. Traditional psychological analyses focus on the internal nature and causes of these women's problems. Latoya might be viewed as having brought on the rape by her seductive behavior. Suzanne might be viewed as having personal problems of adjustment. Feminists are critical of analyses that assume women's problems are caused by internal or personal factors. Feminists instead view the *sources of women's problems as being external.* Latoya's problem is recast as having its roots in a society that condones, indeed encourages, male aggression. Suzanne's problem is recast as having its roots in a society that attaches little value and recognition to being a housewife and mother. This theme of external factors will recur in Chapter 15 in the discussion of the theoretical basis of feminist therapy.

Consciousness Raising   In the late 1960s and early 1970s, as the modern feminist movement gained momentum, consciousness-raising (C-R) groups were popular. Ideally, such groups begin with a small group of women sharing their personal feelings and experiences; they then move to a feminist theoretical analysis of these feelings and experiences, and from this should flow action, whether it involves an individual woman restructuring her relationship with her partner, or a group of women lobbying for a new law to be passed. Although C-R groups are not as common as they were in the 1970s, the process of consciousness raising remains central to feminism. As one theorist put it,

> Consciousness raising is the major technique of analysis, structure of organization, method of practice, and theory of social change of the women's movement. (MacKinnon, 1982, p. 5)

Thus consciousness raising is central to the feminist perspective for a number of reasons. First, it is a means for women to get in touch with their experiences and understand themselves. Previously, the only tools women had for understanding themselves were various psychological theories, such as psychoanalytic theory, that were male centered and defined women from a male point of view. Through the sharing of personal feelings and experiences, women in C-R groups can come to know and understand women from a female point of view. But consciousness raising does not stop with sharing. It proceeds to theoretical analysis. Women come to see that what they had perceived as individual problems are actually common and are rooted in external causes. For example, Linda has been beaten by her husband. In the C-R group, she discovers that three of the other women have also been beaten by husbands or lovers. In so doing, she comes to recognize two central points: that the personal is political (the individual beating by her husband is part of a larger pattern of power in society), and that the sources of her problems are external, rooted in the power structure of society, rather than a result of her own internal deficiencies. Finally, the C-R group becomes the power base for political action. Linda and the other three women might decide to found a shelter for battered women.

Varieties of Feminism   One of the difficulties in writing this section on the feminist perspective is that there are actually several different kinds of feminism, differing in everything from their theoretical analysis to their model for social change to their vision of the ideal society. One method of categorization is to conceptualize five major types of feminism: (1) liberal or moderate feminism, (2) cultural feminism, (3) Marxist or socialist feminism, (4) radical feminism, and (5) postmodern feminism (Enns & Sinacore, 2001; Tong, 1998).

Liberal feminism holds that women should have opportunities and rights equal to those of men. Basically, liberal feminists believe in working within the system for reform. The liberal feminist position is exemplified by organizations such as NOW (National Organization for Women), which is the major group that lobbied for passage of the Equal Rights Amendment. The notion here is that American society is founded on basically good ideals, such as justice and freedom for all, but the justice and freedom need to be extended to women. Some would argue that liberal feminism can be credited with many of the educational and legal reforms that have improved women's lives in the United States over the last several decades (Tong, 1998).

Unlike the claims of liberal feminism, which sees men and women as basically alike but in need of equal rights, *cultural feminism* argues that women have special, unique qualities that differentiate them from men. The crucial task is to elevate and value those special qualities, which have been devalued in our patriarchal society. The special qualities include nurturing, connectedness, and intuition. Gilligan's theorizing about moral development is a clear example of cultural feminism.

Marxist or *socialist feminism* argues that the liberal feminist analysis of the problem is superficial and does not get to the deeper roots of the problem. Marxist feminism views the oppression of women as just one instance of oppression based on class, oppression that is rooted in capitalism. Marxist feminists, for example, point out the extent to which the capitalist system benefits from oppressing women in ways such as wage discrimination. What would happen to the average American corporation if it had to start paying all of its secretaries as much as plumbers earn? (Both jobs require a high school education and a certain amount of manual dexterity and specific skills.) The answer is that most corporations would find their economic structure ruined. Women's situation will not improve, according to this point of view, without a drastic reform of American society, including a complete overhaul of the capitalist economic system and the concept of private property.

Radical feminists such as Shulamith Firestone (1970), Kate Millett (1969), and Andrea Dworkin (1987) view liberal feminism and cultural feminism as entirely too optimistic about the sources of women's oppression and the changes needed to end it. Patriarchal values have saturated society to such an extent that radical change is necessary in everything from social institutions to patterns of thought. Patriarchal values produce the concepts of masculinity and femininity and other kinds of dichotomous thinking, with the result that one of the categories becomes valued more than the other. This kind of polarized, dichotomized thinking must be abolished. Consciousness-raising groups and the naming of oppression are important aspects of radical feminism. Collective political and social action are essential. Given the difficulty of changing social institutions, radical feminists sometimes advocate separatist communities in which women can come together to pursue their work free of men's oppression.

Postmodern feminists have been influenced by the postmodern movement, which questions rationality and objectivity as methods for getting at truth, whether in the humanities or the sciences. Postmodern feminism is not focused on social action, but rather is an academic movement that seeks to reform thought and research within colleges and universities. It is particularly concerned with the issue of **epistemology,** which is the question of how people—whether laypeople or scientists—know. How do we know about truth and reality? Traditional science has been based on positivism as its epistemology. Positivism claims that we can know reality directly through rational, objective scientific methods. Postmodernism questions that claim and instead advocates social constructionism as an epistemology, to be discussed in a later section.

> **Epistemology:** Concerning the origin and methods of human knowledge.

The point here is that not all feminists and not all feminist theories are alike. Instead, there is a wide spectrum of belief and practice. Most of the academic feminist psychologists who have contributed to the psychology of women would be classified as liberal feminists or postmodern feminists, but certainly there is also a sprinkling of cultural feminists, socialist feminists, and radical feminists.

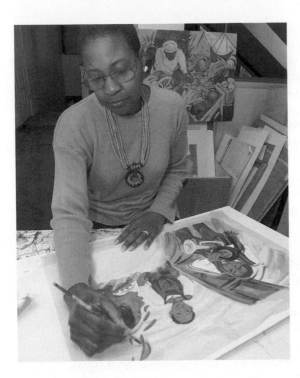

A key point of feminist theory is that not only gender, but also race and class, shape one's life experiences profoundly.

Gender, Race/Ethnicity, and Class   Feminist theories emphasize the critical importance of gender. But feminist theorists argue that gender cannot be understood as a social variable in isolation; it can be understood only in the context of race and social class as well (e.g., Dugger, 1988). That is, feminist theories place emphasis on the simultaneous importance of gender, race, and social class, as these shape everything from social institutions to individual behavior.

We will take up these concepts in more detail in Chapter 4, "Women of Color." As a brief example here, women's attitudes about gender roles and feminist issues vary as a function of their race or ethnicity (Dugger, 1988). Feminists of any race or ethnicity, for instance, have readily recognized that white men oppress white women. Black feminists, on the other hand, have emphasized that the oppression of Black women by Black men can be understood only in the context of the fact that Black men themselves are oppressed by Whites. Gender and race interact in powerful ways when we discuss feminist issues. As one scholar put it,

> A necessary next step is the development of theoretical and conceptual frameworks for analyzing the interaction of race and gender stratification. Separate models exist for analyzing race, ethnic or gender stratification. Although the "double" (race, gender) and "triple" (race, gender, class) oppression of racial ethnic women are widely acknowledged, no satisfactory theory has been developed to analyze what happens when these systems of

oppression intersect. . . . Race, gender and class interact in such a way that the histories of white and racial ethnic women are intertwined. . . . The situation of white women has depended on the situation of women of color. White women have gained advantages from the exploitation of racial ethnic women. (Glenn, 1985, pp. 87, 105)

The Social Construction of Gender   Feminist theorists view gender not as a biologically created reality, but as a socially constructed phenomenon (Beall, 1993; Hare-Mustin & Marecek, 1988). The basic position of *constructivism* is that people—including scientists—do not discover reality; rather, they construct or invent it (Watzlawick, 1984). According to **social construction-ism,** we do not experience reality directly. Instead, we actively construct meanings for events in the environment based on our own prior experiences and predispositions. This theoretical view, then, shares much in common with schema theory, discussed earlier in the chapter.

> **Social constructionism:** A theoretical viewpoint that humans do not discover reality directly; rather, they construct meanings for events in the environment based on their own prior experiences and beliefs.

The extent to which we socially construct gender becomes clearer if we view the issues through the lenses of other cultures. In Euro-American cultures it is perfectly obvious—a clear reality—that there are two genders, males and females. However, among some American Indians, such as the Sioux, Cheyenne, and Zuni, there is a third category, the **Two-Spirit** (also called *berdache*), people who dress as and completely take on the role of the other gender. Some of these tribes con-

> **Two-Spirit:** Among Native Americans, a third gender category.

sider the Two-Spirit to be a third gender, and it is perfectly clear in their culture that there are three genders (Beall, 1993; Kessler & McKenna, 1985). The Navajo in the United States and the Hijara of India believe that there are males, females, and intersexed individuals who are both male and female (Martin & Voorhies, 1975). Again, the belief is that there are three genders. What seems like an obvious reality to Euro-Americans, that there are only two genders, turns out to be a social construction, which becomes clear when we see that other cultures have constructed the categories differently.

Processes closely related to gender are also socially constructed. For example, Americans are quite sure of the reality that women typically feel tired after giving birth, because they have gone through a physically exhausting process. Other so-cieties, though, have the **couvade,** which is practiced among the Ainu of Japan and the Timbira of Brazil (Gregersen, 1996). The couvade consists of elaborate rituals that are based on the as-sumption that the father, not the mother, is the main contributor of effort in childbirth. After the mother gives birth, the baby is given to the father, and he rests for several days to overcome his

> **Couvade:** A custom in which the man is assumed to be the major contribu-tor to childbirth, and therefore suffers symp-toms such as fatigue.

fatigue, whereas the mother returns to work immediately because she is believed not to need rest. The contribution of the father to childbirth, and his fatigue fol-lowing it, is a clear reality to people in these cultures. Again, our Euro-American notions of women's contributions to childbirth are challenged, and we see the extent to which such events are socially constructed.

Feminist psychologists have noted that gender is not only a person variable (as traditional psychology has maintained) but also a stimulus variable (e.g., Grady, 1979). By saying that gender is a person variable, I mean that gender is a characteristic of the individual; this point of view leads to the study of gender differences, a pursuit that has occupied some traditional psychologists and some feminist psychologists (see Chapter 3). By saying that gender is also a stimulus variable, I mean that a person's gender has a profound impact on the way others react to that person. Our understanding of an individual—that is, our social construction of that individual—is in part determined by our knowledge of that individual's gender. This point of view stimulated an area of research in which participants are led to believe that a particular piece of work was done by a male or a female, or that a particular infant is a male or female; their responses to the work or the infant can then be studied as a function of the gender they believe it to be (see Chapters 7 and 9 for examples). Therefore, gender is both a personal characteristic and a stimulus variable.

Social constructionism, then, argues that these processes occur in at least three areas: (1) The individual engages in social constructions, for example, reacting to another person differently depending on whether that person is male or female; (2) the society or culture provides a set of social constructions of gender, for example, whether there are two genders or more; and (3) scientists socially construct gender by the way they construct their research.

Among other things, this view that notions of gender are socially constructed challenges the belief that science is fundamentally objective (Hare-Mustin & Marecek, 1988), a point that was discussed in Chapter 1. Scientific knowledge, like all other knowledge, is shaped by the values and presuppositions of the perceiver—in this case, the scientist.

Social constructionism is sometimes contrasted with *biological essentialism* (DeLamater & Hyde, 1998). Biological essentialism maintains the belief that certain phenomena, such as gender differences, are natural, inevitable, and biologically determined. Sociobiology and evolutionary psychology reflect biological essentialism.

Attitudes Toward Feminism What do American women think about the feminist movement? An answer is provided by the General Social Survey (GSS), a well-sampled national survey conducted annually by the University of Chicago. In 1996 the GSS included questions about feminism, and the responses give us a window onto American women's thinking about these issues (General Social Survey, 2002). Of the 1,444 women surveyed, 21 percent said that they think of themselves as feminists. Clearly feminism is more than a tiny splinter group.

When asked about the impact of the feminist movement on women with working-class jobs, 75 percent said that it had improved their lives, as did 82 percent of the respondents when the question was about women with management or professional jobs. And 38 percent reported that the feminist movement had improved their own lives. Thus positive views of the feminist movement are widespread, even among women who do not consider themselves to be feminists.

Support for feminist issues is also widespread. In another survey, when asked "Which issues are very important to women?" 94 percent agreed that equal pay for equal work was important, 90 percent agreed for day care, 88 percent agreed on the issue of rape, 84 percent agreed for maternity leave at work, 82 percent agreed on the issue of job discrimination, and 74 percent agreed for abortion (*Time*, December 4, 1989). Interestingly, four of the top five issues are work/family issues (for more details, see Chapter 9, "Women and Work").

The feminist movement is not the same as it was in 1970, and the issues have shifted to some extent. But there is no evidence in these statistics that the feminist movement or feminist issues are dead!

Summary   Feminist theories generally highlight a number of points: (a) Gender is a status and power variable, with men having power over women; (b) gender roles and gender-role socialization are powerful forces in any culture; (c) many of women's problems are better conceptualized as being caused by external forces than internal ones; (d) consciousness raising is an essential process for women to get in touch with themselves; (e) gender, race, and class interact in influencing the behavior of individuals as well as social institutions; and (f) knowledge, in particular our understanding of gender, is socially constructed.

Evaluation of Feminist Theories   One criticism of the feminist perspective comes from the New Right and other conservative groups (see, for example, Eisenstein, 1982). They believe that women's roles and status are rooted in biology, perhaps ordained by God, and certainly "natural." They therefore find the feminist viewpoint just plain wrong. These arguments involve basic questions of value and cannot be addressed at a scientific level.

Feminist theories span many disciplines and were not specifically proposed as scientific theories. This means that some of their propositions are difficult to evaluate scientifically. The notion of men as a class having power over women will recur in several studies mentioned later in this book; an example is the sexual harassment of women (see Chapter 14). Also, the data on issues of sexuality for women are the focus in several later chapters (10, 11, 12, and 13). Feminists' concepts about gender roles and socialization are supported by anthropologists' evidence, as discussed earlier. I don't mean to evade the question, but it seems to me that the issues raised by feminist theory are so broad that it is best to wait until you have read the rest of this book before attempting an evaluation.

In Conclusion

In this chapter I have presented six major theoretical perspectives: psychoanalytic theory, sociobiology and evolutionary psychology, social learning theory, cognitive-developmental theory, gender schema theory, and feminist theories. They operate from vastly different underlying assumptions and provide considerably different views of women. Psychoanalytic theory and sociobiology both see the nature of women and gender differences as rooted in biology: evolution, genes, and anatomy. Social learning theory falls at the other end of the nature-nurture continuum, seeing gender differences and gender roles as products of the social environment. Feminist theories, too, emphasize society as the creator of gender roles. Cognitive-developmental theory is an interactionist theory, emphasizing the interaction between the state of the organism (stage of cognitive development) and the information available from the culture. Gender schema theory also emphasizes the cognitive aspects of gender typing and the interaction between the knowledge structures in the individual and the incoming information from the environment.

With regard to scientific evidence for the various theories, certainly there are far more studies supporting social learning theory and cognitive-developmental theory than there are supporting psychoanalytic theory. The evidence concerning the tenets of sociobiology is quite mixed. And gender schema theory has much supporting evidence.

Because our basic purpose is to understand women and gender-role development, we should ask, What insights do these theories give us? No one theory by itself is adequate for understanding women—there is no "right" theory. Yet no theory is completely wrong. Each contributes something to our understanding. Freudian theory was important historically in emphasizing the notion of psychosexual development, highlighting the notion that an individual's gender identity and behavior have their roots in previous experiences. To understand an individual's gender identity as an adult (or at any age, for that matter), one must look at the person's life history. A second important contribution from psychoanalytic theory is the concept of *identification*. Though one might dispute the factors Freud postulated as creating identification, the fact remains that children usually do identify strongly with the same-gender parent, and this identification is an important force in gender-role development.

Social learning theory is important in its emphasis on the social and cultural components of gender-role development—the importance of society in shaping gender-typed behaviors. It points out, quite correctly, that boys and girls are treated differently. Social learning investigators have contributed some very impressive laboratory demonstrations of the power of reinforcements in shaping children's behavior, in particular gender-typed behaviors. Social learning theory also highlights the importance of modeling in the acquisition of gender role. Modern mothers who are concerned about freeing their children from

EXPERIENCE THE RESEARCH

GENDER SCHEMA THEORY

Ask six friends to participate, individually, in a memory study that you are conducting. Collect the data in a quiet place, free from distractions. Before giving the memory task, write on the back of the paper whether this friend is male or female, and whether, knowing this person, you would categorize the person as feminine, masculine, or androgynous. Then give the following set of instructions to the person:

> I am going to read to you a list of 12 words. As soon as I finish, I would like you to recall the words for me, in any order. I want to see how many words you remember.

Then read the following words out loud, in exactly this order:

gorilla	(M)	stepping	(N)
Daniel	(M)	butterfly	(F)
blushing	(F)	trousers	(M)
hurling	(M)	bikini	(F)
ant	(N)	bull	(M)
Susie	(F)	dress	(F)

Read the words slowly and clearly, with about one second between each. Write the words down as your friend recalls them, in exactly the order they are recalled. If the person responds quickly, you may need to abbreviate the words.

Does the pattern of results for your friends look like those that Sandra Bem obtained for her research on gender schemas? That is, did people cluster the words into groups on the basis of gender associations ("butterfly" and "dress" close together, "trousers" and "bull" close together), or on the basis of other categories ("trousers" and "dress" together, "butterfly" and "bull" together)? Did gender-typed people (masculine or feminine) seem to do more clustering on the basis of gender than androgynous people?

gender-role restrictions might do well to keep these forces in mind. It is axiomatic that children do as you do (they imitate). If a mother wants to avoid restrictive gender-role stereotypes for her daughter, it will help to encourage her to be a doctor or a lawyer; but in the end, the mother's own behavior may have a much greater impact than her verbal encouragements. I found myself assembling a child's rocker one Christmas Eve for these very reasons. My daughter Margaret, age 4 at the time, was watching, and the rocker needed to be put together in order to be her little brother Luke's present the next morning. I started to call my husband to do "his" job. But then I realized the meaning of such an action. I stiffened my upper lip, got the screwdriver, and started following the instructions. A half-hour later, the rocker was in one beautiful piece, I felt triumphant, and Margaret was impressed. I don't know what the long-term consequences for her may be, but I do know that I didn't want her to acquire low self-efficacy.

The feminist perspective shares with social learning theory an emphasis on external, social, and environmental shaping of gender roles. Ironically, it shares with psychoanalytic theory an emphasis on sexuality as a critical issue in the lives of humans. Feminism adds the concepts of power, status, race, and class in male-female relations. It also emphasizes the importance of the social construction of gender.

Finally, cognitive-developmental theory emphasizes that gender-role learning is a part of the rational learning processes of childhood (as contrasted with the libidinal motivations postulated by psychoanalytic theory). Gender schema theory shares the emphasis on cognition, or the intellectual processes underlying gender typing. It points out the extent to which we process information in terms of gender and distort information that is not consistent with our gender-typed expectations. Further, cognitive-developmental theory emphasizes that gender-role learning results not solely from externally imposed forces of society, but at least in part from internal motivation. Children actively seek to acquire gender roles, sometimes to the dismay of parents who want their children to be untouched by gender-role stereotypes. Gender roles seem to be helpful to children in structuring and understanding the reality of the world about them.

Suggestions for Further Reading

Bem, Sandra L. (1993). *The lenses of gender.* New Haven, CT: Yale University Press. Presented in this book is Bem's latest theorizing, in which she argues that three lenses—androcentrism, gender polarization, and biological essentialism—shape how people perceive social reality.

Gilligan, Carol. (1982). *In a different voice.* Cambridge, MA: Harvard University Press. This is the original book articulating Gilligan's reconstruction of moral-development theory from a female point of view.

Hrdy, Sara B. (1999). *Mother nature: Maternal instincts and how they shape the human species.* New York: Ballantine. Hrdy, a primatologist, presents a feminist version of sociobiology, integrating data from dozens of species and many human cultures, to explain women's patterns of mothering. Hrdy is a fabulous writer.

Tong, Rosemary, P. (1998). *Feminist thought,* 2nd ed. Boulder, CO: Westview. This is the authoritative textbook on feminist theories.

Gender Stereotypes and Gender Differences

3

Man should be trained for war and woman for the recreation of the warrior.

— NIETZSCHE

In the 2001 film *Legally Blonde*, Elle Woods (played by Reece Witherspoon) initially revels in her life as a happy sorority sister in Delta Nu at California University, Los Angeles. Seized with ambition and armed with brains and gutsy hard work, she wins admission to Harvard Law School. Once there, no one—students or faculty—will take her seriously because she is stereotyped as a dumb blonde. Blonde she is, but dumb she is not. She is forced to work 10 times as hard as other students in her class to earn the respect she deserves. This fictional portrayal captures vividly the power of stereotypes in people's lives and the struggles that individuals must wage to overcome stereotypes.

In this chapter we consider research on the nature of gender stereotypes and their impact on girls and women. Then we examine research on gender differences in various personality characteristics and behaviors, to see whether some gender stereotypes are accurate.

Stereotypes, Real Differences, and the Nature-Nurture Issue

It is important to make a distinction among the following: gender-role stereotypes; psychological gender differences that have been empirically determined to exist ("real" differences); and the causes of gender differences, whether biological or environmental.

Gender-role stereotypes are simply a set of shared cultural beliefs about males' and females' behavior, personality traits, and other attributes. Research shows that even in modern American society, and even among college students, there is a belief that males and females do differ psychologically in many ways (Bergen & Williams, 1991; Rosenkrantz et al., 1968; Spence & Buckner, 2000; Twenge, 1999). A list of these stereotyped traits is given in Table 3.1.

Gender-role stereotypes: A set of shared cultural beliefs about males' and females' behavior, personality traits, and other attributes.

Although these gender stereotypes persist in modern American culture, there is evidence that overall attitudes about gender roles have changed considerably over the last 30 years, becoming considerably more liberal (Loo & Thorpe, 1998; Twenge, 1997). Table 3.2 shows some data on this trend.

TABLE 3.1
Gender-Role Stereotypes

Americans believe that the following are characteristics of men and women.

	Masculine Characteristics	Feminine Characteristics
Personality	Independent	Warm
	Competitive	Gentle
	Decisive	Understanding
	Active	Devoted to others
	Self-confident	Helpful to others
	Stands up to pressure	Aware of others' feelings
	Never gives up	Emotional
Occupations and Leisure Interests	Auto mechanic	Art teacher
	Carpenter	Dental assistant
	Civil engineer	Nurse
	Jet pilot	Social worker
	Team sports	Talking to friends
	Computers/hacking	Aerobics
	Chess	Shopping
Social and Non-verbal Behaviors	Expansive posture when sitting	Smiling

SOURCES: Spence & Buckner (2000); Twenge (1999).

The data seem to present a paradox. Table 3.1 shows the evidence of continuing gender-role stereotypes, the same old stereotypes from 30 years ago. Table 3.2, in contrast, shows that gender-role attitudes are changing. So which is it? The answer is, both. Americans are deeply committed to the principles of equality and justice, and when feminists posed the issue of women's rights within that framework, people were persuaded and changed their attitudes in the equal-rights direction shown in Table 3.2. Yet gender stereotypes remain powerful, and people still believe privately that women are warm and gentle and that men are independent and competitive. Sarah is a woman so she is gentle and emotional, and she has every right to run for president.

To add one more nuance, research by social psychologist Kay Deaux indicates that adults view the male stereotype and the female stereotype as two overlapping categories rather than as two separate and distinct categories. For example,

TABLE 3.2
Changes over Time in Gender-Role Attitudes

Question	Percentage Agreeing	
	1972–1982	1998
1. It is much better for everyone involved if the man is the achiever outside the home and the woman takes care of the home and family.	65%	34%
2. Women should take care of running their homes and leave running the country up to men.	33%	15%
3. Most men are better suited emotionally for politics than are most women.	44%	22%

SOURCE: General Social Survey (2000).

people no longer think that men are strong and women are weak. Rather, they believe that men are likelier to be stronger than women. To get at this idea, Deaux has research participants estimate probabilities that a fictitious character will have a certain characteristic. For example, if participants are given only the gender cue (the person is a man, or the person is a woman), they estimate the probability that a man is strong as 0.66 and that a woman is strong as 0.44 (Deaux & Lewis, 1983).

Deaux's research also indicates that as we learn more information about a person, gender per se has less influence on our impressions of that person (Deaux & Lewis, 1984). We are not totally ruled by gender stereotypes. They are most important in the very first impression we form of a person. Stereotypes are also influential when we are thinking about strangers or some category of people. But as we learn more about an individual, that is, about his or her actual behavior and personality, this information becomes far more important in our opinion of that person.

One of the essential points of feminist theory (see Chapter 2) is that gender and ethnicity interact. For example, stereotypes about women and men may be different for different ethnic groups. In one study, college students at the University of Houston—51 percent of whom were Euro-American and the rest of whom were, in order of frequency, Hispanic, African American, Asian American, and Native American—were asked to list ten adjectives that came to mind when they thought of members of the following groups: Anglo-American males, Anglo-American females, African American males, African American females, Asian American males, Asian American females, Mexican American males, and Mexican American females (Niemann et al., 1994). The most frequently listed adjectives are shown in Table 3.3.

Two important patterns can be seen in Table 3.3: (1) Within an ethnic group, males and females have some stereotyped traits in common, but also some that differ.

TABLE 3.3
Gender and Ethnicity: Stereotypes of Males and Females from Different Ethnic Groups

Males	Females
Anglo-American	**Anglo-American**
Intelligent	Attractive
Egotistical	Intelligent
Upper class	Egotistical
Pleasant/friendly	Pleasant/friendly
Racist	Blond/light hair
Achievement oriented	Sociable
African American	**African American**
Athletic	Speak loudly
Antagonistic	Dark skin
Dark skin	Antagonistic
Muscular appearance	Athletic
Criminal activities	Pleasant/friendly
Speak loudly	Unmannerly
	Sociable
Asian American	**Asian American**
Intelligent	Intelligent
Short	Speak softly
Achievement oriented	Pleasant/friendly
Speak softly	Short
Hard workers	
Mexican American	**Mexican American**
Lower class	Black/brown/dark hair
Hard workers	Attractive
Antagonistic	Pleasant/friendly
Dark skin	Dark skin
Non-college education	Lower class
Pleasant/friendly	Overweight
Black/brown/dark hair	Baby makers
Ambitionless	Family oriented

Source: Niemann et al. Personality and Social Psychology Bulletin, 1994, 20.
Copyright © 1994, reprinted by permission of Sage Publications, Inc.

FOCUS 3.1

STEREOTYPES AND POWER

Social psychologist Susan Fiske (1993) has proposed an insightful analysis of the ways in which power and stereotypes influence each other. Two processes are involved. First, stereotyping exerts control or power over people, thus justifying and maintaining the status quo. Second, powerful people stereotype the less powerful. Given that gender is an important status or power variable, you can read "men" for "powerful people" and "women" for "less powerful people." The theory, of course, extends to other categories, such as ethnic groups.

First, stereotyping exerts control over people. Some stereotypes are descriptive; that is, they describe how most people in the group supposedly behave. Stereotypes claim that women are emotional, that African Americans are athletic, and that Jews are academically talented. These stereotypes then exert pressure on people in the group to conform to them.

Other stereotypes are prescriptive; that is, they tell how people of a certain group *should* behave. For example, women should be nice, Asian Americans should be good at math, adolescent boys should be athletic. If one fails to meet the demands of the stereotype, penalties can be severe (Eagly, Makhijani, & Klonsky, 1992). Again, stereotypes exert control over people.

Let us now turn to the second process: The powerful group stereotypes the less powerful group. Generally, less powerful people pay more attention to powerful people than the reverse; less powerful people therefore have more information about the powerful and tend to stereotype them less. Less powerful people need to pay attention because powerful people control important aspects of their lives and bear close watching. Servants know far more about their employers than the reverse, for example. In contrast, powerful people pay less attention to the less powerful, for three reasons: (1) The less powerful do not control outcomes of the powerful very much, so the powerful do not need to pay attention; (2) the powerful tend to be overloaded with information, and therefore have less attention to devote to the less powerful; and (3) powerful people who have a high need for dominance (not every powerful person does) may not want to pay attention to the less powerful. Because the powerful pay less attention, they have little information about the less powerful, and therefore the powerful rely on stereotypes of the less powerful.

According to Fiske's analysis of power and stereotypes, powerful people pay little attention to less powerful people, whereas the less powerful pay great attention to the powerful. Here the men focus on each other, ignoring the woman, while she pays close attention to them.

Fiske (1993) has conducted many clever experiments to test various aspects of her theory. In one, undergraduates were given the power to evaluate the summer job applications of high school students. Some undergraduates were given more power in the final decision, and others were given less power. The students who were given more power actually paid less attention to the applicants, consistent with Fiske's theory.

Fiske's theory and research were influential in an important Supreme Court case, *Price Waterhouse* v. *Hopkins.* Ann Hopkins was denied a partnership in the prestigious accounting firm of Price Waterhouse. Compared with her male colleagues who were being considered for partnership, she worked more billable hours, was well liked by clients, and brought in millions of dollars in accounts. She was denied partnership not because her performance was inadequate (it was in fact superb), but rather because she was not considered feminine in the way she dressed, walked, and talked.

(continued on next page)

Stereotype violation, in short, was seen as legitimate grounds for the denial of a promotion.

Based on Fiske's analysis, we can see how the power of stereotypes operated at several levels in this case. Men were in power at Price Waterhouse, and women were outnumbered. The powerful men were therefore likely to hold stereotyped expectations about the women. Hopkins, by being a successful woman in a male-dominated profession, management, was a stereotype violator and received punishment for it. The senior partners were probably overloaded with work, evaluating 88 partner candidates that year on top of an otherwise grueling workload, contributing to their lack of attention to Hopkins's qualifications.

The Supreme Court ruled in favor of Hopkins, and the brief filed by the American Psychological Association, reporting Susan Fiske's research, was highly influential in the decisions. As of this writing Ann Hopkins is a partner at Price Waterhouse.

SOURCE: Fiske (1993)

For example, both Mexican American males and Mexican American females are stereotyped as pleasant and friendly; however, Mexican American females are stereotyped as overweight but Mexican American males are not. (2) Within a gender, some stereotyped traits are common across ethnic groups, but others differ. For example, females from all ethnic groups are stereotyped as pleasant and friendly; however, Anglo-American and Asian American females are stereotyped as intelligent, whereas African American and Mexican American females are not.

When data are collected on the actual behavior and personality of females and males, the stereotypes turn out to be true in some cases ("real" differences), but not in others. For example, there is a stereotype that males are more aggressive than females; this turns out to be a real difference, as we will see later in this chapter. On the other hand, women are stereotyped as less intelligent than men, although actual research shows this not to be true; there are no gender differences in IQ. In this case, the stereotype is false. A *real difference*, then, is a gender difference that has been found to exist based on data collected on the personality or behavior of males and females.

Finally, if a gender difference (a real difference) is found, it requires one more step of analysis—and a very difficult one—to determine *whether the difference is biologically or environmentally caused.* For example, because there is a well-documented gender difference in aggression, we cannot automatically infer that this gender difference is biologically caused (e.g., by sex hormones), nor can we automatically decide that it is produced by environmental factors (e.g., socialization). Gender differences may be caused by environmental factors, biological factors, or an interaction between the two. Sophisticated research is necessary to uncover the complex interplay of biological and environmental forces at work.

Stereotype Threat

Stereotypes are more than just abstract ideas. They can really hurt. Psychologist Claude Steele has discovered a phenomenon he calls **stereotype threat,** and it documents the kind of subtle damage that stereotypes can inflict (Steele, 1997; Steele & Aronson, 1995). His original work concerned ethnic stereotypes—specifically, the stereotype that African Americans are intellectually inferior. In one experiment, he administered a test of verbal intelligence to Black and White college students, all of whom were highly talented Stanford students. Half of each group were told that the test was diagnostic of intelligence and half were told it was not diagnostic of intelligence. The Black students who believed that the test measured intelligence performed worse than the Black students who believed it didn't, whereas White students' performance was unaffected by the instructions they received. The effect for the Black students demonstrates stereotype threat. Steele believes that a negative stereotype about one's group leads to self-doubt because one may confirm the stereotype, which then damages performance. In this way, stereotypes really can hurt academic achievement.

> **Stereotype threat:** Being at risk of personally confirming a negative stereotype about one's group.

Other researchers then quickly moved to test whether stereotype threat applies to gender stereotypes—in particular, the stereotype that women are bad at math (Brown & Josephs, 1999; Quinn & Spencer, 2001; Spencer et al., 1999; Walsh et al., 1999). In one experiment, male and female college students with equivalent math backgrounds were tested (Spencer et al., 1999). Half were told that the math test had shown gender differences in the past and half were told that the test had been shown to be gender fair—that men and women had performed equally on it. Among those who believed that the test was gender fair, there were no gender differences in performance, but among those who believed it showed gender differences, women underperformed compared with men. Stereotypes about women and math hurt women's performance. In another experiment by the same researchers, women performed worse on the math test even when there was no mention of gender differences. The stereotype about women and mathematics apparently was well known to them, and it did not even have to be primed by the experimenters. The stereotype is simply there for women any time they encounter difficult mathematics problems.

What about the intersection of gender and ethnicity? The case of Asian American women and mathematics is particularly interesting. As women, they are stereotyped as being bad at math, but as Asian Americans they are stereotyped as being talented at math. Research shows that when Asian American women's ethnic identity is primed they perform better on math problems, and when their gender identity is primed they perform worse, compared with a control group that has had neither identity primed (Shih et al., 1999). The same positive and negative effects of stereotype activation have been found in children as young as kindergarten age (Ambady et al., 2001).

Latinas face a different set of challenges than Asian American women, because both their gender and their ethnic group are stereotyped as lacking in math ability. In an interesting experiment, Latino men and women and White men and women were randomly assigned to either a stereotype-threat condition (they were told that the math test they were about to take was "diagnostic" of their "actual abilities and limitations") or a no-threat condition (no reference to their ability was made) (Gonzales et al., 2002). They then completed a difficult math test. The results are shown in Figure 3.1. Notice that the performance of

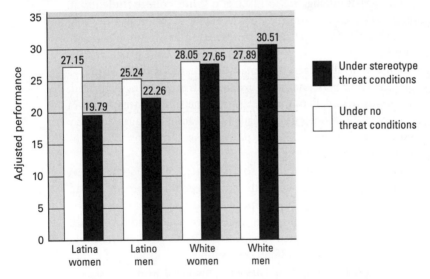

FIGURE 3.1

Results of a study measuring the performance of Latino and White women and men on a difficult math test under stereotype-threat conditions (diagnostic) versus no-threat conditions (nondiagnostic).

Source: Gonzales, Patricia M., Blanton, H., & Williams, K. (2002). "The Effects of Stereotype Threat and Double-Minority Status on the Test Performance of Latino Women," *Personality and Social Psychology Bulletin, 28*, pp. 659–670. Copyright © 2002 by Sage Publications, Inc. Reprinted by permission of Sage Publications, Inc.

Latino men is hurt somewhat under the stereotype-threat (diagnostic) condition, but the performance of Latinas is hurt more. Being the object of two stereotypes seems to hurt their performance twice as much. Notice also that stereotype threat actually helps the performance of White men, something that has been found in numerous studies but is rarely noticed by the researchers. (How would you interpret that result?)

In summary, then, the research on stereotype threat demonstrates the impact that both gender and ethnic stereotypes can have on people's performance.

We now turn to research that looks not at stereotypes but at actual gender differences in personality and behavior. In the process, we will see which of the gender stereotypes are accurate and which are not.

Gender Differences Versus Individual Differences

Suppose we say that a particular study of kindergarten children showed boys to be more aggressive than girls. Just what does that mean?

Such a statement generally means that there were average differences between males and females, and that these differences were statistically significant. It most certainly does not mean, however, that all the boys were more aggressive than all the girls. With data on gender differences, the distributions, although showing average differences, generally overlap to a great extent (see Figure 3.2). Typically there is a great deal of variability among members of one gender (individual differences). Therefore, one should not be surprised to find an aggressive little girl in the kindergarten in such a study. There may be some very aggressive little girls, but on average, the boys are more aggressive. And particularly if the number of people is large, a statistically significant gender difference may be found even though the average scores of males and females are fairly close.

The point is that even when there are average gender differences in a particular trait, almost always there are still large individual differences—differences from one female to the next and from one male to the next. Often these individual differences are more important than the average gender differences. A finding that females are less aggressive than males should certainly not lead one to expect that all females are unaggressive.

Often in this book I will make a statement such as "Males are more aggressive than females" as a kind of shorthand for the more precise—but awkward—"Males, on average, are more aggressive than females." Individual differences and the great overlap of distributions should always be kept in mind, however.

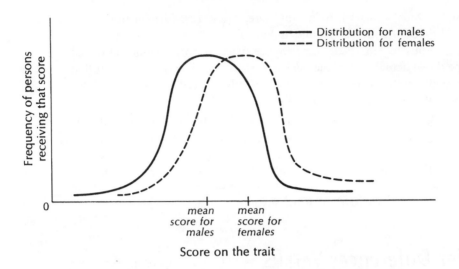

FIGURE 3.2
Examples of distributions of scores for males and females that might lead to statistically significant gender differences in the trait.

Meta-Analysis

At this point, there are literally thousands of studies investigating psychological gender differences. These studies have attempted to document the "real differences," using the terminology introduced earlier. This should mean that we have a thorough understanding of which behaviors show gender differences and which do not. Unfortunately, things are a bit more complicated than that. Often the results of different studies contradict one another. For example, some studies of gender differences in infants' activity levels find that boys are more active, whereas others find no differences. In such cases, what should we conclude?

Another problem is that sometimes a single study that finds a gender difference will be widely cited and included in textbooks, and the five other studies of the same behavior that found no gender difference will be ignored. It seems likely that this occurs particularly when a finding of gender differences confirms the stereotypes held by authors and the general public.

Meta-analysis is a technique that allows researchers to bring order out of this seeming chaos of sometimes contradictory studies (Hyde & Linn, 1986). Meta-analysis is a statistical technique. It allows the researcher to statistically combine the results from all previous studies of the question of interest to determine

Meta-analysis: A statistical technique that allows a researcher to combine the results of many separate research studies.

what, taken together, the studies say. In conducting a meta-analysis, the researcher goes through three steps:

1. The researcher locates all previous studies on the question being investigated (e.g., gender differences in aggression). This step can often be done today using computerized searches of databases such as PsycINFO.

2. For each study, the researcher computes a statistic that measures how big the difference between males and females was, and what the direction of the difference was (males scoring higher or females scoring higher). This statistic is called *d*. The formula for it is

$$d = \frac{M_M - M_F}{s}$$

where M_M is the mean or average score for males, M_F is the mean or average score for females, and s is the average standard deviation of the male scores and the female scores. If you've studied statistics, you know what a standard deviation is. For those of you who haven't, the standard deviation is a measure of how much variability there is in a set of scores. For example, if the average score for females on test Q is 20 and all the scores fall between 19 and 21, then there is little variability and the standard deviation would be small. If, on the other hand, the average score for females is 20 and scores range from 0 to 40, then there is great variability and the standard deviation will be large. The *d* statistic, then, tells us, for a particular study, how big the difference between the male and female means was, relative to the variability in scores. If *d* is a positive value, then males scored higher; if *d* is negative, females scored higher; and if *d* is zero, there was no difference.

3. The researcher averages all the values of *d* over all the studies that were located. This average *d* value tells, when all studies are combined, what the direction of the gender difference is (whether males score higher or females score higher) and how large the difference is.

   Although there is some disagreement among experts, a general guide is that a *d* of 0.20 is a small difference, a *d* of 0.50 is a moderate difference, and a *d* of 0.80 is a large difference (Cohen, 1969).

A substantial number of meta-analyses of gender differences are now available, most of them based on large numbers of studies. Meta-analyses, whenever available, will form the basis for the conclusions presented in this chapter.

We shouldn't leave this discussion without noting a moral that emerges. Often a very interesting gender difference will be found in a study, and the study will be given a great deal of publicity, including being discussed in textbooks and professors' lectures. Students need to develop a critical attitude in such cases. The first question one should ask when hearing such a report is, Has this finding been replicated? **Replicated** means that the study has been repeated independently by other scientists and the same results obtained. A single study that finds a gender difference is not very convincing. Are there other studies of the same behavior that find no difference? Or have many different scientists all found this difference consistently?

> **Replicate:** To repeat a research study and obtain the same basic results.

Now let us proceed to see whether there is evidence for gender differences in a variety of personality characteristics and behaviors.

Aggressive Behavior

Gender Differences   One of the most consistently documented psychological gender differences is in aggressive behavior, with males being more aggressive than females (Maccoby & Jacklin, 1974). Psychologists generally define **aggression** as behavior intended to harm another person. This gender difference holds up for every one of the many different kinds of aggression that have been studied, including physical aggression and verbal aggression (Hyde, 1984b). Furthermore, this gender difference has been found in all cultures in which the appropriate data have been collected (Maccoby & Jacklin, 1974).

> **Aggression:** Behavior intended to harm another person.

Gender differences in aggressiveness appear early.

Developmentally, this difference appears about as early as children begin playing with one another, around the age of 2 or 2½. The difference continues consistently throughout the school years. Of course, as people get older they become less aggressive, at least in the physical sense. It is rare to see adults rolling around on the floor as they punch each other, compared with the frequency with which that occurs on an elementary school playground. We have less information available on gender differences in adult aggression, but we do know that the vast majority of crimes of violence are committed by men (although female crime is on the increase). According to the results of social psychologists' research on aggression (most of it done in the laboratory with college students), there are some situations in which there are no gender differences; but it is rare for women to be more aggressive than men (Frodi et al., 1977). In particular, women are likely to be as aggressive as men when it appears that it would be justified or even prosocial to be aggressive. It also seems that men and women react differently to provocation: What angers a man (and leads him to be aggressive) tends to make a woman anxious, not angry or aggressive.

Because I was interested in finding out how large gender differences in aggression are, I reviewed a large number of studies (143, to be exact) of gender differences in aggression, using the technique of meta-analysis (Hyde, 1984b; see also Eagly & Steffen, 1986). I found that gender differences in aggression do appear consistently. The value of d computed in the meta-analysis was 0.50, which is a moderate difference—in fact, the size of the difference is approximately as large as that shown in Figure 3.2. The analysis also showed that gender differences in aggression are largest among preschoolers; gender differences become smaller with age and are quite small among college-age participants.

What Causes the Gender Difference?   The causes of the gender difference in aggressive behavior have been hotly debated, with the nature and nurture teams battling against each other. The nature team attributes gender differences in aggressiveness to the greater size and muscle mass of males and/or differences in the levels of the sex hormone testosterone. These factors will be discussed in detail in Chapter 10.

On the nurture side, a number of environmental forces might produce the observed gender difference: (1) Aggressiveness is a key part of the male role in our society, and unaggressiveness or passivity a key part of the female role. Following the logic of cognitive-developmental theory, as soon as children become aware of gender roles, girls realize that they are not supposed to be aggressive and boys know that they should be. As noted in Chapter 2, this logic does not work very well in explaining how gender differences develop so early, but it may be helpful in explaining gender differences among older children. (2) Children imitate same-gender adults more than opposite-gender adults, and they see far more aggression in men than in women, particularly on TV and in movies. In short, boys imitate men, who are aggressive, and girls imitate women, who are unaggressive. (3) Boys

FOCUS 3.2

HOW ACCURATE ARE PEOPLE'S GENDER STEREOTYPES?

We sometimes hear a person say, "It's only a stereotype," meaning that stereotypes about gender differences are not real differences, or that stereotypes are not at all accurate. Yet the evidence indicates that sometimes stereotypes correspond to real differences. For example, there is a stereotype that males are more aggressive than females and, as we saw earlier in this chapter, there is a moderate gender difference in aggression.

Psychologist Janet Swim (1994) devised a clever technique to determine the accuracy of people's gender stereotypes. She had research participants estimate how large gender differences were for a list of behaviors for which meta-analyses are available. The participants estimated whether males or females scored higher, and they made their estimates along the scale shown in Figure 3.3. Using that scale, they were told that 0 meant no gender difference, 0.20 was a small difference, 0.50 was a moderate difference, and 0.80 was a large difference, and that they could go even higher for a really large difference.

The results indicated that people are fairly accurate about or, if anything, tend to underestimate the magnitude of gender differences. That is, they don't

receive more rewards for aggression and less punishment for it than girls do. These reinforcements and punishments might be in a physical form, such as spanking, or in a verbal form, such as comments from adults like "Boys will be boys" in response to a boy's aggression and "Nice young ladies don't do that" to a girl's aggression. Boys may also be rewarded in the form of status or respect from their peers for being aggressive, whereas girls receive no such reward. Research, however, indicates that boys are punished more for aggression than girls are by both parents and teachers (Maccoby & Jacklin, 1974; Serbin et al., 1973), thus posing a problem for this explanation. At the same time, psychologists believe that some kinds of punishments for aggression may actually increase a child's aggression rather than decrease it. Therefore, the punishments that boys receive may make them more aggressive. (4) A somewhat more complex cultural argument takes into account the fact that, simply because of the way our culture organizes child-care, the major disciplinarians of small children are women—mothers and teach-

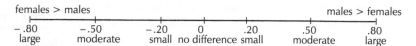

FIGURE 3.3

The rating scale used in Swim's study of the accuracy of people's gender stereotypes.

> SOURCE: From *Journal of Personality and Social Psychology,* 1994, vol. 66, pp. 21–36. Copyright © 1994, the American Psychological Association. Reprinted with permission.

hold stereotypes that blow the differences way out of proportion. For example, the average estimate of the size of the gender difference in aggression was 0.51, and the meta-analysis discussed earlier in this chapter found $d = 0.50$ (Hyde, 1984b). The actual size of the gender difference on the SAT-Math is 0.39 (Hyde et al., 1990), but participants estimated 0.12; that is, they underestimated.

The results, then, indicate that people—or at least college students—do not have wildly inflated notions about how large psychological gender differences are.

> SOURCE: Swim 1994.

ers. Research indicates that children's identification with a punishing adult is important in determining the effects the punishment will have. If the child is highly identified with the adult, punishment will decrease aggression, whereas if the child is not identified with the adult, punishment will increase aggression (Eron et al., 1974). Little girls are more highly identified with their mothers and female teachers than boys are. Hence punishment by mothers and female teachers would decrease the aggression of girls and increase the aggression of boys. One implication of this line of reasoning is that if we want to reduce the aggressiveness of boys, or increase the aggressiveness of girls, or minimize gender differences, we will need to get fathers more involved in caring for their children and encourage more men to be preschool and elementary school teachers.

One interesting experiment tested the first hypothesis stated above, that gender roles are a powerful force creating gender differences in aggression (Lightdale & Prentice, 1994). The researchers used the technique of deindividuation to produce a situation that removed the influences of gender roles. **Deindividuation** refers to a state in which the person has lost his or her individual identity; that is, the person has become anonymous. Under such conditions, people feel no obligation to conform to social norms such as gender roles; deindividuation essentially places the individual in a situation free of gender roles. Half the participants were placed in an individuated condition by having them sit close to the experimenter, identify themselves by name, wear large name tags, and answer personal questions. Deindividuated participants sat far from the experimenter and were simply told to wait quietly. All participants were also told that the experiment required information from only half the participants, whose behavior would be monitored, and that the other half would remain anonymous. Next, the participants played an interactive video game in which they first defended and then attacked by dropping bombs. The number of bombs dropped was the measure of aggressive behavior.

> **Deindividuation:** A state in which a person has become anonymous and has therefore lost his or her individual identity.

The results indicated that, in the individuated condition, men dropped significantly more bombs (31.1, on average) than women did (26.8, on average). In the deindividuated condition—that is, in the absence of gender roles—there were no significant gender differences. In fact, females dropped somewhat more bombs (41.1, on average) than males did (36.8, on average). In short, the significant gender differences in aggression disappeared when the influences of gender roles were removed.

The question of what causes gender differences in aggressiveness is a complex one that has not been completely resolved by scientific data. Perhaps the best conclusion to make at this point, and the one that seems to agree best with the existing data, is that there are probably rather small biologically based gender differences in aggressiveness and that cultural forces act to magnify these differences considerably.

Self-Esteem

Popular best-sellers like Mary Pipher's *Reviving Ophelia* (1994) have spread the word that girls have major self-esteem problems beginning in early adolescence—and, by implication, that boys do not. Meta-analysis is perfectly suited to determining whether these claims are accurate, and so Kristen Kling and I conducted one on studies of gender differences in self-esteem (Kling et al., 1999; see also Major et al., 1999).

We located data on 216 different samples, representing the testing of more than 97,000 people. Averaged over all samples, the average effect size was $d = 0.21$. Males scored higher, on average, but the difference was small—certainly not huge as one would expect from the popular press.

Pipher and others have also argued that the pattern of gender differences changes developmentally with age. Elementary school girls may have self-esteem equal to that of boys, but the problems begin in early adolescence. To test this hypothesis, we computed effect sizes for different age groups. The results showed that for elementary school children (ages 7 to 10), $d = 0.16$; for middle-school children (ages 11 to 14), $d = 0.23$; and for high-schoolers, $d = 0.33$. That is, in early adolescence the gender difference is still small, and it grows larger in high school. Interestingly, for adults who are 23 to 59 years old, $d = 0.10$, and for those who are 60 and over, $d = 0.03$. In other words, the gender difference is close to zero in adulthood.

We were also interested in the combined effects of gender and ethnicity. For White samples the effect size was 0.20, whereas for Black samples it was −0.04. (For other ethnic groups, too few studies were available to compute effect sizes.) These results lead to a rather unsettling conclusion: The female deficit in self-esteem that has caused so much concern is true for Whites (and even then it is small) but not for Blacks, among whom there is no gender difference. Psychology has been a psychology of Whites.

In sum, males on average score higher on self-esteem measures, but the gender difference is small and may be true only for Whites. The gender difference is tiny in the elementary school years and largest in the high school years, but even then it is not huge. On the other hand, it probably is large enough to be concerned about, in which case at least two of Mary Pipher's explanations ring true—that girls in the United States are subjected to a sex-saturated media environment that objectifies them, and that they are victims of peer sexual harassment. Adolescent girls deserve a better environment.

Self-esteem is different from self-confidence. **Self-esteem** refers to the level of global regard that one has for oneself and is measured by items such as "Overall, I feel good about who I am." **Self-confidence,** in contrast, refers to a person's belief that she or he can be successful at some task. Self-confidence tends to vary depending on the task. Latisha may feel confident about math problems but may lack confidence about spelling.

> **Self-esteem:** The level of global positive regard that one has for oneself.

> **Self-confidence:** A person's belief that she or he can be successful at a task.

Let's return to an example we considered in Chapter 1. Suppose a group of students take their first exam in Introductory Psychology. Immediately after they complete the exam and before they receive their grades, we ask them to estimate how many points (out of a possible 100) they think they got on the exam. Most studies indicate that we will find a gender difference, with females estimating that they will get fewer points than males estimate (Beyer, 1999; Mednick & Thomas, 1993). Psychologists interpret this as indicating that females have lower self-confidence than males do.

The gender difference in self-confidence is an important one. People with low expectations for success avoid engaging in challenging tasks. Thus this gender difference may have important effects on women's careers and accomplishments, a point to be discussed further in Chapter 8.

Although the gender difference in self-confidence is fairly consistent, we need to place some qualifications on the general result (Lenney, 1977, 1981; Mednick & Thomas, 1993). First, whether females give lower estimates of their expectancies depends on the kinds of tasks involved. For example, females do not give lower estimates if they are made to think a task is gender appropriate for them. Second, the gender difference depends on the kind of feedback given to people about their performance. If females are given clear and unambiguous feedback about how well they are doing, or how good their abilities are, then their estimates are not lower than males'. Finally, the gender difference depends on the presence or absence of social comparisons or social evaluations. If other people are present and everyone is being compared with one another, then women give low estimates; but if they work alone or in situations where they do not expect their performance to be compared with others', then their estimates are not lower. In short, women have lower self-confidence than men in some situations, but not in others.

Before leaving the topic of self-confidence, I need to note one further complication, namely, interpretation of the results. The objective, statistical result in the studies we have been discussing is that males estimate they will get more points on the exam or some other task. To use the terminology of Chapter 1, the *interpretation* of this result is that males have more self-confidence than females, or that *females are lacking in self-confidence.* This is a *female-deficit* interpretation. Would it be possible to make a different interpretation that would still be consistent with the data? An alternative interpretation is that males' estimates are too high (rather than females' being too low) and that males are unrealistically overconfident. This alternative is just as reasonable an interpretation of the gender difference, but it implies a problem for males. As it turns out, with tasks such as these it is possible to decide which interpretation is more accurate, because we can find out how students actually did on the exam. In fact, males do tend to overestimate their performance by about as much as females underestimate theirs, although some studies find females' estimates to be accurate and males' to be inflated (Beyer, 1999; Mednick & Thomas, 1993). Hence, there is some truth in each interpretation—men are probably a bit overconfident and women a bit underconfident.

Also, girls are socialized for *modesty*—that is, they are socialized not to brag about their accomplishments, but rather to be modest about them. According to this interpretation, women give lower estimates of their expected performance than they may actually think they will achieve in order to conform to the social norm of modesty. In a study designed to test this hypothesis, first-year college students estimated their first semester grade point averages (GPAs) either in public conditions (the student reported it out loud to the student experimenter) or in private conditions (the student wrote it on an index card out of sight of the experimenter and then sealed it in an envelope) (Heatherington et al., 1993). In the public conditions, in which women presumably would feel the pressure of the modesty norm, a significant gender difference in prediction of grades was found, with women predicting lower grades for themselves than men did. However, there was no significant gender difference in the private condition. It seems that when there is no need to be modest, there is no gender difference. In a second experiment by the same researchers, college students were asked to predict their GPAs publicly either to a nonvulnerable person or to a vulnerable person (a person who revealed he or she had earned a low GPA). Women's estimates were lower than men's only in the second condition, that is, when reporting to the vulnerable person. This result suggests that there is more than modesty at work here—namely, empathy for others.

In summary, then, women give lower estimates of their achievements than men do. However, men may overestimate by as much as women underestimate. And women may simply be conforming to norms that they be modest about their achievements and that they not hurt the feelings of someone who may have achieved less. Given all these findings, one would be mistaken to conclude that women lack self-confidence in achievement situations.

Activity

Psychologists have debated whether gender differences in activity level exist. Certainly if you ask the average parent or teacher, they will tell you that boys are more active, and most child psychology texts have maintained the same.

A major meta-analysis found that d was approximately 0.50—that is, that there is a moderate gender difference, with males having the higher activity level (Eaton & Enns, 1986). Among infants, d was 0.29; it was 0.44 for preschoolers and 0.64 for older children. Thus the difference is present from infancy and seems to get larger with age, at least among children.

The findings for gender differences in activity level parallel those for many other gender differences in an important way: They depend on the *situation* in which the activity is measured. For example, the gender difference is significantly larger when peers are present ($d = 0.62$) than when they are absent ($d = 0.44$). That is, the activity level of boys, relative to that of girls, seems to increase when other kids are there.

This meta-analysis was based on samples of children from the general population. In samples of hyperactive children, about 80 percent are boys (Holborow & Berry, 1986).

What causes this gender difference? The arguments are similar to those made about aggressive behavior, and the issue has not been resolved in either case. What we do not know is how much the developmental precocity of girls contributes to this difference. Stated briefly, girls are ahead of boys in development. As children grow older, they learn to control their activity more. It might be, then, that the lower activity level of girls represents simply a greater ability to control activity because of their being somewhat more mature than boys.

Helping Behavior

Social psychologists have studied helping behavior extensively. A meta-analysis of studies of gender differences in helping behavior found that $d = 0.34$ (Eagly & Crowley, 1986). The positive value indicates that males, on average, helped more than females and that the gender difference is somewhere in the small-to-moderate range. This finding may be somewhat surprising because helping or nurturing is an important part of the female role, and therefore we might have expected a negative value for d. To clarify this finding, the researchers, Alice Eagly and Maureen Crowley, probed into those kinds of situations that produced more helping by males and those that produced more helping by females. They noted that some kinds of helping are part of the male role and some are part of the female role. Helping that is heroic or chivalrous falls within the male role, whereas nurturance and caretaking fall within the female role.

Consistent with these predictions from social roles, Eagly and Crowley found that the tendency for males to help more was especially pronounced when the situation might involve danger (such as stopping to help a motorist with a flat tire). The tendency was also stronger when the helping was observed by others (rather than when the person needing help and the research participant were alone together). Helping that involves danger and that carries with it a crowd of onlookers has great potential for heroism, and that kind of helping is part of the male role.

The plot thickens because social psychologists have spent most of their time studying precisely these kinds of helping behaviors—the ones that occur in relatively short-term encounters with strangers. They have devoted little research to the kind of caretaking and helping that is characteristic of the female role—the kind of behavior that more often occurs in the context of a long-term relationship, such as a mother helping her child. Therefore, the gender difference found by Eagly and Crowley, showing that males help more, is probably no more than an artifact of the kinds of helping that psychologists have studied and the kinds of helping that they have overlooked.

Again we see that patterns of gender differences are highly dependent on the situation in which they are observed.

Anxiety

Most studies show that girls and women are more fearful and anxious than boys and men. A meta-analysis found $d = -0.30$ for general anxiety (Feingold, 1995). The difference is significant, but not large. Girls also report more fears than boys do (Brody et al., 1990; Gullone & King, 1992). Once again, though, the difference is not simple. Most of the studies that find differences are based on self-reports, but studies based on direct observations often find no gender difference (Maccoby & Jacklin, 1974). To illustrate the difference between self-reports and direct observations, suppose a psychologist is trying to determine whether girls are more fearful of dogs than boys are. If the psychologist is using the self-report method, he or she would interview children and ask them if they are afraid of dogs. Using the method of direct observation, the psychologist would bring a dog into the room and see whether the children behave fearfully.

What we know, then, is that girls and women are more willing to admit that they have anxieties and fears. It is possible that these self-reports reflect higher levels of fear and anxiety in females than in males. But it is also possible that males and females experience the same levels of fear and anxiety and that females are only more willing to admit them. This might be a result of gender-role stereotypes, which portray women as fearful and timid and men as fearless and brave. Such stereotypes would encourage women to admit their feelings and men to pretend not to have them. At this point, however, studies have not been able to resolve this issue.

Most of the studies just discussed are based on samples of the general population and concern the kinds of fears and anxieties most of us experience routinely. If, in contrast, we consider psychiatrically diagnosable phobias, women clearly outnumber men (Robins et al., 1984; Russo, 1990).

Empathy

Empathy means feeling the emotion another person is feeling. It essentially involves putting yourself in another's place emotionally. Females are considered more empathic than males, as part of the general stereotype of emotional expressivity in females and emotional inexpressivity in males. Does this stereotype reflect a real difference?

Psychologists Nancy Eisenberg and Randy Lennon (1983) reviewed studies of empathy and found that the results on gender differences were rather mixed. Gender differences in empathy seem to depend on the way in which they are measured. When people respond to self-report questionnaires containing items like "Seeing people cry upsets me," the gender difference is large, with females showing more empathy. When researchers use a different measure, designed to measure "empathy" in newborn infants, girl infants are more likely to cry when they hear a tape recording of another infant crying, but the size of this gender difference is only moderate. Finally, when actual psychological measures of emotional responding are used, or when researchers unobtrusively observe actual behavior (facial expressions, tone of voice), gender differences are small. Perhaps gender differences are largest with the questionnaires because the questions tap gender-stereotyped responses. For example, the item mentioned earlier, "Seeing people cry upsets me," sounds a lot like the stereotypes of women as being emotional and aware of the feelings of others, discussed in the first section of this chapter. Such items may measure stereotypes more than reality. Although the evidence does indicate that females are somewhat more empathic than males are, the difference is a small one.

Beyond Gender Stereotypes: Androgyny?

With the last 30 years of feminist thought has come a desire for new models of human behavior that overcome gender stereotypes. One prominent alternative that has been suggested is **androgyny,** the combining of masculine and feminine characteristics in an individual. Psychologists quickly moved to develop tests to measure androgyny (e.g., Bem, 1974). But to understand these tests, we must first go back several more decades and examine psychologists' traditional understandings of masculinity and femininity (M-F) and how they measured them before androgyny arrived on the scene.

> **Androgyny:** The combination of masculine and feminine psychological characteristics in an individual.

Psychologists' Traditional Views of M-F   Psychologists' traditional view was that masculinity and femininity were at opposite ends of a single scale—that is, that a unidimensional, bipolar continuum described variations in M-F (see Section 1 of Figure 3.4).

One of the traditional tests to measure M-F is the FE (for femininity) scale of the California Psychological Inventory (Gough, 1957). It is a simple paper-and-pencil test, with a person responding *true* or *false* to items, depending on whether the items describe the person or not. (A sample item is "I am somewhat afraid of the dark.") Then a score is computed that places the person at some point along the bipolar continuum.

Items were chosen for such tests in a simple way—the criterion being that they must differentiate biological males from biological females. That is, an item was chosen if it showed marked gender differences, meaning that a much different proportion of males as compared with females respond *true* to it. Therefore, an item such as "I prefer a tub bath to a shower" can appear on such tests, not because it reflects anything profound about the essence of masculinity or femininity, but simply because males tend to prefer showers and females tend to prefer tub baths. The implicit assumption, then, is that "femininity" is the quality of women that differentiates them from men.

Feminist psychologists raised a number of criticisms of M-F tests (e.g., Constantinople, 1973). A serious question is whether M-F is so simple that it can be scored on a single scale or dimension or whether, instead, it might require two or several scales to capture its complexity. A second criticism is that

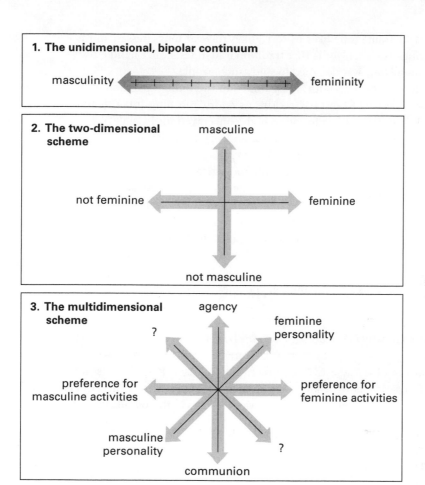

FIGURE 3.4
Progressive conceptualizations of masculinity-femininity.

the psychologists who constructed M-F tests never really defined precisely what they meant by "femininity" or "masculinity." They typically settled for the definition of gender differences when they chose items, with an implicit definition that femininity is whatever women are that men aren't. This may be a practical definition, but it does not give us much insight into what femininity or masculinity is.

The Concept of Androgyny   The question that needs to be raised is, Why can't a person be both feminine and masculine? In fact, most of us know people who are both. An example would be a woman who has strong achievement drives, is very successful at her career, plays tennis very well, and likes to wear jeans, and who at the same time likes to cook, likes to wear long dresses, and is sensitive and caring. The problem is that traditional M-F tests can't handle her. The research on androgyny was designed to study such people.

Androgyny means having both masculine and feminine psychological characteristics. It is derived from the Greek roots *andro,* meaning "man" (as in *androgens*—sex hormones that are found in high concentrations in males), and *gyn,* meaning "woman" (as in *gynecologist*). An androgynous person, then, is a person who has both masculine and feminine psychological characteristics.

As shown in Figure 3.4, the concept of androgyny is based on a two-dimensional model of masculinity-femininity. The idea is that instead of masculinity and femininity being opposite ends of a single scale, they are two separate dimensions, one running from not feminine to very feminine, and the other from not masculine to very masculine. This would allow for androgynous people, that is, people who are high in both femininity and masculinity. It would also allow for feminine people and for masculine people. In the second diagram of Figure 3.4, the androgynous people would be the ones falling in the upper-right-hand quadrant.

Measuring Androgyny   Psychologist Sandra Bem (1974) constructed a test to measure androgyny (see also Spence & Helmreich, 1978) that is shown in Table 3.4. It consists of 60 adjectives or descriptive phrases. Respondents are asked to indicate, for each, how well it describes them on a scale from 1 (never or almost never true) to 7 (always or almost always true). Of the 60 adjectives, 20 are stereotypically feminine,[1] 20 are stereotypically masculine, and 20 are neutral, that is, not gender typed. Items 1, 4, 7, and so on in Table 3.4 are masculine; items 2, 5, 8, and so on are feminine; and 3, 6, 9, and so on are neutral. Therefore, *self-reliant* is a masculine characteristic, *yielding* is feminine, and *helpful* is neutral.

Once the test has been taken, people are given two scores: a masculinity score and a femininity score. The masculinity score is the average of their self-ratings of the masculinity items, and their femininity score is the average of their self-ratings of the femininity items. This will give each person a score on each of the two scales shown in the two-dimensional scheme in Figure 3.4. The androgynous people should be in the upper-right-hand part, which means they should be high in masculinity and high in femininity. Bem (1977) defines "high" as being above the median (the median is a kind of average). Therefore, people are androgynous if they are above the median on masculinity and above the median on femininity (the median on each of these scales is generally about 4.9). A feminine person who scores high (above the median) on femininity but low (below the median)

---

[1]Unlike the constructors of the M-F tests, Bem did not avoid defining M and F by simply relying on gender differences. Instead, she defined femininity as those characteristics that are considered socially desirable for women in our culture, and similarly for masculinity.

TABLE 3.4
Are You Androgynous?

The following items make up the Bem Sex Role Inventory. To find out whether you score as androgynous on it, first rate yourself on each item, on a scale from 1 (never or almost never true) to 7 (always or almost always true).

1. self-reliant	22. analytical	41. warm
2. yielding	23. sympathetic	42. solemn
3. helpful	24. jealous	43. willing to take a stand
4. defends own beliefs	25. has leadership abilities	44. tender
5. cheerful	26. sensitive to the needs	45. friendly
6. moody	of others	46. aggressive
7. independent	27. truthful	47. gullible
8. shy	28. willing to take risks	48. inefficient
9. conscientious	29. understanding	49. acts as a leader
10. athletic	30. secretive	50. childlike
11. affectionate	31. makes decisions easily	51. adaptable
12. theatrical	32. compassionate	52. individualistic
13. assertive	33. sincere	53. does not use harsh
14. flatterable	34. self-sufficient	language
15. happy	35. eager to soothe hurt	54. unsystematic
16. strong personality	feelings	55. competitive
17. loyal	36. conceited	56. loves children
18. unpredictable	37. dominant	57. tactful
19. forceful	38. soft-spoken	58. ambitious
20. feminine	39. likable	59. gentle
21. reliable	40. masculine	60. conventional

SCORING:

(a) Add up your ratings for items 1, 4, 7, 10, 13, 16, 19, 22, 25, 28, 31, 34, 37, 40, 43, 46, 49, 52, 55, and 58. Divide the total by 20. That is your masculinity score.

(b) Add up your ratings for items 2, 5, 8, 11, 14, 17, 20, 23, 26, 29, 32, 35, 38, 41, 44, 47, 50, 53, 56, and 59. Divide the total by 20. That is your femininity score.

(c) If your masculinity score is above 4.9 (the approximate median for the masculinity scale) and your femininity score is above 4.9 (the approximate femininity median), then you would be classified as androgynous on Bem's scale.

SOURCE: Bem (1974, 1977), Hyde & Phillis (1979).

on masculinity would fall in the lower-right-hand quadrant in Figure 3.4. Similarly, a masculine person who scores high on the masculinity scale but low on the femininity scale would fall in the upper-left-hand quadrant. Finally, people who score low on both scales fall in the lower-left-hand quadrant and are called "undifferentiated" because they don't rate themselves very highly on any of the adjectives, masculine or feminine. Therefore, having taken the Bem Sex Role Inventory, an individual can be placed in one of four categories: masculine, feminine, androgynous, or undifferentiated.

In her work with college students, Bem typically finds that about one-third of them are androgynous, according to her scale.

Is It Better to Be Androgynous?   As an ideal, androgyny sounds good. It permits freedom from gender-role stereotypes and allows people to express their opposite-gender tendencies. But what are androgynous people like in reality? Do they function well psychologically? Does society view them suspiciously because of their gender-role nonconformity? A number of studies give us answers to these questions.

Good-Listener Study   Bem has done several studies to find out how androgynous people, as compared with masculine or feminine people, actually behave in various demanding situations (Bem, 1975; Bem & Lenney, 1976; Bem et al., 1976). Her general prediction in these studies is that androgynous people should do better in a wider variety of situations, because they are capable of being feminine or masculine when the situation calls for it. Masculine or feminine people, on the other hand, may do well when stereotyped behavior is required, but in situations demanding nonstereotyped behavior, they will do poorly.

The good-listener study was one such experiment (Bem, 1975). The participant listened as a lonely transfer student (who was actually a confederate of the experimenter's) poured out a list of troubles in adjusting to college life (Bem, 1975). The interaction was watched from behind a one-way mirror, and participants were scored for their responsiveness and sympathy for the talker, as a measure of their nurturance.

The idea is that the "feminine" quality of nurturance is what is called for in this situation. Bem predicted that feminine people would be more nurturant than masculine people. Androgynous people, able to be either masculine or feminine, should do what is appropriate, namely, be nurturant. The results turned out as predicted: Feminine people and androgynous people of both genders did not differ from each other, and both groups were significantly more nurturant than masculine people.[2]

---

[2]If you are a psychology student, you might want to note that this study was a means by which Bem could establish the *validity* of the Bem Sex Role Inventory. That is, to be valid, the scale should be able to differentiate various groups of people based on theoretical predictions. That is precisely what this study does.

Androgyny and Self-Esteem The traditional assumption in psychology was that gender typing was a good thing in terms of personal adjustment. That is, it was thought that the well-adjusted person would be appropriately gender typed (feminine if a female, masculine if a male) and that people who were not gender typed would be poorly adjusted.

With a test to measure androgyny available, we are in a position to see how well adjusted androgynous people are, and how their adjustment compares with that of gender-typed people. Research indicates that androgynous people and masculine people tend to be high in self-esteem, in comparison with feminine people and undifferentiated people, who tend to be lower in self-esteem (Bem, 1977; Spence et al., 1975). The ordering of groups, from highest to lowest in self-esteem, has been found consistently to be as follows: androgynous, masculine, feminine, undifferentiated (Spence & Helmreich, 1978). These results, then, indicate that androgynous people have high self-esteem, an important psychological characteristic. The point that masculine people tend to have higher self-esteem than feminine people is certainly worth noting. The implications of this finding will be discussed further in Chapter 15.

Two conclusions have emerged from research on the psychological implications of androgyny (Taylor & Hall, 1982). First, there is no support for psychologists' traditional assumption that masculinity is best for men and femininity is best for women. For example, masculinity is highly correlated with self-esteem for men, but masculinity is also highly correlated with self-esteem for women. Thus the purely gender-typed feminine woman is at a disadvantage in terms of psychological health. Second, although both masculinity and femininity are positively correlated with self-esteem, masculinity shows a consistently higher correlation. In short, whether one is a man or a woman, one's masculine characteristics seem most related to self-esteem and other measures of psychological health.

Criticisms Androgyny sounds wonderful, but are there any problems with it? Several criticisms have been raised. (For a summary of feminist criticisms of androgyny, see Lott, 1981.)

First, androgyny is advantageous in freeing people from the restrictions of rigid gender-role stereotypes. In so doing, however, it may be setting up an extraordinarily demanding, perhaps impossible, ideal. For example, in the good old days, a woman could be considered reasonably competent ("successful") if she could cook well. To meet new standards and be androgynous, she not only has to cook well, but also has to repair cars. That is, androgyny demands that people be good at more diverse things, and that may be difficult. Indeed, the characteristics required to be androgynous sometimes seem almost mutually contradictory. For example, on the Bem Sex Role Inventory, in order to be androgynous, one needs to be forceful and dominant ("masculine" items) and also shy and soft-spoken ("feminine" items). It is hard to see how a person could be all of those at once. Of

course, the ideal androgyn would display different characteristics in different situations, depending on what was most appropriate; but knowing what is most appropriate can be difficult.

Some feminist scholars have also raised a second criticism of androgyny
(Orloff, 1978). They regard it as essentially a "sellout" to men. That is, to become
androgynous, women need to add masculine traits to their personalities, or
become more like men. Reflecting cultural feminism (see Chapter 2), the argument has been made that what we should do, rather than to encourage women
to become more like men, is to concentrate on valuing those things that women
do and are. To these scholars, rediscovering and cherishing womanhood would
be preferable to encouraging androgyny. This, of course, is a matter of personal
values.

A third criticism is that the very definition of androgyny rests on traditional
assumptions about masculinity and femininity. To be classified as androgynous,
the person merely scores high on two scales that consist of stereotyped masculine
and feminine traits. As such, the concept of androgyny is hardly radical or liberating (Bem, 1981).

Other scholars have pointed out that we need to be careful about generaliz-
ing from androgyny in *personality* traits (as measured by the Bem Sex Role Inventory) to expecting androgyny in actual *behavior* or in *attitudes* about gender roles
(Spence & Helmreich, 1980). That is, just because a person is rated as androgynous on the Bem Sex Role Inventory does not mean he or she will necessarily behave flexibly in all situations, or that he or she will have liberal attitudes about
women's roles.

Stages of Gender-Role Development

A friend of mine recounted the following story. Both she and her husband hold
Ph.D.'s and are professors of political science. Both are feminists, and they try to
have an egalitarian marriage and run an egalitarian household. Yet one day their
son came home from kindergarten, glibly telling them how women could be
nurses and not doctors, and men could be doctors and not nurses. To say the
least, my friend was quite dismayed by this. She had certainly never told her son
such things, and in fact had told him quite the opposite. Probably some of you
have had similar experiences, or know of people who have, and can appreciate
the frustration parents feel when, after all their efforts to teach their children
about gender-role equality and freedom, the children still keep coming up with
the same tired old stereotypes. However, some research and theory in psychology provide an explanation for this phenomenon, not to mention a ray of hope
for parents.

Psychologist Joseph Pleck (1975) has proposed that children go through
stages in their understanding of gender roles. Basically, he has applied cognitive-

developmental theory to children's understanding of gender roles, much as Kohlberg did (as discussed in Chapter 2). Kohlberg, however, stopped his theoretical descriptions when children were five or six; Pleck has extended the theory to describe older children and adults.

According to Pleck's theory, children pass through three stages of gender-role development, and these stages parallel the stages of moral development. In the first stage of moral development in children, the premoral or preconventional phase, children are dominated by their desire to gratify their own impulses, and seek to be good only to avoid punishment. In the corresponding *first stage of gender-role development,* the child's gender-role concepts are disorganized. The child may not even know her or his own gender yet, and has not yet learned that only men are supposed to do certain things, only women others. (In Kohlberg's terms, such children have not yet acquired the concepts of gender identity or gender constancy.) In the second stage of moral development, conventional role conformity, children understand rules and conform to them mostly to get approval from others, particularly authorities. In the corresponding *second stage of gender-role development,* children know the rules of gender roles and are highly motivated to conform to them themselves and also to make others conform to them. This stage begins in childhood and probably reaches its peak in adolescence when gender-role conformity is strongest. In the third stage of moral development, the postconventional phase, moral judgments are made on the basis of internalized, self-accepted principles rather than on the basis of external forces. In the corresponding *third stage of gender-role development,* people manage to go beyond (transcend) the limitations of gender roles imposed by society; such individuals develop psychological androgyny in response to their own inner values. Pleck, then, views androgyny as a stage of development.

Of course, many adults never make it out of the second stage of moral development to move on to the third stage. An example would be the man who donates a lot of money to a charity because doing so will earn him respect and approval from important people, rather than because of an internalized belief that the charity is a good cause and he should support it. So, too, some people never go beyond the second stage of gender-role development and move on to androgyny; they remain for their entire lives restricted by tight limitations of gender roles.

Pleck's theory is informative in answering the question originally posed, namely, Why do children who should have very flexible ideas about gender roles instead have rigid—sometimes absurdly rigid—ideas? This theory suggests that children, as part of their cognitive development and their attempts to understand how the world works, must go through a stage of gender-role fundamentalism. Essentially, they must first learn the common preconception that only men can be doctors and only women can be nurses. Then they can learn that there are exceptions to this rule and that girls can become doctors. Feminist parents probably cannot realistically expect that their children will skip the second stage of gender-role development. What they can hope for, and provide encouragement for, is their children eventually reaching the third stage and androgyny.

In Conclusion

In this chapter I first discussed the nature of gender stereotypes in the United States and how these stereotypes may vary as a function of race/ethnicity. I also considered the potential effects of stereotypes, including stereotype threat. Then I presented the evidence regarding gender differences in some important psychological characteristics, basing the conclusions primarily on the results of meta-analyses. For some characteristics—particularly for aggressive behavior and activity level—there was good evidence of a difference. For others—self-esteem, anxiety, helping, and empathy—there seemed to be a gender difference, but a smaller one, and the gender difference depended more on the situation or on the way in which the trait was measured.

The danger in focusing so much on gender differences is that we will start to think that males and females have entirely different personalities. Although there are some differences, as we have seen, what is perhaps more impressive are the similarities. Even for aggressive behavior, the gender difference is not large. And we have not even begun to discuss a long list of characteristics that have probably never shown a gender difference in anyone's research and have, therefore, been omitted from mention—for example, honesty, optimism, sincerity. It is important to remember that *gender similarities* are more the rule than gender differences.

It is equally important to remember that gender differences often depend heavily on the *situation* or *context*. For example, as we saw in the section on helping behaviors, males are more likely than females to help in a situation that involves some personal danger, whereas females are more likely to engage in nurturant helping with children. Therefore, it makes no sense to refer to women as "the helping sex" or to men as "the aggressive sex." The gender difference found in one situation may not be found in another.

In the last sections of the chapter, we discussed androgyny as an alternative to traditional standards of masculinity and femininity. Thirty years after the concept of androgyny was introduced into psychology, I think we can say two things about it. First, it challenges our traditional notions of masculinity-femininity and suggests new ways of behaving that may be more adaptive and satisfying. That is good. Second, androgyny is not an instant remedy for all the gender-related injustices in society. Although it is an interesting and important concept, we cannot expect too much of it. Research and theorizing must move on.

EXPERIENCE THE RESEARCH

HOW ACCURATE ARE PEOPLE'S BELIEFS ABOUT GENDER DIFFERENCES?

Ask four people you know to provide you, individually, with some data. When you interview them, tell them that you want to determine how accurate people are in estimating the size of some psychological gender differences. Have them fill out the following form, explaining what they are to do. Be sure that they understand that they can give any number they want; that is, they do not have to answer just 0.20 or 0.50, but could give an answer like 0.34. Also be sure that they understand the importance of the difference between negative numbers and positive numbers. Negative numbers on this scale mean that females score higher than males, and positive numbers mean that males score higher than females. This is the form to use:

1. Aggressive behavior among preschoolers.

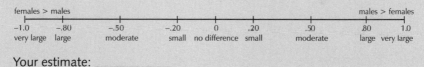

Your estimate: _____

2. Math computations by elementary school children, such as "What is 5 × 7?"

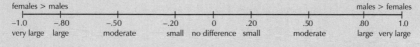

Your estimate: _____

3. Approval of a couple engaging in sexual intercourse when they are only casually acquainted.

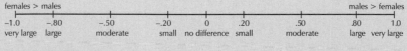

Your estimate: _____

How accurate were your respondents? Meta-analyses show that among preschoolers, males are more aggressive, $d = 0.58$. For accuracy of math computations by elementary school children, $d = -0.20$; girls do somewhat better. For approval of a couple engaging in sexual intercourse when they are only casually acquainted, $d = 0.81$; males are more approving.

SOURCE: Based on Swim (1994). From *Journal of Personality and Social Psychology, 20*, pp. 697–706. Copyright © 1984 by the American Psychological Association. Reprinted with permission.

Suggestions for Further Reading

Fiske, Susan T. (1993). Controlling other people: The impact of power on stereotyping. *American Psychologist, 48,* 621–628. This article describes the Supreme Court case on sex discrimination, *Price Waterhouse* v. *Hopkins,* and how Fiske's research on gender stereotyping was relevant.

Steele, Claude M. (1997). A threat in the air: How stereotypes shape intellectual identity and performance. *American Psychologist, 52,* 613–629. Steele explains his theory of stereotype threat and the evidence for it—including both racial stereotypes and gender stereotypes.

Women of Color

4

An odd thing occurs in the minds of Americans when Indian civilization is mentioned: little or nothing. As I write this, I am aware of how far removed my version of the roots of American feminism must seem to those steeped in either mainstream or radical versions of feminism's history. . . . I am intensely conscious of popular notions of Indian women as beasts of burden, squaws, traitors. . . . How odd, then, must my contention seem that the gynocratic tribes of the American continent provided the basis for all the dreams of liberation that characterize the modern world.

— FROM PAULA GUNN ALLEN, THE SACRED HOOP:
RECOVERING THE FEMININE IN AMERICAN INDIAN TRADITIONS

Introduction

We must confront a serious problem: Much of the scholarship on "the psychology of women" is, in reality, a psychology of White, middle-class, American women. But are phenomena such as difficulties balancing work and family common among all women? When we consider women of diverse racial and ethnic origins in the United States, it quickly becomes apparent that the different and complex social forces acting on them may result in different patterns of gender roles and behaviors. Among these forces are higher rates of poverty, discrimination, variations in family structures, identification with ethnic liberation movements, and evaluation of appearance by White, dominant-culture standards of beauty.

In this chapter we will focus on women in four major U.S. ethnic groups: African Americans, Hispanics, Asian Americans, and American Indians. The purpose of the chapter is to provide important background information about the cultures and heritages of these ethnic groups as well as an overview of gender roles in these cultures. This background and overview will provide the context for more specific discussions of research on ethnic minority women that occur in other chapters throughout the book.

Hispanics: People of Spanish descent, whether from Mexico, Puerto Rico, or elsewhere.

Before we proceed, though, we need a brief discussion of terminology. The term **Hispanics** refers to all people of Spanish origin, whether from Puerto Rico, Cuba, Mexico, or elsewhere. **Chicanos** are Americans of Mexican origin. *Chicano* also refers specifically to men and **Chicana**[1] to women, an example of the familiar male-as-normative problem in language. Another

Chicanos: Americans of Mexican descent; may also refer specifically to male Mexican Americans.

Chicana: A female of Mexican descent.

---

[1]"Chicana" has negative connotations to some, so the broader term "Latina" is generally preferable. "Hispanic" is also not favored by some because it was a term imposed by the U.S. Bureau of the Census.

general term is **Latinos,** which refers to Latin Americans. Again, the term *Latino* refers both to all Latinos and to males, whereas **Latina** refers to females. Most recently, the term **Americanos** has been introduced to refer to Latinos living in the United States (Comas-Diaz, 2001).

Latinos: Latin Americans.

Latina: A female Latin American.

For Americans of African origin, there has been a steady evolution in terminology. Prior to the 1960s, *Negro* was the respectful term. With the 1960s, the Black Power movement was ushered in, and its followers urged the use of the term *Black* to connote pride in the very qualities that were the basis of discrimination, and promoted slogans such as "Black Is Beautiful." In the late 1980s, as ties to Africa and pride in one's heritage came to be emphasized, there was a shift to the term *African Americans.*

Asian Americans[2] (replacing terms such as *Orientals*) and *American Indians* or *Native Americans* are additional terms that are preferred, replacing various slang or older terms that are now considered disrespectful.

Asian Americans: Americans of Asian descent.

Even the terms *White* and *Caucasian* can be problematic. For example, many Hispanics are white in skin color, yet when most people use the term *White* they don't mean to include Hispanics in the category. They really mean "White, not of Hispanic origin," but that phrase is too long to be convenient. The alternative that has been proposed for *White* is **Euro-American.** It has the advantage of being parallel to other terms, such as Asian American and African American, and places the emphasis on the group's cultural heritage.

Euro-Americans: White Americans of European descent. An alternative to the term *Whites.*

Two themes will recur throughout this chapter. One is the theme of similarities and differences. Just as we have approached the issue of gender differences by emphasizing that there are both differences and similarities, so, too, will we approach the topic of ethnicity by recognizing both *differences* and *similarities.* As we look at African American women, Latinas, Asian American women, American Indian women, and Euro-American women, we will see that there are some similarities, some common experiences such as childbirth and motherhood that women from all these cultures share. However, we will also see that there are some profound differences, some resulting from differences in culture in the land of origin, others resulting from the greater poverty and discrimination experienced by members of some ethnic groups. These twin themes, then—similarities and differences—must always be kept in mind.

A second recurring theme in this chapter is simultaneous *oppression and strength.* Women in all these groups have a heritage of oppression, including slavery for African American women and internment in U.S. prison camps during

---

[2]Usually people of Asian heritage are grouped with people of Pacific Islander heritage (e.g., those from the Philippines). Rather than using the long and complicated phrase "Asian and Pacific Islander," I'll use "Asian" with the understanding that it includes Pacific Islanders.

World War II for Japanese American women. Current oppression, in the form of race discrimination and sex discrimination, persists. In the midst of this oppression, though, it would be a mistake to regard these women as victims. Instead, one sees enormous strength in them and in their lives. Thus strength in the face of oppression is another continuing theme.

An Ethnic/Cultural Critique of Psychological Research

In Chapter 1 we considered a gender-based critique of possible sources of sex bias in psychological research. In this section we will consider a parallel critique, namely, an ethnic/cultural critique that examines psychological research for sources of race bias (Landrine et al., 1995; Yoder & Kahn, 1993).

First, the very concept of **race**, as it has been used in psychology over the last 100 years, is problematic (Betancourt & Lopez, 1993; Jones, 1991). The biological concept of race implies a group of people with a common set of physical features, such as skin color, hair texture and color, and so on, who have mated exclusively with other members of their race and not with members of other races. The minute that interbreeding with members of another race occurs, there is no "pure" race. Interbreeding, of course, has been the rule rather than the exception in many countries around the world. For example, in the case of an African American woman in the United States, whose skin color is black, 50 percent of her ancestors may be of African heritage and 50 percent of European heritage. The existence of such people renders the concept of race useless. Nonetheless, this woman may have grown up in the culture of an African American community and may identify herself as African American. For this reason, terms such as culture and ethnicity are generally preferable to race. The term **ethnic group** refers to a group that shares a common culture and language.

> **Race:** A biological concept referring to a group of people with a common set of physical features who have mated only within their race.

Second, just as males have been the norm in psychological research, so have Euro-Americans been the norm. As one critic put it, "Even the rat was white" (Guthrie, 1976). Basing studies exclusively on samples of White college students or other samples of Euro-Americans has been considered perfectly acceptable methodology. In part, this is just bad science. It involves making an unjustified inference from an all-White sample to all people. In addition, the experience of persons of other ethnic groups then becomes invisible. The consequence is that Whites represent "people," and everyone else becomes "subcultures" (Landrine et al., 1995).

> **Ethnic group:** A group of people who share a common culture and language.

Third, psychological research has ignored the different meanings that may be attached to different words, gestures, and so on by people from different ethnic groups (Landrine et al., 1995). The culture in which we grow up teaches us the meaning of various words. Therefore, two different ethnic groups (for example,

African Americans and Euro-Americans) may have different understandings of the meanings of words even though both groups speak the same language (English). This language issue quickly becomes a radical critique of methods in psychological research, because it means that standardized tests, many of which were normed on exclusively White samples, may contain terms that are defined differently by other ethnic groups. The tests, then, might measure something quite different for African Americans or Hispanic Americans. To demonstrate this problem, Hope Landrine and her colleagues (1995) administered the Bem Sex Role Inventory (BSRI), which measures androgyny (see Chapter 3), to 71 White women and 67 women of color. The women first rated themselves on each adjective, and then chose, from among several choices, the phrase that best defined that term for them. Overall, there were no differences between the Euro-American women and the women of color in their scores on the BSRI—that is, there were ethnic group similarities. However, there were major differences between the groups in the definitions chosen. For example, for the term *passive,* White women most frequently chose the definition "am laid-back/easy-going," whereas women of color most frequently chose "don't say what I really think." That is, there were large ethnic or cultural differences in the meanings that the women attached to the terms. Such findings imply that we need to go back to the very beginning with many psychological tests to determine how people from various ethnic groups understand the terms used in the tests.

Ethnocentrism: The tendency to regard one's own ethnic group as superior to others and to believe that its customs and way of life are the standards by which other cultures should be judged.

A fourth criticism concerns possible bias in interpretation of results. If Euro-Americans are the norm, then the behavior and experiences of people of color are interpreted as being deficient—much as we have seen in examples of female deficit models. Just as the latter bias is often called androcentrism, so the former bias can be called **ethnocentrism** or, more specifically, **Eurocentrism.** As an example of such bias, viewed through the eyes of White researchers, the African American family has generally looked deficient.

Eurocentrism: The tendency to view the world from a Euro-American point of view and to evaluate other ethnic groups in reference to Euro-Americans.

As we look at psychological research on women of color in the United States, then, we must bear in mind that both androcentrism and Eurocentrism have permeated much of the traditional research and that new research is badly needed that is both gender fair and race/ethnic fair.

Psychological researchers who are people of color have now proposed guidelines for research with ethnic minority communities (McDonald, 2000; Myers et al., 2000; Santos de Barona & Barona, 2000; Sue & Sue, 2000). Underlying all these guidelines, which are listed below, is the assumption that conducting research with people of a specific ethnic group is valuable.

1. *Collaboration:* Researchers from the ethnic group under study should be included as collaborators. All-White teams of researchers can get it wrong.

2. *Theory:* The theory that is the basis for the research should be examined for its appropriateness for this ethnic group. If it is inappropriate, it should be revised or a new theory should be formulated.

3. *Measurement:* Psychological measures should be tested for reliability and validity in this ethnic group. If a measure does not meet standards, it should be revised or a new measure devised.

The measurement issue is quite complex. Scales and the constructs they are designed to measure should demonstrate *equivalence.* Experts distinguish between conceptual equivalence and translational equivalence (Sue & Sue, 2000). **Conceptual equivalence** refers to the consistency of psychological constructs across different cultures. It is important that a concept developed by, say, a Euro-American psychologist actually exists and has the same meaning in whatever other cultures are being studied. For example, some cultures have no concept of "homosexuality" (Herdt, 1984). And in other cultures, behaviors considered to be homosexual differ considerably from what most Euro-Americans would assume. Among Mexicans, for instance, if two men engage in anal intercourse, the inserting partner is not considered homosexual because his behavior is like the man's in heterosexual intercourse. The man who takes the receptive role is the only one who is considered homosexual (Magaña & Carrier, 1991). Asking about homosexuality in these cultures either may not compute or may lead the respondent to answer with a very different idea in mind than the researcher intended.

> **Conceptual equivalence:** In multicultural research, the construct measured by a scale has the same meaning in all cultures being studied.

Translational equivalence refers to consistency of meaning between languages. For example, a scale written in English and translated into Spanish has to have the same meaning in the second language. The technique used to check this involves both translation and back-translation. That is, the scale would be translated from English to Spanish by a fluently bilingual person, and then translated from Spanish *back* to English by another fluently bilingual person. If the back-translated version matched the original, that would be evidence for translational equivalence.

> **Translational equivalence:** In multicultural research, whether a scale written in one language and translated into another has the same meaning in both languages.

4. *Subcultural variations:* Be aware of subcultural variations. Do not assume, for example, that Chinese Americans and Japanese Americans have the same views on a topic.

5. *Cultural heritage:* Researchers must understand the cultural heritage of the group being studied, including the values of the culture of origin (Japan for Japanese Americans) and the history of that ethnic group in the United States. In short, researchers must be "culturally competent."

6. *Deficit interpretations:* Do not assume that differences between a particular ethnic minority group and Euro-Americans reflect deficits on the part of the ethnic minority group.

7. *Race versus social class:* In many research designs, race and social class are confounded, largely because many ethnic minority groups in the United States are more likely to live in poverty. When race differences are found in research, often it is unclear whether such differences are due to race or to social class. Researchers should remove this confound from their research designs or at least be very cautious in interpretations of findings of ethnic group differences.

Cultural Heritages of Women of Color in the United States

Before we can consider current gender roles and women's issues for women of color, we must first understand the cultural, historical heritage of these women. This heritage includes the cultures in the lands of origin (Africa, Asia, Latin America), the impact of the process of migrating to the United States, and the impact of the dominant Euro-American culture of the United States.

The Cultural Heritage of Asian American Women   Chinese—almost all of them men—were recruited first in the 1840s to come to America as laborers in the West and later in the 1860s to work on the transcontinental railroad (for excellent summaries of the cultural heritage of Asian Americans, see Root, 1995; Tsai & Uemura, 1988). Racist sentiment against the Chinese grew, however, and there was a shift to recruiting first Japanese and Koreans, and then Filipinos. An immigration control law passed in 1924 virtually ended the immigration of Asian Americans until the act was revoked in 1965. Then in the late 1960s and the 1970s, there was a mass exodus to the United States of refugees from war-torn Southeast Asia.

Today, Asian Americans make up 4 percent of the U.S. population and are composed of 21 percent persons of Chinese heritage, 20 percent Filipinos, 15 percent Japanese, 12 percent Vietnamese, 11 percent Koreans, 10 percent Asian Indians, and many smaller groups (Humes & McKinnon, 1999; Tsai & Uemura, 1988).

Examples of racism directed against Asian Americans are many. Perhaps the most blatant was the internment of Japanese Americans during World War II. Japanese Americans had their property confiscated and were forcibly moved to prison camps in the United States.

Research indicates that there are six core Asian values (Kim et al., 2001):

1. *Collectivism:* Others' needs, especially those of the family, should be considered before one's own needs.

2. *Conformity to norms:* The individual should conform to the expectations of the family and society.

3. *Emotional control:* Emotions should not be openly expressed.

4. *Family recognition through achievement:* One's educational failure brings shame to the family, and one's educational success brings honor.

5. *Filial piety:* Children must show deep respect for their parents.

6. *Humility:* One should be humble and never boastful.

For Asian Americans, the family is a great source of emotional nurturance; for them, the family includes not only the nuclear family but ancestors and the family of the future as well. One has an obligation to the family, and the needs of the family must take precedence over the needs of the individual. Maintaining harmonious relations with others, especially one's family, is important. Shame and the threat of loss of face, which can apply both to the individual and to his or her family, are powerful forces shaping good behavior. Often what may appear to be passivity in Asian Americans more accurately represents conscientious efforts to maintain dignity and harmony.

Asian American women have a high interracial marriage rate (Lott, 1990). This pattern began when U.S. servicemen married Asian women in World War II, the Korean War, and the Vietnam War. In second and later generations the interracial marriage rate can be as high as 50 percent.

Subcultural Variations   You would not expect all Europeans—say, French, Germans, and Italians—to be alike and have similar cultures. Similarly, although Asians share some similarities in culture, there are also great variations. One Asian American woman is a Chinese American who is a fourth-generation descendant of a man brought to work on the transcontinental railroad, and who is herself a physician, as is her father. Another is a woman who escaped from Vietnam in a leaky boat in 1975, nearly died several times, and is heroically coping with a new language and a new culture. There are great subcultural variations among Asian American women.

Research on these cultures has begun to appear. One example is a study of Khmer refugee women (Thompson, 1991). (For a similar study of Vietnamese refugee women, see Kibria, 1990; see also Tien, 1994.) The Khmer are an ethnic group from Cambodia, in Southeast Asia. Many fled to the United States in the 1970s when Cambodia was invaded during the Vietnam War. The research began with understanding the role of women in Cambodia before the war, the culture in which these women had grown up and been socialized. Peasant women had responsibility for childcare and household work, but they also tended fish traps and were co-workers in the important activities involved in cultivating the rice fields. Buddhism, a dominant religious influence, assigns a superior status to men.

A Hmong refugee woman in the United States. Large subcultural variations exist among Asian American women. Refugee women, for example, would have very different experiences from Chinese women who are fifth generation in the United States.

Many marriages were arranged, and the women felt that they had been sexually assaulted on their wedding night.

The women had experienced many forms of war-related and refugee-related trauma, including rape, abduction, and torture. The ethics of feminist research posed a dilemma for the researchers in this project, because they wanted to learn more about the traumatic experiences, but questioning the women about them itself seemed to cause pain by reactivating traumatic memories. The researchers tried to achieve a balance between the goal of giving voice to these women's experiences and the goal of not traumatizing them further.

The researchers were particularly impressed by the fact that these women were survivors who possessed incredible strength. The women had survived severe traumas—both physically and mentally—and were now successfully coping with a vastly different culture.

The Cultural Heritage of Latinas   Hispanic Americans are currently the nation's second largest minority, constituting 12 percent of the population, and they are expected to be the largest within a few years (Thierren & Ramirez, 2000). Of those living on the mainland, their backgrounds are as follows: 66 percent Mexican, 9 percent Puerto Rican, 4 percent Cuban, and 15 percent from other Central and South American countries.

When we speak of the cultural heritage of Latinos, we must first understand the concept of acculturation. **Acculturation** is the process of incorporating the beliefs and customs of a new culture (Vasquez & Baron, 1988). The culture of Chicanos is different from both the culture of Mexico and the dominant Euro-American culture of the United States. Chicano culture is based on the Mexican heritage, modified through acculturation to incorporate Euro-American components.

> **Acculturation:** The process by which one takes on the beliefs and customs of a new culture as one's own.

In understanding Latino culture, two factors are especially significant: (1) bilingualism and (2) the importance of the family. **Bilingualism,** or knowing two languages, is important because Latino children often grow up learning two languages and thus two cultures. Spanish is more often the language of home and family, and English the language of school and job. Those Latinas who are immigrants often know no English at first, and therefore the language barrier is a problem in finding employment and in other areas of daily life.

> **Bilingualism:** Knowing two languages.

The family is the central focus of Latino life. Traditional Latinos place a high value on family loyalty and on warm, mutually supportive relationships. Family solidarity is highly valued, as are ties to the extended family (Ginorio et al., 1995; Segura & Pierce, 1993). For Latinos, "familism" has three components: obligation to the family, support from the family, and family as referents (i.e., as role models) (Sabogal et al., 1987). A Hispanic girl is likely to be "mothered" not only by her own mother, but by aunts or grandmothers as well. This emphasis on family is in many ways at odds with the dominant culture's emphasis on individualism. Furthermore, this emphasis on family places especially severe stresses on employed Latinas, who are expected to be the preservers of family and culture and to do so by staying in the home.

The process of *migration* is also critical in understanding the background of Hispanic women. While the majority of Latinos were born in the United States, 39 percent are foreign born (Thierren & Ramirez, 2000). The process of migration can be extremely stressful (Espin, 1987a; Salgado de Snyder et al., 1990). For a woman who leaves her homeland and friends, acute feelings of loss and grief are to be expected.

The Cultural Heritage of American Indian Women   American Indians and Alaska Natives constitute 1.5 percent of the population of the United States (Ogunwole, 2002). To understand the heritage of American Indian women, one needs to understand the cultures of traditional Indian societies. Just as we have recognized subcultural variations for women of other ethnic groups, we must do the same for Indian women, this time recognizing tribal variations, which are in some cases great. Indian societies, however, were invaded by Euro-Americans, so that many current Indian practices resemble Euro-American culture as a result of forced acculturation, Christianization, and economic changes (LaFromboise et al., 1995).

The Spirit World is essential to Indian life, and especially to the life of Indian women. Women are seen as extensions of the Spirit Mother and as keys to the continuation of their people (LaFromboise et al., 1994).

A harmonious relationship with the Earth is an important part of Indian life. Interestingly, the Earth is referred to as Mother Earth, so that women are seen as connected with this important part of existence.

Thus Indian women see themselves as part of a collective, fulfilling harmonious roles in the biological, spiritual, and social realms: Biologically, they value being mothers; spiritually, they are in tune with the Spirit Mother; and socially, they preserve and transmit culture and are the caretakers of their children and relatives (LaFromboise et al., 1990).

The Cultural Heritage of African American Women   Two factors are especially significant in the cultural heritage of African American women: the heritage of African culture and the experience of slavery in America and subsequent racial oppression (Greene, 1994). Two characteristics of the African woman's role are maintained today: an important economic function, and a strong bond between mother and child (Greene, 1994). African women have traditionally been economically independent, functioning in the marketplace and as traders. Black women in the United States continue to assume this crucial economic function in

Mother-child bonds are very important in African American culture.

the family to the present day. Mother-child bonds also continue to be extremely important in the structure of Black society.

African American culture, like that of the other ethnic groups discussed earlier, but in contrast to Euro-American society, emphasizes the collective or tribe over the individual (Fairchild, 1988). It recognizes the important connections between generations, and it is concerned with the individual's harmonious relationship with others (Myers et al., 2000), in contrast to the "me generation" of contemporary White culture and contemporary White psychology.

In the 1800s, when it was popular in the United States to put White women on a pedestal, Black women were viewed as beasts of burden and subjected to performing the same demeaning labor as Black men (Dugger, 1988). Angela Davis has argued that this heritage created an alternative definition of womanhood for Black women, one that includes a tradition of "hard work, perseverance and self-reliance, a legacy of tenacity, resistance, and an insistence on sexual equality" (1981, p. 29).

Gender Roles and Ethnicity

Against this background of the cultural heritages of women of color in the United States, let us consider the gender roles that have evolved in these various ethnic communities. A basic tenet of feminist theory is that gender and ethnicity interact as social norms are formed and as they affect behavior. Thus gender roles are defined in the cultural context of a particular ethnic group, and it is not surprising that there are variations in gender roles from one ethnic group to another.

Gender Roles Among American Indians   It is clear today that the early work of anthropologists misrepresented women's roles in Indian culture (LaFromboise et al., 1990). The tale is an interesting one of how sex bias and race bias can easily pervade research in the social sciences. The researchers were male and non-Indian. As such, they focused on male activities and had greater access to male informants. A stereotyped dichotomy of Indian woman as either princess or squaw emerged, much like the saint/slut dichotomy that was drawn for Victorian White women. Furthermore, because the anthropologists were non-Indians and therefore outsiders, they were able to observe only public behaviors and how Indians interacted with outsiders, thereby missing private interactions. In some tribes, dealing with outsiders was an activity assigned to men. Therefore, researchers overestimated male power within the tribe because they did not observe Indian women's powerful roles within the private sphere. In some tribes, for example, there was a matrilineal system of inheritance, meaning that women could own property and that property passed from mother to daughter. Indian women, doubtless wary after the legacy of White violence against Indians, were unlikely to share their intimate rituals or feelings with these outsiders.

As an example of the problems with this early research, scholars claimed that there was a pattern of isolating menstruating women from the tribe and its activities, keeping them in a secluded menstrual hut, based on the Indian view that women were contaminated at this time (e.g., Stephens, 1961). Firsthand accounts from Indian writers, however, provide a different interpretation (LaFromboise et al., 1990). Menstruating women were not shunned as unclean, but rather were considered extremely powerful, with tremendous capacities for destruction. Women's spiritual forces were thought to be especially strong during menstruation, and women were generally thought to possess powers so great that they could counteract or weaken men's powers. The interpretation makes all the difference—shifting from a view of a shunned, powerless woman to that of a too-powerful woman.

A woman's identity and gender roles in traditional Indian culture were rooted in her spirituality, extended family, and tribe (LaFromboise et al., 1990). The emphasis was on the collective and on harmony with the spiritual world, the world of one's family and tribe, and the natural world.

The evidence shows that some North American Indian tribes had a system of egalitarian gender roles, in which separate but equally valued tasks were assigned to males and females (Blackwood, 1984). It is important to remember tribal variations, for not all tribes had such egalitarian patterns, but certainly some—for example, the Klamath—did.

For American Indian women, status increased with age. Older women were respected for their wisdom and for their knowledge of tribal history, herbal medicine, and the sacred (LaFromboise et al., 1995). Some American Indian women today advocate a return to these traditional values associated with women's roles,

Four generations of Arapaho women. In traditional Native cultures, women's status increased with age.

while at the same time cultivating the skills of the dominant Euro-American culture—a combination known as *bicultural competence* (LaFromboise et al., 1995).

Some tribes—such as the Canadian Blackfeet—had institutionalized alternative female roles. There was the role of the "manly hearted woman," a role that a woman who was exceptionally independent and aggressive could take on. And there was a "warrior woman" role among the Apache, Crow, Cheyenne, Blackfoot, and Pawnee tribes (e.g., Buchanan, 1986). In both cases, women could express "masculine" traits or participate in male-stereotyped activities while continuing to live and dress as a woman.

Gender Roles Among African American Women   As noted earlier, a methodological point must be recognized, one that is apparent in research on African Americans but is a problem with research on other ethnic groups as well. The problem in much of the research to be cited is the *confounding of ethnicity and social class*. Because Blacks tend to be overrepresented in the lower class and Whites in the middle class, it is generally not clear whether differences between Blacks and Whites should be attributed to race or to social class. Research techniques generally have not been powerful enough to conquer this ambiguity. As you read this material on gender and ethnicity, you should keep in mind that much of what seem to be ethnic group differences may actually be due to social class differences.

Multiple gender roles—mother, worker, head of household, wife—have been a reality for African American women for generations, in contrast to the situation for White middle-class American women, for whom these multiple roles are more recent. Reflecting on the absurdity of defining women's role on the pedestal in White middle-class Victorian terms, the Black abolitionist Sojourner Truth commented at a women's rights convention in the 1800s:

> That man over there says that women need to be helped into carriages, and lifted over ditches, and to have the best place everywhere. Nobody ever helps me into carriages, or over mud puddles, or gives me any best places. . . . And ain't I a woman? Look at me! Look at my arm! . . . I have plowed and planted, and gathered into barns, and no man could head me—and ain't I a woman? I could work as much and eat as much as a man (when I could get it), and bear the lash as well—and ain't I a woman? I have borne thirteen children and seen most of them sold off into slavery, and when I cried out with a woman's grief, none but Jesus heard—and ain't I a woman? (Abolitionist, 1831)

Although motherhood is still a prime gender-role definer, African American women have taken on additional roles, such as worker and head of household. Black women generally expect that they must hold paying jobs as adults (Greene, 1994), and this expectation has important consequences for their educational and occupational attainments, as we shall see later. Indeed, since 1986 the number of employed Black women in America has exceeded the number of employed Black men (Dickson, 1993).

The role of the African American woman as head of household has received a great deal of publicity under the term *Black matriarchy,* suggesting that the Black woman has greater power than the man does in the Black family and culture. The high frequency with which Black households, as compared with White households, are headed by women is usually given as evidence for this phenomenon. In 1999, 45 percent of Black households were maintained by women, compared with 13 percent for White families (McKinnon & Humes, 1999). This pattern has increased over time. For example, in 1999, 45 percent of Black families were headed by women, compared with only 25 percent in 1965 (Dickson, 1993).

A number of factors contribute to the greater rates of female-headed households among African Americans (Dickson, 1993; Raley, 1996).

1. *Lower marriage and higher divorce rates among Blacks.* Among Black women between the ages of 30 and 34 in 2000, only 36 percent were married and living with a husband, compared with 65 percent in 1960. In 1990, the divorce ratio was 28.2 divorces per 100 marriages among Blacks, compared with 13 divorces per 100 marriages among Whites. This pattern of lower marriage rates and higher divorce rates in turn is a result of many of the factors listed below.

2. *The obstacles African American men have encountered in seeking and maintaining jobs necessary to support their families (Raley, 1996).* Since World War II, the number of manufacturing jobs in the United States has declined dramatically. These jobs were a major source of employment for working-class Black men. The result has been a decline in the Black working class and an expansion of the Black underclass. Joblessness among Black men contributes to low marriage rates and high divorce rates.

3. *The unequal gender ratio among African Americans.* In 2000, among 30- to 34-year-olds, there were only 84 Black men for every 100 Black women, compared with 100 White men per 100 White women and 104 Hispanic men per 100 Hispanic women (U.S. Census Bureau, 2000).

4. *Interracial dating and marriage patterns of Black men.* Black men are far more likely to marry White women than Black women are to marry White men.

In short, there are just not enough men—particularly not enough good men—to go around, so many African American women find themselves as single-parent heads of households.

On the other hand, the stereotype of matriarchal domination of African American families ignores the fact that if 45 percent of Black households are headed by women, then 55 percent must be headed by men and women jointly or by men. Thus, the female-headed household, although more common among

Blacks than Whites, is not the only pattern—in fact, the majority of Black house-holds are headed jointly by men and women or by men. Furthermore, there is a clear trend toward an increase in the number of female-headed households among Whites.

The unequal gender ratio among African Americans deserves further com-ment, because it is likely to have far-reaching psychological implications. The im-portant theorizing and research of Guttentag and Secord (1983) found that, in cultures in which men are in short supply, men essentially become a scarce and therefore precious resource. Some have argued that this applies among African Americans and that, as a result, Black men hold the power in an emotional rela-tionship (Dickson, 1993). They do not have to work at a relationship or even commit to one. They can always find another woman. On the other hand, this en-courages self-reliance in women, including a drive for more education and a de-sire to be self-supporting.

Among the elderly, too, the role of Black women differs from that of White women. The feelings of uselessness and the lack of roles experienced by White women in their youth-oriented culture are not so common among African Amer-icans. The extended-family structure among Blacks provides a secure position and role for the elderly. The "granny" role—helping to care for young grandchil-dren, giving advice based on experience—is a meaningful and valued role for the elderly Black woman (Greene, 1994). Elderly Black women seem to have a more purposeful and respected role than elderly White women do. This pattern of see-ing elderly women as wise and respected is also found among American Indians.

Gender Roles Among Asian American Women   It is common to think of Asian Americans as the "model minority." In 1998, for example, 33 per-cent of Asian American families had incomes over $75,000, compared with 29 percent for Whites. Currently, 42 percent of Asian Americans graduate from col-lege, compared with 28 percent of Whites. Nonetheless, feminist Asian Americans believe that Asian American women are victims of both racism and sexism. For example, the model minority stereotype hides the plight of recently arrived refugees, as the earlier discussion of Khmer refugee women illustrated. And dis-torted stereotypes remain in the mass media (Sue & Morishima, 1982), such as the Asian man as the violent Kung Fu warrior.

Five stereotypes about Asian American women are widespread (Root, 1995). The first is female subservience, deriving in part from the lower status of women compared with men in China and Japan. This stereotype fuels a mail-order bride business in which Euro-American men seek Asian wives. The second stereotype is that Asian American women are exotic sex toys. The third is the Dragon Lady stereotype, in which the Asian American woman is seen as a diabolical wielder of power. The dichotomy between the subservient stereotype and the Dragon Lady stereotype reinforces good girl/bad girl dualities, and Asian American women who fail to be subservient may be quickly cast as Dragon Ladies. The fourth stereotype is the sexless worker bee, which includes women who work as domestics or garment workers. The fifth stereotype is the China doll, the idea that Asian American women are fragile and innocent.

The expectations from traditional culture—for family interdependence, preservation of group harmony, and stoicism—are associated with Asian American women specifically. As part of their bicultural existence, Asian American women experience gender-role conflict, the gender roles expected in traditional culture being considerably different from those expected in modern Euro-American culture, which increasingly prizes independence and assertiveness for women. Another conflict involves the Euro-American emphasis on equality in male-female relationships, an emphasis that is at odds with the traditional Asian focus on female subservience (Tsai & Uemera, 1988).

Gender Roles Among Latinos   In traditional Latin American cultures, gender roles are rigidly defined (Comas-Diaz, 1987; Gowan & Treviño, 1998). Such roles are emphasized early in the socialization process for children. Boys are given greater freedom, are encouraged in sexual exploits, and are not expected to share in household work. Girls are expected to be passive, obedient, and weak, and to stay in the home.

These rigid roles are epitomized in the concepts of machismo and marianismo (Comas-Diaz, 1987). The term **machismo,** or *macho,* has come to be used rather loosely in American culture today. Literally, *machismo* means "maleness" or "virility." More generally, it refers to the "mystique of manliness" (Ruth, 1990). The cultural code of machismo among Latin Americans mandates that the male must be the provider and the one responsible for the well-being and honor of his family. Males hold a privileged position and are to be treated as authority figures. In extreme forms, machismo has come to include glorification of sexual conquests and the sometimes violent physical domination of women.

> **Machismo:** The ideal of manliness in Latino cultures.

Marianismo is the female counterpart of machismo (Comas-Diaz, 1987). The term derives from the Catholic worship of Mother Mary, who is both virgin and madonna. According to the ideal of marianismo, women, like Mary, are spiritually superior and therefore capable of enduring the suffering inflicted by men. Latin American culture attributes high status to motherhood. The woman is expected to be self-sacrificing in relation to her children and the rest of her family, but Latino culture at the same time holds mothers in high esteem. Although superficially these roles may seem to endorse male domination and female submissiveness, the true situation is complex. Women who do exceptionally well in the marianista role come to be revered as they grow older and their children feel strong alliances with them, so that they wield considerable power within the family.

> **Marianismo:** The ideal of womanliness in Latino cultures.

Most Latin American cultures assign the healing role to women. The majority of *espiritistas* (spiritual healers) are female (Comas-Diaz, 1987). According to research on Hispanic female healers in the United States, the role is associated with power and status (Espin, 1987a).

Thus, although the traditional role for Latinas involves passivity and subservience, this generalization masks the powerful roles that these women play within the family and that they may gain in certain specialized roles, such as that of *espiritista*. Recent research on Latino families has found that there is a great deal of variability, ranging from patriarchal to egalitarian family forms (Segura & Pierce, 1993). Moreover, roles are changing as Latinos press for equality (Ginorio et al., 1995).

Education

Immigrants to the United States have long realized that education is the best avenue for improving their job success, their status, and their standard of living. Worldwide, education and literacy are critical issues for women. Therefore, as we examine women's achievements, it is important to look at education.

Table 4.1 shows the educational attainments of Americans as a function of gender and ethnicity. Focusing first on the section of the table that deals with high school graduation, you can see that although there is some problem with high school dropouts among Whites and Asian Americans, basically about 80 to 90 percent of each group do graduate from high school. Graduation rates are considerably lower for African Americans and Latinos. This pattern is not partic-

TABLE 4.1
Educational Attainments as a Function of Gender and Ethnicity (Ages 25 and Over)

Ethnic Group	Less Than High school		High School Graduate		Some College		College Graduate or More	
	M	F	M	F	M	F	M	F
Asian Americans	13%	17%	20%	25%	21%	19%	46%	39%
Blacks	23	23	38	34	25	27	14	16
Whites	12	12	32	36	25	26	31	25
Latinos*	[43]		[46]				[11]	

*For Hispanics, the census reports do not report educational attainment by gender, nor do they separate high school graduates from those with some college.

SOURCES: McKinnon & Humes (2000); Therrien & Ramirez (2000); U.S. Census 2000, as reported in Humes & McKinnon (2000).

Asian Americans, like middle-class Euro-Americans, emphasize the importance of education, including education for women. In fact, a larger percentage of Asian American women graduate from college than do White men.

ularly gender differentiated, though: The graduation rate for females is about the same as the rate for males.

Examining the section on those who complete some college but do not graduate, you can see that the rates are about the same for all ethnic groups, ranging around 19 to 27 percent, except for Latinos, who have a lower rate of attendance. Many of these prospective Latino students are themselves immigrants and may have come from an impoverished school system and be dealing with the problems of a second language as well. Again, the rates for attending college are not gender differentiated.

The section on those who graduate from college (four or more years of college) indicates that a gender differentiation begins for Whites, with fewer women than men graduates. For the other groups, though, women's rates of graduating from college are as high as men's. Notice, too, that Asian Americans graduate from college at a considerably higher rate than Whites.

There has been much discussion of the dynamics behind Black women's educational parity with Black men (e.g., Sanders, 1988). African American women are somewhat ahead of African American men in educational achievements, as well as in professional achievements. For every Black professional man, there are nearly two Black professional women (Sanders, 1988), although it should be remembered that nursing and teaching are counted in the professions and women are often limited to such professions. In explaining these successes, Paula Giddings commented:

> Prejudice against their race and sex forced Black women to work and simultaneously limited the kinds of work they could perform. The only choice Black women had were the professions—where until recently there was less competition from White women—or domestic work. Since education is the key to the more attractive occupations, Black women have a history of striving for education beyond what their gender or their color seemed to prescribe. Black men, on the other hand, have not had the same motivation, historically, because they had a greater range of options—including blue-collar work, which often pays better than the traditional women's professions (teaching, social work, nursing, and so on). (Giddings, 1984, p. 7)

American Indian women, in contrast, are often the most conflicted about pursuing a college education (Gloria & Kurpius, 2001; LaFromboise et al., 1990). It is difficult for them to adapt to the competitive nature of higher education. Furthermore, family and community members often discourage Indian women from going to college. In one survey of Indian women undergraduates, 90 percent said that they felt they were going against their culture by attending college (Kidwell, 1976).

Beyond these statistics are also important issues of campus climate (Moses, 1989). In terms of classroom dynamics, women of color suffer double prejudice based on both their race and their gender. Leadership and academic competence are associated with White males, and so women of color are doubly distanced from possessing these admirable qualities. Furthermore, women of color are often exposed to stereotypical comments unwittingly made by faculty. As one researcher commented,

> Black students often report that the professors' tone of voice or facial expressions display disbelief or surprise when they respond correctly or otherwise show good performance. . . . Black students report that professors offer little guidance and criticism of Black students' work. . . . Professors will often make stereotypical comments about Blacks without being aware of the hurtful impact that these comments can have on Black students, particularly when they imply that Blacks are less competent than whites. (Katz, 1983, p. 36)

In predominantly White institutions, women of color often experience the paradox of underattention and overattention. On the one hand, their comments may be ignored or they may not receive the help they need in a lab. On the other hand, if the discussion focuses on women of color, they may be called on to represent the views of all women of their ethnic group. (If you are a White student, how would you like it if the class asked you to tell them what all White women, or all White men, think about issue X?)

As we consider the educational experiences of women of color, it is important to recall the important research of Claude Steele on stereotype threat, discussed in detail in Chapter 3 (Steele, 1997; Steele & Aronson, 1995). According to that research, every time a Black woman takes a calculus test, she is likely to experience double stereotype threat because women—and Blacks—are stereotyped as bad at math. Even if she is academically talented, she may be seized with worries that she will confirm stereotypes, and as a result, her performance suffers. The same is true for Latinas and American Indian women. Stereotype threat poses a serious barrier to educational attainment for women of color.

In summary, in this section on education we have examined the interaction of race and gender at two levels: the microlevel (classroom interactions and stereotype threat) and the macrolevel (statistics on degrees awarded to people of color in the United States). Two important points emerge from this discussion:

1. Gender and race are powerful factors in classroom dynamics, whether in elementary school or college. Women of color may receive stereotypical responses that encourage neither their academic achievement nor their sense of their own academic competence.

2. With the exception of Asian Americans, women of color in the United States are not graduating from college or pursuing graduate education at a rate comparable to that of Whites. This lack of education in turn precludes many occupations and limits earnings. Therefore, the recruitment and retention of women of color in higher education need to be a top priority.

Mental Health Issues

The history of clinical psychology and its treatment of people of color in the United States is heavily laden with racial stereotypes and downright racism. For example, the census of 1840 reported that Blacks in the Northern states had far higher rates of psychopathology than Blacks in the slave states. Psychiatrists of the day interpreted this finding as indicating that the supervision and control of Blacks that slavery provided were essential to Blacks' well-being; thus, the data and methods of social science were used to defend slavery as good for Blacks (Deutsch, 1944). That part of the census data was later demonstrated to have been fabricated, but the record remained uncorrected.

Psychologists in the early 1900s—among them the greats such as G. Stanley Hall—advanced theories that perpetuated racial stereotyping. For example, it was thought that Blacks were innately happy-go-lucky and therefore immune to depression (Landrine, 1988b; Thomas & Sillen, 1972).

Contemporary clinicians may perpetuate these stereotyped views, although in fancier social science jargon than their predecessors used. For example, immunity to depression has been attributed not to happy-go-luckiness, but rather to a belief that Blacks have nothing to lose—no jobs, property, or self-esteem (Prange & Vitols, 1962). Such views may be caused by and in turn may cause depressed Blacks to be misdiagnosed, often as schizophrenics (Landrine, 1988b; Simon & Fleiss, 1973). Indeed, contemporary research demonstrates that experiences of racism may contribute significantly to psychiatric symptoms among people of color (Klonoff et al., 1999).

Definitions of the term *normal* given in psychology texts often include such characteristics as emotional control, independence, the capacity for abstract and logical thinking, the ability to delay gratification, happiness, a concern with developing one's own potential to the fullest, and a sense of the self as an autonomous individual who is able to exert control over the environment (e.g., Jourard, 1974). The problem is that this definition is based on White middle-class males' experience of the self and health. It may not reflect the experience of women or of people of color. Women often have less power and control over their environment. And for the ethnic groups we have discussed, there is often more of a concern for relations with one's family and community than for advancing oneself as an individual. Thus the very definitions that psychology offers for normalcy may not be appropriate for women of color (Landrine, 1988b).

For American Indians, the definition of well-being and the method of treating disturbances are at odds with mainstream psychotherapy in the United States. In most Indian cultures, a person is considered to be in a state of well-being when she or he is peaceful and is exuding strength through self-control and adherence to Indian cultural values (LaFromboise et al., 1990). When a person is troubled, traditional healing systems are used, which involve a community process that helps the troubled individual while also reaffirming the norms of the community; the process is holistic and naturalistic (LaFromboise et al., 1995).

Whether on the reservation or off, Indian women experience intense stressors, but they appear to be reluctant to use mental health services (LaFromboise et al., 1995). In part, this reluctance is caused by the fact that they view the existing services as unresponsive to them and their needs (Medicine, 1982). Indians who do use mental health services often express concern that these services shape their behavior in a direction that is incompatible with Indian culture.

Asian American women also experience stresses from racism and sexism, and refugees have been exposed to particularly extreme stresses. Yet statistics indicate that Asian Americans, compared with Euro-Americans, underutilize mental health services (Sue, 1977). The traditional explanation was that Asian Americans simply have a low rate of mental disturbance. Yet it now seems more accurate to say that Asian American culture attaches stigma and shame to mental disturbance, so that individuals do not seek help until a true crisis has developed and all family and community resources have been tried. Furthermore, when

Asian Americans do seek therapy, they often find that it is not sensitive to the values of Asian American culture (Root, 1995).

Latinos, too, are underrepresented in the use of mental health facilities, and Hispanic women are less likely to use them than Hispanic men are (Ginorio et al., 1995; Russo et al., 1987). A number of factors have been proposed to explain why Hispanics are less likely to use these services: existing services may be inaccessible to Hispanics; some segments of the Hispanic population may use traditional methods for dealing with problems, rather than mainstream psychotherapy; and Spanish-speaking clinicians may be lacking.

This discussion indicates that an important task for clinical psychology in the future will be to develop culturally sensitive methods of psychotherapy (Landrine, 1995; True, 1990). An additional task is to increase the number of ethnic minority psychologists, who bring important cultural sensitivities with them.

Feminism and Women of Color

Women of color have emerged as powerful forces in the feminist movement, shaping feminism to reflect their experiences and priorities (Comas-Diaz, 1991). Their writings recognize that the oppression of women of color results from intertwined systems of race, gender, and class oppression. Women of color feminism tends to be critical of White feminists who focus on universal female experi-

Women of color have emerged as a powerful force in the feminist movement.

ences while ignoring racial diversity in women's experiences as well as their own privileged status as Whites (Enns & Sinacore, 2001).

An example is *Black feminist thought* (Collins, 1989; James & Busia, 1993; Ransby, 2000; Tong, 1998). Not a new invention, it has historic origins in activists such as Sojourner Truth, Ida Wells-Barnett, and Fannie Lou Hamer. Indeed, Sojourner Truth attended the famed Seneca Falls convention that shaped the feminist manifesto of the 1800s.

Nor is Black feminist thought purely the product of scholars and activists; its origins lie also in the actions of common Black women and their everyday acts of resistance, beginning in the days of slavery (Collins, 1989). It seeks to recognize and validate the lived experience of African American women, in the belief that this experience has been ignored by the traditional academic disciplines, as well as by White women's studies scholars and male African American studies scholars.

Black feminism values an ethic of caring (see the parallels in the work of Gilligan, Chapter 2). Emotions are appropriate and should be validated, not repressed. Empathy should be cultivated. Black feminist thought also holds that viewpoints and opinions are personal rather than objective (recall the feminist critique of the objectivity of science, Chapter 1), and that individuals are also personally accountable for their beliefs. Thus a psychologist whose theorizing perpetuates racial stereotypes or racism is held responsible for those effects and cannot hide behind the mask of scientific objectivity. Finally, and perhaps most importantly, Black feminist thought recognizes that both racism and sexism affect the lives of Black women.

Chicana feminism has emerged as well (see, for example, Garcia, 1989). In the 1960s, at much the same time as the Black Power movement was very active, a Chicano liberation movement was also a vital force. Probably the best-known facet of this movement was the unionization of the United Farmworkers. Chicanas were an important part of this movement. Like African American women in the Black liberation movement, they gained experience with activism, but at the same time became disturbed at the male dominance and sexism within the Chicano movement. Chicana feminism grew from these roots. Chicana feminists thus have the dual goals of cultural nationalism (liberation for Hispanics) and feminism (liberation for women).

A particularly inspiring story is found in *American Indian feminism*. First, it is important to provide some background on one of the new discoveries in American history. There is now good evidence that the foundation for our American democracy as shaped by the "fathers" of our country in the Constitution lay not in the government of Britain—after all, the patriots were not exactly thinking kind thoughts about the British right then—but in the government of the great Iroquois nation (Grinde, 1977). The founding fathers had a good deal of contact with the nearby Iroquois and apparently observed their system of governance with interest. The Iroquois system was composed of local or "state" bodies, plus a federal government consisting of legislative, executive, and judicial branches. There were important differences, however. Iroquois women had the vote, that is, had an equal say in the choice of leaders; and the executive branch consisted of a Council of Matrons, that is, wise women elders (Allen, 1986). The idea of women having power was taken for granted. Therefore, the roots of the structure of American government may well lie in the government and social structure of an American Indian group, the Iroquois.

EXPERIENCE THE RESEARCH

GENDER ROLES AND ETHNICITY ON PRIME TIME

Identify three current television series (i.e., not reruns) that focus on an African American family. Then identify three comparison series that focus on a Euro-American family. Ideally, choose comparison series that air at the same time as, or perhaps are shown immediately following, the shows about the African American families but on a different station. Observe each program twice, on two consecutive weeks. As you observe the programs, answer the following questions:

1. How are gender roles portrayed on the program? Does the main female character have a paying job? What kind of job is it? Does the main male character have a paying job? What is it? Who does the cooking? Who does the grocery shopping?

2. How is the family portrayed on the program? Is it a traditional married couple with children, or is it a female-headed household or some other kind of family?

3. How is emotional expressiveness portrayed on the program? What emotions do women express? What emotions do men express?

After you have completed your observations, compare the results for the African American family shows and the Euro-American family shows. What are the differences? What are the similarities? What impact do you think these programs have on African American and Euro-American viewers?

Finally, locate three comparable programs that focus on Asian American families, Hispanic families, and Native American families. Were you able to do it? If so, how are gender roles portrayed on those programs?

The latest development is *global feminism* (Acosta-Belén & Bose, 2000; Barlow, 2000; Oyewumi, 1997, 2000; Tong, 1998), which agrees with women of color feminism in the United States that definitions of feminism need to be broadened, but goes beyond it by emphasizing global systems of oppression. In particular, global feminism focuses on political and economic oppression, especially the oppression of Third World people by First World people, including First World women.

The topic of women of color and feminism is a delicate one. Many believe that American feminism has been dominated by White middle-class women who have put their issues at the top of the agenda while ignoring issues that are more important to women of color. At the same time, many women of color feel that feminism divides their loyalties within their own community and that they should put their energies into fighting racism (Comas-Diaz, 1991). They may feel that feminism creates conflicts for them with their men; for example, African American men often feel that African American women should provide support for them when they experience instances of racism. The feeling among some is that African Americans should unite and that feminism only divides them along gender lines.

The important point, however, is that the feminist movement should be for all women and that all have essential contributions to make, whatever the color of their skin. Only by combining the perspectives and scholarship of women of all ethnic groups and nations can we achieve a women's movement that is effective in promoting the equality of all women with all men.

In Conclusion

One of the fundamental points of feminist theory is that we must examine not only gender but also ethnicity as powerful forces in people's lives. To do this, we must go far beyond acknowledging race differences, although we should recognize them when they exist. Similarities across ethnic groups—and there are many—deserve recognition as well. Most importantly, each ethnic group has its own cultural heritage, including its own definitions of gender roles and feminism, and all such heritages exert profound influences on the women from those cultures.

Suggestions for Further Reading

Allen, Paula Gunn. (1986). *The sacred hoop: Recovering the feminine in American Indian traditions.* Boston: Beacon Press. This collection of essays includes poetry, mythology, and literary analyses, all defining the identities of American Indian women.

Giddings, Paula. (1984). *When and where I enter: The impact of black women on race and sex in America.* New York: Bantam Books (Paperback). This modern classic is a sweeping history of Black women in the United States, including portraits of such greats as the antilynching journalist Ida Wells-Barnett and presidential candidate Shirley Chisholm. Important reading for those who wish to understand the social and political context of contemporary African American women.

James, Stanlie, & Busia, Abena. (Eds.). (1993). *Theorizing Black feminisms: The visionary pragmatism of Black women.* New York: Routledge. This collection of essays provides a current view of Black feminism.

Marchetti, Gina. (1993). *Romance and the "yellow peril": Race, sex, and discursive strategies in Hollywood fiction.* Berkeley: University of California Press. This is a fascinating analysis of images of Asian women and men in American film.

Many novels and autobiographies are available that help the reader to grasp more profoundly the experience of women of color. A list of important ones, to name but a few, includes Maxine Hong Kingston's *The Woman Warrior,* Wong's *Fifth Chinese Daughter,* and Amy Tan's *Joy Luck Club* (Asian American women); Toni Morrison's novels such as *Beloved* and *The Bluest Eye* (African American women); and Louise Erdrich's *Bingo Palace* and *Love Medicine* (Native American women).

Women and the Web

Health Information for Minority Women, Office on Women's Health, U.S. Department of Health and Human Services

http://www.4women.gov/minority/index.cfm

Women of Color Health Data Book from the U.S. Department of Health and Human Services

http://www.4women.gov/owh/pub/woc/toc.htm

Women of Color Resource Center

http://www.coloredgirls.org/

National Asian Women's Health Organization

http://www.nawho.org/

5 Gender and Language

Women are the decorative sex. They never have anything to say, but they say it charmingly.

— OSCAR WILDE

Suppose you found the following caption, torn from a cartoon: "That sunset blends such lovely shades of pink and magenta, doesn't it?" If you had to guess the gender of the speaker, what would you say? Most people would guess that the speaker was a woman. Most of us have ideas about what is "appropriate" speech for males and females, and *lovely* and *magenta* just don't sound like things a man would (or should) say. In this chapter we will explore the evidence on the differences between how women and men speak and communicate nonverbally, and on how women are treated in the English language.

Gender Differences in Language Use

The example given above illustrates certain stereotypes about men's and women's speech—namely, that women use adjectives like *lovely* and *magenta* and men don't. Linguist Deborah Tannen, in her widely read books such as *You Just Don't Understand: Women and Men in Conversation* (1991), has popularized the belief that women's and men's patterns of speaking are vastly different, so different that women and men essentially belong to different linguistic communities or cultures. That is, in some sense, they don't speak the same language, leading to painful communication problems. Tannen believes that communication between women and men is as difficult as communication between people from different cultures—say, a person from the United States and a person from Japan.

According to Tannen and others, men and women have different goals when they speak. Women aim to establish and maintain relationships, whereas men aim to exert control, preserve their independence, and enhance their status (Tannen, 1991; Wood, 1994). Women try to show support by matching or mirroring experiences ("I've felt that way, too"), whereas men try to display their knowledge, avoid disclosing personal information, and avoid showing the slightest vulnerability. Women engage in conversation maintenance, trying to get a conversation started and keep it going ("How was your day?"), whereas men engage in conversational dominance (e.g., interrupting). And women display tentative speech whereas men display forceful, authoritative speech.

In terms of the discussion of psychological gender differences in Chapter 3, Tannen's hypothesis holds that there are large gender differences in language behavior. Let's examine what the data say.

According to linguist Deborah Tannen, women and men have different goals
when they speak. Women aim to establish and maintain relationships,
whereas men aim to exert control.

Tentativeness   Tentativeness in women's speech is said to be indicated by
greater use of tag questions, disclaimers, and hedges.

Linguist Robin Lakoff (1973) originally hypothesized that
women use more tag questions than men. A **tag question** is a
short phrase at the end of a declarative sentence that turns it into
a question. An example would be "This is a great game, isn't it?"

> **Tag question:** A short
> phrase added to a sen-
> tence, which turns it into
> a question.

In a classic study, college students participated in a group
problem-solving task in either same-gender or mixed-gender groups of five to
seven people (McMillan et al., 1977). The discussions, which involved solving a
mystery and which lasted 30 minutes, were tape-recorded, and later were coded
and analyzed by the experimenters. They found that the women used about twice
as many tag questions as the men.

Using the terminology of Chapter 1, we have a statistical result that women
use significantly more tag questions than men do. How should that finding be interpreted? The standard interpretation has been that men's tendency not to use
tag questions indicates the self-confidence and forcefulness of their speech.
Women's tendency to use tag questions is interpreted as indicating uncertainty,
tentativeness, or weak patterns of speech. This interpretation implies that
women's speech is somehow deficient, reflecting undesirable traits such as uncertainty. Are other interpretations possible? To interpret this difference in a way
that would be more favorable to women, we might say that the tag question is in-

tended to encourage communication, rather than to shut things off with a simple declarative statement. The tag question helps maintain the conversation and encourages the other person to express an opinion. Rather than reflecting uncertainty, then, women's greater use of tag questions may reflect greater interpersonal sensitivity and warmth (McMillan et al., 1977).

The researchers in the experiment discussed above attempted to determine which of these interpretations was more accurate (McMillan et al., 1977). They did this by comparing the use of tag questions in same-gender versus mixed-gender groups. They reasoned that if tag questions reflect uncertainty, then women should use more tag questions when men are present (mixed-gender groups) than when only women are present (all-female groups). This hypothesis was confirmed by the data, thus supporting the "greater female uncertainty" interpretation. However, the men in the study also used more tag questions in the mixed-gender groups than they did in the all-male groups. The researchers had not hypothesized this, as it did not seem that men should be more uncertain when women were present. Thus the interpretation of this gender difference is still unclear, and more sophisticated research will be necessary before a definitive statement can be made. The most important point to keep in mind, however, is that often alternative interpretations, one favoring men, the other favoring women, can be made of the same statistical results.

Psychologist Elizabeth Aries (1996) reviewed over two decades of studies on gender and tag questions.[1] She found that results across studies were inconsistent. Some studies report more tag questions by women, whereas others report more tag questions from men and still others report no gender difference. Other studies found that the pattern of gender differences depended on the context, as occurred in the study discussed above. When differences are found, they tend to be small. For example, in one analysis of a large body of natural speech, women produced 57 percent of the tag questions, men 43 percent (Holmes, 1984). Tannen's hypothesis finds no support here.

Analysis of that same large body of natural speech also indicated that tag questions could have one of three meanings: uncertainty, expression of solidarity ("You must feel really tired, don't you?"), and politeness (a direct order is softened by the tag question, as in "Close the door, would you?") (Holmes, 1984). These results question the interpretation that women's use of tag questions indicates uncertainty.

Hedges and disclaimers have also been taken as indicators of tentativeness in women's speech. **Disclaimers** are phrases such as "I may be wrong, but. . . ." **Hedges** are expressions such as "sort of" or "kind of." The evidence here is more limited than it is with tag questions, but some research shows that women use more disclaimers and hedges, both of which might indicate tentativeness

Disclaimers: Phrases such as "I may be wrong, but...."

Hedges: Phrases, such as "sort of" that weaken or soften a statement.

---

[1]You may be amazed that two decades of research have been devoted to this apparently narrow issue, but it really captured the attention and imagination of researchers in the field.

(Carli, 1990). Yet, again, the gender difference depended on context: Women used more hedges and disclaimers than men when in mixed-gender groups, but not in single-gender groups.

To summarize:

1. Findings of gender differences in indicators of tentativeness such as tag questions are inconsistent across studies, and the gender differences are at most small. The Tannen hypothesis receives little support (for critiques, see Aries, 1996; Bergvall, 1999; Crawford, 1995; Kunkel & Burleson, 1998; Waldron & DiMare, 1998). Gender similarities seem to be the rule, as they are in many other realms of behavior.

2. The pattern of gender differences in tentative speech varies considerably depending on the context, again refuting notions of "men's speech" and "women's speech."

3. Interpretation of the gender difference, if it exists, is complex. Tag questions do not always indicate uncertainty. They can have other functions such as expressing solidarity or politely softening a command (Holmes, 1995).

Many people read Tannen's books and think that they ring true, yet the scientific data say that she isn't right. Why the discrepancy? I think there are two reasons. One is people's love affair with gender differences, and Tannen's hypothesis reflects the differences model. Many people seem to have a strong desire to see women and men as quite different. The second has to do with gender schemas. As we saw in Chapter 2, gender schemas cause us to filter out or distort information that is inconsistent with the schema. People who hold the view that women and men communicate quite differently are likely to filter out all the instances of similarities. A person who holds the view that women's speech is tentative, is likely to hear all the tag questions and disclaimers that come from women, each time thinking "Aha, I'm right about the way women talk." But that person probably doesn't notice when a man uses a tag question and so the schema is never challenged.

Intensifiers   Robin Lakoff (1973) claimed that women used more intensifiers—words like *very, really,* and *vastly* (e.g., "The governor is really interested in this proposal"). A number of studies indicate that women use these intensifier adverbs more than men do (Aries, 1996; Mulac, 1998). Beyond that, the interpretation of the difference is unclear. Do the intensifiers indicate women's attempts to make their speech more powerful? Do they express more emotion? Research has not yet sorted out the possible interpretations.

Interruptions   Researchers have found that men interrupt women considerably more often than women interrupt men (McMillan et al., 1977; West & Zimmerman, 1983; Zimmerman & West, 1975). To give an idea of the magnitude of the difference, some data from one study are shown in Table 5.1. Notice that women interrupt women about as often as men interrupt men. However, women very seldom interrupt men, whereas men frequently interrupt women.

Once again, we have a statistical result that men interrupt women considerably more than women interrupt men. How should this gender difference be interpreted? The typical interpretation made by feminist social scientists involves the assumption that interruptions are an expression of *power* or *dominance.* That is, the interrupter gains control of a conversation, and that is a kind of interpersonal power. The gender difference, then, is interpreted as indicating that men are expressing power and dominance over women. This pattern may reflect the subtle persistence of traditional gender roles; it may also help to perpetuate traditional roles.

Later researchers have suggested that interruptions can have multiple meanings (Aries, 1996). Some interruptions are requests for clarification. Others express agreement or support, such as an *mm-hmm* or *definitely* murmured while the other person is speaking. Some interruptions express disagreement with the speaker, and other interruptions change the subject. These last two types of interruptions are the ones that express dominance. Most interruptions in fact turn out to be agreements or requests for clarification and have nothing to do with dominance. Women engage in more of this supportive interrupting, particularly when they are in all-female groups (Aries, 1996).

Overall, then, to say that men interrupt more than women do, and that this indicates men's expression of dominance, is not accurate (Aries, 1996). Patterns of gender differences in interruption vary considerably depending on context (mixed-gender group versus same-gender group, natural conversation versus laboratory task), and interruptions can have many meanings besides dominance. More sophisticated research will be needed to focus specifically on the dominance interruptions and the situations in which men use them more than women.

TABLE 5.1
Mean Number of Interruptions per Half Hour in Mixed-Gender Groups

Gender of Interruptee	Gender of Interrupter	
	Female	Male
Female	2.50	5.24
Male	0.93	2.36

SOURCE: McMillan et al. (1977).

Can You Tell Who's Speaking?   Anthony Mulac (1998) has conducted a series of studies in which the speech of men and women (or boys and girls) is transcribed, masked as to the identity of the speaker, and then presented to university students to see whether they can tell whether the speaker was male or female. If Tannen's hypothesis is correct, the task should be a snap and students should be able to identify the gender of the speaker with a high degree of accuracy. In fact, though, students perform no better than chance on the task. These findings support the notion of gender similarities in communication.

Other studies, though, find significant differences between women's and men's speech *when highly trained coders look for specific details* such as intensifiers, tag questions, and references to emotions (Mulac, 1998). The differences must therefore be subtle, detectable by scientifically trained coders but not by the average person.

Other studies by Mulac (1998) indicate that, although students cannot tell whether speech was produced by a man or a woman, significant differences emerge when they rate the speeches on several gender-related dimensions. Speech by females (even when the rater doesn't know the speaker's sex) is consistently rated as showing a more esthetic quality and more social intelligence, and speech by males is rated as showing more dynamism. Mulac calls this the *gender-linked language effect*. Moreover, the nature of the differences is remarkably similar to gender stereotypes: women as esthetically focused and skilled at social interactions, and men as forceful and dynamic. Mulac argues, then, that although women's and men's speech is quite similar, subtle differences exist that create an overall pattern leading people to react differently to the qualities of women's speech compared with men's speech. Women's speech patterns are evaluated differently than men's, and that can be important in situations such as a job interview.

Electronic Talk   Much of the "talk" we do today is on e-mail—that is, it's electronic talk. Does it show gender differences?

In one study, participants sent e-mail messages to a fictitious "netpal" of the same gender (Thomson & Murachver, 2001). Trained raters found significant differences between women's and men's e-talk in terms of expressing emotion (women expressed more), disclosure of personal information (women disclosed more), and hedges and intensifiers (women used more), but no significant gender differences for nine other aspects, including insults, self-derogatory comments, and oppositions. The findings are therefore similar to those for spoken language, in that a few reliable differences appear but many similarities are also found. Untrained raters were able to guess correctly whether the message was written by a man or a woman about 88 percent of the time.

In another experiment by the same team, participants conducted e-mail correspondence with two fictitious netpals and received responses that, in actuality, came from the experimenter (Thomson et al., 2001). For each participant, one netpal responded with female-linked language (more emotion references, more inten-sifiers, and so on) and the other netpal responded with male-linked language (more opinions, fewer emotions, and so on). Interestingly, participants—whether male or female—responded differently depending on the gendered content coming from the netpal, shifting their e-talk to be like that of their netpal. This is a perfect illustration of how gender is constructed in social interactions and how gender pat-terns depend heavily on social context. Social constructionists would be so happy!

Body Language: Nonverbal Communication

The popularizers of the "body language" concept have pointed out that we often communicate far more with our body than with the words we speak. For exam-ple, suppose you say the sentence "How nice to see you" while standing only six inches from another person or while actually brushing up against him or her. Then imagine, in contrast, that you say the sentence while standing six feet from the person. The sentence conveys a much different meaning in the two instances. In the first, it will probably convey warmth and possibly sexiness. In the second case, the meaning will seem formal and perhaps cold. As another example, a sen-tence coming from a smiling face conveys a much different meaning from that of the same sentence coming from a stern or frowning face.

Here I will present the evidence on whether there are differences between women and men in nonverbal styles of communication, and what those differ-ences mean (for meta-analyses, see Hall, 1998).

Interpersonal Distance   Generally it seems that in the United States, men pre-fer a greater distance between themselves and another person, whereas there tends to be a smaller distance between women and others. For example, one study found that women stand closer to other women in public exhibits than men do to men (Baxter, 1970). In another study, subjects seated themselves an average of 4.6 feet from a female stimulus person and an average of 8.5 feet from a male—that is, they sat about twice as far from the male as from the female (Wittig & Skolnick, 1978).

Meta-analyses indicate that these gender differences are moderately large. For women approaching others, $d = -0.54$ (to use the statistics introduced in Chapter 3), and for others approaching women, $d = -0.86$ (Hall, 1984).

How should these results be interpreted? One possibility is that women es-sentially have their personal space, or "territory," violated, and that this expresses dominance over them. An alternative interpretation would be that women have a small interpersonal distance as a result of, or in order to express, warmth or friendliness (Wittig & Skolnick, 1978).

Smiling   Women smile more than men. Meta-analysis indicates that the differ-ence is moderately large ($d = -0.60$) (Hall, 1984, 1998). Once again, however, it is

Men tend to keep a larger interpersonal distance between each other than women do.

not clear how this difference should be interpreted (LaFrance, 1981; Ragan, 1982). Smiling has been called the female version of the "Uncle Tom shuffle"— that is, rather than indicating happiness or friendliness, it may serve as an appeasement gesture, communicating, in effect, "Please don't hit me or be nasty." Others see smiling as a status indicator: Dominant people smile less and subordinates smile more, so women's smiling reflects their subordinate status (Henley,

Smiling is a part of the female role. Do women's smiles indicate happiness and friendliness, or are they forced because of role expectations?

1977). A number of studies, however, contradict this status interpretation. Although women consistently smile more than men in these studies, lower-status people (e.g., employees in a company) do not smile more than higher-status people (e.g., supervisors) (Hall & Friedman, 1999; Hall et al., 2001).

Still other researchers note that smiling is a part of the female role. Most women can remember having their faces feel stiff and sore from smiling at a party or some other public gathering at which they were expected to smile. The smile, of course, reflected not happiness, but rather a belief that smiling was the appropriate thing to do. Women's smiles, then, do not necessarily reflect positive feelings and may even be associated with negative feelings. This pattern of smiling varies as a function of ethnicity; the pattern is more characteristic of white women than African American women (Halberstadt & Saitta, 1987).

In one study, participants were given a written description of a person, accompanied by a photograph of a male or female who was smiling or not smiling (Deutsch et al., 1987). The results indicated that the women who were not smiling were given more negative evaluations: They were rated as less happy and less relaxed in comparison with men and in comparison with women who were smiling. The results indicate that people react negatively when women fail to perform this part of the female role.

Eye Contact   Eye contact between two people when speaking to each other reflects patterns of power and dominance. In North American cultures, higher-status people tend to look at the other person while they (the dominant people) are speaking. Lower-status people tend to look at the other person while listening. Researchers in this area compute a *visual dominance ratio,* defined as the ratio of the percentage of time looking while speaking relative to the percentage of time looking while listening (Dovidio et al., 1988).

Social psychologist John Dovidio has done a series of studies investigating the connection between visual dominance and social power. His research indicates, for example, that patterns of visual dominance are expressed across different levels of military rank and different levels of educational attainment (e.g., Dovidio et al., 1988).

One of these experiments investigated visual dominance as a function of both gender and power (Dovidio et al., 1988). College students were assigned to mixed-gender dyads. Each pair discussed three topics in sequence. The first discussion was on a neutral topic and there was no manipulation of power. For the second topic, one member of the pair evaluated the other member and had the power to award extra credit points to that person. For the third topic, the roles were reversed, and the person who had been evaluated became the evaluator.

In the control condition, men looked at their partner more while speaking and women looked more while listening, as predicted based on considerations of the relative status or power associated with gender. However, in the second and third discussions, when women were in the powerful role, they looked more than men while speaking, and men looked more while listening. That is, when women were given social power, they became visually dominant. These results again support a power or status interpretation of gender differences in visual dominance. And, as women gain more power in society, patterns of visual dominance may well change.

How Women Are Treated in Language

To this point I have discussed women's communication styles, both verbal and nonverbal. The other aspect that needs to be addressed is how women and gender issues are treated in our language. Feminists have sensitized the public to the peculiar properties of terms like *man* used to refer to the entire species.[2] Here we will discuss patterns that emerge in the way the English language treats women and concepts of gender.

Male as Normative   One of the clearest patterns in our language is the normativeness of the male, a concept discussed in Chapter 1 (Hamilton, 1991). The male is regarded as the normative (standard) member of the species, and this is

[2]Someone once commented cutely that feminists have a bad case of "pronoun envy" (Key, 1975).

expressed in many ways in language: for example, the use of *man* to refer to all human beings, and the use of *he* for a neutral pronoun (as in the sentence "The infant typically begins to sit up around six months of age; he may begin crawling at about the same time"). The male-as-normative principle in language can lead to some absolutely absurd statements. For example, there is a state law that reads, "No person may require another person to perform, participate in, or undergo an abortion of pregnancy against his will" (Key, 1975).

At the very least, the male-as-normative usage introduces ambiguity into our language. When someone uses the word *men,* is the reference to males or to people in general? When Dr. Karl Menninger writes a book entitled *Man Against Himself,* is it a book about people generally, or is it a book about the tensions experienced by males?

Some people excuse such usage by saying that terms like *man* are generic. Such an explanation, however, is not adequate. To illustrate the flaw in the "generic" logic, consider the objections raised by some men who joined the League of Women Voters. They complained that the name of the organization should be changed, for it no longer adequately describes its members, some of whom are now men. Suppose in response to their objection they were told that by *woman* is meant "generic woman," which of course includes men. Do you think they would feel satisfied?

The male-as-normative principle is also reflected in the **female-as-the-exception phenomenon.** A newspaper reported the results of the Bowling Green State University women's swimming team and men's swimming team in two articles close to each other. The headline reporting the men's results was "BG Swimmers Defeated." The one for the women was "BG Women Swimmers Win." As another example, when the University of Wisconsin chose a new chancellor, the headline read, "UW Picks Woman Chancellor." It is hard to believe that had a man been chosen, the headline would have been "UW Picks Man Chancellor." His maleness would not have been considered newsworthy. We consider athletes and prestigious professionals to be normatively male. In cases where they are female it seems important to note this fact as an exception.

> **Female-as-the-exception phenomenon:** If a category is considered normatively male and there is a female example of the category, gender is noted because the female is the exception. A byproduct of androcentrism.

Parallel Words   Another interesting phenomenon in our language is how parallel words for males and females often have quite different connotations (Key, 1975; Lakoff, 1973; Schulz, 1975). For example, consider the following list of parallel male and female words:

Male	*Female*
dog	bitch
master	mistress
stud	slut

Note that the female forms of the words generally have negative connotations and that these negative connotations are often sexual in nature. For example, a man who is a *master* is good at what he does or is powerful, but a woman who is a *mistress* is someone who is financially supported in return for her sexual services.

Many of these parallel words originally had equivalent meanings for male and female. This point, too, is illustrated by *master* and *mistress,* terms originally used to refer to the male and female heads of the household. Over time, however, the female term took on negative connotations. Linguist Muriel Schulz (1975) has argued that this process is caused simply by prejudice. That is, terms applied to women take on negative meanings because of prejudice against women (see also Allport, 1954).

Undergraduates were asked to list as many slang terms as they could for either *woman* or *man* (Grossman & Tucker, 1997). Fully 93 percent of men listed *bitch* as a term for woman! But then, so did 73 percent of the women. Overall, the terms listed for *woman* were more likely to carry a sexual meaning than the words listed for *man;* roughly 50 percent of the slang terms for *woman* were sexual, compared with 23 percent of the terms for *man.*

Euphemisms   Generally when there are many euphemisms for a word, it is a reflection of the fact that people find the word and what it stands for to be distasteful or stressful. For example, consider all the various terms we use in place of *bathroom* or *toilet.* And then there is the great variety of terms such as *pass away* that we substitute for *die.*

Feminist linguists have argued that we similarly have a strong tendency to use euphemisms for the word *woman* (Lakoff, 1973; Schulz, 1975). That is, people have a tendency to avoid using the word *woman,* and instead substitute a variety of terms that seem more "polite" or less threatening, the most common euphemisms being *lady* and *girl.* In contrast to the word *man,* which is used frequently and comfortably, *woman* is used less frequently and apparently causes some discomfort or we wouldn't use euphemisms for it.

Infantilizing   A 25-year-old man wrote to an advice columnist, depressed because he wanted to get married but had never had a date. Part of the columnist's response was

> Just scan the society pages and look at the people who are getting married every day. Are the men all handsome? Are the girls all beautiful?

This is an illustration of the way in which people, rather than using *woman* as the parallel to *man,* substitute *girl* instead. As noted in the previous section, this in part reflects the use of a euphemism. But it is also true that *boy* refers to male children, and *man* to adult males. Somehow *girl,* which in a strict sense should refer only to female children, is used for adult women as well. Women are called by a term that seems to make them less mature than they are; women are thus *infantilized* in language. Just as the term *boy* is offensive to Black activists, so *girl* is offensive to feminists.

There are many other illustrations of this **infantilizing** theme. When a ship sinks, it's "Women and children first," putting women and children in the same category. Other examples in language are expressions for women such as *baby,* *babe,* and *chick.* The problem with these terms is that they carry a meaning of immaturity.

> **Infantilizing:** Treating people, for example, women, as if they were children or babies.

How Important Is All This?   Although many of the tenets of the women's movement—such as equal pay for equal work—have gained widespread acceptance, the importance of changing our language to eliminate sexism has not. Many people regard these issues as silly or trivial. Just how important is the issue of sexism in language?

Language reflects thought processes. This being the case, sexism in language may be the symptom, not the disease (Lakoff, 1973). That is, things like the generic use of *man* and *he* may simply reflect the fact that we do think of the male as the norm for the species. The practical conclusion from this is that what needs to be changed is our thought processes, and once they change, language will change with them.

On the other hand, one of the classic theories of psycholinguistics, the **Whorfian hypothesis** (Whorf, 1956), states that the specific language we learn influences our mental processes. If that is true, then things like the generic use of *man* make us think that the male is normative. This process might start with very young children when they are just beginning to learn the language. If such processes do occur, then social reformers need to pay careful attention to eliminating sexism in language because of its effect on our thought processes.

> **Whorfian hypothesis:** The theory that the language we learn influences how we think.

An important study demonstrated that even when *he* and *his* are used in explicitly gender-neutral contexts, people tend to think of males (Moulton et al., 1978). College students were asked to make up stories creating a fictional character who would fit the theme of a stimulus sentence. The students were divided into three groups; the stimulus sentence was as follows:

> In a large coeducational institution the average student will feel isolated in _____ introductory courses.

One of the groups received *his* in the blank space, another received *their,* and the third received *his or her.*

Averaging the responses of all groups, when the pronoun was *his,* only 35 percent of the stories were about females; for *their,* 46 percent were about females; and for *his or her,* 56 percent were about females. The important point is that even though a sentence referred to "the average student," when *his* was used most people thought of males. Many other studies have replicated these findings (e.g., Gastil, 1990). Though a linguist may say that *he* and *his* are gender neutral, they are certainly not gender neutral in a psychological sense.

It seems likely that both processes—thought influencing language and language influencing thought—occur to some extent. Insofar as language does have the potential for influencing our thinking, sexism in language becomes a critical issue.

I became interested in a related question raised earlier—namely, the effect of sexist language on children—and so I began a series of studies to investigate the question (Hyde, 1984a). First, I generated an age-appropriate sentence like the one used by Moulton and asked first-, third-, and fifth-grade children to tell stories in response to it:

When a kid goes to school, _____ often feels excited on the first day.

As in the study by Moulton, one-third of the children received *he* for the blank, one-third received *they,* and one-third received *he or she.* The results were even more dramatic than those of Moulton with college students. When the pronoun was *he,* only 12 percent of the stories were about females. In fact, when the pronoun was *he,* not a single elementary school boy told a story about a girl. Clearly, then, when children hear *he* in a gender-neutral context, they think of a male. I also asked the children some questions to see if they understood the grammatical rule that *he* in certain contexts refers to everyone, both males and females. Few understood the rule; for example, only 28 percent of the first-graders gave answers showing that they knew the rule.

I also had the children fill in the blanks in some sentences such as the following:

If a kid likes candy, _____ might eat too much.

The children overwhelmingly supplied *he* for the blank; even 72 percent of the first-graders did so.

This research shows two things. First, the majority of elementary school children have learned to supply *he* in gender-neutral contexts (as evidenced by the fill-in task). Second, the majority of elementary school children do not know the rule that *he* in gender-neutral contexts refers to both males and females and have a strong tendency to think of males in creating stories from neutral *he* cues. For them, then, the chain of concepts is as follows: (1) The typical person is a "he." (2) *He* refers only to males. Logically, then, might they not conclude that (3) the typical person is a male? Language seems to contribute to androcentric thinking in children.

In a final task, I created a fictitious, gender-neutral occupation: wudgemaker.

Few people have heard of a job in factories, being a wudgemaker. Wudges are made of plastic, oddly shaped, and are an important part of video games. The wudgemaker works from a plan or pattern posted at eye level as _____ puts together the pieces at a table while _____ is sitting down. Eleven plastic pieces must be snapped together. Some of the pieces are tiny, so that _____ must have good coordination in _____ fingers. Once all eleven pieces are put together, _____ must test out the wudge to make sure that all of the moving pieces move properly. The wudgemaker is well paid, and must be a high school graduate, but _____ does not have to have gone to college to get the job.

One-quarter of the children received *he* in all the blanks, one-quarter received *they*, one-quarter received *he or she*, and one-quarter received *she*. The children then rated how well a woman could do the job on a 3-point scale: 3 for very well, 2 for just okay, and 1 for not very well. Next, they rated how well a man could do the job, giving ratings on the same scale. The results are shown in Figure 5.1.

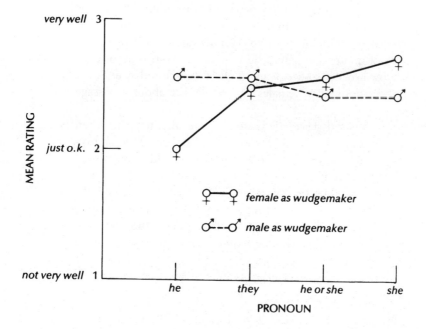

FIGURE 5.1

Children's ratings of the competence of women and men as wudge-makers, as a function of the pronoun they heard repeatedly in the description of the wudgemaker. Women are rated as having only medium competence when the pronoun is *he*, but their ratings rise for *they* and *he or she*. When *she* is used in the description, women are rated near the top of the scale.

SOURCE: "Mean Rating Graph" by Janet Hyde. *Developmental Psychology, 20,* 697–706. Copyright © 1984 by the American Psychological Association. Reprinted with permission.

Which pronoun the children were given didn't seem to affect their ratings of men as wudgemakers, but the pronoun had a big effect on how women were rated as wudgemakers. Notice in the graph that when the pronoun *he* was used, women were rated at the middle of the scale, or just okay. The ratings of women rose for the pronouns *they* and *he or she,* and finally were close to the top of the scale when children heard the wudgemaker described as *she.* These results, then, demonstrate that pronoun choice does have an effect on the concepts children form; in particular, children who heard *he* in the job description thought that women were significantly less competent at the job than children who heard other pronouns did.

Other experiments show that men and boys remember material better when it is written with generic masculine forms, but girls and women remember it better when it is written with gender-neutral or feminine forms (Conkwright et al., 2000; Crawford & English, 1984).

In answer to the original question of whether this pronoun business is really important, I think it is. We need to be concerned about the effects that sexist pronoun usage has on children; research demonstrates that it can affect the children's concepts of occupations, and I think there is also reason for concern about its effect on broader issues, such as girls' self-confidence. Sexist language can even affect how much females can remember about a passage they've read.

One final bold experiment deserves discussion. To see what happens when pronoun usage changes away from the traditional sexist use of *he,* a psychologist used *she* as the generic pronoun with two of her child development classes, and compared the student responses with those of students in a class in which she did not follow this practice (Adamsky, 1981). Strikingly, students in the experimental group started using the generic *she* in their written essays. Although many people think that the sexist usage of pronouns in English cannot be changed, this study demonstrates convincingly that it can be. Here are some student responses (all are from female students) to use of the generic *she:*

> Once I started using the "she" I found it hard to stop. I liked using the generic "she"—it gave me a sense of equality—power even.
>
> I felt surprisingly proud when I used it.
>
> I could picture a female in roles so often pictured as strictly male. (Adamsky, 1981, pp. 777–778)

You might try using *she* as the generic form for a day and try to analyze the reactions, both in yourself and in others. It's a wonderful consciousness-raising device.

Some Practical Suggestions

Some people believe in theory that it would be a good idea to eliminate sexism from language, but in practice they find themselves having difficulty doing this in their speaking or writing. Here we discuss some practical suggestions for avoiding sexist language (American Psychological Association, 2001; Miller & Swift, 1995) and for dealing with some other relevant situations.

Toward Nonsexist Language   The use of generic masculine forms is probably the most widespread and difficult problem of sexist language. The following are some ways to eliminate or avoid these usages.

One possibility is to switch from the singular to the plural, because plural pronouns do not signify gender, at least in English. Therefore, the generic masculine in sentence 1 can be modified as in sentence 2:

1. When a doctor prescribes birth control pills, he should first inquire whether the patient has a history of blood clotting problems.

2. When doctors prescribe birth control pills, they should first inquire whether the patient has a history of blood clotting problems.

Another possibility is to reword the sentence so that there is no necessity for a pronoun, as in this example:

3. A doctor prescribing birth control pills should first inquire whether the patient has a history of blood clotting problems.

One of the simplest solutions is to use *he or she* instead of the generic *he, him or her* instead of *him,* and so on. Therefore, the generic masculine in sentence 1 can be modified as follows:

4. When a doctor prescribes birth control pills, he or she should first inquire whether the patient has a history of blood clotting problems.

Many feminist scholars, however, believe that the order should be varied, so that *he or she* and *she or he* appear with equal frequency. If *he or she* is the only form that is used, women still end up second!

One final possibility is the singular use of *they* and *their*. For years people have been saying sentences like "Will everyone pick up their pencil?" and English teachers have been correcting them, saying that the correct form is "Will everyone pick up his pencil?" Actually, singular *they* was standard usage in English until the late 1700s, when a group of grammarians decided it was wrong (Bodine, 1975b). Because it is so natural to use the plural in this situation, and to do so eliminates the sexism, why not go ahead and do it?

FOCUS 5.1

WOMEN AND HUMOR

Women have a funny relationship with humor. Jokes are often sexist and involve put-downs of women. Thus they can contribute to a cultural milieu in which women are devalued.

At the same time, women—especially feminists—are accused of being humorless, and who wants to be humorless? Women are stereotyped as not "getting" the joke, as not being able to "take" a joke, and as flubbing the punch line when they try to tell a joke. When 200 top executives were asked to give ten reasons why women should not be placed in leadership positions in corporations, "lack of a sense of humor" was high on the list. Did it ever occur to anyone that women may find lots of jokes unfunny precisely because they are sexist?

Some experts suggest that, rather than becoming humor victims, women should learn how to use humor to their advantage, using it to respond to sexist comments. Molly Carnes, a faculty member in the Medical School at the University of Wisconsin, collected examples from women faculty of times when they had used humor as a strategic tool. Here are some of the real gems.

Space does not permit a complete discussion of all possible practical problems that may arise in trying to avoid sexist language. Usually, however, a little thought and imagination can solve most problems. For example, the salutation in a letter, "Dear Sir," can easily be changed to "Dear Madam or Sir," "Dear Sir or Madam," "Dear Colleague," or simply "To Whom It May Concern." The tendency

The Challenge	Women's Strategic Use of Humor in Responding
Infantilizing "Well hello there, young lady."	"Right back at you, middle-aged man."
Race/Ethnicity After 3 years in a department, a senior White male colleague said: "You know, after all this time of knowing you I can see that you really are different" (referring to my race/ethnicity).	"That's interesting. I knew the first minute I met you that you were different."
Irrelevant Beauty Department Chair (to big-wig at a company that might give donations of equipment to the department): "We have these two beautiful assistant professors who could utilize . . ."	"Well you know, I never thought of XX and YY (two male assistant professors in the department) as beautiful, but you're right."
Power and Roles A friend reported what a male colleague said about me in a meeting: "He said he would see you tenured over his dead body."	"It works for me!"
"You are not perceived to be a team player."	I was stunned and had no response. In retrospect, I wish I'd said: "I love to play on a team, as long as I get to be captain."

SOURCES: Adapted from Carnes (2001); see also Berraca (1991).

to use euphemisms for *woman* can be changed by becoming sensitive to this tendency and by making efforts to use the word *woman*.

One other solution to the problem of generic masculine pronouns should also be mentioned—namely, the creation of some new singular pronouns that are gender neutral. Unfortunately, at least ten alternatives for these new pronouns have been proposed, confusing the situation somewhat (Blaubergs, 1978). One set that has been proposed is *tey* for "he" or "she," *tem* for "him" or "her," and *ter* for "his" or "her." Thus one might say, "The scientist pursues ter work; tey reads avidly and strives to overcome obstacles that beset tem." Entire books have been written with this usage (e.g., Sherman, 1978). Although in an ideal sense these new pronouns have a great deal of merit, they have not caught on. Probably they would need to be adopted by a number of respected, widely circulated sources in order to find their way into the ordinary person's language. If the *New York Times,* the *Washington Post, Time, Newsweek,* Stone Phillips, and the president all started using *ter, tey,* and *tem,* these terms would have a chance. Such widespread adoption does not seem to be a very immediate possibility, however.

This brings us to the topic of institutional change in language use.

Institutional Change   A number of institutions have committed themselves to using and encouraging nonsexist language. For example, most textbook publishers have guidelines for nonsexist language and refuse to publish books that include sexism. (Two examples are Scott, Foresman and McGraw-Hill, which initiated this policy in 1972 and 1974, respectively.) The American Psychological Association requires the use of nonsexist language in articles in the journals it publishes (APA, 1994, 2001). And the new *Webster's Dictionary* now has a policy of avoiding masculine generics and other forms of sexist language ("No sexism please," 1991). These are all good sources for the reader wanting more detail on how to eliminate sexist language.

Many occupational titles, particularly in government agencies, have also changed. It is worth noting that some of the changes introduce definite improvements. For example, *firemen* has been changed to *firefighters.* In addition to being nonsexist, the newer term makes more sense, because what the people do is fight fires, not start them, as one might infer from the older term.

Language, Women, and Careers   The discussion of gender differences in language use in the first part of the chapter raises an important practical question for women aspiring to careers in male-dominated occupations such as business executive. Which styles of speaking will work best for them?

One interesting experiment assessed the impact of women using stereotyped patterns of tentative speech compared with assertive speech (Carli, 1990). Participants listened to an audiotape of a persuasive speech delivered by either a woman or a man. On one of the tapes, the woman used many tag questions ("Great day, isn't it?"), hedges ("sort of"), and disclaimers ("I'm no expert, but . . . "), indicating tentativeness. On another tape, she used no tag questions, hedges, or disclaimers, thus indicating assertiveness. In the third tape, a man used tentative speech, and in a fourth tape, a man used assertive speech. The results indicated that the female speaker who used tentative speech was more influential to men

EXPERIENCE THE RESEARCH

GENDER AND CONVERSATIONAL STYLES

Recruit four students, two men and two women not in this class, to participate. Pair one man and one woman together alone in a room and tell them that you are going to give them a topic to discuss and that you want to tape-record their discussion to analyze it for a class. Be sure to obtain their permission to record the conversation, and assure them that you will not reveal to anyone the identity of your participants. Then give the pair a controversial topic to discuss—perhaps a current controversy on your campus or in national politics. Be sure that the topic is not gender stereotyped so that one person will feel superior to the other. For example, "How good is the new quarterback on the football team?" would not be a good topic. "Would you vote for the new crime bill before Congress and why?" is a good topic. Tell them that you will record their discussion for about ten minutes. You should remain in the room and note any observations you have of their discussion. Specifically, count the number of times each person nods in response to what the other is saying.

Repeat this procedure with the second male-female pair. You now have two tapes for data. Analyze the tapes in the following ways:

1. Count the number of times the man interrupted the woman and the woman interrupted the man. Did men interrupt women more than the reverse?

2. Count the number of tag questions (see text for explanation). Did women use more tag questions than men did? Having listened to their conversation, how would you interpret the difference you found? Were the women indicating uncertainty, or were they trying to encourage communication and maintain the relationship?

3. Count the number of hedges (e.g., "sort of"). Did women use more hedges than men?

4. Did women nod more in response to what men were saying or the reverse?

than the assertive female speaker. For women listeners, the effect was just the reverse: They were more influenced by the woman using assertive speech than by the woman with tentative speech. Interestingly, men were equally influential whether their speech was tentative or assertive. Apparently men acquire their status and influence simply by being male; speech style makes little difference. But to return to the implications for women and careers, the results of this study indicate that changing from tentative to forceful speech for women is likely to have different effects, depending on whether the woman is speaking to a man or a woman. Tentative speech seems to work best with men, and assertive speech works best with women.

In Conclusion

In the first section of this chapter, we considered Tannen's hypothesis and the evidence on gender differences in communication styles. Research indicates that gender differences generally are small and depend considerably on the context. Moreover, the meaning or interpretation of the gender differences is often unclear: They may indicate males' greater power, but they may also indicate greater politeness or interpersonal sensitivity on the part of females.

Analyses of the way women are treated in language reveal patterns in which the male is normative. Research with adults as well as children shows that so-called gender-neutral words like *he* and *man* are not psychologically gender neutral, but rather evoke images of men. Gender-biased language may contribute to the early social construction of gender for children.

Suggestions for Further Reading

Aries, Elizabeth (1996). *Men and women in interaction: Reconsidering the differences.* New York: Oxford University Press. Aries does a superb job of assembling and analyzing all the research on gender differences in communicating and, in the process, thoroughly debunks Tannen's hypothesis that women and men belong to different language cultures.

Miller, Casey, & Swift, Kate (1995). *The handbook of non-sexist writing for writers, editors, and speakers.* London: Women's Press. The authors, both professional journalists, provide very useful suggestions for nonsexist language.

Gender and Emotion

6

By talking and discussing things you never get to the point of going to slit your throat or getting angry about some minor thing. . . . That's how I deal with all of my negative problems, whether it's death or anger, or anything. I talk and talk and then it's over with.

— DENISE

I try to minimize feeling envious because you just can't do anything about it— it just aggravates you.

— FRANK

Denise and Frank have different ways of dealing with their emotions, showing remarkable similarity to gender stereotypes. Denise expresses her emotions, talks about them, and then feels better. Frank, in contrast, "minimizes" his feelings—that is, he avoids expressing his emotions (Brody, 1999, p. 260).

Emotions and how we deal with them are extraordinarily important to our mental and physical health, to our interactions with others, and to the way others respond to us in important situations. Suppose that, on a first date with Rick, Samantha flashes anger when someone cuts her off and grabs her parking space. What will Rick think of her? Suppose the situation was reversed and Rick was the one who was driving and displayed anger. What would Samantha think of him?[1] Angry Samantha probably doesn't look very good to Rick as a long-term romantic partner. Who wants an angry woman? In contrast, Samantha may hardly notice it if Rick displays anger because it is so gender-appropriate for him. In this chapter we will consider what is known about gender stereotypes of emotions, differences between women and men in the experience and expression of emotion, and how emotion is shaped by gender socialization.

Gender Stereotypes About Emotions

Emotionality   Females are stereotyped as the emotional sex (Brody & Hall, 2000; Broverman et al., 1972). This stereotype is found not only in the United States, but in most other cultures (Fischer & Manstead, 2000).

The stereotype that women are emotional can hurt women as they try to succeed in education and in the workplace. Since it was founded, Virginia Military Institute (VMI), a state university supported by taxpayers' money, had been

---

[1]Notice that we aren't even touching on the question of the major gender-role violation involved if Samantha is the driver and Rick is the passenger. That gendered behavior seems to be set in stone.

for men only. VMI is very prestigious within Virginia, setting up networks for its graduates that lead them into the halls of power. Women were denied access to all this. When the men-only policy was challenged in the 1990s, the case went all the way to the Supreme Court, which ruled that women must be allowed admission. The interesting aspect for us is the argument made by VMI in the courts, defending their policy (Shields, 2000). One expert gave testimony that VMI "was not suitable for most women, because, compared with men, women are more emotional, less aggressive, suffer more from fear of failure, and cannot withstand stress as well" (Greenberger & Blake, 1996, p. A52). If that expert were right, women would have difficulty succeeding at any competitive university or demanding job. Fortunately, the expert was wrong and was simply mouthing stereotypes. But the point is that stereotypes about emotions can have a huge impact on women's lives.

Specific Emotions Beyond the general stereotype of emotionality, stereotypes specify particular emotions as appropriate for females and others as appropriate for males. A list of these stereotypes for 19 distinct emotions is provided in Table 6.1. This list was obtained by asking undergraduates, as well as adults from

TABLE 6.1
Americans' Gender Stereotypes of Emotions

"Female" Emotions	"Male" Emotions	Gender-Neutral Emotions
Awe	Anger	Amusement
Disgust	Contempt	Interest
Distress	Pride	Jealousy
Embarrassment		
Fear		
Guilt		
Happiness		
Love		
Sadness		
Shame		
Shyness		
Surprise		
Sympathy		

SOURCE: From Ashby E. Plant, Hyde, J. S., Keltner, D., & Devine, P. G. (2000). "The Gender Stereotyping of Emotions," *Psychology of Women Quarterly, 24,* pp. 81–92. Reprinted by permission from Blackwell Publishers.

the community, to rate how much men and women are expected to experience each emotion in our culture (Plant et al., 2000).

Several points emerge from Table 6.1. First, the great majority of emotions—13 of the 19—are stereotyped as characteristic of women, consistent with the stereotype of greater female emotionality. Second, the female-stereotyped emotions encompass both positive emotions (love, happiness, sympathy) and negative emotions (sadness, fear, guilt). Third, all three masculine emotions—anger, contempt, and pride—are associated with dominance and are consistent with men's dominant position in society. In Chapter 16 we will explore the consequences of the fact that just about the only emotion men and boys are allowed to express is anger.

The stereotypes listed in Table 6.1 reflect what participants say when asked about stereotypes in American culture, and the samples of participants were mainly White. We wondered whether those same stereotypes were true in various ethnic groups in the United States. We reasoned that different cultures hold quite different views on the experience and expression of emotion. Asian cultures, for example, value great restraint in the expression of emotion. Might ethnicity interact with gender in constructing stereotypes?

Amanda Durik and I asked African Americans about gender stereotypes of emotion among African Americans, Hispanics about gender stereotypes among Hispanics, and Asian Americans about gender stereotypes among Asian Americans (Durik et al., 2002). The results indicate, for example, that African Americans stereotype African American women as expressing almost as much anger as African American men, and the level for African American women is about the same as for White men. Of the four groups, White women are the ones who are stereotyped as not expressing anger. A comparison among the four ethnic groups for pride and love is shown in Figure 6.1. Notice that Euro-Americans are highly gender stereotyped about pride, whereas African Americans are not; they report that African American women express about as much pride as African American men do. Euro-Americans and African Americans are particularly gender stereotyped about love, whereas Asian Americans are less gender differentiated, probably because of the cultural norm of nonexpression of emotions, which results in a restraint in women's expression of love. In fact, Asian Americans rate women of their group as expressing about as much love as Latinos (a far more emotionally expressive group) rate Latino men as expressing. The larger point is that there is substantial variation from one ethnic group to the next in their rules about which emotions can be expressed by women and which can be expressed by men.

We should not focus only on ethnic-group differences. Many similarities across ethnic groups emerged as well. All ethnic groups, for example, expect women to express more embarrassment and guilt than men.

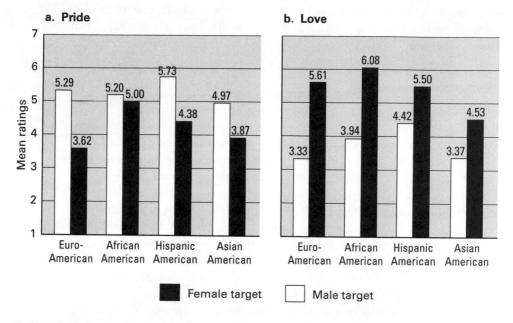

FIGURE 6.1
Gender stereotypes of emotions in four ethnic groups.
Source: Durik et al. (2002).

The Importance of the Emotion Stereotypes As noted in previous chapters, stereotypes play a major role as we process information about the world of people around us. In general, stereotypes make us see all the confirmations of them and filter out exceptions to the stereotypes (see Chapter 2). When a really major stereotype violation occurs that we cannot ignore, we are likely to respond negatively to the stereotype violator. All these processes occur in the specific realm of gender and emotion.

In one study, we showed slides of two men's and two women's faces displaying specific emotions (Plant et al., 2000). In some of the slides, the poser displayed anger, in others sadness, and in some, an ambiguous combination of anger and sadness. The posers were experts, graduate students who were emotion researchers and had been trained to contract exactly the right facial muscles to display particular emotions.

We hypothesized that gender stereotypes would exert their influence when emotional expressions were ambiguous, such that in the anger-sadness blend, a man would be rated as angry (a male-stereotyped emotion) and a woman would be rated as sad (a female-stereotyped emotion). Consistent with this hypothesis, participants rated men's blends as significantly more angry than women's, and women's blends as significantly more sad than men's. Stereotypes affect the emotions we see people displaying, even when the facial expressions are identical.

There was a surprise in the results, though. We had predicted that stereotypes would play a role when emotions were ambiguous, but we had not thought that they would do so when an emotional expression was clear and unambiguous. Yet participants rated women's unambiguous anger poses as significantly less angry than men's unambiguous anger poses. The raters simply saw less anger in women's anger than in men's anger. And as if that weren't enough, participants saw sadness in women's anger poses but not in men's. Anger is just not an acceptable emotion for women. People fail to see it in women's faces, or they misinterpret it as sadness. How difficult for women, not to have their anger be perceived, much less taken seriously. Gender stereotypes of emotions are powerful, then, because they can lead us to misperceive another's feelings.

Turning now to the implications of the findings on ethnicity and gender stereotypes, consider the case of African American women and anger. In African American culture, it is acceptable for women to express anger about as much as men do. Among Whites, it is not acceptable for women to express anger. At work, an African American woman might express anger over some issue in a way that is completely appropriate in her culture, but her White male boss reacts to her as being completely inappropriate because, to him, women are not supposed to express anger. He may see her as a "problem" employee, or he may find confirmation of his stereotype that African Americans are angry. Gender stereotypes of emotion, then, can have a powerful impact on interpersonal interactions in highly important situations.

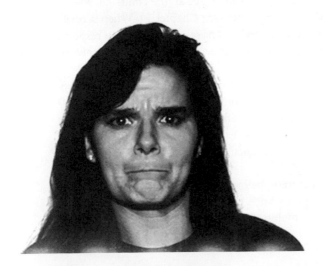

What emotion is this woman experiencing? Research indicates that when women display an ambiguous blend of anger and sadness, as observed in this photo, people believe that women are sad, not angry, whereas a man with a similar ambiguous expression is seen as angry (Plant et al., 2000).

Gender and Emotional Experience and Expression

To this point the focus has been on gender stereotypes of emotion. But what of the real emotional lives of women and men? Are they similar or different?

Display Rules   Emotion researchers distinguish between the *experience* of emotion and the *expression* of emotion. Every day you may experience some emotions that you express and others that you do not express. **Display rules** are a culture's rules for what emotions can be expressed or displayed. In American culture, for example, it is acceptable for people to express happiness; in fact, they are encouraged to do so.

> **Display rules:** A culture's rules for what emotions can be expressed or displayed.

In contrast, expressions of grief are discouraged. Gender stereotypes contribute to display rules, so that it is acceptable for women to express sympathy but not anger, and for men to express anger but not fear. Two distinct questions emerge, then: Do women and men differ in their experiences of emotion, and do they differ in their expressions of emotion? Before those questions can be answered, though, you need to know how psychologists go about measuring emotion.

Measuring Emotion   Emotion researchers have measured emotional experience and expression in a variety of ways. There is no one best way to measure emotion. Instead, the different methods are more like different pieces of the puzzle of emotions in all their complexity.

One approach is to measure physical, biological signs of emotion. In addition to being governed by display rules, gender roles, and other cultural factors, emotions have biological foundations. You have no doubt noticed that, in a situation that provokes intense fear, your heart pounds and your palms sweat. A pounding heart can also go with anger. The pattern of facial muscles that contract when a person experiences anger, or disgust, or happiness, is present from infancy and is universal across cultures (Ekman & Oster, 1979). Different regions of the brain are active depending on the emotion a person is experiencing. Emotional stimuli trigger the firing of neurons in the amygdala (a small region deep within the temporal lobes of the brain), which activates neurons in the brain stem, which in turn triggers the autonomic nervous system—reflected, for example, in changes in heart rate (LeDoux, 1994). The prefrontal cortex (the very front of the brain) and hippocampus (a small structure lying close to the amygdala) are activated as well (Davidson et al., 2000).

Modern neuroscientists are miles away from saying that, because brain regions are activated with the experience of emotions, emotions are "hard-wired" or biologically determined. Rather, neuroscientists today emphasize the *plasticity* of the brain (Davidson et al., 2000). Activation of a certain brain region may create a particular psychological state, but the reverse process occurs as well:

Behavior and experience can create changes in the brain. The brain is plastic and capable of change. For example, patients with posttraumatic stress disorder (PTSD) show some atrophy or deterioration of the hippocampus, as do patients with depression (Davidson et al., 2000). The trauma experienced by the person literally causes some brain cells to die in that person.

Following in the biological tradition, some emotion researchers study *biological measures* of emotion. These measures may include heart rate and skin conductance.[2]

In contrast to these biological aspects are people's own subjective experience of emotion, which typically is measured by *self-reports*. The reports may take a variety of forms, from checklists on which respondents identify the emotions they have experienced in the past week, to daily diary methods in which participants record their emotional responses to events at the time they occur. Self-report measures assume that people recognize and are aware of the emotions they experience, yet it seems likely that some people are better than others at recognizing their emotions. Emotional experience, though, is inherently internal and subjective, and self-reports are able to capture that aspect in a way that biological measures cannot.

Other researchers focus on the *expression* of emotion, captured in measures such as the number and kind of emotion words that people use in their language (verbal expressiveness) or facial muscle contractions (facial expressiveness).

Gender Differences in Emotional Experience and Expression   One study provides a particularly nice example of research on gender differences in these multiple aspects of emotion (Kring & Gordon, 1998). Undergraduates viewed brief film clips designed to stimulate either happiness, sadness, or fear. While the participants viewed the film, their skin conductance was measured and their facial expressions were videotaped. At the end of each clip, they rated how much they had experienced each of four emotions: sadness, fear, disgust, and happiness. In short, biological, self-report, and expression measures were collected.

The results showed that women were significantly more facially expressive than men for all emotion clips. Men and women did not differ significantly in their self-reports of the emotion experienced, but men showed significantly higher skin conductance reactivity to the fear films than women did. Men also showed more skin conductance reactivity to the happy clips, as did women to the sad clips, although the differences were not quite significant. In short, patterns of gender differences can reverse themselves depending on the aspect of emotion that is measured. Women tend to be more facially expressive than men (Hall, 1984), with the

---

[2]Skin-conductance tests assess activation of the autonomic nervous system—getting at, essentially, whether you have sweaty palms.

possible exception of anger. But men, at least for some emotions, show more autonomic nervous system reactivity. How interesting that in this study, men showed more fear—that unmanly emotion—than women when measured physiologically.

Overall, in this study women were more likely to be externalizers (facially expressive but with a low skin conductance response) and men were more likely to be internalizers (facially inexpressive but with a higher skin conductance response) (Kring & Gordon, 1998). Other researchers argue that, although men are more likely to show the internalizer pattern, women are more likely to be generalizers—that is, to express emotions on all measures (Brody & Hall, 2000). The internalizer pattern of men corresponds, of course, to the gender regulation that men should not express emotion.

In a follow-up experiment by the same group, the first experiment was replicated but with different film clips and, in addition, the measurement of participants' gender-role identity using the Bem Sex Role Inventory, discussed in Chapter 3 (Kring & Gordon, 1998). Again, women were more facially expressive than men across all film clips. In terms of skin conductance, men showed more reactivity to the anger and fear films and women showed more reactivity to the sadness and disgust films. Interestingly, gender-role identity showed larger effects than gender on emotion responses: Androgynous people were more facially expressive than masculine people. This finding provides evidence of the key role of gender roles in what emotions we express or do not express.

Another way to measure emotional expression is through language. Whether in conversations or in writing samples, girls and women use more emotion words and talk about emotions more than boys and men do (Brody & Hall, 2000; Goldschmidt & Weller, 2000).

Researchers, using self-report measures, consistently find gender differences in the intensity of emotional experience and expression, with women reporting the greater intensity (Brody & Hall, 2000). Paradoxically, women are both happier and sadder than men. They also demonstrate more awareness of their own emotions and seem to encode their emotional experience in more detail in memory than men do (Barrett et al., 2000; Seidlitz & Diener, 1998).

Anger is an important emotion and one of the few that is male stereotyped. Fourth- and fifth-grade children do not show gender differences in their self-reports of experiencing anger (Buntaine & Costenbader, 1997). They do differ, though, in how they express the anger: Girls are more likely to report sulking and pouting, whereas boys are more likely to report physical expressions such as hitting or kicking. When asked what they do to get over being angry, girls, as expected, are more likely to talk about it or to spend quiet time alone, whereas boys are more likely to do something physical. Lots of men and boys play basketball to cure their emotional ills.

The gender difference in intensity of emotion has been linked to gender roles (Grossman & Wood, 1993). For women, endorsement of gender stereotypes

and reports of intensity of personal emotional experiences are positively correlated: The more that women believe in stereotypes, the more intense they report
their own emotions to be. For men, the correlation between endorsement of gender stereotypes and reports of emotional intensity is negative: The more that
men believe in gender stereotypes, the less intense their emotions. Stereotypical
men don't express emotions and stereotypical women do. In a related
experiment, researchers removed gender-role pressures by exerting pressure for
both men and women to be emotionally expressive—specifically, by telling
participants that research showed a positive correlation between emotional responsiveness and psychological adjustment (Grossman & Wood, 1993). In the
control condition no such instructions were given, and presumably gender-role
pressures were in force as usual. Under the control condition, women gave more
extreme emotional responses to negative slides than men did, but under the
instructions encouraging emotional expressiveness, men's responses were the
same as women's. Women's greater emotionality is thus not a biologically determined Natural Law. This study shows powerfully that it is determined by society's gender rules.

By elementary school, girls are better than boys at controlling their emotions
and displaying socially appropriate emotions. For example, cultural display rules
dictate that, when children are presented with a disappointing gift, they should
not display their negative feelings, but rather should mask them and feign positive feelings. First- and third-grade girls, when presented with a disappointing
gift, display less negative emotion and more positive emotion than their male
peers (Davis, 1995).

Context and Gender Differences in Emotion   Consistent with much
other research on psychological gender differences, patterns of gender differences
in emotion vary depending on the context.

Even gender stereotypes are context dependent to some extent. Overreaction to happy or sad events is seen as more characteristic of women when the
context is interpersonal (a friend is hurt in a car accident), but as more characteristic of men in an achievement context (Chris invents a great new computer
chip but is not given credit for it) (Kelly & Hutson-Comeaux, 1999). Interestingly, overreaction to angry events is seen as more characteristic of men, regardless of context.

In one clever study that gets at actual emotional experience, mothers and fathers carried pagers for one week while going about their normal daily activities
at work and at home (Larson et al., 1994). When signaled at random times, they
immediately filled out a report about their current activity and emotional state.
The results indicated that fathers were happier than mothers when at home.
Mothers, in contrast, were happier than fathers when at work. The pattern of
gender differences in emotion, then, depended profoundly on the situation or
context.

The Socialization of Gendered Emotions

An 18-month-old, frustrated at not being allowed to play with a captivating toy that is in plain view, will not say, "I'm angry." Instead, the child experiences frustration and rage and expresses these emotions facially and in other ways. The parent may respond by saying, "You're angry, aren't you?" or "You're sad, aren't you?" or "Don't get mad." The child learns differently depending on the parent's response—in the first case, learning to label her feelings as anger; in the second, to misinterpret them as sadness; and in the third, to restrain or regulate her feelings. Between 18 and 36 months (3 years) of age, children rapidly learn to label their own emotions and those of others (Bretherton et al., 1986). Parents socialize their children about how to label and interpret their feelings and what to do with them (Eisenberg et al., 1998). In the process, parents are likely to impose gender stereotypes. Here we consider both the family and peers as early socializers of gendered emotions, as well as the ways in which gender continues to be socialized in interpersonal interactions in adulthood.

Socialization in the Family   Beginning at birth, mothers display a greater variety of emotions and more intense facial expressions of emotion to daughters compared with sons, and this pattern continues in the first year of life

The socialization of emotion: Mothers display more intense facial expressions of emotion to infant daughters compared with infant sons.

(Malatesta et al., 1989). Although there are no gender differences in infants' facial displays of emotion at birth, differences have appeared by one year of age, and the more expressive the mother, the more expressive the baby.

A number of studies demonstrate that parents talk about emotions differently with sons compared with daughters (Cervantes & Callanan, 1998; Fivush, 1989). In general, mothers talk about emotions more with daughters than with sons (Brody, 2000; Dunn et al., 1987; Flannagan & Perese, 1998). These interactions form the heart of gender socialization. In one study, mothers were asked to engage their almost-3-year-old child in a conversation about specific events that they thought the child would remember (Fivush, 1989). Mothers used more positive than negative emotion words with their daughters, but used approximately equal numbers of positive and negative emotion words with their sons. Strikingly, mothers never discussed anger with their daughters, but did so with their sons.

In conversations with their children, mothers use more emotion words than fathers do (Fivush et al., 2000). This raises the possibility of modeling effects as specified by social learning theory. If daughters model their mothers and sons model their fathers, girls will express more emotion in language and boys will express less, because their parents are models of this differentiation. Consistent with these socialization forces, by 4 or 5 years of age, girls use more emotion words in talking about past events than boys do (Dunn et al., 1987; Fivush et al., 2000).

Mothers actively encourage boys, more than girls, to respond to angry situations with anger and retaliation (Brody, 1996). Boys get the message and expect their mothers to react more warmly to them when they express anger than when they express sadness (Brody, 1996).

Why do parents socialize children's emotions in stereotypic directions? Parents' patterns of socialization probably reflect the roles that they anticipate sons and daughters will hold in adulthood (Brody, 1999). Men's roles focus on employment, where competition, power, and control are thought to be functional. Boys are therefore shaped not to express their emotions, especially emotions that would reveal vulnerability. The exceptions are anger, contempt, and pride, which boys and men are allowed to express and which seem consistent with high-status work roles. Women's roles focus on caregiving, whether as mothers or in occupations such as teacher or nurse. Girls are therefore socialized for qualities such as warmth and empathic distress. At the same time, in their anticipated lower-status roles, they can express vulnerability by revealing fear and sadness.

Importantly, these differences in emotional expression then serve to perpetuate power and status differences between women and men. An openly fearful person can scarcely be the CEO of a corporation, and a person who is too ready to express anger and contempt can scarcely be a preschool teacher.

In a classic experiment, a videotape was made of a baby's emotional responses to a jack-in-the-box popping open (Condry & Condry, 1976). The baby stared and then cried. The videotape was shown to adults, half of whom were told the baby was a boy and half of whom were told it was a girl. Those who thought the baby was a boy labeled the emotions "anger"; the other half called the "girl's" emotions "fear." In short, the adults "read" the emotions differently depending on the baby's gender. This partly explains why parents socialize children's emotions in gender-stereotyped directions: The parents, filtering a child's behavior through gender-colored lenses, perceive the child experiencing gender-linked emotions.

Interestingly, when fathers become more involved with their children, patterns of gendered emotions are different (Brody, 1999). Girls with more involved fathers express less fear and sadness, compared with girls whose fathers are less involved. Boys with more involved fathers express more warmth and fear. Consistent with Nancy Chodorow's theory (see Chapter 2), fathers' involvement in the family seems to be crucial to breaking down stereotypes in the next generation.

Socialization by Peers   A college student recalled to me how, around fifth grade, his expressions of sadness were literally beaten out of him by other boys. Some sad events happened in his family that year, and that in turn made him more emotional at school. He learned that if he cried in front of his peers, they would ridicule him and engage in dominance behaviors such as punching him. That only made him feel sadder and more like crying; but he learned, painfully yet quickly, never to cry, no matter how hard he was hurting, emotionally or physically.

In a study of first-, third-, and fifth-graders, children reported that they would control their expressions of sadness, anger, and pain more when they were with peers than when they were with their parents (Zeman & Garber, 1996). The reasons they gave focused on anticipated negative reactions from peers, including rejection and ridicule.

In an observational study of elementary school children, those who expressed stereotype-violating emotions were less popular with their peers (Adler et al., 1992). Boys who cried easily were called "sissies" and were less popular. Popular boys suppressed vulnerable feelings. Popular girls, in contrast, were verbally expressive and sensitive to others' feelings. Popularity is a powerful socialization force.

Gender and Emotion Socialization in Adults' Interactions   Gender socialization does not stop in childhood. It continues in adulthood, perpetuated by interactions between women and men. In one study, women who responded with fear to a horror movie were rated as more sexually attractive by a male partner than women who conquered their fear. And men who conquered their fear were rated as more sexually attractive by their female partners than men who did not (Zillmann et al., 1986).

Marital interactions are another stage on which gendered emotions play themselves out. Research has repeatedly shown that, in a marital conflict situation with its associated negative emotions, women on average want to keep talking and to work through to a resolution of the conflict, whereas men often withdraw from the discussion (Levenson et al., 1994). Why does this occur? One explanation is that **emotion work** is part of the female role (Hochschild, 1990). That is, women are expected to be responsible for the emotional quality of relationships, whether between spouses, mother and child, or preschool teacher and student. In a marital conflict, then, women perform their job of trying to work out the emotions.

> **Emotion work:** Taking responsibility for the emotional quality of relationships, which is part of the female role.

A second, intriguing possibility is that the pattern has to do with the differing relationship between physiological arousal and emotion in women compared with men. As noted earlier in this chapter, during the experience of intense emotions, the autonomic nervous system is in a state of high alert, indicated by increased heart rate, higher skin conductance, and so on. For husbands during marital conflict, autonomic arousal is correlated with intensity of negative emotions, whereas for wives the correlation is not significant (Levenson et al., 1994). It may be, then, that men withdraw in order to reduce their physiological arousal and the unpleasant feelings it evokes. This strategy has worked repeatedly for them, and they continue to use it. Women, in contrast, don't feel as bad in this state of physiological arousal, and so are able to stay with the discussion to try to resolve it. In any case, we are left with the typical scene of women talking about and expressing their emotions and husbands withdrawing into emotional nonexpression.

Men's withdrawal or stonewalling in marital conflict situations may serve more purposes than just getting their nervous systems chilled out, of course. Withdrawal controls the situation and the woman. Stonewalling preserves the status quo—and the status quo is generally advantageous to men.

Putting It All Together: Brody's Model   Psychologist Leslie Brody (1999) has proposed a comprehensive model for the development of gender differences in emotional expression. According to her model, the process begins in infancy with slight differences in temperament between girls and boys. Girls have better and earlier language skills than boys. Boys are more active than girls, from infancy onward. And girls develop self-control earlier than boys. Either in response to their daughters' language abilities or because of their own gender stereotypes, mothers then use more emotion words with their preschool daughters than with their preschool sons. Thus by 24 months, girls produce more emotion words than boys, and by 4 or 5 years, they use more emotion words in discussing past events than boys do (Dunn et al., 1987; Fivush et al., 2000).

As children grow older, peers play a larger role in gender socialization, including the socialization of emotional expression. We have just seen that peers from preschool to middle school exert powerful pressures in favor of gender-stereotyped expressions of emotion. Gender-segregated patterns of play are influential as well. Boys play with other boys, and none of them express emotion. Girls play with other girls and freely express emotion with each other.

The culture at large plays a role as well. The media, for example, portray women and men displaying different emotions. And, as we have seen, different cultures and ethnic groups have different expectations about gendered emotions.

EXPERIENCE THE RESEARCH

THE GENDER SOCIALIZATION OF EMOTIONS

In this exercise, you are going to investigate the differences in two mothers' emotion words, comparing the conversations of a mother of a daughter and the mother of a son. Find two mothers with kindergartners, one a boy and one a girl. Obtain their permission to tape-record a conversation between them and their children. Ask each mother to think of two specific events her child has experienced and would be likely to remember and then to engage the child in conversation about first one event and then the other. Tape-record the conversations, which should last between five and ten minutes. After you have completed the data collection, transcribe the tapes—that is, type up exactly what was said on each. Make a count of the number of positive emotion words and negative emotion words that each mother used. As you do this, consider these questions: How are you going to define which words count as emotion words? Did the mother of the daughter use more emotion words than the mother of the son? Were there any other differences in patterns? For example, was anger discussed with the son but not the daughter?

In Conclusion

Women are stereotyped as expressing a wide variety of both positive and negative emotions, including fear, sadness, sympathy, happiness, and love. Men, in contrast, are supposed to express only anger, contempt, and pride. Such stereotypes not only reflect women's and men's roles in adulthood, but also help to perpetuate these differentiated roles.

Although there is great similarity across U.S. ethnic groups in gender stereotypes of emotion, there are also some notable differences. Blacks, for example, believe that Black women express anger nearly as much as Black men do. Gender stereotypes of emotions can have important consequences, leading people to misread others' emotions.

Beyond the stereotypes, the issue of gender differences in actual emotional experience and expression is complex. Emotion manifests itself in many ways, including facial expressions, subjective feelings captured in self-reports, and arousal of the autonomic nervous system. Patterns of gender differences may be inconsistent across these various contexts, thus, highlighting how oversimplified the stereotypes are.

Gender socialization shapes emotions, beginning with parental socialization from infancy. Later, peers play an important role in enforcing gender rules. Girls and women are more facially expressive of emotion and talk about emotions more than boys and men do. And gendered patterns of emotional expression continue to be maintained by interactions between women and men in adulthood.

Suggestions for Further Reading

Brody, Leslie R. (1999). *Gender, emotion, and the family*. Cambridge, MA: Harvard University Press. Brody reviews a mountain of studies on gender stereotypes and gender differences in emotion, and discusses how socialization processes shape these gender differences.

From Infancy to Old Age: Development Across the Lifespan

7

At age twelve I was among the first of my friends to begin to menstruate and to wear a bra. I felt a mixture of pride and embarrassment. For all of my life I had been a chubby, introspective child, but a growth spurt of a few inches, along with my developing breasts, transformed me one summer into a surprisingly slim and shapely child-woman. The funny thing was that on one level I had always known this would happen. Yet it was as if a fairy godmother had visited me. I felt turned on, but I was mostly turned on to myself and the narcissistic pleasure of finding I was attractive to boys.

— FROM OUR BODIES, OURSELVES

When my daughter was 5, she loved to look at the family photograph albums. She begged to see the pictures of herself as a baby or a 2-year-old and to hear the stories of the funny things she had done or said at that age. She nagged to see the pictures of me dressed in my cowgirl outfit at age 5 and to hear how I had wanted to be Dale Evans (Roy Rogers's other half) when I grew up. Then she triumphantly announced, "But you didn't, you're a professor." She saw the picture of me as an awkward-looking 8-year-old, dressed in a ballet costume for my first dance recital, and we laughed together at how I still didn't dance very well. She was fascinated, as most people are, with the process of psychological development—how different she was at 5 from the way she had been at 2, how different adults are from what they as children thought they would be, how predictable some things are from childhood to adulthood. In this chapter we will consider the development of female behavior and roles across the lifespan.

Infancy

Psychologists have spent an extraordinary amount of time studying children, particularly preschoolers and infants. Studies of gender differences have been extensive. Investigations of infant gender differences have had two primary motives. First, it has been thought that if gender differences were found in newborns—say, when they are only one day old—those differences must surely be due to biological factors, because gender-role socialization can scarcely have had time to have an effect. The idea, then, was to try to discover the biological causes of gender differences by studying newborns. Second, many investigators think it is important to study the way parents and other adults treat infants, in order to discover the subtle (and perhaps not-so-subtle) differences in the way adults treat boy babies and girl babies, beginning the process of socialization at a tender age. I review research in these two areas below.

Infant Gender Differences　Most infant behaviors do not show gender differences. That is, *gender similarities* are the rule for most behaviors. Boys and girls, for example, are equally sociable (Maccoby, 1998). Nonetheless, a few gender differences appear early.

One difference is in *activity level,* with boys having the higher activity. In small infants, this may be measured by counting the number of times they swing their arms or kick their legs. In older babies, it might be measured by counting the number of squares the baby crawls across on a playroom floor. A major meta-analysis found that $d = +0.29$ for gender differences in infants' activity level (Eaton & Enns, 1986.) That is, male infants are more active, but the difference is small. The difference is larger among preschoolers ($d = 0.44$) and older children ($d = 0.64$).

Adults' Treatment of Infants　The other area of interest in infant research concerns whether, even at this early age, parents and other adults treat males and females differently.

Once again, *gender similarities* seem to be the rule; for the most part parents treat male and female babies similarly (Maccoby & Jacklin, 1974). Nonetheless, there do seem to be some differences. Boys are handled more roughly (Maccoby & Jacklin, 1974), and boys generally receive more positive responses for playing with male-stereotyped toys (Fagot & Hagan, 1991).

It's important to bear in mind, however, that not only do parents influence infants, but infants also influence parents. Therefore, if there are differences in the behavior of boys and girls, these may cause the differences in parental treatment rather than the reverse. For example, if boys are more active, that may explain why they are handled more roughly.

A classic experiment, the *Baby X Study,* controlled these factors (Seavey et al., 1975; for a review of similar studies, see Stern & Karraker, 1989). The adult participants (all nonparents) were told they were taking part in a study on infants' responses to strangers. They were brought into an observation room and a 3-month-old infant (actually a female) in a yellow jumpsuit was put on the floor in the room with them. One-third of the adults were told the baby was a boy, one-third were told she was a girl, and the other third were given no gender information. Three toys were near the baby—a small rubber football (a "masculine" toy), a Raggedy Ann doll (a "feminine" toy), and a plastic ring (a "neutral" toy). The interactions between the adult and the baby were observed from behind a one-way mirror for three minutes. The frequency of using each of the toys was recorded, and ratings were made of the behavior of the adults toward the infant. Afterward, the adults also rated their own impressions of the infant.

A number of interesting results emerged. With regard to choice of toy, there was an interaction between the gender of the adult and the gender-label of the baby. The results are shown in Table 7.1. The football was not really very popular in any condition, probably because a football does not seem to be an appropriate toy for such a small baby. As expected, the doll was used most frequently when

TABLE 7.1
Mean Frequency of Toy Choices for Babies by the Adults in the Baby X Study

| Gender of Adult | Baby Labeled | Toy | | |
		Football	Doll	Teething Ring
Male	Boy	0.33	0.72	0.61
	Girl	0.50	1.61	0.94
	No label	0.85	0.71	1.42
Female	Boy	0.57	0.71	1.00
	Girl	0.50	1.27	1.05
	No label	0.40	1.23	0.70

SOURCE: From "Baby X: The effects of gender labels on adult responses to infants," by Carol Seavey et al., 1975, *Sex Roles,* 1. Published by Plenum Publishing Corporation. Reprinted by permission.

the baby was introduced as a girl. On the ratings of the interactions, and on the adults' ratings of the babies, however, there were no significant differences depending on the label given to the baby. Some of the most interesting results came from the neutral-label group. Many of these adults inquired what the baby's gender was. Most of them had formed an opinion of what the baby's gender was by the end of the session (57 percent of men and 70 percent of women thought that it was a boy) and had stereotyped rationales for their beliefs. Those who thought the baby was a boy noted the strength of the grasp or lack of hair, whereas those who thought it was a girl remarked on the baby's roundness, softness, and fragility. Gender is a crucial part of information when we form impressions of others, and we "make up" a gender when we don't know for sure.

What can we conclude from this study? It would seem that gender is important in adults' interactions with children, something that is particularly evident when adults are not told a child's gender. However, the effects are not simple, and they may not be large. None of the ratings of the interactions showed gender-label effects. For example, the adults did not automatically give a football to the "boy." Furthermore, the effects depended not only on the gender-label given the baby, but also on the gender of the adult.

Gender Learning   Infants begin learning about and responding to gender at amazingly young ages. By 6 months, infants can distinguish the category of female

voices from the category of male voices (Miller, 1983). And by 9 months, infants are sensitive to the distinction between male faces and female faces (Leinbach & Fagot, 1993). Infancy researchers use a set of clever techniques to ascertain these capabilities in infants. One is the *habituation paradigm*, in which an infant is shown the same stimulus (e.g., a picture of a face) repeatedly. The infant habituates or gets used to it. If a new stimulus is presented, the infant responds with interest and a change in heart rate. Thus, for example, a researcher could habituate a baby to a set of pictures of female faces. When a new female face is presented, the baby still acts habituated. But if a new male face is presented, the infant shows interest and a change in heart rate. Such a pattern of responding would show that the baby responds to male faces as being in a different category than female faces.

Much more gender learning occurs in the toddler and preschool years, as we will discuss in the next section.

Childhood

Gender Learning   Children typically know whether they are a boy or girl—that is, they have acquired a gender identity—by 2 years of age (Kohlberg, 1966). By age 3, they can accurately label other children as boys or girls (Fagot et al., 2000; O'Brien et al., 2000). Also by 3 years of age, children identify an angry-looking character as male (Leinbach, 1993). Children are sensitive to and learn gender categories very early, and they quickly learn to associate certain attributes—for example, anger—with gender. By kindergarten, they associate certain occupations with men and others with women and give a gender-stereotyped preference for their own future occupation (Helwig, 1998).

Childhood Gender Differences   Already by the early preschool years, several reliable gender differences have appeared. One is in *toy and game preference*. Preschool children between the ages of three and five have a strong preference for gender-typed toys and same-gender playmates (Martin & Little, 1990). Girls seem to develop this preference first and boys show it just a little later (Maccoby, 1998). The result is strong gender segregation in childhood, a point we will explore in more detail below.

Another difference that appears early is in *aggressive behavior*. About as soon as aggressive behavior appears in children, around the age of 2, gender differences are found; boys are more aggressive than girls. This difference persists throughout the school years (see Chapter 3).

Socialization   The forces of gender-role socialization become more prominent in childhood (Lips, 1989). **Socialization** refers to the ways in which society conveys to the individual its expectations for his or her behavior.

> **Socialization:** The process by which society conveys to the individual its expectations for his or her behavior, values, and beliefs.

Socialization begins in the *family*. Parents may begin to have different expectations for the child depending on gender. For example, girls may be expected to help with the dinner dishes, boys to take out the garbage. A major meta-analysis of parents' gender-role socialization found that, for the most part, parents treat boys and girls similarly (Lytton & Romney, 1991). However, there was one major exception: encouragement of sex-typed activities, where the difference was large ($d = 0.71$ for preschoolers). The evidence is strong, then, that parents socialize their children toward sex-typed activities. Parents also seem to convey their gender schemas to their children (Tenenbaum & Leaper, 2002).

Parents talk differently with their daughters compared with their sons. Mothers talk more and use more supportive speech with daughters than with sons, perhaps creating a greater emphasis for daughters on verbal interactions and relationships (Leaper et al., 1998). And, as we saw in Chapter 6, parents talk differently about emotions with daughters and sons.

Parents also play differently with sons compared with daughters in the preschool years. Parents engage in more pretend play with girls than with boys, and fathers in particular engage in more physical play with sons than with daughters (Lindsey et al., 1997, 2001). What is unclear, however, is whether parents engage in these different types of play because of their own gender-stereotyped ideas, or because they are responding to the lead of the child and boys and girls initiate different kinds of play.

Children catch on to these direct and indirect messages from their parents. In a study of 4-year-olds, nearly half of the boys said that their fathers would think it was "bad" if they played with girls' toys (Raag & Rackliff, 1998).

Not all families are the same, of course. "Liberated" parents may take great pains to give trucks to their daughters and dolls to their sons and to make sure that the mother and father share equally in childcare duties. A more traditional family will probably encourage more traditional roles.

The research on gender socialization within the family has been based almost exclusively on White middle-class samples (Reid et al., 1995). Yet, as we saw in Chapter 4, there is good reason to think that gender-role socialization varies across different ethnic groups in the United States. For example, gender roles are less differentiated among Blacks, and Black children are exposed to Black women who are assertive, express anger openly, and are independent (Reid, 1995). The version of the female that these children observe and model is different from the version displayed by many White, middle-class women.

As children grow older, schools, the media, and peers become increasingly important sources of gender socialization.

The *schools,* whether purposely or unwittingly, often transmit the information of gender-role stereotypes (Lips, 1989). I recently heard the story of a second-grade teacher urging on a little girl balking at doing a mathematics problem by saying, "You must learn to do your arithmetic so you'll be able to do the marketing for your husband when you grow up." Research based on classroom observations in preschools and elementary schools indicates that teachers treat boys and girls differently. Teachers, on average, pay more attention to boys (De-Zolt & Hull, 2001; Golombok & Fivush, 1994). When teachers praise students, the compliments go to girls for decorous conduct and to boys for good academic performance (Dweck et al., 1980; Golombok & Fivush, 1994). When children make mistakes, boys are given more precise feedback and are encouraged to keep trying until they get it right; girls are more likely to be told not to worry about the mistake, and teachers spend less time with them suggesting new approaches. Girls are more often not told even whether their answers are right or wrong (Sadker & Sadker, 1985). Fortunately, when teachers are given gender-equity training to sensitize them to these issues, they respond with more equitable treatment (DeZolt & Hull, 2001).

As we have seen repeatedly, both gender and ethnicity are factors—in this case, in predicting teachers' interactions with students (e.g., Irvine, 1985, 1986). One study replicated the finding that White girls receive significantly less communication from teachers than White boys do (Irvine, 1985). In contrast, in the early elementary grades (K through 2), Black girls receive as much feedback from the teacher as Black boys do (Irvine, 1986). However, by the later grades (3 through 5), Black girls are receiving less attention than Black boys; they have been molded into the invisibility found among White girls. The researcher suggested that this developmental pattern occurs because Black girls are not socialized by their parents to be passive in the same way that White girls are, so that Black girls are assertive when they enter school in kindergarten. However, by the later grades they have assumed the same passive roles as White girls.

The *media* are powerful socializing agents as well. Many people assume that things have changed dramatically since the 1970s and that gender stereotypes are a thing of the past. The evidence indicates that some change has occurred, yet the same stereotyped gender roles are in plentiful supply. An analysis of picture books for children published between 1995 and 1999 documented substantial progress (Gooden & Gooden, 2001). Girls were the main character as often as boys were, in contrast to the pattern 30 years ago, when boys were the main character 11 times as often as girls (Weitzman et al., 1972). Nonetheless, in the contemporary books, characters were still predominantly engaged in traditional gender roles. Males were rarely shown caring for children and were never seen doing household chores (Gooden & Gooden, 2001).

Analyses of comics and cartoons indicate this same pattern of some change yet much maintenance of traditional roles (Brabant & Mooney, 1997; LaRossa et al., 2001). Women are shown working outside the home more now; by 1994, Blondie had her own catering business. Yet males still appear more often as the main character and females continue to be more likely shown as passive background participants.

An analysis of the content of *Seventeen* magazine—a prime socializer of preteen and teen girls—from 1945 to 1995 indicated that the women's movement had had some impact, but that the changes were slight (Schlenker et al., 1998). Articles were classified as conveying traditional messages (focus on appearance, male-female relations, or domestic skills) or feminist messages (focus on personal development, career development, or political or world issues). The percentage of articles with feminist themes was 52 percent in 1945, 26 percent in 1955 and 1965, 40 percent in 1975, 35 percent in 1985, and 40 percent in 1995. These trends correspond closely to feminist activism: nontraditional roles during World War II, followed by the very traditional 1950s extending into the 1960s, then the Second Wave of the women's movement in the 1970s, a return to conservatism in the 1980s, and then the emergence of the Third Wave of feminism in the 1990s. Career development should be an important topic for teenage girls. In 1955, 10 percent of the articles were about career development; by 1995 that figure had risen almost imperceptibly to 14 percent.

But picture books, cartoons, and magazines are old-fashioned media. One would expect the new media to be less stereotyped. To the contrary, however, video games show patterns of extreme gender stereotyping. According to one analysis, there were no female characters at all in 41 percent of the video games that had characters (Dietz, 1998). Children Now, a nonprofit organization that advocates for children, announced in 2000 that the top-selling video games are "unhealthy" for girls (Children Now, 2000). It had a number of reasons for reaching this conclusion, including the sexualized portrayals of female characters. For example, among the games that contained female characters, 23 percent showed them with exposed breasts or cleavages and 15 percent showed exposed buttocks.

MTV, a prime example of current media, features more male characters than female characters, and shows the female characters in more sexy and skimpy clothing (Signorielli, 1994). Even computer Clipart images are highly gender stereotyped (Milburn et al., 2001).

Research indicates that children's books continue to show children in traditional gender-stereotyped activities, such as boys doing outdoor work (top left) and girls doing household chores (top right). More illustrations are needed showing children involved in nontraditional activities (bottom).

Are the media as stereotyped as they were in 1970? Some are less stereotyped, but stereotypes are still at saturation levels in many types of media.

The stereotyping of television messages has been demonstrated to have an actual effect on children's behavior. In one study, 4- to 6-year-old children viewed a film similar to "Sesame Street" shows in which Muppet-like characters said that a set of toys belonged to a boy; another group of children saw the same film, except that the characters said the toys were a girl's; and a third group of children saw a version of the film in which the characters said the toys could be for either boys or girls (Cobb et al., 1982). After viewing the film, children played more with the toys that had been described as gender appropriate for them. In the condition in which the toys were described as being appropriate for both boys and girls, the children preferred those toys (compared with toys not shown in the film). This result suggests that children can respond positively to nonstereotypical messages on television.

Meta-analysis indicates that amount of television viewing is correlated with acceptance of gender stereotypes (Herrett-Skjellum & Allen, 1996). That is, the more a child watches TV, the more likely he or she is to hold traditional gender-role views.

Peers and the Gender Segregation Effect   The eminent developmental psychologist Eleanor Maccoby, in her book *The Two Sexes: Growing Up Apart, Coming Together* (1998), concludes that gendered patterns of behavior are not solely the result of socialization by forces such as parents and the media. By 3 years of age, children have a tendency to seek out and play with other children of their own gender, and to avoid playing with children of the other gender. The tendency grows stronger by the time children are in elementary school. It occurs regardless of the gender socialization principles in their families, and in villages in developing nations as much as in the United States. The all-female and all-male groups differ in terms of their activities. Boys' play is rougher and involves more risk, confrontation, and striving for dominance. The members of all-girl groups are more likely to use conflict-reducing strategies in negotiating with each other and to engage in more self-disclosure. Girls' groups also tend to maintain communication with adults, whereas boys separate themselves from adults, test the limits, and seek autonomy.

The gender segregation and the different play styles in these groups essentially egg each other on. Boys are attracted to boy groups in part because they adore the rough play, and girls avoid boy groups because they dislike rough play. Once in a boy group, boys are encouraged to play roughly. Boys may be attracted to rough, active play by their higher activity level, which, as we have seen, is present from infancy and may have a biological basis. Engaged in rough play, they become even more active. Girls are attracted to girl groups because they like the positive social network and the self-regulated style of play. Once they are in the group, self-regulation is encouraged.

Much of the gender segregation of childhood, then, results from forces within the child—whether biological or psychological. (An example of the latter is the child's desire to maintain a positive gender identity by engaging in gender-typed activities.) Peer play groups rapidly create the next generation of gender-typed children (Maccoby, 2002).

Interestingly, as Maccoby notes, when children play alone, gender differences in behavior are minimal. When in their same-gender group, the gender differences are large and striking. Again we see evidence of the importance of context in shaping gender differences in behavior.

With all this gender segregation in childhood, how do males and females get back together in adulthood, to form relationships, work cooperatively, and so on? The answer is that, in some cultures, they don't. That is, in some cultures even the adult world is highly gender segregated, leaving contact between husbands and wives as the only intergender contact. In 2001 we learned about such a culture in Afghanistan under Taliban rule. In societies that do allow open contact between males and females, sexual attraction helps bring the sexes together. The process is not without pitfalls, though, as boys' much-practiced dominance style meshes with girls' conflict-reducing style. As men and women come together, whether in romantic relationships or at work, they pursue common goals and their behavior becomes more similar.

Is this gender segregation in childhood, and the male dominance it encourages, inevitable? Maccoby suggests that, as long as we allow children freedom to choose their playmates, the pattern will continue. Nonetheless, schools could take steps to ensure that, in the classroom, children have multiple experiences of working cooperatively in mixed-gender groups. Such practices reduce the extreme gender differentiation of childhood and should foster better male-female relationships in adulthood.

School   Girls make the adjustment to school with greater ease than boys do. Boys are referred to principals, psychologists, or guidance counselors for serious behavioral problems about ten times more frequently than girls are (Golombok & Fivush, 1994). This is due in part to the fact that the incidence of hyperactivity is far higher in boys than in girls; the common estimate is that boys outnumber girls by about four to one (Holborow & Berry, 1986). Girls' interactions with teachers, in contrast, are more pleasant and less full of conflict. Girls are more likely to do their homework than boys are, and girls earn better grades than boys at all grade levels and in all subjects (DeZolt & Hull, 2001).

Tomboys   Despite the pressures of gender socialization, not every girl conforms. Surveys have repeatedly shown that about two-thirds of girls were tomboys in childhood (Hyde et al., 1977; Morgan, 1998). Not every girl, then, is staying at home playing with dolls. In fact, the majority are engaging in active play—perhaps not as active as in boys' groups, but active nonetheless. Tomboyism may simply be childhood's version of androgyny (Hemmer & Kleiber, 1981).

One study of three generations of women (Gen Xers, Baby Boomers, and Senior Citizens) found that tomboy behavior started on average at age 5 and stopped around age 12 (Morgan, 1998). The twilight of tomboyism at age 12 is significant because that age marks the transition to adolescence and a new set of gender pressures.

Although many social critics emphasize the restrictiveness of girls' socialization, stereotype-inconsistent behavior is in fact far less tolerated for boys than it is for girls. Many parents tolerate their daughters climbing trees and playing baseball, but get upset at a son playing with dolls. It is seen as far worse to be a sissy than to be a tomboy.

In childhood, then, some gender differences in behavior are found, and gender-role socialization occurs to some extent. However, gender similarities are the rule, and many girls are allowed a great deal of freedom and are encouraged to achieve in school. Adolescence then marks a turning point.

Adolescence

If the behavior and development of girls and boys are similar for about the first ten years of life, how do the gender differences in adulthood arise? In the early years, girls do better in school and have fewer adjustment problems than boys. Yet adult women, on average, have lower-status jobs than men (see Chapter 9) and have a higher incidence of depression (see Chapter 15). Although the groundwork for these differences is prepared in childhood, the real precipitating factors occur in adolescence.

Gender Intensification   Adolescence researchers agree that pressures for gender-role conformity increase dramatically at the beginning of adolescence, a process known as **gender intensification** (Crouter et al., 1995). The pressure, then, is for girls to become more feminine and less masculine, beginning around 11 or 12 years of age. Research shows that boys actually do increase in masculinity and girls increase in femininity over the transition to adolescence (Galambos et al., 1990; Petersen et al., 1991). As part of this process, girls become more identified with and spend more time with their mothers and boys do the same with their fathers (Crouter et al., 1995). Gender intensification may also shift the focus of girls' attention from school achievement to attractiveness and popularity.

> **Gender intensification:** Increased pressures for gender-role conformity beginning in early adolescence.

Femininity-Achievement Incompatibility   In adolescence, a cultural rule starts to be enforced on the girl: **femininity-achievement incompatibility**—that is, to achieve is gender inappropriate. If the girl continues to achieve she will be unfeminine, and to be feminine is not to achieve. The girl is caught in a situation in which two equally important systems of values are in conflict. One is the desire for a positive sense of self, the sense that one is a worthwhile, productive person. Achieving, getting good grades, and excelling have been encouraged and rewarded so far, providing a major avenue for establishing the self as having worth and value. But the reward system changes abruptly at adolescence. The competing system is the desire to be a good female, to conform to gender-role expectations, and to be feminine, with whatever rewards that carries. The desire to be a competent, worthwhile person is now incompatible with the desire to be good in the female role; but society at large does not value the female role. Even today, adolescent girls' disclosures of achievement are viewed negatively and boys' are viewed positively (Daubman & Sigall, 1997).

> **Femininity-achievement incompatibility:** The cultural belief that, beginning in adolescence, achievement is not appropriately feminine for girls.

The situation is actually a bit more complex in that not all achievements are considered gender inappropriate for girls. It is perfectly acceptable to be preparing to be a nurse or teacher, but achievement in male-stereotyped areas—such as

In early adolescence, gender intensification occurs, and girls learn that their status will be determined by their attractiveness, not their achievements.

being a welder or car mechanic—is inappropriate and subject to sanctions (e.g., Cherry & Deaux, 1978).

The reward system may change in adolescence for either or both of two reasons. First, heterosexual relationships, popularity, and dating rise to importance; thus the peer group begins enforcing the rules of the femininity-achievement incompatibility. And, second, parents may change their teachings as they begin to see popularity and marriageability as important for their daughter. The timing of the change in the parents' emphasis, of course, varies greatly from one family to the next. In one, the girl may be urged to stop studying and to start having boyfriends when she is in sixth grade, whereas in another, achieving a college education will be viewed as far more important than dating, and the parents do not begin asking about marriage prospects until the young woman announces that she is going to go to graduate school and get a Ph.D.

Certainly the origin of the *double-bind* for females lies in the conflict between achievement and femininity (Horner, 1970a, 1972). The adolescent girl is caught in a classic double-bind situation in which she wants both of two alternatives—to be feminine and to achieve—but the two are perceived as being incompatible. In this we see one source of the adjustment problems some adult women have.

Friendship and Dating   It has been said that, in their friendships, girls and women stand "face to face" and boys and men stand "shoulder to shoulder" (Winstead & Griffin, 2001). That is, girls are face to face as they talk and self-disclose, whereas boys are shoulder to shoulder, engaged in some common activity such as a sport.

The origins of these different friendship styles certainly lie in early childhood and the gender-segregated play groups with their different playstyles. By fourth or fifth grade, gender differences in same-gender friendships have appeared that resemble those found in adulthood (Winstead & Griffin, 2001). Girls are more likely than boys to talk and self-disclose. And girls' talk is more often about personal concerns or other people, whereas boys' talk is more likely to be about sports and leisure activities. Not wanting to emphasize gender differences, though, we should note that girls and boys are similar in their friendships in qualities such as honesty, straightforwardness, mutual activities, and loyalty (Buhrmester, 1998).

Despite plentiful research on adolescent sexuality, there are few studies on heterosexual romantic relationships in adolescence. Yet we know that these relationships touch off strong emotions including love, jealousy, anger, and anxiety (O'Sullivan et al., 2001). These relationships also serve a developmental function in the transition to adulthood. They provide a context for learning about the self, including a consideration of one's gender identity and sexual orientation.

Perhaps most importantly for our purposes, adolescent dating is the stage for the enactment of heterosexual, gendered scripts (O'Sullivan et al., 2001). Girls are valued for their appearance, boys for their achievements (Jackson, 1992). Around 10 to 12 years of age, girls begin paying more attention to their hair, clothing, and makeup, in efforts to make themselves more attractive to boys. Boy-girl parties include games with sexual content, such as Spin the Bottle and Seven Minutes in Heaven. Pairwise dating develops out of group dating.

Dating relationships typically involve power differentials between the boy and the girl (O'Sullivan et al., 2001). Girls may be more invested in maintaining the relationship, giving boys more power. Often, too, boys assume decision-making authority.

Sexual Harassment   Although we consider sexual harassment in detail in Chapter 14, it is worth addressing here briefly because it is such a prominent feature of girls' experience in middle school and high school today. The American Association of University Women, in a national survey of students in the eighth through eleventh grades, found that most boys (79 percent) and girls (83 percent) had experienced sexual harassment by peers (AAUW, 2001). Harassing behaviors included sexual touching, forced kissing, and spreading sexual rumors about the person. The rates for boys and girls sound like gender equality, but the inequality lies in the feelings that result from the harassment. Girls are considerably more likely than boys to feel self-conscious (44 percent vs. 19 percent), embarrassed (53 percent vs. 32 percent) and less confident (32 percent vs. 16 percent) because of the incident. Girls are also more likely than boys to change their behavior as a result—for example, by talking less in class. The problem of peer sexual harassment is serious.

Even in a study of third- and fifth-graders in rural Ohio, girls reported being the objects of sexual harassment (Murnen & Smolak, 2000). And again, although about the same percentage of girls as boys reported sexual harassment, the meaning of the events was quite different for girls and boys. Girls thought of such events as frightening, whereas boys thought of them as flattering.

Weight Worries   Many studies have found that adolescent girls have more negative body esteem than adolescent boys (Mendelson et al., 2001; Polce-Lynch et al., 2001). Body esteem or body image has many components, of course, including feelings about one's weight, face, hair, and shape. Beginning in late elementary school, girls are more dissatisfied with their weight than boys are (Smolak & Striegel-Moore, 2001). In one study of sixth-, seventh-, and eighth-grade girls, 72 percent said they were dieting (Levine et al., 1994). The emphasis on thinness is so strong, and the dissatisfaction with weight so great among American girls and women, that it has been termed a "normative discontent" (Rodin et al., 1985).

Dissatisfaction with weight and shape can lead adolescent girls to a number of unhealthy and potentially dangerous behaviors such as dieting and cosmetic surgery, including liposuction and breast enlargement (Smolak & Striegel-Moore, 2001). Girls' weight worries are no small thing—they can actually become life-threatening.

There is little doubt that girls' dissatisfaction with their bodies is powerfully shaped by the media and their displays of hyper-thin models (Martin & Gentry, 1997). Experimental research shows that as little media exposure as viewing ten slides from women's magazines such as *Glamour* leads to increased weight concern (Posavac et al., 1998; see also Lavine et al., 1999). This effect holds true only for women with more initial body dissatisfaction, though. That leads us to consider how these beliefs are internalized, as discussed in Focus 7.1.

In regard to ethnicity, White women and Latinas generally express more weight concern compared with Black women, who express less (Bay-Cheng et al., 2002). Consistent with this finding, Black adolescent girls are more likely to be proud of their body (60 percent) than White (38 percent), Hispanic (45 percent), and Asian American (50 percent) girls (Story et al., 1995).

Transgressions: Athletics and Anger   Traditionally, adolescent girls were the cheerleaders, not the athletes. And they never expressed anger. What happens when these traditional boundaries are transgressed?

FOCUS 7.1

OBJECTIFIED BODY CONSCIOUSNESS

According to feminist theorists, the weight worries of adolescent girls and adult women result from more complex forces than simple gender-role pressures and media bombardment. Using a social constructionist approach, these theorists argue that the feminine body is socially constructed. In particular, the feminine body is constructed as an object to be looked at, an object of the male gaze and male desire. Thus girls learn to view their own bodies as if they were outside observers. This experience of one's own body as an object to be viewed and evaluated is termed *objectified body consciousness*. The higher the level of a woman's objectified body consciousness, the more negative she feels about her body.

Objectified body consciousness has three components. The first is *body surveillance*, a constant self-surveillance to make sure that one's body conforms to feminine standards, which it can never do perfectly. The second is *internalization of cultural standards* for the feminine body: Media images and gender-role standards are internalized by the individual so that she comes to believe that they are her personal standards. At that point, girls and women want to be beautiful; they do not have to be forced to have that desire. The internalization of these cultural standards can be a source of intense *shame* when one's appearance does not measure up. The third component is *control beliefs*. Girls and women come to believe that they can control their appearance and, given enough effort, can achieve cultural standards of beauty and the perfect body. Control beliefs have their good side, in that girls and women feel competent when they look good. The downside is that control beliefs lead women to diet excessively in order to

Until the 1970s, "athlete" meant "male athlete." Athletic teams for girls were rare or nonexistent in high schools. But things began to change in the early 1970s, spurred on by the women's movement and passage of Title IX of the Civil Rights Act (1972), which made it illegal to exclude people from educational programs—including athletic teams—on the basis of sex (Gill, 2001). More

force their unruly bodies to match a cultural ideal. Taken to the extreme, the result is anorexia.

Research shows that higher scores on body surveillance and body shame are associated with negative body esteem, supporting the theory of objectified body consciousness. Moreover, control beliefs are associated with dieting as predicted by the theory. This theory gives insight into the psychological dynamics that underlie girls' internalization of cultural messages about their bodies.

The following are some items from each of the subscales measuring the components of objectified body consciousness (McKinley & Hyde, 1996). Each is rated on a 6-point scale from *strongly disagree* to *strongly agree*. How do you score?

Surveillance

1. During the day, I think about how I look many times.

2. I often worry about whether the clothes I am wearing make me look good.

Body Shame

1. I would be ashamed for people to know what I really weigh.

2. I feel ashamed of myself when I haven't made the effort to look my best.

Control Beliefs

1. I think a person can look pretty much how they want to if they are willing to work at it.

2. I can weigh what I'm supposed to when I try hard enough.

SOURCE: Fredrickson & Roberts (1997), McKinley (1998), McKinley & Hyde (1996).

recently, the U.S. women's soccer team won the World Cup. What amazing progress in just 30 years!

These massive changes have opened up new opportunities for adolescent girls. Today, about one-third of high school athletes in the United States are girls (Gill, 2001). What are the consequences?

Research with college women shows that those who participated in sports before coming to college had higher self-esteem than those who did not (Richman & Shaffer, 2000). Participating in sports seems to have beneficial effects for girls by fostering a sense of physical competence, a positive body image, and more flexible attitudes about gender roles. Athletic participation is also associated, for girls, with lower rates of sexual activity (Miller et al., 1998). Reduced sexual activity and postponement of intercourse are generally considered to be beneficial for adolescent girls, since they reduce the risk of unwanted pregnancy. Athletic participation probably has this effect for a number of reasons. Athletic participation violates the traditional female script, which then has the broader effect of calling into question the equating of girls' worth with their sexual attractiveness. Girl athletes have other methods of attracting attention. And, insofar as they gain status through athletic participation, girls are less reliant on sexual allure for establishing their status. Athletic participation for girls may end up being one of the most powerful forces overturning traditional gender roles.

Gender stereotypes hold that girls should not express anger (see Chapter 6). And many have said that adolescent girls, in Gilligan's language, have lost their

Participating in sports has beneficial effects for girls by fostering a sense of physical competence, a positive body image, and more flexible attitudes about gender roles.

voice (Brown & Gilligan, 1992; Gilligan, 1982). These portrayals miss a transgressive side to adolescent girls, captured by psychologist Lyn Mikel Brown in her book, *Raising Their Voices: The Politics of Girls' Anger* (1998). Some adolescent girls are active resisters, struggling against traditional gender roles. Their voices reflect strength and they experience anger, although they learn to control it. One middle-class 13-year-old girl said,

> Junior high is the virus that causes stupidity. . . . I really get mad at people because they don't want to learn or because they're just dumb. . . . I can't imagine anybody wanting to be stupid and not learn. . . . I used to do a lot of talking. I don't talk as much anymore in class. . . . I usually do something destructive like shave part of my head. . . . I express my anger in my writing and my art and stuff. (quoted in Brown, 1998, p. 157)

Our understanding of adolescent girls should be complex, encompassing not only recognition of the difficult forces of gender intensification and peer sexual harassment, but also acknowledgment of the strength and successes of these girls, and how they are breaking barriers in areas such as athletics.

The Search for Identity and a Future   According to the great developmental theorist Erik Erikson (1950), adolescence is the stage in which the primary developmental crisis is a quest for identity. The focus in his model was on males and, traditionally, their adult identity has been defined largely in occupational terms (Angrist, 1969): "I am a doctor." Adolescence and the emerging identity then become a preparation for this adult identity: "I must start taking science courses and become a responsible student in order to become a doctor." The emphasis for males, therefore, is on developing autonomy and a separate identity.

What happens to girls? Originally, Erikson and others said that girls were in a state of identity suspension, postponing identity formation until marriage, which in itself created identity for them. Additionally, they were thought to shape their identity to the husband's, and therefore had to remain flexible before that. Before 1970, girls simply did not anticipate that work outside the home would be a major source of identity (Douvan, 1970).

Researchers later began to question this cramming of female identity development into an Erikson-shaped box. They suggested, instead, that females define their identities more in interpersonal terms, in a sense of self that is connected to others (Douvan & Adelson, 1966).

Current research indicates that adolescent girls progress by developing both an interpersonal identity and an autonomous identity, whereas boys' identity development focuses mainly on autonomous identity (Lytle et al., 1997). In short, adolescent girls balance the two sources of identity, whereas boys grow in autonomous identity considerably more than in interpersonal identity. It may be, of course, that girls today develop both aspects of identity because real career options are available to them that simply were not there 40 or more years ago.

Girls in late adolescence also vary considerably among themselves in what components they believe will shape their identities. A recent study of women at a Southern university found that 22 percent anticipated a balanced identity with equal emphasis on career, marriage, and parenthood; 57 percent anticipated a family-oriented identity, with little emphasis on career and much on marriage and parenthood; 9 percent anticipated a career-oriented identity with less emphasis on marriage and parenthood; and 12 percent anticipated a career-and-marriage-oriented identity, with little emphasis on motherhood (Kerpelman & Schvaneveldt, 1999). Even today, then, the majority thought that career would not be the major definer of their identity. Yet substantial numbers held other views, in which career was a major definer. In this study, women and men did not differ in their ratings of the salience of career in defining their identity, nor did they differ in their ratings of marriage; but women anticipated, more than men, that parenthood would be salient in their identity.

Girls from different ethnic groups hold somewhat different views about when—and the order in which—these identities will unfold. On average, Hispanic girls anticipate earlier marriage (at 22.1 years of age on average), compared with Black girls (24.5), White girls (23.2), and Southeast Asian girls (24.0) (East, 1998). Black girls are the most likely to anticipate nonmarital childbearing. And with the exception of Hispanics, girls' school and job aspirations are negatively correlated with their estimation of the likelihood of nonmarital childbearing—that is, the more education they are striving for and the better the job they hope for, the less they anticipate nonmarital childbearing. Ethnicity and culture are thus important in shaping girls' views of their future, although some factors are consistent across all groups.

Early Adulthood

Women and Work   The work role is increasingly important for adult women. For that reason, I have devoted an entire chapter to the topic of women and work (Chapter 9) and will postpone discussion of that topic until then.

Heterosexual Marriage   Approximately 92 percent of American women marry heterosexually (U.S. Census Bureau, 2000). Women today marry at later ages than they did 50 years ago. In 1950, the average age of first marriage for women was 20.3 years, whereas today it is 25 (Costello & Stone, 2001). Cohabitation, though, has become a new phase in the process, such that young women often begin cohabiting around the same age as women married a generation ago.

Is marriage good for women or bad? That turns out to be a more complex question than it seems. In 1972, the eminent sociologist Jesse Bernard published a book in which she coined the phrase *his and hers marriage,* meaning that mar-

Will this marriage last? Statistics indicate that 50 percent of today's marriages will end in divorce. One implication is that women need to acquire the education and skills necessary to support themselves.

riage has different consequences for husbands and wives. She concluded that marriage was definitely good for men. The evidence came from comparisons of married men and never-married men on mental health and physical health outcomes. The married men consistently scored better. Married women scored worse than married men, yet never-married women scored better than never-married men. She concluded that marriage benefits men but hurts women. This idea became popularized with the general public and persists today. Yet much has changed. For example, when Bernard conducted her research, the majority of married women were home full time, but today the majority of married women are employed. Do modern data still support Bernard's idea?

In fact, recent data show that, compared with their married counterparts, unmarried women have 50 percent greater mortality rates and unmarried men have 250 percent greater mortality (Ross et al., 1990). That is, marriage "benefits" both women and men, although it benefits men more. Current data also indicate that marriage benefits women as well as men, in terms of both physical health and mental health (Kiecolt-Glaser & Newton, 2001; Waite & Gallagher, 2000).

Not all marriages are alike, though. Some are happy, characterized by mutual support, good communication, equality, and respect. Others are miserable, with the partners sharing little in common, intentionally degrading each other, and perhaps committing physical abuse. Research consistently shows that the quality of marriage is far more important to people's mental and physical health than simply whether one is married (Barnett & Hyde, 2001; Steil, 2001a). Equality between husband and wife in decision making is an important aspect of the quality of marriage (Steil, 2001b). Good marriage is good for women. Bad marriage isn't.

The Housewife Role Sociologist Ann Oakley (1974) did a major study on housewives and their feelings about housework. The basic assumption of her study—that housework could be thought of and analyzed as work—was an unusual one because the general public, as well as social scientists, has tended to think that housework is not really work. The traditional logic goes like this:

1. Women belong in the family, whereas men belong "at work."

2. Therefore men work, and women do not work.

3. Therefore housework is not a form of work. (Oakley, 1974, p. 25)

Oakley believes that housework is a form of work just like any other job, except that it is not paid. She found that housewives are sensitive to the categorization of their work as nonwork. As an ex-typist put it:

> I think housewives work just as hard. I can't stand husbands who come home and say, "Oh look you've done nothing all day, only a bit of housework and looked after the child." But I reckon that's tiring myself, well, not tiring, it's just as hard as doing a job—I don't care what any man says. . . . My husband says this—that's why I feel so strongly about it. (Oakley, 1974, p. 45)

In general, Oakley found that housework evokes a mixture of feelings, but dissatisfaction predominates: 70 percent of the London housewives she interviewed were dissatisfied with housework. The common reasons for dissatisfaction were monotony, loneliness, lack of structure, and long hours. Some women also commented on the unconstructive nature of housework—for example, every morning the housewife makes the beds, which will only be unmade that evening and have to be made again the next morning.

Autonomy—being one's own boss—was the most valued part of the housewife role. An ex–computer programmer put it this way:

> To an extent you're your own master . . . you can decide what you want to do and when you want to do it . . . it's not like being at work when somebody rings you up and you've got to go down and see them or you've got to do this and that within half an hour. (Oakley, 1974, p. 42)

The women's previous experiences with jobs outside the home were related to their satisfactions or dissatisfactions with housework. Specifically, women who had previously held high-status jobs (computer programmer, fashion model) were all dissatisfied with housework.

A more recent study of houseworkers (a few of whom were men) compared with paid workers reached generally similar conclusions (Bird & Ross, 1993). Housework was reported to seem very routine and to offer little intrinsic gratification. Neither did it yield many extrinsic rewards such as money or recognition. The most positive aspect reported by houseworkers was a sense of autonomy.

The women in Oakley's study differed from one another in the extent of their personal identification with the housewife role. Those who were highly identified with it tended to structure the job by establishing routines (Monday is the day we wash our clothes, Tuesday we iron them . . .) and by setting high standards for the work. A critical factor in shaping high or low identification with housework was the identification with that role modeled by the woman's own mother. Many women have told me of the guilt they experience as they walk out the door, leaving a messy kitchen; the guilt is related to an almost tangible ghost of one's own mother sitting on one's shoulder saying, "Bad, bad, bad." Women need to analyze their own identification with the housewife role and how this was shaped by their mothers. They can then begin to analyze how they might experience more satisfaction—or at least less guilt—in regard to housework. Personally, I am very grateful that my own mother was a feminist long before it was fashionable to be one. She saw housework as something to be gotten done as quickly as possible, through using one's wits, so that one could do more satisfying things, like playing the piano. As a result, I think, I rarely experience the housework "guilt ghost." Right on, Mom!

Motherhood   Research shows that although marriage and employment are both generally associated with positive adjustment for women, parenthood is generally associated with greater psychological distress (McLanahan & Adams, 1987).

Motherhood is so basic an assumption of the female role that it is easy to forget that society pressures women to be mothers; indeed, the pressure is so strong that the situation has been called the **motherhood mandate** (Meyers, 2001; Russo, 1979). And, in fact, 90 percent of ever-married American women have had at least one child (Etaugh, 1993). Consistent with the idea of a motherhood mandate, research indicates that people who choose to be childless tend to be viewed as poorly adjusted and misguided (Peterson, 1983; but see Shields & Cooper, 1983, for contradictory evidence).

> **Motherhood mandate:** The cultural belief that all women should have children, that is, be mothers.

Today, women are expected to be not only mothers, but exceptional mothers—a norm called *intensive mothering* (Arendell, 2000). Mothering should be emotionally involving, time-consuming, and completely child-centered, according to this norm.

One option that is being recognized increasingly is *voluntary childlessness.* Terminology makes a difference here. Some reject the term *childless,* which may seem to imply some sort of deficit, in favor of *child-free*. Research shows that women arrive at the decision to remain childless through different paths. Some women arrive at the decision fairly early in life, perhaps even before marriage; they are called "early articulators" (Houseknecht, 1979). Others marry and postpone the decision many times, finally deciding for childlessness relatively late; these are called "postponers." Both of these groups of voluntarily childless women tend to be high in autonomy and achievement orientation (Houseknecht, 1979). A high level of autonomy or independence would be expected from these women because they have been able to make a decision that goes against a great deal of societal pressure. The high levels of achievement orientation also make sense: These women tend to want high levels of achievement in their careers, which may seem incompatible with having children. Early articulators differ from postponers in some ways. In particular, early articulators tend to report less warmth in their families when growing up and less compatibility of attitudes with their parents. Perhaps they have no desire to re-create a family situation that was not particularly pleasant for them, and thus they make the decision to remain childless early. Research also shows that a supportive reference group is extremely important to women making the decision to remain childless (Houseknecht, 1979). For example, a young woman in her second year of medical school may begin to think that it would be impossible to maintain a medical practice and rear children. If she has many women friends who are also medical students and are also reaching similar conclusions, and who offer her positive support for her decision, she is more likely to decide to be child-free.

Psychology has a history of mother blaming—that is, of holding mothers responsible for everything from schizophrenia to eating disorders (Caplan, 2001). Psychologists have been slow to ask what role fathers might play in their offspring's problems, or about the role of peers and other social forces.

Research with mothers and fathers shows that there is a double standard of criticism for mothering compared with fathering (Deutsch & Saxon, 1998). Mothers are more likely than fathers to report that they are criticized for too little involvement at home or too much involvement in paid work. Fathers report the reverse—that they are criticized for too much involvement at home and too little involvement in paid work.

Divorce   Between 1970 and 1980, the divorce rate in the United States more than doubled, rising to more than one million divorces each year (Arendell, 1987). But after peaking in 1980, the divorce rate fell, so that by 1998 it was nearly back to 1970 levels (Costello & Stone, 2001). Among marriages today, approximately 50 percent will eventually divorce (Cherlin, 1992). On the other hand, remarriage rates are high; 70 to 75 percent of divorced women remarry (Amato, 2000; Norton & Moorman, 1987). These statistics vary as a function of ethnicity. For example, among women born in the 1950s, 91 percent of White women, compared with 75 percent of Black women, will ever marry (Cherlin, 1992). Divorce rates also differ: 47 percent of married Black women separate or divorce within ten years of marriage, compared with 28 percent of non-Hispanic Whites and 26 percent of Mexican Americans (Cherlin, 1992). For remarriage rates, 32 percent of Black women remarry within ten years of divorce or separation, compared with 72 percent of non-Hispanic Whites and 53 percent of Mexican Americans. Black women, then, are less likely to marry, more likely to divorce, and less likely to remarry (Cherlin, 1992).

Research on whether divorce is harder, psychologically, on women or men is mixed. Some studies show that women suffer worse effects, others show no difference, and still others show that men experience worse effects (Amato, 2000). The economic consequences, however, are not in doubt.

A study of women and divorce by sociologist Lenore Weitzman (1986) attracted a great deal of attention. She found that divorced women and their children are becoming the new underclass: Whereas divorced men experience a 42 percent increase in their standard of living, divorced women experience a 73 percent decrease. These are the unintended consequences of no-fault divorce, which in the 1970s was thought to be positive for women. The problem is that divorce settlements often make the liberated assumption that women will go out and become self-sufficient earners, ignoring the great disparity between women's wages and men's wages in the United States. In short, no-fault divorce has been an economic disaster for those women who do not have professional training, job skills, or strong work experience. I don't mean to suggest, of course, that no-fault divorce is all bad for women. For example, it makes it easier for a woman to get out of a marriage in which she is battered. Weitzman's statistics have also been criticized for exaggerating divorced women's economic decline (Faludi, 1991). A decline of 35 percent—not 73 percent—is probably more accurate (Amato, 2000). But a 35 percent decline in standard of living is not exactly pleasant, either.

Financial stress is not the only difficulty experienced by divorced women (Etaugh, 1993). Divorced people are generally perceived somewhat negatively and are considered to be less stable, less reliable, and less satisfied than married people. And, indeed, divorced women do typically experience an emotional upheaval in the months leading up to, and the year following, a divorce. They report feeling anxious, depressed, angry, rejected, and incompetent.

They also may experience role strains and role overload. They may have to manage a household by themselves, including doing tasks such as repairs that the husband may have done previously. Divorced women with children may feel that their social life has become extremely limited and that they are socially isolated from other adults.

Support from family and friends is extremely important in helping women adjust following divorce (Etaugh, 1993).

Single Women   It is difficult today to comprehend how radical the concept of the "Mary Tyler Moore Show" was when it began in 1970 (Atkin, 1991). This

TV show was about an attractive, bright woman in her 30s who was *happily single* and who never, in the course of the series, got married. The concept of a woman being purposely single and being happy was a new one.

Today, 20.5 percent of American women are single, never married (Costello & Stone, 2001). By ethnicity, the never married comprise 18 percent of White women, 37 percent of Black women, and 24 percent of Latinas. These statistics are up from 1960, a result of trends toward not marrying and toward marrying later.

Two advantages are typically mentioned in discussions of being a single woman (Donelson, 1977; Etaugh, 1993). One is freedom. There is no necessity to agree with someone else on what to have for dinner, what TV program to watch, or how to spend money. There is the freedom to move when doing so is advantageous to one's career—or to stay put and not to move to follow a husband's career. The other advantage is a sense of self-sufficiency and competence. The single woman has to deal with the irritation of fixing the leaky faucet herself, but having done so, she gains a sense that she is competent to do such things. Among single women, life satisfaction is correlated with having good health, not being lonely, living with a female housemate, having many casual friends, and being highly involved with work (Loewenstein et al., 1981).

In a society as marriage oriented as ours, it is not surprising that there are disadvantages to being a single woman. Most of the social structures for adults involve couples' activities, and the single person is often excluded. Loneliness is another disadvantage that is mentioned frequently.

In one study, one-quarter of childless single women expressed regret at not having had children—but that means that three-quarters expressed no such regret (Loewenstein et al., 1981).

Middle Age

For women, middle age (roughly the period from age 40 to 65) involves both biological and social changes. Hormone levels decline with menopause (Chapter 11) and children leave home. What are the psychological consequences?

Empty Nest or Prime of Life?   During a woman's middle age her children may leave home—to go to work, to go away to college, to get married. For the middle-aged woman, a major source of identity—motherhood—has been taken away. The term **empty nest syndrome** has been used to describe the cases of depression in women at this time. Sociologist Pauline Bart (1971) investigated the empty nest syndrome. Her research indicates that it is the "supermothers," not those who chose careers, who are most susceptible to this depression. The supermothers have invested so much of themselves in the mother role that they have the most to lose when it has ended.

Empty nest syndrome: Depression that middle-aged people supposedly feel when their children are grown and have left home, leaving an empty nest.

Although traditional stereotypes held that women lapse into empty nest depression in middle age, research shows this not to be true. The women's movement has helped many women find new opportunities. Here, a woman runs in the Senior Olympics.

Sociologist Lillian B. Rubin (1979) challenged many ideas about the empty nest syndrome. Her results were based on a study of 160 women, a cross-section of White mothers aged 35 to 54, from the working, middle, and professional classes. To be included in the sample, they had to have given up work or careers after a minimum of three years and to have assumed the traditional role of housewife and mother for at least ten years after the birth of their first child. Therefore, this group should be the most prone to the empty nest syndrome. Typically these women said, "My career was my child." Contrary to the empty nest, Rubin found that, although some women were momentarily sad, lonely, or frightened, they were not depressed in response to the departure or impending departure of their children. The predominant feeling of every woman except one was a feeling of relief. Rather than experiencing an immobilizing depression, most of the women found new jobs and reorganized their daily lives. Rubin felt that the women's movement had helped many of the women by raising their sights to other careers and opportunities.

Psychologists Valory Mitchell and Ravenna Helson (1990) went one step further, arguing that the early 50s are the *prime of life* for women. In a sample of college graduates between 26 and 80, women in their early 50s were the group most likely to describe their lives as "first rate." There were more empty nests (but they may not be so bad), there was better health, and there was higher income compared with other ages. Women at this age displayed confidence, involvement, security, and depth in their personalities.

What should we conclude, then? Probably some women experience empty nest depression, but they are not the majority, and among those who do experience such depression, it may be brief. What is more important is the ability of the majority of women to adjust to the changes that occur in their lives and roles at this time. A feminist reframing of the issues suggests that the early 50s may indeed be the prime of life.

Mothers and Daughters   The topic of the mother-daughter relationship has attracted much attention, with books such as journalist Nancy Friday's *My Mother, My Self* (1977) chalking up big sales. In psychological theory, too, the mother-daughter relationship is thought to be critical, whether the theory is psychoanalytic, as is Nancy Chodorow's (see Chapter 2), or social learning theory.

A major review of research on the mother-daughter relationship concluded that popular views of it as conflict ridden are inaccurate (Boyd, 1989). Although there are conflicts in the relationship when the daughter is in adolescence, the relationship undergoes many transitions as the daughter grows older and moves through life stages herself. Early conflicts give way to reports of increased closeness, greater empathy, and greater mutuality. The adult mother-daughter relationship is described as rewarding and close; mothers and daughters help and care for each other. Thus mothers and daughters, rather than being their own worst enemies, generally contribute positively to each other's psychological well-being.

Old Age

There is a **double standard of aging** (Bazzini et al., 1997; Berman et al., 1981; Etaugh, 1993). That is, as a man reaches middle age and beyond, he may appear more distinguished and handsome, but a woman of the same age does not seem to become more beautiful. As we saw in a previous section, a woman's value in her youth is often judged by her appearance, which may decline with age. Here I will examine some of the research on elderly women.

Double standard of aging: Cultural norms by which men's status increases with age but women's decreases.

Physical Health   Despite the fact that women live longer than men, women have more chronic (long-term) illnesses (Crose et al., 1997). Compared with elderly men, elderly women have higher rates of arthritis and rheumatism (both of which can be extremely painful), diabetes, hypertension, osteoporosis (brittle bones), and vision problems (Crose et al., 1997; Etaugh, 1993).

Do women actually have more illnesses than men, or do they just report them more? Again, there is a finding of a gender difference and two possible interpretations. The first is that women are neurotic and whiny, complaining over slight aches and pains, whereas men are tough and brave and don't let little things get them down. This is a female-deficit interpretation. The alternative interpretation is that men deny illnesses when they have them, which can be quite dangerous and may even lead to death (and men's higher mortality rate), whereas women are sensitive to danger signs and report them to a physician (Etaugh, 1993).

Grandmotherhood   The stereotype of a grandmother is a white-haired lady baking cookies for the little ones. However, women can become grandmothers at vastly different ages. One woman becomes a grandmother at age 30, and another does so at age 65. Nonetheless, because a great many elderly women are grandmothers, we will discuss the topic in this section on elderly women.

In one study of grandparents, most of them women, five aspects of their experience of grandparenthood emerged: (1) centrality, in which grandparenthood is a central part of the woman's life and identity; (2) valued elder, in which the woman passes on family traditions and ethnic or cultural traditions; (3) immortality through the clan, in which the woman has a sense that she lives on through her descendants; (4) reinvolvement with personal past, in which the woman relives her earlier life, when she was the age of her grandchildren, and identifies with her own grandmother; and (5) indulgence, in which the woman is lenient with and "spoils" her grandchildren (Kivnick, 1983).

The grandparenting role is likely to differ for different ethnic groups as a result of different family structures and cultural traditions. Unfortunately, this question has received little research, but I can mention a few relevant studies. One found that African American grandparents were much more likely to assume an authoritative or influential role with grandchildren than were Euro-American grandparents (Cherlin & Furstenberg, 1985). According to another, Mexican American grandparents had more contact with their grandchildren and reported more satisfying relationships with them than did White or Black grandparents (Bengtson, 1985).

In some cases, grandmothers end up rearing their grandchildren. In one sample of Black grandmothers, 10 percent lived in the same home with their grandchildren (Pearson et al., 1990). In some cases, of course, the mother and father were also present. But in other cases they were not, and the grandmother then was responsible for raising the grandchildren. Grandmothers raising children because the parent or parents are drug addicted report that it is rewarding to raise their grandchildren, but research also shows heightened levels of stress in this group as evidenced by signs such as heart attacks and depression (Burton, 1992).

Retirement   Most of the studies of retirement have been based on all-male samples (Etaugh, 1993), no doubt based on the researchers' assumption that women do not hold paying jobs and therefore cannot retire from them. Nothing could be further from the truth, of course (see Chapter 9). Women are committed to their jobs, and retirement has important consequences for them, just as it does for men (George et al., 1984).

Women are more likely than men to retire because of a spouse's retirement—particularly because women tend to be married to men who are somewhat older than they are—and because of a spouse's ill health (Shaw, 1984). Professional women and self-employed women are less likely to retire early than are other women (Shaw, 1984).

Income is a concern for retired women. Women are more likely than men to report that their retirement incomes are not adequate (Etaugh, 1993). One reason is that retired women, on the average, receive considerably smaller Social Security checks than retired men do. This occurs because Social Security payments are based on one's preretirement earnings, and the gender gap in wages ensures that women receive smaller payments.

Gender Ratios   Gender ratios become more and more lopsided with advancing age. Among Americans between the ages of 65 and 69, there are 119 women for every 100 men. By 85–89 there are 220 women for every 100 men, and for those 95 and older, there are 384 women for every 100 men (Costello & Stone, 2001). As a result, elderly women stand a good chance of living alone. Among those 85 and over, 62 percent live alone (Costello & Stone, 2001); by ethnicity, they comprise 63 percent of Whites, 47 percent of Blacks, and 34 percent of Latinas in that age group. (Latinas are much more likely than other groups to live with extended family.)

Widowhood   Women are far more likely to be widowed than men are. In the United States today, among those over 65, 2,000,000 men are widowed, compared with 8,500,000 women—a ratio of more than 4 to 1 (Fields & Casper, 2001). This is the result of two trends: the longer life expectancy of women, and the tendency of women to marry men older than themselves. Opportunities for remarriage are limited because there are so few men compared with women in the "appropriate" age group. Therefore it is fairly common for women to face the last 15 years or so of their lives alone.

A number of factors affect how women respond following the death of a spouse, including the woman's age, whether the death was anticipated or unexpected, and her financial and social resources (Etaugh, 1993). Older widows tend to have an advantage over younger widows (say, widows under 45), because older widows tend to be more financially secure and are not responsible for young children. Older widows also tend to have friends in the same circumstances and tend to be psychologically prepared for a husband's death.

Two problems are especially common among widows: loneliness and financial strain (Etaugh, 1993). Widows may become socially isolated; contact with their children, and especially with friends, is important. Financial strain can be severe. There is loss of the husband's income, and the couple's savings may have been depleted by medical expenses associated with the husband's illness. Elderly women are more likely than elderly men to live in poverty, and older minority women are even more likely to be poor than White women.

The death of a spouse is harder on men than it is on women, whether measured by depression, illness, or death (Stroebe et al., 2001). Put another way, women seem to cope better with widowhood. One possible reason for this is that women are more likely to have deep friendships that they have developed over the years and from which they can draw social support. In one study of people over 65, women had 38 percent more friends than men did (Fischer & Phillips, cited in Peplau et al., 1982). Another possibility is that women are better than men at "grief work"—that is, at expressing their emotions and then going on to cope and readjust (Stroebe et al., 2001).

Gender Roles and Androgyny   Some scholars have suggested that gender roles become more relaxed or even reversed among the elderly. With the children grown, the woman is less restricted to the mother role. In some marriages, because the husband is older than the wife, he may have retired while she continues to hold a job. Thus he may do many of the household chores while she is the breadwinner.

This shifting of gender roles might suggest that the elderly are more androgynous than younger adults. To see whether this is true, people from age 13 to 86 were asked to complete the Bem Sex Role Inventory, discussed in Chapter 3 (Hyde et al., 1991). Based on their scores, they were categorized as androgynous, feminine, masculine, or undifferentiated. The results, shown in Table 7.2, indicate that older men are more androgynous than younger men.[1] In contrast, the percentage of feminine women increased in the oldest age categories. Perhaps this means that both men and women become more feminine with age, resulting in more androgynous men and more feminine women.

TABLE 7.2
Percentages of Males and Females Who Are Classified as Androgynous in Four Age Groups

	Age			
Gender	13–20	21–40	41–60	61 and over
Females	36	12	17	23
Males	18	13	15	41

Source: Hyde et al. (1991).

[1]These data were cross-sectional (collected on many different people at different ages) and not longitudinal (collected on the same group of people repeatedly as they grew older). Therefore, it is important to be cautious in concluding from them too much about actual developmental changes.

EXPERIENCE THE RESEARCH

ELDERLY WOMEN

For this exercise, interview an older woman, over the age of 65. You might choose a female relative or a woman from a local senior citizens center. Record her age, marital status, and ethnic group. Ask her the following questions, and either tape-record or take notes on her answers:

1. What does she feel were the three major events in her life? Why?

2. Did she spend most of her life as a homemaker or having a job or career? Reflecting back on that role, what were the good things about it? What were the negative things?

3. If she is single, is she lonely? Why or why not?

In Conclusion

We have traced female development across the lifespan. In infancy, gender similarities are the rule, except that boy babies are more active than girl babies. Parents generally treat boy and girl babies similarly, although they tend to encourage some sex-typed behaviors. Infants begin processing information by gender early on, categorizing male versus female voices by 6 months of age.

Gender differences in toy and game preferences emerge in the preschool years. Parents continue to socialize gender-appropriate behavior, and the media and peers gain influence. By age 3, children's play is highly gender segregated.

Gender intensification occurs at the beginning of adolescence, and girls are sent the message that femininity and achievement are incompatible. Sexual harassment in the schools is a problem for adolescent girls, and negative body esteem and weight worries become issues. Yet not all girls conform; one example is girls who are athletes. In late adolescence, girls move toward an adult identity, balancing an autonomous identity with an interpersonal identity.

In adulthood, 92 percent of women marry. Marriage—at least good marriage—benefits women's mental and physical health. Motherhood is a valued role for most adult women. Research on the empty nest syndrome and depression in middle age indicates that, in fact, most women fare well during this time, and some researchers believe that the early 50s are the prime of life for women.

Men on average die younger than women do, but women suffer from more chronic health problems such as arthritis. The grandmother role is an important and meaningful one for many women. Most women live a decade or more as widows, and the gender ratio becomes more lopsided with each passing decade.

Suggestions for Further Reading

AAUW. (2001). *Hostile hallways: Bullying, teasing, and sexual harassment in school.* Washington, DC: American Association of University Women. The AAUW's shocking report on sexual harassment in the nation's schools should be read by all parents and educators.

Maccoby, Eleanor E. (1998). *The two sexes: Growing up apart, coming together.* Cambridge, MA: Harvard University Press. Maccoby, a noted developmental psychologist, advances the thesis that psychological gender differences arise not only or even mainly because of forces such as parental socialization, but rather through children's active preferences for gender-segregated play in childhood.

Women and the Web

Girl Power is part of an initiative by the U.S. Department of Health and Human Services, begun by Secretary Donna Shalala, to encourage and motivate 9- to 14-year-old girls to make the most of their lives.
http://www.girlpower.gov/

UNICEF's Voices of Youth: The Girl Child represents the concerns of girls worldwide.
http://www.unicef.org/voy/meeting/gir/girhome.html

Advocates for Youth is a wonderful organization devoted to bettering the lives of adolescents in the United States. Topics on this website include adolescent sexual behavior and health, dating violence, teen pregnancy prevention, and young women of color.
http://www.advocatesforyouth.org/

The **TeenZone** section of the Global Reproductive Health Forum is sponsored by the Harvard School of Public Health.
http://www.hsph.harvard.edu/organizations/healthnet/teenzone.html

National Center for Women and Retirement Research
http://www.agingfocus.com/

Senior Women web site
http://www.seniorwomen.com/

8 Abilities, Achievement, and Motivation

When Samuel Johnson was asked which is more intelligent, man or woman, he replied, "Which man, which woman?"

Part of the lore of the culture is that women are less intelligent than men. Put bluntly, they are dumb—witness the expressions *dumb broad* and *dumb blonde*. An additional stereotype is that women's thought processes are less rational, more illogical than men's, more influenced by emotion. A familiar scene in movies and comics is the man shaking his head over his inability to understand the mind of his wife or girlfriend.

Is there any scientific evidence to support the notion that women are less intellectually competent than men? In this chapter we will explore empirical evidence regarding the intellectual and achievement characteristics of women, and whether they differ from those of men. It is important to remember that the finding of a gender difference does not say anything about what causes it, that is, whether biological or environmental factors are responsible. We will then examine motivational differences between females and males with the goal of better understanding the relationship between women's abilities and their achievements.

Abilities

General Intelligence   There is no evidence to support the hypothesis that females are less intelligent than males. In fact, research has consistently shown that there are no gender differences in general intelligence (Maccoby & Jacklin, 1974).

These results need to be interpreted with some caution because of the nature of IQ-test construction. It became clear to the early test constructors that boys would do better on some kinds of items, whereas girls would do better on others. They decided to balance these subtests so that there would be no gender differences in overall measured intelligence. Therefore, saying that there are no gender differences in tested intelligence essentially means that the test constructors succeeded in their goal of eliminating gender differences.

Rather than looking at global assessments, it is more revealing to analyze patterns of specific abilities in males and in females, such as mathematical ability or verbal ability.

For years, psychology textbooks have told students that there were gender differences in three basic abilities: verbal ability, spatial ability, and mathematical ability. Often these conclusions were based on an important review by Eleanor

Maccoby and Carol Jacklin (1974). However, we now have modern meta-analyses to give us a more accurate and detailed understanding of whether there are gender differences in these abilities and, if so, how large the differences are.

Verbal Ability   Although it was traditionally thought that females showed better verbal ability than males, a meta-analysis found that the gender difference in verbal ability is so small that we can say there is no gender difference (Hyde & Linn, 1988). Overall, $d = -0.11$, indicating a slight female superiority, but one that is so small it can be called zero. The analysis also looked at different types of verbal ability, such as vocabulary, analogies, reading comprehension, and essay writing. The gender difference was small for all types of verbal ability.

Another interesting finding emerged: There was evidence that gender differences had grown smaller over time. For studies published in 1973 or earlier, $d = -0.23$, whereas for studies published after 1973, $d = -0.10$. That is, the gender difference was cut approximately in half. We can't be certain what has caused this narrowing of the gender gap. One possibility is that gender-role socialization practices have become more flexible in the past two decades, and the result is a reduction in the size of gender differences. Another is that those who produce standardized tests have become more sensitive about gender-equity issues, resulting in tests that show no gender differences.

Spatial Ability   Two major meta-analyses of gender differences in spatial ability discovered that there are actually three different types of spatial ability, each showing a different pattern of gender differences (Linn & Petersen, 1985; Voyer et al., 1995). The first type, which the researchers called *spatial visualization,* involves finding a figure in a more complex one, like the hidden-figures games you may have played as a child. This type of spatial ability shows a gender difference favoring males, but the difference is so small that we can consider it zero: $d = +0.13$ (Linn & Petersen, 1985). The second type of spatial ability, *spatial perception,* requires a person to identify a true vertical or true horizontal line when there is distracting or misleading information around it. This type of spatial ability showed a moderate gender difference favoring males: $d = +0.44$. The third type of spatial ability, *mental rotation,* requires the test taker to mentally rotate an object in three dimensions in order to obtain a correct answer. A sample of such an item is shown in Figure 8.1. This is the type of spatial ability that shows a large gender difference favoring males: $d = +0.73$ in the Linn and Petersen analysis and $d = +0.56$ in the Voyer et al. analysis.

Although many occupations do not rely heavily on spatial ability of the last kind, there are some in which it is very important, such as those in engineering. It might therefore be tempting to attribute the small number of women in engineering to women's lower spatial ability. However, the gender difference in spatial ability is not nearly large enough to account for the fact that only 10 percent of the bachelor's degrees in engineering in the United States go to women (Snyder & Hoffman, 2000).

The test below is made up of pictures of blocks turned different ways. The block at the left is the reference block and the five blocks to the right are the answer blocks. One of these five blocks is the same as the reference block except that it has been turned and is seen from a different point of view. The other four blocks could not be obtained by turning the reference block. For example:

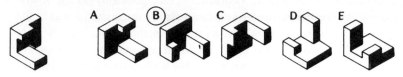

The illustration below shows that "B" is the correct answer.

FIGURE 8.1

Sample item and solution from a test of spatial ability.

Source: From R. E. Stafford, *Identical Blocks*, form AA, 1962. Reprinted with the permission of R. E. Stafford and Harold Gulliksen.

Scores on spatial ability tests can be improved by training (Newcombe et al., 2002; Vasta et al., 1996). The schools generally offer little training in spatial performance in the curriculum; it would be an important addition to a truly gender-fair curriculum for girls.

Mathematics Ability   A major meta-analysis of gender differences surveyed 100 studies, representing the testing of more than 3 million persons (Hyde et al., 1990; also Hedges & Nowell, 1995, for similar results). The results were surprising, because psychologists have said for so long that boys are better at math than girls. In fact, the average effect size was $d = -0.05$ averaged over all samples of the general population. That is, there was a slight female superiority, but basically the gender difference was zero.

The results were a bit more complex, though. Mathematics tests differ in the difficulty of the problems. They may tap simple computation, or deeper understanding of mathematical concepts, or, at the highest cognitive level, problem solving such as word problems or story problems that ask the student to go beyond memorized math facts. The meta-analysis indicated that girls outperformed boys in computation in elementary school and middle school, and the difference was zero in high school. In understanding of concepts, the gender difference was close to zero at all ages. In problem solving, the difference was zero in the elementary and middle school years, but then became more noticeable in high school ($d = +0.29$) and college ($d = +0.32$), with the difference favoring males. Therefore, although the results indicated that there were generally no gender differences in math performance, the gender difference in problem solving that emerges in high school is a cause of concern, because problem solving of that type is important for success in courses and careers in the sciences. It is just in the high school years that boys are more likely than girls to choose math and science courses, and this difference in course taking no doubt accounts for a good part of the gender difference in tested performance. (We will return to this issue of choosing to take math courses later in the chapter.) An encouraging trend is that the gender gap in taking advanced math courses has narrowed in recent years. In 1998, 11.2 percent of boys graduating from high school had taken calculus and 7.3 percent had taken AP calculus (Snyder & Hoffman, 2000). For girls, this compares with 10.6 percent and 6.4 percent, respectively.

One final result of the meta-analysis is also worth noting. Like the results for verbal ability mentioned earlier, the size of the gender difference in math performance has declined over the years. For studies published in 1973 or earlier, $d = +0.31$, whereas for studies published in 1974 or later, $d = +0.14$. That is, this gender difference declined to about half its former size. Again, this may be a result of changes in gender-role socialization practices.

TABLE 8.1
The Magnitude of Gender Differences in Mathematics Performance in Other Nations: International Assessment of Educational Progress

	9-Year-Olds	13-Year-Olds
Country	*d*	*d*
Hungary	−0.03	−0.02
Ireland	−0.06	0.19
Israel	0.16	0.15
Korea	0.28	0.10
Spain	0.01	0.18
United States	0.05	0.04
Type of Problems (Averaged Across All Countries)		
Conceptual understanding	0.02	0.11
Problem solving	0.04	0.13

SOURCE: Beller & Gafni (1996).

Similar results for the magnitude of gender differences in mathematics performance have been found in many other nations. The International Assessment of Educational Progress involves testing 9-year-olds and 13-year-olds in twenty countries (Beller & Gafni, 1996). Results for six of these countries are shown in Table 8.1. Notice that the effects fluctuate somewhat from one country to another, but all are small and many are close to zero.

Perceptual Speed The ability known as perceptual speed involves being able to perceive details quickly and accurately and to shift attention from one item to the next rapidly. Tests of perceptual speed are generally timed and involve comparison of two strings of letters or numbers to see whether they are identical (Table 8.2). This seems to be the basic aptitude necessary for most forms of clerical work.

TABLE 8.2
Sample Items from a Test of Perceptual Speed

Instructions: Compare each line of the COPY at the bottom of the page with the corresponding line of the ORIGINAL at the top. Each *word* or *abbreviation* or *digit* in the copy that is not exactly the same as in the original is one error. In each line, mark every word or abbreviation or figure that is wrong. Then count the errors you have marked in the line and enter the total number in the column at the right. The first line has been done correctly to show you just how to mark and where to enter the total number of errors in the line. Work quickly and accurately.

ORIGINAL

Name	Address	Amount	
Mr. Kevin Johnson	Auburn, ME	$2783.78	
Miss Janine Adams	Austin, TX	4784.12	

COPY

Name	Address	Amount	Number of Errors
Mr. Kevin Johnston	Auburn, AL	$2788.78	3
Dr. Janige Adams	Austing, TX	4784.11	5

SOURCE: Sample item from the *General Clerical Test.* Copyright © 1969 by The Psychological Corporation. Reproduced with permission. All rights reserved.

Women perform consistently better than men on these tests. A meta-analysis indicated that $d = -0.32$; that is, the difference is in the small-to-moderate range (Feingold, 1988).

Physical Performance and Athletics   Gender differences in physical and athletic characteristics provide a contrast to the findings for cognitive abilities (Linn & Hyde, 1990). For example, $d = +2.60$ for physical height, a difference that is about four times greater than any of the differences in cognitive abilities (Thomas & French, 1985).

Large gender differences in athletic performance tend to emerge in adolescence (Eaton & Enns, 1986). For example, for speed in the 50-yard dash, $d = +0.63$ when averaged over all ages, but $d = +2.5$ for adolescence and beyond. For throwing distance, $d = +1.98$. For some other aspects of athletic performance, though, gender differences are small or zero; for example, on tests of balance, $d = +0.09$.

Athletic performance is also strongly responsive to training and diet, as we have seen in the past 25 years with the great advances made in these areas. Figure 8.2 shows record performance in the Olympics over the years for males and

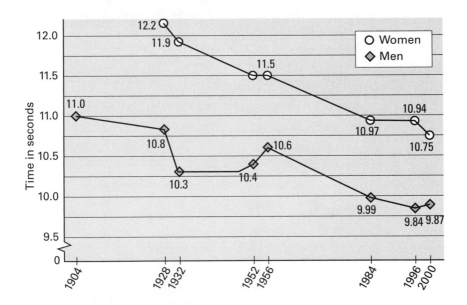

FIGURE 8.2
Gold-medal performance of men and women on the 100-meter dash in the Olympic Games. Women were not permitted to compete in track and field events until 1928.
SOURCE: www.ex.ac.uk/cimt/data/olympics.

females for the 100-meter dash. As you can see, the women who win today run faster than the record-breaking men of 1928, and the gender gap has narrowed.

Summary   A number of conclusions emerge from this discussion of gender differences in abilities:

1. There are no gender differences in verbal ability.

2. There are no gender differences in mathematical performance except in problem solving beginning in the high school years, and this may be accounted for by girls not taking as many math and science courses as boys.

3. There are gender differences in one type of spatial ability, mental rotations— an ability that is important in career fields like engineering. However, spatial ability can be improved by training.

4. Gender differences in some kinds of athletic performance are large beginning in adolescence.

5. The evidence suggests that gender differences in abilities have become smaller in the past 25 years.

6. Gender differences in cognitive abilities are so small as to be irrelevant in practical situations such as job counseling. It would be a great mistake, for example, to urge a high school girl against pursuing an engineering career just because females on average score lower than males on tests of spatial ability. There is too much variability from one female to the next to predict that an individual woman will not have adequate spatial ability for such a career. A far better indicator would be her own score on a spatial ability test.

Choosing Courses: How to Avoid Math

I hope that you didn't begin reading this section thinking that I would tell you how to avoid math courses, because that is not my intention at all. What I am going to tell you is that, beginning in high school, girls stop taking math courses—or they avoid math courses—and that the consequences are serious, keeping them out of many attractive careers.

I am convinced that the traditional approach of looking at gender differences in abilities (e.g., math ability) is not productive. Whether or not a significant gender difference is found, where does that approach get us, either in terms of better scientific understanding or in terms of helping women? Not very far. Psychologist Jacquelynne Eccles has broken ground with what I think is a much more productive approach—understanding why students choose or do not choose to take certain courses (e.g., Eccles, 1994; Meece et al., 1982).

Eccles points out that gender differences in math performance do not appear consistently until the tenth grade. That is just about the time when females become less likely than males to enroll in high school math courses. By the time women emerge from college, they have fewer mathematical skills than men, probably because they have not been taking math.

This in turn is significant because mathematical skills are important to success in many attractive occupations. Indeed, mathematics has been called the "critical filter" (Sherman, 1982) keeping women out of careers in engineering, computer science, the physical sciences, business, and finance. The point that should be investigated by researchers, then, is not whether females have less mathematical ability than males, but rather why it is that females stop taking math courses. If we understood the reasons behind this choice, it might be possible to help women to take more math courses and perhaps to help them expand their career options.

Eccles has proposed an elegant model to explain why students choose or avoid certain courses, such as math courses. A diagram of the model is shown in Figure 8.3. The final behavior Eccles is trying to predict is achievement behavior—specifically, choosing a math course—and it is shown in the box on the bottom in Figure 8.3. The multiple factors feeding into the choice of a course are shown in the other boxes in the diagram.

In overall terms, Eccles has used an *expectation × value model* of achievement (course choice). That is, any particular achievement behavior is a product of the person's expectations and the person's values. Kim is a high school sophomore contemplating taking an optional course in geometry. The model says that she will sign up for geometry only if she has both positive expectations for success in the course (if she thinks she'll get an F, she won't sign up) and positive values with respect to the course (if she thinks the course will be of value to her both now and in the future; but she may instead think that geometry will be of no value if she expects to spend the rest of her life as a housewife). The values part of the model is shown in the right half of Figure 8.3, and the expectancies part is shown in the left half.

Many factors shape Kim's values regarding math courses and her expectations for success in them. In the area of values are the following:

1. The cultural milieu—Kim probably perceives the division of labor by gender in the United States and notes that women are not found in math-related jobs. Furthermore, math as a subject is stereotyped as a masculine domain. And success in an advanced math course may seem competitive to Kim, and competitiveness is not regarded as feminine.

2. Goals and self-schema—Kim has already formed a self-schema or self-concept and has some tentative occupational goals. If these involve being a secretary or a journalist, math courses will not be valued.

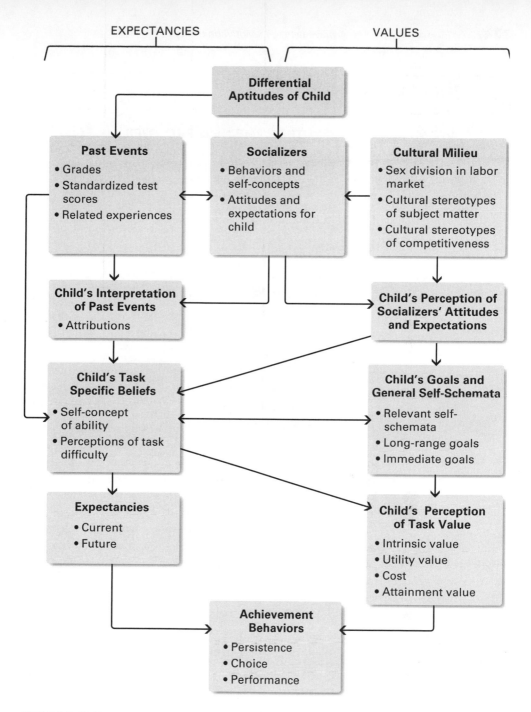

FIGURE 8.3

Eccles's model of academic course choice shows how girls' expectations and values may be shaped such that they do not take math courses in high school.

SOURCE: From "Sex Differences in Math Achievement," 1982, *The Psychological Bulletin, 91.* Copyright © 1982 by the American Psychological Association. Reprinted by permission of Judith L. Meece, Jacquelynne Eccles-Parsons et al. Also from J. E. Parsons et al. in *Achievement and Achievement Motives* edited by Janet T. Spence. Copyright © 1983 by W. H. Freeman and Company. Used by permission.

FOCUS 8.1

WOMEN AND COMPUTERS: THE NEW FRONTIER OF GENDER DIFFERENCES?

It used to be said that mathematics was the "critical filter" keeping women out of many desirable college majors and careers. Today, it may well be that computers are the critical filter keeping women not only out of lucrative and important careers in the computer field, but also out of dozens of other fields in which computers play a major role.

The statistics on women and computers are cause for concern, particularly because they are declining rather than improving. Women went from earning 36 percent of the college degrees in computer science in 1985 to 28 percent in 1995. In 1999, among those students taking the Advanced Placement Computer Science Test, only 17 percent were girls.

Girls' disenchantment with computers increases with age. According to a meta-analysis, there are no gender differences in computer anxiety in elementary school ($d = 0.08$), but the gender difference becomes much larger—with girls being more anxious—by high school ($d = -0.61$) (Whitley, 1997). Girls feel as competent with computers as boys do in elementary school ($d = -0.09$), but by high school, boys feel considerably more competent ($d = 0.66$). Boys feel more competent mostly because they acquire much more computer experience than girls do, beginning in elementary school. Boys are also more likely than girls to have a computer at home.

What leads to girls' and women's disenchantment with computers? Gender stereotypes lead the list of explanations. Computer software is male stereotyped, with games that typically involve violence such as bombing. Boys and girls have different preferences for computer games. For example, boys like the fantasy of arrows popping balloons, which girls dislike; girls like music in a game but boys do not (Malone & Lepper, 1986). Furthermore, computers—and technology more broadly—are stereotyped as a male domain. The very language of computing (e.g., *fatal errors, crashing, aborting*) is violent and may contain emotional associations that are hostile for women. And in the best-selling software for early reading instruction, male central characters are present in 63 percent of the programs but female central characters are present in only 11 percent (Drees & Phye, 2001). Paradoxically, this very new technology relies on very old stereotypes.

Boys and girls are interested in different uses for computers. Boys
are more interested in violent games, and this kind of software domi-
nates the market. (Illustration 1994 by Nicole Hollander)

The computer resources themselves often exist in a masculine environment. Based on observations in high school computer labs, one researcher
noted that they tend to be dominated by unsympathetic male teachers and
unappealing boys who flash their expertise in a way that makes others feel
stupid (Collis, 1985).

What can be done about this situation? Experts recommend the following. First, girls like to join clubs with a group of friends, and they like social
interactions to be part of computer use. Adults organizing computer clubs
should invite groups of girls rather than individuals, and should make sure
that some of the computer activities are collaborative rather than individual

(continued)

FOCUS 8.1
CONTINUED

oriented. Second, adults need to make conscious efforts to encourage girls. Ask a girl to be a computer lab assistant. Ask a girl to help set up new hardware or software. Third, make sure that girls have equal access to computers in the home. Fourth, create computer games for girls that are appealing to them and that feature female characters. Finally, be sure that female role models who are competent with computers are available and visible. Most elementary school teachers—the great majority of whom are women—are given little training in computer use in the classroom. Increasing their competence is important for all children in the classroom, but especially for girls.

As computers become more and more entrenched in our way of life, as well as a prerequisite for many important careers, we must move quickly to reverse sex bias.

SOURCES: Campbell (2000); Collis (1985); Comber et al (1997); Cooper & Stone (1996); Drees & Phye (2001); King et al. (2002); Lanius (2002); McNair et al. (2001); Nelson & Cooper (1997); Terry & Calvert (1997); Whitley (1997).

In the area of expectancies for success are the following factors:

1. Aptitudes and grades—Kim has some idea of her aptitude for math from a variety of sources, including her grades in past courses and her scores on standardized achievement tests. It is strange that in elementary school and junior high, girls' grades in math are as good as those of boys, yet in high school, girls stop taking math courses and boys don't. This tendency is explained in part by the next factor.

2. Interpretations or attributions—Kim may have gotten B's in all her math courses, but may fail to attribute the good grades to her own abilities (see the section on attributions later in this chapter). She may think that the courses so far have just been easy. As a result, she has low expectations for success in future math courses.

Eccles and her colleagues have done a number of studies testing various links in the model, and they have reviewed numerous pertinent studies done by others (Eccles, 1994; Meece et al., 1982). Space does not permit me to review all of this research, but the model has generally been upheld. For example, research shows that by junior high, boys have higher perceptions of their math ability than girls do, and self-concept of math ability is related to one's decisions to enroll in optional math courses. These findings support key points in the model. Like most models, this one isn't perfect, but I think it is very good.

The most recent studies show that boys' sense of their own math competence is only slightly higher than girls' in early elementary school, and that the gender gap narrows over the course of development, so that by high school, girls and boys do not differ in their sense of math competence (Jacobs et al., 2002). This finding is consistent with the narrowed gender gap in taking math courses in high school and with the overall small gender difference in math performance. These trends are very encouraging. The problem is that the scientific results haven't gotten out—that is, the general public continues to hold stereotypes that boys are superior at math.

As an interesting exercise, you might want to trace through Eccles's model, thinking of yourself, trying to see how it predicts why you did or did not continue taking math courses.

What are the practical implications of Eccles's model? Suppose that our goal were to get more girls enrolled in math courses to expand their career options. How would we do that? We could work on the expectancies side of the model or on the values side or on both. On the expectancies side, we would try to get high school girls to have higher expectancies for success in math courses. This could be done in a number of ways: by stressing that there are no average gender differences in math ability prior to high school, by pointing to an individual girl's pattern of success in math courses, and by encouraging girls to attribute their previous good grades in math to their own abilities. On the values side, we would need to increase the value that girls attach to math and math courses. Girls are probably not aware of the wide variety of careers that require math. Individual counseling sessions might examine each girl's anticipated career and the math required for it.

In sum, Eccles has provided a detailed model for why girls choose or avoid math courses. In general, data support the model, although it needs to be tested further by independent researchers. It provides exciting avenues for intervening to get girls into math classes, which should have the beneficial result of expanding their career options.

The SAT

The **SAT** is probably the most publicized and marketed test in the United States today. It is a sturdy gatekeeper of admission to the most selective colleges and universities in the nation. Although its creators claim that it is an ability test, in fact it is an achievement test, measuring information learned in school.

SAT: A standardized academic achievement test taken by many college-bound high school students. Some colleges and universities use it in making admissions decisions.

Let's take a look at the 2001 data on the SAT as a function of gender (College Board, 2001). (The 2001 results were quite similar to those in other recent years.) On the SAT Verbal, males' average score was 509 and females' was 502. On the SAT Math, males averaged 533 and females averaged 498. That translates to $d = 0.06$ for Verbal and $d = 0.31$ for Math.

On the Verbal test, there is basically no gender difference. Note, however, that males on average get 7 more points than females, even though meta-analyses show a tiny female advantage on verbal tests generally. How is it, then, that males score slightly higher than females on the SAT Verbal, a pattern that has been consistent over several decades? There is something odd about the SAT.

The gender gap on the SAT Math is a major cause for concern, showing a small-to-moderate difference favoring males. Not every high school senior takes the SAT. It is taken only by those who are college-bound. When we dig deeper into the data, we find that more females (689,000) than males (597,000) took the SAT in 2001. This is consistent with the fact that today more women than men attend college. What that probably means is that the group of female test takers dips farther down into the pool of female talent and family advantages than does the group of male test takers. Supporting this idea, of the 46,000 test takers whose parents did not have a high school diploma, 61 percent of them were females. That is, the female test takers were more likely to come from a disadvantaged family background. This finding could be part of the explanation for the gender gap on the SAT. In addition, there are many possible sources of sex bias on the SAT, as with many other tests (see Chapter 1).

Another odd feature of the SAT has been termed the **female underprediction effect** (Hyde & Kling, 2001; Willingham & Cole, 1997). The whole point of the SAT is that it is supposed to predict college performance, that is, grades. Insofar as it does that well, college admissions officers should want to use it to select the students who will actually perform the best once they are in college—and perhaps to weed out those who won't be able to make it. Overall, the correlation between SAT scores and first-year college grades is 0.52, which is fairly strong. So far, so good. But we know that women on average score lower than men on the SAT, yet they earn higher grades in college than men do. That is odd. Statistical analyses indicate that, for women, SAT scores underpredict their college grades. That is, women get higher grades than their SAT scores would indicate. Men's grades, in contrast, are lower than their SAT scores predict. The disturbing implication is that each year perhaps thousands of women are denied admission to selective colleges even though those women would have performed as well at the college as the men who were admitted. One study analyzed this issue in more detail, focusing on students applying for admission to the University of California, Berkeley (Leonard & Jiang, 1999). The results indicated that, although the female underprediction effect is small, each year between 200 and 300 women are denied admission to Berkeley because of gender bias in the SAT. The researchers con-

> **Female underprediction effect:** The phenomenon that females' SAT scores predict lower grades in college than they actually get.

cluded that the Educational Testing Service (ETS) should publicly label the test as underpredicting women's grades and warn colleges that they should apply corrections in making admissions decisions.

Achievement

School Achievement   At all grade levels, girls consistently get better grades than boys, even in those areas in which boys score higher in ability tests (e.g., Kimball, 1989). The school progress of girls is also superior to that of boys. Girls less frequently have to repeat a grade and are more frequently accelerated and promoted.

Vocational Achievement   Stop for a moment and think of the name of a famous woman scientist. Write it down. Probably at least 90 percent of you wrote "Marie Curie," and the rest of you wrote nothing because you couldn't think of her name. Who else is there? This illustrates how few women have achieved real eminence in science and how little recognition we give to those who have. (Other examples would be Anna Freud, Jane Goodall, Dian Fossey, and Margaret Mead.)

Even in fields traditionally assigned to women, the top-ranking, most prestigious positions are held by men. Professional interior decorating and clothing design are dominated by men. The chefs who achieve renown and "greatness" are men. Teachers are women, but principals and superintendents of schools are more likely to be men.

In more recent years, there still remains a gap between the accomplishments of women and those of men. We will discuss women and work in far greater detail in Chapter 9. Suffice it to say here that the majority of women are concentrated in a relatively narrow range of female-dominated occupations (occupations in which 80 percent or more of the workers are female); these include librarians, health technicians, secretaries, nurses, bank tellers, telephone operators, childcare workers, and dental assistants. In contrast, the majority of men are spread out over 229 occupations that are at least 80 percent male, including natural scientists, dentists, airplane pilots, and carpenters. There is a great deal of difference between the status of the male-dominated occupations and that of the female-dominated occupations.

This situation is compounded by the fact that women who do make exceptional achievements often remain invisible. For example, when you think of the discovery of the structure of the genetic molecule DNA, you probably think of the two male scientists Watson and Crick. Lost from the story told to the public was the essential contribution of their female colleague, Rosalind Franklin (Sayre, 1978). Examples of a number of women who contributed to major advances in psychology were given in Chapter 1. It is important not only to remove barriers to women's achievement, but also to recognize the work of those who have achieved.

FOCUS 8.2

THE STORY OF A GIFTED WOMAN: BEATRIX POTTER

Beatrix (Helen B.) Potter is best known as the author and illustrator of *The Tale of Peter Rabbit*. But her biography reveals a great deal about the struggles of a gifted woman trying to express her talent in the field of biology.

She was born in 1866 and, by the age of 8, was already carefully drawing and labeling caterpillars. She became particularly interested in fungi, and through her teens and 20s she devoted as many hours as possible of every day to a search for new species she had not previously observed. She then painted each one that she saw.

By 1894, her studies of fungi and lichens were sufficiently advanced for her to take an interest in research from abroad suggesting that lichens result from symbiosis, a relationship between two organisms in which each is necessary for the other's survival. To test this hypothesis, she enlisted the help of her uncle, a distinguished chemist. On the basis of her research, Potter discovered the intimate interdependency between the fungus and alga which together formed the lichen.

It was through her uncle that she gained her first audience with the scientific establishment. He took her to the Royal Botanic Gardens to present her work. One after another of the scientists greeted her with apathy. The director dismissed her paintings of fungi as being too artistic to meet scientific criteria. Although repeatedly rebuffed by the scientific community, she continued her work on lichens, began work on spores, and started drafts of a paper describing her findings. As such, she was the first Briton to explain the symbiotic relationship involved in a lichen and to begin to understand the germination of spores.

Her uncle became increasingly furious over her rejections by the scientific establishment and determined that her views would be heard. In 1897 a paper entitled "On the Germination of the Spores of Agaricineae" by Helen B. Potter was read to the Linnaean Society of London. It was read by a friend; Beatrix Potter was not present because only men were allowed to attend the meetings.

Beatrix Potter's genius is shown in her superb scientific drawings; she encountered such obstacles to a career in science, however, that she channeled her talents into writing and illustrating children's books.

But the prospects for her work to be appreciated remained nonexistent. Two years later she gave up her study of spores, finding the response of children to the books she wrote and illustrated to be much more satisfying. Her first book, complete with illustrations, was about a rabbit. Unable to get a publisher, she paid to have it printed. *The Tale of Peter Rabbit* has been on the list of children's best-sellers ever since its publication 100 years ago. Many of the psychological themes of Potter's own life are reflected in the characters, most notably frustration, a sense of being kept from a desired goal. For example, Peter Rabbit can't roam the garden at will because of the upraised rake of the pursuing gardener, MacGregor. Gifted in both science and art, Beatrix Potter finally found a socially acceptable, gender-appropriate way to express her creativity, by writing and illustrating children's books.

At the age of 47 she married, for the first time, a lawyer and spent her last 30 years living happily in the country. One wonders what great contributions she might have made to science had she not been so thwarted in her efforts. But then where would we be without Peter Rabbit?

SOURCE: From Naomi Gilpatrick, "The Secret Life of Beatrix Potter." Used by permission from *Natural History,* Vol. 81, No. 8. Copyright © 1982, the American Museum of Natural History.

In fact, women's educational achievements have increased dramatically in the last three decades. In 1970, women earned 43 percent of the bachelor's degrees conferred; by 1996, that figure had risen to 55 percent (U.S. Department of Education, 2000). In addition to attending college at higher rates, women have made substantial inroads into areas that were previously male dominated. For example, women earned 9 percent of the undergraduate business degrees attained in 1970 compared with 48 percent in 1996 (U.S. Department of Education, 2000).

To summarize, then: In terms of achievement, girls surpass boys in school achievement in all areas, but in terms of career achievement, females lag behind males. This deficit in achievement is particularly surprising in view of girls' school successes and intellectual abilities; it is probably a result of a variety of forces, including discrimination and gender-role socialization. In the next sections of this chapter we will explore various motivational factors that may also help to account for the lesser professional achievements of women.

Achievement Motivation

A striking paradox has emerged in this chapter. Women start out in life with good abilities, yet they end up in adulthood with lower-status jobs and less recognized achievement than men. Girls also do better in school, yet in adulthood we find them in unpaid occupations such as housewives, or in lower-status, lower-paying ones such as clerks. Why?

There is currently a high consciousness about discrimination against women, and certainly discrimination is an important source of women's low achievement. (See Chapter 9 for a more complete discussion.)

However, psychologists believe that discrimination on the basis of gender is not the entire explanation for the *ability-achievement gap.* Society has subtler ways of achieving its goals, ways in which some women may internalize low drives to achieve. Some of the personality factors that have been proposed to explain this gap are achievement motivation, the motive to avoid success, and expectations about success. We will examine these processes in women in this and the following sections.

Achievement motivation is the desire to accomplish something of value or importance through one's own efforts, to meet standards of excellence in what one does. There are several methods for measuring it. The most commonly used is a projective technique in which participants' stories in response to an ambiguous cue are scored for achievement imagery (McClelland et al., 1953). Participants are shown a series of pictures and are asked to write a story about each picture after being told that this is a test of creative imagination. They are told to cover such questions as the following: What is happening? What

Achievement motivation: The desire to accomplish something of value or importance through one's efforts; the desire to meet standards of excellence.

has led up to this situation? What will happen? What is being thought? One of the pictures shows a young man standing on a sidewalk with a broom in his hand, looking off into the distance. Below are two stories written by different respondents about this picture:

> The boy works in the grocery store. He has just graduated from high school and hasn't enough money to go to college. He is standing there thinking about how long it will take him to save enough to get his education. He doesn't want to remain a store clerk all his life, and wants to make something of himself.

> It seems that this young man has been told by his father to clean up the sidewalk. This has prevented him from going off to the beach for the day with his pals. He is watching them go off in their car and is feeling left out and sore at his father.

The first story would be scored as indicating a high achievement motive, whereas the second indicates a low achievement motive.

Most of the classic literature on gender differences asserted that females have a lower level of achievement motivation than males (Hoffman, 1972; Tyler, 1965). These gender differences are of considerable interest because achievement motivation is related to achievement behaviors such as test performance and occupational choice. Thus, the lower achievement motivation of females might help to explain their lesser occupational achievement and might therefore represent a kind of "internalized barrier to achievement." Theories were constructed to explain the developmental forces, such as socialization, that might lead females to have low achievement motivation (Hoffman, 1972). It was also believed that although females were not motivated for achievement, they were motivated by social concerns, or by a need for affiliation. That is, females were thought to be motivated not by internalized standards of excellence (achievement motivation), but rather by a desire for approval from other people (Hoffman, 1972). Some authors even suggested that girls' achievement behavior (for example, in school) was motivated not by achievement motivation, as it was for boys, but rather by a need for affiliation (the teacher's approval).

These ideas need to be reassessed, however. Later reviews of available research found little evidence for lower achievement motivation in females (Maccoby & Jacklin, 1974; Mednick & Thomas, 1993; Stewart & Chester, 1982). The results are complex because achievement motivation may be tested under any of several conditions. In the simplest case (the "neutral" or "relaxed" condition), participants are simply given the test. Under such conditions, females actually show higher achievement motivation than males. The test may also be given under "achievement arousal" conditions. For example, before taking the test of achievement motivation, participants might be given an anagrams test that they are told measures not only intelligence, but also capacity to organize, to evaluate situations quickly and accurately, and to be a leader. Under these conditions, males' achievement motivation increases sharply, whereas females' does not. However, these studies have been criticized for sex bias in their designs (Stewart & Chester, 1982). Therefore, the research on gender and achievement motivation is muddled, but gender similarities seem to be the rule.

Consistent with the pattern of gender similarities is research indicating that women's achievement motivation has increased over time. One study found increases in American women's achievement motivation from 1957 to 1976, and another study found increases from 1967 to 1981 (Jenkins, 1987; Veroff et al., 1980). It seems likely that the opening of educational opportunities and career options for women over the last several decades has increased girls' achievement motivation as they anticipate jobs with exciting possibilities for achievement. Indeed, a related finding shows that achievement motivation scores of women who were seniors in college predicted their employment in achievement-oriented occupations 14 years later (Jenkins, 1987). In adulthood, moreover, women's achievement motivation may increase with their experiences in achievement-oriented careers. For example, women employed as business entrepreneurs and college professors showed significant increases in their achievement motivation compared with their scores in college, whereas those in other occupations showed no change in achievement motivation (Jenkins, 1987).

Motive to Avoid Success

In 1969 Matina Horner reported on the results of research on an anxiety about success called **motive to avoid success,** or *fear of success,* among bright, high-achieving women.

Motive to avoid success: A hypothesized fear of success that leads people to avoid being successful.

In attempting to understand the basis of gender differences in achievement motivation, Horner first observed that achievement situations, such as test taking, were more anxiety provoking for females than for males. To measure this phenomenon, Horner devised a projective test in which respondents were asked to complete a story that begins: "After first-term finals, Anne (John) finds herself (himself) at the top of her (his) medical-school class." Females wrote about Anne, males about John.

Males' stories generally indicated happiness and feelings of satisfaction over achievement. For example:

> John is a conscientious young man who worked hard. He is pleased with himself. John has always wanted to go into medicine and is very dedicated. . . . John continues working hard and eventually graduates at the top of his class.

Females' responses, on the other hand, were often bizarre:

> Anne starts proclaiming her surprise and joy. Her fellow classmates are so disgusted with her behavior that they jump on her in a body and beat her. She is maimed for life.

The negative imagery expressed by females generally fell into one of three categories—fear of social rejection, worries about maintaining womanhood, and denial of the reality of success. For example:

Social rejection fears:

> Anne is an acne-faced bookworm. She runs to the bulletin board and finds she's at the top. As usual she smarts off. A chorus of groans is the rest of the class's reply. . . .

Worries about womanhood:

> Unfortunately Anne no longer feels so certain that she really wants to be a doctor. She is worried about herself and wonders if perhaps she isn't normal. . . . Anne decides not to continue with her medical work but to take courses that have a deeper personal meaning for her.

Denial of reality:

> Anne is a code name of a nonexistent person created by a group of medical students. They take turns writing exams for Anne.

In her sample of undergraduates at the University of Michigan, Horner found that 65 percent of the females, as compared with fewer than 10 percent of the males, told stories that fell into one of these three categories.

Presumably the motive to avoid success is related to the perceived conflict between achievement and femininity and the perceived connection between achievement and aggressiveness, which is also gender inappropriate for females. Thus, for women, the rewards of achievement are contaminated by the accompanying anxiety.

Horner collected her original data in 1965 for her doctoral dissertation. The results were published in a 1969 *Psychology Today* article. They attracted quite a bit of attention, to put it mildly. The *New York Times* and other newspapers featured stories about the research. The article was required reading for many students. The research was—and is—appealing for a number of reasons. It appeared just at the time of rising interest in women and the women's movement. In particular, it seemed to offer a sensible explanation for why more women had not succeeded in high-status occupations—they simply feared success.

In the cold light of day some 40 years later, the research doesn't seem to provide the surefire answers it originally did. Horner's research has been criticized on a number of grounds (Mednick, 1989; Shaver, 1976; Tresemer, 1974; Zuckerman & Wheeler, 1975): (1) Other studies using Horner's techniques often find men having fear-of-success imagery as much as or more than women. Thus, there is no reason to believe that the motive to avoid success is found only in women, or even that it is more frequent in women. If that is the case, then it cannot be used to explain the lesser occupational achievements of women. (2) Anne's success was in a stereotype-inappropriate field, namely, medical school. Therefore, the research may indicate not a generalized fear of success, but rather a fear of being successful at something that violates stereotypes. Perhaps if Anne were presented as doing well in nursing school, she would not evoke much anxiety. One study showed just that (Cherry & Deaux, 1978). (3) Women are responding to another woman, Anne, not themselves, in writing the stories. Perhaps they feel anxious about Anne's success, but would not feel anxious about their own success. (4) In technical language, Horner's technique confounds gender of participants with gender of the stimulus cue. That is, women write about Anne, men about John. From this, we cannot tell whether women are higher in fear of success than men, or whether successful women (as cues) arouse more anxiety than successful men. Perhaps if men wrote about Anne, they too would indicate bizarre reactions to her. In fact, one study showed that to be exactly what happens (Monahan et al., 1974). This suggests that Horner's techniques may simply measure cultural stereotypes about women rather than murky unconscious conflicts.

Where does this leave us? Is there a motive to avoid success that keeps some women from achieving, or that at least makes them miserable if they do? My belief is that there probably is such a phenomenon, but I must also say that there is not much scientific evidence for it. In Chapter 1, I noted that one of the critical steps in psychological research is *measurement*. That is, when a researcher has some phenomenon to study, she or he must first devise a way to measure it. In Horner's case, she chose to measure the motive to avoid success by using a **projective test.** The idea is that people are given an ambiguous cue. Their stories about that cue presumably reflect a projection of their own unconscious motives. Many psychologists now consider projective tests to be poor methods of measurement and might prefer some more direct method, perhaps a paper-and-pencil checklist (such as Bem used in measuring androgyny, as discussed in Chapter 3). Thus, as noted, my belief is that the motive to avoid success probably exists in some people, but no one has been able to measure it adequately as yet (Macdonald & Hyde, 1980), and it may affect both women and men.

Projective test: A method of psychological measurement that uses ambiguous stimuli; the person's responses are thought to reflect his or her personality based on the assumption that one's personality is projected onto the ambiguous stimulus.

Attributions: When a Woman Succeeds, Is It Just Luck?

Suppose a college woman gets an A on a calculus exam. When she thinks about her success, or when others think about it, what will they believe caused it? To what will she or others attribute her success? This is called the **attribution** process, and it has been studied in detail by social psychologists. Typically four kinds of causes have been studied: ability, effort, luck, and task difficulty. Applied to the example given here, people might think that the woman got an A because

Attribution: The process by which people make judgments about the causes of events.

of her own high mathematical ability, because she studied hard (effort), simply because she was lucky, or because the exam was easy. These four kinds of causes can be further categorized into two groups, those attributing the event to *internal* sources (factors within the individual, that is, ability and effort) and those attributing the event to *external* sources (forces outside the individual, that is, luck and task difficulty).

Early research in this area tended to document gender differences in attribution patterns. Women were found to be more likely than men to attribute their own success to external sources, in particular, luck; men, in contrast, attributed their success to their own abilities (e.g., Simon & Feather, 1973). These results were also found when people explained the performance of another person; they thought that a woman succeeds because of luck and that a man succeeds because of his skill or ability (Deaux & Emswiller, 1974). The early research also showed that, when people are explaining their failures, women are more likely than men to attribute failure to internal sources, namely, to their own lack of abilities (McMahan, 1971, 1972).

Irene Frieze and her colleagues (1982; see also Sohn, 1982; Whitley et al., 1986) then conducted a meta-analysis of all available studies on attribution patterns to see whether gender differences appeared consistently. Their results indicated that the size of the gender differences described above is essentially zero. Once again, gender similarities are the reality.

Research may yet uncover important gender differences in causal attributions if the study designs become more complex, particularly if attention is given to situational factors, such as the type of task that is used (McHugh et al., 1982). For example, if the task involves spatial ability problems or some kind of athletic performance, women might attribute their successes to luck, whereas if the task involves establishing a friendship with a new person or establishing a nurturant relationship with someone in need, then women might be more likely to attribute their successes to ability. But for now it must be said that there are no gender differences in causal attributions, at least as studied so far.

In Conclusion

In this chapter I reviewed evidence on gender differences in abilities, noting that there are no gender differences in verbal ability or mathematical performance, except that boys start doing better in problem solving beginning in high school; and there are gender differences favoring males on only one type of spatial ability, mental rotations. Girls do better in school, yet men achieve higher-status positions in the world of work. There is a disparity, then, between the abilities and school achievement of females, on the one hand, and the status of their jobs in adulthood, on the other.

EXPERIENCE THE RESEARCH

GIRLS, BOYS, AND COMPUTERS

This exercise has two parts:

1. Visit a local store that sells computer games. Examine ten games that are currently being sold. Based on the information on the package and what you know about the games, classify each game as male oriented, female oriented, or neutral. To do this, you will have to specify your criteria for each of these categories. For example, you might decide that any game that involves violence is male oriented. Specify your criteria clearly and write them down. If there is not enough information on the package to classify a game, ask a salesperson in the store to give you more details about it.

     Overall, what were your findings? What percentage of the games were male oriented? Female oriented? Neutral? What are the implications of your findings?

2. Find out whether the local high school has an after-school computer lab. If it does, visit the lab twice to make observations. On each occasion, count the number of male students and female students who are there. Next, observe the computer activity in which each student is engaging, such as playing a game (what kind of game?) or programming.

     Do the boys' computer activities differ systematically from the girls'? Do there seem to be power dynamics in the lab, with some people dominating over others? What is the pattern of those power dynamics?

Two general classes of factors help to explain this discrepancy: (1) external[1] barriers to achievement and (2) internal (or intrapsychic) barriers to achievement. External barriers are factors such as job discrimination and, as noted in Chapter 9, there is ample evidence that this exists, in both obvious and subtle forms. Internal barriers or intrapsychic factors—such as low expectations for success and the low value placed on some areas such as developing math skills—also seem to exist. Of course, the internal barriers may be caused by external forces; for example, a woman may have low expectations for success on her job because she has experienced job discrimination. Thus, a combination of external and internal factors is important in explaining the work achievements of women. It is also important to recognize both sets of factors when trying to bring about the social change necessary to allow women to achieve more.

Suggestions for Further Reading

Holland, Dorothy C., & Eisenhart, Margaret A. (1990). *Educated in romance: Women, achievement, and college culture.* Chicago: University of Chicago Press. The authors used anthropologists' methods to study a predominantly White, southern university and a southern historically Black college. They found that the faculty and administration had relatively little impact. Rather, it was the peer culture stressing romance that led women to abandon their career plans.

Mednick, Martha T. (1989). On the politics of psychological constructs: Stop the bandwagon, I want to get off. *American Psychologist, 44,* 1118–1123. Discusses the demise of the concept of fear of success and some other popular constructs in the psychology of women, and why these constructs failed to deliver as promised.

Women and the Web

Association for Women in Mathematics. This website includes links to research on girls and math.
   http://www.awm-math.org/

Girl Tech: Getting Girls Interested in Computers
   http://math.rice.edu/~lanius/club/girls.html

Women in Engineering: Programs and Advocates Network
   http://wepan.cecs.ucf.edu

---

[1]The use of *external* and *internal* here should not be confused with the references to external and internal in the previous section's discussion of causal attributions.

9

Women and Work

The token woman is a black Chicana fluent in Chinese
Who has borne 1.2 babies
(not on the premises, no child care provided)
owns a Ph.D., will teach freshmen English
for a decade and bleach your laundry
with tears, silent as a china egg.
Your department orders her from a taxidermist's catalog
and she comes luxuriously stuffed with goose down
able to double as sleeping
or punching bag.

— FROM MARGE PIERCY, THE TOKEN WOMAN*

The majority of American women hold paying jobs. Among women between the ages of 25 and 54, 77 percent hold jobs (Women's Bureau, 2000). The working woman, then, is not a variation from the norm; she *is* the norm. Women today constitute 46 percent of the American labor force—very close to half—compared with 30 percent in 1950 (Costello & Stone, 2001).

Stereotypes About Women and Work

There are many stereotypes about women and work. Below I will consider two of them, and what the actual data say.

Stereotype 1: Women are working only for a little extra money. The idea behind this stereotype is that most women are only providing a second income, that the husband supports the family, and that the wife is working only to provide a few frills. In fact, however, most women work because of stark economic necessity. Of the 71 million families in the United States, 13 million (18 percent) are maintained by women and their earnings (i.e., there is no husband present) (Women's Bureau, 2000). In 1999, the average income of married-couple families with the wife in the paid labor force was $63,750, compared with $37,000 for those without the wife in the labor force (Women's Bureau, 2000).

Stereotype 2: A woman who is really ambitious and qualified can get ahead anyway. It is true that some women get ahead, but many others do not. All other factors aside, what the woman worker must often face is simple job discrimination. For example, the average woman worker is as well educated as the average man worker—both have a median of 12.6 years of schooling—but she makes

The majority of American women (77 percent) hold jobs outside the home.

only 72 cents for every dollar he earns when both work full-time, year-round (U.S. Department of Labor, 2002). Most investigators agree that women are discriminated against in employment. Given the same education, job, experience, and so on, they are given less pay and are promoted more slowly (e.g., Betz, 1993; Gutek, 2001b).

Sex Discrimination in the Workplace

Sex discrimination in the workplace may take a number of forms, including discrimination in the evaluation of women's work, discrimination in pay, discrimination in hiring and promotion, the glass ceiling, and people refusing to work for a woman boss.

Discrimination in the Evaluation of Women's Work   Psychologists have contributed some interesting experiments that investigate whether discrimination occurs in the evaluation of women's work. A classic study demonstrated that even when the work of a female was identical to that of a male, it was judged to be inferior (Goldberg, 1968; replicated by Pheterson et al., 1971). Female college students were asked to evaluate scholarly essays in a number of academic fields. All of the students rated the same essays, but half of them rated essays bearing the names of male authors (e.g., John T. McKay), whereas the other half

"AS FAR AS I'M CONCERNED, THE REAL EROGENOUS
ZONE IS WALL STREET!"

rated the same essays with the names of female authors (e.g., Joan T. McKay). The essays were identical except for the names of the authors. The results were that the essays were rated higher when the author was male, even when the essay was in a traditionally feminine field such as dietetics. It appears that the work of males is valued more even if it is identical to that of females. It is interesting to note that the raters in this study, those who gave lower value to female work, were themselves women.

In another study of gender and discrimination in the evaluation of work, the opposite effect was found; it was called the "talking platypus effect" (Abramson et al., 1977). Undergraduates read a one-page biography of a stimulus person. Half of them read about a male, and half about a female; further, in half of the biographies the person was a lawyer, and in the other half the person was a paralegal. Interestingly, the female attorney was rated as *more* competent than the male attorney. The authors believed that with public awareness of the obstacles to achievement that women face, people actually overvalue a woman who has demonstrated a high level of achievement: If you hear a platypus talking, it doesn't much matter what it says; it is simply a wonder that it can say anything at all.

How can we resolve these two apparently contradictory studies, one showing discrimination against women and one showing discrimination against men? A meta-analysis reviewed 106 articles reporting studies of this type (Swim et al., 1989). The authors concluded that there was little evidence of bias in the evaluation of women's work; the average effect size d was -0.07, the negative sign indicating that women's work was given slightly lower ratings than men's work, but the d was so small that we could say it was zero. Notice that—in contrast to other meta-analyses I have reported, in which *d* reflected the difference between the performance of males and the performance of females—here the effect is for the difference between evaluations of work with a man's name on it and evaluations of work with a woman's name on it. The effect size *d*, in this instance, is a measure of the extent of sex bias or discrimination.

It would be a happy conclusion to say that there is no bias in the evaluation of women's work. However, there were complexities in the meta-analysis. First, the effect size depended quite a bit on the kind of material that was rated, and it was larger when that material was an employment application ($d = -0.25$) than when it was something else, such as written work ($d = -0.14$). Thus discrimination against women was greatest for employment applications, and that is a serious matter.

The other complexity was that the effect size (amount of sex bias) depended on the amount of information given to the rater. When raters were given only a small amount of information—just a male or female name—bias was greatest ($d = -0.38$), whereas when raters were given a paragraph or more of information, the effect size was small ($d = -0.08$). This is consistent with a general finding in social psychology, that people stereotype others less the more they know about them. This is an optimistic finding in that it means we do not always have to be ruled by stereotypes. On the other hand, there are some very important situations, such as job interviews, when an interviewer makes a critical decision based on a first impression and a small amount of information, and that is just when stereotyping and bias are most likely to occur.

A serious limitation to the meta-analysis was that virtually all the studies reviewed were laboratory experiments with college students serving as the raters. In short, the studies do not directly measure what is of most concern: sex discrimination in the actual evaluations of the work of real women, that is, evaluations by their actual supervisors, by people actually making hiring decisions, or by other powerful persons. The studies in the meta-analysis provide only analogies to the real situation, and for that reason they are called *analog studies.* We are left wondering, then, whether there is more or less discrimination in the real world of work.

A real-world study investigated the impact of both gender and race on evaluations of work (Greenhaus & Parasuraman, 1993). A total of 1,628 managers in corporations (814 African Americans and 814 Whites) and their supervisors participated. Supervisors gave an attribution rating—that is, to what extent they thought the satisfactory performance of the manager was due to ability. The results indicated that, among the most highly successful managers, the performance of the women was less likely to be attributed to ability than it was for men. The performance of African American managers was less likely to be attributed to ability and effort and was more likely to be attributed to help from others than was the performance of White managers. However, the effects were generally small; for example, for race differences in attributions to ability, $d = 0.18$. Furthermore, these attribution effects were strongest when the manager and supervisor had little experience with each other. With longer experience, the race differences in attributions became smaller. This study, then, provides evidence of gender bias and race bias in evaluations of work in a real-world setting; however, the effects are small, and they become smaller when the supervisor and manager have had more experience together.

Pay Equity Sex discrimination in pay is another serious issue. For many women, especially those who are single heads of households, it is literally a bread-and-butter issue. By 1999, women's earnings had climbed to an average of $26,324 for full-time, year-round workers, compared with $36,476 for men (U.S. Department of Labor, 2002). And this occurs despite the fact that, on average, women are as educated as men.

The wage gap is not only a gender issue, but a race issue as well. Table 9.1 shows annual earnings as a function of both gender and ethnicity. These statistics clearly demonstrate that both women and minorities have lower wages than White men.

What causes the wage gap? One clear factor is job segregation, to be discussed in the next section. Very few jobs have a 50:50 male:female ratio. Most are held predominantly by one sex or the other, and the higher the percentage of women in an occupation, the lower the pay. In extreme cases, when the gender ratio shifts so that women take over a formerly male-dominated occupation, wages drop. An example in the United States is pharmacy, which was once a predominantly male occupation in which men owned their own stores and were businessmen as well as pharmacists, bringing in high earnings. These stores are now being replaced by chain drugstores, where women pharmacists dispense drugs and earn smaller incomes (Bernstein, 1988).

TABLE 9.1
Median Annual Earnings for Full-Time, Year-Round Workers, 1997

	Women	Men	Ratio* (wage gap)
All races	$25,362	$34,199	0.74
Whites	$25,726	$35,741	0.72
Blacks	$22,378	$26,844	0.83
Hispanics	$19,269	$21,952	0.88
Asians/Pacific Islanders	$28,214	$35,222	0.80

*This ratio gives women's earnings as a percentage of white males' earnings.
Source: Costello & Stone (2001, p. 273).

FOCUS 9.1

GENDER, ENTITLEMENT, AND THE WAGE GAP

Among full-time, year-round workers, women earn only 72 cents for every dollar earned by men (U.S. Department of Labor, 2002). This is a gross injustice. Why are women not rioting in the streets, protesting this massive problem?

Psychologist Brenda Major has developed a theory of entitlement that helps to explain both the wage gap and why women tolerate it. *Entitlement* refers simply to the individual's sense of what she or he is entitled to receive (e.g., pay). Major's model is shown in Figure 9.1.

The process begins with inequalities in the social structure in the United States. These include the gender segregation of most jobs, the chronic underpay-

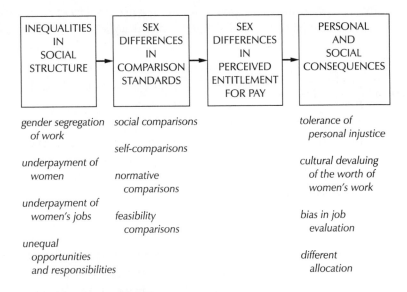

FIGURE 9.1

Major's model of the causes of gender differences in the sense of entitlement and how this gender difference contributes to the wage gap.

SOURCE: From "Gender differences in comparison and entitlement: Implications for comparable worth" by Brenda Major, *Journal of Social Issues 45,* 4, p. 101. Reprinted by permission of the author and the Society for the Psychological Study of Social Issues.

ment of women and of women's jobs, and the lack of equal opportunities for women. These inequalities in the social structure then lead women and men to have different standards of comparison, that is, standards against which they compare their own pay when deciding whether it is equitable. The result is that women compare their pay with that of other women and with others in their typically female-dominated occupation. Women see other women and those in their own occupation as the appropriate comparison group because of a proximity effect—that is, those are the people who are around them and about whom they have information. The average telephone operator is unlikely to have information on what electricians earn. Self-protective factors may also play a part. An underpaid female librarian who is a college graduate does not want to know what a male high school graduate working in a skilled trade earns. It will just make her feel bad. Her tendency will be to compare her pay with that of other female librarians, and then she won't be doing so badly.

These gender differences in standards of comparison then have a great impact on women's and men's perceptions of their entitlement to pay. Many women do not feel entitled to high pay for their work in the way that men do because (1) their pay is reasonable relative to those with whom they compare themselves; (2) their pay is reasonable compared with their own past pay; and (3) their pay is reasonable according to what is realistically attainable given restricted job opportunities for women.

The result is that women have less of a sense of entitlement to high pay than men do. This in turn leads them to tolerate wage injustice. Another consequence is that others come to believe that women will settle for less in pay, precisely because many women do, leading to further bias in setting wage rates. And so the cycle continues.

What evidence is there to support this theory? Many experiments have been conducted testing various aspects of it, and virtually all of them support it. I will discuss two examples here (Major, 1989). In one, female and male undergraduates worked on a gender-neutral task in a research laboratory for a fixed amount of time. Afterward, they paid themselves privately from a pot containing $4.00. In one of the experimental groups, the participants simply paid themselves what they thought their work was worth, in the absence of any social comparison information. In the other group, participants were given bogus information about how much money

(continued)

previous participants had paid themselves for the same work. In the first condition, with no information about others' pay, women paid themselves an average of $1.95, whereas men paid themselves an average of $3.18. However, when comparison information was given, there were no gender differences; men and women both matched their pay to the comparison standard.

Another study, closer to a real-world situation, found that female and male management students who had equal qualifications had different perceptions of what graduates in their field earned; women thought the pay was lower.

As I noted in Chapter 1, we must be careful of interpretations of these phenomena, so that this theory does not become another female deficit model. One interpretation is that women have a low sense of personal entitlement compared with men, that is, that women have a deficit in their sense of entitlement. The other possible interpretation is that men have too great a sense of entitlement—a sense that they are entitled to more than they are worth. An inflated sense of entitlement characterizes many dominant groups, including men, Whites, and those from the upper social classes.

This theory is an excellent example of the ways in which social institutions, such as the gender segregation of occupations (an external factor) interact with psychological processes such as a sense of entitlement (an internal factor) to create gender bias.

On a hopeful note, a real-world study of women in high-achieving occupations indicated that only 29 percent of them compared themselves to other women, whereas 24 percent compared themselves to men and 48 percent compared themselves to both (Steil & Hay, 1997). The women who compared themselves to men earned more than those who compared themselves to other women. These results show that the cycle of women comparing their wages to other women's, and being contented with their low pay, can be broken.

SOURCES: Desmarais (1997), Major (1989, 1994), Steil & Hay (1997), Steil et al. (2001).

"*We can still be friends, Roger. I just don't want you to be one of my vice-presidents anymore.*"

It was the recognition of the gender gap in wages, and the fact that it was an outgrowth of gender-segregated occupations, that led, in the late 1970s, to the concept of **comparable worth.** The idea behind compara- ble worth is that people should be paid equally for work in comparable jobs—that is, jobs with equivalent responsibility, educational requirements, level in the organization, and re- quired experience. As an illustration of the need for principles of comparable worth, in one state both liquor store clerks and librarians are employed by the state government. Liquor store clerks are almost all men, and the job requires only a high school education. Librarians are al- most all women, and the job requires a college education. But in this state, liquor store clerks are paid more than librarians. The principle of comparable worth argues against this pattern. It says that librarians should be paid at least as much as, and probably more than, liquor store clerks because librarians must be college graduates.

> **Comparable worth:** The principle that people should be paid equally for work that is comparable in responsibility, educational requirements, and so forth.

Several states—including my own, Wisconsin—have enacted comparable- worth legislation, stating that at least all government employees must be paid on a comparable-worth basis. This necessitates extensive job analyses by industrial/ organizational psychologists to determine which jobs—ignoring gender—have equivalent requirements in terms of responsibilities, education, and so on. Pre- liminary results in states that have legislated this principle are promising. Despite dire predictions from the business community, it turns out not to be terribly ex- pensive for employers to pay on a comparable-worth basis.

A second factor that seems to be related to the gender gap in wages is women's family roles (Steil et. al., 2001). Marriage and children raise the amount of home-related work for both women and men, but the effect is much greater for women, as we will discuss further in the section on work and family issues. The important point for this discussion of pay equity is that women's greater family responsibilities may lead them to make certain choices (or force them to make certain choices) that will result in lower wages. For example, to be a successful partner in a law firm or to earn tenure as a college professor requires considerably more than 40 hours of work per week—often 60 to 80 hours. Some (though certainly not all) women in this situation may choose not to commit the extra hours, because they want to spend them with their family, or family commitments simply prevent work beyond 40 hours per week. These women then choose or settle for the lower and less well paid levels of their occupations—lawyer but not partner, lecturer but not tenured professor. There is much questioning of why women's family responsibilities should interfere with their job advancement, a point to which we will return later in this chapter.

Discrimination in Hiring and Promotion   As noted earlier in this chapter, there is some evidence of gender bias in the evaluation of employment applications. Here we will focus on discrimination in promotions.

A series of studies by Laurie Larwood and her colleagues (Larwood et al., 1988; Trentham & Larwood, 1998) demonstrates the continuing existence of sex discrimination in the selection of people for work assignments. The research showed that managers (half of them men, half women) were more likely to select a man than a woman for an important assignment (e.g., a "major sale"). They gave reasons for their choice such as "My own experience with customers is that many of them prefer to deal with men" (Trentham & Larwood, 1998, p. 16). On some measures, it was male managers, not female managers, who gave the choice assignment to men, with explanations such as "Males project trust and believability" (Trentham & Larwood, 1998, p. 17).

Most of what has been said here about sex discrimination also characterizes race discrimination. For example, the same studies by Larwood and her colleagues (1988) showed that a Black woman is preferred for an assignment if the client is a Black woman, but that a White man is preferred if the client is a White man—and in most of the business world, the client is a White man.

On a purely logical basis, discrimination in hiring and promotion doesn't make sense. All companies ought to benefit the most from hiring and promoting the best-qualified individuals, regardless of gender or race. Why, then, does discrimination continue?

According to a complex theory advanced by Larwood and her colleagues (1988; Trentham & Larwood, 1998), discrimination occurs because managers who are in charge of making assignments or granting promotions behave in a highly self-interested way. Furthermore, these managers generally perceive that the norms of the business world *support* discrimination. Thus managers essentially believe that it is in their best interest to behave the way the bosses of the corporation want them to—assigning women to stereotyped jobs, keeping them out of important assignments, and so on. Of course, managers may misperceive the beliefs of top executives, but the research shows that if they are unsure about those beliefs, they will discriminate.

Are there any solutions to these thorny problems? Larwood's research does offer some helpful suggestions. It demonstrates quite clearly that if a client or the president of the company has spoken out against discrimination, that action affects the behavior of managers, who are then less likely to discriminate in making assignments. Perhaps most important, therefore, is establishing a corporate climate in which it is clear that those at the top are opposed to discrimination. Managers, still operating out of self-interest, will then be more likely to engage in gender-fair practices.

The Glass Ceiling   The term **glass ceiling** refers to the phenomenon that, in many instances, women seem to be promoted and to advance well in their company up to a certain point, and then there seems to be a barrier or ceiling that prevents them from rising further (Morrison et al., 1992; Task Force on the Glass Ceiling Initiative, 1993; U.S. Department of Labor, 1992). For example, some women make it to the upper levels of management, but can't seem to break into executive positions—they can see the executive suite through the glass, but they can't crack through the barrier.

> **Glass ceiling:** "Invisible" barriers to the promotion of women and ethnic minorities into upper management and executive levels.

What evidence is there that a glass ceiling exists? A study of Fortune 500 companies found that, although 39 percent of all employees in these companies were women, women comprised only 11.9 percent of corporate officers (see Table 9.2). At the highest level of the company, women were fewer than 1 percent of CEOs. The higher one goes in corporations, the fewer women and people of color there are, and that is exactly what is meant by the glass ceiling.

TABLE 9.2
Statistics on the Glass Ceiling: Percentage of Women at Different Levels of Fortune 500 Corporations

All employees	39.3
Executives and managers	39.8
Corporate officers	11.9
CEOs	<1

SOURCE: Wellington & Giscombe (2001).

Although women constitute over 40 percent of medical students today, only 24 percent of full-time medical school faculty are women. Women are fewer than 10 percent of the full professors in medical schools and only 4 percent of department chairs (Kirschstein, 1996).

In a survey of women in management in Wisconsin, we found that 58 percent of the women reported the existence of a glass ceiling at their current or previous companies (Task Force on the Glass Ceiling Initiative, 1993). Among those women who said there was a glass ceiling at their previous company, 80 percent said it was an important reason why they left. Typically either these women moved to a company with a more equitable environment for women, or they started their own business. The study found that women-owned businesses were thriving. This phenomenon is evidence of **women's resistance.** Many talented women do not stay and passively suffer with a glass ceiling; instead, they move to another company or start their own business, and those women-owned businesses often compete successfully with ones they left. Today in the United States there are 5.4 million women-owned businesses.

Women's resistance: Occurs when women do not passively accept discriminatory treatment, but instead take active steps to resist it.

Leadership Issues   Social psychology studies have documented that it is difficult for a woman to assume and be recognized in a leadership role. For example, a classic study investigated this by using the phenomenon that the person seated at the head of a table is usually recognized as being the leader of a group (Porter et al., 1978). Participants were shown photographs of groups seated around a table and were asked to rate the leadership attributes of each member of the group. A man seated at the head of the table in a mixed-gender group was clearly seen as the group's leader, but a woman occupying that position was ignored. Women at the head of the table were recognized as leaders only when the group was all-female.

When women occupy positions of leadership—for example, as a supervisor—the evidence, then, indicates that they tend to be stereotyped as not having the right characteristics to be successful leaders. In real-world job situations, there are three possible reasons that women leaders might be viewed in this way. One is that they are truly lacking in the abilities, personality traits, interpersonal skills, and so on that are necessary in the supervisory role. A second reason is that people simply are biased in their evaluations of women who are leaders. A third reason is that women supervisors, as part of the complex network in a corporation, have less power than their male counterparts do (Nieva & Gutek, 1981). Power involves such things as being able to grant pay raises or promotions to subordinates or being able to influence the decisions of those higher up the corporate ladder. If workers perceive women supervisors as having less power, it should be no surprise if they are unenthusiastic about working for them.

In regard to the first hypothesis—whether women have the right stuff—research generally shows no gender differences in the effectiveness of leaders.

*Women aspiring to nontraditional careers may face various forms of psycho-
logical discrimination; for example, some people have difficulty recognizing a
woman in a leadership role. This photograph shows a woman executive inter-
viewing a man. When you saw the picture, did you perceive him as being her
boss?*

Psychologist Alice Eagly and her colleagues (1995) conducted a meta-analysis of
studies of the effectiveness of leaders. (Note that effectiveness can be measured either subjectively, as when a manager's skills on relevant dimensions are rated by
other managers, or objectively, as when the productivity of a leader's group is assessed.) Averaged over all studies, the magnitude of the gender difference in leadership effectiveness was $d = -0.02$; that is, there was no gender difference. The results were similar regardless of whether subjective measures ($d = 0.05$) or
objective measures ($d = -0.02$) were used. However, male leaders were more effective when the leadership position was consistent with the male gender role,
and female leaders were more effective when the leadership position was consistent with the female gender role. Depending on the situation, then, female leaders
may be more effective than male leaders, and vice versa. Averaged over all situations, there is no gender difference.

The second hypothesis is that people simply are biased in their evaluation
of women leaders. A meta-analysis was performed on laboratory studies in
which women and men occupying leadership roles were evaluated, with all
other factors controlled (Eagly et al., 1992). The results indicated that, overall,
there was little evidence of gender bias; women and men leaders were given sim-

ilar evaluations in general ($d = 0.05$). However, under certain conditions women received notably worse evaluations. If women used an autocratic leadership style (a dictatorial style rather than a more democratic, nurturant one), they received lower evaluations ($d = 0.30$). It may be, then, that it is not so much a question of bias against women leaders as bias against women leaders who behave in a counterstereotyped, masculine style. People have trouble with autocratic, pushy women, although the same behaviors would probably not seem nearly so pushy coming from a man. Other research shows that, perhaps fortunately, women are more likely to use a democratic style of leadership and men are more likely to use an autocratic one (Eagly & Johnson, 1990). These are important findings for women as they assume leadership roles and consider the management style they adopt.

Social psychologist Alice Eagly has proposed a *role congruity theory* of prejudice toward female leaders (Eagly & Karau, 2002). The theory holds that people tend to perceive an incongruity or incompatibility between leadership roles and the female gender role. This perceived incongruity in turn leads to two forms of prejudice. First, people perceive women less favorably than men as potential occupants of leadership positions. This gives women less access to leadership opportunities. Second, when women engage in leadership behavior, the behavior is evaluated less favorably than the same behavior enacted by a man. Research provides considerable evidence supporting this theory. One study, for example, showed that female managers described as successful were rated by participants as more hostile and less rational than male managers described in the same way (Heilman et al., 1995). One implication is that female managers who engage in behaviors that, objectively, represent effective leadership may nevertheless be ineffective as leaders because subordinates react negatively to that kind of behavior coming from a woman.

The third hypothesis above—that women as leaders have less power in organizations—implies that women also need to find ways to increase their power (for an excellent summary and analysis, see Smith & Grenier, 1982). Some of this will involve women's getting specific instruction—for example, assertiveness training or instruction on how to plan careers. But women also need to learn how to use the structural bases of power that exist within organizations. Legitimate power can come from any of three sources (Smith & Grenier, 1982): (1) participating in activities critical to the organization's survival or its current pressing problems; (2) participating in activities that control uncertainty (if the computer breaks down frequently at inopportune moments, then the computer repairperson has power); and (3) controlling resources such as money, people, or information. Women can learn to use any or all of these strategies for gaining power. (There are, of course, many illegitimate sources of power, such as sexual harassment and threats; however, I can't recommend that women learn to use these.)

Feminist psychologists have also suggested new models of leadership (Astin & Leland, 1991; Denmark, 1993). Specifically, they suggest a new model of

empowerment. Replacing the old belief that leaders have the power to control, this new model suggests that leaders have the power to empower. This view "treats power as an expandable resource that is produced and shared through interaction by leader and followers alike" (Astin & Leland, 1991, p. 1). In a study of successful women leaders, their strategies for empowerment included the following: communicating with others on their own level, listening, employing strong people and not feeling threatened by them, offering positive feedback, and working through consensus and collegiality (a democratic style) (Astin & Leland, 1991).

> **Empowerment:** Helping people to find their own strength.

In summary, then, women face some barriers when they assume leadership roles. Although women's effectiveness as leaders is equal to that of men, people may be biased in their evaluation of women leaders, particularly women who adopt an autocratic style. And women may lack power in their organization, so that employees are less enthusiastic about working for them. Feminist psychologists have suggested strategies for women to gain power in their organization, and they have proposed a new model of leadership that involves empowerment.

Occupational Segregation

Most occupations are segregated by gender. Some relevant statistics are shown in Table 9.3. Notice that most occupations are highly segregated by gender, with 90 percent or more of the workers coming from one gender. Men dominate as airline pilots, auto mechanics, carpenters, and welders. Women dominate as childcare workers, dental assistants, and registered nurses. Only a few occupations come close to a 50 to 50 gender ratio: bus drivers, editors and reporters, social workers, and college and university teachers.

Occupational segregation is a critical issue for two reasons. First, the stereotyping of occupations severely limits people's thinking about work options. A man might think himself well suited to being a registered nurse, or a woman might love carpentry, but they are discouraged from following their dreams because certain occupations are not considered gender appropriate for them. Second, occupational segregation is a major contributor to the gender gap in wages. As I noted earlier, women earn only 72 cents for every dollar earned by men. Statistics indicate that about 30 to 45 percent of that wage gap is due to occupational segregation (Reskin, 1988). Occupations that are predominantly female are almost invariably low paying.

Are We Making Any Progress? As we have reviewed evidence of continuing sex discrimination and occupational segregation, you might be wondering whether any progress has been made as the women's movement has pressed its case for equality. The answer is yes, in some areas. For example, in certain fields, women have quickly risen to earn substantial numbers of professional degrees.

TABLE 9.3
Women as a Percentage of All Workers in Selected Occupations, 1975, 1989, and 1998

Occupation	Women as Percentage of Total Employed		
	1975	1989	1998
Airline pilot	0	3.8	3.4
Auto mechanic	0.5	0.7	0.8
Bus driver	37.7	54.8	41.7
Carpenter	0.6	1.2	1.2
Childcare worker	98.4	97.1	97.1
Dentist	1.8	8.6	19.8
Dental assistant	100.0	98.9	98.1
Editor, reporter	44.6	49.2	51.0
Elementary school teacher	85.4	84.7	84.0
College/university teacher	31.1	38.7	42.3
Lawyer, judge	7.1	22.3	28.6
Librarian	81.1	87.3	83.4
Physician	13.0	17.9	26.6
Registered nurse	97.0	94.2	92.5
Social worker	60.8	68.1	68.4
Telephone installer, repairer	4.8	10.8	12.0
Welder	4.4	6.6	5.1

SOURCES: Costello & Stone (2001); U.S. Bureau of Labor Statistics (1976, 1990, 1999).

Some statistics from professions in which women have made the greatest advances are shown in Table 9.4. Now that women are earning so many of the professional degrees in these areas, occupational segregation will surely decrease. It is particularly interesting to note that all of these are high-paying, high-status occupations. I speak with some feeling when I say that education can be one of the most important solutions to the problems women face in the work force.

Some interesting patterns of ethnicity have emerged in relation to these advances in professional degrees. Of the degrees in dentistry awarded to women, only 64.8 percent go to White women, an underrepresentation compared with the percentage of White women in the population. But 21.2 percent of the dentistry degrees awarded to women go to Asian American women—a considerable

TABLE 9.4
**Percentages of Professional Degrees Awarded to Women
in Selected Professions in Which There Have Been Substantial Advances,
1970, 1980, and 1996**

Field	1970	1980	1996
Dentistry	0.9%	13.3%	36.0%
Medicine (M.D.)	8.4%	23.4%	41.0%
Law	5.4%	30.2%	43.6%

SOURCES: Costello & Stone (2001), Rix (1988).

overrepresentation. Asian American women have fueled the drive of women to-ward more medical and dental degrees (Costello & Stone, 2001). And, currently, 9.8 percent of the law degrees awarded to women are awarded to Black women—a bit of an underrepresentation, but a dramatic increase from three decades ago.

Work and Family Issues

Women have traditionally been responsible for maintaining the family, and partic-ularly for caring for children. As women marched into the paid work force in the 1970s and 1980s, they added the responsibilities of their new jobs, but they didn't give up their family obligations. Therefore, combining work and family—both for women and for men—is one of the most important social issues of the twenty-first century. Work and family issues rank high on the feminist agenda, and corpo-rate executives realize their importance. Even the U.S. government has recognized this fact; legislation on parental leave went into effect in 1993 (see Focus 9.2).

Work and Women's Psychological Well-Being   The American woman today holds a full-time job while managing a household and marriage and raising a preschooler or caring for an elderly parent. Is she on overload, stressed out with all her responsibilities, prone to physical and mental illness? Or is she supermom, able to have it all and be happy?

Within the framework of the social sciences, we are asking questions about the effects of multiple roles (e.g., worker, mother, wife) on health. Researchers in this area have taken two major the-oretical approaches (Barnett & Hyde, 2001; Baruch et al., 1987):

1. The **scarcity hypothesis**—This approach assumes that each human has a fixed amount of energy and that any role makes

Scarcity hypothesis: In re-search on women and multiple roles, the hypoth-esis that adding a role (e.g., worker) creates stress, which has negative consequences for mental health and physical health.

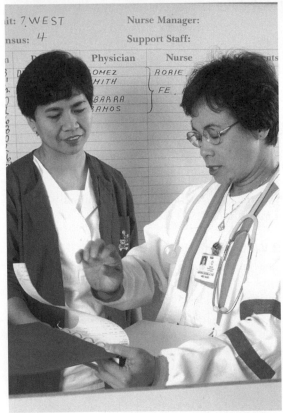

Most occupations are gender segregated. (Above) Male autoworkers. (Below) Female nurses.

demands on this pool of energy. Therefore, the greater the number of roles, the greater the stress and the more negative the consequences on health. The conclusion from this view, then, is that as women take on increased work responsibilities in addition to their family responsibilities, stress and negative health consequences must result.

2. The **expansionist hypothesis**—This approach assumes that people's energy resources are not limited, just as a regular program of exercise makes one feel more energetic, not less energetic. According to this approach, the more roles one has, the more the opportunities for enhanced self-esteem, stimulation, social status, and identity (Barnett & Hyde, 2001). Indeed, one might be cushioned from a traumatic occurrence in one role by the support one is receiving in another role.

Expansionist hypothesis: In research on women and multiple roles, the hypothesis that multiple roles are good for mental health, because they provide more opportunities for stimulation, self-esteem, and so on.

If the second theoretical approach is correct, we need not worry about stress from women's combining work and family roles. The combination might actually enhance mental and physical health rather than threaten it. It might also be true that both theoretical approaches have some validity.

Actual research on the effects of paid employment on women's health shows a generally positive, but also complex, picture (Barnett & Hyde, 2001; Perry-Jenkins et al., 2000). Employment does not appear to have a negative effect on women's physical and mental health. In fact, employment seems to improve the health of both unmarried women and married women who hold positive attitudes toward employment. By being employed, women generally gain social support from colleagues and supervisors as well as opportunities for success or mastery (Christensen et al., 1998), and these factors seem to be important to the health-enhancing effects of employment for women. Many women, of course, are not in such rosy situations; the woman whose work situation exposes her to sexual harassment or the frustrations of discrimination in pay and promotion will probably not enjoy positive health benefits from employment.

Childcare is another critical factor when one considers the relation between employment and women's mental health. If a woman cannot find childcare, or if she feels that such resources do not offer high-quality care for her child or are so expensive that she cannot afford them, then combining work and motherhood becomes stressful. If, on the other hand, the childcare is excellent, then work and family roles are more likely to enhance each other. In one study, the investigators found that children increased depression among nonemployed wives. In contrast, for employed mothers, if childcare was accessible and husbands shared in childcare, depression levels were low. However, employed mothers without accessible childcare and with sole responsibility for the children had extremely high levels of depression (Ross & Mirowsky, 1988).

FOCUS 9.2

PSYCHOLOGY AND PUBLIC POLICY: THE PARENTAL LEAVE DEBATE

In Sweden at the time of the birth of a baby, the parents have a right to 12 months of leave from work at 80 percent of normal pay (up to a certain maximum). The parents can split the leave however they wish. They can have an additional 3 months' leave at pay that is further reduced, and they can have yet an additional 3 months' leave (taking them up to the baby's 18th month) at pay that is still further reduced. At 18 months, each baby in Sweden is entitled to a place in a childcare center. Furthermore, Swedish parents are entitled to work at 75 percent time at 75 percent pay, if they so choose, until the child is 8 years old. This sounds to me like a true profamily policy.

Until 1993, the United States was one of only two industrialized nations in the world (the other being South Africa) that did not have a nationally legislated policy on parental leave. The term *parental leave* refers to leave from work for purposes of recovering from childbirth and/or caring for a child at the time of the birth (or possibly adoption) of a child. An even broader term, *family leave,* refers to leave from work to care for a new baby, an ill spouse, or an elderly parent. With the exception of a few states that passed parental leave legislation around 1987, in most states until 1993 a woman could give birth to a baby, return to work quickly—say, a month later—and find that she had lost her job, and it was perfectly legal for her employer to have fired her. There was an urgent need for legislation that ensured mothers and fathers the right to care for their newborn infant and know they had their jobs waiting for them; among other things, they obviously need the income to support the baby.

The federal legislation—the Family and Medical Leave Act—that went into effect in 1993 mandates that employers must allow mothers and fathers a minimum of 12 weeks of job-guaranteed, unpaid leave at the time of a birth or adoption. This legislation has several important features. First, it is gender fair—that is, fathers and mothers have equal rights to take the leave, and some couples might choose to take the leaves back-to-back, so that one parent would be home with the baby for a total of 24 weeks, or nearly 6 months. I think this is unlikely right now for most couples, for reasons I will describe below. A second feature is that the leave is job guaranteed, which means that the employee has a right to return to the same or a comparable job (in terms of pay and responsibilities). A third feature is that the leave is unpaid, at least as a minimum standard. Most couples cannot afford to lose the wife's income for very long, if at all, and even fewer couples can afford to lose the husband's income, which generally is higher. It is for that reason that I think it is not very likely that many couples would take back-to-back leaves totaling 24 weeks. A fourth feature is that the legislation sets a minimum standard. Employers may be more generous. It's like the minimum wage—if it is $5.80 per hour, employers are perfectly free to pay a highly skilled person $20 per hour; they just can't pay anyone less than $5.80. In the same way, employers can be more generous with parental leave. They can allow more than 12 weeks, or they can provide paid leave. Some progressive corporations have realized that it is beneficial to provide paid leave and are already doing so.

Clearly the legislation could be improved in a number of ways. Providing paid leave is a major necessary improvement. Employers worry about how costly this would be to them, but there are rather simple methods for paying for the leaves. Both Canada and the state of New Jersey have a system using a small payroll tax shared by employer and employee, and functioning much like the Social Security tax. This creates a fund, and employees on leave are paid from the fund. A second improvement needed is to have more employers and employees covered. The legislation applies only to employers with 50 or more employees; that is, small employers don't have to follow the rules. Women work disproportionately for small businesses, and it is important to extend the coverage to all mothers and fathers. A friend of mine recently told me that she had been fired in the first week after returning to work after having a baby. I exclaimed in outrage, "But that's illegal!" She replied that it was perfectly legal because there were only 12 employees at this company and they weren't covered by the legislation.

We have made enormous strides in the last decade with legislation that supports women as they combine work and family. And yet there is always a catch—in this case, some women are still legally fired after taking parental leave.

Where does psychology come into the picture? Often as Congress considers legislation, it calls on expert witnesses, such as psychologists, who can provide evidence on the kind of impact the legislation—or lack thereof—might have. Psychologists' research on this topic can have one of two foci: effects on infants and effects on parents. The consensus that has emerged among

(continued)

developmental psychologists is that infants need to spend approximately the first 4 months of life with a stable caregiver—usually the mother, but equally well the father or some other caring adult, such as a grandparent. This pattern allows infants to form strong and stable attachments to the caregiver and to establish self-regulation of body processes, such as sleeping regularly through the night, feeding at regular times, and learning that they can trust that the food will be there. Therefore, psychologists such as Edward Zigler testified before Congress that legislation should provide 4 months of parental leave to meet the important developmental needs of an infant. This expert testimony on psychological research was influential in the passage of the bill.

As a specialist in the psychology of women, I immediately noticed that the well-being of mothers was invisible in the debate. Therefore, my colleagues and I conducted a large-scale research project that adds a second focus to the psychological research: the effects of parental leave, or the lack of it, on mothers and fathers. Our study was begun before the federal legislation, but there was legislation in Wisconsin that provided 6 weeks of parental leave. Under those conditions, men took an average of 5 days of leave and women took an average of 8 weeks. We are studying the impact of taking a short leave (6 weeks or less) compared with a long leave (12 weeks or more) on women's mental health. We have found that a short leave seems to act as a risk factor for problems such as depression when the short leave is combined with some other risk factor such as a stressful marriage or stressful job. For example, women who took short leaves and had many concerns about their marriage had elevated levels of depression, compared with women who took longer leaves or who took short leaves but had happy marriages. We also found that many of the women in our sample wished they could have taken a longer leave than they did. The leading reason why they didn't take a longer leave was that they could not afford to do so.

This research and the research of developmental psychologists on infants' attachment needs illustrate how important psychological research can be in framing legislation that will have an impact on most of us at some time in our lives.

SOURCES: Hyde & Essex (1991); Hyde, Essex, & Horton (1993); Hyde et al. (1995); Kamerman (2000); Zigler & Frank (1988).

Work/family issues are among those at the top of the feminist agenda. Does combining work and motherhood serve as a source of stress, or does it enhance women's well-being?

The Second Shift   In 1989, sociologist Arlie Hochschild published a book entitled *The Second Shift: Working Parents and the Revolution at Home.* The title reflects her finding that most employed women put in a full day of work on the job and then return home to perform a second shift of house and family work.

Studies in the 1970s found that if work is defined to include work for pay outside the home plus work done in the home, then women work, on average, 15 hours more per week than men do (Hochschild, 1989). Over the course of a year, women work an extra month of 24-hour days. In earlier sections of this chapter, we have discussed the wage gap between women and men. Here what we see is a leisure gap.

The problem of the dual duty for women—job and family work—is more than just a question of hours, though. Hochschild found that women were also more emotionally torn between the demands of work and the demands of family. In addition, the second shift creates a struggle in some marriages. The wife, in many cases, struggles to convince the husband to share the housework equally; alternatively, she does almost all of it and resents the fact that she does. And even when husbands share slightly or equally in doing the housework, women are still *responsible* for all of it.

Hochschild concluded that we are living in a time of transition amidst a social revolution in which gender roles have changed and women have been catapulted into the world of paid work. In this period of transition, we have not yet arrived at stabilized social structures. In a sense, the revolution seemed to have stalled in 1989. On the one hand, we no longer had the mythical, stable but patriarchal, White, middle-class family, with the wife at home, having no economic power. On the other, we had not yet achieved a system in which women have equal relationships with men at work and at home.

Hochschild's arguments have been challenged by some researchers (e.g., Gilbert, 1993; Pleck, 1992). These researchers raise two basic issues: First, Hochschild may have taken insufficient account of changes over the last 20 or 30 years. The evidence shows, for example, that men's contributions to family work have increased from 1970 to the present time, although gradually, and there is still not equity. Women have also altered the way they spend their time. Women today spend as much time with their children as they did in the 1960s: 5.3 hours per day in 1965, compared with 5.5 hours per day in 1998 (Bianchi, 2000). The dramatic change has been in the amount of time spent in housework. In 1965, employed women spent 23.6 hours per week in housework and nonemployed women spent 37.4 hours; today, employed women spend only 17.6 hours per week in housework and nonemployed women spend 25.0 (Bianchi, 2000). So, that's more like half of a second shift than a full second shift. (Remember, too, that many women work part time rather than full time, so they may have a half shift at work and a half shift at home.) Attitudes have also changed. In 1977, 57 percent of American adults agreed that "it is more important for a wife to help her husband's career than to have one herself"; by 1996, only 21 percent agreed.

Second, Hochschild did not sufficiently recognize the diversity of arrangements that couples make in regard to sharing household tasks. For example, research by Lucia Gilbert on dual-career couples shows that they fall into three types: traditional/conventional, modern/participant, and egalitarian/role-sharing (Gilbert, 1985; Gilbert & Dancer, 1992). In the conventional dual-earner family, both partners are involved in careers, but the woman keeps all the responsibility for household work and childcare. Typically both members of the couple agree that work within the home is "women's work," and that men should be free of these obligations to pursue their careers, although they may "help out" a bit if time permits. Typically the man earns a much higher salary than the woman. These sound like the people in Hochschild's study. However, there are other types as well.

In the modern/participant type of relationship, parenting is shared between husband and wife, but household work is still the woman's responsibility. There is less male dominance and less division of labor by gender. Most of the men in these couples are highly motivated to be active fathers and to have close relationships with their children, but they are less interested in other aspects of family work.

The egalitarian/role-sharing couples participate equally in pursuing their careers, in parenting, and in household work. This is the most egalitarian pattern, and the one toward which many couples aspire. However, only approximately one-third of dual-career couples fall into this category, with one-third in the modern/participant and one-third in the traditional/conventional category.

In conclusion, then, the picture may not be as bleak as Hochschild painted it. Some men are contributing more toward home and family work, although more toward family than home. And Hochschild's portrait may still be accurate for a large number of dual-earner couples—just not all of them.

In Conclusion

What directions do we need to take for the future? In my view, we need a combination of private change and public change. In the private realm, gender roles must continue to change so that men contribute equally to and feel equal responsibility for household and childcare tasks. In the public realm, we need new social policies planned by the government that provide real support for two-earner

EXPERIENCE THE RESEARCH

ENTITLEMENT

In this exercise you will investigate Brenda Major's notion of entitlement and how it is related to the gender gap in wages.

Interview four psychology majors, two men and two women, preferably seniors. In each case, read them the following paragraph:

Imagine that you have just graduated with your degree in psychology. You want to get some research experience before deciding whether to go to graduate school. You manage to land a job as a full-time research assistant in the laboratory of a professor at the University of Wisconsin. What do you think your pay would be for your first year at that full-time job? How did you come up with that number—that is, what factors did you take into account?

Write down the gender of your respondent, his or her estimate of pay (be sure to get it in terms of an annual salary, not an hourly wage), and his or her reasoning about the pay.

Were your results consistent with Major's theory of entitlement? Did the men estimate higher salaries than the women? What factors did the women take into account in deciding on the salary? Were these factors different from the men's?

families—policies that are truly profamily. If our society wants to continue to have children reared within the nuclear family, it will have to offer some supports to that family. The U.S. government urgently needs to promote high-quality, affordable childcare. It also needs to devise a system to provide paid parental leave for new mothers and fathers, and opportunities for part-time work, flextime, and job sharing. Finally, we must have a uniform policy of pay equity so that women are paid fairly for the work they do. Many women, for example, would gladly work at 75 percent time if their full-time wage was decent, thereby easing some work and family tension. Only through this combination of private change and public change can we arrive at a new kind of social stability.

Suggestions for Further Reading

Barnett, Rosalind C., & Rivers, Caryl. (1996). *She works/he works: How two-income families are happier, healthier, and better-off.* San Francisco: Harper-SanFrancisco. Barnett, a psychologist who is prominent in work-family research, and Rivers, a journalist, teamed up to produce a very readable book that argues for the expansionist perspective—that women are better off when they combine multiple roles.

Costello, Cynthia B., & Stone, Anne J. (Eds.). (2001). *The American woman, 2001–2002: Getting to the top.* New York: Norton. Updated every two years, this book contains a wealth of statistical information on women and work, as well as many other women's issues.

Women and the Web

Women's Bureau of the U.S. Department of Labor. This website provides a wealth of up-to-date statistics on women's employment.
   http://www.dol.gov/dol/wb/

National Partnership for Women and Families. Formerly the Women's Legal Defense Fund, this organization "uses public education and advocacy to promote fairness in the workplace, quality health care, and policies that help women and men meet the dual demands of work and family."
   http://www.nationalpartnership.org/

National Institute for Occupational Safety and Health. This web site addresses women's safety and health issues at work.
   http://www.cdc.gov/niosh/womsaft.html

Biological Influences on Women's Behavior

10

. . . an extraordinarily important part of the brain necessary for spiritual life, the frontal convolutions and the temporal lobes are less well developed in women and this difference is inborn. . . . If we wish a woman to fulfill her task of motherhood fully, she cannot possess a masculine brain. If the feminine abilities were developed to the same degree as those of the male, her maternal organs would suffer, and we should have before us a repulsive and useless hybrid.

— FROM MOEBIUS, CONCERNING THE PHYSIOLOGICAL INTELLECTUAL FEEBLENESS OF WOMEN, 1907

The human brain is a spectacular organ, containing over 100 billion neurons. It is constantly rearranging its more than 100 trillion connections between neurons in response to learning and exposure to new stimuli. Spectacular though the human brain is, scientists have wondered, for more than 100 years, whether men's brains weren't more spectacular than women's. The psychologist quoted above, writing in 1907, is one example. Women have also been thought to be the victims of their "raging hormones." In this chapter we will examine the evidence on whether biological gender differences create psychological gender differences, and on whether women's behavior is controlled by biological forces.

The biological factors that may influence women and gender differences fall into three major categories: genetic factors, basic physiological processes, sex hormones, and brain differences.

Genes

Normal humans possess a set of 46 chromosomes in each cell of the body. Because chromosomes occur in pairs, there are 23 pairs, classified as 22 pairs of autosomes (nonsex chromosomes) and one pair of sex chromosomes. The female has a sex chromosome pair denoted XX, whereas the male sex chromosome pair is XY. Thus there are no genetic differences between males and females except for the sex chromosomes.

Traits that are controlled by genes on the sex chromosomes are called **sex-linked traits** (for an excellent explanation of sex-linked genetic effects as related to the psychology of women, see Wittig, 1979). For such traits, the female will have a pair of genes controlling a particular sex-linked trait, but the male will have only one gene for that trait, because he has only one X chromosome. The Y chromosome is small, containing fewer than 50 genes, compared with the

Sex-linked trait: A trait controlled by a gene on the X chromosome (and occasionally on the Y chromosome).

There is no evidence that genes influence math ability or other abilities, but the media are delighted by images of genetic female inferiority at math.

X chromosome, which contains between 1,000 and 2,000 genes (Wizemann & Pardue, 2001).

Rapid advances in genetic research during the past decade, including the Human Genome Project, have given us much better information about what's happening with the X and Y chromosomes. The Y chromosome, possessed only by males, contains a few especially interesting genes. One is the SRY (Sex-determining Region, Y chromosome) gene, which, during the prenatal period, directs the fetus's gonads to differentiate in a male direction, forming testes and then producing testosterone. It also contains a few genes related to male fertility (Lahn & Page, 1997).

The X chromosome, with its large number of genes, influences many aspects of the functioning of cells, growth, and development. It contains several genes responsible for differentiation of the ovaries during fetal development. But there is a difference between males and females in "gene dosage" from the X chromosome: Females have twice as many genes because they have two X chromosomes. This extra gene dosage is compensated for by a process called **X-chromosome inactivation**, in which one of the X chromo-

X-chromosome inactivation: In females, the process in which one of the two X chromosomes is inactivated or silenced in nearly every cell, so that only one chromosome functions.

somes is inactivated or silenced in almost all cells, so that only one X chromosome functions (Percec et al., 2002). The same X chromosome is not inactivated in every cell—in some cells the X chromosome from the mother is silenced, and in other cells it is the X chromosome from the father that is silenced. **Genomic imprinting** is the term for this process in which, in females, some genes from the maternal X chromosome and some genes from the paternal X chromosome are expressed (Ezzell, 1994; Wizemann & Pardue, 2001). In a few cells, no X inactivation occurs, so higher levels of the products of those chromosomes are present in those cells.

> **Genomic imprinting:** In females, the process in which some genes from the maternal X chromosome and some genes from the paternal Y chromosome are expressed.

Note that, in the case of the autosomes, both males and females have them in pairs, and both males and females receive one from their mother and one from their father. Therefore, the autosomes should not be a source of male-female differences in basic physiological processes—only the sex chromosomes should be. The autosomes, then, are sources of genetic gender similarities—and there are thousands of genes on the autosomes—whereas the sex chromosomes are sources of genetic gender differences.

Basic Physiological Processes

Males and females differ in a few basic physiological processes, including metabolism and drug absorption (Wizemann & Pardue, 2001). After puberty, males have more muscle mass and, on average, a lower percentage of body fat than females. Muscle tissue metabolizes faster than fat tissue, so males have larger energy requirements—they need more food. Stated conversely, women add fat if they consume the same food as that eaten by a man who does not add fat—even if the two have the same body size. Another example concerns P glycoprotein (Pgp), a protein found in the intestine and the liver that actively transports many drugs out of cells. Males have about twice the level of Pgp in the liver that females have (Schuetz et al., 1995). This suggests that some drugs may have an effect faster in males than in females. Physiological processes such as these are important as we consider women and health issues (see Chapter 11).

Although these gender differences in basic physiological processes are important to health, there is little evidence that they have behavioral or psychological effects. Yet there are exceptions. For example, meta-analyses show that females are more sensitive to pain than males are, an effect that is found across many species (Berkley & Holdcroft, 1999; Riley et al., 1998) and is thought to be related to gender differences in levels of testosterone and estrogen (Wizemann & Pardue, 2001). This brings us to another biological factor that may influence gender differences.

Sex Hormones

Hormones are powerful chemical substances manufactured by the various endocrine glands of the body. Endocrine glands secrete hormones into the bloodstream so that they can have effects throughout the body, including effects on target organs far from the endocrine gland that secreted them. Among the endocrine glands are the gonads (ovaries and testes), pituitary, thyroid, and adrenal glands.

The "male" sex hormone is called **testosterone.** It is one of a group of "male" hormones called **androgens,** which are manufactured by the testes. The "female" sex hormones are **estrogen** and **progesterone,** which are manufactured by the ovaries. If these hormones influence behavior, then they may create gender differences.

Testosterone: A "male" sex hormone; one of the androgens.

Actually, it is a mistake to call testosterone the "male" sex hormone and estrogen and progesterone "female" hormones. Testosterone, for example, is found in females as well as males. The difference is in amount, not presence or absence. In women, testosterone is manufactured by the adrenal gland and the ovaries, and the level in women's blood is one-tenth or less that in men's (Janowsky et al., 1998). "Female" hormones are also found in men's blood.

Androgens: A group of "male" sex hormones, including testosterone, produced more abundantly in males than in females.

Estrogen: A "female" sex hormone produced by the ovaries; also produced in smaller quantities in males.

The differences in levels of sex hormones may affect behavior at two major stages of development: prenatally (the time between conception and birth), and during and after puberty (adulthood). Endocrinologists refer to the effects that occur prenatally or very early in development as *organizing effects,* because they cause a relatively permanent effect in the organization of some structure, whether in the nervous system or the reproductive system. Hormone effects in adulthood are called *activating effects* because they activate or deactivate certain behaviors. To understand the **prenatal** effects, we need to examine the process of prenatal gender differentiation first.

Progesterone: A "female" sex hormone produced by the ovaries; also produced in smaller quantities in males.

Prenatal: Before birth.

Prenatal Gender Differentiation   Gender differences exist at the moment of conception. If the fertilized egg contains two X chromosomes, then the genetic gender of the individual is female; if it contains one X and one Y chromosome, the genetic gender is male. The single cell then divides repeatedly, becoming an embryo, then a fetus. Interestingly, during the first six weeks of human prenatal development, the only differences between females and males are in genetic gender. That is, anatomically and physiologically, males and females develop identically during this period. Beginning approximately during the sixth week of

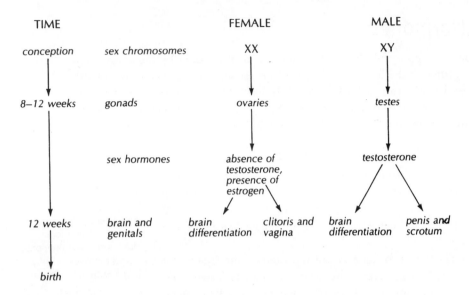

FIGURE 10.1
The sequences of prenatal differentiation of females and males.

pregnancy, and continuing through about the sixth month, the process of prenatal gender differentiation occurs. First, the sex chromosomes direct the differentiation of the gonads (Figure 10.1). An XX chromosome complement directs the differentiation of ovaries; an XY complement produces testes. The gonads then begin secreting sex hormones. Thus the internal environment becomes different for females and males because of hormonal differences.

The sex hormones further affect the course of fetal differentiation. The male testes produce testosterone. If testosterone is present, a penis forms. If testosterone is not present, a clitoris and vagina differentiate. Research indicates that the presence of estrogen may also be critical for the development of female sexual organs (Fausto-Sterling, 1992; Wilson et al., 1984). In addition to influencing the process of anatomical gender differentiation, the sex hormones influence the developing brain. The structure most affected seems to be the hypothalamus. The importance of this differentiation will be discussed later in the chapter.

Prenatal Sex Hormone Effects   Male fetuses and female fetuses, then, live in different hormonal environments. Does this have any effect on later behaviors?

Most of the evidence in this area is based on experiments done with animals. It may be that the effects on humans would not be the same. But let us consider the animal experiments, and then see what is known about similar processes in humans. (For a review, see Ehrhardt & Meyer-Bahlburg, 1981.)

Prenatal sex hormone exposure seems to affect mainly two behaviors: *sexual behavior* and *aggressive behavior*. The organizing effects of sex hormones on sexual behavior have been well documented. In a classic experiment, testosterone was administered to pregnant female guinea pigs (Phoenix et al., 1959). The female offspring that had been exposed to testosterone prenatally were, in adulthood, incapable of displaying female sexual behavior (in particular, lordosis, which is a sexual posturing involving arching of the back and raising the hindquarters so that the male can insert the penis). It is thought that this occurred because the testosterone "organized" the brain tissue (particularly the hypothalamus) in a male fashion. These female offspring were also born with masculinized genitals, and thus their reproductive systems had also been organized in the male direction. But the important point here is that the prenatal doses of testosterone had masculinized their sexual behavior. Similar results have been obtained in experiments with many other species as well (Hines & Collaer, 1993).

In adulthood, these hormonally masculinized females displayed mounting behavior, a male sexual behavior. When they were given testosterone in adulthood, they showed about as much mounting behavior as males did. Thus the testosterone administered in adulthood *activated* male patterns of sexual behavior.

The analogous experiment on males would be castration at birth followed by administration of female sex hormones in adulthood. When this was done with rats, female sexual behavior resulted. These male rats responded to mating attempts from normal males the way females usually do (Harris & Levine, 1965). Apparently the brain tissue had been organized in a female direction during an early critical period when testosterone was absent, and the female behavior patterns were activated in adulthood by administration of ovarian hormones.

Similar effects have also been demonstrated for aggressive behavior (Beatty, 1992). Early exposure to testosterone increases the fighting behavior of female mice (Edwards, 1969). Female rhesus monkeys given early exposure to testosterone show a higher incidence of rough-and-tumble play (Young et al., 1964). Thus early exposure to testosterone also organizes aggressive behavior in a "masculine" direction.

What relevance do these studies have for humans? (For a review, see Collaer & Hines, 1995.) It would be unethical, of course, to do experiments like the ones discussed above on human participants. Nonetheless, a number of "natural" experiments and "accidental" experiments of this sort occur. The natural experiments are the result of a few genetic conditions that cause abnormal hormone functioning prenatally. The accidental experiments have occurred when pregnant women were given drugs containing hormones. (These drugs are no longer administered during pregnancy.) We will consider one of the genetic syndromes.

Congenital adrenal hyperplasia or **CAH** (also known as adrenogenital syndrome or AGS) is a rare recessive genetic condition that causes the fetus's adrenal glands to produce abnormally large amounts of androgens beginning about three months after

Congenital adrenal hyperplasia (CAH): A rare genetic condition that causes the fetus's adrenal glands to produce abnormally large amounts of androgens. In genetic females, the result may be a girl born with masculinized genitals. Also called adrenogenital syndrome.

conception. CAH is most interesting in genetic females, for whom the testosterone exposure is particularly abnormal. Researchers have studied the behavior of CAH girls (Collaer & Hines, 1995; Hines & Kaufman, 1994). CAH girls are significantly more likely, compared with a control group of non-CAH sisters, to choose male-stereotyped toys for play and to prefer active, rough play. These outcomes with humans, then, look much like the experiments with animals, although the effects with humans seem to be smaller and more subtle.

Some cautions must be sounded about the research with humans. First, CAH girls are born with masculine-appearing genitals and generally must undergo surgery to correct the problem. We have no idea how traumatic that might be, nor whether that trauma would have an effect on behavior. Second, the girl's parents know about the genetic condition. Might parents of CAH girls treat them differently than they would normal daughters?

Hormone Effects in Adulthood   The effects of sex hormones in adulthood that are of interest to us fall into two categories. First, sex hormone levels in women fluctuate over the menstrual cycle. This raises the question of whether these hormone fluctuations cause fluctuations in mood or other psychological characteristics. (See Chapter 11 for a detailed discussion of this topic.) Second, levels of sex hormones differ in men and women. For example, as noted earlier, women have only about one-tenth the level of testosterone in the blood that men do. Could it be that these different levels of hormones "activate" different behaviors in men and women?

As noted above, studies done with animals indicate that sex hormones in adulthood have effects on both aggressive behavior and sexual behavior. Are there similar effects in humans? Testosterone has well-documented effects on libido or sex drive in humans (Carani et al., 1990; Carter, 1992; Everitt & Bancroft, 1991). For example, men deprived of their main source of testosterone by castration show a dramatic decrease in sexual behavior in some, but not all, cases. Testosterone therefore has an activating effect in maintaining sexual desire in adult men. Research indicates that androgens, not estrogen, are related to sexual desire in women (Bancroft, 1987; Hutchinson, 1995; Sherwin, 1991). If all sources of androgens in women (the adrenals and the ovaries) are removed, women lose sexual desire. For example, one study investigated the sexual functioning of women who had marked androgen deficiencies because they had undergone either chemotherapy for cancer or an oophorectomy (surgical removal of the ovaries) (Kaplan & Owett, 1993). These women showed a marked decline in sexual desire. Women who seek sex therapy for low sexual desire have, on average, lower androgen levels than age-matched controls (Guay & Jacobson, 2002). Moreover, androgens have been used successfully in the treatment of women with low sexual desire (Kaplan & Owett, 1993). Androgen levels decline with age in women, and research shows that administration of DHEA (an adrenal androgen) to women over 60 results in increased sexual desire (Baulieu et al., 2000). Interestingly, these androgen effects in women were overlooked for decades and have been uncovered only recently in research. Perhaps researchers had trouble believing that "male" sex hormones existed in women, and it would have been a huge stretch to imagine that such hormones actually had effects.

One innovative study examined the behavior of both male-to-female and female-to-male transsexuals before and after they began hormone treatments for their sex change (Van Goozen et al., 1995). When androgens were administered to the female-to-male transsexuals, their aggression proneness and sexual arousability increased. When anti-androgen drugs were given to the male-to-female transsexuals, their aggression proneness and sexual arousability decreased. These results are consistent with the notion that sex hormones have activating effects on aggressive and sexual behaviors in humans.

To summarize, sex hormone levels probably do have some effects on adult human behaviors, particularly aggressive and sexual behaviors. It is also likely that these effects are not as strong as they are in animals, and that they are more complex and interact more with environmental factors.

More Complex Hormone Models   The traditional model in psychology has maintained that "hormones influence behavior"—in other words, that the influence goes in one direction only. Feminists have been critical of this model. Recall from Chapter 1 that feminists urge researchers to consider bidirectional models: "A influences B, but B may also influence A." As it turns out, hormone researchers have been working on exactly these sorts of effects. For example, if women engage in resistance exercise, it raises their testosterone levels (Nindl et al., 2001). That is, behavior influences hormones! We shouldn't settle for simple, biologically deterministic models that assume that hormones determine behavior, or that biological factors such as hormones are fixed and unchanging. Nor should we ignore hormones completely. In short, we need more complex models that will help us understand how hormones and behavior influence each other.

The Brain

In this section we will consider various hypotheses that have been proposed about differences between male and female brains and what effects those differences might have on behavior.

Brain Size   A century ago, scientists discovered that human males had somewhat larger brains than human females. In the culture of the time, they concluded that this brain difference was the cause of the well-known lesser intelligence of women. The hypothesis was later discredited when other scientists found that males' larger brain size was almost entirely accounted for by their

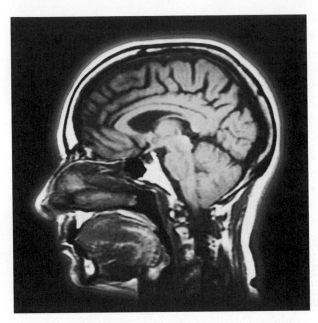

The female brain, a magnificent organ.

greater body size. Elephants have pretty big brains, too, but you wouldn't want to use that as a basis for putting them in charge of the space program.

Amazingly, this same brain-size hypothesis resurfaced in the 1990s. Two different scientists found that men's brains were larger in volume and weighed more than women's, and they argued that this brain difference had an impact on gender differences in intelligence (Ankney, 1992; Rushton, 1992). Interestingly, the same scientists also claimed that Caucasian Americans had larger brains than African Americans and that Asian Americans had larger brains than either group (Rushton, 1992)—so the argument had racial dimensions as well, but here we will focus on the argument about gender.

Feminist biologist Anne Fausto-Sterling provided a detailed critique of this work (Fausto-Sterling, 1993, 2000). First, there is disagreement among scientists about how large the difference in brain size is—estimates range between 10 percent and 17 percent. Second, some of the studies have not actually measured brain size directly. Some have measured the inside volume of skulls, but there is more inside the skull than just the brain, so this isn't a good measure of brain size. And Rushton, the leading proponent of the brain-size argument, actually just measured the outside of people's heads. Third, Rushton used a complicated and questionable formula that indicated that men had larger brains relative to

Differences between male and female brains have been much publicized. However, research evidence is ambiguous and inconsistent.

body size than women did; however, according to Fausto-Sterling's computations, if you simply take the ratio of brain size to body weight, women actually had relatively larger brains. Finally, the question still remains whether brain size has anything to do with intelligence. No one has good evidence—pro or con—on whether it does. Therefore, there doesn't seem to be any reason to stay awake at night worrying about women's somewhat smaller brains.

The Hypothalamus Gender differences do exist in the hypothalamus, a tiny region of the brain on its lower side (Collaer & Hines, 1995). These differences are the result of differentiation of brain tissue in the course of fetal development, much as is the case for the reproductive organs (see Figure 10.1). Additional differentiation occurs in the days immediately after birth. Recall that the sequence of normal development consists of the sex chromosomes directing the differentiation of gonadal tissue into ovaries or testes. The gonads then secrete appropriate-gender hormones, which cause further reproductive-system differentiation. The fetal sex hormones also cause gender differentiation of the hypothalamus (Breedlove, 1994; Fitch & Bimonte, 2002).

Hypothalamus: A part of the brain that is important in regulating certain body functions, including sex hormone production.

Basically, then, brain differentiation in the fetus is a process much like reproductive-system differentiation.

One of the most important organizing effects of prenatal sex hormones is the determination of the estrogen sensitivity of certain cells in the hypothalamus, called *estrogen receptors* (Choi et al., 2001; McEwen, 2001; Taleisnik et al., 1971). If testosterone is present during fetal development, certain specialized receptor cells in the hypothalamus become insensitive to estrogen; if estrogen is present, these cells are highly sensitive to levels of estrogen in the bloodstream. This is important because of the hypothalamic-pituitary-gonadal regulating feedback loop (see Chapter 11). In this process, gonadal hormone output is regulated by the pituitary, which is in turn regulated by the hypothalamus. The hypothalamus responds to the level of gonadal hormones in the bloodstream. Male hypothalamic cells are relatively insensitive to estrogen levels, whereas female hypothalamic cells are highly sensitive to them. We also know that estrogen (and progesterone as well) lowers the threshold of central nervous system (CNS) excitability in adults. Hence, the estrogen-sensitivity effect amounts to a greater increase in CNS excitability in response to estrogen in the female than it does in the male. The estrogen-sensitivity effect is a result of the organizing effect of hormones. Hormones administered in adulthood activate male and female nervous systems differentially depending on early determination (organizing effects) of estrogen sensitivity.

What are the observable consequences of these gender differences in the hypothalamus? One consequence is the determination of a cyclic or acyclic pattern of pituitary release of hormones (Barraclough & Gorski, 1961). The hypothalamus directs pituitary hormone secretion. A hypothalamus that has undergone female differentiation will direct the pituitary to release hormones cyclically, creating a menstrual cycle, whereas a male hypothalamus directs a relatively steady production of pituitary hormones.

The gender differences in the hypothalamus may have some consequences for behavior, too (for a review, see Collaer & Hines, 1995). As discussed earlier, the organization of the hypothalamus in a male or a female direction may have some influence on both sexual and aggressive behavior.

The Callosal Issue   Some researchers claim that there are differences between males and females in the corpus callosum, a region in the central part of the brain containing fibers that connect the right hemisphere and left hemisphere. The original report, based on research with 9 male and 5 female humans, documented a larger corpus callosum (CC)—actually, one larger subsection of the corpus callosum, the splenium—in women than in men (Delacoste-Utamsing & Holloway, 1982). But these findings have been disputed (Bishop & Wahlsten, 1997; Fausto-Sterling, 2000). Later studies found inconsistent results. Finally, researchers conducted a meta-analysis. What it revealed is that men have a slightly larger CC overall ($d = 0.21$), probably because men are slightly larger,

Compared with men, women show significantly better recovery of language following damage to the left hemisphere as a result of a stroke.

but that there are no gender differences in the size or shape of the splenium (Bishop & Wahlsten, 1997). Once again, gender similarities are the rule, even when it comes to brain anatomy.

To make matters more complicated and interesting, certain regions of the corpus callosum increase in size in women through their 50s, whereas for men the size peaks in their 20s to 30s and then declines (Cowell et al., 1992). These findings defy the notion that brain anatomy is fixed and unchanging. They also challenge simple characterizations of gender differences. One might even conclude that women's brains continue to develop longer than men's do!

What does all this have to do with behavior? One finding is that women show significantly better recovery of language following damage to the left hemisphere—for example, following a stroke (Fitch & Bimonte, 2002). This outcome may be related to the corpus callosum, or it may result from the direct effects of estrogen on the cortex. Estrogen has very nice protective effects on the adult and aging brain (Wise et al., 2001). Some have argued—and others have disputed—that the gender difference in the corpus callosum may also be related to gender differences in use of the right hemisphere of the brain versus the left hemisphere (for a review, see Fausto-Sterling, 2000). But as we just saw, according to a meta-analysis, gender differences in the CC are at most tiny.

Right Hemisphere, Left Hemisphere The brain is divided into two halves, a right hemisphere and a left hemisphere. It is thought that these two hemispheres carry out somewhat different functions. In particular, in right-handed, normal persons, the left hemisphere is specialized for language and verbal tasks, and the right hemisphere for spatial tasks. The term **lateralization** refers to the extent to which a particular function, say, verbal processing, is handled by one hemisphere rather than both. Thus, for example, if verbal processing in one person is handled entirely in the left hemisphere, we would say that that person is highly lateralized or completely lateralized. If another person processes verbal material using both hemispheres, we would say that that person is bilateral for verbal functioning.

> **Lateralization:** The extent to which one hemisphere of the brain organizes a particular mental process or behavior.

Based on the old belief that there are gender differences in both verbal ability and spatial ability (see Chapter 8), various theories have been proposed using gender differences in brain lateralization to account for the supposed differences in abilities. We will consider one of these theories and the evidence for it below (for detailed reviews, see Halpern, 1992; Sherman, 1978).

The *cognitive crowding hypothesis* was proposed by psychologist Jere Levy (Levy, 1976; Levy-Agresti & Sperry, 1968). Levy believes that spatial ability is optimized when it is strongly lateralized in one hemisphere. Furthermore, she believes that when verbal processes are lateralized completely in one hemisphere, and spatial processes in the other, the neural connections function the best and performance is best. If lateralization is not strong, then the processes for two different abilities (verbal ability and spatial ability) will occur in the same hemisphere, but essentially there is not enough "neural space" for this to work well, and performance is impaired. Levy argues that, in such cases, verbal processes dominate and spatial ability therefore suffers.

Levy also believes that females are less lateralized than males and are therefore more likely to be bilateral for verbal ability. More neural space is devoted to verbal ability; therefore, females outperform males on tests of verbal ability. At the same time, spatial performance suffers. So, in one neat package, Levy explains both females' superior verbal performance and their inferior spatial performance.

What evidence is there for the cognitive crowding hypothesis? Psychologists typically use two types of tasks in brain lateralization research. One is the dichotic listening task. The researcher presents different stimuli to each ear through headphones. As it turns out, people have ear—or hearing—dominance on the same side as hand dominance. If you are right-handed, you are also right-eared! That is, your right ear is more ready, willing, and able to process stimuli than your left ear is. This, in turn, relates to the hemispheres of the brain. Researchers in this field believe that the more dominant your right ear is (in accuracy and speed of processing stimuli), the more lateralized you are; the same would be true if you were very left-ear dominant. The other task used in this research is the split visual field, in which different stimuli are presented to different sides of your eyes, much like the different stimuli to different ears.

What does the evidence for the cognitive crowding hypothesis say? According to some studies, dichotic listening tasks tend to show that males have a greater right-ear dominance for verbal stimuli than females do, indicating that males are more lateralized for verbal processes (for a review, see Halpern, 1992). The studies are conflicting, though. Fortunately, a meta-analysis is available, based on 266 studies. It shows that—whether measured in the visual or auditory mode, and whether verbal or nonverbal tasks are used—gender differences in lateralization are close to zero, $d = 0.06$ (Voyer, 1996). Clearly, then, statements such as "women are left-brained, men are right-brained" are far from the truth.

The other serious criticism of the hypothesis is that it is designed to explain gender differences in verbal abilities and spatial abilities, yet the results of meta-analyses indicate that currently there are no gender differences in verbal ability, and there are large gender differences in only one type of spatial ability (see Chapter 8).

Brain lateralization is an active area of research, and there are often flashy newspaper or magazine articles on a scientist who has discovered *the* cause of gender differences in abilities based on right-hemisphere/left-hemisphere differences. Thus it is worthwhile for you to know the kinds of theories that have been proposed and the meta-analytic results based on 266 studies (Voyer, 1996).

EXPERIENCE THE RESEARCH

BIOLOGY AND GENDER DIFFERENCES IN THE MEDIA

Search through old issues of *Time, Newsweek, U.S. News & World Report,* or your local newspaper to find at least two articles that report on gender differences. Do the articles report on a psychological gender difference or a biological one? If it is a psychological gender difference, what explanation does the author of the article offer—does the author imply that it is biologically caused or environmentally caused, or is there a balanced discussion of both possibilities? If the article is about a biological gender difference, what is it? Is the information consistent with what you have learned in this chapter?

In Conclusion

We have considered four major classes of biological influences on gender differences and women's behavior: genes, basic physiological processes, hormones, and brain factors. Genes are not likely to be sources of gender differences, except when the genes are on the Y or X chromosome, such as the gene that directs prenatal differentiation of the testes. Hormones have effects prenatally as well as in adulthood, particularly on sexual and aggressive behaviors, and possibly on behaviors related to the menstrual cycle. Regarding brain factors, males have slightly larger brains than females, but it is unclear whether this means anything. Gender differentiation of the hypothalamus in a female direction controls the cyclic functioning of the menstrual cycle and may be related to both aggressive and sexual behaviors. And, finally, gender differences in the size and shape of the corpus callosum are tiny, as are gender differences in hemispheric lateralization.

Suggestions for Further Reading

Angier, Natalie. (1999). *Woman: An intimate geography.* Boston: Houghton Mifflin. Angier, a Pulitzer Prize–winning journalist, uses lush prose to describe the female body and its functioning in new and insightful ways.

Fausto-Sterling, Anne. (2000). *Sexing the body: Gender politics and the construction of sexuality.* New York: Basic Books. Fausto-Sterling, a brilliant feminist biologist, has put together a revealing history of biologists' attempts to understand gender and sexuality and the misadventures along the way.

Women and the Web

Does Sex Matter? This report, developed by a blue-ribbon commission of the National Academy of Sciences, is charged with understanding biological sex differences and their impact on health and disease.

http://www.nimh.nih.gov/wmhc/doessexmatter.pdf

Psychology and Women's Health Issues

11

[There is] an imperative need for women everywhere to learn about our bodies in order to have control over them and over our lives. We seek to communicate our excitement about the power of shared information; to assert that in an age of professionals, we are the best experts on ourselves and our feelings; to continue the collective struggle for adequate health care.

— FROM OUR BODIES, OURSELVES

One of the most important parts of the feminist movement of the past decades has been the women's health movement. It is based on the belief that women need to know more about their bodies in order to have more control over them. One of the best books to come out of that movement is *Our Bodies, Ourselves,* written by the Boston Women's Health Book Collective (1976, 1998).

In this chapter we will consider some of the topics that are important in the women's health movement—menstruation, menopause, abortion, breast cancer, and AIDS. I will give brief information on the physical and medical aspects of each of these topics and concentrate on the psychological research that has been done on them. But first, I will review the overall statistics on gender and health and how women fare in the health care system.

Gender and Health

At every moment from conception to death, males have a higher death rate than females (Strickland, 1988). Approximately 125 male fetuses are conceived for every 100 female fetuses (it is thought that the Y chromosome–bearing sperm are a bit lighter and swim faster to the egg), yet only 106 live male babies are born for every 100 female babies. At the other end of the lifespan, among those who are 100 or older, there are five women for every man. For a baby born in the United States today, the average life expectancy is 79 years for women and 72 years for men (Collins et al., 1994).

Data on the ten leading causes of death for males and females are shown in Table 11.1. Some patterns are strikingly gender differentiated. Suicide is on the "Top Ten" list only for males, not females. The same is true for death by homicide. Accidents are far more likely to be killers for males than for females.

Gender similarities are also striking. Heart disease and cancer are the top two causes of death for both males and females, for all ethnic groups. Despite the stereotype that heart attacks are a male problem, heart disease is the leading killer of women from nearly every ethnic group. We will return to this issue of women and heart disease in a later section.

TABLE 11.1
Life Expectancy and Ten Leading Causes of Death for Females and Males, by Ethnicity (number of deaths per 100,000 people in the population)

	Females					Males				
	Whites	Blacks	Amer. Indians	Asian/ Pacific Islanders	Hispanics	Whites	Blacks	Amer. Indians	Asian/ Pacific Islanders	Hispanics
Life expectancy (years)	80.0	74.8				74.5	67.6			
Causes of death:										
Heart disease	287	224	91	70	79	279	227	110	99	86
Cancers	201	159	73	74	61	224	198	80	89	68
Cerebrovascular diseases (e.g., stroke)	79	60	26	29	20	50	48	20	29	18
Respiratory diseases	51	19	17	7	8	52	27	17	14	10
Pneumonia and influenza	28	17	14	7	7	22	*	12	9	*
Accidents	26	22	36	10	13	48	53	75	19	42
Alzheimer's disease	26	*	*	*	*	*	*	*	*	*
Diabetes	25	39	33	11	18	23	*	27	10	15
Liver diseases	*	*	18	*	5	13	*	25	*	14
Suicide	*	*	*	*	*	19	*	20	9	9
Kidney diseases	13	20	10	5	5	12	18	*	6	*
Septicemia	12	18	7	4	*	*	*	*	*	*
HIV	*	13	*	*	*	*	33	*	*	*
Assault (homicide)	*	*	*	*	*	*	38	15	4	15
All other causes	177	171	106	52	70	169	192	113	65	83

* Not in the top ten for this group.

SOURCE: National Center for Health Statistics (2001), Table 1 (causes of death) and Table 12 (life expectancy).

Notice, too, that some ethnic variations are substantial. White and Black women are highly likely to die from heart disease, whereas American Indian and Asian American women and Latinas have far lower death rates from heart disease. These differences are largely due to the different age distributions of people in these ethnic groups. Asian Americans and Latinas are, on the whole, younger than Whites and Blacks, partly because of immigration of young people. Heart disease is a disease of the middle-aged and elderly, so there are simply more Blacks and Whites in the age range for heart disease. Differences in diet are another likely factor.

Heart Disease   Heart disease is influenced by genetics, age, and behavior (Wizemann & Pardue, 2001). High cholesterol levels and high blood pressure are two of the leading risk factors for heart disease, and cholesterol levels are genetically influenced. In addition, estrogen has positive effects on cholesterol so that, before menopause, estrogen is a protective factor against heart disease for women (Gura, 1995). In terms of behavioral factors, cigarette smoking is a major risk, and men are more likely to be smokers, although, unfortunately, women are catching up. Another behavioral factor is diet, which can raise or lower cholesterol levels. Regular exercise is a behavior that protects against heart disease.

Typically women manifest heart disease ten years later than men do (Wizemann & Pardue, 2001). Men are more likely to first present with heart disease by having a myocardial infarction (MI, or heart attack), but MIs are more often fatal for women, especially Black women (Knox & Czajkowski, 1997). The problem, then, is that women are more likely to have a "silent" form of heart disease that doesn't manifest itself in the flashy way men's heart disease does, with a collapsing-on-the-ground, painful heart attack that absolutely everyone notices. Women, in contrast, are more likely to experience angina, or chest pain, which is often ignored both by them and by their physicians.

Coronary artery bypass graft (CABG) is a surgical intervention that can substantially reduce the risk of fatal heart attacks. Gender appears to be a factor in physicians' decisions about the use of this procedure (Travis & Compton, 2001). Women are considerably less likely to receive this intervention than men are. Women may be more likely to have a medical condition, such as diabetes, that makes CABG inadvisable. But that is only part of the story. Women are more likely to be poor, and income is a factor in whether a person receives this surgery. Stereotypes about gender and heart disease probably play a role as well. The evidence indicates that women are also less likely to receive a number of other crucial interventions for heart disease (Knox & Czajkowski, 1997; Schulman et al., 1999).

In short, women with heart disease are more likely to go undiagnosed and untreated so that, when they do finally have a heart attack, they die from it. The combination of different body functioning and societal stereotypes can be lethal.

Discrimination and Health Emerging evidence is beginning to indicate that stereotypes and discrimination can be hard on your health! In one study, researchers used Claude Steele's stereotype-threat manipulation (discussed in Chapter 3). African American and White college students were placed in either a stereotype-threat condition or a control condition and then worked on some difficult tests (Blascovich et al., 2001). African Americans under stereotype threat not only performed worse but also exhibited larger increases in blood pressure compared with Whites or with African Americans not under stereotype threat. And high blood pressure, of course, is a major risk factor for heart disease. In another study, African American and White women were asked to imagine that they had been wrongfully accused of shoplifting in a department store and then to speak in their own defense (Guyll et al., 2001). African American women, but not White women, reacted with elevated blood pressure.

Stereotype threats and incidents of discrimination may be chronic, repeated stressors in the lives of women, particularly ethnic minority women, that pose serious risks to their health.

Women and the Health Care System

Feminists have been critical of the treatment of women in the health care system. These criticisms can be summarized in the following four points (Landrine & Klonoff, 2001; Travis, 1988a, 1993; Travis & Compton, 2001).

1. The physician-patient relationship reflects the subordinate status of women in society, with the physician (usually male) having power and control over the female patient. Research shows that women's visits with female physicians are much more egalitarian (Roter & Hall, 1997).

2. The medical profession has actively discriminated against women as practitioners (Walsh, 1977). Around 1900, most medical schools refused to admit women. Women were not admitted to the American Medical Association until 1915. Although women now earn 41 percent of M.D. degrees (Costello & Stone, 2001), they still often receive their medical training in an atmosphere that is hostile to women. For example, in a study done on the treatment of women in the medical school at my own university, it was found that women doing their residency in surgery were often referred to by the male surgeons as "skirts." The status of nurses (over 90 percent of whom are women) in relation to physicians also reflects the higher status of male-dominated professions and the lower status of female-dominated professions.

3. Medical care offered to women is often inadequate, irresponsible, or uncaring. As many as 70 percent of **hysterectomies** (surgical removal of the uterus) are unnecessary (Broder et al., 2000).

   Hysterectomy: Surgical removal of the uterus.

Women are 55 percent more likely than men to receive a prescription for an anti-anxiety drug or an antidepressant during an office visit with a physician (Simoni-Wastila, 1998; Svarstad, 1987), leading some to conclude that women's health problems are likely to be misdiagnosed as psychological.

4. Medical research conducted on women is often irresponsible or simply missing. For example, far more contraceptives have been developed for females than for males, and thus the health risks associated with them have been borne disproportionately by women. One notorious example is the Dalkon Shield, an IUD (intrauterine device) that was withdrawn from the market after 17 women died of pelvic inflammatory disease directly traceable to the IUD (Travis, 1988a). Ethnicity is another factor relating to risky research. For example, the initial field trials for the birth control pill, whose risk was unknown at the time, were conducted among poor women in Puerto Rico. Also serious is the fact that women often have not been included in clinical trials of drugs or other medical interventions, and even when they have been, gender has not been analyzed so it is impossible to tell whether the drug is as effective in women as it is in men (Sherman et al., 1995).

Regarding the last point, these problems with clinical trials were documented in a scathing 1992 report by the U.S. Government's General Accounting Office. A number of women in Congress, such as Pat Schroeder, successfully introduced legislation, passed in 1993, requiring that clinical trials involving a disease found in both women and men be carried out in a way that allows the researchers to determine whether the treatment affects women or members of ethnic minority groups differently from others. This represents an enormous and powerful change in public policy (Helmuth, 2000).

Health Needs of Poor and Minority Women   Feminist theory emphasizes the importance not only of gender, but of ethnicity and social class as well. That principle is important as we consider the health care system.

Ethnic minority women have a number of special health concerns (Adler, 1997; Travis & Compton, 2001; Zambrana, 1988):

1. Poor and ethnic minority women experience higher rates of infant mortality than White women. This in turn is related to higher rates of low-birth-weight babies among ethnic minority women. And this in turn is related to more frequent adolescent childbearing among ethnic minorities. That is, adolescent mothers are more likely to have low-birth-weight babies, who have a higher death rate.

2. Chronic diseases are more prevalent among ethnic minority women than among White women. Examples include diabetes, high blood pressure, heart disease, and cervical cancer.

3. The life expectancy of ethnic minority women is five to seven years less than that of White women. This is a result, at least in part, of less access to medical care that would allow early detection and prevention of many diseases.

Ethnic minority women are overrepresented among the poor. We have, then, a combination of ethnicity and poverty contributing to reduced access to necessary health care. This is turn creates more health problems for these women. There is an urgent need for equal access to health care.

Menstruation

Biology of the Menstrual Cycle   The human female is born with approximately 400,000 primary follicles in her ovaries, each follicle containing an egg or **ovum.** (The term **follicle** here refers to a group of cells in the ovary that encapsulates an egg and has nothing to do with the term *hair follicle.*) A single menstrual cycle involves the release of one egg from a follicle, allowing it to move down the fallopian tube for possible fertilization and implantation in the uterus. Hence not more than 400 eggs are ovulated from puberty through menopause. The remaining follicles degenerate. (See Figure 11.1 for a diagram of women's reproductive anatomy.)

Ovum: An egg.

Follicle: The capsule of cells surrounding an egg in the ovary.

A menstrual cycle can be separated into four phases, each describing the state of the follicle and egg within that phase (see Figure 11.2). It would be most convenient to call the period of menstruation the first phase, because it is easily identifiable, but physiologically it represents the last. The first phase, called the **follicular phase,** extends approximately from day 4 to day 14 after menstruation begins. (In counting days of the cycle, day 1 is the first day of menstruation.) During this phase, a follicle matures and swells. The termination of this phase is marked by the rupturing of the follicle and the release of the egg (**ovulation**). During the next phase, the **luteal phase,** a group of reddish-yellow cells, called the corpus luteum, forms in the ruptured follicle. The final phase, marked by **menstruation,** represents a sloughing off of the inner lining (endometrium) of the uterus, which had built up in preparation for nourishing a fertilized egg.

Follicular phase: The first phase of the menstrual cycle, beginning just after menstruation.

Ovulation: Release of an egg from an ovary.

Luteal phase: The third phase of the menstrual cycle, after ovulation.

Menstruation: A bloody discharge of the lining of the uterus; the fourth phase of the menstrual cycle.

These cyclic phases are regulated by hormones that act in a negative feedback loop with one another (Figure 11.3), so that the production of a hormone increases to a high level, producing a desired physiological change. The level is then automatically reduced through the negative feedback loop. Here we are concerned with two basic groups of hormones—those produced by the

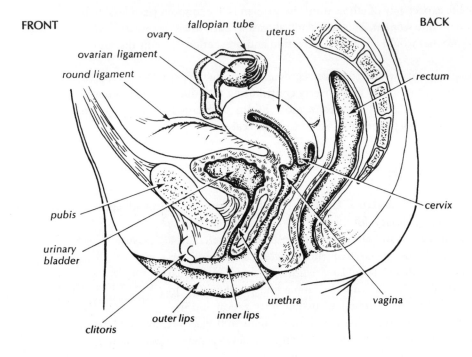

FIGURE 11.1
Schematic cross-section of the female pelvis, showing sexual and reproductive organs.

ovaries, most importantly estrogen and progesterone, and those produced by the pituitary gland, most importantly **follicle-stimulating hormone (FSH)** and **luteinizing hormone (LH).** We also need to consider control of the activity of the pituitary by the hypothalamus, an important region of the brain on its lower side (Figure 11.3), by Gn-RH **(gonadotropin-releasing hormone).** The overall pattern of the negative feedback loop is that the activity of the ovary, including its production of estrogen and progesterone, is regulated by the pituitary, which in turn is regulated by the hypothalamus, which is sensitive to the levels of estrogen produced by the ovaries.

The regulation of the menstrual cycle involves interactions among the levels of these hormones. The follicular phase of the cycle is initiated by the pituitary gland sending out follicle-stimulating hormone (FSH), which signals the ovaries to increase production of estrogen and to bring several follicles to

Follicle-stimulating hormone (FSH): A hormone secreted by the pituitary; in females it stimulates follicle and egg development.

Luteinizing hormone (LH): A hormone secreted by the pituitary; in females it triggers ovulation.

Gonadotropin-releasing hormone (Gn-RH): A hormone secreted by the hypothalamus that regulates the pituitary's secretion of hormones.

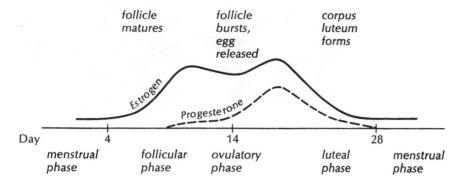

follicle
matures

follicle
bursts,
egg
released

corpus
luteum
forms

Estrogen

Progesterone

Day   4   14   28

menstrual   follicular   ovulatory   luteal   menstrual
phase   phase   phase   phase   phase

FIGURE 11.2
Changes in hormone levels over the phases of the menstrual cycle.

maturity. The resulting high level of estrogen, through the feedback loop, signals the pituitary to decrease production of FSH and to begin production of luteinizing hormone (LH), whose chief function is to trigger ovulation. Temporarily, FSH and LH induce even more estrogen production, which further lowers the amount of FSH. At this point the LH becomes dominant, causing the follicle to rupture and release the egg. The corpus luteum then forms in the ruptured follicle. The corpus luteum is a major source of progesterone. When progesterone levels are sufficiently high, they will, through the negative feedback loop, inhibit production of LH, and simultaneously stimulate the production of FSH, beginning the cycle over again.

Estrogen has a number of functions and effects in the body. It maintains the lining of the vagina and uterus and provides the initial stimulation for breast growth. Its nonreproductive functions include increasing water content and thickness of skin and retarding growth rate. At the beginning and the end of the menstrual cycle, estrogen is at a low level. In between these two times, it reaches two peaks, one immediately prior to and during ovulation, the other in the middle of the luteal phase (Figure 11.2).

Progesterone is especially important in preparing the uterus for implantation of the fertilized ovum and maintaining pregnancy. Because the corpus luteum is a major source of progesterone, progesterone level peaks during the luteal phase and is otherwise low.

A Health Function for Menstruation?   Biologist Margie Profet (1993) argues that menstruation, rather than being just a pain in the abdomen, has a disease-preventing function. Sperm can carry bacteria; bacteria from either the male or female genitals regularly attach themselves to the tails of sperm. With this free ride, during heterosexual intercourse they are transported not only into the

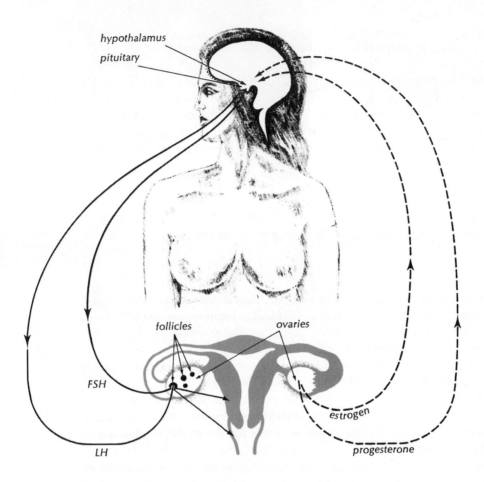

hypothalamus
pituitary
follicles
ovaries
FSH
estrogen
LH
progesterone

FIGURE 11.3

Schematic diagram illustrating the negative feedback loops controlling hormone levels during the menstrual cycle. FSH and LH are produced by the pituitary gland and influence production of estrogen and progesterone in the ovaries. The hypothalamus is sensitive to levels of these hormones and, in turn, regulates levels of FSH and LH. (See text for further explanation.)

vagina, but also into the uterus and fallopian tubes. Menstruation cleans out the uterus and also delivers large numbers of immune cells into the uterus. Menstruation, then, may have a bacteria-fighting function.

If Profet is right, then there is cause for concern about a number of situations in which women do not menstruate, such as women who exercise strenuously and are very lean, anorexic women, and postmenopausal women. These women, if they engage in heterosexual intercourse, should consider using a barrier method such as a condom or diaphragm to reduce the risk of infection.

Menstrual Problems: Cramps Painful cramps during menstruation are called **dysmenorrhea.** Some women experience them regularly, some women experience them some of the time, and some women don't experience them at all. It is very difficult for a man, or for a woman who does not experience severe dysmenorrhea, to understand precisely how it feels to those who do experience it, a point that is expressed poignantly in Focus 11.1, "A Woman Describes Her Experiences with Menstrual Pain."

> **Dysmenorrhea:** Painful menstruation; cramps.

Traditional medical remedies have not been completely successful in treating the problem. Over-the-counter drugs such as Midol help some people some of the time, but they do not help everyone. In fact, until a few years ago, it seemed that the best treatment was plain old aspirin. Then came a major breakthrough in understanding the biology of cramps and corresponding advances in treating them.

Prostaglandins are thought to be the culprit responsible for cramps (Budoff, 1981; Golub, 1992). Prostaglandins are hormone-like substances produced by many tissues of the body, including the lining of the uterus. Prostaglandins cause smooth muscle to contract and can affect the size of blood vessels. Women with severe menstrual pain have unusually high levels of prostaglandins. The high levels cause intense uterine contractions, which are painful; these contractions in turn choke off some of the uterus's supply of oxygen-carrying blood, a painful process that somewhat resembles what occurs in a heart attack. Prostaglandins may also cause greater sensitivity in nerve endings. The combination of the uterine contractions, lack of oxygen, and heightened nerve sensitivity produces cramps.

> **Prostaglandins:** Hormone-like biochemicals that stimulate the muscles of the uterus to contract.

As a result of this analysis of the causes of cramps, a new treatment is the use of *antiprostaglandin drugs*. The drug is mefanamic acid and is sold under brand names such as Ponstel. Other, similar drugs are Motrin, Naprosyn, and Anaprox. Interestingly, its application to menstrual cramps was discovered by a woman physician, Dr. Penny Wise Budoff (1981). In her research, 85 percent of the women tested reported significant relief from menstrual pain and symptoms such as nausea, vomiting, dizziness, and weakness. Not coincidentally, one of the traditional cures for cramps, aspirin, is a weak antiprostaglandin.

In 1982 the Nobel Prize in medicine was awarded to the three scientists who pioneered prostaglandin research (*Time*, October 25, 1982). The news coverage focused on the physiology of prostaglandins and discussed applications in the treatment of ulcers, arthritis, and pain associated with heart attacks. Only fleeting mention was made of the application of prostaglandins to the treatment of menstrual pain. Millions of women who are sufferers might say that the menstrual-pain application is just as important.

FOCUS 11.1

A WOMAN DESCRIBES HER EXPERIENCES WITH MENSTRUAL PAIN

I started to menstruate when I was 12. The pain did not occur the first few times. The first time it happened I was in the kitchen getting tea for my mother. Suddenly, a terrible pain doubled me over, and I could hardly get my breath. I could not stand straight and when I reached my mother she told me to sit on my bed, and that it would pass. She was quite nice that time and told me that sometimes it had been bad for her, too. Later on, after a half-year had passed, she was fed up with me. She began to hate my crying and twisting in pain. . . . Finally, one day when I was thirteen she told me that if I didn't stop crying that instant, she would walk out on me and leave me alone. I sat there and shuddered, but I didn't make any more noise. My mother made it plain. I learned that I could not cry out or she and other people would withdraw from me.

When I got older, this lesson was reinforced. I could mention my problem once, maybe twice, but then the school nurses and personnel all turned a deaf ear. Teachers would not help me cope; they shook their heads at such absurdity, believing that I had suddenly turned into a goldbrick. . . . Past history also seemed to count for nothing. I always loved basketball and participated enthusiastically in gym. Once a month, however, I would incur the wrath of my gym teacher who decided that I suddenly just didn't want to improve my basketball skills. Her attitude cooled the attitudes of the girls in my class for me, also. Who would want to associate with such an unreliable person? . . .

When I was 18, I had a horseback-riding accident in which I broke my back in the middle. The first doctor who examined me failed to X-ray the middle back and said there was nothing wrong but some bruises. I seemed to have too much pain for bruises. . . . Two weeks later my father, who did not like the way I was moving, sent me to Knickerbocker Hospital for more

Psychological Aspects of the Menstrual Cycle   "Why do I get so emotional?" screams the ad for Midol PMS in *Teen* magazine. The notion that women experience changes in personality or mood depending on the phase of the menstrual cycle is well known. In this section we will examine the evidence on the nature and extent of these moods and behavior shifts and their relationship to the hormone cycles occurring during the menstrual cycle.

X-rays. There they found out that my spine had been broken (in addition to my coccyx) and proceeded to put me in a wheelchair and tell me that I must not take another step, which I thought was pretty funny (except for the pain) because for two weeks I had been walking, cleaning, living on my own, and even hiking in that condition. As you know, Knickerbocker is a busy New York City hospital, used to seeing plenty of the rougher side of life. Yet that night, the resident who had examined me and taken the X-rays stopped by my room to speak to me. He said, "I just wanted to see how the bravest girl I've ever met is getting along." His kindness surprised me, but so did the fact that he thought my talking calmly, normally, and not crying or fainting with the enormous pain I was in, was surprising. . . . The rest of the hospital staff also found my behavior very surprising. . . .

There was one thing they did not know, however, about my ability to take pain. It's not that I don't feel it; I have the same number of nerve endings per square foot as anyone else. The difference is that I had been in training for years to endure it. I was used to coping through a haze of nauseating pain, used to having a conversation when every nerve in me was screaming out, used to getting dressed and getting on a bus when I felt as though a red-hot iron was going to knock my stomach out. I got my training every month without fail, when my period came.

I, of course, developed such techniques as I could for enduring this experience, such as mentally talking myself through something, step by step. . . .

These great techniques were not much. Obviously they only helped me to endure what I had to endure anyway to live up to our society's conviction that this condition does not exist and need not be remedied.

SOURCE: From *No More Menstrual Cramps and Other Good News,* by Penny Wise Budoff, Putnam Publishing. Copyright © 1981

In 1931, Robert Frank gave the name *premenstrual tension* to the mood changes that occur during the three or four days immediately preceding menstruation (approximately days 23 to 26 or 28 of the cycle). By now we have an extensive body of research on this phenomenon, as well as on the more general one of fluctuations in mood and behavior corresponding to the menstrual cycle (see Golub, 1992, and Parlee, 1973, for critical reviews).

Three types of studies have been used to document the existence of a premenstrual syndrome. First, attempts have been made to correlate observable behaviors with cycle phase. For example, one study found that a large proportion of the suicides and criminal acts of violence committed by women occur during the four premenstrual and four menstrual days of the cycle (Dalton, 1964). The premenstrual syndrome, then, may have important and far-reaching consequences. On the other hand, the eight premenstrual and menstrual days do constitute 36 percent of the total days in a cycle. Hence a statistic like "49 percent of criminal acts committed by women occur during this time," which appears impressive considered by itself, may not represent a substantial or meaningful increase over the 36 percent expected randomly. And even with these presumed hormone effects, women commit far fewer crimes than men do.

A second type of study used to document the premenstrual syndrome is based on questionnaires requesting that women report retrospectively their symptoms and moods at various phases of the cycle. Such studies are largely useless because retrospective accounts, particularly of such subjective phenomena as moods in relation to menstrual cycle, are notoriously unreliable and have not been demonstrated to correlate with other indicators of premenstrual symptoms (Marván & Cortés-Iniestra, 2001).

A third type of study uses daily self-reports made by women throughout the cycle. Such studies generally find positive moods around the time of ovulation, and various symptoms, such as anxiety, irritability, depression, and headaches, premenstrually (Parlee, 1973; Woods et al., 1999). On the other hand, the fluctuations are not large, on average. In one study, the mean depression score of women was 6.84 around ovulation and 9.30 premenstrually, compared with a mean of 16.03 for depressed psychiatric patients (Golub, 1992). Women are not ready for the psychiatric ward premenstrually!

In summary, the results of the research using all these approaches do seem to indicate that there are fluctuations in mood corresponding to the phases of the menstrual cycle, at least in some women—although even this modest conclusion is contested by some (e.g., Hardie, 1997).

It is tempting to speculate that these mood changes are related to, or perhaps even caused by, changes in hormone levels occurring during the cycle. In particular, it seems that high levels of estrogen (at ovulation) are associated with positive moods, whereas low levels of estrogen and progesterone premenstrually are associated with negative moods.

As suggested earlier, such a conclusion has been criticized on a number of counts (Hardie, 1997; Parlee, 1973; Stanton et al., 2002). First, virtually all the data (with some exceptions discussed below) presented to support this contention are correlational in nature; causal inferences are then made from these data, an unwise procedure at best. That is, the data simply demonstrate a correlation between cycle phase or hormone levels and mood. From this it is unwarranted to infer that hormones actually cause or influence mood. From these data an equally tenable conclusion would be that the direction of causality is the reverse—that psychological factors affect hormone levels and menstrual-cycle phase. For example, stress may delay menstruation or precipitate its onset; many women in concentration camps during World War II ceased menstruating. Social factors may also have an influence; studies have found that women living together in a college dormitory came to have menstrual cycles more closely synchronized as the academic year progressed (Graham, 1991; McClintock, 1971; Weller et al., 1995). In sum, the inference that hormone level influences mood is not completely justifiable on the basis of the available data, although further data may yet substantiate this conclusion.

One study that partially answers the objection about correlational data involved scoring the spoken stories of 102 married women four times during a single menstrual cycle: on days 4, 10, 16, and two days before the onset of menstruation (Paige, 1971; for similar results, see Oinonen & Mazmanian, 2001). Other data were also collected to try to disguise the purpose of the study. The women were classified into three groups: (1) those who were not taking oral contraceptives and never had; (2) those who were taking a combination pill (combination pills provide a steady high dose of both estrogen and progestin, a synthetic progesterone, for 20 or 21 days); and (3) those who were taking sequential-type pills (which provide 15 days of estrogen, followed by 5 days of estrogen-progestin, similar to the natural cycle, but at higher levels). Nonpill women experienced statistically significant variation in their anxiety and hostility levels over the menstrual cycle, as previous studies had shown. Women taking the sequential pill showed the same mood changes that nonpill women did, which agrees with the predicted outcome, because their artificial hormone cycle parallels the natural one. Combination-pill women showed *no* mood shifts corresponding to the menstrual cycle: Their hostility and anxiety levels remained constant. Therefore, it appears that the steady high level of both hormones leads to a steady level of mood. This study serves as a quasi-experiment with respect to hormone levels, thereby answering, in part, the objections with regard to causal inferences on hormone-behavior relations.

A second criticism of this area of research is that the term **premenstrual syndrome (PMS)** is only vaguely defined (Hardie, 1997; Ulssher, 1996). For instance, some authors have defined it so broadly as to include "any combination of emotional or physical features which occur cyclically in a female before menstruation" (Sutherland & Stewart, 1965, p. 1182). While it would be worthwhile to know what percentage of the female population is afflicted with premenstrual symptoms, estimates of this percentage vary between 25 and 80 percent in various studies (Stanton et al., 2002). In view of the vagueness of the definition, it is not surprising that these estimates are not consistent, and until the "syndrome" is more clearly defined, we can have no really accurate

Premenstrual syndrome (PMS): A combination of severe physical and psychological symptoms (such as depression) occurring in some women for a few days before menstruation.

FOCUS 11.2

THE SOCIAL CONSTRUCTION OF PMS

"Why do I get so emotional?" asks the young woman in the ad for Midol PMS. You can bet the emotion she's talking about is not happiness—more likely anger, irritability, or sadness. As we discussed in Chapter 2, feminist theory emphasizes the social construction of gender phenomena—that is, the way we interpret our experiences is shaped in large part by social and cultural forces. PMS, it has been argued, is socially constructed.

The expression of emotions is carefully regulated by social norms. You wouldn't, for example, laugh heartily in the middle of a funeral, and if you did, you would certainly receive negative responses from those around you. As we saw in Chapter 6, there are gender norms for emotions. For most emotions— love, sadness—it is far more acceptable for women to express them than for men. Anger is the exception. The expression of anger by men is tolerated; it is not for women. A woman who expresses anger is violating a social norm.

The expression of anger in women is unacceptable in large part because it interferes with the performance of their social roles. Women's family roles call for them to provide nurturance and emotional support to others. An angry person cannot be nurturant and emotionally supportive. The same is true for work roles. Women are found disproportionately in service occupations, and again anger interferes with performance of the job. No one wants to be cared for by an angry nurse.

On the other hand, many women have plenty to be angry about— low-status jobs, unequal pay for equal work, and battering, to name just a few examples.

In sum, then, many women feel angry or irritable, but feeling these emotions—much less expressing them—is a serious deviation from social norms.

estimate of its incidence. At least from these data it seems fair to conclude that the premenstrual syndrome is far from universal among women. It is possible that 50 percent or more of women have no premenstrual symptoms.

A third problem with this area of research is the problem of participants' expectations. Research participants may report more negative feelings premenstrually because such feelings are culturally prescribed—brainwashing through

This leads the woman herself and those around her to seek some socially acceptable explanation for her emotions. Enter PMS.

From a psychological or social constructionist point of view, PMS can be seen as an attribution (attributions were discussed in Chapter 8). A woman experiences or expresses a particular emotion. To what does she attribute it? If the emotion is a socially unacceptable one, such as anger or irritability, she and others seek a socially acceptable attribution, and society makes PMS a readily available attribution. Magically, she isn't really angry; she is just in that temporary state of insanity, PMS. With a single stroke of attribution, her emotion no longer violates social norms; but at the same time, any real feelings of true anger she may have, perhaps toward her husband or her boss, are also brushed away.

Interestingly, PMS became a popular concept beginning in the 1980s, just as the feminist movement was urging women to discover their anger.

There may be a bit of a paradox here, though, from the viewpoint of feminist theory. The theory argues, on the one hand, that PMS is a social creation but, on the other hand, that we should accept and validate the lived experiences of women. A lot of women truly believe that they experience the emotional symptoms of PMS in a profound way. How can this paradox be resolved? The answer is that these women do experience the emotions they report, but that society has created a particular explanation or attribution for them in the few days before menstruation. When a woman experiences these negative emotions at some other time in the cycle, she may ignore them or seek some other attribution, such as just being in a bad mood that day, or perhaps being truly angry at her boss as a result of something he or she said to her. The PMS attribution, then, becomes a self-fulfilling prophecy.

SOURCES: Pugliesi (1992), Rodin (1992), Ussher (1996).

menstrual drug ads—or because they feel the experimenter expects those feelings, for the women must certainly be aware of the investigator's interest in their menstrual cycle.

Psychologist Diane Ruble (1977; see also Klebanov & Jemmott, 1992) did a clever experiment to determine whether people's expectations influence their reporting of premenstrual symptoms. College students were tested on the sixth or seventh day before the onset of their next menstrual period. They were told that they would participate in a study on a new technique for predicting the expected date of menstruation using an electroencephalogram (EEG), a method that had already been successfully tested with older women. After the EEG had been run, the woman was informed of when her next period was to occur, depending on which of three experimental groups she had been assigned to: (1) She was told she was "premenstrual" and her period was due in one or two days, (2) she was told she was "intermenstrual" or "midcycle" and her period was not expected for at least a week to ten days, or (3) she was given no information at all about the expected date of menstruation (control group). The women then completed a self-report menstrual-distress questionnaire. The results indicated that those who had been led to believe they were in the premenstrual phase reported significantly more water retention, pain, and changes in eating habits than those who had been led to believe they were around midcycle. (In fact, the women in these groups did not differ significantly in terms of when their periods actually arrived.) There were no significant differences between the groups in ratings of negative moods, however. This study indicates that, probably because of learned beliefs, women overstate the changes in body states that occur over the menstrual cycle. When they think they are in the premenstrual phase, they report more problems than when they think they are at midcycle.

A subtle problem of interpretation exists in menstrual-cycle research. A typical conclusion is that symptoms increase or that mood is negative premenstrually. Perhaps, however, the premenstrual state is the "usual" one, and what occurs is really a decrease in symptoms, or a positive mood shift, at ovulation. This is essentially a problem of establishing a baseline of behavior—and what should that be? Should it be the average for males? Or are males irrelevant to this research? These are complex questions.

Also noteworthy are the tremendous cultural influences on menstrual-cycle mood shifts (Woods et al., 1995). In many preliterate societies and religions, a menstruating woman is seen as unclean, and many taboos arise to prevent her uncleanness from spreading to others (Golub, 1992). For example, she may not be permitted to cook while menstruating, or she may even be isolated from the rest of the community in a separate hut outside the village. Such superstitions become subtler in modern America, but they still persist. For example, many couples abstain from sexual intercourse during the woman's period. A survey of 960 California families showed that half the men and women had *never* had sex during menstruation (Paige, 1973). There is also considerable evidence of cultural influences on menstrual distress. An analysis of over 200 advertisements for menstrual products in popular women's magazines indicated that the common theme was heightening insecurities (Simes & Berg, 2001). The ads talk about the possibility of "accidents," embarrassment, "getting caught" having your period (i.e., others find out), feeling dirty or unclean, and odor. Drug ads, of course, emphasize pain and their products' ability to relieve PMS. The sign over the aisle in Walgreen's

Does advertising for menstrual drugs contribute to the social construction of PMS?

calls them "feminine hygiene" products—"hygiene" meaning practices such as cleanliness that preserve health. A menstruating woman must be unclean if she has to use hygiene products. Is all this so different from the menstrual hut?

Just as feminist approaches to science often point up alternative interpretations of phenomena, the perspectives of different ethnic groups can suggest new interpretations. American Indian women believe that menstruation is a time of centering and balancing oneself (Hernandez, 1990). The flow out of the body washes away impurities and the negative things that have occurred during the month. Reflecting the close connection of the Indian people to nature, Indian women refer to the menstrual period as being "on the moon," which is considered a positive time.

Practical Implications In assessing the practical implications of research on mood shift and menstrual phase, some important considerations should be kept in mind. First, the *magnitude* of the mood shift depends on the individual woman. Certainly in practical situations, the magnitude of the mood shift is most significant. For instance, it is much more essential to know that a particular woman experiences mood shifts so small as to be unnoticeable in her work and interpersonal relations than it is to know that she experiences slight mood shifts detectable only by sensitive psychological tests. Hence the most important characteristics are individual ones, just as they are for men.

Second, in making practical decisions about hiring people, *performance* is certainly more crucial than mood. Research on performance—such as intellectual or athletic performance—generally shows no fluctuations over the cycle (Golub, 1992; Stanton et al., 2002). Research has found no fluctuations in academic performance, problem solving, memory, or creative thinking (Golub, 1992). Thus there is no evidence of cycle fluctuations in the kinds of performance that are important on the job.

In one particularly interesting study, female pilots were tested in a flight simulator to assess their performance in the mid-luteal and menstrual phases (Mumenthaler et al., 2001). The results indicated no significant difference between performance in the two phases, and no significant correlation between performance and estradiol (an estrogen) or progesterone levels. The flying public should be happy to know about this one.

The one exception to this pattern of no fluctuations in performance is in three-dimensional spatial ability (discussed in Chapter 8). Some studies do find fluctuations across the cycle in performance on spatial tests (Hausmann et al., 2000; McCormick & Teillon, 2000). Spatial performance is highest during menstruation, when estradiol and progesterone levels are low. Interestingly, spatial performance is positively correlated with women's testosterone levels, and negatively correlated with their estradiol levels (Hausmann et al., 2000). And in one study, women's spatial scores during the menstrual phase did not differ significantly from men's (McCormick & Teillon, 2001). This research is new, and it will take a while to sort it out and determine whether the effects are reliable. It is also important to acknowledge that three-dimensional spatial ability is unimportant for performance in most occupations, such as newspaper reporter or lawyer, but crucial to a few, such as engineering and architecture.

In addition, it is likely that monthly hormonal cycles exist in men as well (Delaney et al., 1976; Hersey, 1931; Parlee, 1978; Ramey, 1972), but until quite recently such cycles have not been the subject of scientific investigation—probably because they produce no obvious physical changes like menstruation. One study in fact found no differences between men and women in day-to-day mood changes—men were no more nor less changeable than women (McFarlane et al., 1988; see also McFarlane & Williams, 1994).

In summary, research suggests that menstrual-cycle changes in hormone levels may be related to corresponding changes in mood. Mood is generally positive at ovulation or midcycle, when estrogen levels are high, whereas it is negative, with feelings of depression, anxiety, and irritability, at the time of low estrogen levels premenstrually. The existing research has many problems: Most of it is correlational in nature, and expectations complicate interpretations. Cultural factors may also contribute to mood shifts. Probably a substantial proportion of women either do not experience such mood cycles, or their cyclic fluctuations are so small as to be undetectable. In addition, there is no evidence of fluctuation in performance.

Other Menstrual-Cycle Fluctuations   Research has demonstrated that there are menstrual-cycle fluctuations in the sensitivity of the senses: vision, smell, hearing, taste, and touch (Parlee, 1983). For example, sensitivity to the smell of certain compounds is greatest around the time of ovulation and is reduced during menstruation. According to laboratory tests, women's pain sensitivity fluctuates across the cycle; women are least sensitive during the follicular phase (Riley et al., 1999). In the search for psychological characteristics that are controlled by biological factors fluctuating over the menstrual cycle, these basic sensory processes may be a better place to look than more diffuse attributes such as moods, which are far more influenced by environment, socialization, and cognitions.

Menopause

Physical and Psychological Changes   A number of physical changes occur during the climacteric. *Climacteric* refers to the gradual aging of the ovaries over the years, leading to a decline in their efficiency. Most importantly, estrogen production declines, leading to the most obvious symptom of the climacteric, menopause (the ceasing of menstruation), which occurs on average around the age of 51. Another effect is the loss of elasticity of the vagina and shrinking of the breasts.

A number of symptoms occur at this time: physical symptoms such as "hot flashes" and psychological symptoms such as depression, irritability, and difficulties with concentration.

How common are these symptoms? The Massachusetts Women's Health Study followed a large sample of middle-aged women for several years, beginning when they were premenopausal and continuing through menopause to the postmenopausal period (Avis & McKinlay, 1995; McKinlay et al., 1992). The peak in reporting of hot flashes and night sweats occurred just before actual menopause, with 50 percent of women reporting them. About one-quarter (23 percent) did not report a hot flash at any of the interview times. And 69 percent of the women reported not being bothered by the hot flashes and night sweats. So, about one-quarter of women do not experience hot flashes and 50 to 75 percent of women do, but the majority report that they are not bothered by them.

In regard to mental health, this same study found that 85 percent of women were never depressed during the menopausal years, 10 percent were depressed occasionally, and just 5 percent were persistently depressed (McKinlay et al., 1987). In short, the evidence indicates that the incidence of depression is no higher during menopause than at other times in a woman's life.

Ethnic groups differ somewhat in their reporting of symptoms. In one study of menopausal women, 39 percent of African American women reported hot flashes, compared with 26 percent of Latinas, 24 percent of White women, and 12 percent of Japanese American women (Avis et al., 2001). Interestingly, soy—

which is found, for example, in tofu—is a natural source of estrogen, and diet has been proposed as an explanation for the low incidence of symptoms in Japanese American women.

In sum, the evidence indicates that menopause does not bring on an avalanche of problems, whether one looks at well-sampled studies of middle-aged women or compares middle-aged women with other age groups. A few limited symptoms do appear, particularly hot flashes.

Biology, Culture, or Both?   The difficulties associated with menopause are attributed to biology (in particular, to hormones) by some and to culture and its expectations by others. In this discussion, we must distinguish between physical symptoms (e.g., hot flashes) and psychological symptoms (e.g., depression). As we saw in the previous section, there is an increase at menopause in physical symptoms, but not in psychological symptoms. It therefore makes no sense to debate whether increased depression is due to biology or culture if there is no increase in depression.

From the biological perspective, menopausal problems appear to be due to the woman's hormonal state. In particular, the symptoms appear to be related either to low estrogen levels or to hormonal imbalance. The former hypothesis, called the **estrogen-deficiency theory,** has been the subject of the most research. Proponents of this theory argue that the physical symptoms, such as hot flashes, are caused by declining amounts of estrogen in the body.

> **Estrogen-deficiency theory:** The hypothesis that the symptoms of menopause are due to low levels of estrogen.

The best evidence for the estrogen-deficiency theory comes from the success of **estrogen-replacement therapy (ERT),** such as Premarin, or **hormone-replacement therapy (HRT),** which involves both estrogen and progesterone, and possibly testosterone as well. HRT is successful in relieving low-estrogen menopausal symptoms like hot flashes, night sweats, osteoporosis (brittle bones), vaginal discharges, and vaginal dryness (Golub, 1992; Wright et al., 2002). (Osteoporosis increases the risk of broken bones, such as hip fractures, which may lead to death in elderly women, so it is a serious condition.) Moreover, HRT protects women from cardiovascular diseases such as heart attack and stroke (Hedblad et al., 2002; Ross & Stevenson, 1993).

> **Estrogen-replacement therapy (ERT):** Replacement doses of estrogen given to some women to treat menopausal symptoms.

> **Hormone-replacement therapy (HRT):** Replacement doses of estrogen and progesterone and possibly testosterone, given to some women to treat menopausal symptoms.

Any possible benefits of HRT should be weighed against the dangers. HRT increases the risk of breast cancer and endometrial cancer (Chen et al., 2002; Rosenberg, 1993; Steinberg et al., 1991; Wright et al., 2002). However, in one study, women using ERT or HRT had a lower rate of death than women who did not (Grodstein et al., 1997). A woman's risk of death between the ages of 50 and 94 is 31 percent from heart disease and only 2.8 percent from breast cancer and 2.8 percent from hip fractures (Brinton & Schairer, 1997). Therefore, HRT protects women against the more serious risk.

In a startling move in 2002, the National Institutes of Health (NIH) stopped a clinical trial of Prempro with menopausal women (Enserink, 2002). Prempro contains a combination of estrogen and progesterone. The NIH did not stop the other treatment group in the study, who were taking estrogen only. The reason for the dramatic action was that women in the Prempro group had a higher incidence of heart attack, stroke, breast cancer, and blood clots, compared with the placebo control group. That is, Prempro was increasing rather than decreasing the rates of heart attack and stroke. Does this mean that all women should stop HRT? Not necessarily. The trial involved a particular drug—Prempro—but some other formulation of estrogen and progesterone might be fine. And the estrogen-only group was doing well, so no concerns were raised about estrogen. The study was investigating long-term use of HRT and stopped the Prempro group at five years. Short-term use of HRT for one or two years is probably safe for most women. Moreover, the increase in risk from Prempro might seem small to women who are having serious difficulty with menopausal symptoms. The study found that, per 10,000 women on Prempro, the increased risk amounted to seven more women with heart disease compared with the control group.

The picture on ERT and HRT is complex and speaks to the importance of individualized evaluation and treatment for each woman, taking into account her particular pattern of symptoms and how distressed she is by them.

Advocates of the environmental point of view note the cultural forces that act to produce psychological stress in women around the time of menopause. The aging process itself may be psychologically stressful in our youth-oriented culture. The menopausal years remind a woman forcefully that she is aging. Menopause also means that the woman can no longer bear children. For women who have a great psychological investment in motherhood, this can be a difficult realization. In Chapter 7 we reviewed research on the empty nest syndrome and found that some investigators question whether this is a time of depression among women. Further, I noted that menopausal symptoms do not occur in women in cultures where women's status rises at this time (Bart, 1971).

We have a strong cultural bias toward expecting menopausal symptoms. Thus any quirk in a middle-aged woman's behavior is attributed to the "change." It simultaneously becomes the cause of, and explanation for, all the problems and complaints of the middle-aged woman. Given such expectations, it is not surprising that the average person perceives widespread evidence of menopausal symptoms. Ironically, idiosyncrasies in women of childbearing age are blamed on menstruation, whereas problems experienced by women who are past that age are blamed on the *lack* of it.

As a way of resolving this biology-culture controversy, it seems reasonable to conclude that the physical symptoms of menopause, such as hot flashes, are due to declining estrogen levels, and that the belief that there are psychological symptoms, such as depression, is a product of culture.

Contraception

Detailed information on the various methods of contraception is available elsewhere (e.g., Hyde & DeLamater, 2003). What I want to do here is concentrate on the psychological aspects of contraceptive use—or, more accurately, of nonuse.

Each year in the United States one million teenagers, or one out of every eight women aged 15 to 19, become pregnant (Hatcher et al., 1998). Approximately 30 percent of these pregnancies are terminated by abortion, 50 percent result in live births, and the remainder end in miscarriage (Hatcher et al., 1998). In an era when highly effective contraceptives are readily available, why should so many unwanted pregnancies occur? The basic answer is that lots of women have sexual intercourse while using no contraceptive, even though they are single and don't want to get pregnant. For example, among sexually active teenage girls, 21 percent use no method of contraception (Forrest & Singh, 1990). Similar statistics are reported at many universities.

Why? Why is there such widespread nonuse of contraceptives, and so many resulting unwanted pregnancies? Two traditional theories were used to explain this phenomenon (for a summary, see Luker, 1975). One is the *contraceptive ignorance theory*. It holds that women fail to use contraceptives and have unwanted pregnancies because they lack knowledge about or access to contraceptives. The theory goes on to say that if women had more information about contraceptives, about their advantages, disadvantages, and so on, they would use them. That is probably true for some women, but not for the majority in the United States. In one study of women who were undergoing abortions, more than half reported having previously used a prescription method of contraception (usually the pill), and the majority displayed some or considerable knowledge about birth control when interviewed (Luker, 1975).

A second theory is the *intrapsychic conflict theory*. It holds that women generally have adequate skills in contraception, but that they fail to use contraceptives because of internal psychological conflicts. According to this view, a woman might use an "accidental" pregnancy to trap a man into marrying her, or to get back at parents whom she feels have not given her enough love. This model portrays women as neurotic and manipulative. Stereotypes strike again!

Sociologist Kristin Luker (1975) formulated an excellent alternative theory about why unwanted pregnancies occur, in her book *Taking Chances: Abortion and the Decision Not to Contracept*. The cause of unwanted pregnancies, she argues, is *contraceptive risk taking*, which results from conscious decision-making processes about whether to use contraceptives in any given sexual encounter. She believes that the decision not to use contraceptives is analogous to the decision not to fasten one's seat belt when driving.

According to Luker's theory, the woman engages in an informal cost-benefit analysis (although she might not be able to articulate it) in which she weighs the costs and benefits of contraception against the costs and benefits of pregnancy. The woman must assess the risk or probability of pregnancy (which is actually unknown, even to scientists), and she generally decides that it is very low. Thus if there are many costs associated with contraception, the woman begins to engage in risk taking. Luker's model is based on data she collected at an abortion clinic in northern California, by analyzing the medical records of 500 women treated at the clinic and by doing in-depth interviews with 50 women undergoing abortions at the clinic.

What are the costs of contraception? First, there are a number of social-psychological costs. Using, and planning to use, contraceptives involves acknowledging that one is a sexually active woman, and this is difficult for many women, even today. Using a contraceptive such as the pill signals that one is always sexually available, and this may be seen as decreasing the woman's right to say no. Some methods, such as the diaphragm, decrease the spontaneity of sex, which for some people is a psychological cost. Second, there are structurally created costs— women must call for an appointment with a physician for some methods, and they may be told that no appointments are available for several weeks. They are

The introduction into the United States, in the late 1990s, of RU-486, the "abortion pill," created a major new option for early abortions. RU-486 means that a woman does not have to go to an abortion clinic, with the potential for harassment by pro-life protesters; instead, she can be treated privately in any doctor's office. Planned Parenthood placed these ads in subways trains in New York to educate women about this new option. The ads were protested by The Catholic League.

expected to have high motivation and to use abstinence or to call repeatedly for appointments. Even the "drugstore" methods (foam or condoms) involve going into the store and openly acknowledging to the world—or at least to the people in the store—that one is sexually active. Third, there may be costs to the relationship—the woman may fear negative reactions from the man if she uses a contraceptive such as foam or a diaphragm, or rejection if she asks him to use a condom. Finally, there are biological-medical costs, particularly fears of side effects from the pill.

Luker also points out that the woman may anticipate benefits from pregnancy. Some people view pregnancy as proof of womanhood, and this may be particularly important in a society with a fluctuating view of gender roles. Pregnancy may enhance one's feeling of self-worth, proving that one is a valuable person who can produce children. Unarguably, pregnancy is a proof of fertility, and some women may feel a need for this proof—fully two-thirds of the women interviewed by Luker said that their gynecologists had told them they would have trouble getting pregnant because of problems in their reproductive systems. Pregnancy can be a way of accomplishing something with a significant other, perhaps forcing a man to define the relationship more clearly or perhaps going from living together to marriage. Finally, the pure excitement of risk taking itself may be fun for some.

Given all this, Luker argues, the woman weighs the costs and benefits and often decides to take the risk. The costs and benefits, of course, vary from one woman to the next and at different times in a woman's life. The costs of pregnancy to a single college student are probably far greater than they are to a married woman with two children who would rather have no more. Risk taking, if successful, may foster more risk taking: "I got away with it once; surely I can again." And so the cycle goes, eventually ending in an unwanted pregnancy. But the costs of this failure are not terribly high, as long as abortion is legal and available. Accordingly, many women leave the abortion clinic with no plans to use an effective method in the future, and the risk taking begins again.

On a more hopeful note, Luker argues that as women become more aware of their own decision-making processes, they will become more effective in using contraceptives to achieve the goals they truly desire.

Abortion

A number of methods of abortion are available (see Hyde & DeLamater, 2003, for a more complete discussion). The most commonly used method, accounting for 97 percent of abortions in the United States today (Hatcher et al., 1998), is **vacuum aspiration,** also called vacuum suction. It is done on an outpatient basis with a local anesthetic. The procedure itself takes only about ten minutes and the woman stays

Vacuum aspiration: A method of abortion that is performed in the first trimester.

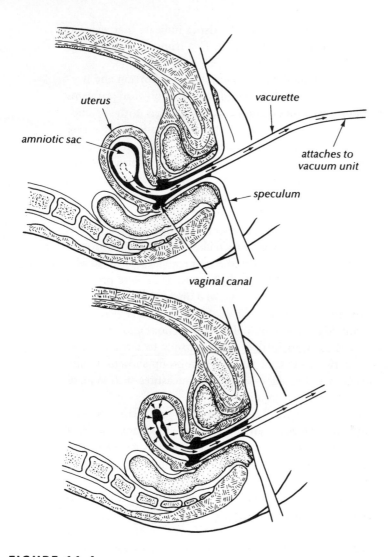

FIGURE 11.4
The procedures involved in vacuum aspiration abortion. A tube is inserted through the vagina and the cervix and into the uterus. The uterine contents are then suctioned out.

in the doctor's office, clinic, or hospital for a few hours. The woman is prepared as she would be for a pelvic exam, and an instrument is inserted into the vagina (Figure 11.4). The instrument dilates (stretches open) the opening in the cervix. A tube is then inserted through the opening until one end is in the uterus. The other end is attached to a suction-producing machine, and the contents of the uterus, including the fetal tissue, are sucked out. Statistics indicate that vacuum aspiration is the safest method of abortion during the first trimester (Centers for Disease Control, 1985).

It is a common belief that making the decision to have an abortion and having one are times of extreme psychological stress and that psychological problems may result. A major review of the methodologically sound studies of the psychological responses of U.S. women having legal abortions concluded that severe problems are rare and that, in fact, the worst stress occurs before the abortion (Adler et al., 1990, 1992). For example, in one study women were interviewed two weeks after first trimester abortions (Lazarus, 1985). The most common feeling was relief, reported by 76 percent of the women; the most common negative feeling was guilt, reported by 17 percent.

In one particularly well done study, 360 adolescents seeking pregnancy tests were interviewed (Zabin et al., 1989). They were then classified into three groups: (1) those whose test was negative, meaning they weren't pregnant; (2) those who were pregnant and carried the baby to term; and (3) those who were pregnant and had an abortion. The women were then interviewed one year later and again two years later. After two years, the women who had had abortions were more likely to have graduated from high school or still to be in school and in the appropriate grade than either those who carried the pregnancy to term or those who were not pregnant. And two years later the abortion group showed, if anything, a more positive psychological profile—in terms of measures such as anxiety and self-esteem—than the other two groups.

In January 1989, then–Surgeon General C. Everett Koop released a report reviewing studies on the psychological effects of abortion. He, too, concluded that there was no scientific evidence that abortion had negative effects on mental health (Holden, 1989). In the antiabortion Reagan administration, the report was quickly suppressed (Roberts, 1990).

It is also important to consider the possible consequences of restricting abortion, that is, denying abortions to some women, and the implications for children born to women in this situation. Such research is impossible to conduct in the United States, because abortion has been legal since 1973 (although recent Supreme Court decisions giving states the right to limit access to abortion may again give us a population of women denied permission for abortion). In some other countries, access to abortion depends on obtaining official approval. In Czechoslovakia, for example, researchers followed the situations of 220 children born to women denied abortion (the "study group") and 220 children born to women who had not requested abortion; the children were studied when they were 9 years old, again when they were 14 to 16 years old, and again in their 20s (David, 1992; David & Matejcek, 1981). By age 14, 43 children from the study group, but only 30 from the control group, had been referred for counseling. Although there were no differences between the groups in tested intelligence, children in the study group did less well in school and were more likely to drop out.

At age 16 the boys (but not the girls) in the study group more frequently rated themselves as feeling neglected or rejected by their mothers and felt that their mothers were less satisfied with them. In their early 20s, the study group reported less job satisfaction, more conflicts with co-workers and supervisors, and fewer and less satisfying friendships. Several other studies have found results similar to the Czechoslovakian one (David et al., 1988). These results point to the serious long-term consequences for children whose mothers would have preferred to have an abortion.

In sum, legal first-trimester abortion does not seem to be dangerous to mental health, on average. The evidence also indicates that there may be long-term negative consequences for children born to women denied access to abortion.

Breast Cancer

Breast cancer is the second most common form of cancer in women, exceeded only by skin cancer. It is rare in women under 25, and a woman's chances of developing it increase every year after that age. About one out of every nine American women has breast cancer at some time in her life. Every year, 40,600 women in the United States die of breast cancer (American Cancer Society, 2000).

Because breast cancer is relatively common, every woman should do a breast self-exam monthly, around midcycle (*not* during one's period, when there may be natural lumps). Unfortunately, psychological factors such as fear prevent some women from doing the self-exam or, if they discover a lump, from seeing a doctor immediately. This is unfortunate because the more quickly breast cancer is discovered and treated, the better the chances of recovery. If the cancer has not spread beyond the breast, the survival rate is 94 percent five years after treatment (American Cancer Society, 1995).

In fact, not all breast lumps are cancerous. There are three kinds of breast lumps: cysts (fluid-filled sacs, also called fibrocystic disease or cystic mastitis), fibroadenomas, and malignant tumors. The important thing to realize is that 80 percent of breast lumps are cysts or fibroadenomas and are therefore benign, that is, not dangerous. Most physicians feel that the most definitive method for diagnosis is the excisional biopsy, in which a small slit is made in the breast, the lump is removed, and a pathologist determines whether it is cancerous. Other diagnostic techniques include needle aspiration and mammography.

If a malignancy is confirmed, what is the best treatment? The treatment usually is some form of mastectomy, that is, surgical removal of the breast. In **radical mastectomy,** the most serious form of the surgery, the entire breast, as well as the lymph nodes and underlying muscles, is removed. Advocates of this procedure argue that it is best to be as thorough as possible, and that the muscle and lymph nodes should be removed in case the cancer has spread to them.

Radical mastectomy: A surgical treatment for breast cancer in which the entire breast, as well as underlying muscle and lymph nodes, is removed.

■ WHY DO THE BREAST SELF-EXAM?

There are many good reasons for doing a breast self-exam each month. One reason is that it is easy to do and the more you do it, the better you will get at it. When you get to know how your breasts normally feel, you will quickly be able to feel any change, and early detection is the key to successful treatment and cure.

Remember: A breast self-exam could save your breast—and save your life. Most breast lumps are found by women themselves, but, in fact, most lumps in the breast are not cancer. Be safe, be sure.

Finger Pads

■ WHEN TO DO BREAST SELF-EXAM

The best time to do breast self-exam is right after your period, when breasts are not tender or swollen. If you do not have regular periods or sometimes skip a month, do it on the same day every month.

■ NOW, HOW TO DO BREAST SELF-EXAM

1. Lie down and put a pillow under your right shoulder. Place your right arm behind your head.

2. Use the finger pads of your three middle fingers on your left hand to feel for lumps or thickening. Your finger pads are the top third of each finger.

3. Press firmly enough to know how your breast feels. If you're not sure how hard to press, ask your health care provider. Or try to copy the way your health care provider uses the finger pads during a breast exam. Learn what your breast feels like most of the time. A firm ridge in the lower curve of each breast is normal.

4. Move around the breast in a set way. You can choose either the circle (A), the up and down line (B), or the wedge (C). Do it the same way every time. It will help you to make sure that you've gone over the entire breast area, and to remember how your breast feels.

5. Now examine your left breast using right hand finger pads.

6. If you find any changes, see your doctor right away.

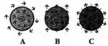
A   **B**   **C**

■ FOR ADDED SAFETY:

You should also check your breasts while standing in front of a mirror right after you do your breast self-exam each month. See if there are any changes in the way your breasts look: dimpling of the skin, changes in the nipple, or redness or swelling.

You might also want to do a breast self-exam while you're in the shower. Your soapy hands will glide over the wet skin making it easy to check how your breasts feel.

In *modified radical mastectomy,* the entire breast and lymph nodes, but not the muscles, are removed. In *simple mastectomy,* only the breast, and possibly a few lymph nodes, is removed. In partial mastectomy, or **lumpectomy,** only the lump and some surrounding tissue are removed. Research indicates that in cases of early breast cancer, lumpectomy or quadrantectomy (removal of the quarter of the breast containing the lump), followed by radiation therapy, is as effective as old-fashioned radical mastectomy (Henahan, 1984; Veronesi et al., 1981) and obviously much preferable.

> **Lumpectomy:** A surgical treatment for breast cancer in which only the lump and a small bit of surrounding tissue are removed.

Social class is an issue in breast cancer. Although breast cancer is more common among higher income women, low-income women have higher rates of mortality from it (Miller et al., 1993; Segnan, 1997). It seems likely that this pattern is a result of higher-income women's greater knowledge about and access to mammography. Breast cancer is diagnosed later in the disease progression for low-income women, resulting in a higher death rate. Being poor can literally kill you.

What are the psychological consequences of breast cancer and the treatments for it? Approximately 30 to 40 percent of women report feeling increased depression and anxiety around the time of diagnosis (Compas & Luecken, 2002). Although there is great variation from one woman to the next, the majority show good adjustment after mastectomy (Jamison et al., 1978; Meyerowitz, 1980). Interestingly, the postmastectomy period is not rated as the most difficult psychologically; rather, the period immediately following discovery of the lump is reported as being the worst (Jamison et al., 1978). Research also shows that, compared with more radical surgeries, lumpectomy is associated with better body image and sexual functioning following surgery (Moyer, 1997).

One study compared breast cancer survivors with matched controls (Cordova et al., 2001). The cancer survivor group did not differ from the controls on measures of depression and well-being, indicating overall good adjustment. The researchers added an important innovation. Rather than just studying possible problems of adjustment, they considered the possibility of *posttraumatic growth,* defined as positive life changes following highly stressful experiences. The breast cancer survivors showed significantly more posttraumatic growth than the controls, particularly in relationships with others, appreciation of life, and spiritual growth. The stress lenses are not the only ones through which to view life events such as breast cancer. We must also remain open to seeing the potential for growth in the midst of trauma.

Nonetheless, many women suffer considerable psychological distress in the process from discovery of a lump through diagnosis and treatment. It is important for them and their partners to have counseling available. In many towns, the American Cancer Society organizes support groups for breast cancer patients. Support groups, of course, are popular today for dealing with just about every situation, including writing a dissertation. As a psychologist, I must raise the question, Are support groups effective—in this case, for breast cancer patients? Surprisingly, it is not clear that peer support groups are beneficial (Helgeson & Cohen, 1996). One study compared the effects of peer support groups for women with breast cancer with the effects of educational classes focused on relevant information (Helgeson et al., 1999, 2001). The results indicated that peer support groups yielded no benefits to quality of life, compared with no intervention, but the education intervention provided both immediate and long-term benefits to quality of life. Peer support groups may be helpful to some women, but may actually be harmful to others so that, averaged over everyone, they provide no benefit (Helgeson et al., 2000).

For women who are more severely distressed, cognitive behavioral therapy with a trained therapist can be very effective (Antoni et al., 2001).

Women and HIV

AIDS refers to acquired immunodeficiency syndrome, a disease that destroys the body's natural immunity to infection, so that the person is susceptible to and may die from diseases such as pneumonia and cancer. *HIV* stands for human immunodeficiency virus, the virus that causes AIDS. The disease is spread by exchange of body fluids, which occurs, specifically, through (1) sexual intercourse (either penis-in-vagina intercourse or anal intercourse); (2) contaminated blood (blood transfusion with HIV-contaminated blood); (3) contaminated hypodermic needles (a risk for those who abuse intravenous drugs); and (4) passage from an infected pregnant woman to her baby during pregnancy or childbirth. There is about a 30 percent chance that a baby born to an infected woman will be infected (Gentry, 1993).

In the first decade of the disease, approximately 90 percent of the cases of AIDS in the United States were men (most of them gay men or male injection drug users); for this reason, most attention has been focused on them. However, in Africa AIDS infects men and women nearly equally, and so it is clear that women can and do become infected. Moreover, the number of infected women in

---

FOCUS 11.3

AIDS: HOW IT CHANGED ONE WOMAN'S LIFE

I met Michael the summer after I graduated from college. I was on vacation and was in good spirits and ready to take hold of anything life handed me. I first encountered Michael when he asked me to dance in a bar. A few dances turned into a few drinks, which led to hours of talking. We fell for each other instantly.

I knew immediately that Michael was the type of man I had always wanted to marry. He was intelligent, funny, handsome, masculine, sensitive, and so romantic. Two days after we met, we made love. Michael was insistent that we use a condom, because I wasn't on any birth control. I was comforted by the fact that he was responsible about sex. Most men I had had sex with didn't want anything to do with condoms.

Two days later he told me he loved me and wanted to marry me. But I felt I couldn't commit myself to him yet. So when I returned home from vacation our long-distance relationship began. There were many expensive phone calls, long letters, and plane rides.

the United States is rising rapidly; today, 25 percent of new AIDS cases are women (Centers for Disease Control, 2002). Thus there is an increasing need to address the needs of women with AIDS (Amaro, 1995; Fox-Tierney et al., 1999; Morokoff et al., 1997).

Among women diagnosed with AIDS in 2000, 38 percent were infected through heterosexual intercourse (Centers for Disease Control, 2002). Another 25 percent were infected through injection drug use.

AIDS is an issue for women on several counts. First, it is an issue for women who themselves become infected. In addition, because women are disproportionately in caregiving roles such as nursing, they bear a huge burden in the care of HIV-infected patients. Women also are the mothers, wives, and sisters of infected men and suffer with the suffering of the infected person. Focus 11.3, "AIDS: How It Changed One Woman's Life," provides one woman's story about the impact of AIDS on her.

HIV-infected women are more likely than infected men to be unemployed or to be employed in situations in which they feel vulnerable to being fired (Gentry, 1993). They have serious fears that they will lose their job if their HIV status

---

As the months went by, I found myself falling in love with Michael. When I called him and told him this, he asked me to marry him. I said yes. We bought the engagement ring that weekend, and it was gorgeous. Hours before we were to leave for the airport, we realized we had run out of condoms. We decided to risk it that one time and have sex without protection.

When I kissed Michael goodbye at the airport, I thought of what we had talked about after our lovemaking that day. We had talked about how scary AIDS is, and how we had both thought about getting tested. We had talked about how many partners we had both had. Although we didn't talk about actual numbers, we joked that I could count mine on my fingers and he could count his on his fingers and toes. He also told me that he had had an operation four years ago that had required two units of blood. I knew this put him at a higher risk for the AIDS virus, but I didn't really think about it because, after all, he was my fiancé. He *couldn't* be infected. But even so, our talk had disturbed me enough that I decided to get tested for the HIV antibody.

(continued)

When I told Michael what I had done, he went in for his own test. A few weeks later, I found out that my test was negative. I called Michael and I could hear him crying. He had tested positive for the HIV antibody.

I comforted Michael the best I could, reassuring him that I loved him. I fell to my knees after I hung up the phone and started crying. My heart was pounding as my whole world died.

My first thought was "I love you, Michael, but I can't marry you," and my second one was "Oh my God, I'm going to get AIDS."

Christmas with my family was hell. I wanted to die when I was given a place setting in my silver pattern and the card was for Michael and me. It killed me to watch my nieces and nephews and think that Michael and I would never have children. The questions my family asked about Michael and me, the wedding, our jobs, our plans for children—all these were like scissors cutting up my insides. I felt I couldn't tell my family the truth because I didn't want to hurt or scare them. I was so overwhelmed with it all. I was scared, so scared.

After the holidays, I went back to the clinic and told the nurse the news. She told me to come back 14 weeks after the date Michael and I had last had unprotected sex. I flew to visit Michael and we sat down and made rules about our lovemaking. We wouldn't French kiss, I would not perform fellatio, and Michael would use two rubbers and pull out before he ejaculated. At times I wondered if the rules were too extreme, but it was the only way I could feel even fairly safe.

Physically and mentally, I felt awful. I caught a cold that lasted two weeks, followed by a urinary tract infection. I lost weight. When I finally told Michael I did not think I could marry him, we both cried. Michael was, for the most part, pretty understanding of my feelings. I felt as if I were abandoning him when he needed me most. I felt immense guilt but, most of all, I felt frightened. I didn't know if I was HIV positive or negative yet.

For many days, all I could do was cry, sleep, eat a little, and cry some more. I was angry with God for doing this to Michael and me. I felt immense jealousy when I heard about friends of mine getting married.

After the 14 weeks, I got retested. After the test, I had to wait another 7 days to get the results. During that time, I flew up to see Michael again. As before, we were very careful during sex . . . but then it happened. When Michael pulled out, the rubbers were still inside me. It was then I realized that even though I loved him very, very much, I could not have sex with him again. It was making me crazy.

When I returned home, I found out that my test results had come back negative. I told the nurse what had happened to us with the rubbers the weekend before, and she told me to come back in another 14 weeks. She said that, most likely, my results would be negative again, because Michael and I had been so careful. She also said that if I did not have sex with Michael or anyone else in the next 14 weeks, and if my test came back negative again, then I would not have the virus.

Right now I do not know what the result of my next test will be. Michael knows that if it is negative, I will leave him. Considering the circumstances, he has been very loving and supportive of my decision. Sometimes I feel very guilty and selfish, but I know I cannot mentally handle having sex with him and being constantly worried about whether we have been careful enough. I know in my heart that I am doing the right thing for myself.

I will never, ever have unprotected sex again. And if I ever get married, my future husband will have to get tested, because I will never put myself through this again.

Now I must go on with my life and think about my future, not the past. But this doesn't stop me from thinking about all the beautiful, dark-haired, blue-eyed babies we could have had together.

SOURCE: Personal communication to the author.

EXPERIENCE THE RESEARCH

WOMEN'S EXPERIENCE OF PMS

Interview four women friends on the topic of PMS. Ask each the following questions and record their answers:

1. Do you experience PMS? (Continue with questions 2 through 7 if the answer is yes; use questions 8 through 11 if the answer is no.)

2. How do you define PMS?

3. What symptoms of PMS do you experience? Include both physical symptoms and psychological symptoms.

4. About how frequently do you experience PMS? That is, out of ten menstrual periods, for how many of them do you experience PMS?

5. About how long do the symptoms of PMS last for you? How many days before your period do they begin? For how many days do they last?

6. How much does the PMS interfere with your functioning? Do you continue pretty much as you normally would, or do you have to stay in bed for a while?

7. How do you treat the PMS? Do you take any medication for it? If so, what? Is it effective? What symptoms does it relieve? If you do not take any medication, how do you try to relieve the PMS symptoms?

[This ends the questions for those with PMS.]

8. How do you define PMS?

9. Do you have any ideas about why you don't have PMS?

10. Do you experience any symptoms or changes over your menstrual cycle? Do you experience any symptoms during your menstrual period, such as cramps?

11. How do you feel about women with PMS?

What can you conclude from your interviews? How common is PMS? What are its symptoms? How do women cope with it? How do they define it?

becomes known. Moreover, HIV-infected women are more likely than infected men to have sole responsibility for their children, and they worry about what will happen to their children if they die. Or they may fear losing custody of their children if they become seriously ill and have difficulty caring for them. They may also worry that their children will be ostracized at school if the mother's infection becomes known.

Race and ethnicity are also important issues in AIDS (Amaro, 1988; Mays & Cochran, 1987; Peterson & Bakeman, 1988). Approximately 40 percent of AIDS cases in the United States are found among non-Whites, which is greatly disproportionate to non-Whites' representation in the general population. For example, African Americans make up about 12 percent of the American population, but they constitute 55 percent of AIDS cases among women (Morokoff et al., 1997). Hispanics represent 12 percent of the general population, but 20 percent of women with AIDS (Morokoff et al., 1997). The pattern of transmission of HIV tends to be different in minority populations from its pattern among Whites. Among African Americans, for example, transmission occurs more often by heterosexual contacts, whereas in the White population it occurs more often through male-male sexual contacts. Inequalities in power between women and men are at the heart of women's heterosexual infection with HIV (Ickovics et al., 2000).

Programs of AIDS intervention and education for women of color need to be culturally sensitive. For example, programs need to be designed for low-income women. Such women may need to be reached for education in special ways, such as working through social welfare agencies. Educational programs need to be sensitive to different attitudes about contraception in different ethnic groups and to the resistance of some to using condoms. Prevention efforts will work best if they involve the entire community, including Spanish radio and television programs, bilingual telephone hot lines, tenant groups, church groups, and neighborhood organizations.

In our efforts to address the needs of men with AIDs, we must not forget that women, too, are at risk.

In Conclusion

In this chapter we have discussed the psychological aspects of some key issues considered important by the women's health movement. In particular, we reviewed statistics on gender and health and examined how women are treated by the health care system.

We also considered the evidence on whether women experience menstrual-cycle fluctuations in mood and whether these shifts are caused by fluctuating hormone levels. Although much research has been done on these questions, there are fundamental problems with much of the mood research. My conclusion is that some, though not all, women experience menstrual-cycle fluctuations in mood. There is evidence of both hormonal and cultural influences on the fluctuations.

At menopause many women experience hot flashes, but research on psychological symptoms such as depression and irritability indicates no increases compared with other stages of life. The physical symptoms such as hot flashes are related to declines in estrogen levels.

Research on psychological aspects of contraception indicates that many young women fail to use contraceptives and engage in contraceptive risk taking.

Research on the psychological consequences of having an abortion indicates that it is generally not a traumatic experience. However, children born to women who were denied an abortion do show problems of adjustment.

Women with breast cancer report the most depression and anxiety around the time of diagnosis. Following treatment, most women do well psychologically, and there is some evidence of posttraumatic growth.

AIDS is not just a gay men's disease. It affects women, too, in growing numbers, either because they are infected or because they are the wives, mothers, sisters, or caretakers of infected men. Heterosexual transmission of HIV to women involves basic issues of power between women and men.

I believe that, in all these cases, as women inform themselves more about the functioning of their bodies, they should inform themselves about the *psychological* aspects of these processes.

Suggestions for Further Reading

Boston Women's Health Book Collective. (1998). *Our bodies, ourselves for the new century: A book by and for women.* New York: Touchstone. This is the latest edition of the classic and best book on women's health.

Hatcher, Robert A., et al. (1998). *Contraceptive technology* (17th ed.). New York: Ardent Media. This is the authoritative book on contraceptive methods, updated every two years.

White, Evelyn C. (Ed.). (1994). *The Black women's health book.* Seattle: Seal Press. This book provides information on the special concerns of Black women.

Women and the Web

National Women's Health Information Center. This website was established by the Office on Women's Health, U.S. Department of Health and Human Services.
http://www.4woman.gov

Pro Choice Forum. This website provides detailed scientific information on abortion, including a section devoted to psychological issues and research.
http://www.prochoiceforum.org

Society for Women's Health Research. This website is provided by a scientific society devoted to women's health.

http://www.womens_health.org

Alan Guttmacher Institute. The Alan Guttmacher Institute is a not-for-profit organization for reproductive health research, policy analysis, and public education. It produces many excellent publications. One is the journal *Family Planning Perspectives*, which is online at this website.

http://www.agi_usa.org

Planned Parenthood. Planned Parenthood is the nation's largest family planning agency. Its website contains a wealth of information.

http://www.plannedparenthood.org

American Cancer Society. The American Cancer Society offers accurate information on cancer, treatment, and support.

http://www.cancer.org

National Abortion and Reproductive Rights Action League. The National Abortion and Reproductive Rights Action League (NARAL) is a political action organization dedicated to preserving a woman's right to safe and legal abortion.

http://www.naral.org

The Society for Menstrual Cycle Research. This is the website of a multidisciplinary organization that provides a network of communication on menstrual cycle research.

http:/www.pop.psu.edu/smcr

The North American Menopause Society. This website provides information on perimenopause, menopause, and a wide variety of therapies to enhance women's health during midlife and beyond.

http://www.menopause.org/

12

Female Sexuality

> *Let us assume that the clitoris exists to give us pleasure, and that pleasure provides the spur to seek sex—that without the promise of great reward we'd be content to stay home and catch up on our flossing. Then we must revisit the matter of disappointment, the frequency with which the clitoris fails us. Why do we have to work much harder for our finale than men do? The clitoris is an idiot savant: it can be so brilliant, and so stupid.*
>
> — FROM NATALIE ANGIER, WOMAN: AN INTIMATE GEOGRAPHY

It is not coincidental that the women's movement and the sexual revolution grew together. Historically, sex for women always meant pregnancy, which meant babies and a life devoted to motherhood. For the first time in the history of our species, because of the development of highly reliable methods of contraception, we are now able to separate sex from reproduction, both in theory and in practice.

In the 1970s, because of advances in contraception, women came to see themselves as free to be sexy without incurring a surprise pregnancy. The AIDS and herpes epidemics of the 1980s and 1990s have complicated the picture of sexual freedom. Nonetheless, female sexuality has been let out of the bag and shows no signs of returning.

Physiology

Much of our contemporary knowledge of female sexual physiology is due to the pioneering work of William Masters and Virginia Johnson (1966).

Masters and Johnson distinguished four phases in sexual response, although these stages actually flow together. The first phase is *excitement.* In the female, the primary response is **vasocongestion** or engorgement of the tissues surrounding the vagina. This simply means that a great deal of blood flows to the blood vessels of the pelvic region. A secondary response is the contraction of various muscle fibers (termed **myotonia**), which results, among other things, in erection of the nipples.

Vasocongestion: An accumulation of blood in the blood vessels of a region of the body, especially the genitals; a swelling or erection results.

Myotonia: Muscle contraction.

Perhaps the most noticeable response in the excitement phase is the moistening of the vagina with a lubricating fluid. This seems quite different from the most noticeable response in males, erection of the penis. In fact, Masters and Johnson discovered that the underlying physiological mechanisms are the same, namely, vasocongestion (the blood vessels becoming engorged with blood). The droplets of moisture that appear on the walls of the vagina during sexual excitation are fluids that have seeped out of the congested blood vessels in the surrounding region. The physiological underpinnings are the same in males and in females, although the observable response seems different.

Lubrication marks only the beginning of female sexual response, however. In the excitement phase, a number of other changes take place, most notably in the clitoris. The clitoris, located just in front of the vagina (see Figures 12.1 and 12.2), is, like the penis, a shaft with a bulb, or *glans*, at the tip. The glans is densely packed with highly sensitive nerve endings. The clitoris is therefore the most sexually sensitive organ in the female body. In response to further arousal, the clitoral glans swells, and the shaft increases in diameter, due to increasing vasocongestion. The clitoris is interesting because it is the only exclusively sexual organ in the human body; all the others, such as the penis, have both sexual and reproductive functions. The clitoris is purely for sexual pleasure.

The vagina also responds in the excitement phase. Think of the vagina as an uninflated balloon in the unaroused state, divided into an outer third (or lower third, in a woman standing upright) and an inner two-thirds (or upper two-thirds). During the successive stages of sexual response, the inner and outer portions react in different ways. In the latter part of the excitement phase, the inner two-thirds of the vagina undergoes a dramatic expansion, or ballooning (see Figure 12.3).

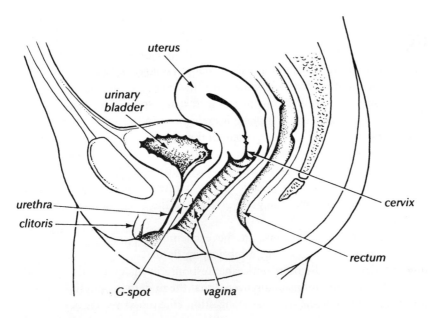

FIGURE 12.1
Female sexual and reproductive anatomy.

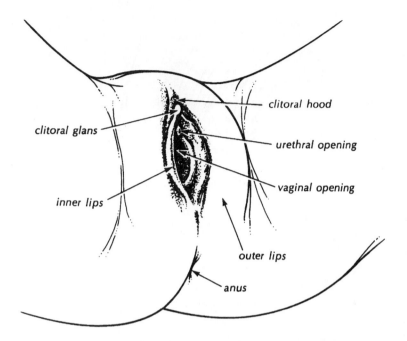

FIGURE 12.2
The vulva, or external genitals, of the human female.

In the second phase of the woman's sexual response, the *plateau phase*, the major change is the appearance of the "orgasmic platform" (Masters & Johnson, 1966). This refers to the outer third of the vagina when it swells and is engorged with blood, with its diameter reduced by as much as 50 percent (Figure 12.3). Whereas the upper portion of the vagina expands during excitement, the lower or outer portion narrows during the plateau phase. The orgasmic platform therefore grips the penis (if there happens to be a penis in the vagina at that point), resulting in a noticeable increase in the erotic stimulation experienced by the male.

The other major change occurring during the plateau phase is the elevation of the clitoris. The clitoris retracts and draws into the body, but continues to respond to stimulation. A number of autonomic responses also occur, including an increase in pulse rate and a rise in blood pressure and in rate of breathing.

Once again, these complex changes are the result of two basic physiological processes, vasocongestion and increased myotonia or muscular tension, which occur similarly in both men and women. Readiness for orgasm occurs when these two processes have reached adequate levels.

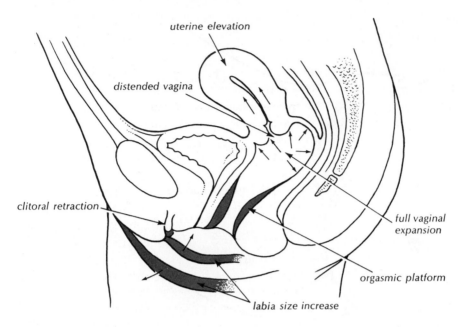

uterine elevation

distended vagina

clitoral retraction

full vaginal expansion

orgasmic platform

labia size increase

FIGURE 12.3
Female sexual and reproductive organs during the plateau phase of sexual response. Notice the ballooning of the upper part of the vagina, the elevation of the uterus, and the formation of the orgasmic platform.

Orgasm, the third phase of sexual response, consists of a series of rhythmic muscular contractions of the orgasmic platform. Generally there is a series of 3 to 12 contractions, at intervals of slightly less than a second. The onset of the subjective experience of orgasm is an initial spasm of the orgasmic platform preceding the rhythmic contractions.

Orgasm: An intense sensation that occurs at the peak of sexual arousal and is followed by the release of sexual tensions.

The sensations of orgasm in the female have been described as follows:

> In the female, orgasm starts with a feeling of momentary suspension followed by a peak of intense sensation in the clitoris, which then spreads through the pelvis. This stage varies in intensity and may also involve sensations of "falling," "opening up," or even emitting fluid. Some women compare this stage of orgasm to mild labor pains. It is followed by a suffusion of warmth spreading from the pelvis through the rest of the body. The experience culminates in characteristic throbbing sensations in the pelvis. (Katchadourian & Lunde, 1972, p. 58)

In the fourth phase, or *resolution phase,* of sexual response, the major physiological changes are a release of muscular tensions throughout the body and a release of blood from the engorged blood vessels. In the female, the breasts, which were formerly enlarged with nipples erect, return to the unaroused state. The clitoris returns to its normal, unretracted position and shrinks to normal size. The orgasmic platform relaxes, and the ballooned upper portion of the vagina shrinks. The return of the female to the unstimulated state may require as long as a half-hour following orgasm. If the woman reaches the plateau phase without having an orgasm, the restoration process takes longer, often as much as an hour. Indeed, prostitutes who habitually experience arousal without orgasm may suffer cumulative physiological effects, resulting in chronic engorgement of vaginal tissues (Masters & Johnson, 1966).

Criticisms of Masters and Johnson's work have been raised (e.g., Tiefer, 1991; Zilbergeld & Evans, 1980). One of the most important of these criticisms is that Masters and Johnson's model focuses exclusively on physiological processes and ignores cognition and affect—that is, what we are thinking and feeling emotionally during sexual response.

An alternative model to address this criticism, the *triphasic model,* was proposed by the eminent sex therapist Helen Singer Kaplan (1979). According to her, there are three components to sexual response: sexual desire, vasocongestion, and the muscle contractions of orgasm. The vasocongestion and orgasm components are consistent with Masters and Johnson; the new component is sexual desire, which refers to an interest in or motivation to engage in sexual activity. Without this psychological component of desire, sexual activity is not apt to take place, or if it does, it is less likely to be pleasurable. The desire component is also important in understanding some sexual dysfunctions, to be discussed later in this chapter.

Common Fallacies

Because sexuality has so often been the subject of superstition and so seldom the subject of scientific research, even modern American culture is filled with distorted ideas about it. A discussion of several misconceptions about female sexuality and the results of relevant scientific research follow.

Clitoral and Vaginal Orgasm   Freud believed that women can experience two different kinds of orgasm— clitoral and vaginal. According to his view, little girls learn to achieve orgasm through stimulation of the clitoris during masturbation. However, in adulthood they have to learn to transfer the focus of their sexual response from the clitoris to the vagina, and to orgasm from intercourse. Because some women fail to make this transfer, they can experience only clitoral orgasm, and are therefore "vaginally frigid." Freud thought that the only mature female orgasm was vaginal.

Masters and Johnson dispelled this myth by showing convincingly that, physiologically, there is only one kind of orgasm. The major response is the contraction of the orgasmic platform. That is, physiologically an orgasm is the same whether it results from clitoral stimulation or from vaginal stimulation. Some women are even able to have orgasms through breast stimulation—and the physiological response is identical to that occurring from vaginal intercourse (Masters & Johnson, 1966).

Although it is well established that orgasms resulting primarily from vaginal and clitoral stimulation are physiologically the same, psychologically they may be experienced differently. The sensations arising from heterosexual intercourse and clitoral masturbation, for example, may be quite different. Physiologically, the orgasm is the same, but the context (presence of the male and contact with his body) may lead to quite different perceptions of the sensation.

The Single, Satiating Orgasm   Traditionally it was thought that women, like men, experience only one orgasm, followed by a *refractory period* of minutes or even hours when they are not capable of arousal and orgasm. Research shows that this is not true and that in fact women can have multiple orgasms. Alfred Kinsey and his colleagues (1953) discovered this a half century ago, reporting that 14 percent of the women they interviewed experienced multiple orgasms. The scientific establishment dismissed these reports as unreliable, however.

Observations from the Masters and Johnson laboratory provided convincing evidence that women do indeed experience multiple orgasms within a short time period. Moreover, these multiple orgasms do not differ from single ones in any significant way except that there are several. They are not minor experiences.

Physiologically, after an orgasm, the vaginal region loses its engorgement of blood. However, in the female, but not in the male, this process is immediately reversible. That is, under continued or renewed erotic stimulation the region again becomes engorged, the orgasmic platform appears, and another orgasm is initiated. This is the physiological mechanism that makes multiple orgasms possible in females.

Most frequently, multiple orgasms are attained through masturbation rather than vaginal intercourse, because it is difficult for a male to postpone his orgasm for such long periods.

As Natalie Angier put it, regarding the clitoris, penis, and multiple orgasms, "Who would want a shotgun when you can have a semiautomatic?" (Angier, 1999, p. 58).

Sexuality and the Elderly   It is a popular belief that a woman's sexual desire is virtually gone by the time she is 60 or so, and perhaps ceases at menopause. Some people believe that sexual activity is a drain on their health and physical resources, and they deliberately stop all sexual activity in middle age to prevent or postpone aging. These, too, are myths that Masters and Johnson have exploded.

As they concluded, "There is no time limit drawn by the advancing years to female sexuality." For the male, also, under conditions of good health and emotional adjustment, there is "a capacity for sexual performance that frequently may extend beyond the eighty-year age level." A major survey of people over 50, conducted by the American Association of Retired Persons (AARP, 1999), found that 24 percent of the women between 60 and 74 had sexual intercourse at least once a week. That declined to 7 percent for women over 75, but about 80 percent of them had no sexual partner, so the problem is mainly one of lack of a partner.

It is true that certain physiological changes occur as women age that influence sexual activity. The ovaries sharply reduce their production of estrogen at menopause, causing the vagina to lose much of its resiliency, and the amount of lubrication is substantially reduced. However, it is common for women to be given hormone-replacement therapy after menopause, which minimizes these changes. Application of lubricants is also helpful. Sexual performance depends much more on the opportunity for regular, active sexual expression and physical and mental health than it does on hormone imbalance (Masters & Johnson, 1966).

A study of healthy women in their 60s, all with a male partner, found differences between those who were sexually active and those who were not (Bachmann & Leiblum, 1991). Those who were sexually active reported intercourse an average of five times per month. A pelvic exam by a physician who was unaware of which women were sexually active found less atrophy of the genitals in the women who were sexually active. If you don't use it, you lose it.

The G-Spot?

A great deal of publicity has been given to the discovery of the G-spot. The **G-spot** (short for **Gräfenberg spot**, named for a German obstetrician-gynecologist who discovered it originally in 1944, although his work was overlooked) is a small organ located on the top or front side of the vagina, about halfway between the pubic bone and the cervix (see Figure 12.1 on p. 324). It is thought to be an anatomical structure rather like the prostate in the male.

Gräfenberg spot (G-spot): A small gland on the front wall of the vagina, emptying into the urethra, which may be responsible for female ejaculation.

There are two reasons that the G-spot is thought to be important. First, the researchers who have investigated it believe that it is the source of *female ejaculation* (Addiego et al., 1981; Belzer, 1981; Ladas et al., 1982; Perry & Whipple, 1981). Traditionally, it was thought that men ejaculate and women don't. However, sex researchers John Perry and Beverly Whipple (1981) reported that they discovered fluid spurting out of the urethra of some women during orgasm. According to one study, the fluid is chemically similar to the seminal fluid of men, but contains no sperm. Perry and Whipple estimate that 10 to 20 percent of women ejaculate during orgasm. This is an important discovery, because given the old wisdom that women don't ejaculate, many women who did ejaculate suffered extreme embarrassment and anxiety, thinking that they were urinating during sex.

There is a second reason that the G-spot might be important. Based on its discovery, Perry and Whipple theorized that there is a *uterine orgasm*. They believe that there are two kinds of orgasm: vulvar orgasm (the kind studied by Masters and Johnson, produced by clitoral stimulation, and named for the vulva, or external genitals, of the female) and uterine orgasm (felt more deeply and produced by stimulation of the G-spot). This sounds like the old argument about clitoral versus vaginal orgasm, and certainly we should withhold judgment on the G-spot until there can be independent replication by other scientists.

In one study designed to test Perry and Whipple's hypotheses, two female gynecologists examined 11 women, 6 of whom claimed to be ejaculators. The gynecologists found an area like the G-spot in only 4 of the 11 women, but not in the rest, and the G-spot was not found more frequently among the ejaculators. Analysis of the ejaculate indicated that it was chemically like urine, not like semen (Goldberg et al., 1983). Yet a large survey of women found that 40 percent reported having experienced an ejaculation at the time of orgasm at least once, and 66 percent reported having an especially sensitive area on the front wall of the vagina (Darling et al., 1990). Evidence on the G-spot is thus mixed.

Psychological Aspects

Gender Differences in Sexuality It is a traditional stereotype in our culture that female sexuality and male sexuality are quite different. Women were reputed to be uninterested in sex and slow to arouse. Men, in contrast, were supposed to be constantly aroused. What is the scientific evidence on gender differences in sexuality?

Mary Beth Oliver and I conducted a meta-analysis of studies reporting data on gender differences in sexuality (Oliver & Hyde, 1993). Two gender differences were particularly large: the incidence of masturbation and attitudes about casual sex. Women are less likely to have masturbated than men are ($d = 0.96$), and women are considerably less approving of sex in a casual or uncommitted relationship than men are ($d = 0.81$). Notice that the sizes of these gender differences, 0.96 and 0.81, are enormous compared with some of the other gender differences we have examined, such as gender differences in abilities (see Chapter 8).

Let's first consider the gender difference in masturbation. Kinsey, based on his massive survey conducted in the 1940s, found that 92 percent of the men in his sample reported having masturbated to orgasm at least once in their lives, compared with 58 percent of the women (Kinsey et al., 1953). More recent surveys have found percentages very close to these (Laumann et al., 1994). That is, this gender difference doesn't seem to have disappeared in recent years with the sexual revolution. In fact, every year I survey the students in my human sexuality course and find statistics on masturbation very close to Kinsey's.

One question we must ask, however, is whether this is a real gender difference or just an inaccuracy resulting from the use of self-reports. In our culture, particularly in previous decades, more restrictions have been placed on female sexuality than on male sexuality. It might be that these restrictions have discouraged females from ever masturbating. On the other hand, they might simply lead women not to report masturbating. That is, perhaps women do masturbate but are simply more reticent to report it on a sex survey than men are. I tend not to believe this argument. On today's sex surveys, women report all kinds of intimate behaviors, such as fellatio and cunnilingus. More of them report having engaged in fellatio and cunnilingus than report having masturbated. It is hard to believe that these women honestly report about oral-genital sex and suddenly get bashful and lie about masturbation.

The other large gender difference was in attitudes about casual sex, such as sex in a "one-night stand." Men are more approving and women are more disapproving. Investigating this idea, Janell Carroll, Kari Volk, and I surveyed a random sample of students at Denison University (Carroll et al., 1985). The responses to the question "How would you feel about sex in a 'one-night stand'?" are shown in Table 12.1. Notice that virtually all the women said they would feel either guilty or anxious, whereas about half the men said they would feel comfortable, relaxed, or satisfied. This gender difference can be a source of great conflict between women and men.

Related to this finding is the stereotype that men and women differ in their motives for having sex. Men—at least according to the stereotype—are more interested in the physical aspects of sex and have a "love 'em and leave 'em" attitude. Women, in contrast, are thought to be most interested in love and romance and to be concerned with the interpersonal more than the physical aspects of the relationship. We investigated this stereotype in the same survey of students discussed earlier. The results generally confirmed the stereotype as being a real

TABLE 12.1

Percentages of Males and Females Giving Different Responses to the Question "How Would You Feel About Sex in a 'One-Night Stand'?"

	Guilty	Anxious	Comfortable/ Relaxed	Satisfied
Males	28	22	22	28
Females	68	23	6	3

SOURCE: Carroll et al. (1985).

difference between women and men. In one open-ended question, we asked, "What would be your motives for having sexual intercourse?" These were some of the typical answers from women:

> emotional feelings that were shared, wonderful way to express LOVE!!

> my motives for sexual intercourse would all be due to the love and commitment I feel for my partner

> to show my love for my partner and to feel loved and needed

> love, to feel loved, to express love to someone

These responses clearly indicate the importance most women attach to love and a close relationship as part of their sexual expression. Contrast those quotations with these typical responses from men:

> need it

> to gratify myself

> for the pleasure or the love

> to satisfy my needs

> when I'm tired of masturbation

These responses reflect the greater importance men—at least in this college-aged group—attach to physical gratification from sex.

Of course, not every respondent gave typical responses. For example, a response to that same question from one woman was "to enjoy myself physically, for experimentation, exercise, fun, and to get to know someone better." And this atypical answer came from a male: "Intercourse makes me happy, and people enjoy doing things that make them happy. I express myself oftentimes better physically. I have lots of love to give, and it's one way that is a better avenue of expressing my feelings for others."

Another stereotype is that a gender difference exists in arousal to erotic materials, men being much more responsive to them than women are. Is there any scientific evidence that this is accurate?

A meta-analysis of laboratory studies on gender differences in arousal to erotic materials found that men are more aroused, but the difference is not large, $d = 0.31$ (Murnen & Stockton, 1997). Interestingly, the difference was largest among college students ($d = 0.38$) but was nonexistent among adults beyond the college years ($d = -0.04$). This finding points to the importance of looking at changing patterns of gender differences in sexuality across the lifespan.

An interesting study by psychologist Julia Heiman (1975) provides insight into the responses of males and females to erotic materials. Her participants were sexually experienced university students, and she studied their responses as they listened to tape recordings of erotic stories. Not only did Heiman obtain people's self-ratings of their arousal, as other investigators had done, but she also got objective measures of their physiological levels of arousal. To do this, she used two instruments: a penile strain gauge and a photoplethysmograph. The penile strain gauge is used to get a physiological measure of arousal in the male; it is a flexible loop that fits around the base of the penis. The photoplethysmograph measures physiological arousal in the female; it is an acrylic cylinder that is placed just inside the vagina. Both instruments measure vasocongestion in the genitals, which is the major physiological response during sexual arousal.

Participants heard one of four kinds of tapes. The stereotype is that women are more turned on by romance, whereas men are more aroused by "raw sex," or the physical aspects of sex. The tapes varied according to which of these kinds of content they contained. The first group of tapes was *erotic;* they included excerpts from erotic material and popular novels giving explicit descriptions of heterosexual sex. The second group of tapes was *romantic;* a couple were heard expressing affection for each other, but they did not actually engage in sex. The third group of tapes was *erotic-romantic;* these tapes included erotic elements of explicit sex and also romantic elements. Finally, the fourth group of tapes served as a *control;* a couple were heard engaging in conversation but nothing else. The plots of the tapes also varied according to whether the male or the female initiated the activity and whether the description centered on the female's physical and psychological responses or on the male's. Thus the tapes were male-initiated or female-initiated and female-centered or male-centered. Three important results emerged from the study:

1. Explicit sex (heard in the erotic and erotic-romantic tapes) was most arousing, both for women and for men. The great majority of both males and females responded most, both physiologically and in self-ratings, to the erotic and erotic-romantic tapes. Women, in fact, rated the erotic tapes as more arousing than men did. Neither men nor women responded—either physiologically or in self-reports—to the romantic tapes or to the control tapes.

2. Both males and females found the female-initiated, female-centered tape to be the most arousing.

3. Women were sometimes not aware of their own physiological arousal. Generally there was a high correlation between self-ratings of arousal and objective physiological measures of arousal, both for men and for women.

When men were physically aroused, they never made an error in reporting this in their self-ratings—it's pretty hard to miss an erection. But when the women were physically aroused, about half of them failed to report it in their self-ratings. (One might assume that women who were sophisticated enough to volunteer for an experiment of this sort and who were willing to insert a photoplethysmograph into their vagina would not suddenly become bashful about reporting their arousal; that is, it seems likely that these women honestly did not know when they were aroused.)

In sum, then, Heiman's study indicates that females and males are quite similar in their responses to erotic materials, but that women can sometimes be unaware of their own physical arousal. This study, however, dealt only with the preliminary stages of arousal; perhaps women vary in the point at which they recognize their arousal.

An additional gender difference in sexuality is found in orgasm consistency. According to one major survey, 75 percent of men, but only 29 percent of women, always have an orgasm during sex with their partner (Laumann et al., 1994, p. 116). The gap is narrower for orgasm consistency during masturbation, but even here men seem to be more effective: 80 percent of men, compared with 60 percent of women, report that they usually or always have an orgasm when masturbating (Laumann et al., 1994, p. 84).

Sexual Development   Sexual development in childhood and adolescence involves a complex interplay between the developing body, early experiences with masturbation, and messages from the media, parents, and peers (Hyde & Jaffee, 2000).

The earliest sexual experiences many people have are in masturbation. But as we have seen, the data indicate that substantial numbers of females never masturbate, and many of those who do, do so later in life than males do. This may have important consequences in other areas of sexuality as well.

Childhood and adolescent experiences with masturbation are important early sources of learning about sexuality. Through these experiences we learn how our bodies respond to sexual stimulation and what the most effective techniques for stimulating our own bodies are. This learning is important to our experience of adult, two-person sex. Perhaps the women who do not masturbate, and who are thus deprived of this early learning experience, are the same ones who do not have orgasms in sexual intercourse. This is exactly what Kinsey's data suggested: 31 percent of the women who had never masturbated to orgasm before marriage had not had an orgasm by the end of their first year of marriage, compared with only 13 to 16 percent of the women who had masturbated (Kinsey et al., 1953, p. 407). Girls' lack of experience with masturbation in adolescence, then, may be related to their problems with having orgasms during heterosexual intercourse.

It is interesting to note from the Kinsey data that boys and girls seem to learn about masturbation in different ways. Most males reported having heard about it before trying it themselves, and a substantial number had observed others doing it. Most females, on the other hand, learned to masturbate by accidental discovery of the possibility. Apparently communication about sexual behavior is not so free among girls as it is among boys, or perhaps girls are not so eager to pursue this information. At any rate, it appears that most males have learned to associate the genital organs with pleasure by the time of puberty, whereas many females have not.

Not only may women's relative inexperience with masturbation lead to a lack of sexual learning, but it may also create a kind of "erotic dependency" on men. Typically, boys' earliest sexual experiences are with masturbation. They learn that they can produce their own sexual pleasure. Girls typically have their earliest sexual experiences in heterosexual petting. They therefore learn about sex from boys, and they learn that their sexual pleasure is produced by the male. As sex researcher John Gagnon commented:

> Young women may know of masturbation, but not know *how* to masturbate—how to produce pleasure, or even what the pleasures of orgasm might be. . . . Some young women report that they learned how to masturbate after they had orgasm from intercourse and petting, and decided they could do it for themselves. (1977, p. 152)

An illustration of the way in which masturbation can expand female sexuality is given by what one young woman student wrote in an essay:

> At twelve years old, I discovered masturbation. . . . I was almost relieved to have, quite by accident, discovered this practice. This actually was one of the nicest discoveries that I've ever made. I feel totally comfortable with this and have actually discussed it with some of my friends. One of my favorite theories centers around this. When men have asked me to have intercourse with them and I felt that I was basically going to only serve the purpose of being an instrument to produce their orgasm, I usually tell them that I'm sure that they'd "have a better time by themselves." Masturbation does produce a better, more controlled, orgasm for me. I've read Shere Hite's study on male sexuality that the same is true for men. I'm not saying that it's better than sexual contact with a man for me but I do think it's more satisfying than waking up next to someone I don't care about and feel comfortable with. I'm surprised that according to Kinsey, only 58 percent of women masturbate at some time in their lives. I thought everyone did. It's very creative for me. I've tried several techniques and it certainly helps me in my sexual experiences. I know a great deal about my sexual responses and I think that in knowing about myself, some of it relates to men and their sexual responses.

Experiences with masturbation—or lack of such experiences—then, may be very important in shaping female sexuality and making it different from male sexuality.

Of course, socialization forces on girls' developing sexuality are also important. Our culture has traditionally placed tighter restrictions on women's sexuality than it has on men's, and vestiges of these restrictions linger today. It seems likely that these restrictions have acted as a damper on female sexuality, and thus they may help to explain why some women do not masturbate or do not have orgasms. In an essay one woman student recalled one of her childhood socialization experiences as follows:

> A big part of my childhood was Catholic grammar school. The principal and teachers were nuns of the old school. . . . I remember one day the principal called all of the girls (third grade to eighth) to the auditorium. "I can't blame the boys for lifting your skirts to see your underwear," she scolded, "you girls wear your skirts so short it is temptation beyond their control." I had no idea what she was talking about, but throughout school the length of our skirts was of utmost importance. Nice girls did not show their legs.

The differences in restrictions on female and male sexuality are encoded in the **double standard** (Muehlenhard & McCoy, 1991; Sprecher et al., 1987). The double standard says, essentially, that the same sexual behavior is evaluated differently, depending on whether a male or a female engages in it (see Chapter 2). An example is premarital sex. Traditionally in our culture, premarital intercourse has been more acceptable for males than for females. Indeed, premarital sexual activity might be considered a status symbol for a male but a sign of cheapness for a female.

Double standard: The evaluation of male behavior and female behavior according to different standards; used specifically to refer to holding more conservative, restrictive attitudes toward female sexuality.

These different standards have been reflected in behavior. For example, the Kinsey data, collected in the 1940s, indicated that more than twice as many males (71 percent) as females (33 percent) had premarital sex. Apparently, society's message got through to young women of that era. Most of them managed to keep themselves chaste before marriage, whereas their male contemporaries tended to get the experience that was expected of them.

Generally, there seems to be less of a double standard today than there was in former times. For example, people now approve of premarital sex for females about as much as they do for males (Sprecher & Hatfield, 1996). This change in attitude is reflected in behavior. A much higher percentage of women report having engaged in premarital intercourse now than in Kinsey's time. In one sample, 80 percent of the men and 63 percent of the women had engaged in premarital intercourse (Robinson et al., 1991). Thus there is much less of a difference between females and males now than there was in the 1940s and 1950s.

On the other hand, there is still more disapproval of a woman who has many partners than of a man who does. In response to the statement "A man who has had sexual intercourse with a great many women is immoral," 32 percent of men and 52 percent of women agree (Robinson, et al., 1991). But when the statement is about a woman, the percentages agreeing leap up to 51 and 64 for men and for women respondents, respectively.

As I noted in Chapter 7, *ambivalence* is an important theme in the psychology of women. In that chapter I discussed ambivalence about achievement and femininity. Sexuality is another area of ambivalence for women. This ambivalence results from the kind of mixed message that females get from society. Beginning in adolescence, they are told that popularity is important for them, and being sexy increases one's popularity. But actually engaging in premarital intercourse, especially with many different partners, can lead to a loss of status. The ambivalence-producing message is "Be sexy but don't be sexual."

Ambivalence toward sexuality is reflected in the large number of unwanted pregnancies among unmarried women. In the United States, one out of every eight women aged 15 to 19 becomes pregnant (Hatcher et al., 1998). And among sexually active teenage girls, 29 percent use no method of contraception (Hofferth, 1990). Why? Taking a birth control pill every day indicates that the woman thinks intercourse is a real possibility. For unmarried women, particularly those not involved in a long-term relationship, this is a difficult admission to make. Constantly being ready for sexual relations still suggests lack of morals. In fact, the antipathy toward taking a daily measure against conception is apparently so great that it outweighs the undesirability of pregnancy, as discussed in Chapter 11. The woman would much prefer to believe that she was "swept off her feet," rather than the implied alternative, that she was expecting to have sex.

Research on the development of sexuality suggests that discussing gender differences in sexuality is too simple an approach. It is the developmental process of sexuality that differs for males and females (Kaplan & Sager, 1971). In a sense, males and females move through the stages of sexual development in adolescence and adulthood in opposite orders. For males, adolescent sexuality is genitally focused, with strong orgasmic needs—some report four to eight orgasms per day. But by the time a man reaches 50, emphasis has shifted away from genitally centered sensations to include more emphasis on the quality of the relationship with the partner, and two orgasms per week are considered satisfactory. For the female, adolescent sexuality is not genitally focused, with little emphasis on orgasm, but rather is relationship focused. Genital sexuality and orgasmic potential develop later, not reaching a peak until the 30s and 40s. Orgasmic response in women is faster and more consistent in the 40s than it is in the teens or 20s. It appears, then, that early male sexuality is genital and gradually evolves to add a relationship component, whereas female sexuality begins with a focus on the interpersonal and gradually develops the genital component.

Adolescent Girls, Desire, and First Intercourse   Most discussions of teenage girls' sexuality focus on topics such as teen pregnancy and date rape—

that is, on the negatives. Missing from such discussions is any recognition that adolescent girls may actually experience sexual desire. Psychologist Michele Fine (1988) has called this the "missing discourse of desire."

A study of eleventh-grade girls, representing multiple ethnic groups, some urban and some suburban, gives us insight into these girls' experience of sexual desire (Tolman & Szalacha, 1999). About two-thirds of the sample said that they felt desire. As they described it, the desire had a power, intensity, and urgency. It was grounded in the body, challenging beliefs that girls' sexuality is purely relational. At the same time, the girls questioned their entitlement to their own sexual feelings.

Differences emerged between the urban and suburban girls in how they responded to feelings of desire. The urban girls expressed agency with a goal of self-protection. They exercised self-control and caution about their body's feelings, recognizing their own vulnerability to AIDS, pregnancy, and getting a bad reputation. The suburban girls, in contrast, expressed agency with a goal of pleasure. They were curious about sex and were less restrained by feelings of vulnerability, although cultural messages about appropriate female sexuality still exerted controls. One suburban girl expressed her complicated feelings as follows:

> I don't like to think of myself as feeling really sexual. . . . I don't like to think of myself as being like someone who needs to have their desires fulfilled. . . . I mean I understand that it's wrong and that everybody has needs, but I just feel like self-conscious when I think about it, and I don't feel self-conscious when I say that we do these things, but I feel self-conscious about saying I need this kind of a thing. (Tolman & Szalacha, 1999, p. 16)

Many girls have their first experience of heterosexual intercourse during high school or the early college years. Their own desire is one of many reasons for this significant event. In one well-sampled national survey, 71 percent of women reported that their first intercourse was wanted, another 25 percent said that it was not wanted but was not forced, and 4 percent reported that it was forced (Laumann et al., 1994). Among those whose first intercourse was wanted, 48 percent of the women (compared with 25 percent of the men) reported that the main reason for first intercourse was affection for the partner. In contrast, 51 percent of the men reported the main reason was curiosity and a feeling that they were ready for sex (compared with 24 percent of women). Thus the motivation and emotions that teens bring to the experience is considerably different for girls and boys. Girls typically bring affection and boys bring curiosity.

Girls also tend to experience less pleasure at first intercourse than boys do. In a large national sample of college students, women reported significantly less pleasure and significantly more guilt about first intercourse than men did (Sprecher et al., 1995). On a pleasure scale ranging from 1 (*not at all*) to 7 (*a great deal*), women gave an average rating of only 2.95 for first intercourse. Despite, or perhaps because of, our culture's romanticized vision of first intercourse, adolescent girls typically find it disappointing. Nonetheless, they persist.

Gender, Race, and Sexuality

The topic of the meeting of gender, race, and sexuality is a large and complex one that could easily fill several books. Many historical issues are involved. For example, during the period of slavery in the United States, White masters assumed that they had the right to sexual intercourse with African American slave women. In sharp contrast, the reverse—an African American slave man having sex with a White woman—was not only forbidden but grounds for death.

Here we will focus on contemporary data collected by social scientists that allow us to compare the sexual behavior of women of various ethnic groups. Some of these data are summarized in Table 12.2. The data show evidence of both differences and similarities. African American women, on average, have intercourse for the first time somewhat earlier than White women do, although the gap is not large. Women of all ethnic groups are about equally likely to have had sex with a same-gender partner, except for Asian Americans. And White, African American, and Latina women are all about equally likely to terminate a pregnancy with an abortion, but Asian American women are considerably more likely to do so. Asian countries typically do not have the taboos on abortion found in American society.

Earlier in the chapter I noted that females tend to begin masturbating at later ages than males do. When the data are broken down by ethnicity, however, it becomes clear that this statement is true for Whites but not for African Americans. On average, Black women begin masturbating at an earlier age than Black men do and considerably earlier than White women do (Belcastro, 1985). This finding

TABLE 12.2

A Comparison of the Sexuality of American Women of Different Ethnic Groups

	Whites	African Americans	Latinas	Asian Americans
Mean age of first intercourse*	17.4	16.8	17.6	NA
Percent who masturbated in the last year**	44%	32%	35%	NA
Percent who have performed oral sex**	75%	34%	60%	NA
Percent of conceptions terminated by abortion**	10%	9%	11%	21%
Percent who have had sex with a same-gender partner**	5%	3%	4%	0

NA = Not available in that study.
SOURCES: Day (1992)*; Laumann et al. (1994)**.

One factor affecting African American women's romantic relationships is an imbalance in the gender ratio: There are more Black women than Black men.

is a good reminder that we shouldn't look simply at gender differences, but should remember that gender often interacts with ethnicity.

Sexual Dysfunction and Therapy

The term **sexual dysfunction** refers to various disturbances or impairments of sexual functioning, such as inability to have an orgasm (orgasmic dysfunction) or premature ejaculation. Let us now look at some specific examples of sexual dysfunction in women.

> **Sexual dysfunction:** A problem with sexual responding that causes a person mental distress; examples are erection problems in men and orgasm problems in women.

Orgasmic Dysfunction   Orgasmic dysfunction (also termed **anorgasmia,** female orgasmic disorder, or inhibited female orgasm) is the condition of being unable to have an orgasm. In *primary orgasmic dysfunction* the woman has had intercourse but

> **Anorgasmia:** The inability to have an orgasm; orgasmic dysfunction.

has never experienced an orgasm (for a review, see Anderson, 1983). Sex therapists do not use the term *frigidity*, because it has a variety of imprecise, negative connotations.

   In *situational orgasmic dysfunction*, the woman has orgasms in some situations, but not in others. Clearly in this case, there is no organic impairment of orgasm, because the woman is capable of experiencing it. One example of situational orgasmic dysfunction is the case of women who are able to have orgasms through masturbation but not through sexual intercourse. This pattern is so common, however, that it probably shouldn't be classified as a dysfunction (Hyde, 1994).

Orgasmic disorders in general are common among women. According to one survey, 24 percent of the women reported difficulty in the last 12 months with having orgasms (Laumann et al., 1994).

Vaginismus   **Vaginismus** involves a tightening or spasm of the outer third of the vagina, possibly to such an extent that the opening of the vagina is closed and intercourse becomes impossible (Basson et al., 2001; Leiblum & Rosen, 1989). Factors in the woman's history that seem to cause this condition include family background in which sex was considered dirty and sinful, a previous sexual assault, and long experience of painful intercourse due to a physical problem (Masters & Johnson, 1970).

> **Vaginismus:** A strong, spastic contraction of the muscles around the vagina, perhaps closing off the vagina and making intercourse impossible.

Painful Intercourse   Painful intercourse, or **dyspareunia**, may be organic or psychogenic in origin (Meana & Binik, 1994). Too often, the woman's complaints of pain are dismissed, particularly if the physician cannot find an obvious physical problem. However, this is a serious condition and should be treated as such. When pain is felt in the vagina, it may be due to failure to lubricate, to infection, to special sensitivity of the vagina (such as to the contraceptives being used), or to changes in the vagina due to age. Pain may also be felt in the region of the vaginal outlet and clitoris, or deep in the pelvis. In this latter case, the causes may be infection or tearing of the ligaments supporting the uterus, particularly following childbirth.

> **Dyspareunia:** Painful intercourse.

Disorders of Sexual Desire   Sexual desire, or libido, refers to a set of feelings that lead the individual to seek out sexual activity or to be pleasurably receptive to it (Kaplan, 1995). When sexual desire is inhibited, so that the individual is not interested in sexual activity, the dysfunction is termed *low sexual desire* or hypoactive sexual desire (Basson et al., 2001; Beck, 1995; Rosen & Leiblum, 1995a). People with inhibited sexual desire often manage to avoid situations that will evoke sexual feelings. If, despite their best efforts, they find themselves in an arousing situation, they experience a rapid "turnoff" of their feelings. The turnoff may be so intense that some people report negative, unpleasant feelings; others simply report sexual anesthesia, that is, no sexual feeling at all, even though they may respond to the point of orgasm.

A survey of a "normal" (nonpatient) population indicated that 33 percent of the women and 16 percent of the men complained of lack of interest in sex (Laumann et al., 1994).

As with other dysfunctions, disorders of sexual desire entail complex problems of definition. There are many circumstances when it is perfectly normal for a person's desire to be inhibited. For example, one cannot be expected to find

WOMEN'S SEXUAL PROBLEMS: A NEW VIEW

Feminist psychologist and sex therapist Leonore Tiefer (2001), together with a large group of experts, has proposed a new view of women's sexual problems. Tiefer argues that the classification of sexual problems has, for decades, been based on men's problems and the increasing medicalization of their problems encouraged by drug companies that have made billions on Viagra. A new view is needed, Tiefer argues, that focuses on women's sexual experiences. The new view proposes four broad categories for women's sexual problems:

1. *Sexual problems due to sociocultural, political, or economic factors.* These include ignorance and anxiety about sexuality resulting from inadequate sexuality education. In the absence of education, women may lack information about the biology of sexual functioning. And in the absence of information about the impact of gender roles, women may experience sexual avoidance or distress because they feel they cannot meet cultural standards of ideal female sexuality.

2. *Sexual problems relating to partner and relationship.* These include discrepancies in desire or in preferred behaviors between the partners,

every potential partner attractive. Sex therapist Helen Singer Kaplan (1979) recounted an example of a couple consisting of a shy, petite woman and an extremely obese (350 pounds, 5 feet 3 inches tall), unkempt man. He complained of her lack of desire, but one can understand her inhibition and would certainly hesitate to classify her as having a sexual dysfunction. One cannot expect to respond sexually at all times, in all places, and with all persons.

It is also true that an individual's absolute level of sexual desire is often not the problem—rather, the problem is a *discrepancy of sexual desire* between the partners (Zilbergeld & Ellison, 1980). That is, if one partner wants sex less frequently than the other partner wants it, there is a conflict.

The following have been implicated as determinants of low sexual desire: hormones, psychological factors (particularly anxiety and/or depression), cognitive factors (not having learned to perceive one's arousal accurately or having limited expectations for one's own ability to be aroused), and sexual trauma such as sexual abuse in childhood (Pridal & LoPiccolo, 2000; Rosen & Leiblum, 1987).

distress about sexuality because of dislike or fear of the partner, and problems created by poor communication about sex.

3. *Sexual problems due to psychological factors.* These include sexual aversion and inhibition of sexual pleasure due to past experiences of physical, sexual, or emotional abuse; problems associated with attachment issues; and depression and anxiety.

4. *Sexual problems due to medical factors.* These include pain or lack of response during sex that is not due to any of the factors listed above. Problems in this category can result from specific medical conditions such as diabetes; or they may involve side effects of medications.

This classification scheme starting from women's point of view is strikingly different from the traditional one reflected in the American Psychiatric Association's *Diagnostic and Statistical Manual* (DSM-IV). What would happen if we now imposed these categories on men's sexual experience?

Source: Leonore Tiefer, "A New View of Women's Sexual Problems: Why New? Why Now?" *Journal of Sex Research,* 38, pp. 89–96. © 2001. Reprinted with permission of the Society for the Scientific Study of Sexuality.

Therapies for Sexual Dysfunction Masters and Johnson pioneered modern sex therapy (Masters & Johnson, 1970; for a critique, see Zilbergeld & Evans, 1980). Their approach can be seen basically as behavior therapy, grounded in learning theory, although they themselves did not frame it that way.

The treatment program they developed has a number of unusual features. One is that it requires that both partners participate in the therapy. Masters and Johnson maintained that there is no such thing as an uninvolved partner in cases of sexual dysfunction, even if only one person displays overt symptoms. For instance, a woman who does not experience orgasm is anxious and wonders whether there is anything wrong with her, or whether she is unattractive to her partner. The partner, at the same time, may wonder why he (or she) is failing to stimulate her to orgasm. Both partners are deeply involved. Realizing the reciprocal nature of sexual gratification, Masters and Johnson employed the practice of having both partners participate.

The major objective in therapy using the Masters and Johnson method is abolishing goal-directed sexual performance. Most people think that certain things should be *achieved* during sexual activity—for example, that the woman should achieve or attain an orgasm. This emphasis on achieving leads to a fear of failure, which spells disaster for sexual enjoyment. The therapist therefore tries to remove the individual from a spectator role in sex—observing her or his own actions, evaluating their success. Instead, the emphasis is on the enjoyment of all sensual pleasures. Clients use a series of "sensate focus" exercises, in which they learn to touch and to respond to touch. They are also taught to express sexual needs to their partners, which people generally are reluctant to do. For instance, the woman is taught to tell her partner in which regions of her body she enjoys being touched most and how firm or light the touch should be. Beyond this basic instruction, which includes lessons in sexual anatomy and physiology, the therapist simply allows natural sexual response to emerge. Sexual pleasure is natural; sexual response is natural. After removing artificial impediments to sexual response, most people quickly begin joyful, "successful" participation in sex.

Masters and Johnson evaluated the success of their therapy, both during the two-week therapy session and in follow-up studies five years after couples left the clinic. Their research indicated that therapy is successful in approximately 75 percent of the cases (although their results have been disputed—see Zilbergeld & Evans, 1980).

New Therapies for Women's Sexual Dysfunctions   The incidence of women who have problems having orgasms, particularly in intercourse, is so high that it seems that this pattern is well within the range of normal female sexual response. It is questionable whether it should be called a dysfunction, except insofar as it causes unhappiness for the woman. With the growing awareness of the frequency of this problem have come a number of self-help sex therapy books for women, one of the best being Lonnie Garfield Barbach's *For Yourself: The Fulfillment of Female Sexuality* (1975; see also Heiman et al., 1976). Reading and working through the exercises in these self-help books actually has a fancy name—bibliotherapy—and it has been demonstrated to produce significant gains in women's frequency of orgasm (Van Lankveld, 1998).

A common recommendation of Barbach and other therapists (LoPiccolo & Stock, 1986; Rosen & Leiblum, 1995b) is that pre-orgasmic women practice masturbation to increase their capacity for orgasm. The idea is that women must first explore their own bodies and learn how to bring themselves to orgasm before they can expect to have orgasms in heterosexual intercourse. As noted earlier in this chapter, many women have not had this kind of practice, and sex therapists recommend that they get it.

Kegel exercises or *pubococcygeal muscle exercises* are also recommended (Kegel, 1952). The pubococcygeal (PC) muscle

Kegel exercises: Exercises to strengthen the muscles surrounding the vagina; pubococcygeal muscle exercises.

runs along the sides of the entrance to the vagina. Exercising this muscle increases women's sexual pleasure by increasing the sensitivity of the vaginal area. This exercise is particularly helpful to women who have had the PC muscle stretched in childbirth or who simply have poor tone in it. The woman is instructed first to find the PC muscle by sitting on a toilet with her legs spread apart, urinating, and stopping the flow of urine voluntarily. The muscle that stops the flow is the PC. After that, the woman is told to contract the muscle ten times during each of six sessions per day. Gradually she can work up to more.

Feminist Sex Therapy   Sex therapist Leonore Tiefer has pioneered models of feminist sex therapy (Tiefer, 1995; 1996; see also McCormick, 1994). Tiefer questions the medicalization of sexual dysfunctions that results from therapists using DSM "diagnoses" (for further discussion of the DSM, see Chapter 15). She argues that these diagnoses are based on Masters and Johnson's exclusively physiological model of sexual response and that they oversimplify sexuality and ignore the social context of sexuality and sex problems. The advent of Viagra, of course, has only increased the medicalization of sex problems, and the search for a "female Viagra" channels the medicalization toward women's problems.

Tiefer recommends that feminist sex therapy for women include the following components:

1. *Education about feminism and women's issues:* This can be liberating as women realize that their individual problem is common and often is rooted in our culture's negative attitudes about sexuality and women.

2. *Anatomy and physiology education:* Because sexuality education in our nation—whether from parents or schools—is so inadequate, many women have fundamental misunderstandings about their sexual anatomy and its functioning. Education can be a simple solution in many cases.

3. *Assertiveness training:* Women need to learn to be assertive in asking a partner for what they need in a sexual interaction, just as in other areas of life.

4. *Body-image reclamation:* Women need to make a substantial shift away from seeing their bodies as objects to be evaluated (as we saw in the discussion of objectified body consciousness in Chapter 7) to seeing their bodies as sources of sensations and competencies.

5. *Masturbation education:* As noted earlier, many women do not masturbate and some do not even know about masturbation. Masturbation education has proven to be successful in sex therapy for women. From a feminist point of view, it can be seen as empowering women.

EXPERIENCE THE RESEARCH

GENDER DIFFERENCES IN SEXUALITY

Administer the questionnaire below to ten students, five men and five women. Because the information you will collect is sensitive, be sure to explain to each participant that their answers will be anonymous. You must devise some method to ensure anonymity, such as having respondents mail the questionnaire back to you, or having them place it into a large brown envelope that already contains others' questionnaires. Assure your respondents that the questionnaire will take less than five minutes to complete.

SEXUALITY QUESTIONNAIRE

1. Age: _____

2. Gender: _____ Female _____ Male

3. Ethnic heritage (check the one that applies):
   _____ Black/African American
   _____ Hispanic
   _____ Asian American
   _____ Native American
   _____ White (not Hispanic)
   _____ Biracial or multiracial

For each of the questions below, circle the letter that best reflects your response. Remember that your answers will be kept completely anonymous.

4. What is your attitude about a couple engaging in sexual intercourse when they are engaged?
   a. Strongly disapprove
   b. Disapprove somewhat
   c. Neutral
   d. Approve somewhat
   e. Strongly approve

5. What is your attitude about a couple engaging in sexual intercourse when they are only casually acquainted (i.e., a "one-night stand")?
   a. Strongly disapprove
   b. Disapprove somewhat
   c. Neutral
   d. Approve somewhat
   e. Strongly approve

6. Have you ever masturbated to orgasm?
   a. Yes (Go to question 7)
   b. No (Skip question 7 and go to question 8)

7. In the past month, how many times did you masturbate to orgasm?
   Number: _____

8. Have you ever engaged in sexual intercourse?
   a. Yes (continue on to question 9)
   b. No (Skip to the end)

9. With how many different partners have you engaged in sexual intercourse?
   Number: _____

Thank you for completing this questionnaire.

Gender Similarities

In previous chapters I have stressed gender similarities in psychological processes. There are also great gender similarities in sexuality. A few decades ago, at the time of the Kinsey research, there were marked gender differences in several aspects of sexuality. However, more recent research shows that these differences are greatly decreased, or even absent now.

For example, according to Kinsey's data collected in the 1940s, 71 percent of males but only 33 percent of females had premarital intercourse by age 25 (Kinsey et al., 1953). There was, at that time, a marked gender difference in premarital sexual activity. In a recent study, though, 78 percent of men and 70 percent of women had engaged in premarital intercourse (Laumann et al., 1994), representing a clear trend toward gender similarities. In the meta-analysis discussed earlier in this chapter, a number of variables showed no gender difference, including sexual satisfaction and attitudes about masturbation (Oliver & Hyde, 1993). Although there are some large gender differences in sexuality (incidence of masturbation and attitudes about casual sex), there are many gender similarities.

Suggestions for Further Reading

Angier, Natalie. (1999). *Woman: An intimate geography.* Boston: Houghton Mifflin.
   Angier, a Pulitzer Prize–winning science writer, has written an absolutely luscious account of women's bodies.

Barbach, Lonnie G. (1975). *For yourself: The fulfillment of female sexuality*. New York: Anchor Press/Doubleday. This is the classic self-help book on female sexuality and, I think, still the best one around.

Ellison, Carol R. (2000). *Women's sexuality: Generations of women share intimate secrets of sexual self-acceptance*. New York: New Harbinger. Ellison, a noted sex therapist and researcher, has put together a wonderful book in which we truly hear the voices of women of all ages speaking about their sexuality in all its complexity.

Hyde, Janet S., & DeLamater, John D. (2003). *Understanding human sexuality* (8th ed.). New York: McGraw-Hill. Clearly I have a prejudice in favor of this book, but I would like to recommend it if you want more information on sexuality than I could provide in one brief chapter here.

Wyatt, Gail E. (1997). *Stolen women: Reclaiming our sexuality, taking back our lives*. New York: Wiley. Wyatt, a psychologist and expert sex researcher, wrote this book for Black women. It documents historical forces as well as current forces that shape Black women's sexuality, and suggests positive paths for the future.

Women and the Web

Planned Parenthood. The website of the Planned Parenthood Federation of America contains a wealth of valuable information, including this page on women's sexuality.
http://www.plannedparenthood.org/WOMENSHEALTH/sexuality.htm

Sexuality Information and Education Council of the United States. This website, established by the Sexuality Information and Education Council of the United States (SIECUS), is filled with information and resources.
http://siecus.org/

Alan Guttmacher Institute. This website provides information and data on sexual and reproductive health and rights in the United States and worldwide. The Institute's slogan is "confronting ideology and rhetoric with evidence, reason, and practical solutions."
http://www.guttmacher.org

Lesbian and Bisexual Women

13

Between man and woman love is an act; each torn from self becomes other: what fills the woman in love with wonder is that the languorous passivity of her flesh should be reflected in the male's impetuosity; the narcissistic woman, however, recognizes her enticements but dimly in the man's erected flesh. Between women love is contemplative; caresses are intended less to gain possession of the other than gradually to re-create the self through her; separateness is abolished, there is no struggle, no victory, no defeat; in exact reciprocity each is at once subject and object; sovereign and slave; duality becomes mutuality.

— FROM SIMONE DE BEAUVOIR, THE SECOND SEX

With the sexual revolution and the feminist movement has also come the rise of gay liberation. The gay liberation movement can be counted as dating from June 1969, when, in response to police harassment, homosexuals rioted in Greenwich Village in New York. Lesbians have sometimes been united with the women's movement and sometimes in conflict with it. Radical lesbians argue that to be truly liberated, women must become separatists; that is, they must stay separate from men. Among other things, this would argue *against* heterosexuality and *for* lesbianism. More moderate lesbians join in working for the moderate goals of the women's movement, such as an end to job discrimination. A discussion of women today would be incomplete without a discussion of lesbian and bisexual women.

It is important to bear in mind that there is no "typical lesbian" and no single lesbian experience. Lesbians vary tremendously from one to another, just as heterosexual women do. Some are professors and some work on assembly lines. Some are fat and some are thin. Some are White and some are African American.

Sexual orientation is defined as a person's erotic and emotional orientation toward members of her or his own gender or members of the other gender (Hyde & DeLamater, 2003). Sexual orientation is not just an issue of eroticism or sexuality, but also an issue of the direction of one's emotional attachments. It is not just a matter of whom one has sex with, but whom one loves. A **lesbian,** then, is a woman whose erotic and emotional orientation is toward other women. A *bisexual* is a person whose erotic and emotional orientations are toward both women and men.

Sexual orientation: A person's erotic and emotional orientation toward members of her or his own gender or members of the other gender.

Lesbian: A woman whose sexual orientation is toward other women.

Stereotypes and Discrimination

Some experts believe that many Americans' attitudes toward lesbians and gay men can best be described as homophobic. **Homophobia** may be defined as a strong, irrational fear of homosexuals and, more generally, as fixed negative attitudes and reactions to homosexuals. Some scholars dislike the term *homophobia* because, although certainly some people have antigay feelings so strong that they could be called a phobia, what is more common is negative attitudes and prejudiced behaviors. Therefore, some prefer the term **antigay prejudice** or *sexual prejudice* (Herek, 2000a).

Homophobia: A strong, irrational fear of homosexuals.

Antigay prejudice: Negative attitudes and behaviors toward gay men and lesbians. Also called sexual prejudice.

Results of a well-sampled 1998 survey of Americans' attitudes are shown in Table 13.1. Notice that Americans' attitudes have become substantially more tolerant over 25 years. More than twice as many Americans in 1998, compared with 1973, believe that homosexuality is not wrong at all. Nonetheless, a majority of Americans (54 percent) believe that it is always wrong.

Many tangible instances of antigay prejudice exist. There are numerous documented cases of women being fired from their jobs or dishonorably discharged from the armed forces upon disclosure of their sexual orientation (Shilts, 1993), and in 1993 there was a great debate between President Bill Clinton and military leaders about whether the military should continue this practice of dishonorable discharge. The result was a "don't ask, don't tell" policy, in which it was all right to be gay or lesbian as long as one was secretive about it. Court cases have repeatedly upheld the right of employers to fire persons on

TABLE 13.1
Attitudes of Adult Americans Toward Homosexuality, 1973 and 1998

Question and Responses	Percentage of Sample	
	1973	*1998*
Are sexual relations between adults of the same sex:		
Always wrong	74	54
Almost always wrong	7	5
Wrong only sometimes	8	6
Not wrong at all	11	27

Source: From Davis and Smith, *General Social Surveys, 1971–1991, Cumulative Codebook,* published by the National Opinion Research Center and General Social Surveys. *www.icpsr.umich.edu/gss.*

the basis of sexual orientation.[1] Most states do not recognize lesbian partners in matters of health insurance or inheritance.

Another form of discrimination is the prohibition against lesbians rearing children. In most states it is illegal for lesbians to adopt children, and lesbianism may be grounds for a father to regain custody from a lesbian mother of children they had when married. Yet many lesbians desire children, and these issues can be heartbreaking. There is currently a move in several states to modify some of this discrimination against lesbians.

The most extreme expressions of antigay prejudice occur in *hate crimes* against lesbians (Garnets et al., 1993). The following is one case:

> Late one night in July, Heidi Dorow was embracing another woman on the corner of Bleecker and Carmine Streets in the West Village [of New York], when a teenager began to taunt them. As they shoved past him, Ms. Dorow said, "He swung around and punched me in the head."
>
> The youth and 10 other teenagers then jumped on the women, felling them with their fists and kicking them as they lay on the pavement.
>
> Dazed and bleeding, Ms. Dorow and her friend staggered down the street in search of a cab, passing a man who shouted obscenities at them.
>
> At a nearby hospital, both women were treated for cuts and bruises, and Ms. Dorow's friend for a concussion, and released. Then the women, who are lesbians, went to the Sixth Precinct . . . to file a report. As they were leaving, someone on the street shouted more obscenities at them. (Hays, 1990)

Other forms of discrimination are more subtle and psychological, involving the stereotyping of lesbians, who are expected to be unfeminine or even mannish, and certainly to be man-haters. In one study, participants were given written and tape-recorded descriptions of one of the following women: a feminine woman (described as feminine, emotional, warm toward others, and kind) or a masculine woman (described as masculine, competitive, active, feeling superior) with either heterosexual or homosexual feelings (Storms et al., 1981). Then participants rated their perceptions of the woman described to them. The woman who was described as homosexual was rated as being more masculine than the heterosexual woman. The woman who was described as feminine and homosexual was perceived as having a confused, unstable sexual identity. This sort of stereotyping is another unpleasant fact of life for lesbians.

In considering this stereotype of the lesbian as masculine, it is important to make a distinction between gender identity and choice of sexual partner. Most lesbians have a female identification—that is, they are quite definitely women;

---

[1]My own state, Wisconsin, as well as Hawaii and Massachusetts are among the only states in the nation to have laws that ban discrimination on the basis of sexual orientation, in matters such as employment and housing.

they dress and behave like women; but they simply choose to direct emotional, sexual love toward other women. Indeed, a large proportion of them have had heterosexual relations, and many are or have been heterosexually married. According to a well-sampled survey, 0.1 percent of the women reported that all of their sexual experiences had been with women; but 2.5 percent had had some experiences with men and some with women (Johnson et al., 1994, p. 187).

Finally, perhaps the most subtle and simultaneously most powerful discriminatory belief is the assumption that heterosexuality is universal, or what Adrienne Rich (1980) has called *compulsory heterosexuality*. Perhaps you have seen the T-shirts that read "How Dare You Presume I'm Heterosexual?" But that is exactly the assumption that most people make in their day-to-day interactions. As a result, lesbians must tolerate co-workers asking if they have a boyfriend or mothers asking if a husband is on the horizon yet. Just as we have seen in previous chapters that the male is normative, so, too, heterosexuality is normative.

Lesbian Culture

Lesbian Community   Today there is a lesbian community or culture with its own norms and values (Esterberg, 1996). Even for lesbians who are in the closet, this culture has a profound impact on identity and behavior—such as the books they read, or the way they define sex. As one woman put it,

> I have seen lesbian communities all over the world (e.g., Zimbabwe) where the lesbians of that nation have more in common with me (i.e., they play the same lesbian records, have read the same books, wear the same lesbian jewelry) than the heterosexual women of that nation have in common with heterosexual women in the U.S. (Rothblum, 1993)

Participation in the lesbian community can then become a major force in the lives of lesbians who are out of the closet.

Lesbian Relationships   With the 2000 census, the U.S. Census Bureau made an unprecedented change. It allowed as a category in the count of household types same-sex, unmarried-partner households. Previously these households and the relationships that they imply had been literally invisible in the census. In fact, in the 1990 census, if a same-gender couple reported that they were married, the Census Bureau changed the gender of one of the partners and counted them as a heterosexual married couple (Smith & Gates, 2001).

The 2000 census counted 600,000 same-gender-partner households in the United States, although this is likely an undercount (Smith & Gates, 2001). These households were about evenly split between gay male households and lesbian households, and were found in 99 percent of all counties in the United States. There were, for example, 4,129 lesbian households in Alabama and 4,370 in Wisconsin.

Lesbian pop singer Melissa
Ethridge. One important feature
of lesbian culture is music.

What is known psychologically about the relationships in these households? In studies of lesbians, close to 75 percent report being in a steady relationship (Peplau, 1993). Researchers in both the United States and the Netherlands have concluded that two fundamental values are related to the nature of lesbian relationships: attachment to the partner and personal autonomy (Peplau et al., 1978; Schreurs & Buunk, 1996). That is, lesbians vary from one to another in the extent to which they want a strong attachment to the partner, emphasizing emotional closeness, love, and security, and the extent to which they want personal independence. These values shape the kind of relationship that is formed. Feminist lesbians tend to emphasize personal autonomy.

Researchers have found that the average length of lesbian relationships is 6 years, and that these relationships range beyond 20 years—not so different from heterosexual couples (Schreurs & Buunk, 1996). Lesbians report the same level of satisfaction in their relationships as heterosexual couples do (Patterson, 2000). In one study, more than 70 percent of the lesbian women said that they almost always experienced orgasms when having sex with their partner (Peplau et al., 1978).

Lesbians tend to value an equal balance of power in their relationships, although they don't always achieve it (Patterson, 2000). When there is an imbalance, the woman who has more income and more education tends to be the more powerful member of the couple.

One stereotype is that lesbians play "butch" and "femme" roles in their relationships, that is, that they mimic the male and female roles found in traditional marriages. Research shows that this stereotype is rarely true (Peplau et al., 1996). Only a small minority of lesbian couples play such roles. Indeed, the majority of lesbian couples stress flexibility and taking turns—that is, equality—in their relationships.

Boston Marriages　The term **Boston marriage** is used to refer to a romantic but asexual lesbian relationship. Historically, the term had a somewhat different meaning. In the early 1900s, the term was used to refer to two "spinsters" who set up housekeeping together, having failed to find husbands and given up the hope. We can't know whether these relationships were sexual or asexual. The term has been reappropriated today for lesbian relationships that are romantic but asexual.

> **Boston marriage:** A romantic but asexual lesbian relationship.

Research on Boston marriages indicates that the partners typically had been sexual with each other for at least a short time in the past but are no longer (Rothblum & Brehony, 1993). Yet the women still felt sexually attracted to their partner. Their relationship was indistinguishable from other long-term lesbian relationships, with the exception of the lack of genital sex. Most of the couples were "out" in the lesbian community as well as in the workplace. Although some kept their asexuality secret in the lesbian community (it isn't very fashionable to be asexual these days), others were quite open about it.

Boston marriages are interesting in and of themselves, but they also raise some thought-provoking questions. How does one define a couple? For heterosexuals, legal marriage defines couple status, although certainly there are many heterosexual pairs who, though not married, would still be considered a couple. And there are some heterosexual married couples who are asexual. For gay male couples and lesbian couples, usually having a sexual relationship defines two people as being a couple. Where does that leave the Boston marriage, though? There is no marriage license and no sex, but the two women may have purchased a house together, lived together for 15 years, made out joint wills, perhaps raised children together. What defines two people as being a couple? That is a very complex question.

Coming Out

The process of coming out of the closet, or **coming out,** involves acknowledging to oneself, and then to others, that one is gay or lesbian (Coleman, 1982).

> **Coming out:** The process of acknowledging to oneself, and then to others, that one is lesbian or gay.

Before coming out can occur, however, the person must have arrived at a lesbian identity. The process of identity development itself generally proceeds in six stages (Cass, 1979):

1. *Identity confusion.* The woman most likely began by assuming she was heterosexual because heterosexuality is so normative in our society. As same-gender attractions or behaviors occur, there is confusion. She wonders, "Who am I?"

2. *Identity comparison.* The woman now thinks, "I *may* be lesbian." There may be feelings of alienation because the comfortable heterosexual identity has been lost.

3. *Identity tolerance.* The woman now thinks, "I *probably* am lesbian." She seeks out other lesbians and makes contact with the lesbian community, hoping for affirmation. The quality of these initial contacts is critical.

4. *Identity acceptance.* The woman now thinks, "I am lesbian," and accepts rather than tolerates this identity.

5. *Identity pride.* The woman dichotomizes the world into lesbians and gays (who are good) and heterosexuals (who are not). There is strong identification with the lesbian group and increased coming out of the closet.

6. *Identity synthesis.* The person no longer holds an us-versus-them view of homosexuals and heterosexuals, and recognizes that there are some good and supportive heterosexuals. In this stage, the person is able to synthesize public and private identities.

The woman is very vulnerable in the process of coming out, whether in the lesbian community, to her old friends, or to her co-workers. Whether she experiences acceptance or rejection can be critical to self-esteem. The process of coming out can be highly stressful. There may also be fears of losing one's job or custody of one's children. Many lesbians make a decision to be selectively out—that is, to be out with people they know they can trust, and not with others.

Lesbians who are selectively out may face a distinct set of stresses. Consider a common situation in which a woman is not out at work, but is out in the lesbian community. At work, she must take care not to reveal her secret, be careful about the pronoun she uses when referring to her date, or worry that a worker will phone her at home and her partner will answer. On the other side, she may be pressured by the lesbian community to be completely out.

Coming out to one's family is one of the most significant events for gays and lesbians. Research with college students indicates that 59 percent of lesbians have disclosed their identity to their mother, and 25 percent to their father (Savin-Williams, 1998). Parents are usually not the first person to whom lesbians and gays disclose their sexual identity—typically it is a peer. And most disclose to their mother before their father (Savin-Williams, 1998). Mothers are, in fact, more likely to be accepting of the disclosure (Pilkington & D'Augelli, 1995).

Some lesbians remember being lesbian ever since they became sexual, a pattern like that of almost all gay men. However, some lesbians come out in middle age, having been heterosexually married and had a heterosexual identity before that time (Burch, 1993).

Mental Health Issues

Lesbians' Adjustment What scientific evidence is there regarding whether homosexuality is an abnormal form of adjustment? To answer this question, I must first define what is meant by *abnormal*. A variety of definitions are possible (Hyde & DeLamater, 2003). The one that seems most appropriate here is that sexual behavior or identity is abnormal if it is associated with poor psychological adjustment and the person is unhappy about it.

Empirical research supports the view that lesbianism is not a deviant form of behavior (Peplau & Garnets, 2000). Much of the early research on lesbian adjustment studied lesbians who were in psychotherapy (Rosen, 1974). The use of such respondents was not surprising, because these women were easy to recruit, and, with the assumption that lesbianism was an abnormal form of adjustment, the researcher could rationalize the sampling techniques by saying that the "typical" lesbian would be in therapy.

In view of the approach, it is not surprising that some of these early research efforts did find abnormal personality characteristics in lesbians. However, a major breakthrough occurred with the advent of research on *nonpatient* lesbians, recruited through homophile organizations or newspaper ads. Such studies have generally found that lesbian women do not differ psychologically from control groups of heterosexual women in any consistent ways, with the one exception of their choice of sex partner (Peplau & Garnets, 2000). In one particularly well-designed study, the adjustment of lesbians was compared with that of a control group of their heterosexual sisters (Rothblum & Factor, 2001). The results indicated no significant differences between the two groups in adjustment, but the lesbians had higher self-esteem.

Thus the assumption that lesbianism is an inadequate form of adjustment is not supported by the data. The comparative absence of psychological disturbance among lesbians is even more remarkable in view of the social pressures to which they are subject. The notion that lesbianism, and homosexuality more generally, is an adequate form of adjustment is reflected in the 1973 decision of the American Psychiatric Association to remove the term *homosexual* from its official list of diagnostic categories.

Rather than seeing lesbian identity as automatically causing adjustment problems or not causing problems, it is preferable to understand that being a lesbian may be a risk factor for some mental health problems and a protective factor from others. For example, the risk of alcohol use or abuse may be increased for those who socialize in bars, although a study using excellent sampling techniques found no differences between lesbian and heterosexual women in drinking patterns (Bloomfield, 1993). On the other hand, lesbians have fewer eating disorders and less preoccupation with weight than heterosexual women do (Brand et al., 1992).

Coping   Stresses are present in lesbians' lives, some resulting from the kinds of discrimination discussed previously, some from the kinds of problems that everyone, gay and straight alike, must deal with. How do lesbians cope? Far more research is needed in this area, but at least one study provides information.

In this study, 79 lesbians, all working women, responded to a mailed questionnaire (Shachar & Gilbert, 1983). They were questioned about various conflicts they experienced and how they coped with them. Of the interrole conflicts—conflicts between two different roles that women must fulfill—the one most frequently mentioned was that between the lover and worker roles (mentioned by 41 percent of the women). As one woman commented,

> My lover wants the security of staying in one area and spending much time with me; I am very busy with my career . . . and I must move frequently to gain experience/opportunities. (Shachar & Gilbert, 1983, p. 249)

Other interrole conflicts mentioned with less frequency were conflicts between the roles of worker and political activist (13 percent), lover and daughter (7 percent), and lover and political activist (6 percent). Interestingly, certain other potential conflicts—for example, mother versus lover—were reported by no more than one respondent. On the other hand, those conflicts were rated as very stressful.

Intrarole conflicts are internal conflicts within a single role. As an area of intrarole conflict, work was mentioned most frequently (33 percent). One woman said,

> Expectations of co-workers and boss (all male) that I be heterosexual (dress, act, and have evidence of so being) when I really wish I could just be who I am at work. I cannot, usually, because I am afraid of what'd result. (Shachar & Gilbert, 1983, p. 250)

Of course, the fact that one-third of the lesbian respondents reported intrarole conflicts at work implies that two-thirds did not experience such conflicts.

Coping mechanisms for dealing with role conflicts can be placed in three categories (Shachar & Gilbert, 1983):

1. Structural role redefinition—The individual deals directly with those people who communicate role demands and negotiates a change that is mutually acceptable.

2. Personal role redefinition—The individual changes her own perceptions of roles and role demands rather than changing the external environment.

3. Reactive behavior—The individual assumes that role demands are unchangeable and denies or tries to meet all role demands.

Generally, Type 1 or Type 2 coping is more successful, resulting in less stress and greater satisfaction with coping. In dealing with interrole conflicts, 82 percent of the lesbian respondents reported using Type 1 or Type 2 strategies. Further, those who used one of those two strategies had significantly higher self-esteem than those who used the Type 3 strategy. In general, then, the majority of lesbians use healthy strategies for coping with their stresses.

Therapy   Some lesbians seek psychotherapy for psychological distress, just as some heterosexuals do. Unfortunately, however, many psychotherapists are not well educated about sexual orientation issues and may provide inappropriate or inadequate care. In response to this problem, the American Psychological Association has adopted guidelines for psychotherapy with gay, lesbian, and bisexual clients. These guidelines emphasize issues such as the following (Division 44, 2000):

1. It is important for psychologists to understand that having a homosexual or bisexual orientation does not automatically mean that the person is psychologically disturbed. Psychologists, of course, grow up in the same culture as everyone else, and learn the same kinds of myths that lay persons learn.

2. Psychologists need to probe their own personal attitudes about sexual orientation issues as well as their knowledge about these issues. If they discover limitations in their expertise or attitudes that might have a negative impact on the client, they should refer the client to another therapist.

3. Lesbians, gays, and bisexuals (LGBs) are stigmatized in dozens of ways, ranging from subtle prejudice to outright violence, and psychologists must gain a deep understanding of the impact this may have on the mental health of their client. They should also understand that these experiences may affect the client's behavior in therapy.

4. Psychologists should be knowledgeable about relationship issues for LGBs. This includes respecting LGBs' romantic relationships and understanding

how disclosure of sexual orientation may have an impact on the client's relationship with her or his family of origin—and how nondisclosure places a psychological burden on the client.

5. Lesbian, gay, and bisexual persons who are members of ethnic minority groups may face particular challenges because of cultural norms against homosexuality within their group, and psychologists must be sensitive to these issues.

Children of Lesbian Mothers   As noted earlier, lesbian mothers often lose custody of children they had when heterosexually married, and being a lesbian may be grounds for being denied adoption (Falk, 1993). The underlying psychological assumption is that lesbians are bad mothers, in the sense that they will not do a good job rearing their children and the children will grow up poorly adjusted. There also is an assumption that these children will be stigmatized, teased by their peers, and so on. How well adjusted are the children of lesbian mothers?

An important political issue for lesbian couples is the right to have children. The child shown here was born to the woman holding her, as a result of artificial insemination.

Research has compared children of lesbian mothers with children of hetero-sexual parents on measures such as sexual identity, personal development, and social relationships. This research has found evidence that the children of lesbian mothers develop as well as children reared by heterosexual couples (Patterson, 1992, 2000). Research has also shown that the child-rearing practices of lesbian mothers and heterosexual mothers are quite similar (Falk, 1993).

Regarding the issue of stigmatizing, one study found no differences between children from lesbian households and heterosexual households in peer group re-lationships, popularity, and social adjustment (Green et al., 1986).

In summary, the evidence seems to indicate that there is no cause for con-cern about the adjustment of children growing up in a lesbian household.

Another concern is that lesbian parents might work to "convert" their chil-dren to being lesbian or gay or that children might model their mother's lesbian relationship. In fact, the data indicate that the great majority of children growing up with a gay or lesbian parent become heterosexual (Bailey & Dawood, 1998).

Theoretical Views

The Psychoanalytic View   Sigmund Freud was one of the first medical therapists to attempt the treatment of a lesbian, publishing his insights in a paper, "The Psychogenesis of a Case of Homosexuality in a Woman," in 1920.

Freud considered human beings to be bisexual in nature. In this assertion, he recognized that all humans are capable of homosexual behavior. According to Freud, the sources of sexual pleasure in the young are many and diffuse.

As discussed in Chapter 2, at about age 3 the boy encounters the Oedipal complex. In the positive component of the complex, the mother is a love object for the boy and the father is the object of ambivalence. In resolving the Oedipal complex, the boy comes to identify with his father. A *negative Oedipal complex* occurs when the shift to identification with the father is not made, and the boy continues his initial identification with the mother, wanting (like her) to be loved by the father. According to Freud, people in general never really completely shed themselves of this negative component, but homosexual people remain fixated on it.

Freud initially viewed these psychological processes as highly similar for boys and for girls. It was some years before the gap between the logic of the theory and the realities of female development disposed Freud to a revised version of sexual development in women. He finally recognized that the boy's Oedipal develop-ment was far simpler than the girl's. The boy retains his original love object (mother), merely substituting another female for the original. For the girl, the mother is also the original love object, but the father must become the object. Thus presumably the negative Electra situation for the girl—in which she contin-ues to love the same-gender parent, the mother—may well be more intense, last longer, and not be resolved. The lesbian alternative, according to Freud, occurs when the negative Electra component persists, so that mother and, later, other women are the object of love. The masculine component of the woman's personality is retained and the object choice is homosexual.

Freud speculated that the basis for homosexuality in men and in women may well be a matter of self-love, or *narcissism*. The outcome, then, is to love the self and to seek for a sex partner a same-gender person who resembles the self. From this perspective we may be seeing a positive aspect of lesbian development. A problem with "normal" female development is that many women end up with low self-confidence and low regard for other women. Lesbian development may be an alternative in which the self and the female can be loved and valued.

Learning Theory   Learning theory (Ford & Beach, 1951; Hyde & Jaffee, 2000; McConaghy, 1987) emphasizes the point that all animals, including humans, display or are capable of homosexual activities. Thus, animals appear to be innately bisexual, and the environment may have a great influence on whether one or another choice of sex partner is made. Clellan Ford and Frank Beach (1951), in their classic work on sexual behavior in humans and animals, gave detailed evidence of the bisexual inheritance of humans. In some preliterate cultures, a male may be the appropriate sex partner for a young male, whereas in his adulthood the accepted partner is a female (Herdt, 1984).

Therefore humans may have no inborn preference for the other gender as an appropriate sex partner, but conditioning and socialization channel this disposition. That is, cultural pressures channel a generalized drive in a culturally prescribed direction. According to this view, heterosexual behavior too is acquired or learned. We should ask not only Why do lesbians develop? but also Why do heterosexuals develop?

The learning theory view, then, is that humans have a general pool of sex drive that may, depending on experience and circumstance, be conditioned in one direction or another, into heterosexuality or into homosexuality. This model thus readily accommodates lesbianism as a normal form of behavior, in contrast to the psychoanalytic theories, which treat it as deviant or compensatory.

The Feminist and Sociological Perspectives   Feminists and modern sociologists have rather similar things to say about lesbianism, and so I have grouped them here. One of the main points of the feminist perspective is that, when trying to understand the behavior of a woman, the emphasis should be shifted away from *internal factors* (her personality, adjustment, early childhood) to *external factors* (institutions, laws, interactions with others). (See Chapter 2.) Sociological theories share this emphasis on external factors. They agree with the feminist perspective in criticizing previous theories for focusing too much on internal factors, such as disturbances in early childhood. They hold instead that researchers should focus on external forces acting on lesbians: institutions and laws

The Millennium March on Washington for Equality passes the Washington Monument Sunday, April 30, 2000. Thousands of people converged on the National Mall in support of gay and lesbian rights.

discriminating against lesbians and stereotypes that produce unpleasant interactions with others.

Sociologists also focus on *norms*, rules for behavior that are understood by the people in a culture and that guide their behavior. Feminists point out that heterosexuality is a strong—indeed, a coercive—norm in our society. The term *compulsory heterosexuality* has been used to describe this norm (Rich, 1980). Thus lesbians can be understood as norm-violators.

Both sociologists and feminists, then, view lesbians as a minority group (Brooks, 1981). As such, lesbians are denied civil rights, much as African Americans have been denied those rights. They are also prevented from contributing to various social institutions that affect their lives—it is doubtful, for example, that an out-of-the-closet lesbian could be elected to most state legislatures.[2] Lesbians, then, can be seen as occupying two minority statuses.

Existentialism and Lesbianism   Existential philosophy maintains that anyone can change his or her self-view and view of the world at any time and can thus profoundly alter the course of his or her life—that humans are always free to reappraise their own condition and to take action to alter it. People need not rely

[2]One notable exception is the representative to the U.S. House from the district that includes Madison, Wisconsin—the Honorable Tammy Baldwin, an out lesbian.

forever on the "crutches" of morals, social expectations, and past habits, but can in their own lives think for themselves and disavow all those things that they have been in the past. The only dictum is that humans should be authentic, and *authenticity* demands that one accept full responsibility for one's actions.

The existentialist who has commented most on lesbianism is the famous French philosopher Simone de Beauvoir (1952). Exemplifying the existentialist theme, she insisted that "the truth is that homosexuality [lesbianism] is no more perversion deliberately indulged in than it is a curse of fate. It is an attitude *chosen in a certain situation*—that is at once motivated and freely adopted" (p. 398; italics are de Beauvoir's). She viewed female homosexuality not as a compensatory condition of life, but as an instance of self-reappraisal and choice. Furthermore, de Beauvoir agreed with the view that all women have a natural homosexual component. Thus, lesbianism from this viewpoint is the reflection of conscious choice and a willingness to accept the responsibilities for such a choice.

A woman who enters upon heterosexual relations enters upon a social contract that society expects and reinforces. It requires much greater, not less, emotional strength and conviction (authenticity) for a woman to enter a homosexual relationship, risking social rejection. So, according to the existentialists, in some sense it requires a much more integrated woman to make the choice to be a lesbian.

Some Final Thoughts About the Theoretical Perspectives   Psychoanalysts, learning theorists, feminists, sociologists, and existentialists all have rather different things to say about lesbianism. Psychoanalysts and learning theorists focus on what causes lesbianism to develop. Feminists, sociologists, and existentialists reject the search for causes. Instead, they focus on understanding the lesbian's current experiences. Increasingly—though there are exceptions—that is the trend in research: to investigate the experiences of lesbians in trying to build strong romantic relationships, in dealing with co-workers, or in trying to balance love, work, and children.

Why Do Women Become Lesbian, Bi, or Straight?

A fascinating psychological question is: Why do people become homosexual, heterosexual, or bisexual? In the previous section, we examined some theoretical answers to that question. Here we will look at what the data say.

You will notice that older theories and research took it as their task to explain homosexuality. They operated under the assumption that everyone should turn out heterosexual unless some "accident" occurred that shifted the person in a homosexual direction. New theories and research take as their task to explain sexual orientation—not only why people become homosexual, but why people become heterosexual as well.

Biological Explanations Three biological explanations have been proposed: genetics, brain factors, and hormones.

Some have suggested that sexual orientation is genetically determined or influenced. To test this hypothesis, one research team recruited lesbian women who either were members of an identical twin pair or members of a nonidentical twin pair, or had a sister by adoption (Bailey et al., 1993; for a critique, see Byne & Parsons, 1993). The concordance rate for lesbian orientation was 48 percent for identical twins (*concordance* means that if one member of the twin pair is lesbian, so is the other). This was compared with a concordance rate of 16 percent for nonidentical twins and 6 percent for adoptive sisters. The finding that identical twins have a much higher concordance rate than nonidentical twins provides evidence for a genetic basis. At the same time, the 48 percent concordance rate means that 52 percent of the identical twins pairs were *dis*cordant—one was lesbian and the other heterosexual. If sexual orientation were completely genetically determined, the concordance would be 100 percent. Therefore, environmental factors must also exert an influence.

The same researchers conducted a second study using improved methodology (Bailey et al., 2000). This time the concordance rate among women was 24 percent for identical twins and 11 percent for nonidentical twins. This finding suggests some possible genetic contributions, but the results are far less clear than in the earlier study.

In regard to brain factors, a highly publicized study by neuroscientist Simon LeVay (1991) identified differences in the hypothalamus between heterosexuals and homosexuals. The three study groups were gay men, heterosexual men, and heterosexual women. In short, there was no lesbian group, giving us no information about their brains. Much research and theory on sexual orientation has had this problem—lesbians have been invisible.

Investigating the possibility that endocrine imbalance is the cause of homosexuality, researchers have tried to determine whether testosterone levels of male homosexuals might be low compared with those of male heterosexuals, and whether lesbians might have higher testosterone levels or perhaps lower estrogen levels than heterosexual women. Modern research testing these hypotheses has consistently found no differences between lesbian and heterosexual women on a variety of hormones (Byne, 1996; Downey et al., 1987). This hypothesis is not taken seriously anymore.

Others have wondered whether prenatal hormone exposure might be influential. They have, for example, studied CAH girls (discussed in Chapter 10). None of these studies have yielded definitive evidence, either.

Psychological Factors As noted earlier, psychoanalytic theory and learning theory provide hypotheses about experiences and psychological factors that might influence sexual orientation. The evidence does not support psychoanalytic theory (Bell et al., 1981).

Learning theory does no better when tested against the data. For example, children who grow up with a homosexual parent are not themselves likely to become gay (Bailey et al., 1995; Golombok & Tasker, 1996; Patterson, 1992). Modeling therefore does not seem to play a role. In addition, lesbians are no more likely than heterosexual women to have been heterosexually raped (Bell et al., 1981). This counters the hypothesis from learning theory that an unpleasant heterosexual experience should channel sexual orientation in a homosexual direction.

The Bottom Line The bottom line, simply put, is that scientists do not know what causes sexual orientation (Bell et al., 1981). But there may be a good theoretical lesson to be learned from that somewhat frustrating conclusion. It has generally been assumed not only that lesbians are a distinct category, but also that they form a homogeneous category, that is, that all lesbians are fairly similar. Not so. In all likelihood there are many different "types" of lesbians. Some researchers, for example, distinguish between lifetime lesbians (who have been lesbian ever since they became sexual) and adult lesbians (who were heterosexual and became lesbian in midlife) (Valanis et al., 2000). If this is the case, then one would expect not a single "cause" of lesbianism but rather many causes, each corresponding to its type. The important next step in research, then, should be to identify the various types of lesbians—not to mention the various types of heterosexual women—and the different developmental pathways that lead to each.

Differences Between Lesbians and Gay Men

Theorists frequently refer to homosexuality as if there were no difference between male and female homosexuality (or else as if male homosexuality were the only phenomenon of interest). How similar are lesbians and gay men?

There do appear to be some differences between the two groups. First, lesbians place more emphasis on the emotional intimacy of their relationship than gay men do (Peplau & Garnets, 2000). Lesbians are also much less likely than gay men to have sex with a new partner on a first date (Klinkenberg & Rose, 1994), a pattern that is completely consistent with findings of gender differences in sexuality in research based on heterosexual samples (Oliver & Hyde, 1993; discussed in Chapter 12). Furthermore, in their sexuality, lesbians are similar to heterosexual women, and different from gay men (Bailey et al., 1994). Gender, then, seems to be the defining characteristic, not sexual orientation.

Second, many gay men have numerous different sex partners, whereas lesbians more typically form long-term, exclusive relationships, and therefore have fewer different partners. In a well-sampled national study, men who had had at least one same-gender sex partner reported, on average, 44 different sex partners since age 18 (Laumann et al., 1994). This compares to an average of 20 different partners for women in that same category. In a study of couples who had been together more than two years (often many more), 79 percent of the gay men had had sex with an outside partner in the previous year, compared with 19 percent for lesbians, 11 percent for heterosexually married men, and 9 percent for heterosexually married women (Blumstein & Schwartz, 1983).

Third, men with a male partner have sex (defined as genital sex) considerably more frequently than women with a female partner (Peplau, 1993).

Fourth, women tend to be more bisexual than men do (Rust, 2000). In the same well-sampled survey, among people who reported having had at least one same-gender sexual partner, 38 percent of the women had had both male and female partners, compared with 28 percent of the men (Laumann et al., 1994).

Finally, lesbians and gay men are the objects of somewhat different attitudes from the predominantly heterosexual American population. People hold negative attitudes toward both gay men and lesbians, but, on average, they are more intensely hostile to gay men (Herek, 2000b). This trend is driven by men's more hostile attitudes toward gay men than toward lesbians. Women's attitudes toward lesbians and gay men are similar.

In sum, gay men and lesbians appear to be similar only in the superficial sense of same-gender attraction. The differences between the two are logical consequences of psychological differences between the genders and differences in their developmental experiences. Indeed, although research has found that one's gender is a fairly good predictor of a number of psychological characteristics, one's homosexual status is not (Bell, 1974). Therefore, a lesbian is probably more like a heterosexual woman than she is like a gay man.

Lesbians and Ethnicity

Lesbians who are women of color experience triple oppression: discrimination on the basis of gender, race, and sexual orientation. For the individual woman, there may be conflicts between lesbian identity and ethnic identity, because some ethnic groups in the United States have even more negative attitudes toward lesbians than Anglo society does.

As a first example, we will consider Latina lesbians (Espin, 1987b, 1993). Although in Latin cultures emotional and physical closeness among women is considered acceptable and desirable, attitudes toward lesbianism are even more restrictive than in Euro-American culture. The special emphasis on family—defined as mother, father, children, and grandparents—in Latin cultures makes the lesbian even more of an outsider (Espin, 1987b). As a result, Latina lesbians often become part of a Euro-American lesbian community while remaining in the closet with their family and among Latinos, creating difficult choices among identities. As one Cuban woman responded to a questionnaire, "I identify myself as a lesbian more intensely than as Cuban/Latin. But it is a very painful question because I feel that I am both, and I don't want to have to choose" (Espin, 1987b, p. 47).

Lesbians who are women of color may experience multiple forms of discrimination—on the basis of gender, sexual orientation, and ethnicity.

As a second example, we will consider Asian American lesbians (Chan, 1993; Liu & Chan, 1996). In one study, Asian American lesbians felt more strongly identified with their lesbian than with their Asian American identity (Chan, 1993). Some of the issues are the same as for Latina lesbians. In Asian cultures, being lesbian is typically viewed as a rejection of the most important roles for women: being a wife and mother. In addition, if a daughter is lesbian, there is an implication that the parents have failed in their role and that the child is rejecting the importance of family and Asian culture. Indeed, in Asian cultures it is often denied that Asian American lesbians and gay men exist—homosexuality is seen as a White, Western phenomenon (Chan, 1993; Ruan & Bullough, 1992). Asian American lesbians therefore face a conflict between ethnic identity and lesbian identity.

A third example concerns African American lesbians, who regard their ethnic community as extremely homophobic (Greene, 2000). This sexual prejudice probably derives from a belief among Blacks that any sexual behavior outside the norms of the dominant culture in the United States may reflect negatively on Blacks, as they strive for respect and acceptance. In this context, Black lesbians may seem to be an embarrassment to the Black community.

We have seen many times in this book that women have been rendered invisible in everything from history to science. Lesbians who are women of color are, in a sense, triply invisible—invisible because they are women, because they are people of color, and because they are lesbian. They deserve much more attention in psychological research in the future, for their complex identities have much to tell us about the interplay of gender, race, and sexuality.

Bisexual Women

Bisexuality refers to being erotically and emotionally attracted to both males and females. As noted earlier, using this definition, bisexuality is actually more common than exclusive homosexuality is. For example, in a well-sampled study, women were asked about their sexual partners in the past five years (Laumann et al., 1994): 1.4 percent reported having both male and female partners, compared with only .8 percent reporting female partners only. That is, about twice as many were bisexual as were exclusively lesbian. The comparable statistics for men were 2.1 percent and 2.0 percent. Bisexuals are more than just a third category (although they are that) inasmuch as they reveal the enormous variability and complexity of human sexual expression.

> **Bisexuality:** Being erotically and emotionally attracted to both females and males.

The case of Rachel, a bisexual woman, is offered in Focus 13.1 to illustrate the life experience of a bisexual woman.

Sociologists Philip Blumstein and Pepper Schwartz (1976, 1993) conducted interviews with bisexual women. On the basis of these interviews, they concluded that a number of factors contributed to a woman with a lesbian history moving toward bisexuality. Most lesbians have had at least some heterosexual experience, including intercourse. When these are recalled as pleasurable it is reasonable to return to them later in life. Another factor is all the social rewards in our society that go with a heterosexual lifestyle, including having a husband and children. Bisexuality can be a way of avoiding the social ostracism that lesbians must often face, while still engaging in some lesbian activity. However, some forces discourage the movement from lesbianism to bisexuality. Many lesbians receive their major emotional support in a lesbian community, and they stand to lose this if they adopt bisexuality. Some lesbians view bisexual women as cop-outs (Rust, 2000).

Blumstein and Schwartz have also concluded that a number of factors contribute to heterosexual women moving in a bisexual direction. They believe that women learn, as part of learning how to compete with women in being attractive to men, what is attractive in other women. They thereby become aware of erotic qualities in other women. Furthermore, women are more permitted to be emotionally and physically expressive toward one another in our society, once again making a move toward bisexuality easier. As part of the more liberated sexual standards of the last several decades, some people experiment with having sex in groups of more than two persons at once, allowing an opportunity to experiment with lesbianism. Finally, the women's movement has created an environment that is relatively supportive of lesbianism, and some heterosexual women decide to experiment with lesbianism, and thereby become bisexuals, out of feminist convictions.

FOCUS 13.1

A QUEER[3] WOMAN TELLS HER STORY

Despite growing up in a small Midwestern town, I was exposed to homosexuality when several of my close friends came out during high school. At about the same time, I began to date a boy who was a year older than myself and we continued to date on and off for the next three years. By the end of high school I identified myself as bisexual but had had no sexual experiences with women. I considered sexuality to be a continuum and, perhaps idealistically, believed that gender was not a factor in determining whether I was attracted to someone. I felt that I existed on the edge of my gender, not traditionally masculine or feminine but a mixture of the two. I decided to embrace this by learning to ride a motorcycle and teaching myself to box, but kept my hair long and continued to wear makeup.

For the first three years of college I did not date and, instead, chose to maintain a close relationship with my family and to develop intense friendships. Even then, though, I found myself gravitating towards queer-identified people. During my final year of college I began dating again and had a succession of relatively brief encounters with both men and women. Instead of feeling disappointed, I realized that a certain amount of dissatisfaction was acceptable and even inevitable; after all, the process of sifting and winnowing is exactly what dating is about. A year ago I met a women with whom I chose to develop a long-term relationship. The beginning of our relationship was difficult as I struggled to understand how to be intimate with a woman. I found that there was little difference between relationships with men and

[3]*Queer* used to be a derogatory term for gays and lesbians. More recently it has been appropriated by gay activists and scholars to mean the spectrum of gays, lesbians, and bisexuals.

In Conclusion

This chapter has been based on the assumption—supported by the available data—that lesbianism is a normal form of behavior, and that lesbians and bisexual women are just as diverse in their physical attributes, personality characteristics, occupations, ethnicity, and family backgrounds as heterosexual women. I have spent the past year navigating what it means to be in a sexual-emotional relationship with a woman.

Being queer, even in a relatively progressive university community, has its ups and downs. Though personal safety is a concern, I find myself most irritated by the common assumption that women have sexual relationships with each other solely for the benefit and consumption of heterosexual men. Men have approached my girlfriend and me, only to initially assume that we are available heterosexual women (something that would not occur if a man and a woman were sitting together at a bar), and then, upon realizing that we are together, ask if we are interested in engaging in group sex. When heterosexual couples talk about their relationships, people do not automatically think about them having sex. But, when two women talk about being together, people often imagine various sexual permutations or assume that they are asexual, emotional companions (the "Boston marriage" theory). There is not a whole lot of room between these two stereotypes. For many people it is difficult to understand how frustrating these assumptions about sexuality can be. To put this problem in perspective, I have overheard many straight men express their discomfort with gay men, saying things like, "I'm fine with him as long as he doesn't try to flirt with me." The same can be said for my girlfriend and me. I wish that it wasn't necessary to share or advertise my sexual orientation.

I am fortunate, however, to have a family that supports the choices I have made about my sexuality. My parents have taught me a great deal about how to have a healthy, satisfying relationship with an emphasis on clear and open communication. I don't know if I will ever date men again; I am satisfied with the relationship I have now and I don't spend time thinking about who I will date in the future.

SOURCE: Based on an essay written for the author's class.

women. Lesbians frequently are stereotyped and may be the objects of various forms of discrimination, including hate crimes. A lesbian culture or community exists in cities and towns around the world. The process of lesbian identification and coming out proceeds in several stages, beginning with identity confusion and eventually moving to identity synthesis. Theoretical views of the nature of lesbianism are varied. Psychoanalytic theory sees it as an outcome of a persisting negative Electra complex, so that the woman continues to love her mother, and later other women, throughout her life. Learning theory stresses that sex drive is a generalized drive that is channeled toward one or another object through conditioning; thus both heterosexuality and homosexuality are learned. Sociologists and feminists are more concerned with the impact on lesbians of institutions and norms. Existentialism does not concern itself with the developmental origins of lesbianism, but instead treats it simply as a free and legitimate choice. Research on the development of lesbianism suggests that there is probably no one single causal factor. Male and female homosexuality are different in nature as a consequence of psychological and developmental differences between females and males. Women of color who are lesbians experience triple oppression: on the basis of their gender, their race, and their sexual orientation.

Research on lesbianism is in its infancy, and the conclusions we draw must be tentative. Certainly the nature of research on lesbianism is changing as scientists shed the assumption that it is a form of pathology. We now no longer seek to find what disturbances in development would create lesbianism; instead, we ask what developmental factors would lead a woman to develop heterosexuality or homosexuality or bisexuality.

EXPERIENCE THE RESEARCH

LESBIAN COMMUNITY

Does your campus have a gay/lesbian speakers' bureau? (If not, why do you think there is none?) Contact the speakers' bureau and arrange for three lesbians to attend your class to lead a panel discussion. When the speakers attend your class, have them introduce themselves first and then follow a question-and-answer format with the class. Be sure that the following questions are asked of the women:

1. What is your experience of the lesbian community? Explain, for a heterosexual audience, the features of the lesbian community.

2. Have you ever been the object of a hate crime because you are lesbian? What happened?

3. Describe the process of coming out as you experienced it.

Suggestions for Further Reading

Herek, Gregory M., Kimmel, Douglas C., Amaro, Hortensia, & Melton, Gary B. (1991). Avoiding heterosexist bias in psychological research. *American Psychologist, 46,* 957–963. Just as in Chapter 1 we examined the sexist aspect of male-based psychological research, so this article examines how research has been based predominantly on heterosexual models. It also suggest ways to correct this problem.

Hutchins, Loraine, & Kaahumanu, Lani. (1991). *Bi any other name: Bisexual people speak out.* Boston: Alyson. This book explores the often misunderstood and neglected topic of bisexuality by sharing the personal stories of bisexuals.

Peplau, L. Anne, & Garnets, Linda D. (Eds.). (2000). Women's sexualities: New perspectives on sexual orientation and gender. *Journal of Social Issues, 56(2).* This entire special issue of the journal is devoted to articles on women's sexual orientation and reviews the most up-to-date research.

Women and the Web

Healthy Lesbian, Gay, and Bisexual Students Project. This is the website of the Healthy Lesbian, Gay, and Bisexual Students Project at the American Psychological Association.

http://www.apa.org/ed/hlgb.html

Human Rights Campaign. The Human Rights Campaign is a gay and lesbian advocacy organization.

http://www.hrc.org

Llegó. Llegó is also known as the National Latino/a Lesbian, Gay, Bisexual, and Transgender Organization.

http://www.llego.org

The Gay and Lesbian Medical Association. This website provides a wealth of information, including health care referrals for lesbians and gay men.

http://www.glma.org

Lambda Legal Defense and Education Fund. The Lambda Legal Defense and Education Fund is an organization that advances the legal rights of lesbians and gay men.

http://www.lambdalegal.org

14

The Victimization of Women

Eboni's basic education about sex came from what she saw and the direct experiences that she had. When she was 5, she and her brother were wrestling with their uncle. Suddenly her uncle locked her brother out of the room and began taking off Eboni's clothes. He held her down on the bed and began to penetrate her but stopped abruptly. Eboni was frightened of him from then on. She didn't really understand what he intended to do or why he wanted to do it, but she knew that his behavior was unexpected and strange.

. . . Eboni's grandmother and father insisted that she not talk to strangers or take money from them. Eboni understood why—she knew that being molested meant being raped. But strangers were not the predators.

— FROM GAIL WYATT, Stolen Women

The women's movement, beginning in the early 1970s, brought the issue of the victimization of women into the public spotlight. Rape was the first topic to be addressed. Feminists assert that rape is one of the ways in which men exercise power and control over women (e.g., Brownmiller, 1975). More recently, attention has been drawn to the plight of battered women, to girls who are the victims of child sexual abuse, and to the issue of sexual harassment. These topics have moved from being something a woman felt she should hide to being a subject of public debate.

This chapter is about the victimization of women as seen in rape, woman-beating, child sexual abuse, and sexual harassment. A discussion of all aspects of these problems (e.g., legal factors, self-defense) is beyond the scope of this book. Here I will concentrate on the psychological aspects.

Rape

Definition Rape is typically defined, following current laws in many states, as "nonconsensual oral, anal, or vaginal penetration, obtained by force, by threat of bodily harm, or when the victim is incapable of giving consent" (Koss, 1993, p. 1062). Notice that the definition includes not only forced vaginal intercourse, but forced oral sex and anal sex as well. The issue is that the activity is nonconsensual—that is, the victim did not consent to it. One type of nonconsent occurs when the victim is incapable of giving consent, perhaps because she is drunk, unconscious, or high on some type of drug.

Rape: Nonconsenting oral, anal, or vaginal penetration obtained by force, by threat of bodily harm, or when the victim is incapable of giving consent.

Because this book concerns the psychology of women, we will focus on rape of women by men, although certainly there are cases of men raping men and rare reports of women raping men.

A key point of the feminist perspective is that gender
roles have been and continue to be a powerful force
casting women as victims.

Incidence Statistics   In 1999 there were 89,100 cases of reported rape in the
United States; that means there were 65 reported rapes for every 100,000 women
(FBI, 2000). However, according to the FBI, forcible rape is one of the most un-
derreported crimes. One study found that only about one in five (21 percent) of
stranger rapes and only 2 percent of acquaintance rapes had been reported to the
police (Koss et al., 1988).

   A well-sampled national study of women college students found that 28 percent had experienced an act that met the legal definition of rape (Koss et al.,
1987). According to the National Violence Against Women Survey, a woman has a
15 percent chance of being raped over her lifetime (Tjaden & Thoennes, 1998).
Statistics vary somewhat from one study to another, but most find that the lifetime chance of a woman being raped is between 15 and 25 percent (Koss, 1993).

Rape is a highly gendered crime. The national survey mentioned above found that a woman has a 15 percent chance of being the victim of a rape in her lifetime, compared with a 2 percent chance for a man (Tjaden & Thoennes, 1998). Statistics on perpetrators are even more skewed: 99 percent of all persons arrested for rape are men (Rozee & Koss, 2001).

The Impact of Rape   A large number of studies have investigated the psychological reactions of women following rape (see the review by Koss, 1993). This research shows that rape is a time of crisis for a woman and that the effects on her adjustment may persist for a year or more. The term **rape trauma syndrome** has been used to refer to the emotional and physical effects a woman undergoes following a rape or an attempted rape (Burgess & Holmstrom, 1974a).

Rape trauma syndrome: The emotional and physical effects a woman undergoes following a rape or attempted rape.

Emotional reactions immediately after a rape (the acute phase) are generally severe. The high levels of distress generally reach a peak three weeks after the assault and then continue at a high level for the next month. A gradual improvement then begins two or three months after the assault (Koss, 1993; Rothbaum et al., 1992). Many differences between raped and nonvictimized women disappear after three months, except that raped women continue to report more fear, anxiety, self-esteem problems, and sexual dysfunctions. These effects may persist for 18 months or longer (Koss, 1993).

Some women experience self-blame. The woman may spend hours agonizing over what she did to bring on the rape or what she might have done to prevent it: "If I hadn't worn that tight sweater . . ."; "If I hadn't worn that short skirt . . ."; "If I hadn't been dumb enough to walk on that dark street . . ."; "If I hadn't been stupid enough to trust that guy. . . . " This is an example of a tendency on the part of both the victim and others to *blame the victim.*

Researchers are finding increased evidence of the damage to women's *physical health* that results from violence such as rape and battering (Golding, 1999; Heise, 1993; Koss et al., 1991; Koss & Heslet, 1992). The woman may have physical injuries from the rape, such as cuts and bruises. Women who have been forced to have oral sex may suffer irritation or damage to the throat; rectal bleeding and pain are reported by women forced to have anal intercourse. The woman may contract a sexually transmitted disease, such as HIV/AIDS or herpes, from the rape. She may become pregnant; in about 5 percent of rape cases, pregnancy results (Koss et al., 1991). There is strong evidence for long-term health effects as well. A history of having been sexually assaulted is associated with worse general health and a variety of specific problems including chronic pelvic pain, menstrual disturbances, headache and other pain syndromes, intestinal disorders, and sexual disorders (Golding, 1996, 1999).

Recently it has been suggested that, rather than focusing on rape trauma syndrome, a "women's issue," we should recognize that rape victims are experiencing

posttraumatic stress disorder (e.g., Koss, 1993). Posttraumatic stress disorder (PTSD) is an official diagnosis that was originally developed to describe the long-term psychological distress suffered by war veterans, most of whom are men. Symptoms can include anxiety, depression, nightmares, and a lack of feelings of safety. According to the cognitive-behavioral view of PTSD, people who have experienced a terrifying event form a memory schema that involves information about the situation and their responses to it (Foa et al., 1989). Because the schema is large, many cues can trigger it and thereby evoke the feelings of terror that occurred at the time; the schema is probably activated at some level all the time. Schemas also affect how people interpret new events, so that the consequences are far-reaching and long-lasting.

> **Posttraumatic stress disorder (PTSD):** Long-term psychological distress suffered by someone who has experienced a terrifying, uncontrollable event.

Approximately half of college-age women who have been the victims of forced, nonconsensual sexual intercourse do not label the experience as rape, nor themselves as rape victims (Kahn et al., 1994). Why do some women fail to realize that they have been raped? We will call these women "unacknowledged victims," and those who realize that they were raped, "acknowledged victims." The difference lies in their rape scripts (Kahn et al., 1994). Unacknowledged victims are more likely to have a violent, stranger rape script for rape, whereas acknowledged victims are more likely to include acquaintance rape in their rape script. Unac-

Many experts feel that women should learn self-defense skills as a way of combating rape.

knowledged victims often have experienced an acquaintance rape, which does not match their rape script, so they do not label the event as rape.

Rape affects many people besides the victim. Most women perform a number of behaviors that stem basically from rape fears. For example, a single woman is not supposed to list her full first name in the telephone book, because that is a giveaway that she is alone. Rather, she should list a first initial or a man's name. Many women, when getting into their car at night, almost reflexively check the backseat to make sure no one is hiding there. Most college women avoid walking alone through dark parts of the campus at night. At least once in their lives, most women have been afraid of spending the night alone. If you are a woman, you can probably extend the list from your own experience. The point is that most women experience the fear of rape, if not rape itself (Burt & Estep, 1981; Warr, 1985). Furthermore, this fear restricts their activities.

Date Rape In Mary Koss's national study of college women, among those who had experienced an act that met the legal definition of rape, 57 percent of the rapes involved a date (Koss et al., 1988; Koss & Cook, 1994). Date rape is one of the most common forms of rape, especially on college campuses.

In some cases, date rape seems to result from astounding male-female miscommunication. The traditional view in dating relationships has been that if the woman says no, she really means yes. Men need to learn that no means no. Consider this example of miscommunication and different perceptions in a case of date rape:

> Bob: Patty and I were in the same statistics class together. She usually sat near me and was always very friendly. I liked her and thought maybe she liked me, too. Last Thursday I decided to find out. After class I suggested that she come to my place to study for midterms together. She agreed immediately, which was a good sign. That night everything seemed to go perfectly. We studied for a while and then took a break. I could tell that she liked me, and I was attracted to her. I was getting excited. I started kissing her. I could tell that she really liked it. We started touching each other and it felt really good. All of a sudden she pulled away and said "Stop." I figured she didn't want me to think that she was "easy" or "loose." A lot of girls think they have to say "no" at first. I knew once I showed her what a good time she could have, and that I would respect her in the morning, it would be OK. I just ignored her protests and eventually she stopped struggling. I think she liked it but afterwards she acted bummed out and cold. Who knows what her problem was?

> Patty: I knew Bob from my statistics class. He's cute and we are both good at statistics, so when a tough midterm was scheduled, I was glad that he suggested we study together. It never occurred to me that it was anything except a study date. That night everything went fine at first, we got a lot of studying done in a short amount of time, so when he suggested we take a

break I thought we deserved it. Well, all of a sudden he started acting really romantic and started kissing me. I liked the kissing but then he started touching me below the waist. I pulled away and tried to stop him but he didn't listen. After a while I stopped struggling; he was hurting me and I was scared. He was so much bigger and stronger than me. I couldn't believe it was happening to me. I didn't know what to do. He actually forced me to have sex with him. I guess looking back on it I should have screamed or done something besides trying to reason with him but it was so unexpected. I couldn't believe it was happening. I still can't believe it did. (Hughes & Sandler, 1987, p. 1)

Date rape is particularly difficult for women to be effective in resisting because, compared with stranger rape, they have the sense that there is little potential threat during a date (Norris et al., 1996). Alcohol consumption on dates further contributes to women's vulnerability. The social context of dating and psychological factors such as embarrassment and fear of being rejected by a man she really likes all present barriers to women's successful resistance to date rape (Norris et al., 1996).

In summary, studies of date rape have consistently found that such incidents are not rare, but rather are fairly common even in "normal" populations.

Rapists   What is the profile of the typical rapist? The basic answer is that there is no typical rapist. Rapists vary tremendously in occupation, education, marital status, previous criminal record, and motivation for committing rape.

An important program of research by Neil Malamuth, Mary Koss, and their colleagues identified four factors that predispose men to engage in rape of women (Malamuth, 1998; Malamuth et al., 1991):

1. *Violent home environment.* A boy who grows up in a hostile home environment has a higher likelihood of engaging in sexual aggression against women. Factors that contribute to a hostile home environment include violence between the parents and abuse directed toward the child, whether battering or sexual abuse.

2. *Delinquency.* Being involved in delinquency is itself made more likely by coming from a hostile home. But the delinquency in turn increases the likelihood of engaging in rape: The boy associates with delinquent peers who, for example, encourage hostile attitudes and rationalizations for committing illegal acts and reward a tough, aggressive image.

3. *Sexual promiscuity.* The male develops a heavy emphasis on sexual conquests to bring him self-esteem and status with the peer group. Coercion may seem to him a reasonable way of making conquests.

4. *A hostile masculine personality.* This personality constellation involves deep-seated hostility toward women along with negatively defined, exaggerated

masculinity—masculinity defined as rejecting anything feminine such as nurturance, and emphasizing power, control, and macho characteristics.

Surprisingly, this research was based not on convicted rapists but rather on a national representative sample of male college students. The factors that contribute to sexual aggression against women can be present even in such an apparently benevolent population (Abbey et al., 2001).

One factor seems to attenuate or reduce a man's likelihood of raping: empathy (Dean & Malamuth, 1997). That is, a man who has several of the risk factors listed above, but who also is sensitive to others' feelings and needs and is not self-centered, is less likely to rape than a man who has the risk factors and lacks empathy and is self-centered. These research findings have important implications for programs of therapy for convicted rapists. Empathy training should be emphasized, as it is in the most modern programs (Marshall, 1993; Pithers, 1993).

Marital Rape   The possibility that a man could rape his wife was brought to public attention in 1978 when Greta Rideout sued her husband for marital rape. Defining marital rape is complicated by the fact that in many states, rape laws exclude the possibility of marital rape; the assumption has been that sex in marriage is always the husband's "right." This is a legacy of the Hale doctrine, formulated by Lord Matthew Hale in the seventeenth century, which states that "the husband cannot be guilty of a rape committed by himself upon his lawful wife, for by their mutual matrimonial consent and a contract the wife hath given up herself in this kind unto her husband which she cannot retract" (Whatley, 1993).

How common is marital rape? In a random sample of San Francisco women, 12 percent of the married women reported that they had experienced some form of forced sex in marriage (Russell, 1982). Other studies generally find that the prevalence of marital rape in the general population is between 7 and 14 percent (Whatley, 1993).

One phenomenon that emerges in research on marital rape is an association between it and marital violence—that is, the man who batters his wife is also likely to rape her. For example, in a study of 137 women who had reported being physically assaulted by their husbands, 34 percent reported being raped by their husbands (Frieze, 1983). The fact that some women are unwilling to define certain acts as marital rape is evident from the 43 percent of that sample (more than the number who reported being raped) who said that sex was unpleasant because it was forced upon them by their husbands. Asked why they had been raped, 78 percent said the cause was the husband's belief that the act would prove his manhood. An additional 14 percent attributed the rapes to the husband's drinking. The response of the majority of the women was anger toward the husband. However, women who had been frequently raped by their husbands began to experience self-blame. Marital rape also had consequences for the marriage: The raped women were more likely to say that their marriages had been getting worse over time.

Blaming the victim in cases of rape has been a serious problem. This cartoon satirizes that point of view, showing how ridiculous it would be to take this stance in regard to another victim of crime, such as a man whose wallet was stolen.

Thus, research shows that marital rape is a real phenomenon, that it is associated with wife-battering, and that it has negative consequences, both for the woman and for the marriage.

Causes of Rape   Four theoretical views of the causes of rape have been proposed (Albin, 1977; Baron & Straus, 1989):

1. *Victim-precipitated.* This view holds that a rape is always caused by a woman "asking for it." Rape, then, is basically the woman's fault. This view represents the tendency to blame the victim.

2. *Psychopathology of rapists.* This theoretical view holds that rape is an act committed by a psychologically disturbed man. His deviance is responsible for the crime occurring.

3. *Feminist.* Feminist theorists view rapists as the product of gender-role socialization in our culture. They deemphasize the sexual aspects of rape and instead view rape as an expression of power and dominance by men over women. Gender inequality is both the cause and the result of rape.

4. *Social disorganization.* Sociologists believe that crime rates, including rape rates, increase when the social organization is disrupted and social disorganization results. Under such conditions the community cannot enforce its norms against crime. War is an extreme case of social disorganization.

What do the data say? Research indicates that a number of factors contribute to rape, ranging from forces at the cultural level to forces at the individual level. These factors include the following: cultural values, sexual scripts, early family influences, peer group influences, characteristics of the situation, characteristics of the victim, miscommunication, sex and power motives, and masculinity norms and men's attitudes. The data on each of these factors are considered below.

Cultural values can act in support of rape. Cross-culturally, rape is significantly more common in preliterate societies that are characterized by male dominance, a high degree of general violence, and an ideology of male toughness (Otterbein, 1979; Sanday, 1981). In the United States, research has documented widespread acceptance of rape myths and attitudes that foster rape among average citizens and police officers (Burt, 1980; Feild, 1978). R-rated movies and rap music that objectify women also foster rape-permissive attitudes (Milburn et al., 2000; Wester et al., 1997).

Sociologists Larry Baron and Murray Straus (1989), experts in violence research, did an extensive study to test the feminist theory and social disorganization theory described above. Both theories deal with rape as a product of cultural context or values. Baron and Straus collected extensive data on each of the 50 states in the United States, seeing them as representing variations in cultural context (think, for example, of the different cultures of Louisiana, New York, and North Dakota). They collected data on the extent of gender inequality in each state (for example, the gap between men's and women's wages). They also collected measures of social disorganization, such as the number of people moving into or out of the states, and the divorce rate. Their data gave strong support to three conclusions: (1) Gender inequality is related to rape (the states with the greatest gender inequality had the highest rape rates); (2) pornography provides cultural, ideological support for rape (the states with the highest circulation of pornographic magazines had the highest rape rates); and (3) social disorganization contributes to rape (those states with the greatest social disorganization tended to have the highest rape rates). This research shows that many complex factors in the culture may contribute to cultural values that encourage rape.

Sexual scripts play a role as well (Byers, 1996). Adolescents quickly learn society's expectations about dating and sex by culturally transmitted sexual scripts. These scripts support rape when they convey the message that the man is supposed to be the sexual "aggressor." By adolescence, both girls and boys endorse scripts that justify rape (Koss et al., 1994). A study of 1,700 middle school students revealed that approximately 25 percent of the boys said that it was acceptable for a man to force sex on a woman if he had spent money on her (cited in Koss et al., 1994). These findings have been replicated in a number of studies of high school and college students (e.g., Goodchilds & Zellman, 1984; Muehlenhard et al., 1985).

Early family influences may play a role in shaping a man into a sexual aggressor. Specifically, young men who are sexual aggressors are likely to have been sexually abused themselves in childhood (Friedrich et al., 1988; Koss et al., 1994).

The *peer group* can have a powerful influence encouraging men to rape. Anthropologist Peggy Sanday (1990) conducted a detailed ethnographic study of a case of fraternity gang rape at a particular university. According to her analysis, the initiation rituals of many fraternities follow a sequence of creating high levels of anxiety in the new members, followed by a male bonding ritual that makes them "brothers." Essentially the young man's identity as an individual is undermined while loyalty to the group is prized, in fact, enforced. Under these conditions, the peer group of the fraternity brothers becomes an extremely powerful force. In the particular case investigated by Sanday, the XYZ fraternity (she used this name to guard the anonymity of the population being studied, as required by the ethical standard for anthropologists) had a practice called the "XYZ express," referring to an express train. It involved what would be classified as a gang rape in which a woman, typically drunk or surreptitiously drugged so that she was barely conscious, is raped successively by a series of brothers who stand in line to take their turn, just as cars in a train are in a line.

When the case was brought to court, many of the brothers said that they had no idea that their activities were wrong or illegal. The culture of the fraternity— the peer group pressure and peer group norms—had dulled their capacity for rational judgment. And this was not a group of juvenile delinquents in a poor section of the city—it was a group of college students.

Characteristics of the situation play a role. Among these is social disorganization, as noted earlier. An extreme example is war, in which rape of women is common (Brownmiller, 1975). In the 1990s we saw graphic examples of this in the war in the former Yugoslavia. Bosnian women—Croats and Muslims—were frequently raped by the attacking Serbs. Secluded places foster rape, as do parties in which excessive alcohol use is involved (Koss et al., 1994).

Are some women especially likely to be rape victims? That is, are there *characteristics of the victim* that make her vulnerable to being raped? Although many studies have attempted to identify characteristics of women that make them vulnerable to rape—such as certain personality characteristics or appearance—these studies have uniformly failed to find differences between victims and nonvictims (Koss et al., 1994). That is, it doesn't seem to be something about the woman herself that is a key factor. On the other hand, studies have consistently shown that active resistance such as screaming, fleeing, or physically struggling are associated with higher rates of avoiding rape when a man is attempting rape (e.g., Bart, 1981). It pays to fight back.

Miscommunication between men and women is a factor. In the section on date rape, we saw a detailed example of a case in which the man and the woman had totally different understandings of what had occurred. Because many people in the United States are reluctant to discuss sex directly, they try to infer sexual interest from subtle nonverbal cues, a process that is highly prone to errors (Abbey, 1991). Specifically, men are apt to interpret a woman's friendly behavior as carrying a sexual message that she did not intend (Abbey, 1991; Abbey et al., 2001).

Sex and power motives are involved in rape. Feminists have stressed that rape is an expression of power and dominance by men over women (Brownmiller, 1975). Current theorizing emphasizes that sexual motives and power motives are both involved and interact with each other. A number of processes may be involved (Barbaree & Marshall, 1991). For example, rapists may differ from non-rapists in the ability to suppress sexual arousal when it occurs under inappropriate circumstances. Rapists may be capable of experiencing sexual arousal and hostile aggression simultaneously, whereas other men find that hostile aggression inhibits sexual arousal.

Finally, *masculinity norms and men's attitudes* are another factor (Koss et al., 1994). Sexually aggressive men are more likely than nonaggressors to give themselves traditional masculine ratings. Sexually aggressive men are also more likely to endorse attitudes that are tolerant or supportive of rape, including rape myths. These attitudes allow them to believe that a victim wanted or deserved to be raped.

Prevention and Treatment

How can we prevent rape from occurring? Once a rape has occurred, how can we help the victim and treat the rapist so that he does not repeat his offense?

Preventing Rape   Strategies for preventing rape fall into three categories: (1) avoiding situations in which there is a high risk of rape; (2) if the first strategy has failed, knowing some self-defense techniques if a rape is actually attempted; and (3) changing the culture that contributes to rape.

The Association of American Colleges offers the following guidelines for avoiding date rape situations (Hughes & Sandler, 1987):

> *Set sexual limits.* No one has a right to force you to do something with your body that you don't want to do. If you don't want to be touched, for example, you have a right to say, "Don't touch me," and to leave if your wishes are not respected.

> *Decide early if you would like to have intercourse.* The sooner you communicate your intentions firmly and clearly, the easier it will be for your partner to understand and accept your decision.

> *Do not give mixed messages; be clear.* Say "yes" when you mean it and "no" only when you mean "no."

> *Be forceful and firm.* Do not worry about being polite if your wishes are being ignored.

Do not do anything you do not want to do just to avoid a scene or unpleasantness. Do not be raped because you were too polite to get out of a dangerous situation or because you were worried about hurting your date's feelings. If things get out of hand, be loud in protesting, leave, and go for help.

Be aware that alcohol and other drugs are often associated with date rape. They compromise your ability and that of your date to make responsible decisions.

Trust your gut-level feelings. If the situation feels risky to you, or if you feel you are being pressured, trust your feelings. Leave the situation or confront the person immediately.

Be careful when you invite someone to your home or you are invited to your date's home. These are the most likely places for date rapes to occur.

If these avoidance strategies are unsuccessful and a woman is actually the object of a rape attempt, it is important for her to resist loudly and physically. Research has demonstrated that verbal and physical resistance can be effective in preventing rape in the face of an attempt (Rozee & Koss, 2001).

Feminists argue that the whole responsibility for preventing rape should not rest on women's shoulders. Ultimately, the best way to prevent rape is for men not to attempt it. To do this, our society would need to make a radical change in the way it socializes males (Hall & Barongan, 1997). That would mean not pressuring little boys to be aggressive and tough, and not demanding that adolescent boys demonstrate that they are hypersexual.

Rape prevention programs have been attempted over the past several decades. Often they are designed for a mixed-gender audience of, perhaps, first-year college students. Sadly and frustratingly, evaluations of these programs typically show only small changes in attitudes that do not last long, and no changes in actual rape rates (Breitenbecher, 2000; Rozee & Koss, 2001). Experts in the field are developing much better ideas for creating effective prevention programs for both women and men; we need to put our best energies into these efforts (Lonsway, 1996; Rozee & Koss, 2001).

Treating Victims   Some women recover psychologically from rape on their own. But others are severely traumatized and develop PTSD. Psychologists have developed therapies that are effective in treating the symptoms of this condition (Foa et al., 1999). Treatments today typically use cognitive-behavioral methods. Applied to rape survivors with PTSD, one component of therapy is stress inoculation therapy, which teaches clients how to manage trauma-related anxiety using strategies such as relaxation training and cognitive restructuring. A second component is exposure therapy, in which clients relive memories of the traumatic event while relaxing, and confront situations that are being avoided because they trigger distress. PTSD does not have to be a life-long, incurable virus.

Treating Rapists   A number of studies have investigated recidivism in sexual offenders—that is, they analyze whether sex offenders tend to repeat their offense after release from prison. Two meta-analyses of these studies concluded that rates of recidivism tend to be low, even in the absence of treatment beyond serving jail time. Recidivism rates are around 27 percent for untreated offenders and between 13 and 19 percent for treated offenders (Hall, 1995; Hanson & Bussiere, 1998). The problem with these studies, however, is that they lump together a broad range of sexual offenders, ranging from the fraternity man who commits date rape to the serial pedophile. This leaves us with little idea of recidivism rates for rapists specifically. What makes the issue even murkier is the fact that a wide variety of treatments are thrown together. The treatments range from biomedical therapies such as antiandrogen drugs (the idea being that if testosterone levels are lowered, sex drive will decrease) to behavioral and cognitive-behavioral therapy. Both antiandrogen drugs and cognitive-behavioral therapies have been shown to be effective (Hall, 1995). The evidence also indicates that antiandrogen drugs should not be used by themselves; they should always be combined with education and psychotherapy (Prentky, 1997).

These studies leave some big questions unanswered. Chief among them is the fate of the date rapist whose victim or victims never report the rape. He remains unarrested and unjailed, and certainly untreated. What happens to him? Does he go on date raping?

Battered Women[1]

One solution to the rape problem that some people propose is for women simply to stay home, off the streets. However, the data indicate that a woman may actually be less safe in her own home than on the street. Research demonstrates that women are more likely to be attacked, raped, injured, or killed by current or former male partners than by any other type of assailant (Koss et al., 1994). The following statistics give some indication of the extent of domestic violence (Browne, 1993):

- Each year, an estimated 960,000 women in the United States are beaten by their intimate partners (U.S. Department of Justice, 1998).

- Aproximately 84 percent of the victims of domestic violence are women (U.S. Department of Justice, 1998).

---

[1]Battering can occur in situations other than marriage—for example, when a man who is divorced or separated returns to beat the woman, or when battering occurs among couples who are simply living together. To simplify the terminology, I will refer to battered women and intimate violence in the discussion that follows. It is also true that in some cases it is the wife who beats the husband. However, when the violence is physical but not homicidal, the greater physical strength of the male means that far greater damage is done in wife-beating than in husband-beating (Steinmetz, 1977). The focus here will be on battered women.

He beat her 150 times. She only got flowers once.

Every 15 seconds, a woman is beaten in this country.
For as many as four million women, this battering is so severe, they require medical or police attention.
But for nearly 4,000 women each year, the abuse ends. They die.

National Coalition Against Domestic Violence

If you need help or want to help, call 1-303-839-1852. Or write: NCADV, P.O. Box 18749, Denver, CO 80218-0749.

The National Coalition Against Domestic Violence
(Washington, DC) has launched an ad campaign to
reduce domestic violence.

- Approximately 3 percent of women in any one year are *severely* beaten by their intimate partner (punched, kicked, choked, beaten, threatened with or had a gun or knife used on them) (Straus & Gelles, 1990).

- Each year in the United States, approximately 1,800 murders are committed by an intimate, and in three out of four of these cases the victim is the woman (U.S. Department of Justice, 1998).

- Internationally, violence against women by intimates is found in all reporting nations. Depending on the country, from 10 percent to 50 percent of women report being hit or otherwise physically harmed by an intimate at some point in their lives (Heise et al., 1999).

In fact, wife-beating has a long history, and at many times has been considered a legitimate form of behavior, a logical extension of the roles of men and women. For example, in the sixteenth century in France, the Abbé de Brantôme, although reluctant to speak against the teachings of the Catholic Church, felt compelled to ask, "But however great the authority of the husband may be, what *sense* is there for him to be allowed to kill his wife?" (Davis, 1971, p. 261). In Russia during the reign of Ivan the Terrible, the state church supported such practices by issuing a "Household Ordinance" that detailed how a man might most effectively beat his wife (Mandel, 1975, p. 12). The first contemporary book exposing the topic was *Scream Quietly or the Neighbors Will Hear,* by Erin Pizzey (1974), who opened a shelter for battered women in England.

The 1994 case of the murder of Nicole Simpson, allegedly by her exhusband, O. J. Simpson, highlighted to the public that batterers can kill. Battered women's shelters were flooded with women following the murder, apparently because many women realized that their situation was far more dangerous than they realized.

Although the family in America is romanticized as a haven of peace and safety, current estimates are that the incidence of family violence is high. In one study, sociologist Murray Straus (1980; see also Straus & Gelles, 1990) analyzed a probability sample of more than 2,000 families. The data indicated that 16 percent of the couples experienced some violence between themselves (ranging from slapping to actual beating) within the preceding year. Over the duration of a marriage, this would mean that about 28 percent of all couples would be involved in violence between spouses. Straus estimates that in about 5 percent of marriages the wife is actually beaten at some time during the marriage. The average frequency of beating is 2.4 times per year. These statistics doubtless represent an underestimate, because many people are unwilling to admit that beating occurs. In a sample of women at a battered women's shelter, 42 percent had been assaulted once a week or more (Gondolf et al., 1988).

The Batterer: Psychological Aspects What kind of man beats his wife? As with the rapist, I can give no profile of the "typical" wife-beater. Such men are found in all social classes and in a wide variety of occupations.

Research does show, however, that characteristics of the batterer are much better predictors of violence than are characteristics of the woman (Hotaling & Sugarman, 1986). That is, it's something about the man, not something about the woman.

Research shows average psychological differences between violent and nonviolent husbands. Compared with nonviolent husbands, violent husbands are more likely to have an insecure or disorganized attachment style and to be more preoccupied with their wives (Holtzworth-Munroe et al., 1997).

Batterers are a diverse group. To organize this diversity, researchers have identified three types of batterers (Holtzworth-Munroe, 2000; Holtzworth-Munroe & Stuart, 1994). *Family-only* batterers are the least violent and show little violence toward people outside their family. They show little psychopathology—except, of course, for beating their female partners. *Dysphoric-borderline* batterers engage in moderate or severe violence toward their wife but not toward others.

Battered women's shelters are a necessary part of aid to battered women.

They are the most psychologically distressed, exhibiting depression and anxiety and borderline personality characteristics such as extreme emotion fluctuations and intense, unstable interpersonal relationships. *Generally violent–antisocial* batterers are the most violent, both toward their spouse and toward others and are likely to be characterized by antisocial personality disorder.

Another research group has identified two types of batterers, nicknamed "cobras" and "pit bulls"—and you wouldn't want to be in the cage (or home) with either one (Jacobson & Gottman, 1998; Gottman et al., 1995). The pit bulls get angry quickly, their heart rates accelerate, and they become violent. Cobras are far less impulsive, and their heart rates actually slow down as they deliberately threaten and become violent. Cobras use less overt physical abuse, but they are more likely to be deadly.

An important implication of these typologies is that the treatment that works for one type of batterer is unlikely to work for another. Multiple treatments are needed, with a pairing of batterers to the appropriate treatment, as discussed in a later section.

Impact of Battering on the Woman   The physical consequences of being battered can be severe. In relationships with repeated violence, episodes often involve a combination of assault, verbal abuse, rape, and threats (Browne, 1993). Injuries range from bruises, cuts, black eyes, concussions, broken legs or back, and miscarriages to permanent injuries such as damage to joints, partial loss of hearing or vision, or even death.

Assault by a partner can indeed be lethal. Of the 3,000 women murdered in the United States in 2000, 1,000 (33 percent) were murdered by a husband or boyfriend (FBI, 2001).

The psychological impact can be devastating as well (Browne, 1993; Walker, 2001). Reactions of shock, denial, withdrawal, confusion, psychological numbing, and fear are common. Depression and suicide attempts are also common. Chronic fatigue and tension, startle reactions, disturbed sleeping and eating patterns, and nightmares are also often found among battered women. If battering continues over a long period of time, long-term responses include emotional numbing, extreme passivity, and helplessness.

Although the term *battered woman syndrome* was originally coined for these responses, psychologists now favor seeing them, like responses to rape, as instances of *posttraumatic stress disorder* (PTSD) (Browne, 1993; Walker, 1991).

Why do battered women stay with the batterer? A number of reasons have been identified (Glazer, 1993; Walker, 2001): (1) hope that the husband will reform; (2) having no other place to go; (3) fear that there will be reprisals from the batterer and that he may even kill her (as we saw in the O. J. Simpson case); (4) concern about the children (they need a father, the woman cannot support them herself, and so on); and (5) economic dependence (the woman cannot support herself).

Impact on the Children   In addition to the impact on the woman herself, there is an impact on the children. The man who batters his wife is likely to abuse his children as well (Bowker et al., 1988). Just witnessing their mother being beaten can be devastating to children. Research on children and adolescents exposed to domestic violence shows that they exhibit signs of trauma including PTSD, elevated levels of aggressive behavior, and diminished academic functioning (Fantuzzo & Mohr, 1999; Fantuzzo et al., 1997; Kolbo et al., 1996; Levendosky et al., 2002a, 2002b).

Theories of the Causes of Woman-Battering   A number of theoretical perspectives are available for understanding why battering occurs (for reviews, see Straus, 1980; Walker, 1980, 2001). These perspectives in some ways parallel the different theoretical views of the nature of rape described earlier in this chapter.

Several different *psychological theories* are possible. One is that the man who batters his wife is simply a rare, psychologically disturbed individual, perhaps a psychopath. This view does not seem plausible given the high incidence of wife-beating documented by research. A second psychological approach is to say that battering occurs because of the psychopathology of the wife. In this view, the

FOCUS 14.1

A LETTER FROM A BATTERED WIFE

I am in my thirties and so is my husband. I have a high school diploma and am presently attending a local college, trying to obtain the additional education I need. My husband is a college graduate and a professional in his field. We are both attractive and, for the most part, respected and well-liked. We have four children and live in a middle-class home with all the comforts we could possibly want.

I have everything, except life without fear.

For most of my married life I have been periodically beaten by my husband. What do I mean by "beaten"? I mean that parts of my body have been hit violently and repeatedly, and that painful bruises, swelling, bleeding wounds, unconsciousness, and combinations of these things have resulted. . . .

I have been kicked in the abdomen when I was visibly pregnant. I have been kicked off the bed and hit while lying on the floor—again, while I was pregnant. I have been whipped, kicked and thrown, picked up again and thrown down again. I have been punched and kicked in the head, chest, face, and abdomen more times than I can count.

I have been slapped for saying something about politics, for having a different view about religion, for swearing, for crying, for wanting to have intercourse.

I have been threatened when I wouldn't do something he told me to do. I have been threatened when he's had a bad day and when he's had a good day. . . .

Few people have ever seen my black and blue face or swollen lips because I have always stayed indoors afterwards, feeling ashamed. I was never able to drive following one of these beatings, so I could not get myself to a hospital for care. I could never have left my young children alone, even if I could have driven a car.

Hysteria inevitably sets in after a beating. This hysteria—the shaking and crying and mumbling—is not accepted by anyone, so there has never been anyone to call.

My husband on a few occasions did phone a day or so later so we could agree on the excuse I would use for returning to work, the grocery store, the dentist appointment, and so on. I used the excuses—a car accident, oral surgery, things like that.

Now, the first response to this story, which I myself think of, will be "Why didn't you seek help?" I did. Early in our marriage I went to a clergyman who, after a few visits, told me that my husband meant no real harm, that he was just confused and felt insecure. I was encouraged to be more tolerant and un-derstanding. Most important, I was told to forgive him the beatings just as Christ had forgiven me from the cross. I did that, too.

Next time I turned to a doctor. I was given little pills to relax me and told to take things a little easier. I was just too nervous.

I turned to a friend, and when her husband found out, he accused me of either making things up or exaggerating the situation. She was told to stay away from me. She didn't, but she could no longer really help me.

I turned to a professional family guidance agency. I was told there that my husband needed help and that I should find a way to control the incidents. I couldn't control the beatings—that was the whole point of my seeking help. At the agency I found I had to defend myself against the suspicion that I wanted to be hit, that I invited the beatings. Good God! Did the Jews invite themselves to be slaughtered in Germany? . . .

I called the police one time. They not only did not respond to the call, they called several hours later to ask if things had "settled down." I could have been dead by then!

I have nowhere to go if it happens again. No one wants to take in a woman with four children. Even if there were someone kind enough to care, no one wants to become involved in what is commonly referred to as a "domestic situation." . . .

No one has to "provoke" a wife-beater. He will strike out when he's ready and for whatever reason he has at the moment.

I may be his excuse, but I have never been the reason. . . .

I have suffered physical and emotional battering and spiritual rape be-cause the social structure of my world says I cannot do anything about a man who wants to beat me. . . . But staying with my husband means that my chil-dren must be subjected to the emotional battering caused when they see their mother's face or hear her screams in the middle of the night.

(continued)

I know that I have to get out. But when you have nowhere to go, you know that you must go on your own and expect no support. I have to be ready for that. I have to be ready to support myself and the children completely, and still provide a decent environment for them. I pray that I can do that before I am murdered in my own home. . . .

It must be pointed out that while a husband can beat, slap, or threaten his wife, there are "good days." These days tend to wear away the effects of the beating. They tend to cause the wife to put aside the traumas and look to the good—first, because there is nothing else to do; second, because there is nowhere and no one to turn to; and third, because the defeat is the beating and the hope is that it will not happen again. A loving woman like myself always hopes that it will not happen again. When it does, she simply hopes again, until it becomes obvious after a third beating that there is no hope. That is when she turns outward for help to find an answer. When that help is denied, she either resigns herself to the situation she is in or pulls herself together and starts making plans for a future life that includes only herself and her children.

For many the third beating may be too late. . . .

What determines who is lucky and who isn't? I could have been dead a long time ago had I been hit the wrong way. My baby could have been killed or deformed had I been kicked the wrong way. What saved me?

I don't know. I only know that it has happened and that each night I dread the final blow that will kill me and leave my children motherless. I hope I can hang on until I complete my education, get a good job, and become self-sufficient enough to care for my children on my own.

woman is seen as a disturbed individual who brings on the attack and self-destructively stays with the man who batters her. The psychoanalyst might call her masochistic. Note that this view blames the victim.

A third psychological approach is the *learned helplessness theory* of battering proposed by Lenore Walker (1980), a psychologist who has done extensive research with battered women. This explanation rests on the same learned helplessness and hopelessness theory that is used in explaining depression in women in Chapter 15. It is based in learning theory. According to this view, the battered woman has a history of childhood gender-role socialization to passivity and help-lessness. In adulthood, being battered increases her helplessness. This theory ex-plains the depression experienced by battered women. It also explains why bat-tered women stay with their husbands or return to them after having tried to escape. Their conditioning to helplessness is so complete that they cannot act to save themselves.

Sociological theory presents yet another view (Straus, 1980). It focuses on norms and attitudes in our society that condone violence within families, partic-ularly violence by husbands to wives. Sociologists also call attention to the process of gender-role socialization in childhood, in which girls are expected to be passive and boys are expected to be aggressive.

The *feminist perspective* holds that wife-beating is both cause and effect of the inequality of power between men and women (Anderson, 1997; Walker, 1980, 2001). The inequality of power causes wife-beating because it serves as a rationale for a man to "discipline" his wife, much as a parent may discipline a child. But in-equality of power is also affected by wife-beating, because battering serves to per-petuate the dominance of men over women. Feminists also note both the histori-cal and contemporary approval of wife-beating.

What Can Be Done?   The problems of battered women are complex, and no single measure is likely to solve them. If violence in American society could be reduced in general, that would help to a certain degree. Some of the problems of battered women, however, are special and require special solutions. One solution is providing refuge houses. These houses provide the woman with a safe place to go (one of her most immediate needs), with emotional support from those around her, and possibly with job counseling and legal advice. Refuge shelters have sprung up like mushrooms in the past 25 years in the United States. Interest-ingly, these shelters and the paraprofessional and peer counseling they provide are the most successful treatment for battered women (Walker, 1980).

Community social services are also needed to deal with the problem of do-mestic violence. Crisis hot lines are important so that the woman can get imme-diate help. In addition, counseling services for the batterer, the victim, and the children are needed. Feminist therapy (see Chapter 15) should be particularly helpful to the battered woman.

Self-defense training for battered women has also been recommended (e.g., Martin, 1976). The woman who is an expert in karate or some other system can offset the greater strength of her husband and assertively discourage his attacks.

Legal and police reform are important as well (Walker, 2001). One problem is that the American legal system has considered the family and home to be sa-cred and has been loath to interfere with them in any way. Somehow the police officer who intervened in a "family" fight was viewed as violating the sanctity of the family. Police officers were often unwilling to arrest a husband for assault unless they had actually witnessed the attack, which is rare since the police are usually called after the fact.

On a hopeful note, in 1984 Congress passed the Family Violence Prevention and Services Act, which allocated funds for victims of domestic violence. Domestic violence is now a crime in all 50 states (Diehm & Ross, 1988). Many communities have experimented with a "mandatory arrest" or "shock arrest policy" in which the man must be arrested and spend a minimum of one night in jail if the police are called in on a case of domestic violence. The idea is to convey clearly to the man that what he is doing is wrong and illegal. Research has shown mixed results as to how effective mandatory arrest is; it seems to work at least as well as anything else that has been tried (Berk, 1993). In an experiment with new technologies, an ankle bracelet for the batterer is being tried. It contains an electronic device that sounds an alarm if he gets within a block of the woman's house.

At least some of the blame must also rest with traditional gender roles and socialization. Wife-beating, after all, is a way of exerting dominance and thereby of fulfilling the male role. And staying with such a husband is consistent with the submissiveness for which women are socialized. Reforms in gender roles, socialization, and education, therefore, will be necessary to remedy the situation fully.

Sexual Harassment

The sexual victimization of women is not limited to cases of out-and-out rape. Most women have experienced incidents of varying degrees of sexual harassment, what one author called "the little rapes" (Offir, 1982).

Because incidents of sexual harassment differ in the degree of offensiveness and coercion, they can be difficult to define, both in a legal or scholarly sense and in a personal sense. The official definition given by the U.S. government's Equal Employment Opportunity Commission (EEOC) is the following:

> Harassment on the basis of sex is a violation of Section 703 of Title VII (of the United States Civil Rights Act). Unwelcome sexual advances, requests for sexual favors, and other verbal or physical conduct of a sexual nature constitute sexual harassment when
>
> 1. submission to such conduct is made either explicitly or implicitly a term or condition of an individual's employment.
>
> 2. submission to or rejection of such conduct by an individual is used as the basis for employment decisions affecting such individual, or
>
> 3. such conduct has the purpose or effect of unreasonably interfering with an individual's work performance or creating an intimidating, hostile or offensive working environment.

The EEOC definition contains two parts. The first is often termed *quid pro quo harassment* and is captured in points 1 and 2. (*Quid pro quo* is a Latin phrase meaning "I'll give you something if you give me something in return," or "I'll scratch your back if you scratch mine.") Quid pro quo harassment refers to exchanges such as the following: "Have sex with me and I'll hire you," or "Have sex with me and I'll see to it that you get a big raise."

The second part of the definition refers to *hostile environment* and is captured in point 3. For this part of the definition, there does not have to be a requirement of sex in exchange for hiring, promotion, or pay. Rather, the issue is whether the behavior and environment in the workplace is so hostile to women that it interferes with their work performance. The classic example was the Jacksonville Shipyards Supreme Court case (*Robinson* v. *Jacksonville Shipyards,* 1991). In that case, Lois Robinson was employed at the shipyards and felt that her work was impaired by being surrounded by a hostile environment, including pornographic pictures prominently displayed (e.g., a pinup showing a meat spatula pressed against a woman's pubic area), crude and explicit graffiti on the walls, and a dart board covered with a picture of a woman's breast with the nipple as a bull's eye. The Supreme Court found in favor of Ms. Robinson and declared this kind of hostile environment to be illegal.

Sexual harassment can occur in a variety of settings—at work, in education, in psychotherapy (see Chapter 15), on the street.

Sexual Harassment at Work   Sexual harassment at work can take a number of different forms. A prospective employer may make it clear that sexual activity is a prerequisite to being hired. Stories of such incidents are rampant among actresses. On the job, sexual activity may be made a condition for continued employment, for a promotion, or for other benefits, such as a raise. Here is one case:

> June, a waitress in Arkansas, was serving a customer when he reached up
> her skirt. When she asked her manager for future protection against such
> incidents, she was harassed by him instead. "They put me on probation,"
> she recalled, "as if I was the guilty one. Then things went from bad to
> worse. I got lousy tables and bad hours." (Phillips, 1977)

Such an incident is a clear case showing how the man uses his position of power to punish the woman for her noncompliance with sexual requests.

Research indicates that sexual harassment at work is far more common than many people realize. Estimates of its prevalence vary considerably. One recent, well-sampled study found that 12 percent of women experience sexual harassment in their lifetime (Dansky & Kilpatrick, 1997). However, most experts believe that this study underestimated the extent of the problem considerably by not asking sufficient questions about hostile environment harassment. The average over a number of studies is 44 percent when harassment by co-workers—not just supervisors—is counted (Welsh, 1999).

Sexual harassment at work may be blatant, such as making it clear that sexual activity is a prerequisite to being hired; or it may be more subtle, as is the case in this photograph. The woman cannot avoid physical contact. Yet, if the man is her boss, she may feel too intimidated to complain.

Men, too, can be victims of sexual harassment. Same-gender harassment is relatively rare between women but far more common among men (DuBois et al., 1998). And for men, harassment by another man is associated with considerably worse psychological responses than is harassment by a woman (DuBois et al., 1998).

Sexual harassment at work is more than just an annoyance. It can mean the difference between getting a career advancement and not getting one. For the working-class woman who supports her family, being fired for sexual noncompliance is a catastrophe. The potential for coercing her is enormous. Women typically describe the experience as being degrading and humiliating. Sexual harassment has been linked to anxiety, depression, sleep disturbances, nausea, headaches, and PTSD (Fitzgerald, 1993a; Welsh, 1999).

Sexual Harassment in Education   The scene is also set for sexual harassment in an educational setting: The male teacher or professor wields power over the female student (Dziech & Weiner, 1983).

A survey of male professors at a prestigious research university indicated that fully 26 percent admitted to having had a sexual encounter or sexual relationship with a student (Fitzgerald et al., 1988). If anything, of course, that is an underestimate, because this is the kind of behavior that a respondent might hide in a survey.

The data indicate that about 50 percent of female students have been harassed in some way or another by professors, ranging from insults and come-ons to sexual assault (Fitzgerald, 1993a).

> This professor made sexist and derogatory comments about the women in the class, women in public life, women in general:
>
> "You women are going to waste your education raising babies."
>
> "There is no future for women in political science. I don't believe in women in government at all."
>
> "Now if Justice Marshall had been a woman he would have sat down and cried, which is the reason—and a good one—we don't have a woman on the Supreme Court."
>
> "Any husband who is foolish enough to listen to what his wife says politically deserves anything he gets."
>
> I discussed with him the fact that his remarks were at first irritating and then progressively more offensive. I said that some of the women in the class felt intimidated and put down. The point is that if I, with all kinds of positive reinforcement from women professors and feminist friends, was brought down in spirit by this man, then surely so are other women students. (Williams, 1983, pp. 366–367)

The problem, once again, is unequal power. Women students in such a situation hardly have the power to protest, because the professor holds the power of having their grades in his hands. In cases that occur in graduate school, the professor controls critical evaluations and recommendations that affect the course of the woman's career. Women report dropping courses, changing majors, or dropping out of higher education as a result of sexual harassment (Fitzgerald, 1993a).

Harassers   Psychologist John Pryor has developed a person × situation model of sexual harassment (Pryor et al., 1995). According to this model, some men are much more likely to sexually harass than others. Put those men in a situation conducive to harassment and they harass. Pryor measures men's likelihood to sexually harass (LSH) by asking them to imagine a series of situations in which they have the opportunity to exploit an attractive woman sexually and experience no negative consequences; the men are asked to rate, for each situation, their likelihood of behaving in a sexually exploitive way.

Organizational norms play a large role in creating situations conducive to harassment (Pryor et al., 1995; Welsh, 1999). Some restaurants, for example, require the waitresses to wear short, tight skirts—and Hooters is not the only guilty one. These restaurants have created a sexualized atmosphere in which customers and co-workers are given permission to sexually harass the waitresses. Place a man who is high in LSH in that situation and he is likely to harass.

Feminist Analysis   Feminists make several points about sexual harassment. First, traditional thinking often blames the victim, suggesting that the woman behaves provocatively or explicitly initiates sexual activity in the hope of getting a promotion, getting a good grade, and so on. In contrast, the feminist perspective is that such activity is usually initiated by the male in the powerful position. Second, feminist analysis emphasizes issues of power and control. It is precisely because men are so often in positions of greater power—whether at work or in education—that sexual harassment becomes a possibility. Sexual harassment functions as a form of social control; research indicates that women are most at risk in occupations traditionally reserved for men and that women who report harassment commonly experience retribution (Koss et al., 1994). Furthermore, the woman who is the victim of sexual harassment experiences a lack of control over her own life, perhaps much like that of a rape victim.

Child Sexual Abuse

Child sexual abuse (CSA) is another topic that has come out of the closet in recent years. Two decades ago it was considered unmentionable and rare. Today one can flick on the television in the middle of the day and watch victims speak openly on talk shows.

Incidence of Child Sexual Abuse   Traditionally, it was thought that CSA was a rare and bizarre occurrence. Early research seemed to confirm this notion, indicating that the incidence prosecuted through the police and courts in the United States was very low. The catch, though, is that the overwhelming majority of cases go unreported and unprosecuted. Recent well-sampled surveys of the general population indicate that approximately 30 percent of girls are the victims of child sexual abuse in all its forms, including sexual touching; 8 percent experience intercourse as part of the CSA (Bissada & Briere, 2001; Kendler et al., 2000).

Psychological Impact on the Victim   The evidence indicates that child sexual abuse can have serious consequences for victims, both in the short run (while they are still children) and in the long run (when they are adults).

In a major review of studies of children who were sexually abused (this included incestuous abuse by a family member and other forms of abuse such as by a preschool teacher), the researchers concluded that there is strong evidence of a number of negative effects on these children compared with control groups of

Child sexual abuse has become a major concern, as exemplified by this educational poster.

nonabused children (Kendall-Tackett et al., 1993; see also Cosentino et al., 1995). Sexually abused children were significantly more likely to have symptoms of anxiety, posttraumatic stress disorder (PTSD), depression, poor self-esteem, health complaints, aggressive and antisocial behavior, inappropriate sexual behavior, school problems, and behavior problems such as hyperactivity. Victims had more severe symptoms when the perpetrator was a member of the family, when the sexual contact was frequent or occurred over a long period of time, and when the sexual activity involved penetration (vaginal, oral, or anal).

Studies of adults who were sexually abused as children have also found evidence of serious psychological consequences (Fleming et al., 1999; Kendler et al., 2000; Merrill et al., 2001; Rodriguez et al., 1997). One especially well-designed study focued on female adult twins (Kendler et al., 2000). Of particular interest are twins who were discordant for abuse—that is, one member of the twin pair had been sexually abused and the other had not. The results indicated that CSA was associated with increased rates of major depression, generalized anxiety disorder, bulimia, alcohol dependence, and drug dependence. CSA is also associated with PTSD (Rodriguez et al., 1997).

A controversial meta-analysis by psychologist Bruce Rind and his colleagues concluded that the effects of child sexual abuse were slight (Rind et al., 1998). This result contradicted the experience of psychotherapists who treat victims of CSA and are painfully aware of its consequences. The meta-analysis was flawed, though. Chief among the flaws was that it was limited to studies of college students (Hyde, 2003). It seems likely that those individuals who are the most traumatized by CSA never make it to college because they are not functioning well enough. Therefore, the most severely affected victims are missed in studies of college samples.

FOCUS 14.2

FALSE MEMORY SYNDROME? RECOVERED MEMORY?

One of the nastiest controversies in psychology today concerns the issue of what some call recovered memory and what others call false memory syndrome. The issue is sexual abuse or other severe trauma in childhood and whether the child victim can forget (repress) the memory of the event and later recover that memory.

On one side of the argument, the *recovered memory* side, psychotherapists see adult clients who display serious symptoms of prior trauma, such as severe depression and anxiety. Sometimes these clients have clear memories of being sexually abused in childhood and have always known about the events, but never told anyone until they told the therapist. In other cases, the client didn't remember that any abuse occurred but something triggered the memory and the client now recalls the sexual abuse. Psychotherapists are understandably outraged about the psychological trauma that results from childhood sexual abuse.

On the other side, some psychologists believe that these memories for events that had been forgotten and then are remembered are actually *false memories*. They argue that unscrupulous therapists may induce these memories through hypnosis or by strongly suggesting to clients that childhood abuse occurred.

Why is this an issue in feminist psychology? The reason is that a large proportion of cases of child sexual abuse involves a female victim and a male perpetrator, such as a father or other trusted adult such as an uncle or a priest.

On average, then, victims of CSA show greater psychological distress than controls. The effects are variable, though, with some victims showing severe distress and others showing little or no distress. The evidence indicates that the extent of distress is associated with a number of factors including, especially, the severity of the abuse. Patterns of sexual abuse can range from five minutes of fondling by a distant cousin to repeated forced intercourse by a father or stepfather over a period of five years. The effects of sexual abuse are the most severe when it involved intercourse, occurred repeatedly over years, and was committed by a father or stepfather (Cosentino et al., 1995; Fleming et al., 1999; Kendler et al., 2000).

Feminists are concerned that, if the false memory syndrome side wins, women's reports that they were sexually abused in childhood will not be taken seriously.

What do the data say? First, evidence from laboratory studies indicates that, although low levels of stress can enhance memory, high levels of stress disrupt memory (Nadel & Jacobs, 1998). Research directly on the issue of child sexual abuse also provides support for the existence of forgetting in some cases. In one study, 100 women who were known to have been sexually abused as children—they had been brought to a hospital for the abuse and it had been medically verified—were subsequently interviewed; 38 percent could not remember their prior abuse (Williams, 1992, 1994). In a study of adult women who reported being victims of child sexual abuse, 30 percent reported that they had completely blocked out any memory of the abuse for a full year or more (Gold et al., 1994). And in a massive study of adults who were survivors of a variety of traumatic events, delayed recall (forgetting the event for a time and then remembering it) was reported by 20 percent of victims of child sexual abuse and by 16 percent of those who had experienced injuries in combat or witnessed others being injured (Elliott, 1997). Most commonly, the trigger to remembering was a media presentation such as a television show. Therefore, the evidence seems to indicate that in some cases—percentages range between 20 and 38 percent—memories of childhood sexual abuse can be forgotten for a period of time and then remembered again.

The other question is, Can memories of events that did not occur be "implanted" in someone? In one study, the researcher was able to create false memories of childhood events in 25 percent of the adults given the treatment (Loftus, 1993). Certain conditions seem to increase the chances of people

(continued)

thinking that they remember things that did not occur, including suggestion by an authority figure and suggestion under hypnosis.

What is the bottom line? There is evidence that some people do forget memories of childhood sexual abuse and then later remember them. There is also evidence that some people can form false memories based on suggestion by another person. It seems to me likely that most of the cases of recovered memory of child sexual abuse are true, but that a few are false and the product of suggestion. To put the matter in perspective, each year thousands of children are sexually abused; the vast majority of these cases go unreported and the perpetrators go unpunished. It is also probably true that false accusations of child abuse are made, often by a well-intentioned "victim" who is highly suggestible to press reports of other cases or who has been misled by an overly zealous therapist. As a result, an accused person who is actually innocent may be convicted and go to jail. There are errors of justice on both sides. Nonetheless, I believe that, statistically, there are many, many more cases of unreported and unpunished perpetrators than of falsely convicted persons.

SOURCES: Bootzin & Natsoulis (1965); Elliott (1997); Freyd (1996); Gold et al. (1994); Loftus (1993); Moulds & Bryant (2002); Nadel & Jacobs (1998); Williams (1992, 1994).

Feminist Analysis   Feminists make several points about child sexual abuse. First, they warn against blaming the victim—that is, suggesting that a daughter initiates sex with her father by her seductive behavior and that he therefore cannot be held responsible. The evidence indicates that it is usually the father who is the initiator; even if the daughter were the initiator, the father, because of his age and position of responsibility in the family, must certainly refuse her. The most common pattern is for the CSA to begin when the daughter is 8 or 9 years old (Herman, 1981), scarcely an age at which she can be held responsible. Second, feminists point out that this is another instance in which men exercise power and control over women. Approximately twice as many girls as boys are victims of CSA, and 94 percent of perpetrators are men (Bissada & Briere, 2001; Finkelhor, 1984). Third, feminists want to alert the public to the frequency of CSA and the psychological damage it can do to girls and women.

In Conclusion

In this chapter we have considered four situations in which women and girls are victimized: rape, wife-battering, sexual harassment, and child sexual abuse. All have in common the reticence of the victims to report the occurrences and a corresponding difficulty in helping the unknown victims. In all four, the victim traditionally was blamed. Feminists emphasize the basic ways in which rape, wife-battering, sexual harassment, and child sexual abuse represent male expressions of power and dominance over women.

We need to recognize the victimization of women. But we also need to move beyond that recognition. For example, contrast these two terms: *rape victim* and *rape survivor*. The woman who has been raped yet manages to return to a productive life is a survivor, not a victim; she is strong, not weak. Even tragic situations in which women are made powerless can be a means for women to begin to discover and regain their strength and power, both at the individual level and at the level of the larger society.

As an old saying has it, "If it doesn't kill you, it will make you stronger." Some psychologists are now considering this possibility for severe traumas such as the ones discussed in this chapter and have even coined the term *posttraumatic growth*

EXPERIENCE THE RESEARCH

A SCALE TO ASSESS VIEWS ON THE CAUSES OF RAPE

In this exercise, you are going to construct a scale to assess people's beliefs in the four theoretical views of the causes of rape (see page 382 in the text). Generate four statements for each theoretical view; the statements should be ones that can be rated on a scale from *strongly disagree* (1) to *strongly agree* (5). For example, for the victim-precipitated theory, one statement might be "Most rapes occur because the woman really wanted it." For the feminist theory, one statement might be "Men use rape to dominate women." Once you've listed the 16 statements, have another person in this class check them to see whether each really reflects one of the four theoretical views. Then administer your 16-item scale to five women and five men. Compute an average score for each theoretical view for each person; that is, each of your participants will have a score on victim-precipitated beliefs, psychopathology of rapist beliefs, feminist beliefs, and social disorganization beliefs.

Do you see patterns in your data? For example, do most people seem to hold most strongly to psychopathology of rapist beliefs? Are there differences between men's and women's responses? What is the pattern of those differences?

(Tedeschi et al., 1998). In one study of low-income women who were sexually abused as children, approximately half reported some positive outcomes: They were better at protecting their own children from abuse, they were better at protecting themselves, and they felt that they were stronger people as a result (McMillen et al., 1995). Some women survive and even thrive following these traumas, and we should recognize them not as victims but as resilient, remarkably strong survivors.

Suggestions for Further Reading

Bates, Carolyn M., & Brodsky, Annette M. (1989). *Sex in the therapy hour.* New York: Guilford Press. Although sexual harassment in psychotherapy is discussed in Chapter 15, it also deserves mention here. In this book, the first author tells her story of being harassed in therapy. The second author, a feminist therapist, then analyzes the issues involved.

Brady, Katherine. (1979). *Father's days.* New York: Dell (paperback). This autobiography of a CSA victim is both moving and insightful.

Gordon, Linda. (1988). *Heroes of their own lives.* New York: Viking. This noted feminist historian traces the lives of battered women in the early 1900s and concludes that they were remarkable survivors—heroes, indeed.

Koss, Mary P., Goodman, Lisa A., Browne, Angela, Fitzgerald, Louise, Keita, Gwendolyn P., & Russo, Nancy F. (1994). *No safe haven: Male violence against women at home, at work, and in the community.* Washington, DC: American Psychological Association. This remains the most up-to-date, authoritative book on violence against women.

Walker, Lenore E. (1989). *Terrifying love: Why battered women kill and how society responds.* New York: Harper & Row. Walker, a psychologist who is an expert on battered women, has been an expert witness in the trials of more than 150 battered women who eventually killed their batterers. This book gives voice to these women, telling their life stories and how they got to the point of murder.

Women and the Web

The National Coalition Against Domestic Violence. The National Coalition Against Domestic Violence is a not-for-profit organization dedicated to the empowerment of battered women and their children.

   http://www.ncadv.org

Rape, Abuse, and Incest National Network (RAINN). RAINN is the nation's largest antisexual assault organization and operates a hotline, 1-800-656-HOPE.

   http://www.rainn.org

The Minnesota Center Against Violence and Abuse at the University of Minnesota. This is a clearinghouse on all forms of violence and abuse.

   http://www.mincava.umn.edu/

Women and Mental Health Issues

15

I was eighteen when I started therapy for the second time. I went to a woman for two years, twice a week. She was constantly trying to get me to admit that what I really wanted was to get married and have babies and lead a "secure" life; she was very preoccupied with how I dressed, and just like my mother, would scold me if my clothes were not clean, or if I wore my hair down; told me that it would be a really good sign if I started to wear makeup and get my hair done in a beauty parlor (like her, dyed blond and sprayed); when I told her that I like to wear pants she told me that I had a confusion of sex roles. . . . I originally went to her when my friends started to experiment with sex, and I felt that I couldn't make it, and that my woman friends with whom I had been close had rejected me for a good lay. . . .

—FROM PHYLLIS CHESLER, WOMEN AND MADNESS

Stories such as the one told by this woman were all too common among women in 1972 when psychologist Phyllis Chesler wrote her revolutionary book, *Women and Madness*. Today, issues of sexism in psychotherapy are more subtle, just as modern sexism has replaced traditional sexism in many other areas of life. In this chapter, we explore some of the adjustment problems women have, the evidence on whether sexism occurs in traditional psychotherapy, and newly emerging therapies for women.

Gender Ratios and Mental Health

A number of psychological disorders show very lopsided gender ratios. Gender differences are pronounced for alcohol abuse, with a ratio of three men to every one woman. In adulthood, twice as many women as men are depressed, and girls and women constitute 90 percent of those with anorexia. Here we will consider in more detail depression and eating disorders because they so disproportionately affect women, and alcoholism and drug abuse because they are stereotyped as "masculine" problems—for which reason female abusers stand a good chance of being overlooked.

Depression

The symptoms of depression include (1) emotional aspects—a dejected mood; (2) cognitive aspects—low self-esteem and negative expectations about the future; (3) motivational aspects—motivation is low and there is an inability to mobilize oneself to action; and (4) behavioral aspects—appetite loss, sleep disturbance, loss of interest in sex, poor concentration, and fatigue (Beck & Greenberg, 1974).

No matter how you count it, more women than men are depressed. As noted, twice as many women as men are depressed (Blehar & Oren, 1995; Kessler et al., 1993). The 2:1 gender ratio holds up consistently whether the index is diagnosable depression, people seeking therapy for depression, or even depressive symptoms in samples drawn from the general community. Among 15- to 24-year-olds, females have a 21 percent lifetime incidence of major depressive disorder, compared with 11 percent for males (Kessler et al., 1993). And the 2:1 ratio is found in studies of other nations as well (Weissman et al., 1993).

The developmental pattern associated with depression is important to understanding the emergence of this gender difference. Some studies find no gender difference in depression during childhood; others find boys to be more depressed. By ages 13 to 15, though, more girls than boys are depressed (e.g., Hankin et al., 1998). Longitudinal studies indicate that girls' depressive symptoms increase after age 13, whereas boys' symptoms remain relatively constant (Cole et al., 1999; Ge et al., 1994).

Some have argued that these higher rates of depression in women are not cause for concern because the gender difference is an "artifact" rather than a true difference. That is, it is possible that in reality, men and women suffer equally from depression but that women are overrepresented in the statistics, perhaps because they are more willing to admit mood symptoms or to seek help (therapy) for their problems. However, a detailed review of available research has led to the conclusion that the gender difference in depression is a true difference, not an artifact (Weissman & Klerman, 1979). In short, the evidence indicates that women report more depression because they actually experience more depression.

Why do women have more problems with depression? A number of factors seem to be involved, including cognitive vulnerability, body esteem, negative life events, peer harassment in the schools, violence against women, and poverty.

Cognitive Vulnerability Psychologist Lyn Abramson and her colleagues (1989) proposed one of the major theories of depression, **hopelessness theory.** According to this theory, a negative cognitive style makes a person vulnerable to depression. When bad things (negative life events) happen to people, those with a negative cognitive style tend to do three things: (1) They attribute the negative event to stable, global causes. In other words, they believe that whatever caused the negative event is going to continue (stable attribution) and will create more negative events in the future, and that whatever caused the negative event is going to generalize to many other areas of their lives (global attribution). If Jess says to herself "I got the F on that math exam because I'm stupid," she is making a stable attribution (stupidity tends to be permanent) as well as a global attribution

Hopelessness theory: The theory that a negative cognitive style makes a person vulnerable to depression.

(stupidity tends to generalize beyond math to other areas of life). (2) They conclude that the negative event implies bad things about themselves—that is, they make an internal attribution: "I got the F because *I'm* stupid." (3) They believe that the negative event will lead to other negative consequences in the future. Put this all together and you have a hopeless person, one who believes that bad things will continue to happen and that she or he is helpless to control them.

Research with children under 11 indicates no gender difference in cognitive style or boys having the more negative style (Abela, 2001; Gladstone et al., 1997). In contrast, research with adolescents shows a more negative style among girls (Hankin & Abramson, 2001). The teenage years, then, are when the cognitive-vulnerability stage is set for the gender difference in depression to emerge.

Hopelessness theory is a vulnerability-stress theory of depression. That is, people can have the cognitive vulnerability but not actually become depressed unless they experience a stressful life event that touches off their vulnerability. Negative life events are also key to understanding girls' and women's greater depression, as discussed later in this section.

Depression is a major mental health issue for women. Twice as many women as men are depressed, and the gender difference emerges in adolescence.

Psychologist Susan Nolen-Hoeksema (1991b) has introduced an additional aspect of cognitive vulnerability to depression—*rumination*, defined as the tendency to think repetitively about one's depressed mood or about the causes and consequences of negative life events. People who ruminate just can't seem to get these negative thoughts out of their heads. Nolen-Hoeksema finds that girls and women ruminate more than boys and men do. One study indicates a gender difference in rumination as early as age 9 (Broderick, 1998).

Body Esteem   Girls and women have more negative body esteem than boys and men (Mendelson et al., 2001; Polce-Lynch et al., 2001). These negative feelings about the body may contribute to depression. In one study involving a sample of high school students, the gender difference in depression was eliminated when body image and self-esteem were controlled for (Allgood-Merten et al., 1990). In another study, body image measures predicted later increases in depressive symptoms for adolescent girls (Stice & Bearman, 2001).

Negative Life Events   If girls and women experience more negative life events—if more bad things happen to them—this alone, or in combination with greater cognitive vulnerability, could account for the gender difference in depression. In fact, a number of studies have found that girls and women do report more negative life events than boys and men do (see the meta-analysis by Davis et al., 1999). These negative events can include everything from having parents with a high-conflict marriage to experiencing child sexual abuse or rape. One large, well-sampled study found that, among women with a history of child sexual abuse, 29 percent had experienced a diagnosable major depressive disorder, compared with only 9 percent among women with no history of child sexual abuse (MacMillan et al., 2001). The issue of violence against women is discussed in more detail below.

The Timing of Puberty   If we look specifically at the sharp emergence of the gender difference in depression around age 13, one factor may be pubertal timing. Early puberty is just plain disadvantageous for girls (Caspi et al., 1993; Ge et al., 1996). A girl who develops sexy curves and noticeable breasts at 10 or 11 is sexualized and teased by her peers and, compared with other girls, is less able to handle it, precisely because she is young. Early puberty for boys, in contrast, is good news for them. They grow taller and more muscular ahead of their peers and perform better athletically. Research shows that early puberty in girls is associated with elevated depression and anxiety (Ge et al., 1996; Graber et al., 1997).

Peer Harassment in the Schools   Peer harassment in the schools, especially sexual harassment, has become a significant problem. According to a major national survey of students in the eighth through eleventh grades, most boys (79 percent) and girls (83 percent) have experienced such harassment, but girls are far more likely to feel upset about it or to change their behavior (AAUW, 2001). Girls are also considerably more likely than boys to feel self-conscious because of the incident (44 percent versus 19 percent), embarrassed (53 percent versus 32 percent), and less confident (32 percent versus 16 percent). Peer harassment is definitely a likely suspect in the emergence of the gender difference in depression during early adolescence.

Violence and Poverty   Two additional factors contribute to depression in women and help to explain why more women than men are depressed: violence against women and poverty (Belle, 1990; Koss, 1990). Violence against women is discussed in detail in Chapter 14. Suffice it to say here that the experience of being battered, for example, can lead to depression. Regarding the second factor, poverty is becoming increasingly gender-related. An increasing proportion of those living below the poverty line are women or women and their children, a phenomenon known as the **feminization of poverty.** This in turn is related to factors such as the increased proportion of single-parent households headed by women, the inadequacy of child support payments following divorce, and the lack of decent, affordable childcare that would allow these women to work at jobs that could bring them to self-sufficiency (Belle, 1990). Abundant evidence shows a link between poverty and mental health problems (Belle, 1990). Therefore, the feminization of poverty has mental health implications for women. Research indicates that women who are financially stressed and have responsibility for young children experience more symptoms of depression than other women do (e.g., Pearlin & Johnson, 1977). One study found that nearly half the low-income mothers of young children in the sample had sufficient symptoms to be categorized as depressed (Hall et al., 1985). There is little doubt that the higher rates of poverty among women contribute to the higher incidence of depression in women.

> **Feminization of poverty:** The increasing trend over time for women to be overrepresented among the poor in the United States.

Alcoholism and Drug Abuse

Statistics on Gender and Alcohol Abuse   The ratio of males to females with alcohol abuse or dependence problems is approximately 3:1. In the definitive National Comorbidity Survey, 14 percent of men and 5 percent of women between the ages of 15 and 54 met the criteria for a diagnosable alcohol use disorder (Kessler et al., 1994). We can think of drinking behavior as falling along a continuum from abstinence at one end to dependence at the other, with moderate drinking, heavy drinking, and problem drinking falling in between.

In addition to the well-known damage that alcoholism does to women's day-to-day functioning, heavy drinking increases women's mortality rates. In one study, heavy drinking (defined as six or more drinks per day) increased women's risk of death by 160 percent, compared with an increased risk from heavy drinking of 40 percent for men (Klatsky et al., 1992). Alcohol intake, perhaps even in moderate amounts, is associated with an increased risk of breast cancer. It is thought that this may occur because alcohol raises levels of several sex hormones known to increase breast cancer risk (Dorgan et al., 2001).

We can ask two questions here. What causes the gender difference in alcohol disorders? And what factors predispose a woman to develop an alcohol disorder?

Causes of Gender Differences in Alcohol Disorders   Heavy drinking almost always precedes and often predicts the development of an alcohol disorder, and more men than women are heavy drinkers (Dawson et al., 1995). That then leads to the question: Why are more men heavy drinkers? One view is that heavy drinking and drunkenness are more socially disapproved for women than for men (Vogeltanz & Wilsnack, 1997). Women therefore regulate their behavior to avoid this disapproval.

A biopsychology explanation notes that alcohol has greater bioavailability in women than in men. This means that, given equivalent doses of ethanol, a woman will experience a higher blood alcohol level than a man, even when body weight is controlled for (El-Guebaly, 1995; York & Welte, 1994). Women are therefore more sensitive to the effects of alcohol and, according to this explanation, learn to moderate its use, thereby avoiding becoming problem drinkers.

Predictors of Alcohol Disorders in Women   A number of factors have been implicated in the development of alcohol disorders in women: genetic factors, a history of childhood adversity, having a mood disorder, and having a husband or partner who is a problem drinker.

A substantial body of evidence indicates that genetic factors contribute to alcohol problems, although some researchers believe that genetic influence is weaker in women than in men (McGue & Slutske, 1996). Certainly it is true that not all people with an alcoholic parent become alcoholic themselves. One interesting study has found that being in a good marriage substantially protects women with an alcoholic parent from becoming alcoholic (Jennison & Johnson, 2001).

A history of childhood adversity is a strong predictor of alcohol problems in women (Widom et al., 1995). Child sexual abuse is an especially important factor (Wilsnack et al., 1997). In one sample of alcohol- and/or drug-dependent women, 51 percent had experienced child sexual abuse and 39 percent had been exposed regularly to physical abuse by a parent (Berry & Sellman, 2001).

Depression and anxiety are commonly associated with alcohol problems in women. The question is, Are the depression and anxiety the cause or the effect? Do they precede or follow alcohol disorders? Longitudinal research indicates that depression often precedes and is a risk factor for alcohol abuse in women, but that it may also be a consequence (Hartka et al., 1991). In regard to anxiety disorders, agoraphobia and social phobia typically precede alcohol disorders (Kushner et al., 1990). A socially anxious woman may essentially self-medicate by drinking, perhaps heavily, before a social event.

Many studies have shown an association between a woman's drinking and her husband or partner's drinking (Vogeltanz & Wilsnack, 1997). Who drives whom to drink? The answer appears to be "both." That is, each partner probably influences the heavy drinking of the other (Roberts & Leonard, 1997).

Ethnicity, Gender, and Alcohol Abuse   As noted in Chapter 4, it is essential to consider interactions between gender and ethnicity, and alcohol abuse is a good case in point. Among teenage girls, heavy drinking has been found to be most common among American Indian girls (11 percent) and lowest among African American girls (3 percent), with Whites (6 percent), Hispanics (5 percent), and Asian Americans (4 percent) being intermediate (Travis, 1988b). For teenagers, the ratio of male:female heavy drinkers is 2:1 for American Indians, 2.5:1 for Whites, 3:1 for African Americans, 3.6:1 for Hispanics, and 55:1 for Asian Americans (Travis, 1988b). Notice that the gender ratio is always greater than 1:1. That is, there are more male than female heavy drinkers in all these ethnic groups. Nonetheless, the gender imbalance is far greater for Asian Americans than it is for all other ethnic groups.

Other Drugs   Although drug addiction is stereotyped as masculine, there are plenty of women suffering from addictions, and the pattern is not at all new. During the 19th century, the majority of morphine and opium addicts were women (Kandall, 1996). In 1894 Dr. Joseph Pierce proclaimed, "We have an army of women in America dying from the opium habit—larger than our standing army. The profession [medicine] is wholly responsible for the loose and indiscriminate use of the drug" (p. 631).

Today, as Table 15.1 shows, substantial proportions of women have used illicit drugs such as marijuana and cocaine, and the majority have used the licit drugs: alcohol and nicotine (cigarettes). According to another well-sampled survey, 13 percent of women have used cocaine, and of those, 15 percent have a history of dependence on it (compared with 20 percent of men using and 18 percent of those becoming dependent) (Anthony et al., 1994). About 1 percent of women have used heroin, and of those, 13 percent have a history of dependence (compared with 2 percent of men using and 22 percent of those becoming dependent) (Anthony et al., 1994).

As to the factors that increase a woman's risk of developing a substance abuse disorder, the list looks much like the one predicting alcohol abuse. They include genetic factors (parents' drug use), childhood sexual abuse, inadequate parenting, drug use by peers, and adult victimization by domestic violence (Goldberg, 1995; Kilbey & Burgermeister, 2001). In one large, well-sampled study, 6.6 percent of women who had a history of child sexual abuse met criteria for drug abuse or dependence, compared with 1.4 percent of women with no history of abuse (MacMillan et al., 2001).

TABLE 15.1
Percentages of Women and Men Aged 12 or Older Reporting Any Use in Their Lifetime and in the Past 30 Days of Illicit and Licit Drugs

Drug	Lifetime		Past Month	
	Women	Men	Women	Men
Any illicit drug	30.3	41.6	4.5	8.1
Marijuana	27.9	38.5	3.5	6.7
Cocaine	8.2	13.1	0.5	1.1
Hallucinogens	7.4	12.6	0.6	0.8
Inhalants	3.7	7.9	0.2	0.5
Any psychotherapeutic drug	7.6	11.1	0.9	1.4
Alcohol	77.6	85.2	45.1	58.7
Cigarettes	64.7	75.1	25.7	29.7

SOURCE: SAMSHA (1999).

The issue of women and drug addiction is doubly a women's issue because not only do women themselves suffer enormously from dependence on drugs, but increasingly women are being legally charged for damage to a fetus exposed to harmful drugs during a pregnancy (Kandall, 1996).

Eating Disorders

Have you ever heard the saying "A woman can never be too rich or too thin?" I'm not sure about the rich part, but the thin part is a different matter. A woman *can* be too thin. The condition is anorexia nervosa, and it can kill. It is fatal in about 5 percent of cases (Hsu et al., 1993).

Anorexia Nervosa: Symptoms and Diagnosis   Anorexia nervosa is a disorder in which a person essentially starves herself. The pronoun *herself* is used intentionally here because the disorder occurs disproportionately among females: More than 90 percent of anorexics are females, and the great majority are adolescents, the usual age of onset being between 13 and 25. Anorexia is estimated to afflict 0.5 to 1 percent of girls and women if one uses DSM diagnostic criteria, and up to 4 percent if one uses broader criteria (Walters & Kendler, 1995).

According to the DSM-IV (see Focus 15.2), the following are the official criteria for a diagnosis of **anorexia nervosa**:

Anorexia nervosa: An eating disorder characterized by overcontrol of eating for purposes of weight reduction, sometimes to the point of starvation.

This artwork was done by an anorexic woman at the severest stage of her ill-ness. It shows her feelings of isolation and distorted body image.

(a) refusal to maintain weight at or above the minimum normal weight for that person's age and height (usually this means less than 85 percent of normal weight); (b) an intense fear of gaining weight or becoming fat, even though the person is underweight; (c) distorted perception of body weight or denial of the seriousness of the extreme weight loss; and (d) amenorrhea (the absence of men-struation) for three consecutive months.

The extreme weight loss characteristic of anorexia results from the anorexic's compulsive dieting. Although she may begin with "normal" dieting, it soon gets out of control. She limits herself to perhaps 600–800 calories per day. Her thoughts become obsessively focused on food and eating, and rituals develop around eating. She may restrict herself to only a few low-calorie foods, perhaps ex-isting solely on cottage cheese and apples. She eats in private and generally be-comes a loner. One anorexic described her ritualistic behavior to me: At work after her co-workers had eaten their lunches, she looked for opportunities when they were out of the office and then searched through the trash can for the paper wrap-pings from their lunches. She would finger the wrappings and sniff them for odors of food, then quickly return them to the trash can before she was discovered.

The compulsive dieting is a result of a phobia of gaining any weight and a cor-responding drive toward thinness. But the anorexic's body image is severely distorted, so that she believes herself to be fat even though she is emaciated, perhaps 20 percent or more under normal body weight. Despite her low intake of calories, the anorexic typically has abundant energy, to the point of being hyperactive. She often undertakes overly strenuous exercise to try to burn off more calories. The anorexic usually engages in denial: She firmly maintains that she has no problem and that she is not underweight, and she resists undergoing psychotherapy.

Bulimia Bulimia (also known as *bulimia nervosa*) is another eating disorder. It is sometimes called the bingeing-and-purging syndrome because the woman gorges herself by binge overeating, and then, before the calories enter her body, purges herself of the food either by forcing herself to vomit or by abusively using laxatives. The bulimic may consume 4,000 to 5,000 calories per day, yet continue to lose weight.

Bulimia: An eating disorder in which the person binges on food and then purges the body of the calories by vomiting or using laxatives.

According to the DSM-IV, the criteria for a diagnosis of bulimia include (a) recurrent episodes of *binge eating*, which is defined as eating, within a short time (two hours), an amount of food that is definitely more than most people would eat, combined with a feeling of lack of control over the eating; (b) recurrent behaviors to prevent weight gain from the bingeing, such as self-induced vomiting, fasting, excessive exercise, and misuse of laxatives, diuretics, or enemas; and (c) the occurrence of both bingeing and purging at least twice a week for three months.

Surveys of college populations indicate that as many as 13 to 20 percent of the women have engaged in bulimic behaviors that include binge eating followed by vomiting (Russo & Green, 1993). Thus this problem is not rare. Like anorexia, it is primarily a female problem; 90 percent of bulimics are female (American Psychiatric Association, 1994).

The prevalence of this disorder is disturbing, particularly because it has serious health consequences. Some of these are the result of starvation and will be discussed in the next section. In addition, the bulimic may suffer serious damage to her teeth and esophagus, due to the acidity associated with vomiting.

Causes A number of factors have been proposed as causes of or risk factors for eating disorders, including biological factors, personality traits such as perfectionism and low self-esteem, traumatic life events, and a culture that is obsessed with thinness.

It has been proposed that anorexia is a result of *biological causes*. Anorexics do have many disturbances of their biological functioning. But the problem is that physicians never see these people until they are already anorexic. At that point, it is not clear whether the physiological problems are the cause of the anorexia or the result of starvation (Piran, 2001). Research indicates that most likely, the problematic conditions are the result of starvation because most of those conditions reverse themselves and return to normal as the person gains

FOCUS 15.1

AN ANOREXIC TELLS HER STORY

At age 27 I am a recovered anorexic. I am 6 feet tall and weigh 140 pounds, which is just right for me. But things were not always that way.

At age 3 I was already fat. My mother loved to cook and I loved to eat. She was 5 feet 2 inches tall and weighed 180 pounds herself. When I got to school, I found that the other kids rejected me because I was fat. I quickly learned that the only way to get attention and have people like me was to cater to them, doing what they wanted, giving them things, never thinking of myself. When I was 14, my mother dieted down to 120 pounds. When my sister was 15 and I was 18, she became anorexic. I swore that would never happen to me.

At age 23 I weighed 187 pounds and had never had a date. One day a co-worker casually commented to me, "We both need to lose some weight." The comment instantly triggered something in me, and I started dieting. Within a few months, I was down to 140 pounds. I was asked on my first date. People said, "You look great, don't lose any more." I found that good things happen when you diet.

At that point, things were going so well that I decided, just to be on the safe side, that I should take off a few more pounds. I cut out sweets entirely. In the next three months, I went from 140 to 113 pounds. My menstrual period stopped.

When I reached 113 pounds, I decided to set 100 pounds as my goal. Dieting became an obsession. It was everything to me. I bought calorie counters, including seven copies of one of them. I cut almost all foods. Typically I consumed 500 calories per day maximum. Breakfast would be a slice of toast with a dab of peanut butter (I couldn't give up peanut butter). I skipped lunch. I ate dinner "out" so my family wouldn't know what I was doing. Usually it would be one bowl of chili, which has 280 calories. I drank lots of tea and chewed on ice so I could chew on something with no calories. Sometimes I also skipped breakfast, but got up early, before the rest of my family, and banged around the kitchen, pretending to fix breakfast but eating nothing. When I did eat, I always ate alone, never with others. I baked for my family, but then ate none of it. Everything was ritual and compulsion. I thought of nothing but food. Life with my family was a constant battle. The more they told me they wanted me to eat, the less I wanted to eat. When they asked me what I had for supper, I said, "I ordered a hamburger, french fries, and a milkshake." And I did. I ordered them at a fast food place, picked them up at the drive-through window, and then threw all of it in the trash can without eating any of it.

I never did make it to 100 pounds. The lowest I reached was 110. At that point, I missed work (I work as a dental assistant) and didn't care. I was perpetually cold and had my electric blanket on "high" in the middle of the summer. In the winter I would typically dress in panty hose, thermal underwear, two pairs of slacks, and several sweaters, and still be cold. Despite the small number of calories I consumed, my energy level was high. I sometimes woke up in the middle of the night and did sit-ups. I exercised while my co-workers were out at lunch.

Then I started having dizzy spells. That scared me. I got glasses, thinking my eyes were the problem and that glasses would help me. Needless to say, they didn't. Then I went to a physician. He told me to start eating. I didn't.

Soon after that I read a magazine article on anorexia. It triggered a rather dull click in my head. Some of the things that woman did sounded like me. The article contained the address of a national agency that made referrals for help.* I wrote to the address. They referred me to a nearby support group for anorexics. I went to it only twice. I didn't want to be with all of those thin people when I was so fat, as I saw myself.

The support group leader told me that I couldn't continue in the support group unless I also went for individual psychotherapy. Obedient person that I was, catering to her wishes as I always did to everyone's, I went to a therapist at a nearby community mental health clinic. I didn't want to go. At the first session I told him I didn't know why I was there. The first session converted me. Therapy was wonderful. Dr. G didn't tell me I had to eat or that I had to gain weight, as everyone else in my life was doing. He said, "We won't talk about weight. We'll talk about you." He helped me find out what my own wants were, a first for me because I had spent my life catering to others. After that first session, there was no doubt in my mind—I definitely wanted to continue therapy. In later sessions I learned to be assertive, doing something about my own wants. I learned how I had had no control of things in my life, and so chose to control one thing within my power—my weight. I came to realize

*One such organization is the National Anorexic Aid Society, 1925 East Dublin Granville Rd., Columbus, OH 43229. They make referrals to therapists, support groups, and hospitals, as well as offering many other services.

(continued)

FOCUS 15.1
CONTINUED

that I had had chronically low self-esteem, and I learned that I was a worthy human being. Previously I had been afraid to be anything but an angel with other people. With Dr. G, I could be myself, and our relationship was still okay. I learned to take that out to the rest of the world. I made new friends and started dating. In sessions with Dr. G, I had his undivided attention.

In all, I was in intensive therapy for about seven months, once per week. I still go in for a session occasionally if I feel particularly stressed or feel like I need a "booster shot." After the first session, I decided that eating was safe. I ate, and it was the first thing I'd ever done for myself. I added one thing a day to my eating. After three months I was still eating only small amounts, but it was progress and I had gained 7 pounds. My eating habits were still rigid, though. Then I got up to 127 pounds and stayed there for a year. I was less of a loner and had more of a social life. After that I got up to 140 pounds, and I have been there ever since.

I'm confident that I will never be anorexic again. Occasionally, if I am under great stress, I stop eating. But I instantly recognize the signs, I remember how horrible it was to be anorexic, and I start eating again.

SOURCE: Based on an interview conducted by the author.

weight. The functioning of the hypothalamus in the anorexic is disturbed. The hormones LH and FSH are at very low levels, comparable to those of a girl before puberty. Electrolytes are important for the proper functioning of the nervous system, and electrolyte levels (e.g., potassium) are disturbed in anorexics. Low potassium levels are a particular problem in bulimics, resulting from the vomiting and misuse of laxatives. Convulsions, low blood pressure, low heart rates, and irregular heartbeats are other results of the starvation. It seems, though, that all these biological abnormalities are results, rather than causes, of the anorexia.

Perfectionism has been identified as a risk factor for both anorexia and bulimia (Fairburn et al., 1999). Not all perfectionists develop eating disorders, of course. Perfectionism is a vulnerability that, combined with just the right stressor—such as a dawning belief that one is overweight or a comment from a gymnastics coach that one is getting too heavy to be successful in the sport—leads to the development of an eating disorder (Joiner et al., 1997b).

Traumatic life events may predispose a girl to an eating disorder, or may pre-cipitate an eating disorder in a girl who is vulnerable for some other reason. Pa-tients with eating disorders are considerably more likely (35 percent) to have a history of child sexual abuse than healthy controls (11 percent) (Fairburn et al., 1997). Those with eating disorders are also considerably more likely (50 percent) to have been teased repeatedly about their weight or appearance compared with healthy controls (28 percent).

Finally, it's important to note that a major factor in eating disorders is our culture's obsession with thinness. This issue is discussed in detail in the section on the feminist perspective later in the chapter.

Treatments   A *behavior therapy* approach, based on learning theory, treats anorexia as an eating phobia (e.g., Brady & Rieger, 1975). The idea is that, for an anorexic, eating causes anxiety. Therefore, fasting causes anxiety reduction, which is a powerful reinforcer. An understanding of these principles can be useful in the hospital treatment of anorexics, the goal being to get them to eat. This may be an extremely important short-term goal because, as noted previously, there is some risk of death due to starvation or to complications resulting from it, such as organ failure or electrolyte imbalance. Behavior therapy can be used to reduce the anxiety that the patient associates with eating. Simultaneously, the patient may be taught to associate positive reinforcers with eating (Garfinkel & Garner, 1982). Unfortunately, when patients treated this way return to their old home environ-ment, they often revert to their previous anorexic behavior patterns.

Bulimia might seem difficult to explain using learning theory. Vomiting is so inherently aversive, why would anyone do it repeatedly? The answer, once again, lies in anxiety. The bulimic wants to lose weight; therefore, an eating binge creates a high level of anxiety. Vomiting reduces the anxiety, and thus actually becomes a positive reinforcer.

Cognitive-behavioral therapy has now largely replaced the simpler behavioral therapies in many areas of psychotherapy, recognizing the importance of cogni-tions or thought processes in psychological disorders (e.g., Srebnik & Saltzberg, 1994). Cognitive-behavioral therapy helps people to change not only their behav-iors, but also the way they think about themselves and the world around them. Research shows that people with eating disorders have a variety of dysfunctional thought processes (Butow et al., 1993). They have distorted perceptions of their own bodies, often believing themselves to be fat when they are emaciated. They believe that weight gain is a sign of indulgence or lack of control. They are almost morbidly fascinated with weight control, so that it enters their thoughts when food and eating are not an issue (e.g., while taking an exam). They base their own feelings of self-worth on how well they are controlling their eating and their weight. Typically they think of themselves as worthless and inadequate. And as if all this were not enough, they are extremely rigid in holding onto these ideas, making therapy difficult.

Pharmacotherapy or treatment with drugs is sometimes used with anorexics and bulimics (Ellingrod, 2000). No drug has been developed specifically for the treatment of eating disorders. Rather, antidepressants are used, based on the belief that depression (as seen in the feelings of worthlessness and inadequacy) contributes to the eating disorder.

Research has been done on the effectiveness of cognitive-behavioral therapy and drug therapy in the treatment of eating disorders (Mitchell et al., 1993; Wilson et al., 2000). Antidepressants seem to be somewhat successful in some, but certainly not all, cases. For example, the frequency of binge eating is typically reduced by about 70 percent, but only about 24 percent of bulimics abstain from binge eating by the end of treatment (Mitchell et al., 1993). Antidepressants may help some, but they aren't the "quick fix" for all, or even most, of those with eating disorders. Most experts agree that drugs by themselves are relatively ineffective and are best used together with a treatment such as cognitive-behavioral therapy (Herzog et al., 1992).

Cognitive-behavioral therapy has been shown to be effective (Wilson et al., 2000). It, too, is more effective in reducing the frequency of binge eating and less successful at bringing about complete abstinence from bingeing. Success rates vary widely, but typically 30 to 50 percent of clients are abstinent by the end of therapy (Mitchell et al., 1993). The eating disorders are difficult to treat, and no treatment to date has come close to a 100 percent success rate.

Systems theory and *family therapy* represent yet another approach to anorexia. Systems theory regards the anorexic not as an isolated, disturbed individual, but rather as a person embedded in a complex system that includes her family and society at large (Minuchin et al., 1978). Her parents may have done things in her early childhood to predispose the girl to anorexia. Family interaction and communication patterns trigger and then perpetuate the problem in adolescence. But the girl's problem behavior also has disastrous effects on the functioning of the family. Her pathology becomes the focus of the family, and if she were to get well, a whole new family organization would be required. The predominantly upper-middle-class families of anorexic girls tend to emphasize or place importance on beauty (and therefore thinness) and externally visible signs of success, such as good grades. The girl thus learns to subordinate herself. As one team of researchers commented,

> Her expectation from a goal-directed activity, such as studying or learning
> a skill, is therefore not competence, but approval. The reward is not
> knowledge, but love. (Minuchin et al., 1978, p. 59)

Dieting produces external, tangible signs of "success" and simultaneously allows the girl to gain a sense of control.

In following the systems theory approach, family therapy is necessary. Therapy for the girl alone will not work, because she remains embedded in the family that maintains her illness. Thus both the family and the anorexic must participate in therapy.

Feminist Perspective   The *feminist perspective* emphasizes not the pathology of the individual, but rather the socialization practices and messages of our society (e.g., Boskind-Lodahl, 1976). The anorexic shows an extreme reaction to the socialization messages that all women in American society hear while growing up. The emphasis is on thinness—as the saying quoted earlier put it, "A woman can never be too thin." High-fashion models, *Playboy* centerfolds, and Miss America contestants present images of slimness that are difficult to live up to. Just as wealthy Chinese for centuries bound the feet of their daughters to achieve a culturally defined standard of beauty, so a particular standard of appearance of thinness is enforced in American society, not through physical methods but rather by socialization (Garfinkel & Garner, 1982).

The media feature models who are unrealistically thin, which contributes to a culture that fosters eating disorders in women.

Here are some of the data: Whereas a generation ago, female models weighed only about 8 percent less than the average American woman, today they weigh 23 percent less (Wolf, 1991). The average model, dancer, or actress today weighs less and looks thinner than 95 percent of the female population in the United States (Wolf, 1991). In the 1950s, the average body mass index (BMI) of Miss America winners was 19.4; by the late 1980s it had declined to 18.0 (Spitzer et al., 1999). (The BMI is an index of weight relative to height, so lower scores mean thinner.) *Playboy* centerfolds in the 1990s had a BMI averaging 18. The World Health Organization's cutoff for anorexia is a BMI less than 17.5. Meanwhile, the average actual BMI of American women aged 18 to 24 went from a little over 22 in 1970 to a bit over 24 in 1990 (Spitzer et al., 1999). Despite decades of emphasis by the women's movement on these issues, the gap between ideal and actual women's bodies has only increased.

College women rate their ideal figure as considerably thinner than their actual figure (Lamb et al., 1993). In fact, dissatisfaction with weight is so common among adolescent girls and women that it has been termed a "normative discontent" (Rodin et al., 1985). In one study of sixth-, seventh-, and eighth-grade girls, 72 percent dieted (Levine et al., 1994). And in another study, among fourth graders (10-year-olds), 51 percent of White girls and 46 percent of Black girls selected an ideal body size, from an array of drawings, that was thinner than their current size (Thompson et al., 1997). These standards of attractiveness are attached to Euro-American culture. For example, researchers found that Ugandans rated somewhat overweight and fat figures as being significantly more attractive than British respondents did (Furnham & Baguma, 1994).

In yet another study, college students watched one of four videotapes of a woman eating a meal (Basow & Kobrynowicz, 1993). The woman and her behavior were the same on each videotape. The tapes differed only in the meal she ate. Videotape 1 showed her eating a small salad and a glass of seltzer. Videotape 2 showed a large Greek salad and a diet soda. Videotape 3 showed her eating a half-size meatball sandwich, six mozzarella sticks, and a large Coke. Videotape 4 showed her eating a full-size meatball sandwich (approximately 1 foot in length), six mozzarella sticks, large fries, a piece of cake, and a large Coke. The woman in Videotape 1 was rated as having significantly better eating habits and as having significantly more social appeal than the same woman in the other videotapes. We have developed not only powerful cultural norms about the proper, thin body for women, but also norms about what women should eat.

Feminist therapists also note that anorexia is often precipitated by breaking up with a boyfriend or some other perceived rejection by a male (Boskind-Lodahl, 1976). The problem here is that the anorexic has given males the power to define her life and control her self-esteem.

Psychologist Eric Stice (2001) put many of these factors into a model of the development of bulimic symptoms (see Figure 15.1) and tested the model with a sample of girls initially assessed when they were in ninth or tenth grade and then

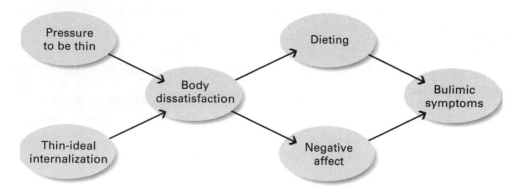

FIGURE 15.1

A model of the factors that contribute to the development of bulimia.

SOURCE: Stice, E. (2001). A Prospective Test of the Dual-pathway Model of Bulimic Pathology: Mediating Effects of Dieting and Negative Effect, *Journal of Abnormal Psychology, 110,* 124–135. Copyright © 2001 by the American Psychological Association. Reprinted with permission.

followed up 10 months later and 20 months later. According to the model, the initial force is cultural pressure to be thin. This cultural pressure is internalized, leading the girl to become dissatisfied with her body. This dissatisfaction in turn leads to two outcomes: She engages in dieting, and she experiences increased negative affect (moodiness and feelings of depression). Dieting further contributes to the negative affect. The dieting and negative affect in turn lead to actual bulimic symptoms. Stice's results with the high-school sample indicated significant support for every link in the model.

Sexism and Psychotherapy

With the rise of the women's movement in the late 1960s, psychotherapists and the institution of psychotherapy became the object of sharp attacks for sexism (e.g., Chesler, 1972). What evidence is there that sexism in psychotherapy was and continues to be a problem?

The Broverman Study   By far the most frequently cited study used as evidence of sexism in psychotherapy is one done by psychologist Inge Broverman and her colleagues (1970). They investigated the judgments of clinicians (psychiatrists, clinical psychologists, and social workers) on criteria of mental health for males and females. The clinicians in the sample were given a personality questionnaire with a series of rating scales of gender-typed personality characteristics, for example:

very	*not at all*
aggressive	*aggressive*

FOCUS 15.2

GENDER AND THE POLITICS OF PSYCHIATRIC DIAGNOSIS

The American Psychiatric Association publishes a thick book called the *Diagnostic and Statistical Manual* (DSM). The latest edition, DSM-IV, came out in 1994. Why is this book important? It contains the listing of all the official labels or diagnoses that psychiatrists and psychologists can give to people's mental disorders, together with a list of the criteria or symptoms that a patient must show in order to be given a particular diagnosis. Money is involved because, in order for your health insurance to pay for psychotherapy, the therapist must give you an official diagnosis from this book, which then becomes part of your record.

The DSM-IV contains a new diagnosis, not present in previous editions: Premenstrual Dysphoric Disorder (PMDD). ("Dysphoria" is the opposite of "euphoria"; "dysphoria" means unhappiness or depressed mood.) To be diagnosed with PMDD, a woman (and obviously only women can get this diagnosis) must display

> symptoms such as markedly depressed mood, marked anxiety, marked affective lability, and decreased interest in activities. These symptoms have regularly occurred during the last week of the luteal phase in most menstrual cycles during the past year. The symptoms begin to remit within a few days of the onset of menses . . . and are always absent in the week following menses. . . . This pattern of symptoms must have occurred most months for the previous 12 months. (American Psychiatric Association, 1994, p. 715)

Clearly this is the American Psychiatric Association's attempt to incorporate PMS into its diagnoses. Although this might sound like an innocent enough idea, gender politics are involved.

One-third of the clinicians were instructed to indicate on each item the pole to which a mature, healthy, socially competent *male* would be closer. Another third were told to do this for a *female,* and the remaining third were told to do so for an *adult.* Three interesting results emerged. First, although no significant differences were seen between the standards for males and for adults, there were

The PMDD diagnosis may do harm to women in several ways. For example, if a woman is diagnosed with PMDD, an ex-husband might use this to argue that he should get custody of their children because she has psychiatric problems. As another example, physicians may fail to properly diagnose and treat serious pelvic problems—such as pain resulting from an untreated sexually transmitted disease—because their focus is shifted to "treating" psychological issues following the PMDD diagnosis. One should generally be suspicious of a psychiatric diagnosis that can be applied to one gender only.

Another cause for suspicion about PMDD is that it has little or no scientific evidence backing it. The DSM is supposed to contain only diagnoses that have been validated scientifically. However, in an important study, a group of women reporting severe premenstrual symptoms was compared with a group of women with no symptoms (Gallant et al., 1992). The women responded to a checklist that contained the symptoms listed in the criteria for PMDD. There were no differences between the two groups! That is, the PMDD criteria failed to differentiate between a group of women who believed they had PMS and a group of women who did not. To establish the validity of PMDD, it would be essential to demonstrate differences between the two groups. Therefore, there is serious question about the scientific validity of PMDD.

What about women who do feel depressed just before their period? Don't we need a diagnosis for them? There already is one—depression. They can be treated for it, with no need for gender-stereotyped and potentially harmful labels of premenstrual dysphoria.

Even a process as seemingly innocent as psychiatric diagnosis may involve gender stereotypes and practices that can be harmful to women.

SOURCE: Caplan (1995).

differences between the standards for females and for adults. This is a good example of the male-as-normative principle in psychology. The standards for human mental health are for males, and females are a deviation from them—or, as one feminist put it, the Broverman results show that "a normal, average, healthy woman is a crazy human being." A second result was that socially desirable personality characteristics tended to be assigned to males, undesirable ones to females. For example, a mature, healthy, socially competent woman was supposed to be more submissive, more excitable in minor crises, have her feelings more easily hurt, and be more conceited about her appearance than a mature, healthy, socially competent man. A third result was that there was no difference in the results depending on whether the clinician-rater was a man or a woman (more than one-third of the clinicians were women). Apparently female clinicians were no more exempt than males from these views of "healthy" womanhood.

As evidence of sexism in psychotherapy, there are some problems with the Broverman study. The basic problem is that it does not provide a direct measure of what we are concerned with: whether therapists, in their treatment of clients, act in a sexist manner. This study does not measure what therapists actually do in therapy, but rather what their attitudes are, based on their responses to a paper-and-pencil questionnaire. What we need are data on therapists' actual treatment of clients (Stricker, 1977), but such information is in short supply. (In a later section I will review those data that are available.) Another problem with the Broverman study is that it is now more than 30 years old. It is possible that therapists have changed their attitudes substantially in the past 30 years, in response to changing attitudes about gender roles in our culture. In sum, the Broverman study does not provide strong evidence of sexism in psychotherapy today.

Currently, three areas are causes for concern about sex bias in therapy: gender bias in diagnosis, gender bias in treatment, and sexual misconduct by therapists with their clients. Each of these is discussed below.

Gender Bias in Diagnosis   Gender stereotypes may influence clinicians' diagnoses of women who come to them for help (Hartung & Widiger, 1998). For example, in one study clinicians labeled a stereotyped description of a single, middle-class White woman as an hysterical personality (Landrine, 1987). But clinicians given the same description for a *married,* middle-class woman labeled her depressed. As another example, a female client might be labeled histrionic, but a male client with the same characteristics might be labeled as antisocial (Ford & Widiger, 1989).

Focus 15.2 provides an illustration of the ways in which the very diagnostic labels that are available in the American Psychiatric Association's official *Diagnostic and Statistical Manual* (DSM) are influenced by gender and political considerations.

Diagnostic and Statistical Manual **(DSM):** The American Psychiatric Association's official manual of psychiatric diagnoses.

In short, the diagnosis of a mental disorder is not an objective, value-free process. The therapist's values and gender stereotypes enter the process. On an institutional level, gender considerations affect the very diagnostic categories that are officially available.

Gender Bias in Treatment   Gender bias in psychotherapy may occur in a number of forms, some of them blatant and some of them quite subtle (American Psychological Association, 1975b; Gilbert & Rader, 2001):

1. *A client's concerns are conceptualized stereotypically.* For example, the therapist may assume that a woman's problems will be solved by getting married or becoming a better wife. Or the therapist may expect lesbian and gay relationships to mimic heterosexual relationships with regard to masculine and feminine roles.

2. *The therapist uses essentialist, gender-difference beliefs in working with clients.* For example, in viewing women as especially competent at relationships and less competent in the world of work, the therapist may fail to help the client construct a vision of herself that transcends traditional gender roles.

3. *The therapist misuses the power of the therapist role.* This may include using diagnosis as a means of categorizing and controlling a client and viewing a client who disagrees with the therapist's interpretations as being "difficult." Seduction of a female client is one of the worst abuses of a therapist's power.

Sexual Misconduct by Therapists One of the most serious problems for women in therapy is the possibility of a male therapist initiating sex with a female client (Pope, 2001).

The 1978 revision of the APA's ethical code states: "Sexual intimacies between therapist and client are unethical." This means that under no circumstances is a therapist to have a sexual relationship with a client. A survey investigated the sexual activities of a sample of licensed Ph.D. psychologists with their clients (Holroyd & Brodsky, 1977); 5.5 percent of the male and 0.6 percent of the female psychologists returning the questionnaire admitted having engaged in sexual intercourse with a client during the time the patient was in therapy, and an additional 2.6 percent of male and 0.3 percent of female therapists had intercourse with clients within three months of termination of therapy. These are probably best regarded as minimum figures, because they are based on the self-reports of the therapists and some might not be willing to admit such activity, even though the questionnaire was anonymous. Of those therapists who had intercourse with clients, 80 percent repeated the activity with other clients.

Experts regard this situation as having the potential for serious emotional damage to the client (Pope, 2001). Like other cases of sexual coercion, it is a situation of unequal power, in which the more powerful person, the therapist, imposes sexual activity on the less powerful person, the client. The situation is regarded as particularly serious, because people in psychotherapy have opened themselves up emotionally to the therapist and therefore are extremely vulnerable emotionally. Results from a national survey indicate that about 90 percent of clients who have sex with a therapist are harmed by it (Pope, 2001).

How Traditional Therapies Apply to Women

One of the most important factors influencing a woman's experience in therapy is the theoretical orientation of the therapist and the corresponding type of therapy she or he uses. Below we will consider two kinds of therapy to see how they relate to women and whether they are likely to be biased.

Psychoanalysis   Psychoanalysis is a system of therapy based on Freud's theory (see Chapter 2). Both Freudian theory and psychoanalysis have received sharp criticism from feminists. Some feminists feel that psychoanalysis is inherently, or at least very likely to be, sex biased (e.g., American Psychological Association, 1975b). Others, however, feel that it can be applied in an unbiased way, and even speak of feminist psychoanalysis (e.g., Eichenbaum & Orbach, 1983; Shainess, 1977).

> **Psychoanalysis:** A system of therapy based on Freud's psychoanalytic theory in which the analyst attempts to bring repressed, unconscious material into consciousness.

The problem with psychoanalysis is that some of its central concepts *are* sex biased. For example, women's achievement strivings may be interpreted as penis envy. Women who enjoy orgasm from masturbation may be regarded as immature and thus be urged to strive for the more mature, vaginal orgasm. The evidence indicates that women in psychoanalysis have sometimes been convinced that they are inferior, masochistic, and so on (American Psychological Association, 1975b). Therefore, although feminist or nonsexist psychoanalysis may be a possibility, clients should be sensitized to the potential sexism of psychoanalysis.

Behavior Therapy   Behavior therapy (behavior modification or behavior mod) is a set of therapies based on principles of classical conditioning (usually associated with Pavlov) and operant conditioning (usually associated with Skinner). In contrast to psychoanalysis, behavior therapy attempts no in-depth analysis of the patient's personality or unconscious motives. Instead, the focus is on problematic behavior and how it can be modified by learning principles such as rewarding desired behaviors or punishing undesired ones (for a detailed discussion of behavior therapy and its implications for women, see Bleckman, 1980).

> **Behavior therapy:** A system of treatment based on the principles of learning theory.

A number of specific therapy techniques may be used. One is **systematic desensitization,** which is used in the treatment of phobias. The client and therapist make a list of events that arouse the patient's anxiety, and these are listed in a "hierarchy" from least anxiety-provoking to most anxiety-provoking (Table 15.2) The client is then trained in deep muscle relaxation. Next, the client relaxes and, while relaxed, is asked to imagine the least anxiety-provoking item on the hierarchy; if there is any tension,

> **Systematic desensitization:** A method used by behavior therapists in the treatment of phobias; it involves associating a relaxed, pleasant state with gradually increasing anxiety-provoking stimuli.

TABLE 15.2
A Client's Hierarchy for Systematic Desensitization

Most anxiety-arousing

1. An argument she raises in a discussion is ignored by the group.

2. She is not recognized by a person she has briefly met three times.

3. Her mother says she is selfish because she is not helping in the house (studying instead).

4. She is not recognized by a person she has briefly met twice.

5. Her mother calls her lazy.

Least anxiety-arousing

6. She is not recognized by a person she has briefly met once.

Source: Adapted from Joseph Wolpe and A. A. Lazarus, *Behavior Therapy Techniques: A Guide for the Treatment of Neuroses,* 1966, Pergamon Press. Reprinted with permission.

the patient goes back to concentrating on relaxation. Once the client is relaxed while imagining that situation, the therapist moves on to the next situation on the hierarchy, and so on, until the client is relaxed while imagining the most anxiety-provoking situation. Once clients feel relaxed imagining these events, they are often able to feel relaxed and confident when actually confronting them.

Another therapy technique involves *positive reinforcement,* in which desired behaviors are rewarded. *Observation* and *imitation* can also be used, especially, for instance, in assertiveness training for women, which we will discuss later in this chapter. Finally, *aversive learning procedures*—in which some unpleasant stimulus functions to eliminate an undesired behavior—may be applied. For example, the drug antabuse may be given to alcoholics; if they drink, the drug causes unpleasant body reactions such as nausea and vomiting. Such therapy is called *aversive counterconditioning.*

There is no inherent sexism in the concepts of behavior therapy (Lazarus, 1974). It does not assume that there should be gender differences, or that only women should engage in certain behaviors. Of course, behavior therapy does contain value judgments, but these should be applied equally to females and males. For example, assertiveness is valued by behavior therapists, and it should be valued both for males and for females. Of course, an individual behavior therapist may be sex biased, but there is nothing in the theoretical system itself that is biased.

As an example of the treatment of a particularly common problem for women, the behavior therapist would attack depression by trying to increase the level of positive reinforcement the woman receives in her environment (Beck & Greenberg, 1974). For instance, it might be that her husband is unresponsive, or even that he responds negatively, to her attempts at conversation or her work around the house, or to discussion of her job. Her husband might be trained to be more responsive to her, thus providing more positive reinforcement. Or she may receive little positive reinforcement in her job, in which case she might be encouraged to alter her work or find a different job that would provide more positive reinforcement.

As noted earlier in this chapter, **cognitive-behavioral therapy** has now largely replaced behavior therapy (e.g., Srebnik & Saltzberg, 1994). In cognitive-behavioral therapy, the therapist and client identify not only dysfunctional behaviors, but also dysfunctional thought patterns. As an example of a problem behavior, a woman might have become so concerned that her hips

> **Cognitive-behavioral therapy:** A system of psychotherapy that combines behavior therapy and restructuring of dysfunctional thought patterns.

are fatter than those of the models she sees on TV and in magazines that she refuses to go to the swimming pool because she will have to be seen in a swimming suit, despite the fact that she loves to swim and it's a hot summer. The therapist can help the woman confront such *avoidant behaviors* and substitute adaptive behaviors. In the cognitive realm, the therapist can help the client discover *negative beliefs* (my hips are fat and therefore no one can love me). The client can then discover how irrational those beliefs are and engage in *cognitive restructuring,* in which she substitutes positive beliefs (my hips are just fine, they're just fatter than those of skinny models, and I have lots of lovable qualities that people will notice, rather than staring at my hips).

Again, there is nothing inherently sex-biased about cognitive-behavioral therapy, although certainly an individual therapist could use it in a biased manner. Some feminist therapists are developing feminist cognitive-behavioral therapy (e.g., Srebnik & Saltzberg, 1994).

New Therapies for Women

Feminist Therapy   In response to the critiques of traditional therapies, particularly psychoanalysis, feminist psychologists developed feminist counseling and psychotherapy (e.g.,

> **Feminist therapy:** A system of therapy informed by feminist theory.

Rawlings & Carter, 1977). The assumptions and principles of **feminist therapy** are as follows (Enns, 1997; Worell & Johnson, 2001; Worell & Remer, 1992; Wyche & Rice, 1997):

1. Gender is a salient variable in the process and outcomes of therapy, but it can be understood only in the context of many other factors in a woman's

life. Women have multiple identities defined by gender, race/ethnicity, social class, sexual orientation, and disability.

2. The personal is political: Women's experiences must be understood from a sociocultural perspective that includes an analysis of power relationships as well as intrapsychic or individual perspectives. Women's experiences of sexism and discrimination must also be addressed. "Symptoms" can be seen as a woman's best attempts to cope with a restrictive and oppressive environment. Social activism can help a woman gain a sense of personal strength and control over her life.

3. A major goal of feminist therapy is personal empowerment and helping women to expand their alternatives and choices.

4. The therapeutic relationship is mutual and egalitarian.

5. Therapy focuses on a woman's strengths rather than only on her deficits.

6. The qualities of caring and nurturing are valued and honored. Clients are encouraged to nurture themselves and to bond with other women in a community of support.

Empowerment is a key feature of feminist therapy (Worell & Remer, 2002). This process begins with the declaration that the therapist and client are equal in the therapy process—equal in the sense that both are persons of equal worth. Therapy cannot empower women if it begins by making them less powerful than the therapist. The client is then encouraged to develop two sets of skills, one dealing with the internal and the other with the external. She is empowered in dealing with her personal situation by developing flexibility in problem solving and by developing a wide range of interpersonal and life skills. In addition, focusing on external issues, the woman is empowered by the therapist's encouragement to identify and challenge external conditions in her life that devalue her as a woman and perhaps as a member of an ethnic minority group or sexual minority as well. Rather than "fixing" the client's problems, the feminist therapist encourages the client to discover her strengths and develop new strengths that empower her to deal with situations that have previously caused her distress.

Assertiveness Training   Assertiveness training—a technique of behavior therapy—has become popular among women, and it can take place as a part of formal psychotherapy, in informal self-help groups, or in classes. First, some terms need to be defined.

Assertion, or **assertiveness,** involves standing up for one's basic interpersonal rights in such a way that the rights of another person are not violated. Assertion should be a direct, honest, and appropriate expression of one's feelings. *Aggression,* in this context,

Assertiveness: Standing up for one's basic interpersonal rights in such a way that the rights of another person are not violated.

involves standing up for one's rights in such a way that the rights of the other person are violated. It involves dominating, humiliating, or putting down the other person. *Nonassertion* is failing to stand up for one's rights and, consequently, permitting one's rights to be violated by others (Jakubowski-Spector, 1973).

Women tend to have more problems with being assertive than men do. In part that is because assertiveness is confused with aggressiveness, and aggressiveness is definitely not part of the feminine role—but then neither is assertiveness. Passivity and many of the other traits females are socialized for are contrary to assertiveness. Women are often concerned with maintaining harmonious relationships with others, and they may fear that being assertive will cause friction. The problem is that there is a cost in always swallowing one's feelings—a sense of frustration, ineffectiveness, or hurt. Some therapists believe that depression can result from lack of assertion (Jakubowski, 1977). Because assertiveness is a valuable human quality, many women are taking courses in assertiveness training.

Assertiveness training often consists of role playing in which students respond to people who are being aggressive or infringing on their rights, the idea being that assertiveness is learned through practice and through seeing models of assertive behavior. The following is an example of how high-quality assertion can be used to resolve a conflict.

> A graduate professor often continued evening class ten minutes or more beyond the normal class period. Although many students were irked by this behavior, one student was assertive and approached the professor after class one evening.
>
> STUDENT: I recognize that sometimes we get so involved in the discussion that you may not realize that the class is running overtime. I'd appreciate your ending the class on time because I have several commitments which I need to keep immediately after this class.
>
> PROFESSOR: I don't really think that I've been late so often.
>
> STUDENT: I guess that you haven't noticed but the last three classes have been ten or fifteen minutes late. Is there any way I could help you end it on time?
>
> PROFESSOR: As a matter of fact there is. I'm often so interested in the class that I don't look at my watch. It'd help me if you'd raise your hand five minutes before the end of the class period. If I don't stop in five minutes, signal me again.
>
> STUDENT: I'd be happy to do that. (Jakubowski, 1977, pp. 157–158)

Notice that the student was assertive, expressing her feelings directly, but in a way that showed regard for the professor. She did not show aggression (e.g., "You're so damned inconsiderate of us, making us stay late all the time"). Neither was she nonassertive (in this case, doing nothing and continuing to suffer). The situation proceeded to a satisfactory resolution.

Assertiveness training for girls and women is particularly important today because of victimization issues as well as the AIDS epidemic. Research with university women shows that assertiveness protects against sexual victimization, and experts recommend that assertiveness training be a major component of programs designed to prevent sexual assault (Greene & Navarro, 1998). Assertiveness training is also crucial for women who want to practice safe sex. Some experts advocate beginning assertiveness training with girls in early adolescence (Thompson et al., 1996).

New Directions

As we look to the future of women's mental health, we should bear in mind a central tenet of feminist theory: The primary source of women's pathology is societal, not individual. If we could stop men from battering, there would be no need for therapy for battered women. Therefore, we must continue to press for social change. In regard to the future of therapy for women, one issue seems particularly important: addressing the mental health needs of women of color and poor women.

Addressing the Mental Health Needs of Women of Color and Poor Women
Mental health services have been most available to middle- and upper-middle-class Whites, and the services have been designed to meet their needs. Women of color and poor women have had less access to these services. Furthermore, the services to which they have had access have not been sensitive to their needs (Comas-Diaz & Greene, 1994).

In therapy with women of color, therapists need to assess the woman's degree of identification with her ethnic group and her degree of acculturation (Worell & Remer, 1992). One Mexican American woman, for example, might speak Spanish almost exclusively and live in a Mexican American community in California, whereas another Mexican American woman's family might have been in the United States for four generations, and she might live in a suburb of Minneapolis and speak little Spanish. Such factors affect the cultural values the woman brings to therapy and therefore affect the goals that she and the therapist set for her. In general, feminist therapists need to make themselves familiar with the cultures from which women of color come.

In therapy with women of color, therapists must assess women's experiences not only of sex discrimination, but of race discrimination as well (Worell & Remer, 1992). These experiences can have a profound negative effect on psychological well-being.

Few psychotherapists are women of color. Clients who are women of color may prefer to have a therapist of their own ethnic group, with whom they will feel comfortable and who will understand their cultural background better. One of the important things that psychology as an institution must do is

Therapy for women of color needs to be culturally sensitive.

support more women of color in becoming psychotherapists. In the meantime, in many instances White women therapists will work with clients who are women of color. These therapists need to make extra efforts to provide culturally competent therapy.

As an example, we will consider the particular needs of Asian American women (Bradshaw, 1994; Chin et al., 1993; True, 1990). A number of potential sources of stress exist in their lives. Some stresses arise from traditional Asian cultures, which are patriarchal and expect women to be passive and obedient. Younger, educated Asian American women may embrace modern egalitarian values in the United States and thus may come into conflict with older family members. Interracial dating and marriage can be another source of stress. Although such relationships are common statistically for Asian American women, they are strongly discouraged by Asian families (True, 1990), again producing conflict and stress. There are, of course, stresses such as work-family conflicts that are experienced by White women as well, but Asian American women are likely to experience these stresses more keenly.

Culturally sensitive or culturally adapted therapy for Asian American women involves several features (True, 1990):

1. Use of bilingual therapists for non-English-speaking clients.

2. Use of family-focused rather than individual-focused approaches, with a respect for the women's family ties.

3. Respect for Asian American women who are not verbally or emotionally expressive.

4. Attention to the women's physical (somatic) complaints as possible reflections of psychological distress, knowing that in Asian culture it is more acceptable to have physical health problems than it is to have mental health problems.

5. Recognition that there may be strong sentiment against feminism within the Asian American community.

Just as we have discussed the importance of woman-valuing in a feminist approach to therapy, so an ethnic validity model has been proposed in working with people of color (Chin et al., 1993; Tyler et al., 1985). According to this model, the

EXPERIENCE THE RESEARCH

GENDER STEREOTYPES AND PSYCHOTROPIC DRUGS

In your school's library, locate the medical journals, particularly those in the area of family medicine and psychiatry (e.g., *Archives of General Psychiatry, American Journal of Psychiatry*). If your school's library does not carry these specialty journals, it probably will at least carry the *New England Journal of Medicine* and *Journal of the American Medical Association,* and you can use those for this exercise, too. Inspect three issues. Locate all the ads for drugs for treating psychological disorders. These ads will mostly be for antianxiety drugs (tranquilizers) and antidepressants. For each ad, record the following: the gender of the physician in the ad, the gender of the patient, and the emotion expressed by the patient's facial expression. How does the ad signal which person is the physician and which is the patient? Also analyze the text of the ad. Does it carry a message about the expected gender of patients receiving this drug? How does it describe these patients and their problem?

Are the ads gender stereotyped? That is, do they portray physicians as men and people suffering from depression or anxiety as women? Or do the ads try to break down stereotypes, for example, by showing a woman physician? What kinds of effects do you think these ads might have?

values and lifestyle of people of color must be valued. In addition, the deficit hypothesis, which views ethnic cultures other than Euro-American culture to be deficient, must be abandoned and replaced by a difference hypothesis, which acknowledges differences between cultures while at the same time valuing them equally.

These are important new directions for feminist therapy in the next decade.

Suggestions for Further Reading

Gottlieb, Lori (2001). *Stick figure: A diary of my former self.* New York: Berkley Books. Gottlieb, now a medical student, recounts her early adolescent experiences with anorexia based on her diaries written at the time. The writing is insightful, funny, and poignant.

Lerner, Harriet G. (1985). *The dance of anger: A woman's guide to changing the patterns of intimate relationships.* New York: Harper & Row. Lerner, a psychotherapist, writes wonderful books for the lay public. This one deals with anger. Another good one is *The dance of intimacy* (1989).

Women and the Web

NIMH. This website at the National Institute of Mental Health (NIMH) provides a fact sheet titled "Depression: What Every Woman Should Know."
http://www.nimh.nih.gov/publicat/depwomenknows.cfm

APA. This website at the American Psychological Association contains the proceedings of the October 2000 Summit on Women and Depression.
http://www.apa.org/pi/wpo/women&depression.pdf

National Association of Anorexia and Associated Eating Disorders. This website provides information about eating disorders, as well as a directory of therapists.
http://www.anad.org/

NIDA. This website at the National Institute on Drug Abuse (NIDA) provides summaries of research on women and drug abuse.
http://www.nida.nih./gov/WHGD/WHGDHome.html

Psychology of Men

16

The man controlling his environment is today the prevailing American image of masculinity. A man is expected to prove himself not by being part of society but by being untouched by it, soaring above it. He is to travel unfettered, beyond society's clutches, alone—making or breaking whatever or whoever crosses his path. He is to be in the driver's seat, the king of the road, forever charging down the open highway, along that masculine Möbius strip that cycles endlessly through a numbing stream of movies, TV shows, novels, advertisements, and pop tunes. He's a man because he won't be stopped. He'll fight attempts to tamp him down; if he has to, he'll use his gun.

— FROM SUSAN FALUDI, STIFFED

Perhaps it seems odd to you to have a chapter on the psychology of men in a book on the psychology of women, particularly when I argued earlier that much of traditional psychology has been a psychology of men, one that has, for example, ignored women's issues (menstruation, woman-battering) and done research with male participants only. But even though that is true, traditional psychology was not purposeful in or conscious of being a psychology of men. Emerging from the feminist movement and feminist scholarship of the 1970s has been a self-aware psychology of men. It is rooted in feminism and aware of the power of gender roles, and particularly of how the male role influences the lives of men. It is this emerging feminist psychology of men that we will consider in this chapter.

Male Roles

Just as there are gender-role stereotypes about women, there are such stereotypes about men (Chapter 3). Masculine characteristics include aggressiveness, independence, self-confidence, and being unemotional (Twenge, 1999; Spence & Buckner, 2000).

Several methods have been suggested for organizing the long list of masculine traits. For example, research suggests that there are four major factors in stereotypes about males (Brannon & David, 1976; Fischer et al., 1998):

1. No sissy stuff—Masculinity involves the avoidance of anything feminine. Note that in this aspect of masculine stereotypes, masculinity is defined negatively; it means avoiding femininity.

2. The big wheel—The masculine person is a "big wheel." He is high in status, successful, looked up to, and makes a lot of money, thereby being a good breadwinner.

3. The sturdy oak—Masculinity involves exuding confidence, strength, and self-reliance.

4. Give 'em hell—The masculine person is aggressive (perhaps to the point of violence), tough, and daring.

Research also shows that there are four stereotyped types of men in American culture (Edwards, 1992):

1. The businessman—A professional man, dressed in a suit, who is educated, money-oriented, and success-oriented.

2. The athlete—A muscular jock who is a football player or weightlifter; he is physically fit, coordinated, competitive, and determined, and he talks sports.

3. The family man—He is the father and the breadwinner, working full-time to support his family; he is married, responsible, and devoted to his family.

4. The loser—A jerk or a wimp, he has a bad attitude, has low self-confidence, and is a quitter.

Recent History: Changes in the Male Role   Today there are ambiguities and strains in the male role. For example, men are supposed to be aggressive, yet it is increasingly unacceptable for them to rape or beat their wives. They are expected to be aggressive lions at work in the corporation or on the athletic field, yet they are expected magically to transform themselves into tender, loving pussycats as they walk through the door to their own homes. Men are supposed to possess great physical strength and be active, yet what is adaptive in today's society is to be able to interact intelligently with a computer while sitting quietly at the keyboard.

Psychologist Joseph Pleck (1981) argues that the sources of these ambiguities and strains become clear if we look at the recent history of changes in the male role. Whenever roles change, ambiguities are created because of contradictions

Are modern men caught in the shift from traditional roles to modern roles?

between the old role and the new one. The individual feels a personal sense of strain in the tension between these roles, perhaps having been raised by the standards of the old role and then needing to function as an adult in the new role, and perhaps not even being aware that there is an old role and a new role.

In the late 1800s, the Victorian era in the United States and England, differences between men and women were controlled externally, and very strictly, by institutions (Pleck, 1981). Men went to all-male colleges, lived in fraternities, and drank at the all-male saloon. Later they functioned in the corporate boardroom, where no woman ever entered. Indeed, in those days my own alma mater, Oberlin College, although amazingly progressive in being coeducational, required men to walk on the sidewalk on one side of the street and women to walk on the sidewalk on the opposite side. In those days it was clear—though oppressive to those involved—what a man should do, and no one questioned the meaning of masculinity.

But somehow, in less than a century, we jolted from men and women walking on separate sidewalks to men actually becoming women through transsexual surgery. All-male colleges became coeducational, all-male saloons became singles' bars, and some women even entered the corporate boardroom. In short, external, institutional definition and control of masculinity declined.

Pleck argues that as society loses one kind of control over people's lives, it increases control over other aspects of their lives. Thus, as external, institutional control of masculinity declined, emphasis shifted to internal, psychological masculinity and gender identity. And at that point the psychologists stepped in. Pleck believes it was no accident that the first major work on psychological masculinity-femininity, Terman and Miles's *Sex and Personality* (1936), was published at the height of the Great Depression, just when traditional definitions of masculinity—having a job and being a breadwinner—were threatened most seriously. Thus the shift was from externally defined masculinity to internally defined masculinity—or from what side of the street you were supposed to walk on to what end of a masculinity-femininity scale you score on and what your gender identity is. As Pleck put it, "If holding a job to support a family could no longer be counted on to define manhood, a masculinity-femininity test could" (1981, p. 159).

Paralleling these historical changes from external to internal definitions of masculinity was a shift in the traits and behaviors expected of men. That is, there was a shift from the traditional male role to the modern male role.

The *traditional male role* has been found in all social classes in the United States during the nineteenth century, in most nonindustrial societies studied by anthropologists, and in working-class communities today. In the traditional male role, physical strength and aggression are of primary importance. Tender emotions are not to be expressed, although anger is permitted. The traditional male likes to spend his time with other men and defines his masculinity in the male group. Although he is married, he regards himself as superior to women, and does not value an egalitarian, emotionally close relationship with women.

By contrast, in the *modern male role,* primary importance is given to success on the job and earning a lot of money. Thus, working well in the corporation (which requires interpersonal skills and intelligence) and gaining power over others are far more important than physical strength. The modern male prefers the company of women and validates his masculinity through them. A high-quality intimate relationship with one woman, rather than numerous anonymous conquests, is his goal. Emotional sensitivity may—indeed, should—be expressed with women, but self-control is still the name of the game on the job.

Some men, of course, find even the modern male role to be oppressive and seek new options and liberation from it. Many others are caught in historical change, in the conflicts and strains between the traditional male role and the modern male role.

Traditional Psychology's View of Men and Masculinity

Traditional psychology has been greatly concerned with gender-role identity in males. As noted above, beginning in the 1930s the notions of masculinity and masculine identity were considered critical, and a large body of research, continuing to the present, was spawned. Pleck (1981) sees this body of research as based on the belief in the critical importance of masculine identity, or as based on the **male sex-role identity (MSRI) paradigm.** He has analyzed the set of assumptions involved in this traditional view, as well as whether the data support these assumptions. Some of the most critical assumptions are reviewed below.

> **Male sex-role identity (MSRI) paradigm:** Traditional psychology's approach to the psychology of men, based on the assumption that a masculine identity is essential for good adjustment.

One critical assumption of the MSRI paradigm is that *gender-role identity results from identification/modeling and, to a lesser extent, reinforcement and cognitive learning, and that cognitive learning is more important in males than in females.*[1] This assumption appears to be quite reasonable and certainly is consistent with traditional psychological theories (see Chapter 2). On reviewing the evidence, however, Pleck (1981) concluded that research does not support any of the several parts of this assumption. Let us consider why in a bit more detail.

Both psychoanalytic theory and social learning theory view identification/modeling as the source of gender-role identity in children. The idea is that children identify with and model the same-gender parent (see Chapter 2). But psychoanalytic theory and social learning theory are at odds with each other as to which traits of the father encourage identification. Psychoanalytic theory says the

---

[1]*Gender-role identity* is defined as the psychological structure representing the individual's identification with his or her own gender group; it demonstrates itself in the individual's gender-appropriate behavior, attitudes, and feelings.

boy identifies with his father out of fear of the father's wrath. Therefore, a punishing father should encourage identification. Social learning theory says it is the warm, nurturant, reinforcing father who encourages identification. Research does not support the punishing father idea from psychoanalytic theory. However, there is some support for the notion that boys imitate same-gender models more than other-gender models as early as 3 years of age (Bussey & Bandura, 1992, 1999). The identification/modeling assumption also predicts that sons should be more like their fathers than they are like their mothers, because boys should identify with and model their fathers. For example, if a boy has a talkative, outgoing father and a quiet, shy mother, the theories say that the boy should be talkative and outgoing because he identifies with his father and tries to be like him. But the data don't support this idea either—boys are not very similar to either parent on gender-typed traits (Maccoby & Jacklin, 1974).

The other part of this first assumption is that cognitive learning of gender roles should be more important for boys than it is for girls. The reasoning is something like this. In their formative, preschool years, boys spend most of their time with their mothers and little time with their fathers, because mothers are at home and fathers are off at work. This makes it rather difficult to identify with the father, because he is not there. Thus identification with the father does not work well as a source of masculine identity. The boy must then resort to other means for gaining a masculine identity, specifically, cognitive learning of masculinity (cognitive social learning theory—see Chapter 2) from general cultural sources such as TV and books. Although there is one pair of studies supporting this whole idea (McArthur & Eisen, 1976a, 1976b), far more research on the issue is needed.

In short, we do not really know how males develop a masculine identity. The research is often contradictory or inadequate, much of it having been based on unidimensional measures of masculinity-femininity (see Chapter 3), which do not recognize the possibility of androgyny.

A second assumption of the MSRI paradigm is that *the development of gender identity is risky and prone to errors, particularly in males.* The belief that errors are more likely in the development of a masculine identity is based in part on the point noted above, namely, that fathers are not around often enough for boys to identify with them. Data on transsexuals are also often presented as evidence. Transsexuals are persons who feel they are trapped in the body of the wrong gender; they are the people who seek sex-change operations. The person who has a male body but believes he is truly a woman is called a male-to-female transsexual. Data indicate that, among those people seeking sex-change operations, male-to-female transsexuals outnumber female-to-male transsexuals by a ratio of 3:1 (Abramowitz, 1986). That is, it is more common to have a person with a male body who has failed to form a (correct) masculine identity and instead has a feminine identity. This would be evidence that masculine identity development is more prone to error. The problem is that these data are only for reported cases and may ignore many female-to-male transsexuals who never seek a sex-change operation, in part because the operation in that direction is far more difficult. There is other evidence on the second assumption, but it, too, turns out to be weak. Overall, then, the evidence is poor that males are more vulnerable than females are to problems in the development of their gender identities (Pleck, 1981).

A third assumption of the MSRI paradigm is that *men's negative attitudes and behaviors toward women are a result of problems of gender-role identity that are caused by mothers.* Three possible ideas have been proposed about exactly what feature of the mother-son relationship causes problems; all three include an assumption that fathers do not participate much in rearing their sons. One possibility is that the little boy experiences the power his mother has over him as overwhelming and threatening. In adulthood, then, men try to control and subordinate women in order to defend against their fear of women's (mother's) control of them (this is the idea of Karen Horney, whose theories were discussed in Chapter 2). A second possibility is that the issue is not power, but rather identification. The idea is that the little boy mistakenly identifies with his mother because his father is not around, but he later realizes that he must get rid of this identification and become masculine. Thus men fear the feminine part of their identity and react to this fear by dominating and controlling those who are feminine—namely, women (this is the idea of Nancy Chodorow, whose theory was also discussed in Chapter 2). A third possibility considers mothers as agents of socialization. Socialization of boys frequently consists of punishing feminine behaviors, and mothers, who do most of the socialization, therefore punish boys for femininity. As a result, boys come to dislike their mothers and to generalize this dislike to all women. Actually, the second and third possibilities contradict each other—in the second the problem is that mothers make boys feminine, whereas in the third the problem is that mothers make boys masculine.

Any or all of these possibilities, then, could be used to explain why men have negative attitudes toward women. In extreme cases, they might be used as explanations of rape or woman-battering. What the feminist would note, though, is that in all cases the mother is blamed.

There really is not enough definitive research on this third assumption to decide whether it is accurate or not. But perhaps the more important point is that there are two much simpler explanations about why men hold negative attitudes toward women: (1) Men do so because it is to their advantage (negative attitudes about women justify and perpetuate men's privileged position in society), and (2) such attitudes are widespread in our culture and it is not surprising that each new generation of little boys picks them up.

A fourth assumption of the MSRI paradigm is the school feminization hypothesis: *Boys have academic and adjustment problems in school because schools are feminine* (most teachers are female, teachers encourage femininity, and schools have a feminine "image") *and that only makes boys' identity problems worse.* Once again, the data do not support this assumption (Pleck, 1981). For

Some have argued that boys have more problems in school than girls do because most teachers are women, with whom boys have trouble identifying.
The research, however, does not support this claim; there are no differences
between boys with male teachers and boys with female teachers.

example, research on academic performance shows that there is no difference
between boys who have female teachers and those who have male teachers (Gold
& Reis, 1982).

In summary, none of the assumptions of the MSRI paradigm, which has
been psychology's traditional view of men, has much evidence backing it.

Perhaps you are wondering why I have told you all these things and then told
you each of them is wrong. There are two reasons. First, it is important to understand the assumptions underlying traditional psychology's view of men and to
understand that those assumptions are questionable at best. Second, a significant
conclusion comes out of this discussion, namely, that psychology's obsessive concern with masculine identity is simply not useful and not validated by data. If we
let go of the concept of masculine identity—as a crucial thing and a goal of development—we are in turn freed from some worries, for example, about boys in
father-absent families and whether they will "turn out all right" (which often is
defined as developing a masculine identity).

Although the conclusion here is that the male sex-role identity paradigm is
not a very good one, there is an alternative approach for the future, the sex-role
strain paradigm.

A New View: Sex-Role Strain

Current feminist research on both the female role and the male role is often based on a new set of assumptions, called collectively the **sex-role strain (SRS) paradigm** (Pleck, 1981). Here are some of the assumptions of the SRS paradigm.

The first assumption is that *gender roles are contradictory and inconsistent.* There are multiple aspects of these inconsistencies in gender roles. For example, today's college men are caught in the tension between the traditional norm that men should be intellectually superior to women and the modern norm that men and women should be intellectual equals. As noted earlier in this chapter, some of these inconsistencies are created because gender roles have changed over time. The more general point is that these contradictions in gender-role norms are sources of stress to men, because men may be uncertain as to which role they are to follow, or because in following one they violate another—for example, by establishing an intellectually egalitarian relationship with a woman, a man fails the male superiority test. Note that the SRS paradigm focuses on gender roles as a source of strain to individuals, compared with the MSRI paradigm, which views gender roles and masculine identity as positive goals to be achieved. Research shows that, indeed, the more men experience conflict in the male role, the greater their psychological distress and the lower their self-esteem (Good et al., 1995; Mahalik et al., 2001; Shepard, 2002).

> **Sex-role strain (SRS) paradigm:** Feminist psychology's approach to the male role, based on the assumption that gender roles for men are contradictory and stressful.

A second assumption of the SRS paradigm is that *a large proportion of individuals violate gender roles.* The idea here is that gender roles often become so idealized, so difficult, and so unrealistic that most people cannot live up to them, at least not on all occasions. Therefore, only a few people are actually perfect examples of their gender role, and the rest bumble along in various degrees of failure to live up to it. That gap between what men think they actually are and what they think is expected of them causes strain.

A third assumption of the SRS paradigm is that *violating gender roles has worse consequences for males than it does for females.* The evidence on this point is actually rather mixed. Pleck reviewed some of the relevant studies, and they show that although male-role violators are sometimes viewed negatively, in other cases they are accepted.

A fourth assumption of the SRS paradigm is that *some characteristics that are prescribed by gender roles are actually maladaptive.* That is, some gender-role characteristics do not help a person function well psychologically. The aggressive component of the male role is a prime instance (Pleck, 1981). For example, men's liberationist Marc Fasteau (1974) analyzed the Pentagon Papers and showed how expansion of the Vietnam War was linked to concerns about power, strength, and dominance in the writings of influential male leaders. And more recently, sociologist Michael Kimmel (2000) has traced how right-wing militias in the United States, such as White supremacists, are bound together by an ideology of self-reliant masculinity. He also argues that the El Qaeda terrorists who flew planes into the World Trade Center on September 11, 2001, all had in common the fact that they were educated, middle-class men who were unemployed in their home nations, such as Egypt, where economies were struggling (Kimmel, 2001). Their masculinity was threatened and El Qaeda terrorism restored it. If socialization of males plays a role in creating violence and wars, it seems reasonable to call it maladaptive. It also leads to a whole series of interesting questions about what things would be like if socialization practices were different. If men were not socialized for aggressiveness, would there still be wars?

In this section we have considered the SRS paradigm. It shifts emphasis away from traditional psychology's concern with masculine identity. Instead, it views gender roles as sources of strain for people: Gender roles are contradictory, many individuals violate them, some aspects of gender roles are maladaptive, and males pay a particularly high price for violation of their role. Because this model is relatively new, there are fewer data to test it critically, as has been done with the MSRI paradigm. Until more evidence accumulates, the SRS paradigm will provide new perspectives on gender roles, and particularly on the male role.

Lifespan Development

In this section we will adopt the developmental perspective, tracing issues for males as they arise from infancy to adulthood.

Infancy   Most of the evidence indicates that *gender similarities* are the rule in infancy (see Chapter 7). Yet there is evidence that boy babies have a higher activity level than girls (Eaton & Enns, 1986). The question is, What does that mean in terms of later behavior? Does it predict the higher rate of hyperactivity in boys in the elementary school years? Does it create the higher level of aggressiveness in boys? And what causes the higher activity level in boys? Unfortunately, we do not yet know the answers to these questions.

One experience of male infants that is worth noting and investigating more is circumcision. Circumcision (surgical removal of the foreskin of the penis, usually done within a few days of birth) is routinely done to 59 percent of male infants born in hospitals in the United States, although the procedure has been questioned (Lindsey, 1988). There are several reasons for circumcision. One is religious—it is part of Jewish religious practice, symbolizing the covenant between God and God's people. There are also health reasons. Removal of the foreskin permits better cleaning of the penis. And there is some evidence that uncircumcised babies are more vulnerable to urinary tract infections and that uncircumcised men have a greater risk of infection with the AIDS virus (Moses et al., 1990; Touchette, 1991; Wiswell et al., 1987).

In 1999, in the midst of heated debate about circumcision, the American Academy of Pediatrics declared that there is no medical need for circumcision. The more interesting question for us, though, is what the psychological effects of this early trauma might be. Research actually indicates there is no effect (Brackbill & Schroder, 1980). That is, there appear to be no differences in behavior between circumcised and uncircumcised boy babies.

Childhood   As a boy moves from infancy to childhood, the peer group becomes increasingly important as an influence. School-age children spend considerably more time with their peers than with their parents. Furthermore, children care a great deal about the approval of their peers, so that the peer group is a powerful shaper of behavior through modeling, positive reinforcers, or punishments (Carter, 1987).

Children tend to be gender segregated in their play—that is, boys play with boys, and girls play with girls (Maccoby, 1998). Compared with girls, boys are more sensitive to the reactions of peers and less sensitive to those of teachers (Fagot, 1985).

Gender-segregated play and the gender typing of toys and activities seem to have mutually facilitating effects. That is, the more a boy plays in the all-male group, the more he plays with trucks, and the more he plays with trucks, the more playing house seems alien; thus he avoids playing with girls and shows an even stronger preference for the company of boys, which means more play with trucks, which means more play with boys, and so the pattern spirals.

Boys have more problems in school—in the sense that they are more frequently put in remedial classes and more frequently referred to psychologists than girls are (see Chapter 7). One possible explanation comes from the well-established finding that the incidence of *hyperactivity* is far higher in boys than in girls. The most common estimate is that among hyperactive children the ratio of males to females is about 4:1, or about 80 percent of hyperactive children are male and only 20 percent are female (Holborow & Berry, 1986). Hyperactive children are characterized by an extremely high activity level in situations—such as the school classroom—where it is clearly inappropriate. Hyperactive children characteristically also have problems of attention; that is, their attention span tends to be short. The greater incidence of hyperactivity in boys may help to explain their school difficulties. The attentional problems are likely to create learning problems and referral to remedial classes. The hyperactivity itself is irritating to teachers and probably leads them to refer the children to psychologists. This line of reasoning raises two further questions. First, how would schools change if there were more male elementary school teachers who themselves had been hyperactive as children—would they be more sympathetic, as well as more skillful as teachers of hyperactive boys? Second, why are there so many more hyperactive boys than girls? No one really has an answer to this second question. One speculation is that hyperactivity is a result of a developmental or maturational lag; that is, children gain more control of their activity level with age, and the hyperactive child may simply be a very slow maturer (Wright et al., 1979). If boys generally are slower to mature than girls are, perhaps boys' greater rate of hyperactivity is a result of their slower maturation.

Adolescence   An increase in the intensity of peer demands for conformity to gender roles occurs in adolescence (see Chapter 7). Here we will concentrate on one aspect of the male role that is highly demanding in adolescence: athleticism (Messner, 1990). As the popular song put it, "You've got to be a football hero to get the love of a beautiful girl." Athletic participation is the single most important factor in high school boys' social status (Kilmartin, 2000).

Consider the athlete role from the perspective of the SRS paradigm. In one study, 24 men in their 20s were interviewed. Half of them had been varsity athletes, and the others had not been involved in athletics (Stein & Hoffman, 1978). The study was aimed at identifying sources of male-role strain, based on the SRS paradigm. The sources of strain, of course, varied between the athletes and the

Success in the athlete role is critical for males—but is this little guy ready for it?

nonathletes. The athletes reported a strain resulting from ambiguity as to whether it was most important to succeed as an individual or as a team. A second source of strain resulted from a changing value attached to athletics at different times in the lifespan. In high school, athletics is a supreme, unquestioned value. In college, it continues to be important for some but is less important for most. At age 30, no one cares a bit about one's high school varsity letter in football, nor about the thousand hours that went into earning it. Another source of strain for the athletes was the obsession with winning, expressed so eloquently by Vince Lombardi: "Winning isn't everything. It's the only thing." The problem is that in a contest between two teams, only one can win, and that means that half the players go home losers. Sports, of course, do not have to be structured competitively. Feminists have emphasized "new games" and noncompetitive sports. But the dominant reality in American athletics has been competition, and that produces losers.

In focusing on the psychological strains created by the athlete role, we should not forget that actual physical damage is also part of this reality (Sabo, 1992). For example, I knew one boy who continued to play as a quarterback on the high school football team despite the fact that he had broken several ribs in a previous game. Each year, approximately 15 high school boys in the United States die playing football (Kilmartin, 2000).

The athlete role also creates strain for the male nonathlete (Stein & Hoffman, 1978). The boy who is a nonathlete is essentially flunking part of the masculinity test. Remember how children choose others one by one when forming teams? The uncoordinated or unskilled boy is chosen last. The message can be devastating: "Not only are you a poor athlete, but your peers don't want you on their team." A friend of mine, who spent his high school years being an intellectual, recounted a story about himself that is a perfect illustration of the way the male nonathlete is treated. He was in a football scrimmage in a gym class. The teacher was giving instructions to members of the team as to what to do in the next play. After all the others had been given specific things to do, the teacher looked at the last poor fellow and said, "When the ball is snapped, you fall down and we'll hope that someone on the other team trips over you." The message to the nonathlete is clear: "You're a failure."

In sum, the competitive, success-oriented emphasis on athletics, particularly in high school, creates problems for both the athlete and nonathlete. We need to emphasize a new, noncompetitive, health-oriented vision of athletics. You may get shin problems from jogging or sore muscles from aerobics, but you won't get a bruised ego.

Adulthood   In this section on the period of adulthood for men, we will first consider two traditional roles for men: that of provider and that of soldier. Next, we will discuss a role of emerging interest, fatherhood. Finally, we will consider whether there is a male midlife crisis that is perhaps analogous to the menopause experience for women.

The provider role: Several centuries ago, before the industrial revolution, men and women shared the **provider role** (for a review of this concept, see Doyle, 1989). Men were responsible for providing food, either by hunting or by farming, and shelter, perhaps by building it themselves. But women, too, were expected to be providers. They provided food, in such activities as growing a garden, milling flour, and cooking. They were responsible for other kinds of providing as well, such as producing clothing by spinning, weaving, and sewing it. In short, men and women shared the provider role. In an agricultural society, they shared time and space as well, for men were not off in factories while women remained at home.

> **Provider role:** The male role in preindustrial societies, which required the man to provide food and shelter for his family.

Then came the industrial revolution. Men went out to work in factories, and women stayed home. Thus their roles became far more divided. The work men did became less intrinsically satisfying—for example, forging a particular part for a particular machine is likely to be less satisfying than growing and harvesting one's own grain to become food on the table. Often the only good thing about the work was the money that was earned. Simultaneously, there was a shift for men from the provider role to the **good provider role.** That is, with the shift to an emphasis on earning money, the man was expected to be a good provider for his family—to earn a lot of money. The more money he earned, the more successful and manly he was.

> **Good provider role:** The male role in industrialized societies, in which the man is expected to earn money and provide well for his family.

It is an understatement to say that the good provider role is a high-pressure one. Once again, the SRS paradigm is applicable: The good provider role for men is a source of strain. There is the pressure of being the sole provider, with a great deal of money needed to support the modern family, particularly if the wife does not earn anything. Furthermore, the good provider role is a highly competitive role; a man is in competition with other men to provide for his family better than the way those other men provide for theirs. Finally, it is a role that is destroyed by unemployment, which may occur through no fault of one's own but rather as a result of economic conditions. It is no wonder that the Great Depression shook the foundations of manhood. Nor is it a wonder that one of the slogans of the men's liberation movement is "We're not just success objects."

Current conditions may ease some of the strains of the good provider role for men. Most notably, the majority of wives now hold paying jobs, and the two-paycheck marriage has become the norm. This reduces the pressure on the man of being the sole provider. But other trends may be working in the opposite direction. In contrast to the social activism of the 1960s and 1970s, the decades of the 1980s and 1990s showed every sign of a return to concern over success on the job and making money. With that, the pressure of the good provider role increases. Best-selling self-help books offered ample testimony to the trend, with titles such as *Winning Through Intimidation* and *Looking Out for Number One.* Rather than offering alternatives to the good provider role, these books show men how to go about it more intensely. Perhaps in the aftermath of September 11, with decreased emphasis on materialism, these pressures will ease.

The military: The military experience has been a standard one for American men. All recruits have in common having experienced the rite of passage known as basic training. Most go through the experience when they are between the ages of 17 and 20, a critical junction between adolescence and adulthood and an important time in identity development.

What is the result of the military experience for the individual male? It makes a man out of him, of course. Slogans such as "The Army will make a man out of you" and "The Marines take only a few good men" provide ample testimony to the cultural notion that the military experience turns boys into men. Appeals to masculinity are used as recruiting and training tools (Doyle, 1989; Goldstein, 2001).

Indeed, shame is used to keep men in the military and to keep them fighting during a war, under terrifying conditions (Goldstein, 2001). To succumb to (very justified) fear during battle is to fail the test of manhood; the men who do so are shamed.

To gain a better view of what actually transpires as men go through the military experience, consider one man's recollections of his training:

> I went into the Army like a lot of people do—a young scared kid of 17 told he should join the Army to get off probation for minor crimes. At the time the Army sounded real fine: three meals, rent-free home, adventure and *you would come out a man.* (It's amazing how many parents put this trip on their kids.)
>
> In basic training I met the dregs of the Army. (Who else would be given such an unimportant job as training "dumb shit kids"?) These instructors were constantly making jokes such as "don't bend over in the shower" and encouraging the supermasculine image of "so horny he'll fuck anything." People talked about fucking sheep and cows and women with about the same respect for them all.
>
> Not many 17-year-olds could conform to such hard core experience. You're told the cooks were gay (pieces of ass for your benefit). The "hard core" sergeants with all these young "feminine" bodies (everyone appears very meek, i.e., feminine, when constantly humiliated, by having his head shaved and being harassed with no legitimate way of fighting back) were always dunghole talking ("your ass is grass and Jim's the lawnmower").
>
> These "leaders" are the *men;* that pretty much makes you the "pussy's"—at the very most "boys." You have to conform to a hard core, tough image or you're a punk. And I began to believe it because of my insecure state of mind, which was so encouraged in training. I was real insecure, so I wanted to be a superman and went Airborne, which, unlike most of the Army, is more intense and worse than basic training. The pressures of assuming manhood are very heavy.

Not only are you hard, you're Airborne hard—sharp, mean, ruthless. You have to be having an impressive sexual life or a quick tongue to talk one up. You've got to be ready to fight a lot because you're tough and don't take shit from anyone. All these fronts were very hard for me to keep up because they contradicted everything I felt. I didn't feel tougher than anyone. I was very insecure about my dick size and ability to satisfy women.

All I had was my male birthright ego. I stayed drunk to be able to struggle through the barroom tests of strength and the bedroom obstacle courses. The pressures became heavier and stronger, requiring more of a facade to cover up the greater insecurity. To prove I was tougher I went looking for fights and people to fuck over. To prove I was "cock strong" I fucked over more women and talked more about it. I began to do all the things I was most insecure about doing, hoping that doing them would make me that "real man."

Having survived the initial shock of such a culture I became very capable in such required role-playing as toughest, meanest, and most virile— the last meaning a cold unreproachable lover (irresistible to women and unapproachable by other men). (Anonymous, "Life in the Military," 1974, pp. 127–128)

The military's operational definition of manhood is clear: The real man is hyperaggressive, has no emotions, and treats women as objects. Some scholars have referred to this process, particularly combat training, as "military socialization" (Arkin & Dobrofsky, 1978), a socialization into the male role (at least as defined by the military) at the beginning of adulthood.

The men who came of age during the Vietnam era—the fathers of today's college students—faced a new set of difficulties (Faludi, 1999). World War II had been a righteous war, but the Vietnam War wasn't. About 32 percent of that generation served in the military, about 8 percent in Vietnam, and about 5 percent in actual combat (Faludi, 1999). Those who didn't go were criticized then and later for being unpatriotic draft dodgers. Those who did serve often regretted it, wondered what they were fighting for, and came home with PTSD. During election campaigning in 1992, soon-to-be President Bill Clinton was criticized for not serving and for opposing the war. His successor, President George W. Bush, was in the military during Vietnam, but no one could figure out where (geographically) he had served. Defining one's masculinity by military service became difficult, to say the least, both during and after Vietnam.

In 1973 there was a shift to an all-volunteer army, but in 1980 the draft was reinstituted. Therefore, at this time men in the United States can be drafted and women can volunteer, and the 1981 Supreme Court decision in *Rotsker* v. *Goldberg* says that this is not discriminatory. With the shift to a more modern army, advertising promotions for recruits have a different pitch. Instead of selling the macho marine image, the emphasis is now on presenting military enlistment as a chance to acquire job skills. It has been argued, though, that the male socialization is still powerfully present. The content is no longer toughness, but rather being successful as a breadwinner, and here the good provider role surfaces once more.

The entry of women into the military is a scene set for conflict. As the above excerpt testifies, basic training is not designed to have women be a part of it. Which side of the conflict will emerge triumphant? Will women change the military, making it more humane and androgynous? Or will the military change women recruits, producing platoons of macho women? Only time and research will tell.

Fatherhood: The father role is one of the major adult roles for men. In considering this role, there are two interesting topics for psychologists to investigate. One is to examine the effects of the father on his children, technically called *paternal influence* (e.g., Marsiglio et al., 2000; Phares & Compas, 1992). The other is to consider the father role and its meaning for the man himself—what the satisfactions of being a father are, what the frustrations are, and so on (Cohen, 1993).

What kinds of effects do fathers have on their children? Or do they have much influence at all, given the limited number of hours of father-child contact? Studies indicate that fathers can be as competent in caring for infants and as responsive to them as mothers are (Parke, 1979). It is also clear that, from the earliest interactions, mothers and fathers give different kinds of attention to their children. Specifically, mothers are more likely to engage in caregiving activities, whereas fathers engage in play, particularly rough, stimulating play (Parke & O'Leary, 1976). In short, mothers exchange dirty diapers for clean ones, and fathers give horseback rides. Research also shows that once children pass their first birthday, fathers begin directing more attention to their sons and less to their daughters (Lamb, 1979). Thus children's interest is drawn to the same-gender parent, and children develop a preference for the same-gender parent. This, of course, may be the heart of the whole gender-typing process.

Much of the evidence on the effects of fathers on their children has been based on studies of *father absence.* The logic is that if we compare children in intact (both parents present) families with those in father-absent (usually through divorce) families, any differences between children in the two situations must be indicative of the effects of fathers on children. A meta-analysis of 67 studies of the effects of father absence found little or no evidence of harmful effects (Stevenson & Black, 1988). There was a decided lack of effect for girls. There were some small effects for boys: Preschool father-absent boys were less stereotyped in their choice of toys and activities, in comparison with father-present boys. But there was a slight tendency for older father-absent boys to be more stereotyped than father-present boys.

Notice that the motivation for this line of research is rooted in the MSRI paradigm discussed earlier in this chapter. It is based on the notion that gender identity is essential for development and that males get their gender identity from their fathers. Thus father absence is expected to be dangerous, particularly to sons. However, as Pleck (1981) concluded, the MSRI paradigm is not a particularly good one and is not supported by research evidence. Specifically, researchers fail to find much of a correlation between fathers and sons in terms of masculinity.

A meta-analysis of studies of "nonresidential" fathering—that is, fathering in situations where the father does not live with the mother and child—showed that closeness and encouragement from fathers were predictive of children's psychological well-being (Amato & Gilbreth, 1999). Simple frequency of contact was less important than the quality of the father-child relationship. And research on intact families shows that fathers who are warm, accepting, and loving toward their children contribute to their children's psychological well-being and to decreased rates of aggressive behavior and conduct problems (Flouri & Buchanan, 2002; Rohner & Veneziano, 2001). Fathers can have a positive impact on their sons, but not by being hypermasculine.

When fathers are present, how much time do they spend with their children? In one widely cited study, Freda Rebelsky and C. Hanks (1971) attached tape-recorder microphones to newborn infants. They found that fathers spent an average of only 38 seconds per day talking with their infants. This low level of paternal involvement seemed scandalous. However, there is reason to think that the results of the study may have been idiosyncratic—for example, only ten fathers were sampled. More recent, better-sampled research indicates that fathers spend more than 38 seconds per day on their children. One way to approach questions of how time is spent is the *time diary method,* in which individuals keep a careful record of all their activities for a 24-hour day, usually on a detailed diary form. The results of one such study are shown in Table 16.1 (Sandberg & Hofferth, 2001). Time spent with children was defined broadly in this study, to include time actually interacting with children as well as time accessible to them. Notice that fathers spend only slightly more time with their children when mothers are employed compared with families in which the mother is not employed. Notice also that employed women spend nearly as many hours with their children as women who are not employed. These figures for fathers are up markedly from 1981, when men with working wives spent only 17 hours per

TABLE 16.1
Children's Time with Parents (Hours per Week) in Two-Parent Families

	Father	Mother
Wife employed	23.0	26.5
Wife not employed	22.4	32.0

SOURCE: Sandberg & Hofferth (2001).

week with their children (compared with 23 hours per week today) (Sandberg & Hofferth, 2001).

In another study, a well-sampled national survey, husbands and wives were asked to estimate their time spent on household tasks per week (Shelton & John, 1993). The results are shown in Table 16.2. Note that the pattern of contributions varies as a function of ethnicity. In both White and Hispanic families, wives spend about twice as many hours per week doing household work as husbands do, whereas there is a little more equality among African Americans. Given stereotypes about macho Hispanic men, it is interesting to note that they actually spend somewhat more time than White men do on household work.

The other side of the father role is the way the father perceives and responds to that role. Is it a source of satisfaction, or of inadequacy and frustration? Research shows that parental status per se makes no difference in men's psychological well-being—that is, fathers and men who have no children report about equal well-being (Barnett et al., 1992). What does make a difference is the quality of the father role. Positive relations with their children are associated with fathers' well-being and negative relations with their children are associated with psychological distress (Barnett et al., 1992). There is a stereotype that men get most of their satisfaction from work, whereas women get most of their satisfaction from their families. However, well-sampled studies find that both men and women rate marriage and the family as more satisfying—and more critical to their psychological well-being—than work (Barnett & Hyde, 2001; Veroff et al., 1981).

Male midlife crisis? The midlife period (I will define this roughly as the decade between the ages of 40 and 50) was summed up by one author as follows:

> The hormone production levels are dropping, the head is balding, the sexual vigor is diminishing, the stress is unending, the children are leaving, the parents dying, the job horizons are narrowing, the friends are having their first heart attacks; the past floats by in a fog of hopes not realized, opportunities not grasped, women not bedded [sic], potentials not fulfilled, and the future is a confrontation with one's own mortality. (Lear, 1973)

TABLE 16.2

Hours per Week Spent on Household Labor by Men and Women as a Function of Ethnic Group

	Whites	Blacks	Hispanics
Men	19.6	25.0	23.2
Women	37.3	38.0	41.8

SOURCE: Shelton and John, "Ethnicity, Race, and Difference" in J. C. Hood (ed.), *Men, Work, and Family*, pp. 131–150. Copyright © 1993. Reprinted by permission of Sage Publications, Inc.

This points to the complex forces, biological, personal, and social, that converge on the middle-aged man.

Let us consider in more detail the nature of the changes that were summarized in the above quotation. Testosterone levels decline gradually in midlife men. This time of life has been called **andropause,** a term that refers to declining levels of androgens (Lamberts et al., 1997). Some experts argue that a low-testosterone syndrome occurs in some older men and that testosterone treatments are beneficial, although this view is controversial (Morley et al., 1997; Schow et al., 1997; Tserotas & Merino, 1998).

> **Andropause:** A time of declining testosterone levels in middle-aged men.

Several extensive research programs have investigated various psychological and social factors that are important to the midlife male (Levinson, 1978; Lowenthal et al., 1975; see also the review by Brim, 1976). These factors are discussed below.

Most human beings have a desire to feel good about themselves based on their achievements. For men, this positive sense of self comes mainly from the job or career. Around age 40 many men recognize that there is an *aspiration-achievement gap,* that is, that their actual achievements have not matched the high aspirations they had in their 20s. The question is, How does a man resolve this aspiration-achievement gap for himself? For many men, perhaps the majority, there is a gradual reconciliation, with a downward shift in aspirations until they are at a realistic level, and the man emerges feeling good about himself. For others, the reconciliation is not easy, resulting in a crisis and depression.

Erik Erikson (1950) considered one of the major tasks of adult development to be a resolution of the issue of *stagnation versus generativity.* Most people seem to have a deep-seated desire to feel a sense of growth, or generativity, in their lives. At age 40, with a receding hairline, one finds it difficult to see oneself as continually growing, and a sense of stagnation may set in. It is possible to resolve this issue in adulthood by finding a sense of growth in other sources, such as the growth of one's children or grandchildren, and that represents a positive resolution of this issue. The question arises as to how men with no children can gain a continual sense of generativity. There are, however, many other ways to maintain that sense, such as taking an interest in fostering the careers of one's younger co-workers.

Confrontation with death is another theme of the midlife period. Signs of aging are apparent on the man's own body, and it is likely that one of his close friends will die of a heart attack or other causes. This experience, too, may lead to negative outcomes such as depression. Or it may lead to a positive outcome in which the man comes to terms with the idea of his own death; reorders the priorities of his life, perhaps in some wonderful ways; and recognizes that happiness is not always to be found in the future, but must be sought in the present.

Relationships within the family also shift. The children grow up and move away from home, leaving the husband and wife alone together. Although it is a popular stereotype that this is a difficult time in marriage, producing many divorces, in fact the data indicate that married couples on average rate the post-parental period as one of the happiest in their lives (Ward & Spitze, 1998). The man's own parents may become increasingly dependent on him, requiring a transformation of that relationship. And the man's wife, freed from childcare responsibilities, may seek more education, a new career, or a more active involvement in a career she already has, requiring a renegotiation of the marital relationship.

Systematic, well-sampled research indicates that men in their 40s, compared with men aged 25 to 39 and 50 to 69, do show significantly higher depression scores and more alcohol and drug use; on the other hand, their levels of anxiety are no higher, nor do they report any less life satisfaction or happiness (Tamir, 1982). Thus it seems that men in their 40s have some problems, but the problems are probably not much worse than those men face at other ages.

This section began with the question of whether there is a male midlife crisis. The answer is that things are a bit too complicated to give a yes-or-no answer. First, it is important to question the notion that there are fixed stages of adult development, meaning that there is a "crisis stage" at age 40 or some other age. Popularized books such as Gail Sheehy's *Passages* have given the public the impression that there are specific crises that predictably happen to people at certain ages. But the actual research does not support that idea at all (Kilmartin, 2000). In part, things are not so predictable because different things happen to different people at different times. For instance, if in the 12 months after his 50th birthday a man fails to get a promotion, finds out his best friend has died of a heart attack, has to move his parents to a nursing home, and has frequent episodes of erection problems, he probably will have a crisis. But another man may not experience these things, or they may happen in a different order, or they may be spread out over a period of five or ten years. The changes for such a person will be much more gradual, never reaching a crisis.

Men of Color

Men of color in the United States share some experiences in common. Among these are high unemployment rates and low wages compared with those of White men (although not necessarily compared with those of White women). Data on this point are shown in Table 16.3. Economic adversity due to low wages or unemployment, as well as experiences of race discrimination, are common for men of color. Beyond that, we must look at specific ethnic groups, each with its own history and set of cultural values that shape men's roles.

African American Men   Both theories and research in the social sciences have traditionally viewed the African American man as being downtrodden, having a poor self-concept, and being psychologically castrated. For several reasons, this view is neither very realistic nor very useful. First, the traditional view is

TABLE 16.3
Unemployment Rates and Earnings as a Function of Ethnicity and Gender

Unemployment rates of adults, 1998

	Women	Men
African Americans	9.0%	8.9%
American Indians	11.9%	14.5%
Hispanics	8.2%	6.4%
Whites	3.9%	3.9%

Median earnings for year-round, full-time workers, 1997

	Women	Men
African Americans	$22,378	$26,844
Hispanics	$19,269	$21,952
Whites	$25,726	$35,741
Asian Americans	$28,214	$35,222

SOURCES: Bureau of Labor Statistics (1999); Costello & Stone (2001); LaFromboise et al. (1990). Data for American Indians are from 1987 (LaFromboise et al., 1990), because the Department of Labor reports only on Whites, Blacks, and Hispanics.

based on historical tracing of the African American male role back to the days of slavery. This historical analysis has ignored the strong contributions of Black men to their families, even within the confines of slavery (Staples, 1978). For example, Alex Haley's *Roots* portrayed many male characters who were responsible and strong and who had a good sense of themselves.

A second problem with the notion of the castrated Black male is that it rests on the concept of Black matriarchy. Black matriarchy is an interpretation of the fact that the percentage of female-headed households is larger among Blacks than it is among Whites (see Chapter 4). But this ignores the fact that the *majority* of Black households are headed by men or by men and women jointly. Once again, the Black man's contributions have not been sufficiently recognized. From a feminist point of view, it is interesting that the relatively egalitarian African American family, when viewed by White male social scientists, has appeared matriarchal (Staples, 1978).

The view of African American men as having a poor self-concept ignores the various ways in which people learn to cope with their situations in life. The results of oppression may seem less severe, depending on the context in which one is making judgments. For example, unemployment is often a terribly depressing

Many African American culture heroes are available for African American boys to identify with. (Left) Political activist Jesse Jackson. (Right) Basketball star Shaquille O'Neal.

experience for White men. The Black man may be better able to cope with unemployment if many of his friends are also unemployed, although that scarcely makes unemployment pleasant. Yet African American men have a reference group within their own culture by which they judge themselves, and against which they may come out quite well (Staples, 1978). As attribution theory points out (see Chapter 8), the attributions people make for their successes and failures are important. The civil rights movement has made African Americans aware of discrimination as a force in their lives. Thus a Black man who fails to get a promotion on the job may make the external attribution that the failure was due to discrimination, rather than the internal attribution that the failure was due to his own lack of ability. The former attribution helps to keep one's self-concept intact.

Development Issues   In a 1968 best-seller, *Black Rage*, psychiatrists William Grier and Price Cobbs said, "Whereas the white man regards his manhood as an ordained right, the black man is engaged in a never-ending struggle for its possession." There has been concern within traditional psychology about the development of adequate male identity in African Americans, particularly among youths, given the high percentage of female-headed Black households (e.g., Pettigrew, 1964). Such a view ignores the time fathers may spend with their sons, even though they are not part of the same household, and the contributions of older brothers, uncles, and grandfathers. Furthermore, there are many African American culture heroes with whom Black youth can identify. Depending on his concerns at the time, the young Black male identifies with different heroes from his culture (Taylor, 1976)—for instance, if his passion is sports, his idol may be Shaquille O'Neal, or if his interest is in politics and civil rights, it may be Martin Luther King, Jr. Thus there are many sources of identification for an African American youth besides his own father.

Earlier in this chapter the MSRI paradigm was discussed. The concern over African American male identity is clearly part of this paradigm. Having concluded that the MSRI paradigm is not a very good one and that concerns over gender identity are overblown, we must accept the implication that there has been too much emphasis on Black male identity. If we shift to the SRS paradigm, we see gender roles as sources of psychological strain for Black men, which is a more productive approach.

Roles: Breadwinner, Husband, Father   There is a high unemployment rate among Black men. For example, as the data in Table 16.3 indicate, in 1998 the unemployment rate was 3.9 percent for White males over age 16; for Black males, it was 8.9 percent, more than double the rate for Whites. The high unemployment rate creates a gender-role problem because the role of breadwinner or good provider is an important part of the male role in the United States (Wilson, 1996). Thus Black men, and particularly Black male teenagers (for whom the unemployment rate is 34 percent), may feel that they are not fulfilling this part of their role. From the perspective of the SRS paradigm, we again see gender roles as a source of strain.

Not being able to fulfill this part of the male role may express itself in a number of ways. It may turn into antisocial behavior, violence, and crime, accounting for the high crime rate among male African American teenagers. It has also been suggested that volunteering for the army becomes an alternative means of fulfilling the male role—whereas 8 percent of young White men intend to enlist, 18 percent of young Black men do (Department of Defense, 2001).

The role of husband is closely tied to the breadwinner role. African American men are understandably reluctant to take on the responsibility of marriage when unemployment is such a justified fear. On the other hand, middle-class African American men place an especially strong emphasis on the provider role and on obtaining the education necessary to fulfill that role (Diemer, 2002).

The father role, too, is closely tied to the breadwinner role, and the responsibility of supporting children is a source of stress to the unemployed African American man. On the other hand, fathering children can be a means of fulfilling the male role for the lower-class Black man who is denied much success in the breadwinner role. Interestingly, middle-class Black men father fewer children than any other group in our society and, in particular, father fewer children than lower-class Black men do (McKay, 1978). Research shows that middle-class Black men are very child-oriented and participate more in childrearing than White men do (Daneal, 1975).

In sum, the SRS paradigm seems to be most useful in understanding the experience of the Black male. We can examine, for instance, how the breadwinner role is a source of strain to a group that has such a high unemployment rate. Data are scarce, but the SRS paradigm suggests many interesting and productive approaches for future research—for example, what impact does the "no sissy stuff" part of the male role have on Black men? Does it contribute to their devaluing of women, or does it help them find satisfaction in their role, or is it not relevant in African American culture?

Asian American Men   Asian American men share some things in common with African American men—the experience of racial discrimination and being "the other" in a White-dominated society. Still, there are some substantial differences. Asian Americans do not have the heritage of slavery. And there is great diversity among Asian American groups, from recent refugees who escaped from Vietnam or Cambodia under dangerous and traumatic conditions, to those Japanese Americans or Chinese Americans who are fifth generation in the United States.

U.S. immigration policies and the manner in which some Asian Americans (e.g., Chinese men brought to build the transcontinental railway in the 1860s) came to the United States created a great imbalance in the gender ratio, resulting in far more Asian American men than Asian American women. For example, at one point the ratio of Filipino men to Filipino women in the state of Washington was 33:1 (Bulosan, 1960). In the context of laws and norms prohibiting interracial marriage, this meant a permanently enforced bachelorhood for a great many Asian American men. The problem is confounded by the fact that in many Asian societies, one is a full-fledged adult only when one is married and becomes a parent. Therefore, in the context of their own cultural values, many Asian American men were condemned to a life of perpetual boyhood (Kim, 1990).

Just as the sexuality of African Americans has been stereotyped, so, too, has the sexuality of Asian Americans. The Asian American man has been stereotyped as asexual (lacking in sexuality), whereas the Asian American woman has been stereotyped as exotic and entirely sexual (Kim, 1990).

Asian American men, of course, share many of the same difficulties faced by Asian American women (see Chapter 4), including bilingualism and conflicts between Asian cultural values and the dominant cultural values of America.

Hispanic Men   Hispanic culture is typically viewed as highly patriarchal, with men expected to live up to the ideal of machismo. However, Mexican Americans in the United States are different from Mexicans in Mexico, and it seems that Mexican American family structure is less patriarchal, although the strong emphasis on the importance of *la familia,* the family, remains (Vasquez & Baron, 1988). Recent psychological research refutes the notion of extreme male dominance in Hispanic families (Vasquez-Nuttall et al., 1987). For example, studies of marital decision making by Hispanic couples gives little support to the notion of male dominance (Cromwell & Ruiz, 1979).

In regard to the provider role, less-acculturated Mexican immigrants show the strongest beliefs that the provider role is the man's responsibility (Taylor et al., 1999). Highly acculturated Mexican immigrants show less strong beliefs, and highly acculturated, U.S.-born Mexican Americans show the least support for the belief that the provider role is men's responsibility—but even this last group holds to the traditional view more strongly than White Americans do.

American Indian Men   At least some Indian tribes, including the Cherokee, Navajo, Iroquois, Hopi, and Zuni, traditionally had relatively egalitarian gender roles (LaFromboise et al., 1990). Women had important economic, political, and spiritual roles, and there was even a matrilineal pattern of inheritance. Men tended to have more authority in the public sphere, but women's power in the private sphere of the family was great.

The overwhelming consequence of acculturation resulting from contact with the dominant White culture in the United States has been an increase in male dominance among Indians (LaFromboise et al., 1990). It remains to be seen whether this is beneficial to Indian men. The realities of high unemployment rates probably have a greater impact.

Health Issues

A baby boy born in the United States today can expect to live 74.5 years if he is White and 67.6 years if he is Black; a baby girl can expect to live 80 years if she is White and 75 years if she is Black (National Center for Health Statistics, 2001). In short, men live about 6 fewer years than women do. The argument rages as to whether the difference in life expectancy is due to biological factors or environmental factors. That is, are men more biologically vulnerable, more susceptible to disease, genetic defects, and so on; or are men the victims of their environment, specifically of the male role—the "lethal aspects of the male role," as one psychologist put it? In this section we will examine the evidence on both sides of the issue (for more extended discussions, see Cowdenay, 2000; Theorell & Härenstam, 2000; Turner, 1982).

On the biological side of the argument, it has been found that males have a higher death rate than females, even prenatally. At conception, the ratio of males to females is probably about 120:100.[2] At birth the male:female ratio is down to

---

[2]You may be wondering why males and females are not conceived in equal numbers. The answer seems to be that sperm that bear the Y chromosome (Y-bearing sperm), and therefore produce a male at conception, are lighter than X-bearing sperm. This in turn is because the Y chromosome is smaller than the X chromosome. This allows the Y-bearing sperm to swim faster and makes them more likely to reach the egg.

about 105:100 (Harrison, 1978). That is, even before birth, males have a higher death rate (Kilmartin, 2000). One can scarcely attribute this to socialization into the male role. The higher prenatal mortality rate for males is probably due to sex-linked recessive genetic defects or diseases, such as hemophilia. It has also been found that females have more resistance to infectious diseases than males do, because there are genes on the X chromosome that increase one's immune resistance (Goble & Konopka, 1973).

X-linked diseases probably cause a relatively small proportion of the excess male deaths, though. Of the biological factors, sex hormones are far more important (Kilmartin, 2000). Specifically, heart disease is a leading cause of death for both men and women, but heart disease tends to strike men at much younger ages than women. This contributes to men's shorter life expectancy. Estrogen appears to be a protective factor against heart disease, and so women are more protected. Estrogen seems to have this protective effect because of its action against LDL, the "bad cholesterol" that increases the risk of heart disease.

On the environmental side of the argument, a thorough analysis of the causes of deaths in males and females indicates that about one-third of the male-female difference is due to smoking (Waldron, 1976; Waldron & Johnston, 1976). Of the leading causes of death in which males outnumber females, two are lung cancer and heart attacks, and cigarette smoking is implicated in both (Sue, 2000). Another leading cause of death in which males outnumber females is cirrhosis of the liver, and that is related to excessive drinking, a behavior pattern that is considered more appropriate for males than females. Accidents—specifically, car and truck accidents and shooting accidents during hunting—are another cause of death in which males outnumber females; these kinds of deaths, too, can clearly be linked to patterns of socializing males for such traits as aggressiveness and risk taking. Thus some specific behaviors associated with the male role—smoking, drinking, aggression, and risk taking—are linked to higher death rates in males. It doesn't stretch the data to call these "lethal aspects of the male role." Research shows that, in fact, more masculine men—as measured by psychological tests of masculinity-femininity—die younger than less masculine men (Lippa et al., 2000).

There has been a great deal of publicity about the Type A, or coronary-prone, behavior pattern (Friedman & Rosenman, 1974; Matthews, 1982). Type A behaviors include extremes of aggressiveness and hostility, competitiveness, difficulty in relaxing, impatience, and a chronic sense of urgency about time, or "hurry sickness." Type A behaviors have been linked significantly to coronary heart disease (Matthews, 1982), and, as mentioned earlier, that is a leading cause of the greater number of male deaths. It is hard to avoid noticing that the list of Type A traits reads like a litany of the male role. Insofar as males are socialized into such traits, it seems likely that they will become Type A individuals and will have a greater risk of developing heart disease. In fact, research indicates that extreme masculinity is related to severity of heart attacks and to Type A behaviors (Helgeson, 1990). From a feminist point of view, most of the research on Type A has been conducted with men only, and it is important that the research be extended to women.

An important related question is, What will happen to women as they become increasingly liberated and able to do things formerly reserved for males? If the liberation of women means liberating them to smoke, drink, and be aggressive, competitive, and hurried, will the ultimate reward be an earlier death? The available data indicate that this is not likely. For example, from 1940 to 1977 women's participation in paid jobs and careers increased substantially, yet deaths from coronary heart disease among women fell rapidly during this period (Siegel, 1978)—indeed, the rates for women declined faster than the rates for men did, both declines being due to greatly improved medical techniques. There is also evidence that Type A women who have been in the work force for more than half of their lives are no more likely to have heart disease than Type A homemakers (Haynes et al., 1978). Thus it may be that women can take on some aspects of the male role without too much risk. Nonetheless, I would not want to be part of the group of women who tests whether the female body can survive three packs of cigarettes and four martinis a day.

In conclusion, it seems that neither biological factors nor environmental factors alone can explain the higher mortality rates of males. Male deaths from heart disease and cirrhosis of the liver seem linked to environmental factors, specifically, the male role and smoking and drinking behaviors. But these can scarcely explain the higher rate of male deaths prenatally. Thus the higher male mortality rate is most likely due to a combination of biological factors (sex hormones) and environmental factors (the male role, which encourages smoking, drinking, and risk taking, Byrnes et al., 1999).

Male Sexuality

The research of Masters and Johnson (1966) indicates that men go through the same biological stages in sexual arousal as women do: excitement, plateau, orgasm, and resolution (see Chapter 12). A major process during both male and female arousal is vasocongestion, or increased blood flow into the genitals. In men, the vasocongestion produces erection of the penis. In males past puberty, orgasm is accompanied by ejaculation, the penis emitting a milky fluid containing sperm. One difference between males and females is that males have a refractory period following orgasm. A refractory period is a period of time during which one cannot be restimulated to orgasm. Women have no such refractory period, and thus can have multiple orgasms, whereas men are generally limited to single ones. The length of the refractory period in men varies, depending on a number of factors, including age. In young men, the refractory period may be as short as a few minutes, whereas in men over the age of 65, it might be 24 hours.

What is more intriguing than the biology is the psychology of male sexuality. An important first point is that, according to traditional definitions, sexuality—

FOCUS 16.1

MYTHS OF MALE SEXUALITY

Psychologist and sex therapist Bernie Zilbergeld has provided a superb analysis of male sexuality—and how to cope with it—in his book *The New Male Sexuality* (1999). His central thesis is that men in our culture are taught a "fantasy model of sex," an unrealistic, idealistic set of expectations that put intense performance pressures on them. He captures the message of the fantasy model of sex in the title of one of his chapters: "It's Two Feet Long, Hard as Steel, Always Ready, and Will Knock Your Socks Off," referring to the fantasy model of the enormous, ever-erect, aroused penis. He details the various aspects of the fantasy model in a list of cultural myths about male sexuality, discussed below.

Myth 1: A real man isn't into sissy stuff like feelings and communicating. A central part of the male role is being unemotional. That means that feelings of love, tenderness, and perhaps even vulnerability are inappropriate and unmasculine. Unfortunately, those are precisely the emotions that are essential in developing intimate relationships. They are the emotions that enrich the sexual experience. Is it any wonder that males—particularly adolescent males for whom masculine identity is a key concern—focus mainly on the physical aspects of sexuality and neglect the emotional aspects? It is as though the culture had handicapped them from birth, crippling their tenderness, intimacy, and sensuality. Zilbergeld urges women to understand this problem as a handicap and, rather than resenting men's lack of emotional expressiveness, to help them overcome their handicap and discover their tender, intimate selves.

Zilbergeld argues that it is this myth which leads men to mislabel their feelings and to think that what they are feeling is a sexual need for intercourse, when in fact what they are experiencing is love, or tenderness, or just a need for a good cuddle. Growing up thinking that they experience only lust, men mislabel their feelings. They think they want intercourse when what they are really experiencing is a need for a hug or for someone to say, "I love you."

Myth 2: A real man performs in sex. A man must perform because sex is seen as an achievement situation. Our culture is highly achievement-oriented, and we tend to turn sex into just one more achievement situation. We express this in language such as *achieving* orgasm, and in setting up achieve-

(continued)

ment goals in sex, such as simultaneous orgasms for the man and woman. In addition, achievement is a key feature of the male role.

Myth 3: A man should be able to make the earth move for his partner, or at the very least knock her socks off. Put this myth together with the preceding one, and you have a situation in which sex becomes, for the man, an achievement situation in which he is expected to play the woman's body as skillfully as Itzhak Perlman plays the violin. However, the work of Masters and Johnson (1970) and others indicates that achievement-orientation and performance-orientation contribute importantly to sexual dysfunctions such as erection problems. When one sets up an achievement goal, one is also setting up the possibility of failure. Fear of failure creates anxiety, and anxiety quickly ruins the pleasure of sexual expression and produces sexual dysfunction.

The extent of performance pressures on men is strikingly illustrated in this account by two sex therapists:

> We'll never forget the man who called himself a premature ejaculator even though fairly regularly he lasted for forty-five minutes of vigorous thrusting. We know he lasted this long because his partner confirmed it. Actually, she had never been orgasmic in intercourse and had no desire to become so. She much preferred shorter intercourse because she sometimes became so sore through almost an hour of thrusting that she could barely sit down the next day. That had little influence on the thinking of our client, who was convinced that she would have orgasms if only he could last an hour. (Zilbergeld, 1978, p. 257)

Myth 4: A man is always interested in and always ready for sex. Men are portrayed as always interested in sex and easily arousable. But that is not always true. Men need to learn to acknowledge that sometimes, in certain situations, or when they are tired, or with a certain partner, they are just not in the mood. Men need to learn to say no—something women received more than adequate training for, but men learned was not part of their script.

Myth 5: Sex is centered on a hard penis. In our culture we have learned a script for sexual interactions. The script specifies what should occur and in what order. Touching, kissing, and hugging progress to heavy petting, which progresses to intercourse, at least if everything goes well. As a result, we do not know how to relax and enjoy sex that consists only of kissing and touching. I once gave a talk on sex to a group of adolescent girls whom a social worker considered predelinquents. I was supposed to convey some information or inspiration that would keep them from getting pregnant. I suggested oral-genital sex as a way of having enjoyable sex with no risk of pregnancy. One girl raised her hand and said, with the penetrating honesty of the adolescent, "But that isn't *real* sex." She expressed perfectly the sentiment in our culture. Anything other than intercourse is not "real" sex, or is merely a ritualistic prelude to the real thing. The problem with all of this, from the male point of view, is that an erection is absolutely essential if intercourse is to take place. Erections are nice if they happen on their own; when they are an entrance requirement, things are not such fun. Once again, the stage is set for anxiety, fear of failure, and failure. Part of the remedy is to learn that there are many enjoyable aspects of sex that require no erection—in fact, the only thing that requires an erection is intercourse.

   Myth 6: Good sex is spontaneous with no planning and no talking. Of course, spontaneous sex can be nice, but not all good sex has to be that way. The problem with the emphasis on spontaneity is that it discourages some important things from happening. For example, some people fail to plan for and talk about birth control because they say it interferes with the spontaneity of sex. That logic has a high chance of producing an unwanted pregnancy. In the AIDS era, it is crucial to talk about safer sex. The spontaneity/naturalness myth is also responsible for many men neglecting to educate themselves about sex. It is better to recognize that good sex sometimes does take planning, learning, and talking, which is in contradiction to beliefs that sex is just natural and that men are born sex experts.

   Zilbergeld recommends that men try to shed the sexual scripts that they have learned and to spend some time discovering what is truly pleasing to them sexually, expressing those ideas, and then trying to have sex that way, rather than the way society dictates.

specifically, heterosexuality—is a central aspect of male identity (Herek, 1990). Men are supposed to be very interested in sex and good at it. The increasing recognition of women's interest in sex does not diminish its centrality for men—in fact, it may heighten it. One sex therapist's analysis of the psychology of male sexuality is provided in Focus 16.1.

Sex research has turned up many unexpected findings about male sexuality. For example, men sometimes fake orgasm. They want more emotional involvement in sex. And they feel under great performance pressure (e.g., Shanor, 1978). What is happening is that we are beginning to appreciate the complexity of male sexuality, in part by adopting the feminist perspective of examining the influence of gender roles on male sexuality, and then considering ways in which men can be liberated from some of the restrictions and demands of those roles.

In Conclusion

An important point in this chapter was the distinction between the male sex-role identity paradigm and the sex-role strain paradigm. The MSRI paradigm was part of traditional psychology and was based on the assumption that a man must have a masculine identity in order to be psychologically healthy. But as we saw, the MSRI paradigm is just not borne out by the evidence—boys' masculinity is not correlated with their fathers' masculinity, father absence does not necessarily produce inadequate masculinity, and so on. The alternative model is the SRS paradigm, which

EXPERIENCE THE RESEARCH

CHILDHOOD EXPERIENCES OF THE MOTHER AND MEN'S DESIRE TO CONTROL WOMEN

One assumption of the male sex-role identity (MSRI) paradigm is that men's negative attitudes toward women are a result of problems of gender-role identity caused by mothers. One hypothesis is that little boys experience the mother as overwhelming and therefore try to control and dominate women in adulthood. If this is the case, there should be a correlation between men's ratings of their childhood experiences of their mother and their attitudes, as adults, toward women. Men who experienced their mothers as overwhelming should want to control women, and men who did not experience their mothers as overwhelming should be less interested in controlling women. You will collect data to see whether this is true.

Use the following items to assess men's experience of their mothers in child-hood:

1. When I was a child, my mother seemed overwhelming to me.
2. When I was a child, my mother tried to control me all the time.

Use the following items to assess men's attitudes toward women:

1. The husband should have the final say in family decisions.
2. In the traditional marriage vows, the wife promises to obey the husband, and there is great wisdom in that.

Participants should rate each item on a scale from (1) *strongly disagree* to (5) *strongly agree*, with (3) meaning *neither agree nor disagree*. To make the purpose of these items less obvious, construct at least ten items assessing attitudes on some other topics and intersperse the four critical items among them.

Administer your 14-item scale to five men who are *not* in your class (men who take a psychology of women course are not a random sample of the male popula-tion). If possible, include in your sample several men who are older than traditional college age.

Take the average of the two items on experience of the mother as the man's score on Experience of Mother. Take the average of the two control of women items as the man's score on Control Women. For your five respondents, does there appear to be a correlation between Experience of Mother scores and Control Women scores? That is, do men who have high scores on one tend to have high scores on the other? If you have taken a statistics course, compute the actual correlation be-tween the two scales. You may also put your data together with those of other stu-dents in your class to obtain a larger sample and then compute the correlation.

Do the results support or go against the hypothesis?

views gender roles as sources of strain in our culture. It is useful in understanding some of the topics covered later in the chapter. For instance, it is useful in under-standing the problems created by the emphasis on athletic prowess for males, an emphasis that produces strains for both the athlete and the nonathlete; and it is use-ful in understanding the problem of unemployment for the Black male in a culture that stresses the breadwinner or good provider role as a definition of manhood.

Suggestions for Further Reading

Kilmartin, Christopher T. (2000). *The masculine self* (2nd ed.). New York: McGraw-Hill. A good psychology of men textbook.

Kimmel, Michael S., & Messner, Michael A. (2001). *Men's lives.* (5th ed.) Boston: Allyn and Bacon. An excellent collection of readings about men on topics including work, health, sexuality, and families.

Rotundo, E. Anthony. (1993). *American manhood: Transformations in masculinity from the Revolution to the modern era.* New York: Basic Books. This is an excellent tracing of historical changes in the male role in the United States.

Zilbergeld, Bernie. (1999). *The new male sexuality.* (Rev. ed.). New York: Bantam Books. Zilbergeld's writing is delightful and insightful. This is must reading on the topic of male sexuality.

Men and the Web

American Men's Studies Association. The website of this professional organization of scholars who study masculinity from a gender roles perspective. It provides links to bibliographies and a journal of men's studies.

http://www.mensstudies.org

Society for the Psychological Study of Men and Masculinity. This is the website of the American Psychological Association's Division 51, which is devoted to the psychological study of men and masculinity.

http://www.apa.org/divisions/div51

Retrospect and Prospect 17

Future Research

Re-Visioning Theory

Feminism Revisited

Future Roles for Women

Standing on the ground of common sense and the constitution of the human mind, I deny that anyone knows, or can know, the nature of the two sexes, so long as they have only been seen in their present relation to one another. . . . What is now called the nature of woman is an eminently artificial thing—the result of forced repression in some directions, unnatural stimulation in others.

— JOHN STUART MILL, THE SUBJECTION OF WOMEN (1869)

The great philosopher and feminist John Stuart Mill, quoted here, lived in an era in which there was no science of psychology. He believed that no one could understand the true nature of women and men. More than 100 years—and a great deal of psychological research—later, how can one respond to Mill?

Certainly scientists would not claim to know the "true nature" of woman any more than Mill did. But I would argue that that is not the right question. Rather than trying to establish the "true nature" of woman, we would do better to try to understand how women function psychologically now in our culture, how they function in some other cultures and other times, and what their potential for the future is.

This book has focused particularly on trying to understand how women function psychologically in our contemporary culture. To do this, I have reviewed the existing scientific theories and research. They provide some reasonable ideas that further research will continue to refine.

Several important themes have cropped up repeatedly in this book. One is gender similarities, the notion that women and men are more similar to each other than they are different. Another theme has been ambivalence, as seen in the conflict between motherhood and career, and in ambivalence about sexuality. Finally, it is important to consider both gender and ethnicity as definers of people's identity and roles.

Future Research

In 1974, in writing the first edition of this book, I commented that research on the psychology of women was in its infancy. However, coming away from the most recent (2002) convention of the American Psychological Association, I felt that enormous progress has been made and that research and theory are becoming truly sophisticated. We understand the ways in which gender bias can enter psychological research, and we have some ways to correct it. There are some fairly well-documented differences in the emotional expression of females and males, and research is proceeding to determine exactly what these differences mean.

Three generations of women. Far more research on women of color is needed in psychology.

Feminist therapy is more than a twinkle in some feminist's eye and is now widely practiced. And so the list goes.

Of course, this does not mean that we know everything there is to know about women. Far from it. There is much information that we do not yet have. You may want to spend some time thinking about what the most important questions for future research are. I will suggest a few that I think are important.

Perhaps the most important need is to study women of color. The psychology of women has been too much the psychology of White middle-class women. We need to know far more about African American, Asian American, Latina, and American Indian women, of all social classes. We need to know about those who have become enormously successful despite the odds, and about those who are homeless. We need to know far more about how different ethnic groups in the United States define gender roles and regulate women's sexuality. In doing this, we will always have to keep a balanced perspective between ethnic similarities and ethnic differences.

We need more research on adjustment problems in women, particularly on depression, anxiety, alcoholism, and eating disorders, because they are all so frequent. We need to know what causes depression and what can be done to prevent it (e.g., changing childrearing practices, school policy, violence against women, or family roles). Along with this, we need more work on psychotherapy for women's problems and research on the effectiveness of these therapies. Related research should be directed toward the psychological aspects of women's health issues such as wanted and unwanted pregnancy, HIV/AIDS, and breast cancer.

We need to know more scientifically about feminism. What leads women to become feminists? What happens to women psychologically when they become feminists? How do other people react to women who are feminists? What impact does feminism have on men?

In one relevant study, Adena Bargad and I evaluated the impact of women's studies courses on the students who take them (Bargad & Hyde, 1991; Hyde, 2002). We looked particularly at the development of feminist identity in women taking the courses compared with a group of women not taking women's studies. According to one theory, feminist identity develops in five stages:

Stage 1: Passive Acceptance In this stage, women passively accept traditional gender roles and discrimination and do not question either.

Stage 2: Revelation In this stage, catalyzed perhaps by a crisis or by taking a women's studies course, the woman questions gender roles and sexism. She often experiences great anger and holds a negative view of men.

Stage 3: Embeddedness The woman develops a sense of connectedness with other women and receives affirmation and strength from them.

Stage 4: Synthesis The woman develops a positive feminist identity and tran scends gender roles. She no longer blames men as a group, but evaluates men on an individual basis.

Stage 5: Active Commitment Feminist identity is consolidated and the woman becomes committed to working actively to promote a nonsexist world.

We developed a scale, the Feminist Identity Development Scale (FIDS), to measure women's scores on each of the stages and administered the scale at the beginning and end of the semester. Our research indicated that women taking women's studies courses, compared with the control group, showed significant declines in their degree of passive acceptance. That is, those in women's studies decreased significantly in Passive Acceptance from the beginning to the end of the semester. At the same time, they increased significantly in their scores on Revelation, Embeddedness, and Active Commitment. Women's studies courses do seem to have an impact on women who take them.

In another study, the researcher found that in a women's studies course, the attitudes of both men and women changed, although the women's attitudes changed more than the men's did (Steiger, 1981). The author concluded that it was the consciousness-raising component of the course that changed people's attitudes. Furthermore, he speculated that the consciousness-raising component of the women's movement is having a significant impact on people.

We need to know what impact recent advances in sex-related technology will have on women's lives. Some have argued that the greatest single stimulus to the current liberation of women was the development of the birth control pill. If a single technological advance of that sort can have such far-reaching consequences, what will be the impact of other technologies? What will be the effect of test-tube babies, surrogate mothering, sex-choice technologies? Regarding the last issue, it may be possible within the next decade to choose the gender of one's offspring. In a sense, that is possible now; a woman could have amniocentesis or ultrasound, find out the gender of her child, and have an abortion if it were the "wrong" one. Personally, I would hate to see women abort fetuses on the basis of gender, and I think very few women would do so. But more sophisticated methods of gender choice will be available soon. One study investigated the impact of gender-choice technology by surveying 710 undergraduates (Fidell et al., 1979). As previous surveys had shown, people have an overwhelming preference for a boy as the first child; 85 percent express that preference. Having the second child be a girl was preferred by 73 percent. Given the preference people express as to the size of families, more boys (55 percent) would be born than girls. And given previous findings on differences between first-borns and second-borns, psychological gender differences would probably be magnified. Much more research of this sort is needed.

Re-Visioning Theory

Just as we must press forward with new research, so we must continue to revise androcentric theories in psychology. Carol Gilligan's (1982) revision of moral-development theory is often trotted out as a good example, but that work is now more than 20 years old, and many, many more theories need to be revised. The process of theory revision must continue.

The best example of current feminist revision of theory is UCLA psychologist Shelley Taylor's major challenge to classical theories of stress and her proposed alternative (Taylor et al., 2000). Classical stress theory, originally proposed by Walter Cannon in 1932 and taught as fact in many psychology courses today, argues that the standard human (and animal) response to stress is the *fight-or-flight response*. The body reacts physiologically in ways that help the person stay and fight the attacker or flee with lightning speed. Specifically, the sympathetic nervous system is activated, and the adrenal gland is stimulated, which initiates a cascade of hormones to be produced, including especially norepinephrine and epinephrine. Notice that this theory proposes a *biobehavioral response* to stress: The behavioral response is fight-or-flight, and the activation of the sympathetic nervous system is the biological response, which facilitates the behavioral response.

Taylor noted that most of the research exploring classical stress theory has been conducted on male rats. In human research prior to 1995, women were only 17 percent of the participants in laboratory studies of physiological responses to stress. And, while fighting or fleeing might be very adaptive for males of various species, it may not be for females, who often must protect not only themselves but their young as well. Fight-or-flight leaves babies unprotected.

Taylor's alternative theory of stress for females substitutes *tend-and-befriend* for fight-or-flight. She argues that females' behavioral response to stress is to (1) tend their young and (2) affiliate with (befriend) a social group that, collectively, provides protection from threats. Females' biological responses support these behaviors and involve secretion of oxytocin. Her theory is also biobehavioral, but it specifies different behaviors and a modified understanding of the biological response.

In the classical theory, stress, perceived consciously by the cortex, activates certain centers in the hypothalamus, which secretes corticotropin-releasing hormone (CRH), which in turn stimulates the adrenal gland to secrete epinephrine and norepinephrine. Taylor noted that the "fight" effects of epinephrine are magnified by testosterone, which occurs at higher levels in males and is stimulated by stress.

Females have the same sympathetic nervous system response, paired with increased epinephrine and norepinephrine. However, in females, the hypothalamus secretes oxytocin in response to stress. Oxytocin has two important effects: (1) It interacts with estrogen to reduce epinephrine levels, which leads to a reduction in fear and increased feelings of calm, thereby heading off tendencies to fight or flee. And (2) it stimulates maternal behavior (tending) and affiliative behavior (befriending), as demonstrated in numerous studies.

Stress theory is fundamental in psychology. Taylor has innovatively recognized that women may respond differently to stress than men do and that this different response is adaptive. Moreover, she has constructed a plausible account of the biological basis of women's behavioral response. Her alternative approach is a beautiful example of feminist revision of psychological theory.

Feminism Revisited

In Chapter 1 a short definition of feminism was given: "A feminist is a person who favors political, economic, and social equality of women and men, and therefore favors the legal and social changes that will be necessary to achieve that equality." Your understanding of feminism is now much more complex than that. I hope that your view of feminism has been transformed in reading this book. Feminists are not a bunch of ugly women burning their bras; nor are they a group of screaming picketers protesting discrimination. Feminism, or the femi-

" I'LL PLAY 'DOCTOR' ONLY IF I'M THE DOCTOR. "

Has society changed so that girls understand the complexities of power, gender roles, and occupations?

nist perspective, or the feminist paradigm, whichever term you prefer, offers a substantially different view of the world, and specifically of psychology, than traditional science has offered (see Focus 17.1, "Paradigms, Science, and Feminism"). The feminist paradigm says that the focus of psychology should be on women as much as on men. Issues of concern to women—rape, battering, menstruation—should be given research attention. Scientists must be careful in interpreting outcomes: for example, when they investigate rape, they must not automatically blame it on the victim, the woman. People need to be aware of the power of gender roles in their lives. And so on: We could continue the list for pages. The point is that feminism provides a new view in psychology, a new set of questions, a fresh set of hypotheses. I find that exciting, and I hope you do, also.

FOCUS 17.1

PARADIGMS, SCIENCE, AND FEMINISM

Thomas Kuhn's *The Structure of Scientific Revolutions* (1970) has become a modern classic in the philosophy of science. A consideration of Kuhn's analysis will help us to understand science, and specifically how feminism fits into science.

The general public tends to view science as advancing continually in small steps by accumulating facts. One of Kuhn's fundamental points is that if we look at the history of science, that is not at all the way it works. His analysis indicates that science instead proceeds in occasional revolutionary leaps that disrupt calm periods of data collection. Essential to his conceptualization is the term *paradigm*. As he defines it, a paradigm refers to the set of beliefs, underlying assumptions, values, and techniques shared by a particular community of scientists. In a sense a paradigm is a "worldview," or at least a view of the piece of the world that is the focus of the particular scientific specialty. A new paradigm is usually drastically different from the paradigm that preceded it in its field, but it gains followers because it solves some problems that the old paradigm could not handle; a radical revolution occurs as the science shifts from the old paradigm to the new. A paradigm is also sufficiently open-ended that it creates within it a whole new set of questions that scientists can busy themselves with answering.

A specific example that may clarify these concepts is Copernicus and the Copernican revolution in astronomy. In Europe at the beginning of the fifteenth century, everyone, scientists included, believed that the earth was the center of the universe and that the sun revolved around the earth, a view known as the geocentric (earth-centered) or Ptolemaic view. Copernicus (1473–1543) proposed a new view, or paradigm—namely, that the sun was the center (heliocentric view) around which the earth rotated yearly, while the earth spun on its own axis daily. The Copernican view solved some problems that existed with the old, geocentric view. One of these was that in order for geocentrism to be correct, the other planets must be traveling at irregular speeds around the earth, darting ahead and then slowing down. Using the Copernican view, the planets could be seen as moving at constant speed, while the earth (with the astronomer on it) moved simultaneously. Copernicus's ideas were opposed by the Catholic Church as erroneous and possibly heretical, which is often the case with new scientific paradigms. But eventually his ideas were widely accepted by astronomers, who then used them as the basis for their research. Kuhn's point is clear: Science proceeds in occasional revolutionary leaps as new paradigms, representing radically different ideas, arise.

The general public, as well as many scientists, tends to view science as fundamentally objective. Kuhn also disputes this notion. He believes that there is no such thing as a pure fact in science; rather, there are only facts that exist within the context of a particular paradigm. Once a new paradigm has taken over, the old "facts" will seem wrong or downright stupid. For example, if we had lived before the time of Copernicus, we would naturally have observed the "fact" that the sun rises in the East every morning and sets in the West every evening. We would further have taken this as ample evidence of the "fact" that the sun is revolving around the earth. From our modern, post-Copernican perspective, these do not seem to be facts at all. This illustrates Kuhn's argument that there are no objective facts in science; facts exist only from the point of view of a particular paradigm.

How does all this relate to psychology? Psychology has had several paradigms, the actual number depending on how broad or narrow one wants to be in identifying paradigms. Certainly *learning theory* has been a dominant paradigm in psychology. And Ralph Rosnow (1981) has traced the history of *experimentalism* as a dominant paradigm in social psychology. The belief in social psychology has been that the tightly controlled laboratory experiment is the best, perhaps the only, way to get good "facts" on people's social behavior. Rosnow also documents a crisis that experimentalism faces. Experimenter effects and observer effects (discussed in Chapter 1) mean that scientists may get poor data from their experiments, or only data that conform to their own biases.

Feminists point out that the paradigms of psychology have been *androcentric,* that is, focusing on males and coming from a male perspective.

In the context of Kuhn's arguments, feminism can be seen as a new paradigm in the science of psychology. Feminism fits the definition of a paradigm in that it comprises a set of beliefs, values, and techniques that are shared by a community of scientists, namely, feminist psychologists. Feminism provides a new worldview. Traditional psychology could be viewed as seeing the world revolving around men (androcentrism), just as the pre-Copernicans saw the

(continued)

sun revolving around the earth. Feminists do not want to shift to viewing the world as revolving around women. Rather, the feminist desire is to view the world revolving around men and women jointly.

Another characteristic of a paradigm, according to Kuhn, is that it provides answers to a set of problems that could not be solved by the old paradigm and were creating a crisis. A number of such problems have not been solved by traditional psychology. One of these is the nature of masculinity and femininity (Pleck, 1981). Traditional psychology has viewed masculinity-femininity as an essential personality dimension (see Chapter 3). Furthermore, gender typing was supposed to be essential to mental health. That is, the highly masculine male and the highly feminine female were supposed to be the most well adjusted, according to that paradigm. Actual research, however, shows that this is not true. For example, highly masculine males are prone to risky behaviors and die younger than their less masculine peers (Lippa et al., 2000). Traditional psychology's paradigm cannot handle that result. Feminism provides a framework that answers that difficulty. It suggests the possibility that people can be androgynous and that the androgynous person would be most healthy psychologically.

Paradigms, according to Kuhn, also create a whole new set of research questions because they present a different way of looking at the world. And so the feminist paradigm has created a new set of research topics that had not come to light in traditional psychology: rape, wife-battering, sexual harassment of women at work, how different ethnic groups define gender roles, and sexism in psychotherapy, to name a few.

Feminist psychology, then, fits Kuhn's definition of a paradigm nicely. One final comment is in order, however. It is sometimes argued that feminism has no place in scientific psychology because feminism consists merely of a set of political biases and these biases do not permit objective research. Concerning this point, it is well to remember Kuhn's argument that science is not truly objective and that facts are facts only in the context of a particular paradigm. Thus feminist psychology is neither more nor less objective than other paradigms in psychology. What it does is provide a set of "facts" that make sense in the feminist context.

SOURCES: Kuhn (1970), Pleck (1981), Rosnow (1981).

Future Roles for Women

How will the female role emerge in the United States from the present upheaval in gender roles? In many ways, ours may be an optimal time for gender-role change for women. The de-emphasis on fertility and childrearing may be critical. The nature of the female role is intimately tied to whether a society wants to reproduce at a high rate. With a strong emphasis on reproduction, maternal aspects of the female role are stressed. With the current de-emphasis on fertility, careers for women are much more viable alternatives than they formerly were. Indeed, childlessness has become an option for women, freeing them for substantially different roles than housewife/mother.

On the other hand, we must recognize the emergence of a political movement known as the New Right (for a feminist analysis of the New Right, see Eisenstein, 1982). The New Right abhors recent social change. It claims that its stance is "pro-family," but it narrowly defines the family as a married heterosexual couple with children, with the husband working in the labor force and the wife staying home full-time. The New Right rues the demise of patriarchy and the loss of the father's authority within the family. To say the least, the forces of the New Right act in opposition to the forces of feminism. Focus 17.2, "Backlash!" details some of these anti-women forces. It remains to be seen which will win out. Interestingly, the New Right has lost some key legislative battles; in 1983 it lost a critical Senate vote attempting to put into law a constitutional amendment that would have prohibited abortion. On the other hand, the Equal Rights Amendment also went down to defeat. And today very few medical students and residents are training to perform abortions because they don't want to risk the danger to themselves and their families from far right radicals who bomb abortion clinics.

One problem to be faced is that we really have no adequate measure of social change. There has been a tendency to equate work outside the home with progress for women. Yet working outside the home is the opposite of progress if it must be done in addition to all the housewife and mother tasks. The work of women, whether inside the home or outside the home, must be evaluated in terms of its contributions to society in general and to the growth of the individual in particular. A much more complex and adequate measure of social change would result.

We need, then, to expand our notion of the meaning of equality—it means more than just women holding jobs outside the home, for example. Part of the expansion must include changes in the male role. Equality requires modification of the male role, not only to make true equality possible, but because the male role itself is in need of revision.

But I must add one note of caution, and this is in regard to the values attached to gender roles. Cross-culturally (at least currently) it is a universal phenomenon that the male role is more powerful and the female role is valued less. This devaluing of the female role surely has many consequences, among them psychological ones such as the higher frequency of depression found in women. In my opinion it

FOCUS 17.2

BACKLASH!

Pulitzer Prize–winning author Susan Faludi's 1991 book *Backlash* helped to energize a new surge of feminist activism. The feminist movement that began in the 1960s is now referred to as the "second wave" (the first wave being the suffragettes who won the right to vote for women in the early 1900s), and a new, third wave of feminism became vigorous in the 1990s. Susan Faludi's book is passed around as eagerly today as Betty Friedan's *The Feminine Mystique* was in the 1960s.

Faludi's basic argument is that women have made some progress—legal, economic, political—in the United States in the last two decades and that a counterassault of antifeminism has been launched to attack this progress. This is the backlash against women and feminism.

The basic argument of the backlash forces is that women have made progress yet they are still unhappy, so their unhappiness must be the fault of the feminist movement. The alternative explanation—that women's unhappiness may be related to continued sexism in every place from the bedroom to the boardroom—is ignored.

What evidence does Faludi present for the existence of this backlash movement? Much of it comes from analyses of the popular media's reporting of stories that gnaw away at the psyches of liberated women. For example, there was much publicity in 1986 of a study that found that a single, college-educated woman over the age of 30 had only a 20 percent chance of ever marrying, and a single, college-educated woman of 40 had only a 1.3 percent chance. The clear messages were "If you're a single woman with some education, you're going to end up a miserable old spinster" and "There's a terrible man shortage. Better treat men as precious resources." It turns out that the story originated when a newspaper reporter at the Stamford (Connecticut) *Advocate* wanted to do a Valentine's Day article and phoned the sociology department at Yale. She reached a faculty member, Neil Bennett, who gave her the statistics noted above, which had come from data analyses just completed, and the study was not yet published. These results, which had not even been reviewed by a scientific journal, spread like wildfire. Associated Press picked up the story, and the results were discussed in magazines ranging from *Mademoiselle* to *Cosmo*, on television shows such as "Designing

Women" and "Kate and Allie," and in movies such as *When Harry Met Sally.* As it turned out, the Bennett statistics were flawed (Faludi recounts the flaws in gripping detail, for which there isn't space here). A better study by Jeanne Moorman of the U.S. Census Bureau indicated that at 30, a never-married college-educated woman had a 58 to 66 percent chance of marriage, and at 40, she had a 17 to 23 percent chance. Moorman's findings received only muted publicity, were in fact attacked in op-ed articles in places such as the *New York Times,* and were suppressed by her superiors at the Census Bureau under the Reagan administration.

As another example, in the 1980s there was much publicity over child sexual abuse in daycare centers—toxic daycare, as some said. Working women couldn't help but feel guilty over leaving their children in such dangerous situations. In fact, though, child sexual abuse was verified in relatively few daycare centers. More importantly, statistics indicate that most child sexual abuse occurs in the home, not in daycare centers.

As a third example, in 1982 the *New England Journal of Medicine* published an article on the "infertility epidemic"—women between the ages of 31 and 35 stood a nearly 40 percent chance of being infertile, according to the research. There was a fatherly editorial admonishing women to reevaluate their goals and have their babies before their careers. The findings were on the front page of the *New York Times* the next day and were widely publicized throughout the country. Again, the study was seriously flawed. The participants were French women being treated at artificial insemination centers—that is, their husbands were completely sterile and they were trying artificial insemination, which is far less effective in producing pregnancies than good old-fashioned sexual intercourse. Moreover, the declines in fertility were attributed to women building careers and postponing childbearing. In fact, any increases in women's infertility are far more likely to be a result of the epidemic of sexually transmitted diseases such as chlamydia, which, if not treated, can cause blockage of the fallopian tubes.

The message to women in the publicity in all three examples was "Don't think about developing a career. Marry early, have babies early, or you'll be sorry. And once the babies are born, don't get a job and leave them in daycare, or you'll be even sorrier."

Faludi's evidence includes far more than overpublicized, flawed research. She analyzes images of women on TV and in high fashion, the New Right,

(continued)

Robert Bly's men's movement, and much more. In all cases, the effort is to re-verse the trends set in motion by the women's movement, and the messages are often quite frightening.

The critical question is, Are we now in a time of a resurgence of femi-nism—a third wave—energized by college-age women and young working women, who can fight the backlash and continue to press for women's rights?

Writing in 2001, Faludi updated her account of threats to feminism. She ar-gued that the latest threat to feminism is the hyper-consumerism of the 1990s, which commercialized feminism. Advertisers promoted the idea that liberation meant earning lots of money and buying lots of stuff with it, and that this would make women feel happy and satisfied with their lives. Modern feminism as defined by *Sex and the City* involves buying designer shoes that are about as good for the feet as footbinding was. The freedom to choose became the free-dom to choose expensive liposuction. Feminists, according to Faludi, must chal-lenge the commercialization of feminism and re-emphasize the core values of feminism: the right of women to act responsibly in the world, to build a society that recognizes that caring—not more "stuff"—is what's important.

SOURCE: Faludi (1991, 2001).

is imperative that whatever the reallocation or modification of gender roles, the result must be that the male role and the female role are valued equally.

Although I am emphasizing the need for a higher valuing of the female role, this higher valuing must come not only from without, but also from within. That is, institutional change aimed at raising the value of the female role—for exam-ple, treating childrearing as a profession—and changing male attitudes are not enough. Women must also value themselves. This is an important goal of self-help groups formed by women across the country.

Whatever the reallocation of gender roles in the future, equal respect and value must be attached to both roles. In part, I am suggesting that gender roles in some form will probably continue, and that rather than trying to eliminate them, we might more profitably concentrate on improving the valuation attached to the female role. Much as Blacks shifted from an emphasis on integration and assimilation into White culture to a proclamation that Black is beautiful, so I hope women will increasingly believe that female is good. As Christabel Pankhurst, a British suffragette, said a century ago:

> Remember the dignity
> of your womanhood.
> Do not appeal,
> do not beg,
> do not grovel.
> Take courage,
> join hands,
> stand beside us.

And Maya Angelou, writing in 2000, put it this way:*

> Pretty women wonder where my secret lies.
> I'm not cute or built to suit
>   a fashion model's size
>   But when I start to tell them,
>   They think I'm telling lies.

> I say,
> It's in the reach of my arms,
> The span of my hips,
> The stride of my step,
> The curl of my lips.

> I'm a woman
> Phenomenally.
> Phenomenal woman,
> That's me.

EXPERIENCE THE RESEARCH

FEMINIST IDENTITY

Think about the stages of feminist identity development described in the Bargad and Hyde (1991) study (see page 476). They go from Stage 1, Passive Acceptance, to Stage 5, Active Commitment. You have just taken a psychology of women course. Do you think that you passed through one or several of those stages as the course progressed? What stage would you say you are in now?

*"Phenomenal Woman," from *And Still I Rise* by Maya Angelou. Copyright © 1978 by Maya Angelou. Used by permission of Random House, Inc.

Suggestions for Further Reading

Faludi, Susan. (1991). *Backlash: The undeclared war against American women.* New York: Anchor Books/Doubleday. This book is considered one of the major works of the "third wave" of the women's movement. Must reading.

Taylor, Shelley. (2002). *The tending instinct: Women, men, and the biology of nurturing.* New York: Times Books. In this book, written for the general public, Taylor expands on her tend-and-befriend theory of women's response to stress, discussed in the present chapter.

APPENDIX
Psychology of Women
Resource Directory

Below are listed various organizations that may provide services or information useful to you. All are focused on issues related to the psychology of women.

I. General

American Psychological Association
750 First St., NE
Washington, DC 20002-4242
(202) 336-5500
web: *http://www.apa.org*

This is the major organization of psychologists in the United States. Division 35 of the APA is the Society for the Psychology of Women (*www.apa.org/divisions/div35/*). The APA also has a Women's Program Office (*www.apa.org/pi/wpo*).

Association for Women in Psychology
email: *support@awpsych.org*
web: *http://www.awpsych.org*

The Association for Women in Psychology is a political action group of women psychologists. It sponsors an annual feminist psychology conference.

National Organization for Women (NOW)
1000 Sixteenth St., NW, Suite 700
Washington, DC 20036
(202) 331-0066
email: *now@now.org*
web: *http://www.now.org*

NOW seeks to take action to bring women into full participation in the mainstream of U.S. society, exercising all the privileges and responsibilities thereof in truly equal partnership with men.

Women's Bureau
U.S. Department of Labor
200 Constitution Ave., NW, Frances Perkins Bldg.
Washington, DC 20210
(800) 827-5335
web: *http://www.dol.gov/wb*

The Women's Bureau alerts women about their rights in the workplace; proposes policies and legislation that benefit working women; researches and analyzes information about women and work; and reports findings to the president, Congress, and the public. In 2003, in the Bush administration, this mission was radically changed. Check it out.

II. Health Issues

The Alan Guttmacher Institute
120 Wall Street, 21st Floor
New York, NY 10005
(212) 248-1111
email: *info@guttmacher.org*
web: *http://www.agi-usa.org*

The Alan Guttmacher Institute is a not-for-profit organization dedicated to reproductive health research, policy analysis, and public education. It produces many excellent informational publications.

American Cancer Society
1599 Clifton Road, NE
Atlanta, GA 30329-4251
(800) 227-2345
web: *http://www.cancer.org*

The American Cancer Society offers up-to-date and accurate information on cancer treatment and support. It also funds research on cancer.

National Abortion and Reproductive Rights Action League (NARAL)
1156 15th Street, Suite 700
Washington, DC 20005
(202) 973-3000
web: *http://www.naral.org*

A political action organization working at both state and national levels, NARAL is dedicated to preserving a woman's right to safe and legal abortion and also to teaching its members effective use of the political process to ensure abortion and reproductive rights.

National Association of Anorexia Nervosa and Associated Disorders (ANAD)
P.O. Box 7
Highland Park, IL 60035
(847) 831-3438
email: *info@anad.org*
web: *http://www.anad.org/*

ANAD is the oldest national nonprofit organization dedicated to alleviating eating disorders and promoting a healthy lifestyle.

Division of STD/HIV/TB Prevention
National Center for Prevention Services
Centers for Disease Control
1108 Corporate Square
Atlanta, GA 30329
(404) 639-8040
email: *nchstp@cdc.gov*
web: *http://www.cdc.gov/nchstp/od/nchstp*

This division of the CDC offers the most up-to-date information on sexually transmitted diseases and HIV. It also administers federal programs for the prevention of STD and HIV infection.

National Women's Health Network
514 10th St., NW, Suite 400
Washington, DC 20004
(202) 347-1140
web: *http://www.womenshealthnetwork.org*

This feminist group is concerned with women's health issues. It provides an information clearinghouse, health resource guides, a speakers' bureau, and educational conferences.

Planned Parenthood Federation of America (PPFA)
810 Seventh Avenue
New York, NY 10019
(212) 541-7800
email: *communications@ppfa.org*
web: *http://www.plannedparenthood.org*

PPFA is the nation's oldest and largest voluntary family planning agency. Through local clinics (call 1-800-230-PLAN for the clinic nearest you), it offers birth control information and services, pregnancy testing, voluntary sterilization, prenatal care, abortion, pelvic and breast exams, and other reproductive health services, including sexuality education.

III. Sexuality

Lambda Legal Defense and Education Fund
120 Wall Street, Suite 1500
New York, NY 10005-3904
(212) 809-8585
web: *http://www.lambdalegal.org*

This organization advances the legal rights of lesbians, gay men, and people with AIDS through test case litigation and public education. It also publishes many resource manuals, newsletters, bibliographies, and articles on current topics for lesbians, gay men, and people with HIV/AIDS.

National Gay and Lesbian Task Force (NGLTF)
1325 Massachusetts Avenue, NW, Suite 600
Washington, DC 20005
(202) 393-5177
email: *ngltf@ngltf.org*
web: *http://www.ngltf.org*

NGLTF, the oldest national gay and lesbian civil rights advocacy organization, is involved in lobbying and grassroots organizing. It also provides publications and referrals.

Sexuality Information and Education Council of the United States (SIECUS)
130 West 42nd Street, Suite 350
New York, NY 10036-7802
(212) 819-9770
email: *siecus@siecus.org*
web: *http://www.siecus.org*

SIECUS serves as an enormous source of information on sexuality and sexuality education. It maintains a database of titles of books and journals on human sexuality that currently consists of over 8,000 entries.

Society for the Scientific Study of Sexuality
P.O. Box 416
Allentown, PA 18105-0416
(610) 530-2483
email: *thesociety@inetmail.att.net*
web: *http://www.sexscience.org*

This organization is devoted to promoting quality sex research. It publishes the *Journal of Sex Research,* and its website lists educational opportunities in the field of human sexuality.

Glossary

Acculturation The process by which one takes on the beliefs and customs of a new culture as one's own.

Achievement motivation The desire to accomplish something of value or importance through one's efforts; the desire to meet standards of excellence.

Adrenogenital syndrome *See* Congenital adrenal hyperplasia.

African Americans Americans of African descent.

Aggression Behavior intended to harm another person.

Androcentrism Male centered; the belief that the male is the norm.

Androgens A group of sex hormones, including testosterone, produced more abundantly in males than in females.

Androgyny The combination of masculine and feminine psychological characteristics in an individual.

Andropause A time of declining testosterone levels in middle-aged men.

Anorexia nervosa An eating disorder characterized by overcontrol of eating for purposes of weight reduction, sometimes to the point of starvation.

Anorgasmia The inability to have an orgasm; orgasmic dysfunction.

Antigay prejudice Negative attitudes and behaviors toward gay men and lesbians.

Asian Americans Americans of Asian descent.

Assertiveness Standing up for one's basic interpersonal rights in such a way that the rights of another person are not violated.

Attribution The process by which people make judgments about the causes of events.

Behavior therapy A system of treatment based on the principles of learning theory.

Berdache *See* Two-Spirit.

Bilingualism Knowing two languages.

Bisexuality Being erotically and emotionally attracted to both females and males.

Boston marriage A romantic but asexual relationship between two women.

Bulimia An eating disorder in which the person binges on food and then purges the body of the calories by vomiting or using laxatives.

Care perspective According to Gilligan, an approach to moral reasoning that emphasizes relationships between people and caring for others and the self.

Chicana A female American of Mexican descent.

Chicanos Americans of Mexican descent; may also refer specifically to male Mexican Americans.

Cognitive-behavioral therapy A system of psychotherapy that combines behavior therapy and restructuring of dysfunctional thought patterns.

Coming out The process of acknowledging to oneself, and then to others, that one is lesbian or gay.

Comparable worth The principle that people should be paid equally for work that is comparable in responsibility, educational requirements, and so forth.

Conceptual equivalence In multicultural research, whether a scale measures the same thing or has the same meaning in all cultures being studied.

Congenital adrenal hyperplasia (CAH) A rare genetic condition that causes the fetus's adrenal glands to produce abnormally large amounts of androgens. In genetic females, the result may be a girl born with masculinized genitals. Also called adrenogenital syndrome.

Conventional morality   In Kohlberg's theory, an intermediate level of moral reasoning, in which children and adults understand rules and obey them rigidly.

Couvade   A custom in which the man is assumed to be the major contributor to childbirth, and therefore suffers symptoms such as fatigue.

Deindividuation   A state in which a person has become anonymous and has therefore lost his or her individual identity.

Disclaimers   Phrases such as "I may be wrong, but. . . ."

Display rules   A culture's rules for what emotions can be expressed or displayed.

Double standard   Tolerance of male promiscuity and disapproval of female promiscuity.

Double standard of aging   Cultural norms by which men's status increases with age but women's decreases.

***Diagnostic and Statistical Manual* (DSM)**   The American Psychiatric Association's official manual of psychiatric diagnoses.

DSM   *See Diagnostic and Statistical Manual.*

Dysmenorrhea   Painful menstruation; cramps.

Dyspareunia   Painful intercourse.

Dysphoria   Unhappiness or sad mood.

Electra complex   In psychoanalytic theory, a girl's sexual attraction to and intense love for her father.

Emotion work   Taking responsibility for the emotional quality of relationships, which is part of the female role.

Empowerment   Helping people to find their own strength.

Empty nest syndrome   Depression that middle-aged people supposedly feel when their children are grown and have left home, leaving an empty nest.

Entitlement   The individual's sense of what he or she is entitled to or deserves.

Epistemology   Concerning the origins and methods of human knowledge.

Equivalence   In multicultural research, the construct measured by a scale has the same meaning in all cultures being studied.

Erogenous zones   Areas of the body that are particularly sensitive to sexual stimulation.

Estrogen   A "female" sex hormone produced by the ovaries; also produced in smaller quantities in males.

Estrogen-deficiency theory   The hypothesis that the symptoms of menopause are due to low levels of estrogen.

Estrogen-replacement therapy (ERT)   Replacement doses of estrogen given to some women to treat menopausal symptoms.

Ethnic group   A group of people who share a common culture and language.

Ethnocentrism   The tendency to regard one's own ethnic group as superior to others and to believe that its customs and way of life are the standards by which other cultures should be judged.

Euro-Americans   White Americans of European descent. An alternative to the term *Whites*.

Eurocentrism   The tendency to view the world from a Euro-American point of view and to evaluate other ethnic groups in reference to Euro-Americans.

Expansionist hypothesis   In research on women and multiple roles, the hypothesis that multiple roles are good for mental health, because they provide more opportunities for stimulation, self-esteem, and so on.

Experimenter effects   Some characteristics of the experimenter affect the way participants behave and therefore affect the research outcome.

Female-as-the-exception phenomenon If a category is considered normatively male and there is a female example of the category, gender is noted because the female is the exception. The men's basketball team is called simply the basketball team, whereas the women's basketball team is called the women's basketball team. A byproduct of androcentrism.

Female deficit model A theory or interpretation of research in which women's behavior is seen as deficient.

Female underprediction effect The phenomenon that females' SAT scores predict lower grades in college than they actually get.

Feminine evil The belief that women are the source of evil or immorality in the world, as in the Adam and Eve story.

Femininity-achievement incompatibility The cultural belief that, beginning in adolescence, achievement is not appropriately feminine for girls.

Feminist A person who favors political, economic, and social equality of women and men, and therefore favors the legal and social changes necessary to achieve that equality.

Feminist research Research growing out of feminist theory, which seeks radical reform of traditional research methods.

Feminist therapy A system of psychotherapy informed by feminist theory.

Feminization of poverty The increasing trend over time for women to be overrepresented among the poor in the United States.

Fitness In evolutionary theory, an animal's relative contribution of genes to the next generation.

Follicle The capsule of cells surrounding an egg in the ovary.

Follicle-stimulating hormone (FSH) A hormone secreted by the pituitary; in females it stimulates follicle and egg development.

Follicular phase The first phase of the menstrual cycle, beginning just after menstruation.

Gender The state of being male or female.

Gender constancy In cognitive-developmental theory, a child's understanding that gender is a permanent, unchanging characteristic of the self.

Gender-fair research Research that is free of gender bias.

Gender identity In cognitive-developmental theory, the individual's knowledge that she or he is a female or male.

Gender intensification Increased pressures for gender-role conformity beginning in early adolescence.

Gender-role stereotypes A set of shared cultural beliefs about males' and females' behavior, personality traits, and other attributes.

Gender schema A person's general knowledge framework about gender; it processes and organizes information on the basis of gender-linked associations.

Gender similarities Ways in which males and females are similar rather than different.

Genomic imprinting In females, the process in which some genes from the maternal X chromosome and some genes from the paternal Y chromosome are expressed.

Glass ceiling "Invisible" barriers to the promotion of women and ethnic minorities into upper management and executive levels.

Gonadotropin-releasing hormone (GnRH) A hormone secreted by the hypothalamus that regulates the pituitary's secretion of hormones.

Good provider role The male role in industrialized societies, in which the man is expected to earn money and provide well for his family.

Gräfenberg spot (G-spot) A hypothesized small gland on the front wall of the vagina, emptying into the urethra, which may be responsible for female ejaculation.

Hedges Phrases, such as "sort of," that weaken or soften a statement.

Hispanics People of Spanish descent, whether from Mexico, Puerto Rico, or elsewhere.

Homophobia A strong, irrational fear of homosexuals.

Hopelessness theory The theory that a negative cognitive style makes a person vulnerable to depression.

Hormone-replacement therapy Replacement doses of estrogen and progesterone and possibly testosterone, given to some women to treat menopausal symptoms.

Hypothalamus A part of the brain that is important in regulating certain body functions including sex hormone production.

Hysterectomy Surgical removal of the uterus.

Imitation When people do what they see others doing.

Infantilizing Treating people, for example, women, as if they were children or babies.

Justice perspective According to Gilligan, an approach to moral reasoning that emphasizes fairness and the rights of the individual.

Kegel exercises Exercises to strengthen the muscles surrounding the vagina; pubo-coccygeal muscle exercises.

Lateralization The extent to which one hemisphere of the brain organizes a particular mental process or behavior.

Latina A female Latin American.

Latinos People of Latin American descent.

Learned helplessness theory A theory that depression is caused by a person having learned that he or she is helpless or unable to control important outcomes in life.

Lesbian A woman whose sexual orientation is toward other women.

Lumpectomy A surgical treatment for breast cancer in which only the lump and a small bit of surrounding tissue are removed.

Luteal phase The third phase of the menstrual cycle, after ovulation.

Luteinizing hormone (LH) A hormone secreted by the pituitary; in females it triggers ovulation.

Machismo The ideal of manliness in Hispanic cultures.

Male as normative A model in which the male is seen as the norm for all humans, and the female is seen as a deviation from the norm.

Male sex-role identity (MSRI) paradigm Traditional psychology's approach to the psychology of men, based on the assumption that a masculine identity is essential for good adjustment.

Marianismo The ideal of womanliness in Hispanic cultures.

Masochism The desire to experience pain.

Maternity leave *See* Parental leave.

Measurement *See* Psychological measurement.

Menstruation A bloody discharge of the lining of the uterus; the fourth phase of the menstrual cycle.

Meta-analysis A statistical technique that allows a researcher to combine the results of many separate research studies.

Motherhood mandate The cultural belief that all women should have children, that is, be mothers.

Motive to avoid success A hypothesized fear of success that leads people to avoid being successful.

Myotonia Muscle contraction.

Natural selection According to Darwin, the process by which the fittest animals survive, reproduce, and pass their genes on to the next generation, whereas animals that are less fit do not reproduce and therefore do not pass on their genes.

Observational learning When a person observes someone doing something, and then does it at a later time.

Observer effects When the researcher's expectations affect his or her observations and recording of the data.

Oedipal complex In psychoanalytic theory, a boy's sexual attraction to and intense love for his mother, and his desire to do away with his father.

Orgasm An intense sensation that occurs at the peak of sexual arousal and is followed by the release of sexual tensions.

Overgeneralization A research error in which the results are said to apply to a broader group than the one sampled; for example, saying that results from an all-male sample are true for all people.

Ovulation Release of an egg from an ovary.

Ovum An egg.

Paradigm The set of beliefs, underlying assumptions, values, and techniques shared by a particular community of scientists.

Paradigm shift A radical revolution in science, in which scientists change from one paradigm to another.

Parental investment In sociobiology, behaviors or other investments in the offspring by the parent that increase the offspring's chance of survival.

Parental leave A leave from work for purposes of recovering from childbirth and/or caring for the child, at the time of birth or adoption.

PC exercises *See* Kegel exercises.

Pejoration The process by which a term takes on negative connotations.

Phallic stage The third stage of development in psychoanalytic theory, around 3 to 6 years of age, during which the pleasure zone is the genitals and sexual

feelings arise toward the parent of the other gender.

Phallocentric Male centered, or, specifically, penis centered.

Postconventional morality In Kohlberg's theory, the most mature level of moral reasoning, in which the person understands that rules are not absolute, but rather are part of a social contract; the person behaves from internalized ethical principles.

Posttraumatic stress disorder (PTSD) Long-term psychological distress suffered by someone who has experienced a terrifying, uncontrollable event.

Preconventional morality In Kohlberg's theory, the earliest stage of moral reasoning, in which children do the right thing simply to gain rewards or avoid punishments.

Premenstrual syndrome (PMS) A combination of several physical and psychological symptoms (such as depression) occurring in some women for a few days before menstruation.

Prenatal Before birth.

Progesterone A "female" sex hormone produced by the ovaries; also produced in smaller quantities in males.

Projective test A method of psychological measurement that uses ambiguous stimuli; the person's responses are thought to reflect his or her personality, based on the assumption that one's personality is projected onto the ambiguous stimulus.

Prostaglandins Hormone-like biochemicals that stimulate the muscles of the uterus to contract.

Provider role The male role in pre-industrial societies, which required the men to provide food and shelter for his family. *See also* Good provider role.

Psychoanalysis A system of therapy based on Freud's psychoanalytic theory, in which the analyst attempts to bring repressed, unconscious material into consciousness.

Psychoanalytic theory A psychological theory originated by Freud; its basic assumption is that part of the human psyche is unconscious.

Psychological measurement The process of assigning numbers to people's characteristics, such as aggressiveness or intelligence.

Pubococcygeal muscle exercises (PC exercises) *See* Kegel exercises.

Quasi-experimental design A research design that uses two or more groups, but participants are not randomly assigned to groups so it is not a true experiment. An example is two-group designs comparing males and females.

Race A biological concept referring to a group of people with a common set of physical features who have mated only within their race.

Radical mastectomy A surgical treatment for breast cancer in which the entire breast, as well as underlying muscle and lymph nodes, are removed.

Rape Nonconsenting oral, anal, or vaginal penetration obtained by force, by threat of bodily harm, or when the victim is incapable of giving consent.

Rape trauma syndrome The emotional and physical effects a woman undergoes following a rape or attempted rape.

Reinforcement In operant conditioning, something that occurs after a behavior and makes the behavior more likely to occur in the future.

Replicate To repeat a research study and obtain the same basic results.

SAT A standardized academic achievement test taken by many college-bound high school students. Some colleges and universities use it in making admissions decisions.

Scarcity hypothesis In research on women and multiple roles, the hypothesis that adding a role (e.g., worker) creates stress, which has negative consequences for physical health and mental health.

Schema In cognitive psychology, a general knowledge framework that a person has about a particular topic; the schema then processes and organizes new information on that topic.

Self-confidence A person's belief that she or he can be successful.

Self-efficacy A person's belief in her or his ability to accomplish a particular task.

Self-esteem The level of global positive regard that one has for oneself.

Sex-linked trait A trait controlled by a gene on the X chromosome (or occasionally on the Y chromosome).

Sex-role strain (SRS) paradigm Feminist psychology's approach to the male role, based on the assumption that gender roles for men are contradictory and stressful.

Sexism Discrimination or bias against people based on their gender. Sex bias.

Sexual dysfunction A problem with sexual responding that causes a person mental distress; examples are erection problems in men and orgasm problems in women.

Sexual orientation A person's erotic and emotional orientation toward members of her or his own gender or members of the other gender.

Sexual selection According to Darwin, the processes by which members of one gender (usually males) compete with each other for mating privileges with members of the other gender (usually females), and members of the other gender (females) choose to mate only with certain preferred members of the first gender (males).

Social constructionism A theoretical viewpoint that humans do not discover reality directly; rather, they construct meanings for events in the environment based on their own prior experiences and beliefs.

Socialization The process by which society conveys to the individual its expectations for his or her behavior, values, and beliefs.

Social-structural theory A theory of the origin of psychological gender differences that focuses on the social structure, particulary the division of labor between men and women.

Sociobiology The application of evolutionary theory to explaining the social behavior of animals, including people.

Stereotype threat Being at risk of personally confirming a negative stereotype about one's group.

Superego Freud's term for the part of the personality that contains the person's ideals and conscience.

Systematic desensitization A method used by behavior therapists in the treatment of phobias; it involves associating a relaxed, pleasant state with gradually increasing anxiety-provoking stimuli.

Tag question A short phrase added to a sentence, which turns it into a question.

Testosterone A sex hormone; one of the androgens.

Trait An enduring characteristic of a person, such as extraversion.

Translational equivalence In multicultural research, whether a scale written in one language and translated into another has the same meaning in both languages.

Two-Spirit Among Native Americans, a third gender category.

Vaginismus A strong, spastic contraction of the muscles around the vagina, perhaps closing off the vagina and making intercourse impossible.

Vasocongestion An accumulation of blood in the blood vessels of a region of the body, especially the genitals; a swelling or erection results.

Whorfian hypothesis The theory that the language we learn influences how we think.

Womb envy In Horney's analytic theory, the male's envy of woman's uterus and reproductive capacity.

Women's resistance Occurs when women do not passively accept discriminatory treatment, but instead take active steps to resist it.

X-chromosome inactivation In females, the process in which one of the two X chromosomes is inactivated or silenced in nearly every cell, so that only one chromosome functions.

Bibliography

In the bibliography I have largely followed the style of spelling out first names of authors. I do this to help readers become aware of the scientific contributions made by women.

AAUW. (1991). *Shortchanging girls, shortchanging America*. Washington, DC: American Association of University Women.

AAUW. (2000). *Tech-savvy: Educating girls in the new computer age*. Washington, DC: American Association of University Women.

AAUW. (2001). *Hostile hallways: Bullying, teasing, and sexual harassment in school*. Washington, DC: American Association of University Women.

Abbey, Antonia. (1991). Misperception as an antecedent of acquaintance rape: A consequence of ambiguity in communication between men and women. In A. Parrott & L. Bechhofer (Eds.), *Acquaintance rape: The hidden crime*. New York: Wiley.

Abbey, Antonia, Ross, Lisa T., McDuggie, Donna, & McAuslan, P. (1996). Alcohol and dating risk factors for sexual assault among college women. *Psychology of Women Quarterly, 20*, 147–169.

Abbey, Antonia, et al. (2001). Attitudinal, experiential, and situational predictors of sexual assault perpetration. *Journal of Interpersonal Violence, 16*, 784–807.

Abela, J. (2001). The hopelessness theory of depression: A test of the diathesis-stress and causal mediation components in third and seventh grade children. *Journal of Abnormal Child Psychology, 29*, 241–254.

Abend, Teresa A., & Williamson, Gail M. (2002). Feeling attractive in the wake of breast cancer: Optimism matters, and so do interpersonal relationships. *Personality and Social Psychology Bulletin, 28*, 427–436.

Abramowitz, Stephen I. (1986). Psychosocial outcomes of sex reassignment surgery. *Journal of Consulting and Clinical Psychology, 54*, 183–189.

Abramson, Lyn Y., Metalsky, Gerald I., & Alloy, Lauren B. (1989). Hopelessness depression: A theory-based subtype of depression. *Psychological Review, 96*, 358–372.

Abramson, P. R., et al. (1977). The talking platypus phenomenon as a function of sex and professional status. *Psychology of Women Quarterly, 2*, 114–117.

Abreu, José M., Goodyear, R., Campos, A., & Newcomb, M. (2000). Ethnic belonging and traditional masculinity ideology among African Americans, European Americans, and Latinos. *Psychology of Men and Masculinity, 1*, 75–86.

Acosta-Belén, Edna, & Bose, Christine E. (2000). U.S. Latina and Latin American feminisms: Hemispheric encounters. *Signs: Journal of Women in Culture and Society, 25*, 1113–1120.

Adams, Kathryn A., & Landers, Audrey D. (1978). Sex difference in dominance behavior. *Sex Roles, 4*, 215–224.

Adamsky, Catherine. (1981). Changes in pronomial usage in a classroom situation. *Psychology of Women Quarterly, 5*, 773–779.

Addiego, F., et al. (1981). Female ejaculation: A case study. *Journal of Sex Research, 17*, 13–21.

Adleman, Jeanne, & Enguidanos, Gloria M. (Eds.). (1995). *Racism in the lives of women: Testimony, theory, and guides to antiracist practice*. New York: Haworth.

Adler, D. N., & Johnson, S. B. (1994). Sample description, reporting, and analysis of sex in psychological research. *American Psychologist, 49*, 216–218.

Adler, Nancy E., David, Henry P., Major, Brenda N., Roth, Susan H., Russo, Nancy F., & Wyatt, Gail E. (1990). Psychological responses after abortion. *Science, 248*, 41–44.

Adler, Nancy E., David, Henry P., Major, Brenda N., Roth, Susan H., Russo, Nancy F., & Wyatt, Gail E. (1992). Psychological factors in abortion. *American Psychologist, 47*, 1194–1204.

Adler, Nancy E., & Coriell, Marilee. (1997). Socioeconomic status and women's health. In S. Gallant, G. Keita, & R. Royak-Schaler (Eds.), *Health care for women: Psychological, social, and behavioral influences* (pp. 11–24). Washington, DC: American Psychological Association.

Adler, P., Kless, S., & Adler, P. (1992). Socialization to gender roles: Popularity among elementary school boys and girls. *Sociology of Education, 65,* 169–187.

Alan Guttmacher Institute. (2002). *In their own right: Addressing the sexual and reproductive health needs of American men.* New York: Alan Guttmacher Institute.

Alba, Joseph W., & Hasher, Lynn. (1983). Is memory schematic? *Psychological Bulletin, 93,* 203–231.

Albee, George W. (1977). The Protestant ethic, sex, and psychotherapy. *American Psychologist, 32,* 150–161.

Albin, Rochelle S. (1977). Psychological studies of rape. *Signs, 3,* 423–435.

Alferi, Susan M., et al. (2001). An exploratory study of social support, distress, and life disruption among low-income Hispanic women under treatment for early stage breast cancer. *Health Psychology, 20,* 41–46.

Allen, Paula Gunn. (1986). Who is your mother? Red roots of white feminism. In P. G. Allen, *The sacred hoop: Recovering the feminine in American Indian traditions.* Boston: Beacon Press.

Allgood-Merton, B., Lewinsohn, P., & Hops, H. (1990). Sex differences and adolescent depression. *Journal of Abnormal Psychology, 99,* 55–63.

Allport, G. (1954). *The nature of prejudice.* Reading, MA: Addison-Wesley.

Amaro, Hortensia. (1988). Considerations for prevention of HIV infection among Hispanic women. *Psychology of Women Quarterly, 12,* 429–444.

Amaro, Hortensia, Raj, Anita, & Reed, Elizabeth. (2001). Women's sexual health: The need for feminist analyses in public health in the Decade of Behavior. *Psychology of Women Quarterly, 25,* 324–334.

Amato, Paul R. (2000). The consequences of divorce for adults and children. *Journal of Marriage and the Family, 62,* 1269–1287.

Amato, Paul R., & Gilbreth, J. G. (1999). Nonresident fathers and children's well-being: A meta-analysis. *Journal of Marriage and the Family, 61,* 557–573.

Ambady, Nalini, Shih, M., Kim, A., & Pittinsky, T. (2001). Stereotype susceptibility in children: Effects of identity activation on quantitative performance. *Psychological Science, 12,* 385–390.

American Association of Retired Persons. (1999). *Modern Maturity Sexuality Study.* Washington, DC: AARP.

American Cancer Society. (1991). *Facts on breast cancer.* New York: Author.

American Psychiatric Association. (1994). *Diagnostic and statistical manual,* 4th ed. New York: Author.

American Psychological Association. (1994). *Publication manual* (4th ed.). Washington, DC: Author.

American Psychological Association. (1996). *Research agenda for psychosocial and behavioral factors in women's health.* Washington, DC: Author.

American Psychological Association. (2001). *Publication manual* (5th ed.). Washington, DC: Author.

Anderson, Barbara L. (1983). Primary orgasmic dysfunction: Diagnostic considerations and review of treatment. *Psychological Bulletin, 93,* 105–136.

Anderson, Kristin L., & Leaper, Campbell. (1998). Meta-analyses of gender effects on conversational interruption: Who, what, when, where, and how. *Sex Roles, 39,* 225–252.

Anderson, Kristin L. (1997). Gender, status, and domestic violence: An integration of feminist and family violence approaches. *Journal of Marriage and the Family, 59,* 655–669.

Angelou, Maya. (2000). *Phenomenal woman.* New York: Random House.

Angier, Natalie. (1999). *Woman: An intimate geography.* Boston: Houghton Mifflin.

Angrist, Shirley S. (1969). The study of sex roles. *Journal of Social Issues, 25,* 215–232.

Ankney, C. Davison. (1992). Sex differences in relative brain size: The mis-measure of woman, too? *Intelligence, 16,* 329–336.

Anonymous. (1974). Life in the military. In J. Pleck & R. Sawyer (Eds.), *Men and masculinity.* Englewood Cliffs, NJ: Prentice-Hall.

Anthony, J. C., Warner, L. A., & Kessler, R. C. (1994). Comparative epidemiology of dependence on tobacco, alcohol, controlled substances, and inhalants: Basic findings from the National Comorbidity Survey. *Experimental Clinical Psychopharmacology, 2,* 244–268.

Antoni, Michael H., et al. (2001). Cognitive-behavioral stress management intervention decreases the prevalence of depression and enhances benefit finding among women under treatment for early-stage breast cancer. *Health Psychology, 20*, 20–32.

Arendell, Terry. (1987). Women and the economics of divorce in contemporary America. *Signs, 13*, 5.

Arendell, Terry. (2000). Conceiving and investigating motherhood: The decade's scholarship. *Journal of Marriage and the Family, 62*, 1192–1207.

Argyle, Michael, et al. (1968). The effects of visibility on interaction in a dyad. *Human Relations, 21*, 3–17.

Aries, Elizabeth. (1996). *Men and women in interaction: Reconsidering the differences.* New York: Oxford University Press.

Aries, Elizabeth. (1998). Gender differences in interaction: A reexamination. In D. Canary & K. Dindia (Eds.), *Sex differences and similarities in communication* (pp. 65–82). Mahwah, NJ: Erlbaum.

Arkin, W., & Dobrofsky, Lynne R. (1978). Military socialization and masculinity. *Journal of Social Issues, 34*(1), 151–168.

Astin, Helen S., & Leland, C. (1991). *Women of influence, women of vision: A cross-generational study of leaders and social change.* San Francisco: Jossey-Bass.

Atkin, David. (1991). The evolution of television series addressing single women, 1966–1990. *Journal of Broadcasting & Electronic Media, 35*, 517–523.

Avis, Nancy E., & McKinlay, Sonja M. (1995). The Massachusetts Women's Health Study: An epidemiological investigation of the menopause. *Journal of the American Medical Women's Association, 50*, 45–63.

Avis, Nancy E., et al. (2001). Is there a menopausal syndrome? Menopausal status and symptoms across racial/ethnic groups. *Social Science and Medicine, 52*, 345–356.

Bachmann, G. A., & Leiblum, S. R. (1991). Sexuality in sexagenarian women. *Maturitas, 13*, 43–50.

Baenninger, Maryann, & Newcombe, Nora. (1989). The role of experience in spatial test performance: A meta-analysis. *Sex Roles, 20*, 327–344.

Bailey, J. M., Pillard, R. C., Neale, M. C., & Agyei, Y. (1993). Heritable factors influence sexual orientation in women. *Archives of General Psychiatry, 50*, 217–223.

Bailey, J. Michael, Bobrow, D., Wolfe, M., & Mikach, S. (1995). Sexual orientation of adult sons of gay fathers. *Developmental Psychology, 31*, 124–129.

Bailey, J. Michael, & Dawood, K. (1998). Behavior genetics, sexual orientation, and the family. In C. J. Patterson & A. R. D'Augelli (Eds.), *Lesbian, gay and bisexual identities in families: Psychological perspectives.* New York: Oxford University Press.

Bailey, J. Michael, Dunne, M., & Martin, N. (2000). Genetic and environmental influences on sexual orientation and its correlates in an Australian twin sample. *Journal of Personality and Social Psychology, 78*, 524–536.

Bailey, J. Michael, Gaulin, S., Agyei, Y., & Gladue, B. (1994). Effects of gender and sexual orientation on evolutionarily relevant aspects of human mating psychology. *Journal of Personality and Social Psychology, 66*, 1081–1093.

Baker, Laurence C. (1996). Differences in earnings between male and female physicians. *New England Journal of Medicine, 334*, 960–964.

Bancroft, John. (1987). A physiological approach. In J. H. Geer and W. T. O'Donohue (Eds.), *Theories of human sexuality* (pp. 411–421). New York: Plenum.

Bandura, Albert. (1965). Influence of model's reinforcement contingencies on the acquisition of imitative responses. *Journal of Personality and Social Psychology, 1*, 589–595.

Bandura, Albert. (1986). *Social foundations of thought and action: A social cognitive theory.* Englewood Cliffs, NJ: Prentice-Hall.

Bandura, Albert, Barbaranelli, C., Caprara, G., & Pastorelli, C. (2001). Self-efficacy beliefs as shapers of children's aspirations and career trajectories. *Child Development, 72*, 187–206.

Bandura, A., & Walters, R. H. (1963). *Social learning and personality development.* New York: Holt, Rinehart & Winston.

Barash, David P. (1982). *Sociobiology and behavior* (2nd ed.). New York: Elsevier.

Barbach, Lonnie G. (1975). *For yourself: The fulfillment of female sexuality.* Garden City, NY: Anchor Press/Doubleday.

Barbaree, H. E., & Marshall, W. L. (1991). The role of male sexual arousal in rape: Six models. *Journal of Consulting and Clinical Psychology, 59*, 621–630.

Bargad, Adena, & Hyde, Janet S. (1991). Women's studies: A study of feminist identity development in women. *Psychology of Women Quarterly, 15*, 181–201.

Bargh, John A., Raymond, P., Pryor, J., & Strack, F. (1995). Attractiveness of the underling: An automatic power –> sex association and its consequences for sexual harassment and aggression. *Journal of Personality and Social Psychology, 68,* 768–781.

Barlow, Tani. (2000). International feminism of the future. *Signs: Journal of Women in Culture and Society, 25,* 1099–1105.

Barnett, Rosalind C., & Hyde, Janet S. (2001). Women, men, work, and family: An expansionist theory. *American Psychologist, 56,* 781–796.

Barnett, Rosalind C., & Rivers, Caryl. (1996). *She works/he works: How two-income families are happier, healthier, and better-off.* San Francisco: Harper San Francisco.

Barnett, Rosalind C., Marshall, Nancy, & Pleck, Joseph. (1992). Men's multiple roles and their relationship to men's psychological distress. *Journal of Marriage and the Family, 54,* 358–367.

Baron, Larry, & Straus, Murray A. (1989). *Four theories of rape in American society.* New Haven: Yale University Press.

Barraclough, C. A., & Gorski, R. A. (1961). Evidence that the hypothalamus is responsible for androgen-induced sterility in the female rat. *Endocrinology, 68,* 68–79.

Barreca, R. (1991). *They used to call me Snow White . . . but I drifted: Women's strategic use of humor.* New York: Penguin Books.

Barrett, Lisa F., Lane, R., Sechrest, L., & Schwartz, G. (2000). Sex differences in emotional awareness. *Personality and Social Psychology Bulletin, 26,* 1027–1035.

Barry, H., Bacon, Margaret K., & Child, I. L. (1957). A cross-cultural survey of some sex differences in socialization. *Journal of Abnormal and Social Psychology, 55,* 327–332.

Bart, Pauline B. (1971). Depression in middle-aged women. In V. G. Gornick & B. K. Moran (Eds.), *Women in sexist society.* New York: Basic Books.

Bart, Pauline B. (1981). A study of women who both were raped and avoided rape. *Journal of Social Issues, 37,* 123–136.

Baruch, Grace et al. (1983). *Lifeprints: New patterns of love and work for today's women.* New York: McGraw-Hill.

Baruch, Grace K., Biener, Lois, & Barnett, Rosalind C. (1987). Women and gender in research on stress. *American Psychologist, 42,* 130–136.

Basow, Susan A., & Kobrynowicz, Diane. (1993). What is she eating? The effects of meal size on impressions of a female eater. *Sex Roles, 28,* 335–344.

Basson, R., et al. (2001). Report of the International Consensus Development Conference on female sexual dysfunction: Definitions and classifications. *Journal of Sex and Marital Therapy, 27,* 83–94.

Bates, Carolyn M., & Brodsky, Annette M. (1989). *Sex in the therapy hour.* New York: Guilford Press.

Baulieu, E. E., et al. (2000). Dehydroepi-androsterone (DHEA), DHEA sulfate, and aging: Contributions of the DHEAge Study to a sociobiomedical issue. *Proceedings of the National Academy of Sciences—USA, 97,* 4279–4284.

Baxter, I. C. (1970). Interpersonal spacing in natural settings. *Sociometry, 33,* 444–456.

Bay-Cheng, Liana, Zucker, A., Stewart, Z., & Pomerleau, C. (2002). Linking femininity, weight concern, and mental health among Latina, Black, and White women. *Psychology of Women Quarterly, 26,* 36–45.

Bazzini, Doris G., McIntosh, W., Smith, S., Cook, S., & Harris, C. (1997). The aging woman in popular film: Underrepresented, unattractive, unfriendly, and unintelligent. *Sex Roles, 36,* 531–543.

Beall, Anne E. (1993). A social constructionist view of gender. In A. E. Beall & R. J. Sternberg (Eds.), *The psychology of gender* (pp. 127–147). New York: Guilford.

Beatty, W. (1992). Gonadal hormones and sex differences in nonreproductive behaviors. In A. Gerall et al. (Eds.), *Handbook of behavioral neurobiology* (Vol. 11, pp. 85–128). New York: Plenum.

Beausang, Carol C., & Razor, Anita G. (2000). Young Western women's experiences of menarche and menstruation. *Health Care for Women International, 21,* 517–528.

Beauvoir, Simone de. (1952). *The second sex.* New York: Knopf.

Beck, A. T., & Greenberg, Ruth L. (1974). Cognitive therapy with depressed women. In V. Franks & V. Burtle (Eds.), *Women in therapy.* New York: Brunner/Mazel.

Beck, J. Gayle. (1995). Hypoactive sexual desire disorder: An overview. *Journal of Consulting and Clinical Psychology, 63,* 919–927.

Becker, Gay. (2000). *The elusive embryo: How women and men approach new reproductive technologies.* Berkeley: University of California Press.

Beckman, Linda J., & Harvey, S. Marie. (Eds.). (1998). *The new civil war: The psychology, culture, and politics of abortion.* Washington, DC: American Psychological Association.

Belcastro, P. A. (1985). Sexual behavior differences between black and white students. *Journal of Sex Research, 21,* 56–67.

Bell, Alan P. (1974). Homosexualities: Their range and character. In *Nebraska symposium on motivation 1973.* Lincoln: University of Nebraska Press.

Bell, Alan P., & Weinberg, Martin S. (1978). *Homosexualities.* New York: Simon & Schuster.

Bell, Alan P., Weinberg, Martin S., & Hammersmith, Sue K. (1981). *Sexual preference: Its development in men and women.* Bloomington: Indiana University Press.

Belle, Deborah. (1990). Poverty and women's mental health. *American Psychologist, 45,* 385–389.

Beller, Michal, & Gafni, Naomi. (1996). The 1991 International Assessment of Educational Progress in Mathematics and Sciences: The gender differences perspective. *Journal of Educational Psychology, 88,* 365–377.

Beller, Michal, & Gafni, Naomi. (2000). Can item format (multiple choice vs. open-ended) account for gender differences in mathematics achievement? *Sex Roles, 42,* 1–22.

Belsky, Janet K. (2001). Aging. In J. Worell (Ed.), *Encyclopedia of gender* (pp. 95–108). San Diego: Academic Press.

Belzer, E. G. (1981). Orgasmic expulsions of women: A review and heuristic inquiry. *Journal of Sex Research, 17,* 1–12.

Bem, Sandra L. (1974). The measurement of psychological androgyny. *Journal of Consulting and Clinical Psychology, 42,* 155–162.

Bem, Sandra L. (1975). Sex-role adaptability: One consequence of psychological androgyny. *Journal of Personality and Social Psychology, 31,* 634–643.

Bem, Sandra L. (1977). On the utility of alternative procedures for assessing psychological androgyny. *Journal of Consulting and Clinical Psychology, 45,* 196–205.

Bem, Sandra L. (1981). Gender schema theory: A cognitive account of sex-typing. *Psychological Review, 88,* 354–364.

Bem, Sandra L. (1983). Gender schema theory and its implications for child development: Raising gender-aschematic children in a gender-schematic society. *Signs, 8,* 598–616.

Bem, Sandra L. (1993). *The lenses of gender.* New Haven, CT: Yale University Press.

Bem, Sandra L., & Bem, Daryl J. (1970). Case study of nonconscious ideology: Training the woman to know her place. In D. J. Bem (Ed.), *Beliefs, attitudes, and human affairs.* Belmont, CA: Brooks/Cole.

Bem, Sandra, L., & Lenney, Ellen. (1976). Sex-typing and the avoidance of cross-sex behavior. *Journal of Personality and Social Psychology, 33,* 48–54.

Bem, Sandra L., Martyna, W., & Watson, C. (1976). Sex typing and androgyny: Further explorations of the expressive domain. *Journal of Personality and Social Psychology, 34,* 1016–1023.

Benenson, Joyce F., Morash, D., & Petrakos, H. (1998). Gender differences in emotional closeness between preschool children and their mothers. *Sex Roles, 38,* 975–986.

Bengtson, Vern L. (1985). Diversity and symbolism in grandparental roles. In V. L. Bengtson & J. F. Robertson (Eds.), *Grandparenthood.* Beverly Hills: Sage.

Berenbaum, Sheri A. (Ed.). (1998). *Gonadal hormones and sex differences in behavior.* Hillsdale, NJ: Lawrence Erlbaum.

Bergen, D. J., & Williams, J. E. (1991). Sex stereotypes in the United States revisited: 1972–1988. *Sex Roles, 24,* 413–423.

Berk, Richard A. (1993). What the scientific evidence shows: On the average, we can do no better than arrest. In R. J. Gelles & D. R. Loseke (Eds.), *Current controversies on family violence.* Newbury Park, CA: Sage.

Berkley, K., & Holdcroft (1999). Sex and gender differences in pain. In P. Wall & R. Melzack (Eds.), *Textbook of pain* (pp. 951–965). Edinburgh: Churchill Livingstone.

Berlin, Robin E., et al. (2001). Effects of the menstrual cycle on measures of personality in women with premenstrual syndrome: A preliminary study. *Journal of Clinical Psychiatry, 62,* 337–342.

Berman, Phyllis W., O'Nan, Barbara A., & Floyd, W. (1981). The double standard of aging and the social situation. *Sex Roles, 7,* 87–96.

Bernal, Guillermo, & Scharron-del-Rio, Maria R. (2001). Are empirically supported treatments valid for ethnic minorities? Toward an alternative approach for treatment research. *Cultural Diversity and Ethnic Minority Psychology, 7,* 328–342.

Bernard, Jesse. (1972). *The future of marriage.* New York: Bantam Books.

Bernstein, A. (1988, February 29). So you think you've come a long way, baby? *Business Week.*

Berry, R., & Sellman, J. D. (2001). Childhood adversity in alcohol- and drug-dependent women presenting to out-patient treatment. *Drug and Alcohol Review, 20,* 361–367.

Bervall, Victoria L. (1999). Toward a comprehensive theory of language and gender. *Language in Society, 28,* 272–293.

Betancourt, Hector, & Lopez, Steven R. (1993). The study of culture, ethnicity, and race in American psychology. *American Psychologist, 48,* 629–637.

Bettelheim, Bruno. (1962). *Symbolic wounds.* New York: Collier Books.

Betz, Nancy. (1993). Women's career development. In F. L. Denmark & M. A. Paludi (Eds.), *Psychology of women: Handbook of issues and theories* (pp. 627–684). Westport, CT: Greenwood.

Beyer, Sylvia. (1999). Gender differences in the accuracy of grade expectancies and evaluations. *Sex Roles, 41,* 279–296.

Bianchi, Suzanne M. (2000a). Maternal employment and time with children: Dramatic change or surprising continuity? *Demography, 37,* 401–414.

Bianchi, Suzanne. (2000b). Is anyone doing the housework? Trends in the gender division of household labor. *Social Forces, 79,* 191–228.

Bigler, Rebecca S. (1999). Psychological interventions designed to counter sexism in children: Empirical limitations and theoretical foundations. In W. Swann, J. Langlois, & L. Gilbert (Eds.), *Sexism and stereotypes in modern society: The gender science of Janet Taylor Spence* (pp. 129–152). Washington, DC: American Psychological Association.

Bimonte, Heather, Fitch, Roslyn, & Denenberg, Victor. (2000). Neonatal estrogen blockade prevents normal callosal responsiveness to estradiol in adulthood. *Developmental Brain Research, 122,* 149–155.

Bird, Chloe E. (1999). Gender, household labor, and psychological distress: The impact of the amount and division of housework. *Journal of Health and Social Behavior, 40,* 32–45.

Bird, Chloe E., & Ross, Catherine E. (1993). Houseworkers and paid workers: Qualities of the work and effects on personal control. *Journal of Marriage and the Family, 55,* 913–925.

Bishop, Katherine, & Wahlsten, Douglas. (1997). Sex differences in the human corpus callosum: Myth and reality. *Neuroscience and Biobehavioral Reviews, 21,* 581–601.

Bissada, Angela, & Briere, John. (2001). Child abuse, physical and sexual. In J. Worell (Ed.), *Encyclopedia of women and gender* (pp. 219–231). San Diego: Academic Press.

Blackwood, E. (1984). Sexuality and gender in certain Native American tribes: The case of the cross-gender females. *Signs: Journal of Women in Culture and Society, 10,* 27–42.

Blascovich, Jim, Spencer, S., Quinn, D., & Steele, C. (2001). African Americans and high blood pressure: The role of stereotype threat. *Psychological Science, 12,* 225–229.

Blaubergs, Maija S. (1978). Changing the sexist language: The theory behind the practice. *Psychology of Women Quarterly, 2,* 244–261.

Bleckman, Elaine A. (1980). Behavior therapies. In A. M. Brodsky & R. Hare-Mustin (Eds.), *Women and psychotherapy.* New York: Guilford.

Blehar, Mary, & Oren, D. (1995). Women's increased vulnerability to mood disorders: Integrating psychobiology and epidemiology. *Depression, 3,* 3–12.

Block, Jeanne H. (1978). Another look at sex differentiation in the socialization behaviors of mothers and fathers. In J. Sherman & F. Denmark (Eds.), *Psychology of women: Future directions of research.* New York: Psychological Dimensions.

Bloomfield, Kim. (1993). A comparison of alcohol consumption between lesbians and heterosexual women in an urban population. *Drug and Alcohol Dependence, 33,* 257–269.

Blumenthal, Paul, Johnson, Jane, & Stewart, Felicia. (2000). The approval of mifepristone (RU486) in the United States: What's wrong with this picture? *Medscape Women's Health, 5*(4). Retrieved from *www.medscape.com* on November 8, 2000.

Blumenthal, Susan J., & Wood, Susan F. (1997). Women's health care: Federal initiatives, policies, and directions. In S. Gallant, G. Keita, & R. Royak-Schaler (Eds.), *Health care for women: Psychological, social, and behavioral influences* (pp. 3–10). Washington, DC: American Psychological Association.

Blumstein, Philip W., & Schwartz, Pepper. (1976). Bisexual women. In J. P. Wiseman (Ed.), *The social psychology of sex.* New York: Harper & Row.

Blumstein, Philip W., & Schwartz, Pepper. (1983). *American couples.* New York: William Morrow.

Bodine, Ann. (1975b). Androcentrism in prescriptive grammar: Singular "they," sex indefinite "he," and "he or she." *Language in Society, 4,* 129–146.

Bonaparte, Marie. (1953). *Female sexuality.* New York: International Universities Press. (Reprinted 1965. New York: Grove Press.)

Bond, James T., Galinsky, Ellen, & Swanberg, J. (1998). *The 1997 national study of the changing workforce.* New York: Families and Work Institute.

Bonebright, T., Thompson, J., & Leger, D. (1996). Gender stereotypes in the expression and perception of vocal affect. *Sex Roles, 34,* 429–445.

Bootzin, R. R., & Natsoulas, T. (1965). Evidence for perceptual defense uncontaminated by response bias. *Journal of Personality and Social Psychology, 1,* 461–468.

Boskind-Lodahl, Marlene. (1976). Cinderella's stepsisters: A feminist perspective on anorexia nervosa and bulimia. *Signs, 2,* 120–146.

Boskind-Lodahl, Marlene, & Sirlin, Joyce. (1977, March). The gorging-purging syndrome. *Psychology Today,* p. 50.

Bosselman, Beulah C. (1960). Castration anxiety and phallus envy: A reformulation. *Psychiatric Quarterly, 34,* 252–259.

Boston Lesbian Psychologies Collective. (1987). *Lesbian psychologies.* Urbana: University of Illinois Press.

Boston Women's Health Book Collective. (1976). *Our bodies, ourselves.* New York: Simon & Schuster.

Boston Women's Health Book Collective. (1998). *Our bodies ourselves for the new century: A book by and for women.* New York: Touchstone.

Botkin, Darla R., Weeks, M., & Morris, J. (2000). Changing marriage role expectations: 1961–1996. *Sex Roles, 42,* 933–942.

Bowker, Lee H., Arbitell, Michelle, & McFerron, J. Richard. (1988). On the relationship between wife beating and child abuse. In K. Yllo & M. Bogard (Eds.), *Feminist perspective on wife abuse.* Newbury Park, CA: Sage.

Boyd, Carol J. (1989). Mothers and daughters: A discussion of theory and research. *Journal of Marriage and the Family, 51,* 291–301.

Brabant, Sarah, & Mooney, Linda. (1986). Sex role stereotyping in the Sunday comics: Ten years later. *Sex Roles, 14,* 141–148.

Brabant, Sarah, & Mooney, Linda A. (1997). Sex role stereotyping in the Sunday comics: A twenty year update. *Sex Roles, 37,* 269–282.

Brace, Laura, & Davidson, Jula O. (2000). Minding the gap: General and substantive theorizing on power and exploitation. *Signs: Journal of Women in Culture and Society, 25,* 1045–1050.

Brackbill, Yvonne, & Schroeder, Kerri. (1980). Circumcision, gender differences and neonatal behavior: An update. *Developmental Psychobiology, 13,* 607–614.

Bradshaw, Carla K. (1994). Asian and Asian-American women: Historical and political considerations in psychotherapy. In L. Comas-Diaz & B. Greene (Eds.), *Women of color.* New York: Guilford.

Brady, I. P., & Rieger, W. (1975). Behavioral treatment in anorexia nervosa. In T. Thompson & W. Dockens (Eds.), *Applications of behavior modification.* New York: Academic Press.

Brady, Katherine. (1979). *Father's days.* New York: Dell.

Breedlove, S. M. (1994). Sexual differentiation of the human nervous system. *Annual Review of Psychology, 45,* 389–418.

Breitenbecher, K. H. (2000). Sexual assault on college campuses: Is an ounce of prevention enough? *Applied and Preventive Psychology, 9,* 23–52.

Bremer, Nancy D. McMahon, P., Warren, C., & Douglas, K. (1999). Forced sexual intercourse and associated health-risk behaviors among female college students in the United States. *Journal of Consulting and Clinical Psychology, 67,* 252–259.

Bremner, J. Douglas, Shobe, K., & Kihlstrom, J. (2000). False memories in women with self-reported childhood sexual abuse. *Psychological Science, 11,* 333–337.

Bretherton, Inge, Fritz, J., Zahn-Waxler, C., & Ridgeway, D. (1986). Learning to talk about emotions: A functionalist perspective. *Child Development, 57,* 529–548.

Brewster, Karin L., & Padavic, Irene. (2000). Change in gender-ideology, 1977–1996: The contributions of intracohort change and population turnover. *Journal of Marriage and the Family, 62,* 477–487.

Brim, Orville I. (1976). Theories of the male mid-life crisis. *Counseling Psychologist, 6*(1), 2–9.

Brinton, Louise A., & Schairer, Catherine. (1997). Postmenopausal hormone-replacement therapy—Time for a reappraisal? *New England Journal of Medicine, 336,* 1821–1822.

Britton, Karen T., & Koob, George F. (1998). Premenstrual steroids? *Nature, 392,* 869–870.

Broder, M. S., Kanouse, D., Mittman, B., & Bernstein, S. (2000). The appropriateness of recommendations for hysterectomy. *Obstetrics and Gynecology, 95,* 199–205.

Broderick, P. (1998). Early adolescent gender differences in the use of ruminative and distracting coping strategies. *Journal of Early Adolescence, 18,* 173–191.

Brody, Leslie R. (1993). On understanding gender differences in the expression of emotion: Gender roles, socialization, and language. In S. Ablon et al. (Eds.), *Human feelings: Explorations in affect development and meaning* (pp. 89–121). Hillsdale, NJ: Analytic Press.

Brody, Leslie R. (1996). Gender, emotional expression, and parent-child boundaries. In R. Kavanaugh et al. (Eds.), *Emotion: Interdisciplinary perspectives* (pp. 139–170). Mahwah, NJ: Erlbaum.

Brody, Leslie R. (1997). Gender and emotion: Beyond stereotypes. *Journal of Social Issues, 53,* 369–394.

Brody, Leslie. (1999). *Gender, emotion, and the family.* Cambridge, MA: Harvard University Press.

Brody, Leslie R. (2000). The socialization of gender differences in emotional expression: Display rules, infant temperament, and differentiation. In A. Fischer (Ed.), *Gender and emotion.* Cambridge, UK: Cambridge University Press.

Brody, Leslie R., & Hall, Judith A. (2000). Gender emotion, and expression. In M. Lewis & J. Haviland-Jones (Eds.), *Handbook of emotions.* New York: Guilford.

Brody, Leslie R., Hay, Deborah H., & Vandewater, Elizabeth. (1990). Gender, gender role identity, and children's reported feelings toward the same and opposite sex. *Sex Roles, 23,* 363–387.

Brody, Leslie R., Hay, D., & Vandewater, E. (1990). Gender, gender role identity, and children's reported feelings toward the same and opposite sex. *Sex Roles, 23,* 363–385.

Brooks, Virginia R. (1981). *Minority stress and lesbian women.* Lexington, MA: Lexington Books.

Broverman, Inge K., Broverman, D. M., Clarkson, F. E., Rosenkrantz, P. S., & Vogel, S. R. (1970). Sex role stereotypes and clinical judgments of mental health. *Journal of Consulting and Clinical Psychology, 34,* 1–7.

Broverman, Inge K., Vogel, Susan R., Broverman, D. M., Clarkson, F. E., & Rosenkrantz, P. S. (1972). Sex role stereotypes: A current appraisal. *Journal of Social Issues, 28,* 59–78.

Brown, Lyn M. (1998). *Raising their voices: The politics of girls' anger.* Cambridge, MA: Harvard University Press.

Brown, Lyn M., & Gilligan, Carol. (1992). *Meeting at the crossroads: Women's psychology and girls' development.* Cambridge, MA: Harvard University Press.

Brown, Ryan P., & Josephs, Robert A. (1999). A burden of proof: Stereotype relevance and gender differences in math performance. *Journal of Personality and Social Psychology, 76,* 246–257.

Browne, Angela. (1993). Violence against women by male partners. *American Psychologist, 48,* 1077–1087.

Brownell, K. D., & Foreyt, J. P. (Eds.). (1986). *Physiology, psychology, and treatment of eating disorders.* New York: Basic Books.

Brownmiller, Susan. (1975). *Against our will: Men, women, and rape.* New York: Simon & Schuster.

Buchanan, K. M. (1986). *Apache women warriors.* El Paso, TX: Texas Western Press.

Budoff, Penny W. (1981). *No more menstrual cramps and other good news.* New York: Penguin Books.

Buhrmester, Duane. (1998). Need fulfillment, interpersonal competence, and the developmental contexts of early adolescent friendship. In W. Bukowski et al. (Eds.), *The company they keep: Friendship in childhood and adolescence* (pp. 158–185). New York: Cambridge University Press.

Bulosan, Carlos. (1960). *Sound of falling light: Letters in exile.* Quezon City: University of the Philippines.

Buntaine, Roberta L., & Costenbader, Virginia K. (1997). Self-reported differences in the experience and expression of anger between girls and boys. *Sex Roles, 36,* 625–638.

Burch, Beverly. (1993). *On intimate terms: The psychology of difference in lesbian relationships.* Urbana: University of Illinois Press.

Bureau of Labor Statistics (1999, January). Employment and earnings.

Burgess, Ann W., & Holmstrom, Lynda L. (1974a). Rape trauma syndrome. *American Journal of Psychiatry, 131,* 981–986.

Burt, Martha. (1980). Cultural myths and support for rape. *Journal of Personality and Social Psychology, 38,* 217–230.

Burt, Martha R., & Estep, Rhoda E. (1981). Apprehension and fear: Learning a sense of sexual vulnerability. *Sex Roles, 7,* 511–522.

Burton, Linda M. (1992). Black grandparents rearing children of drug-addicted parents: Stressors, outcomes, and social service needs. *Gerontologist, 32,* 744–751.

Buss, David M. (1989). Sex differences in human mate preferences: Evolutionary hypotheses tested in 37 cultures. *Behavioral and Brain Sciences, 12,* 1–14.

Buss, David M. (1991). Evolutionary personality psychology. *Annual Review of Psychology, 42,* 459–491.

Buss, David M. (1995). Evolutionary psychology: A new paradigm for psychological science. *Psychological Inquiry, 6,* 1–30.

Buss, David M., & Schmitt, David P. (1993). Sexual strategies theory: An evolutionary perspective on human mating. *Psychological Review, 100,* 204–232.

Bussey, Kay, & Bandura, Albert. (1992). Self-regulatory mechanisms governing gender development. *Child Development, 63,* 1236–1250.

Bussey, Kay, & Bandura Albert. (1999). Social cognitive theory of gender development and differentiation. *Psychological Review, 106,* 676–713.

Butow, Phyllis, Beumont, Pierre, & Touyz, Stephen. (1993). Cognitive processes in dieting disorders. *International Journal of Eating Disorders, 14,* 319–329.

Byers, E. Sandra. (1996). How well does the traditional sexual script explain sexual coercion? Review of a program of research. *Journal of Psychology and Human Sexuality, 8,* 7–25.

Byne, William. (1996). Biology and homosexuality. In R. Cabaj & T. Stein (Eds.), *Textbook of homosexuality and mental health* (pp. 129–146). Washington, DC: American Psychiatric Press.

Byne, William, & Parsons, B. (1993). Human sexual orientation: The biologic theories reappraised. *Archives of General Psychiatry, 50,* 228–239.

Byrnes, James P., Miller, D., & Schafer, W. (1999). Gender differences in risk taking: A meta-analysis. *Psychological Bulletin, 125,* 367–383.

Cachelin Fary M., Veisel, Catherin, Barzegarnazari, Emilia, & Striegel-Moore, Ruth H. (2000). Disordered eating, acculturation, and treatment-seeking in a community sample of Hispanic, Asian, Black, and White women. *Psychology of Women Quarterly, 24,* 244–253.

Cameron, Deborah. (1998). Gender, language and discourse: A review essay. *Signs: Journal of Women in Culture and Society, 23,* 945–973.

Campbell, Carole A. (1995). Male gender roles and sexuality: Implications for women's AIDS risk and prevention. *Social Science and Medicine, 41,* 197–210.

Campbell, Katy. (2000). Gender and educational technologies: Relational frameworks for learning design. *Journal of Educational Multimedia and Hypermedia, 9,* 131–149.

Canary, Daniel J., & Dindia, Kathryn. (Eds.). (1998). *Sex differences and similarities in communication.* Mahwah, NJ: Erlbaum.

Caplan, Paula. (1995). *How do they decide who is normal?* Reading, MA: Addison-Wesley.

Caplan, Paula. (2001). Motherhood: Its changing face. In J. Worell (Ed.), *Encyclopedia of gender* (pp. 783–794). San Diego: Academic Press.

Caplan, Paula J., & Caplan, Jeremy B. (1994). *Thinking critically about research on sex and gender.* New York: Harper Collins.

Carani, Cesare et al. (1990). Effects of androgen treatment in impotent men with normal and low levels of free testosterone. *Archives of Sexual Behavior, 19,* 223–234.

Carey, Michael P., et al. (2000). Using information, motivational enhancement, and skills training to reduce the risk of HIV infection for low-income urban women: A second randomized clinical trial. *Health Psychology, 19,* 3–11.

Carli, Linda L. (1990). Gender, language, and influence. *Journal of Personality and Social Psychology, 59,* 941–951.

Carli, Linda L., & Bukatko, Danuta. (2000). Gender, communication, and social influence: A developmental perspective. T. Eckes & H. Trautner (Eds.), *The developmental social psychology of gender* (pp. 295–332). Mahwah, NJ: Erlbaum.

Carlo, Gustavo, Raffaelli, M., Laible, D., & Meyer, K. (1999). Why are girls less physically aggressive than boys? Personality and parenting mediators of physical aggression. *Sex Roles, 40,* 711–730.

Carlson, Rae. (1971). Where is the person in personality research? *Psychological Bulletin, 75,* 203–219.

Carnes, Molly. (2001). Humor. In J. Worell (Ed.), *Encyclopedia of women and gender* (pp. 601–609). San Diego: Academic Press.

Carroll, Janell, Volk, Kari, & Hyde, Janet S. (1985). Differences between males and females in motives for engaging in sexual intercourse. *Archives of Sexual Behavior, 14,* 131–139.

Carter, C. Sue. (1992). Hormonal influences on human sexual behavior. In J. B. Becker et al. (Eds.), *Behavioral endocrinology* (pp. 131–142). Cambridge, MA: MIT Press.

Carter, D. B. (1987). The roles of peers in sex role socialization. In D. B. Carter (Ed.), *Current conceptions of sex roles and stereotyping* (pp. 101–121). New York: Praeger.

Caspi, Avshalom, Lynam, D., Moffitt, T., & Silva, P. (1993). Unraveling girls' delinquency: Biological, dispositional, and contextual contributions to adolescent misbehavior. *Developmental Psychology, 29,* 19–30.

Cass, Vivienne C. (1979). Homosexual identity formation: A theoretical model. *Journal of Homosexuality, 4,* 219–235.

Centers for Disease Control. (2002). HIV/AIDS among US women: Minority and young women at continuing risk. Available online at *www.cdc.gov/hiv/pubs/facts/women.htm.*

Cervantes, Christi A., & Callanan, Maureen A. (1998). Labels and explanations in mother-child emotion talk: Age and gender differentiation. *Developmental Psychology, 34,* 88–98.

Chafetz, Janet S. (1997). Feminist theory and sociology. *Annual Review of Sociology, 23,* 97–120.

Chan, Connie S. (1993). Issues of identity development among Asian-American lesbians and gay men. In L. D. Garnets & D. C. Kimmel (Eds.), *Psychological perspectives on lesbian and gay male experience* (pp. 376–387). New York: Columbia University Press.

Chapman, Heather, Hobfoll, Stevan, & Ritter, Christian. (1997). Partners' stress underestimations lead to women's distress: A study of pregnant inner-city women. *Journal of Personality and Social Psychology, 73,* 418–425.

Chen, C. L., Weiss, N. S., Newcomb, P., Barlow, W., & White, E. (2002). Hormone replacement therapy in relation to breast cancer. *Journal of the American Medical Association, 287,* 734–741.

Cherlin, Andrew J. (1992). *Marriage, divorce, remarriage* (rev. ed.). Cambridge, MA: Harvard University Press.

Cherlin, Andrew, & Furstenberg, Frank F. (1985). Styles and strategies of grandparenting. In V. L. Bengtson & J. F. Robertson (Eds.), *Grandparenthood.* Beverly Hills: Sage.

Cherry, Frances, & Deaux, Kay. (1978). Fear of success versus fear of gender-inappropriate behavior. *Sex Roles, 4,* 97–102.

Chesler, Phyllis. (1972). *Women and madness.* Garden City, NY: Doubleday.

Children Now. (2000). Top-selling video games "unhealthy" for girls. Retrieved from *www.childrennow.org* on January 3, 2001.

Chin, Jean L., De La Cancela, Victor, & Jenkins, Yvonne M. (1993). *Diversity in psychotherapy: The politics of race, ethnicity, and gender.* Westport, CT: Praeger.

Chodorow, Nancy. (1978). *The reproduction of mothering.* Berkeley: University of California Press.

Choi, E. J., et al. (2001). Low-density DNA array-coupled to PCR differential display identifies new estrogen-responsive genes during the postnatal differentiation of the rat hypothalamus. *Molecular Brain Research, 97,* 115–128.

Chrisler, Joan, et al. (1994). Menstrual joy: The construct and its consequences. *Psychology of Women Quarterly, 18,* 375–388.

Christensen, Kimberly A., Stephens, Mary Ann, & Townsend, Aloen L. (1998). Mastery in women's multiple roles and well-being: Adult daughters providing care to impaired parents. *Health Psychology, 17,* 163–171.

Clark, Kenneth B., & Clark, Mamie P. (1947). Racial identification and preferences in Negro children. In T. M. Newcomb & E. L. Hartley (Eds.), *Readings in social psychology.* New York: Holt, Rinehart & Winston.

Clark, Ruth A. (1998). A comparison of topics and objectives in a cross section of young men's and women's everyday conversations. In D. Canary & K. Dindia (Eds.), *Sex differences and similarities in communication* (pp. 303–320). Mahwah, NJ: Erlbaum.

Cobb, Nancy J., et al. (1982). The influence of televised models on toy preference in children. *Sex Roles, 8,* 1075–1080.

Cohen, Jacob. (1969). *Statistical power analysis for the behavioral sciences.* New York: Academic Press.

Cohen, T. F. (1993). What do fathers provide? In J. C. Hood (Ed.), *Men, work, and family.* Newbury Park, CA: Sage.

Cole, David A., Martin, J., Peeke, L., Seroczynski, A., & Fier, J. (1999). Children's over- and underestimation of academic competence: A longitudinal study of gender differences, depression, and anxiety. *Child Development, 70,* 459–473.

Coleman, Eli. (1982). Developmental stages of the coming out process. In W. Paul et al. (Eds.),

Homosexuality: Social, psychological, and biological issues. Beverly Hills: Sage.

Coley, Rebekah L. (2001). (In)visible men: Emerging research on low-income, unmarried, and minority fathers. *American Psychologist, 56,* 743–753.

Collaer, Marcia L., & Hines, Melissa. (1995). Human behavioral sex differences: A role for gonadal hormones during early development? *Psychological Bulletin, 118,* 55–107.

College Board. (2001). College-bound seniors: A profile of SAT program test takers. Available online at *www.collegeboard.com.*

Collins, B. (1985). Psychological implications of sex differences in attitudes toward computers: Results of a survey. *International Journal of Women's Studies, 8,* 207–213.

Collins, Karen S., Rowland, Diane, Salganicoff, Alina, & Chait, Elizabeth. (1994). Assessing and improving women's health. In C. Costello & A. J. Stone (Eds.), *The American woman 1994–95.* New York: Norton.

Collins, Patricia H. (1989). The social construction of Black feminist thought. *Signs: Journal of Women in Culture and Society, 14,* 745–773.

Coltrane, Scott. (2000). Research on household labor: Modeling and measuring the social embeddedness of routine family work. *Journal of Marriage and the Family, 62,* 1208–1233.

Coltrane, Scott, & Messineo, M. (2000). The perpetuation of subtle prejudice: Race and gender imagery in 1990s television advertising. *Sex Roles, 42,* 363–390.

Comas-Diaz, Lillian. (1987). Feminist therapy with mainland Puerto Rican women. *Psychology of Women Quarterly, 11,* 461–474.

Comas-Diaz, Lillian. (1991). Feminism and diversity in psychology: The case of women of color. *Psychology of Women Quarterly, 15,* 597–610.

Comas-Diaz, Lillian. (2001). Hispanics, Latinos, or Americanos: The evolution of identity. *Cultural Diversity and Ethnic Minority Psychology, 7,* 115–120.

Comas-Diaz, Lillian, & Greene, Beverly. (1994). *Women of color: Integrating ethnic and gender identities in psychotherapy.* New York: Guilford.

Comber, Chris, Colley, A., Hargreaves, D., & Dorn, L. (1997). The effects of age, gender, and computer experience upon computer attitudes. *Educational Research, 39,* 123–133.

Compas, Bruce E., & Luecken, Linda. (2002). Psychological adjustment to breast cancer. *Current Directions in Psychological Science, 11,* 111–114.

Condry, J. C., & Condry, S. (1976). Sex differences: A study of the eye of the beholder. *Child Development, 47,* 812–819.

Conkright, Lea, Flannagan, D., & Dykes, J. (2000). Effects of pronoun type and gender role consistency on children's recall and interpretation of stories. *Sex Roles, 43,* 481–498.

Constantinople, Anne. (1973). Masculinity-femininity: An exception to a famous dictum. *Psychological Bulletin, 80,* 389–407.

Conway, Michael, & Vartanian, L. (2000). A status account of gender stereotypes: Beyond communality and agency. *Sex Roles, 43,* 181–200.

Cooper, Joel, & Stone, Jeff. (1996). Gender, computer-assisted learning, and anxiety: With a little help from a friend. *Journal of Educational Computing Research, 15,* 67–91.

Cordaro, L., & Ison, I. R. (1963). Psychology of the scientist: X. Observer bias in classical conditioning of the planarian. *Psychological Reports, 13,* 787–789.

Cordova, Matthew J., Cunningham, Lauren, Carlson, Charles, & Andrykowski, Michael. (2001). Posttraumatic growth following breast cancer: A controlled comparison study. *Health Psychology, 20,* 176–185.

Cortina, Lilia M. (2001). Assessing sexual harassment among Latinas: Development of an instrument. *Cultural Diversity and Ethnic Minority Psychology, 7,* 164–181.

Cortina, Lilia M., Swan, Suzanne, Fitzgerald, Louise F., & Waldo, Craig. (1998). Sexual harassment and assault: Chilling the climate for women in academia. *Psychology of Women Quarterly, 22,* 419–441.

Cosentino, Clare E., Meyer-Bahlburg, Heino, Alpert, Judith, Weinberg, Sharon, & Gaines, Richard. (1995). Sexual behavior problems and psychopathology symptoms in sexually abused girls. *Journal of the American Academy of Child and Adolescent Psychiatry, 34,* 1033–1042.

Costello, Cynthia B., & Stone, Anne J. (Eds.). (2001). *The American woman 2001–2002: Getting to the top.* New York: Norton.

Courtenay, Will H. (2000). Engendering health: A social constructionist examination of men's health beliefs and behaviors. *Psychology of Men and Masculinity, 1,* 4–15.

Cowell, P. E., Allen, L. S., Zalatimo, N. S., & Denenberg, V. H. (1992). A developmental study of sex and age interactions in the human corpus callosum. *Developmental Brain Research, 66,* 187–192.

Craig, Steve. (Ed.). (1992). *Men, masculinity, and the media.* Newbury Park, CA: Sage.

Crandall, Christian S., Tsang, J., Goldman, S., & Pennington, J. (1999). Newsworthy moral dilemmas: Justice, caring, and gender. *Sex Roles, 40,* 187–210.

Crandall, Virginia C. (1969). Sex differences in expectancy of intellectual and academic reinforcement. In C. P. Smith (Ed.), *Achievement-related motives in children.* New York: Russell Sage Foundation.

Crawford, Mary. (1995). *Talking difference.* London: Sage.

Crawford, Mary. (2001). Gender and language. In R. Unger (Ed.), *Handbook of the psychology of women and gender* (pp. 228–244). New York: Wiley.

Crawford, Mary, & English L. (1984). Generic versus specific inclusion of women in language: Effects on recall. *Journal of Psycholinguistic Research, 13,* 373–381.

Crawford, Mary, & Kimmel, Ellen. (1999). Promoting methodological diversity in feminist research. *Psychology of Women Quarterly, 23,* 1–6.

Crawford, Mary, Stark, Amy C., & Renner, Catherine H. (1998). The meaning of Ms.: Social assimilation of a gender concept. *Psychology of Women Quarterly, 22,* 197–208.

Cromwell, R. E., & Ruiz, R. A. (1979). The myth of macho dominance in decision making within Mexican and Chicano families. *Hispanic Journal of Behavioral Sciences, 1,* 355–373.

Crose, Royda, Leventhal, Elaine A., Haug, Marie R., & Burns, Edith A. (1997). The challenges of aging. In S. Gallant, G. Keita, & R. Royak-Schaler (Eds.), *Health care for women: Psychological, social, and behavioral influences* (pp. 221–234). Washington, DC: American Psychological Association.

Crouter, Ann, Manke, B., & McHale, S. (1995). The family context of gender intensification in early adolescence. *Child Development, 66,* 317–329.

Cyranowski, Jill M., Frank, E., Young, E., & Shear, K. (2000). Adolescent onset of the gender differences in lifetime rates of major depression. *Archives of General Psychiatry, 57,* 21–27.

Dalton, Katharina. (1964). *The premenstrual syndrome.* Springfield, IL: Charles C. Thomas.

Dalton, Katharina. (1966). The influence of mother's menstruation on her child. *Proceedings of the Royal Society for Medicine, 59,* 1014.

Daneal, J. (1975). *A definition of fatherhood as expressed by black fathers.* Unpublished doctoral dissertation, University of Pittsburgh.

Dansky, B., & Kilpatrick, D. (1997). Effects of sexual harassment. In W. O'Donohue (Ed.), *Sexual harassment: Theory, research, and treatment* (pp. 151–174). Boston: Allyn & Bacon.

Darling, Carol A., Davidson, J. Kenneth, & Conway-Welch, C. (1990). Female ejaculation: Perceived origins, the Gräfenberg spot/area, and sexual responsiveness. *Archives of Sexual Behavior, 19,* 29–48.

Dasgupta, Shamita D. (1998). Gender roles and cultural continuity in the Asian Indian immigrant community in the U.S. *Sex Roles, 38,* 953–974.

Daubman, Kimberly A., & Sigall, Harold. (1997). Gender differences in perceptions of how others are affected by self-disclosure of achievement. *Sex Roles, 37,* 73–90.

Davey, F. Heather. (1998). Young women's expected and preferred patterns of employment and child care. *Sex Roles, 38,* 95–102.

David, Henry P. (1992). Born unwanted: Long-term developmental effects of denied abortion. *Journal of Social Issues, 48*(3), 163–181.

David, Henry P., Dytrych, Zdenek, Matejcek, Zdenek, & Schuller, Vratislav. (Eds.). (1988). *Born unwanted: Developmental effects of denied abortion.* New York: Springer.

David, Henry P., & Matejcek, Z. (1981). Children born to women denied abortion: An update. *Family Planning Perspectives, 13,* 32–34.

Davidson, Richard J., Jackson, D., & Kalin, N. (2000). Emotion, plasticity, context, and regulation: Perspectives from affective neuroscience. *Psychological Bulletin, 126,* 890–909.

Davis, Angela. (1981). *Women, race and class.* New York: Random House.

Davis, Donald M. (1990). Portrayals of women in prime-time network television: Some demographic characteristics. *Sex Roles, 23,* 325–332.

Davis, Elizabeth Gould. (1971). *The first sex.* New York: G. P. Putnam's Sons.

Davis, M., Matthews, Karen, & Twamley, E. (1999). Is life more difficult on Mars or Venus? A meta-analytic review of sex differences in major and minor life events. *Annals of Behavioral Medicine, 21,* 83–97.

Davis, Teresa L. (1995). Gender differences in masking negative emotions: Ability or motivation? *Developmental Psychology, 31,* 660–667.

Dawson, D. A., Grant, B. F., & Hartford, T. C. (1995). Variation in the association of alcohol consumption and five DSM-IV alcohol problems domains. *Alcoholism: Clinical and Experimental Research, 19,* 66–74.

Day, Randal. (1992). The transition to first intercourse among racially and culturally diverse youth. *Journal of Marriage and the Family, 54,* 749–762.

Dean, Karol E., & Malamuth, Neil M. (1997). Characteristics of men who aggress sexually and of men who imagine aggressing: Risk and moderating variables. *Journal of Personality and Social Psychology, 72,* 449–455.

Deal, Jennifer J., & Stevenson, M. (1998). Perceptions of female and male managers in the 1990s: Plus ça change . . . *Sex Roles, 38,* 287–300.

Deaux, Kay, & Emswiller, T. (1974). Explanations of successful performance on sex-linked tasks: What is skill for the male is luck for the female. *Journal of Personality and Social Psychology, 29,* 80–85.

Deaux, Kay, & Kite, Mary. (1993). Gender stereotypes. In F. L. Denmark & M. A. Paludi (Eds.), *Psychology of women: Handbook of issues and theories.* Westport, CT: Greenwood.

Deaux, Kay, & Lewis, Laurie L. (1983). Components of gender stereotypes. *Psychological Documents, 13,* 25 (Ms. No. 2583).

Deaux, Kay, & Lewis, Laurie L. (1984). Structure of gender stereotypes: Interrelationships among components and gender label. *Journal of Personality and Social Psychology, 46,* 991–1004.

DeBellis, Michael D., et al. (2001). Sex differences in brain maturation during childhood and adolescence. *Cerebral Cortex, 11,* 552–557.

De Judicibus, Margaret, & McCabe, Marita P. (2001). Blaming the target of sexual harassment: Impact of gender role, sexist attitudes, and work role. *Sex Roles, 44,* 401–418.

Delacoste-Utamsing, C., & Holloway, R. L. (1982). Sexual dimorphism in the human corpus callosum. *Science, 216,* 1431–1432.

DeLamater, John D., & Hyde, Janet S. (1998). Essentialism versus social constructionism in the study of human sexuality. *Journal of Sex Research, 35,* 10–18.

DeLamater, John D., & MacCorquodale, Patricia. (1979). *Premarital sexuality: Attitudes, relationships, behavior.* Madison: University of Wisconsin Press.

De Lisi, Richard, & McGillicuddy–De Lisi, Ann. (2002). Sex differences in mathematical abilities and achievement. In A. McGillicuddy–De Lisi & R. De Lisi (Eds.), *Biology, society, and behavior:*

The development of sex differences in cognition (pp. 155–182). Westport, CT: Ablex.

Denmark, Florence L. (1993). Women, leadership, and empowerment. *Psychology of Women Quarterly, 17,* 343–356.

Denmark, Florence L., & Goodfield, Helen M. (1978). A second look at adolescence theories. *Sex Roles, 4,* 375–380.

Denmark, Florence, Russo, Nancy F., Frieze, Irene H., & Sechzer, Jeri A. (1988). Guidelines for avoiding sexism in psychological research. *American Psychologist, 43,* 582–585.

Denzin, N., & Lincoln, Y. (1994). *Handbook of qualitative methods.* Thousand Oaks, CA: Sage.

Department of Defense. (2001). Trends in enlistment propensity. Available online at *www.defenselink.mil.*

Desmarais, Serge, & Curtis, J. (1997). Gender difference in pay histories and views on pay entitlement among university students. *Sex Roles, 37,* 623–642.

Deutsch, A. (1944). The first U.S. census of the insane (1840) and its use as pro-slavery propaganda. *Bulletin of the History of Medicine, 15,* 469–482.

Deutsch, Francine M., LeBaron, Dorothy, & Fryer, Maury M. (1987). What is in a smile? *Psychology of Women Quarterly, 11,* 341–352.

Deutsch, Francine M., & Saxon, Susan E. (1998). The double standard of praise and criticism for mothers and fathers. *Psychology of Women Quarterly, 22,* 665–684.

Deutsch, Helene. (1924). The psychology of women in relation to the functions of reproduction. *International Journal of Psychoanalysis, 6.*

Deutsch, Helene. (1944). *The psychology of women.* New York: Grune & Stratton.

DeZolt, Denise, & Hull, Stephen. (2001). Classroom and school climate. In J. Worell (Ed.), *Encyclopedia of gender* (pp. 246–264). San Diego: Academic Press.

Diamond, Lisa M. (1998). Development of sexual orientation among adolescent and young adult women. *Developmental Psychology, 34,* 1085–1095.

Dickson, Lynda. (1993). The future of marriage and the family in Black America. *Journal of Black Studies, 23,* 472–491.

Diehm, Cynthia, & Ross, Margo. (1988). Battered women. In S. Rix (Ed.), *The American woman 1988–89.* New York: Norton.

Diekman, Amanda B., & Eagly, Alice H. (2000). Stereotypes as dynamic constructs: Women and men of the past, present, and future. *Personality and Social Psychology Bulletin, 26,* 1171–1188.

Diemer, Matthew A. (2002). Constructions of provider role identity among African American men: An exploratory study. *Cultural Diversity and Ethnic Minority Psychology, 8,* 30–40.

Dietz, Tracy L. (1998). An examination of violence and gender-role portrayals in video games: Implications for gender socialization and aggressive behavior. *Sex Roles, 38,* 425–442.

Dinwiddie, S., et al. (2000). Early sexual abuse and lifetime psychopathology: A co-twin-control study. *Psychological Medicine, 30,* 41–52.

Dion, Kenneth L., & Cota, Albert A. (1991). The Ms. stereotype. *Psychology of Women Quarterly, 15,* 403–410.

Division 44/Committee on Lesbian, Gay, and Bisexual Concerns. (2000). Guidelines for psychotherapy with lesbian, gay, and bisexual clients. *American Psychologist, 55,* 1440–1451.

Donelson, Elaine. (1997). Becoming a single woman. In E. Donelson & J. Gullahorn (Eds.), *Women: A psychological perspective.* New York: Wiley.

Dorgan, J. F., et al. (2001). Serum hormones and the alcohol–breast cancer association in postmenopausal women. *Journal of the National Cancer Institute, 93,* 710–715.

Doss, Brian D., & Hopkins, J. R. (1998). The multicultural masculinity ideology scale: Validation from three cultural perspectives. *Sex Roles, 38,* 719–742.

Douvan, Elizabeth. (1970). New sources of conflicts in females at adolescence and early adulthood. In J. Bardwick, E. Douvan, M. Horner, & D. Gutman (Eds.), *Feminine personality and conflict.* Belmont, CA: Brooks/Cole.

Douvan, Elizabeth, & Adelson, J. (1966). *The adolescent experience.* New York: Wiley.

Dovidio, J. F., Ellyson, S. L., Keating, C. F., Heltman, K., & Brown, C. E. (1988). The relationship of social power to visual displays of dominance between men and women. *Journal of Personality and Social Psychology, 54,* 233–242.

Doyle, James A. (1989). *The male experience* (2nd ed.). Dubuque, IA: William C. Brown.

Downey, J., Ehrhardt, A., Schiffman, M., Dyrenfuth, I., & Becker, J. (1987). Sex hormones in lesbian and heterosexual women. *Hormones and Behavior, 21,* 347–357.

Drees, Deanne E., & Phye, Gary D. (2001). Gender representation in children's language arts computer software. *Journal of Educational Research, 95,* 49–55.

DuBois, Cathy L., Knappe, D., Faley, R., & Kustis, G. (1998). An empirical examination of same- and other-gender sexual harassment in the workplace. *Sex Roles, 39,* 731–750.

Dugger, Karen. (1988). Social location and gender-role attitudes: A comparison of Black and White women. *Gender & Society, 2,* 425–448.

Dunn, Judith, Bretherton, I., & Munn, P. (1987). Conversations about feeling states between mothers and their children. *Developmental Psychology, 23,* 132–139.

Durik, Amanda, Hyde, Janet S., Marks, A., Roy, A., Anaya, D., & Schultz, G. (2002). Ethnicity and gender stereotypes of emotion. Submitted for publication.

Dweck, Carol, Goetz, Therese E., & Strauss, Nan L. (1980). Sex differences in learned helplessness: IV. An experimental and naturalistic study of failure generalization and its mediators. *Journal of Personality and Social Psychology, 38,* 441–452.

Dworkin, Andrea. (1987). *Intercourse.* New York: Free Press.

Dziech, Billie W., & Weiner, Linda. (1983). *The lecherous professor: Sexual harassment.* Boston: Beacon.

Eagly, Alice H. (1978). Sex differences in influenceability. *Psychological Bulletin, 85,* 86–116.

Eagly, Alice H. (1987). *Sex differences in social behavior: A social role interpretation.* Hillsdale, NJ: Erlbaum.

Eagly, Alice H., & Carli, Linda L. (1981). Sex of researchers and sex-typed communications as determinants of sex differences in influenceability: A meta-analysis of social influence studies. *Psychological Bulletin, 90,* 1–20.

Eagly, Alice H., & Crowley, Maureen. (1986). Gender and helping behavior: A meta-analytic review of the social psychological literature. *Psychological Bulletin, 100,* 283–308.

Eagly, Alice H., & Johnson, B. T. (1990). Gender and leadership style. *Psychological Bulletin, 108,* 233–256.

Eagly, Alice H., & Karau, Steven J. (2002). Role congruity theory of prejudice toward female leaders. *Psychological Review, 109,* 573–598.

Eagly, Alice H., Karau, S., & Makhijani, M. (1995). Gender and the effectiveness of leaders: A meta-analysis. *Psychological Bulletin, 117,* 125–145.

Eagly, Alice H., Makhijani, M. G., & Klonsky, B. G. (1992). Gender and the evaluation of leaders: A meta-analysis. *Psychological Bulletin, 111,* 3–22.

Eagly, Alice H., Mladinic, A., & Otto, S. (1991). Are women evaluated more favorably than men? An analysis of attitudes, beliefs, and emotions. *Psychology of Women Quarterly, 15,* 103–216.

Eagly, Alice H., & Steffen, Valerie J. (1986). Gender and aggressive behavior: A meta-analytic review of the social psychological literature. *Psychological Bulletin, 100,* 309–330.

Eagly, Alice H., & Wood, Wendy. (1999). The origins of sex differences in human behavior: Evolved dispositions versus social roles. *American Psychologist, 54,* 408–423.

Eagly, Alice H., Wood, Wendy, & Diekman, Amanda B. (2000). Social role theory of sex differences and similarities: A current appraisal. T. Eckes & H. Trautner (Eds.), *The developmental social psychology of gender* (pp. 123–174). Mahwah, NJ: Erlbaum.

East, Patricia L. (1998). Racial and ethnic differences in girls' sexual, marital, and birth expectations. *Journal of Marriage and the Family, 60,* 150–162.

Eaton, Warren O., & Enns, Lesley R. (1986). Sex differences in human motor activity level. *Psychological Bulletin, 100,* 19–28.

Eccles, Jacquelynne S. (1994). Understanding women's educational and occupational choices: Applying the Eccles et al. model of achievement-related choices. *Psychology of Women Quarterly, 18,* 585–610.

Eccles, Jacquelynne S., Freedman-Doan, Carol, Frome, Pam, Jacobs, Janis, & Yoon, K. S. (2000). Gender-role socialization in the family: A longitudinal approach. In T. Eckes & H. Trautner (Eds.), *The developmental social psychology of gender* (pp. 333–360). Mahwah, NJ: Erlbaum.

Eckert, Penelope, & McConnell-Ginet, Sally. (1999). New generalizations and explanations in language and gender research. *Language in Society, 28,* 185–201.

Edwards, Carolyn P., Knoche, Lisa, & Kumru, Asiye. (2001). Play patterns and gender. In J. Worell (Ed.), *Encyclopedia of gender* (pp. 809–816). San Diego: Academic Press.

Edwards, D. A. (1969). Early androgen stimulation and aggressive behavior in male and female mice. *Physiology and Behavior, 4,* 333–338.

Edwards, Gwenyth H. (1992). The structure and content of the male gender role stereotype: An exploration of subtypes. *Sex Roles, 27,* 533–552.

Ehrhardt, Anke A., & Meyer-Bahlburg, Heino. (1981). Effects of prenatal sex hormones on gender-related behavior. *Science, 211,* 1312–1318.

Eisenberg, Nancy, Cumberland, A., & Spinrad, T. (1998). Parental socialization of emotion. *Psychological Inquiry, 9,* 241–273.

Eisenberg, Nancy, & Lennon, Randy. (1983). Sex differences in empathy and related capacities. *Psychological Bulletin, 94,* 100–131.

Eisenstein, Zilla R. (1982). The sexual politics of the New Right: Understanding the "Crisis of Liberalism" for the 1980s. In N. O. Keohane et al. (Eds.), *Feminist theory.* Chicago: University of Chicago Press.

Ekman, Paul, & Oster, H. (1979). Facial expressions of emotion. *Annual Review of Psychology, 30,* 527–554.

El-Guebaly, Nady. (1995). Alcohol and polysubstance abuse among women. *Canadian Journal of Psychiatry, 40,* 73–79.

Ellingrod, Vicki. (2000). Pharmacotherapy of eating disorders. *Clinical Psychopharmacology Seminar.* Retrieved from *www.ch.org/providers/conferences/CPS/44.html* on February 21, 2001.

Elliott, Diana M. (1997). Traumatic events: Prevalence and delayed recall in the general population. *Journal of Consulting and Clinical Psychology, 65,* 811–820.

Ellison, Carol R. (2000). *Women's sexuality: Generations of women share intimate secrets of sexual self-acceptance.* New York: New Harbinger.

Engle, Patrice, L., & Breaux, Cynthia. (1998). Fathers' involvement with children: Perspectives from developing countries. *Social Policy Report: Society for Research in Child Development, 12,* 1–23.

Enns, Carol Z. (1997). *Feminist theories and feminist psychotherapies: Origins, themes, and variations.* New York: Harrington Press.

Enns, Carolyn Z., & Sinacore, Ada. (2001). Feminist theories. In J. Worell (Ed.), *Encyclopedia of women and gender* (pp. 469–480). San Diego: Academic Press.

Enserink, Martin. (2002). The vanishing promises of hormone replacement. *Science, 297,* 325–326.

Epping-Jordan, Joanne, et al. (1999). Psychological adjustment in breast cancer: Processes of emotional distress. *Health Psychology, 18,* 315–326.

Erikson, Erik H. (1950). *Childhood and society.* New York: Norton.

Eron, Leonard, et al. (1974). The convergence of laboratory and field studies of the development of aggression. In J. de Wit & W. W. Hartup (Eds.), *Determinants and origins of aggressive behavior.* The Hague: Mouton.

Espin, Oliva M. (1987a). Psychological impact of migration on Latinas: Implications for psychotherapeutic practice. *Psychology of Women Quarterly, 11,* 489–504.

Espin, Oliva M. (1987b). Issues of identity in the psychology of Latina lesbians. In Boston Lesbian Psychologies Collective, *Lesbian psychologies.* Urbana: University of Illinois Press.

Espin, Oliva M. (1993). Issues of identity in the psychology of Latina lesbians. In L. D. Garnets & D. C. Kimmel (Eds.), *Psychological perspectives on lesbian and gay male experiences* (pp. 348–363). New York: Columbia University Press.

Espiritu, Yen L. (2001). "We don't sleep around like White girls do": Family, culture, and gender in Filipina American lives. *Signs: Journal of Women in Culture and Society, 26,* 415–440.

Esterberg, Kristin G. (1996). Gay cultures, gay communities: The social organization of lesbians, gay men, and bisexuals. In R. Savin-Williams & K. Cohen (Eds.), *The lives of lesbians, gays, and bisexuals* (pp. 377–392). Fort Worth, TX: Harcourt.

Etaugh, Claire. (1993). Women in the middle and later years. In F. L. Denmark & M. A. Paludi (Eds.), *Psychology of women: Handbook of issues and theories.* Westport, CT: Greenwood.

Etaugh, Claire, & Bridges, Judith. (2001). Midlife transitions. In J. Worell (Ed.), *Encyclopedia of gender* (pp. 759–770). San Diego: Academic Press.

Evans, Lorraine, & Davies, K. (2000). No sissy boys here: A content analysis of the representation of masculinity in elementary school reading textbooks. *Sex Roles, 42,* 255–270.

Everitt, Barry J., & Bancroft, John. (1991). Of rats and men: The comparative approach to male sexuality. *Annual Review of Sex Research, 2,* 77–118.

Ezzell, Carol. (1994). Genomic imprinting and cancer: Mama may have and Papa may have. *Journal of NIH Research, 6,* 53–58.

Fagot, Beverly I. (1985). Beyond the reinforcement principle: Another step toward understanding sex-role development. *Developmental Psychology, 21,* 1097–1104.

Fagot, Beverly I., & Hagan, Richard. (1991). Observations of parent reactions to sex-stereotyped behaviors: Age and sex effects. *Child Development, 62,* 617–628.

Fagot, Beverly I., Leinbach, M., Hort, B., & Strayer, J. (1997). Qualities underlying the definitions of gender. *Sex Roles, 37,* 1–18.

Fagot, Beverly, & Patterson, Gerald. (1969). An in vivo analysis of reinforcing contingencies for sex-role behaviors in the preschool child. *Developmental Psychology, 1,* 563–568.

Fagot, Beverly I., Rodgers, Carie S., & Leinbach, Mary D. (2000). Theories of gender socialization. T. Eckes & H. Trautner (Eds.), *The developmental social psychology of gender* (pp. 65–90). Mahwah, NJ: Erlbaum.

Fairburn, Christopher G., Cooper, Zafra, Doll, Helen A., & Welch, Sarah L. (1999). Risk factors for anorexia nervosa. *Archives of General Psychiatry, 56,* 468–476.

Fairburn, Christopher G., Welch, Sarah L., Doll, Helen A., Davies, B A., & O'Connor, M. E. (1997). Risk factors for bulimia nervosa: A community-based case-control study. *Archives of General Psychiatry, 54,* 509–517.

Fairchild, Halford H. (1988). Curriculum design for Black (African American) psychology. In P. Bronstein & K. Quina (Eds.), *Teaching a psychology of people.* Washington, DC: American Psychological Association.

Falk, Patricia J. (1993). Lesbian mothers: Psychosocial assumptions in family law. In L. D. Garnets & D. C. Kimmel (Eds.), *Psychological perspectives on lesbian and gay male experience* (pp. 420–436). New York: Columbia University Press.

Fallon, Patricia, Katzman, Melanie A., & Wooley, Susan C. (Eds.). (1994). *Feminist perspectives on eating disorders.* New York: Guilford.

Faludi, Susan. (1991). *Backlash: The undeclared war against American women.* New York: Anchor Books/Doubleday.

Faludi, Susan. (1999). *Stiffed: The betrayal of the American man.* New York: HarperCollins.

Faludi, Susan. (2001, January 8). Don't get the wrong message. *Newsweek.*

Fantuzzo, John, Boruch, R., Beriama, A., & Atkins, M. (1997). Domestic violence and children: Prevalence and risk in five major U.S. cities. *Journal of the American Academy of Child and Adolescent Psychiatry, 36,* 116–122.

Fantuzzo, John W., & Mohr, Wanda K. (1999). Prevalence and effects of child exposure to domestic violence. *Future of Children, 9*(3), 21–32.

Faragher v. *City of Boca Raton.* S.Ct., 97–282. (1998). Available online at *http://laws.findlaw.com.*

Fasteau, M. F. (1974). *The male machine.* New York: McGraw-Hill.

Fausto-Sterling, Anne. (1992). *Myths of gender* (2nd ed.). New York: Basic Books.

Fausto-Sterling, Anne. (2000). *Sexing the body: Gender politics and the construction of sexuality.* New York: Basic Books.

Fausto-Sterling, Anne. (1993, October). Sex, race, brains, and calipers. *Discover, 14*(10), 32–37.

FBI (Federal Bureau of Investigation). (2000). Forcible rape. *Uniform Crime Reports.* Available online at *www.fbi.gov.*

FBI (Federal Bureau of Investigation). (2001). Murder and nonnegligent manslaughter. *Uniform Crime Reports.* Available online at *www.fbi.gov.*

Feild, Hubert S. (1978). Attitudes toward rape: A comparative analysis of police, rapists, crisis counselors, and citizens. *Journal of Personality and Social Psychology, 36,* 156–179.

Feingold, Alan. (1988). Cognitive gender differences are disappearing. *American Psychologist, 43,* 95–103.

Feingold, Alan. (1995). Gender differences in personality: A meta-analysis. *Psychological Bulletin, 116,* 429–456.

Fidell, Linda, Hoffman, Donnie, & Keith-Spiegel, Patti. (1979). Some social implications of sex-choice technology. *Psychology of Women Quarterly, 4,* 32–42.

Fields, Jason, & Casper, Lynne. (2001). *America's families and living arrangements.* Washington, DC: U.S. Census Bureau. Available online at *www.census.gov.*

Fine, Michelle. (1988). Sexuality, schooling, and adolescent females: The missing discourse of desire. *Harvard Educational Review, 58,* 29–53.

Fine, Michelle. (1992). *Disruptive voices: The possibilities of feminist research.* Ann Arbor: University of Michigan Press.

Fine, Reuben. (1990). Anna Freud (1895–1982). In A. N. O'Connell & N. F. Russo (Eds.), *Women in psychology: A bio-bibliographical sourcebook* (pp. 96–103). Westport, CT: Greenwood Press.

Finkelhor, David. (1980). Sex among siblings: A survey on prevalence, variety and effects. *Archives of Sexual Behavior, 9,* 171–194.

Finkelhor, David. (1984). *Child sexual abuse: New theory and research.* New York: Free Press.

Finkelhor, David, Hotaling, G., Lewis, I., & Smith, C. (1989). Sexual abuse and its relationship to later sexual satisfaction, marital status, religion, and attitudes. *Journal of Interpersonal Violence, 4,* 379–399.

Firestone, Shulamith. (1970). *The dialectic of sex.* New York: Bantam.

Fischer, Agneta H. (1995). Emotion concepts as a function of gender. In J. Russell et al. (Eds.), *Everyday conceptions of emotion* (pp. 457–474). Amsterdam: Kluwer.

Fischer, Agneta H. (Ed.). (2000). *Gender and emotion: Social psychological perspectives.* Cambridge, UK: Cambridge University Press.

Fischer, Agneta H., & Manstead, Anthony. (2000). The relation between gender and emotions in different cultures. In A. Fischer (Ed.), *Gender and emotion* (pp. 71–94). Cambridge, UK: Cambridge University Press.

Fischer, Ann R., & Good, Glenn E. (1998). New directions for the study of gender role attitudes: A cluster analytic investigation of masculinity ideologies. *Psychology of Women Quarterly, 22,* 371–384.

Fischer, Ann R., Tokar, David M., Good, Glenn E., & Snell, Andrea F. (1998). More on the structure of male role norms. *Psychology of Women Quarterly, 22,* 135–155.

Fiske, Susan T. (1993). Controlling other people: The impact of power on stereotyping. *American Psychologist, 48,* 621–628.

Fisher, Seymour. (1973). *Understanding the female orgasm.* New York: Basic Books.

Fitch, Roslyn H., & Bimonte, Heather A. (2002). Hormones, brain, and behavior: Putative biological contributions to cognitive sex differences. In A. McGillicuddy–De Lisi & R. De Lisi (Eds.), *Biology, society, and behavior: The development of sex differences in cognition* (pp. 55–92). Westport, CT: Ablex.

Fitzgerald, Louise F., & Nutt, Roberta. (1986). The Division 17 principles concerning the counseling/psychotherapy of women: Rationale and implementation. *The Counseling Psychologist, 14,* 180–216.

Fivush, Robyn. (1989). Exploring sex differences in the emotional content of mother-child conversations about the past. *Sex Roles, 20,* 675–692.

Fivush, Robyn, Brotman, M., Buckner, J., & Goodman, S. (2000). Gender differences in parent-child emotion narratives. *Sex Roles, 42,* 233–254.

Flaherty, Mary. (2001). How a language gender system creeps into perception. *Journal of Cross-cultural Psychology, 32,* 18–31.

Flannagan, Dorothy, & Perese, San. (1998). Emotional references in mother-daughter and mother-son dyads' conversations about school. *Sex Roles, 39,* 353–368.

Fleming, Jillian, Mullen, P., Sibthorpe, B., & Bammer, G. (1999). The long-term impact of childhood sexual abuse in Australian women. *Child Abuse and Neglect, 23,* 145–159.

Flouri, Eirini, & Buchanan, Ann. (2002). What predicts good relationships with parents in adolescence and partners in adult life: Findings from the 1958 British Birth Cohort. *Journal of Family Psychology, 16,* 186–198.

Foa, Edna B., Dancu, C., Hembree, E., Jaycox, L., Meadows, E., & Street, G. (1999). A comparison of exposure therapy, stress inoculation training, and their combination for reducing posttraumatic stress disorder in female assault victims. *Journal of Consulting and Clinical Psychology, 67,* 194–200.

Foa, Edna B., Steketee, G., & Olasov, B. (1989). Behavioral/cognitive conceptualization of post-traumatic stress disorder. *Behavior Therapy, 20,* 155–176.

Ford, Clellan S., & Beach, Frank A. (1951). *Patterns of sexual behavior.* New York: Harper & Row.

Ford, M., & Widiger, T. (1989). Sex bias in the diagnosis of histrionic and antisocial personality disorders. *Journal of Consulting and Clinical Psychology, 57,* 301–305.

Forrest, Jacqueline D., & Singh, Susheela. (1990). The sexual and reproductive behavior of American women, 1982–1988. *Family Planning Perspectives, 22,* 206–215.

Fox, Greer L., & Murry, Velma M. (2000). Gender and families: Feminist perspectives and family research. *Journal of Marriage and the Family, 62,* 1160–1172.

Fox-Tierney, Rachel, Ickovics, Jeannette, Cerreta, Carrie, & Ethier, Kathleen. (1999). Potential sex differences remain understudied: A case study of the inclusion of women in HIV/AIDS-related neuropsychological research. *Review of General Psychology, 3,* 44–54.

Foy, Michael R., Henderson, V., Berger, T., & Thompson, R. (2000). Estrogen and neural plasticity. *Current Directions in Psychological Science, 9,* 148–152.

Fragoso, José M., & Kashubeck, Susan. (2000). Machismo, gender role conflict, and mental health in Mexican American men. *Psychology of Men and Masculinity, 2,* 87–97.

Fredrickson, Barbara, & Roberts, T. (1997). Objectification theory: Toward understanding women's lived experiences and mental health risks. *Psychology of Women Quarterly, 21,* 173–206.

Freud, Anna. (1926). *Introduction to the technique of child analysis.* Trans. L. P. Clark. (1928). New York: Nervous and Mental Disease Publishing Co.

Freud, Anna. (1936). *The ego and the mechanisms of defense.* Trans. C. Bains (1937). London: Hogarth Press.

Freud, Anna. (1943). *War and children.* New York: Medical War Books.

Freud, Sigmund. (1933). *New introductory lectures in psychoanalysis.* New York: Norton.

Freud, Sigmund. (1948). Some psychical consequences of the anatomical distinction between the sexes. In I. Riviere (Trans.), *Collected papers* (Vol. V, pp. 186–197). London: Hogarth Press.

Freud, Sigmund. (1955). *The interpretation of dreams* (J. Strachey, trans.). New York: Basic Books.

Freyd, Jennifer J. (1996). *Betrayal trauma: The logic of forgetting childhood abuse.* Cambridge, MA: Harvard University Press.

Freyd, Jennifer J., & Quina, Kathryn. (2000). Feminist ethics in the practice of science: The contested memory controversy as an example. In M. Brabeck (Ed.), *Practicing feminist ethics in psychology* (pp. 101–123). Washington, DC: American Psychological Association.

Friedman, M., & Rosenman, R. H. (1974). *Type A behavior and your heart.* New York: Fawcett Books.

Friedrich, W. N., Beilke, R. L., & Urquiza, A. J. (1988). Behavior problems in young sexually abused boys. *Journal of Interpersonal Violence, 3,* 1–12.

Frieze, Irene H. (1983). Causes and consequences of marital rape. *Signs, 8,* 532–553.

Frieze, Irene H., et al. (1982). Assessing the theoretical models for sex differences in causal attributions for success and failure. *Sex Roles, 8,* 333–334.

Frodi, Ann, Macauley, Jacqueline, & Thome, Pauline R. (1977). Are women always less aggressive than men? A review of the experimental literature. *Psychological Bulletin, 84,* 634–660.

Funtowicz, M N., & Widiger, Thomas A. (1999). Sex bias in the diagnosis of personality disorders: An evaluation of the DSM-IV criteria. *Journal of Abnormal Psychology, 108,* 195–201.

Furnham, Adrian, & Baguma, Peter. (1994). Cross-cultural differences in the evaluation of male and female body shapes. *International Journal of Eating Disorders, 15*, 81–89.

Gagnon, John H. (1977). *Human sexualities.* Glenview, IL: Scott, Foresman.

Galambos, N., Almeida, D., & Petersen, A. (1990). Masculinity, femininity, and sex role attitudes in early adolescence: Exploring gender intensification. *Child Development, 61*, 1905–1914.

Gallant, Sheryle J., Popiel, Debra A., Hoffman, Denise M., Chakraborty, Prabir, K., & Hamilton, Jean. (1992). Using daily ratings to confirm premenstrual syndrome/late luteal dysphoric disorder, Part II, What makes a "real" difference? *Psychosomatic Medicine, 54*, 167–181.

Gannon, Linda, et al. (1992). Sex bias in psychological research: Progress or complacency? *American Psychologist, 4*, 389–396.

Garcia, Alma M. (1989). The development of Chicana feminist discourse, 1970–1980. *Gender & Society, 3*, 217–238.

Garfinkel, Paul E., & Garner, D. M. (1982). *Anorexia nervosa: A multidimensional perspective.* New York: Brunner/Mazel.

Garner, Pamela W., Robertson, S., & Smith, G. (1997). Preschool children's emotional expressions with peers: The roles of gender and emotion socialization. *Sex Roles, 36*, 675–692.

Garnets, Linda, Herek, Gregory M., & Levy, Barrie. (1993). Violence and victimization of lesbians and gay men: Mental health consequences. In L. D. Garnets & D. C. Kimmel (Eds.), *Psychological perspectives on lesbian and gay male experience* (pp. 579–598). New York: Columbia University Press.

Garnets, Linda D., & Kimmel, Douglas C. (Eds.). (1993). *Psychological perspectives on lesbian and gay male experiences.* New York: Columbia University Press.

Gastil, J. (1990). Generic pronouns and sexist language: The oxymoronic character of masculine generics. *Sex Roles, 23*, 629–643.

Ge, X., Conger, R., & Elder, G. (1996). Coming of age too early: Pubertal influences on girls' vulnerability to psychological distress. *Child Development, 67*, 3386–3400.

Ge, X., Lorenz, F., Conger, R., Elder, G., & Simons, R. (1994). Trajectories of stressful life events and depressive symptoms during adolescence. *Developmental Psychology, 30*, 467–483.

General Accounting Office. (2001). *Women in management.* Washington, DC: Author. Available online at *www.gao.gov/new.items/d02156.pdf.*

General Social Survey. (2002). Retrieved from *www.icpsr.umich.edu/GSS/rnd1998/merged/cdbk/feminist.htm* on February 26, 2002.

Gentry, Jacquelyn H. (1993). Women and AIDS. In *Psychology & AIDS exchange.* Washington, DC: American Psychological Association.

Gentry, Margaret. (1998). The sexual double standard: The influence of number of relationships and level of sexual activity on judgments of women and men. *Psychology of Women Quarterly, 22*, 505–511.

George, Enitza D. (2000). Estrogen replacement therapy. American College of Physicians— American Society of Internal Medicine Annual Session 2000. Retrieved from *www.medscape.com* on April 6, 2000.

George, Linda K., Fillenbaum, G. G., Palmore, E. (1984). Sex differences in the antecedents and consequences of retirement. *Journal of Gerontology, 39*, 364–371.

Giddings, Paula. (1984). *When and where I enter: The impact of black women on race and sex in America.* New York: Bantam Books.

Gilbert, Lucia A. (1985). *Men in dual-earner families: Current realities and future prospects.* Hillsdale, NJ: Erlbaum.

Gilbert, Lucia A. (1989). *Sharing it all: The rewards and struggles of two-career families.* New York: Plenum.

Gilbert, Lucia A. (1993). *Two careers/one family.* Newbury Park, CA: Sage.

Gilbert, Lucia A., & Dancer, L. S. (1992). Dual-earner families in the United States and adolescent development. In S. Lewis, D. N. Izraeli, & H. Hootsmans (Eds.), *Dual-earner families: International perspectives* (pp. 151–171). Newbury Park, CA: Sage.

Gilbert, Lucia A., & Rader, Jill. (2001). Counseling and psychotherapy: Gender, race/ethnicity, and sexuality. In J. Worell (Ed.), *Encyclopedia of women and gender* (pp. 265–277). New York: Academic Press.

Gilbert, Lucia A., & Scher, Murray. (1999). *Gender and sex in counseling and psychotherapy.* Boston: Allyn and Bacon.

Gilbert, Lucia A., Walker, S., McKinney, S., & Snell, J. (2000). Challenging discourse themes reproducing gender in heterosexual dating: An analog study. *Sex Roles, 42*, 753–774.

Gill, Diane L. (2001). Sport and athletics. In J. Worell (Ed.), *Encyclopedia of gender* (pp. 1091–1100). San Diego: Academic Press.

Gilligan, Carol. (1982). *In a different voice: Psychological theory and women's development.* Cambridge, MA: Harvard University Press.

Gilpatrick, Naomi. (1972). The secret life of Beatrix Potter. *Natural History, 81*(8).

Ginorio, Angela B., Gutierrez, Lorraine, Cauce, Ana Mari, & Acosta, Mimi. (1995). Psychological issues for Latinas. In H. Landrine (Ed.), *Bringing cultural diversity to feminist psychology: Theory, research, and practice* (pp. 241–264). Washington, DC: American Psychological Association.

Ginorio, Angela B., & Martinez, Lorraine J. (1998). Where are the Latinas? Ethno-race and gender in psychology courses. *Psychology of Women Quarterly, 22,* 53–68.

Gladstone, T., Kaslow, Nadine, Seeley, J., & Lewinsohn, P. (1997). Sex differences, attributional style, and depressive symptoms among adolescents. *Journal of Abnormal Child Psychology, 25,* 297–305.

Glazer, Sarah. (1993, February). Violence against women. *CQ Researcher,* 171–192.

Gleason, Jean B., & Ely, Richard. (2002). Gender differences in language development. In A. McGillicuddy–De Lisi & R. De Lisi (Eds.), *Biology, society, and behavior: The development of sex differences in cognition* (pp. 127–154). Westport, CT: Ablex.

Glenn, Evelyn Nakano. (1985). Racial ethnic women's labor: The intersection of race, gender and class oppression. *Review of Radical Economics, 17*(3), 86–108.

Glick, Peter, & Fiske, Susan T. (1997). Hostile and benevolent sexism: Measuring ambivalent sexist attitudes toward women. *Psychology of Women Quarterly, 21,* 119–136.

Gloria, Alberta M., & Kurpius, Sharon E. R. (2001). Influences of self-beliefs, social support, and comfort in the university environment on the academic nonpersistence decisions of American Indian undergraduates. *Cultural Diversity and Ethnic Minority Psychology, 7,* 88–102.

Goble, F. C., & Konopka, E. A. (1973). Sex as a factor in infectious disease. *Transactions of the New York Academy of Science, 35,* 325.

Gold, Delores, & Reis, Myrna. (1982). Male teacher effects on young children: A theoretical and empirical consideration. *Sex Roles, 8,* 493–514.

Gold, Steven N., Hughes, Dawn, & Hohnecker, Laura. (1994). Degrees of repression of sexual abuse memories. *American Psychologist, 49,* 441–442.

Goldberg, Daniel C., et al. (1983). The Gräfenberg spot and female ejaculation: A review of initial hypotheses. *Journal of Sex and Marital Therapy, 9,* 27–37.

Goldberg, Margaret E. (1995). Substance-abusing women: False stereotypes and real needs. *Social Work, 40,* 789–798.

Goldberg, Philip. (1968, April). Are some women prejudiced against women? *Transaction, 5,* 28–30.

Golding, Jacqueline M. (1996). Sexual assault history and women's reproductive and sexual health. *Psychology of Women Quarterly, 20,* 101–122.

Golding, Jacqueline M. (1999). Sexual-assault history and long-term physical health problems: Evidence from clinical and population epidemiology. *Current Directions in Psychological Science, 8,* 191–194.

Goldschmidt, Orly T., & Weller, Leonard. (2000). "Talking emotions": Gender differences in a variety of conversational contexts. *Symbolic Interaction, 23,* 117–134.

Goldstein, Joshua S. (2001). *War and gender.* New York: Cambridge University Press.

Goldstein, Nancy, & Manlowe, Jennifer L. (Eds.). (1996). *AIDS as a gender issue: Perpsectives on the pandemic in the United States.* New York: New York University Press.

Golombok, Susan, & Fivush, Robyn. (1994). *Gender development.* New York: Cambridge University Press.

Golombok, Susan, & Tasker, Fiona. (1996). Do parents influence the sexual orientation of their children? Findings from a longitudinal study of lesbian families. *Developmental Psychology, 32,* 3–11.

Golub, Sharon. (1976). The effect of premenstrual anxiety and depression on cognitive function. *Journal of Personality and Social Psychology, 34,* 99–104.

Golub, Sharon. (1992). *Periods: From menarche to menopause.* Newbury Park, CA: Sage.

Gondolf, E. W., Fisher, E., & McFerron, J. R. (1988). Racial differences among shelter residents: A comparison of Anglo, Black, and Hispanic battered women. *Journal of Family Violence, 3,* 39–51.

Gonzales, Patricia M., Blanton, H., & Williams, K. (2002). The effects of stereotype threat and double-minority status on the test performance of Latino women. *Personality and Social Psychology Bulletin, 28,* 659–670.

Gonzalez-Calvo, Judith T. (1993). *Gender: Multicultural perspectives.* Dubuque, IA: Kendall/Hunt.

Good, G. E., et al. (1995). Male gender role conflict: Psychometric issues and relations to psychological distress. *Journal of Counseling Psychology, 42,* 3–10.

Goodchilds, Jacqueline, & Zellman, Gail. (1984). Sexual signaling and sexual aggression in adolescent relationships. In N. Malamuth & E. Donnerstein (Eds.), *Pornography and sexual aggression.* New York: Academic Press.

Gooden, Angela M., & Gooden, Mark A. (2001). Gender representation in notable children's picture books: 1995–1999. *Sex Roles, 45,* 89–101.

Gordon, Linda. (1988). *Heroes of their own lives.* New York: Viking.

Gordon, R. E., Kapostins, E. E., & Gordon, Katherine K. (1965). Factors in postpartum emotional adjustment. *Obstetrics and Gynecology, 25,* 158–166.

Gottlieb, Lori. (2001). *Stick figure: A diary of my former self.* New York: Berkley Books.

Gottman, John M., et al. (1995). The relationship between heart rate reactivity, emotionally aggressive behavior, and general violence in batterers. *Journal of Family Psychology, 9,* 227–248.

Gough, Harrison G. (1957). *Manual for the California Psychological Inventory.* Palo Alto, CA: Consulting Psychologists Press. (Rev. ed., 1964.)

Gould, Stephen J. (1987). *An urchin in the storm.* New York: Norton.

Gowan, Mary, & Treviño, Melanie. (1998). An examination of gender differences in Mexican-American attitudes toward family and career roles. *Sex Roles, 38,* 1079–1094.

Gowers, S. G., North, C. D., & Byram, C. (1996). Life event precipitants of adolescent anorexia nervosa. *Journal of Child Psychology and Psychiatry, 37,* 469–477.

Graber, Judith, Lewinsohn, P., Seeley, J., & Brooks-Gunn, J. (1997). Is psychopathology associated with the timing of pubertal development? *Journal of the American Academy of Child and Adolescent Psychiatry, 36,* 1768–1776.

Grady, Kathleen. (1979). Androgyny reconsidered. In J. H. Williams (Ed.), *Psychology of women: Selected readings* (pp. 172 177). New York: Norton.

Graham, Cynthia A. (1991). Menstrual synchrony: An update and review. *Human Nature, 2,* 293–311.

Green, Richard, Mandel, J. B., Hotvedt, M. E., Gray, J., & Smith, L. (1986). Lesbian mothers and their children. *Archives of Sexual Behavior, 15,* 167–184.

Greenberger, M. D., & Blake, D. L. (1996, July 5). The VMI decision: Shattering sexual stereotypes. *The Chronicle of Higher Education.*

Greene, Beverly. (1994). African American women. In L. Comas-Diaz & B. Greene (Eds.), *Women of color: Integrating ethnic and gender identities in psychotherapy* (pp. 10–29). New York: Guilford.

Greene, Beverly. (2000). African American lesbian and bisexual women. *Journal of Social Issues, 56,* 239–250.

Greene, Dennis M., & Navarro, Rachel L. (1998). Situation-specific assertiveness in the epidemiology of sexual victimization among university women: A prospective path analysis. *Psychology of Women Quarterly, 22,* 589–604.

Greenhaus, Jeffrey H., & Parasuraman, Saroj. (1993). Job performance attributions and career advancement prospects: An examination of gender and race effects. *Organizational Behavior and Human Decision Processes, 55,* 273–297.

Gregersen, Edgar. (1996). *The world of human sexuality.* New York: Irvington.

Grier, William H., & Cobbs, Price M. (1968). *Black rage.* New York: Basic Books.

Grinde, Donald A. (1977). *The Iroquois and the founding of the American nation.* San Francisco: American Historian Press.

Grodstein, Francine, et al. (1997). Postmenopausal hormone therapy and mortality. *New England Journal of Medicine, 336,* 1769–1775.

Grossman, Aryn L., & Tucket, Joan S. (1997). Gender differences and sexism in the knowledge and use of slang. *Sex Roles, 37,* 101–110.

Grossman, Frances K., Cook, Alexandra B., Kepkep, Selin S., & Koenen, Karestan C. (1999). *With the phoenix rising: Lessons from ten resilient women who overcame the trauma of childhood sexual abuse.* San Francisco: Jossey-Bass.

Grossman, M., & Wood, W. (1993). Sex differences in intensity of emotional experience: A social role interpretation. *Journal of Personality and Social Psychology, 65,* 1010–1022.

Gruenbaum, Ellen. (2001). *The female circumcision controversy: An anthropological perspective.* Philadelphia: University of Pennsylvania Press.

Guay, A., & Jacobson, J. (2002). Decreased free testosterone and dehydroepiandrosterone-sulfate (DHEA-S) levels in women with decreased libido. *Journal of Sex and Marital Therapy, 28*, 129–142.

Guerrero, Laura K., & Reiter, Renee L. (1998). Expressing emotion: Sex differences in social skills and communicative responses to anger, sadness, and jealousy. In D. Canary & K. Dindia (Eds.), *Sex differences and similarities in communication* (pp. 321–350). Mahwah, NJ: Erlbaum.

Guillelmon, Delphine, & Grosjean, François. (2001). The gender marking effect in spoken word recognition: The case of bilinguals. *Memory and Cognition, 29*, 503–511.

Gullone, Eleonora, & King, Neville J. (1992). Psychometric evaluation of a Revised Fear Survey Schedule for children and adolescents. *Journal of Child Psychology and Psychiatry, 33*, 987–998.

Gura, Trisha. (1995). Estrogen: Key player in heart disease among women. *Science, 269*, 771–773.

Gutek, Barbara A. (1985). *Sex and the workplace.* San Francisco: Jossey-Bass.

Gutek, Barbara A. (2001a). Women and paid work. *Psychology of Women Quarterly, 25*, 379–393.

Gutek, Barbara A. (2001b). Working environments. In J. Worell (Ed.), *Encyclopedia of women and gender* (pp. 1191–1204). San Diego: Academic Press.

Guthrie, R. V. (1976). *Even the rat was white: A historical view of psychology.* New York: Harper.

Guttentag, Marcia, & Secord, P. (1983). *Too many women?* Beverly Hills, CA: Sage.

Guyll, Max, Matthews, Karen, & Bromberger, Joyce. (2001). Discrimination and unfair treatment: Relationship to cardiovascular reactivity among African American and European American women. *Health Psychology, 20*, 315–325.

Haan, Norma. (1975). Hypothetical and actual moral reasoning in a situation of civil disobedience. *Journal of Personality and Social Psychology, 32*, 255–270.

Halberstadt, Amy G., & Saitta, M. B. (1987). Gender, nonverbal behavior, and perceived dominance: A test of the theory. *Journal of Personality and Social Psychology, 53*, 257–272.

Hall, Gordon C. N., Sue, Stanley, Narang, David S., & Lilly, Roy S. (2000). Culture-specific models of men's sexual aggression: Intra- and interpersonal determinants. *Cultural Diversity and Ethnic Minority Psychology, 6*, 252–267.

Hall, Gordon C. Nagayama, & Barongan, Christy. (1997). Prevention of sexual aggression: Sociocultural risk and protective factors. *American Psychologist, 52*, 5–14.

Hall, Gordon C. Nagayama. (1995). Sexual offender recidivism revisited: A meta-analysis of recent treatment studies. *Journal of Consulting and Clinical Psychology, 63*, 802–809.

Hall, Judith A., & Friedman, Gregory. (1999). Status, gender, and nonverbal behavior: A study of structured interactions between employees of a company. *Personality and Social Psychology Bulletin, 25*. 1082–1091.

Hall, Judith A. (1984). *Nonverbal sex differences.* Baltimore: Johns Hopkins University Press.

Hall, Judith A. (1998). How big are nonverbal sex differences? The case of smiling and sensitivity to nonverbal cues. In D. Canary & K. Dindia (Eds.), *Sex differences and similarities in communication* (pp. 155–178). Mahwah, NJ: Erlbaum.

Hall, Judith A., LeBeau, Lavonia B., Gordon, Jeannette, & Thayer, Frank. (2001). Status, gender, and nonverbal behavior in candid and posed photographs: A study of conversations between university employees. *Sex Roles, 44*, 677–692.

Hall, Judith, Halberstadt, A., & O'Brien, C. (1997). "Subordination" and nonverbal sensitivity: A study and synthesis of findings based on trait measures. *Sex Roles, 37*, 295–318.

Hall, L. A., Williams, C. A., & Greenberg, R. S. (1985). Supports, stressors, and depressive symptoms in low-income mothers of young children. *American Journal of Public Health, 75*, 518–522.

Halpern, Diane F. (1992). *Sex differences in cognitive abilities* (2nd ed.). Hillsdale, NJ: Erlbaum.

Hamilton, Mykol C. (1991). Masculine bias in the attribution of personhood: People = male, male = people. *Psychology of Women Quarterly, 15*, 393–402.

Hankin, Ben, & Abramson, Lyn. (2001). Development of gender differences in depression: An elaborated cognitive vulnerability-transactional stress theory. *Psychological Bulletin, 127*, 773–796.

Hankin, Ben, Abramson, L., Moffitt, T., Silva, P., McGee, R., & Angell, K. (1998). Development of depression from preadolescence to young adulthood: Emerging gender differences in a 10-year longitudinal study. *Journal of Abnormal Psychology, 107*, 128–140.

Hanson, R. Karl, & Bussiere, Monique T. (1998). Predicting relapse: A meta-analysis of sexual offender recidivism studies. *Journal of Consulting and Clinical Psychology, 66*, 348–362.

Hardie, Elizabeth A. (1997). Prevalence and predictors of cyclic and noncyclic affective change. *Psychology of Women Quarterly, 21*, 299–314.

Hare-Mustin, Rachel T., & Marecek, Jeanne. (1988). The meaning of difference: Gender theory, postmodernism and psychology. *American Psychologist, 43*, 455–464.

Hariton, E. Barbara. (1973, March). The sexual fantasies of women. *Psychology Today, 6*, 39–44.

Harned, Melanie S. (2000). Harassed bodies: An examination of the relationships among women's experiences of sexual harassment, body image, and eating disturbances. *Psychology of Women Quarterly, 24*, 336–348.

Harrigan, Jinni A., & Lucic, Karen S. (1988). Attitudes about gender bias in language: A reevaluation. *Sex Roles, 19*, 129–140.

Harris, G. W., & Levine, S. (1965). Sexual differentiation of the brain and its experimental control. *Journal of Physiology, 181*, 379–400.

Harris, S. (1971). Influence of subject and experimenter sex in psychological research. *Journal of Consulting and Clinical Psychology, 37*, 291–294.

Harrison, J. (1978). Warning: The male sex role may be dangerous to your health. *Journal of Social Issues, 34*(1), 65–86.

Hartka, E., et al. (1991). A meta-analysis of depressive symptomatology and alcohol consumption over time. *British Journal of Addiction, 86*, 1283–1298.

Hartung, C. M., & Widiger, Thomas A. (1998). Gender differences in the diagnosis of mental disorders: Conclusions and controversies of the DSM-IV. *Psychological Bulletin, 123*, 260–278.

Hastings, J. E., & Hamberger, L. K. (1988). Personality characteristics of spouse abusers: A controlled comparison. *Violence and Victims, 3*, 31–48.

Hatcher, Robert A., et al. (1998). *Contraceptive technology* (17th ed.). New York: Ardent Media.

Hausmann, Markus, et al. (2000). Sex hormones affect spatial abilities during the menstrual cycle. *Behavioral Neuroscience, 114*, 1245–1250.

Haynes, S. G., et al. (1978). The relationship of psychosocial factors to coronary heart disease in the Framingham Study. II. Prevalence of coronary heart disease. *American Journal of Epidemiology, 107*, 384–402.

Hays, Constance R. (1990, Sept. 30). Reports of assaults on homosexuals increase. *New York Times.*

Hays, H. R. (1964). *The dangerous sex: The myth of feminine evil.* New York: G. P. Putnam's Sons.

Heatherington, Laurie, et al. (1993). Two investigations of "female modesty" in achievement situations. *Sex Roles, 29*, 739–754.

Hedblad, B., et al. (2002). Incidence of cardiovascular disease, cancer and death in postmenopausal women affirming use of hormone replacement therapy. *Scandinavian Journal of Public Health, 30*, 12–19.

Hedges, Larry V., & Nowell, Amy. (1995). Sex differences in mental test scores, variability, and numbers of high-scoring individuals. *Science, 269*, 41–45.

Heilman, M. E., Block, C. J., Martell, R. F. (1995). Sex stereotypes: Do they influence perceptions of managers? *Journal of Social Behavior and Personality, 10*, 237–252.

Heiman, Julia R. (1975). The physiology of erotica: Women's sexual arousal. *Psychology Today, 8*(11), 90–94.

Heiman, Julia, LoPiccolo, Leslie, & LoPiccolo, Joseph. (1976). *Becoming orgasmic: A sexual growth program for women.* Englewood Cliffs, NJ: Prentice Hall.

Heise, Lori, et al. (1999). Ending violence against women. *Population Reports 27*(4), 1–43.

Helgeson, Vicki, Cohen, S., Schulz, R., & Yasko, J. (2000). Group support interventions for women with breast cancer: Who benefits from what? *Health Psychology, 19*, 107–114.

Helgeson, Vicki, Cohen, S., Schulz, R., & Yasko, J. (2001). Long-term effects of educational and peer discussion group interventions on adjustment to breast cancer. *Health Psychology, 20*, 387–392.

Helgeson, Vicki S. (1990). The role of masculinity in a prognostic predictor of heart attack severity. *Sex Roles, 22*, 755–790.

Helgeson, Vicki S., & Cohen, Sheldon. (1996). Social support and adjustment to cancer: Reconciling descriptive, correlational, and intervention research. *Health Psychology, 15*, 135–148.

Helliwell, Christine. (2000). "It's only a penis": Rape, feminism, and difference. *Signs: Journal of Women in Culture and Society, 25*, 789–816.

Helmuth, Laura. (2000). Reports see progress, problems, in trials. *Science, 288,* 1562–1563.

Helwig, Andrew A. (1998). Gender-role stereotyping: Testing theory with a longitudinal sample. *Sex Roles, 38,* 403–424.

Hemmer, Joan D., & Kleiber, D. A. (1981). Tomboys and sissies: Androgynous children? *Sex Roles, 1,* 1205–1212.

Henahan, John. (1984). Honing the treatment of early breast cancer. *Journal of the American Medical Association, 251,* 309–310.

Hendy, Helen M., Gustitus, Cheryl, & Leitzel-Schwalm, Jamie. (2001). Social cognitive predictors of body image in preschool children. *Sex Roles, 44,* 557–570.

Henley, Nancy M. (1977). *Body politics: Power, sex, and nonverbal communication.* Englewood Cliffs, NJ: Prentice-Hall.

Henley, Nancy M., Meng, Karen, O'Brien, Delores, McCarthy, William J., & Sockloskie, Robert J. (1998). Developing a scale to measure the diversity of feminist attitudes. *Psychology of Women Quarterly, 22,* 317–348.

Herdt, Gilbert H. (Ed.). (1984). *Ritualized homosexuality in Melanesia.* Berkeley: University of California Press.

Herek, Gregory M. (1990). The context of anti-gay violence: Notes on cultural and psychological heterosexism. *Journal of Interpersonal Violence, 5,* 316–333.

Herek, Gregory M. (2000a). The psychology of sexual prejudice. *Current Directions in Psychological Science, 9*(1), 19–22.

Herek, Gregory M. (2000b). Sexual prejudice and gender: Do heterosexuals' attitudes toward lesbians and gay men differ? *Journal of Social Issues, 56,* 251–266.

Herek, Gregory M., Kimmel, Douglas C., Amaro, Hortensia, & Melton, Gary B. (1991). Avoiding heterosexist bias in psychological research. *American Psychologist, 46,* 957–963.

Herman, Judith L. (1981). *Father-daughter incest.* Cambridge, MA: Harvard University Press.

Hernandez, Ines. (1990, April). *American Indian women writers.* Colloquium presented at the University of Wisconsin-Madison.

Herrett-Skjellum, J., & Allen, M. (1996). Television programming and sex stereotyping: A meta-analysis. In B. Burleson (Ed.), *Communication Yearbook 1995* (pp. 157–185). Thousand Oaks, CA: Sage.

Hersey, R. B. (1931). Emotional cycles in man. *Journal of Mental Science, 77,* 151–169.

Hines, Melissa, & Collaer, Marcia L. (1993). Gonadal hormones and sexual differentiation of human behavior. *Annual Review of Sex Research, 4,* 1–48.

Hobfoll, Stevan, et al. (1995). Depression prevalence and incidence among inner-city pregnant and postpartum women. *Journal of Consulting and Clinical Psychology, 63,* 445–453.

Hochschild, Arlie. (1989). *The second shift: Working parents and the revolution at home.* New York: Viking.

Hochschild, Arlie R. (1990). Ideology and emotion management. In T. Kemper (Ed.), *Research agendas in the sociology of emotions* (pp. 117–142). Albany: State University of New York Press.

Hofferth, Sandra L. (1990). Trends in adolescent sexual activity, contraception, and pregnancy in the United States. In J. Bancroft & J. M. Reinisch (Eds.), *Adolescence and puberty.* New York: Oxford.

Hoffman, Lois W. (1972). Early childhood experiences and women's achievement motives. *Journal of Social Issues, 28*(2), 129–155.

Holborow, P. L., & Berry, P. S. (1986). Hyperactivity and learning difficulties. *Journal of Learning Disabilities, 11,* 426–431.

Holden, Constance. (1989). Koop finds abortion evidence "inconclusive." *Science, 243,* 730–731.

Holden, Constance. (1999). MIT issues mea culpa on sex bias. *Science, 283,* 1992.

Holland, Dorothy C., & Eisenhart, Margaret A. (1990). *Educated in romance: Women, achievement, and college culture.* Chicago: University of Chicago Press.

Holmes, Janet. (1984). Women's language: A functional approach. *General Linguistics, 24,* 149–178.

Holmes, Janet. (1995). *Women, men and politeness.* London: Longman.

Holstein, Constance. (1976). Development of moral judgment: A longitudinal study of males and females. *Child Development, 47,* 51–61.

Holtzworth-Munroe, Amy. (2000). A typology of men who are violent toward their female partners: Making sense of the heterogeneity in husband violence. *Current Directions in Psychological Science, 9,* 140–143.

Holtzworth-Munroe, Amy, & Stuart, Gregory L. (1994). Typologies of male batterers: Three subtypes and the differences among them. *Psychological Bulletin, 116,* 476–497.

Holtzworth-Munroe, Amy, Stuart, Gregory, & Hutchinson, Glenn. (1997). Violent versus nonviolent husbands: Differences in attachment patterns, dependency, and jealousy. *Journal of Family Psychology, 11,* 314–331.

Hood, Jane C. (Ed.). (1993). *Men, work, and family.* Newbury Park, CA: Sage.

Horner, Matina S. (1969). Fail: Bright women. *Psychology Today, 3*(6), 36.

Horner, Matina S. (1970a). Femininity and achievement: A basic inconsistency. In J. Bardwick, E. Douvan, M. Horner, & D. Gutman (Eds.), *Feminine personality and conflict.* Belmont, CA: Brooks/Cole.

Horner, Matina S. (1972). Toward an understanding of achievement-related conflicts in women. *Journal of Social Issues, 28*(2), 157–175.

Horney, Karen. (1924). On the genesis of the castration complex in women. *International Journal of Psychoanalysis, 5,* 50–65.

Horney, Karen. (1926). The flight from womanhood. *International Journal of Psychoanalysis, 7,* 324–339.

Hotaling, G. T., & Sugarman, D. B. (1986). An analysis of risk markers in husband to wife violence: The current state of knowledge. *Violence and Victims, 1,* 101–124.

House, W. C. (1974). Actual and perceived differences in male and female expectancies and minimal goal levels as a function of competition. *Journal of Personality, 42,* 493–509.

Houseknecht, Sharon K. (1979). Timing of the decision to remain voluntarily childless: Evidence for continuous socialization. *Psychology of Women Quarterly, 4,* 81–96.

Hoyt, William T., & Kerns, M. (1999). Magnitude and moderators of bias in observer ratings: A meta-analysis. *Psychological Methods, 4,* 403–424.

Hrdy, Sarah B. (1981). *The woman that never evolved.* Cambridge: Harvard University Press.

Hrdy, Sarah B. (1999). *Mother nature: Maternal instincts and how they shape the human species.* New York: Ballantine.

Hsu, L. K. George, Kaye, Walter, & Weltzin, Theodore. (1993). Are the eating disorders related to obsessive compulsive disorder? *International Journal of Eating Disorders, 14,* 305–318.

Hughes, Jean O., & Sandler, Bernice R. (1987). "Friends" raping friends: Could it happen to you? Washington, DC: Association of American Colleges.

Humes, Karen, & McKinnon, Jesse. (1999). *The Asian and Pacific Islander population in the United States.* U.S. Census Bureau. Available online at *www.census.gov.*

Hunt, Morton. (1974). *Sexual behavior in the 1970s.* Chicago: Playboy Press.

Hunter, M., & O'Dea, I. (2001). Cognitive appraisal of the menopause: The menopause representations questionnaire (MRQ). *Psychology, Health and Medicine, 6,* 65–76.

Hutchins, Loraine, & Kaahumanu, Lani. (1991). *Bi any other name: Bisexual people speak out.* Boston: Alyson.

Hutchinson, Ira W. (1999). Alcohol, fear, and woman abuse. *Sex Roles, 40,* 893–920.

Hutchinson, Karen A. (1995). Androgens and sexuality. *American Journal of Medicine, 98* (Suppl. 1A), 1A111S–1A115S.

Hyde, Janet S. (1979). *Understanding human sexuality.* New York: McGraw-Hill.

Hyde, Janet S. (1981). How large are cognitive gender differences? A meta-analysis using ω^2 and *d. American Psychologist, 36,* 892–901.

Hyde, Janet S. (1984a). Children's understanding of sexist language. *Developmental Psychology, 20,* 697–706.

Hyde, Janet S. (1984b). How large are gender differences in aggression? A developmental meta-analysis. *Developmental Psychology, 20,* 722–736.

Hyde, Janet S. (1990). *Understanding human sexuality,* 4th ed. New York: McGraw-Hill.

Hyde, Janet S. (1994). *Understanding human sexuality,* 5th ed. New York: McGraw-Hill.

Hyde, Janet S. (2002). Feminist identity development: The current state of theory, research, and practice. *Counseling Psychologist, 30,* 105–110.

Hyde, Janet S. (2003). The use of meta-analysis in determining the effects of child sexual abuse. In J. Bancroft (Ed.), *Sexual development.* Bloomington: Indiana University Press.

Hyde, Janet S., & DeLamater, John D. (2003). *Understanding human sexuality* (8th ed.). New York: McGraw-Hill.

Hyde, Janet S., & Essex, Marilyn J. (Eds.). (1991). *Parental leave and child care: Setting a research and policy agenda.* Philadelphia: Temple University Press.

Hyde, J. S., Essex, M. J., & Horton, F. (1993). Fathers and parental leave. *Journal of Family Issues, 14,* 616–641.

Hyde, Janet S., Fennema, Elizabeth, & Lamon, Susan J. (1990). Gender differences in mathematics performance: A meta-analysis. *Psychological Bulletin, 107,* 139–155.

Hyde, Janet S., Geiringer, Eva R., & Yen, Wendy M. (1975). On the empirical relation between spatial ability and sex differences in other aspects of cognitive performance. *Multivariate Behavioral Research, 10,* 289–310.

Hyde, Janet S., & Jaffee, Sara R. (2000). Becoming a heterosexual adult: The experiences of young women. *Journal of Social Issues, 56,* 283–296.

Hyde, Janet S., Klein, M., Essex, M. J., & Clark, R. (1995). Maternity leave and women's mental health. *Psychology of Women Quarterly.*

Hyde, Janet S., & Kling, Kristin C. (2001). Women, motivation, and achievement. *Psychology of Women Quarterly, 25,* 364–378.

Hyde, Janet S., Krajnik, Michelle, & Skuldt-Niederberger, Kristin. (1991). Androgyny across the life span: A replication and longitudinal follow-up. *Developmental Psychology, 27,* 516–519.

Hyde, Janet S., & Linn, Marcia C. (Eds.). (1986). *The psychology of gender: Advances through meta-analysis.* Baltimore: Johns Hopkins University Press.

Hyde, Janet S., & Linn, Marcia C. (1988). Gender differences in verbal ability: A meta-analysis. *Psychological Bulletin, 104,* 53–69.

Hyde, Janet S., & Phillis, Diane E. (1979). Androgyny across the lifespan. *Developmental Psychology, 15,* 334–336.

Hyde, Janet S., & Rosenberg, B. G. (1976). *Half the human experience: The psychology of women* (1st ed.). Lexington, MA: D. C. Heath.

Hyde, Janet S., Rosenberg, B. G., & Behrman, JoAnn. (1977). Tomboyism. *Psychology of Women Quarterly, 2,* 73–75.

Ickovics, Jeannette R., Thayaparan, Beatrice, & Ethier, Kathleen. (2000). Women and AIDS: A contextual analysis. In A. Baum et al. (Eds.), *Handbook of health psychology* (pp. 821–839). Hillsdale, NJ: Erlbaum.

Irvine, Jacqueline J. (1985). Teacher communication patterns as related to the race and sex of the student. *Journal of Educational Research, 78,* 338–345.

Irvine, Jacqueline J. (1986). Teacher-student interactions: Effects of student race, sex, and grade level. *Journal of Educational Psychology, 78,* 14–21.

Jackson, Dorothy W., & Tein, J. (1998). Adolescents' conceptualization of adult roles: Relationships with age, gender, work goal, and maternal employment. *Sex Roles, 38,* 987–1008.

Jackson, Linda A. (1992). *Physical appearance and gender: Sociobiological and sociocultural perspectives.* Albany: State University of New York Press.

Jackson, Linda A., Ervin, K., Gardner, P., & Schmitt, N. (2001). Gender and the Internet: Women communicating and men searching. *Sex Roles, 44,* 363–379.

Jacobs, Janis E., Lanza, S., Osgood, D., Eccles, J., & Wigfield, A. (2002). Changes in children's self-competence and values: Gender and domain differences across grades one through twelve. *Child Development, 73,* 509–527.

Jacobson, Neil, & Gottman, John. (1998). *When men batter women: New insights into ending abusive relationships.* New York: Simon & Schuster.

Jadack, Rosemary A., Hyde, Janet S., & Moore, Colleen F. (1995). Moral reasoning about sexually transmitted diseases. *Child Development, 66,* 167–177.

Jaffee, Sara, & Hyde, Janet S. (2000). Gender differences in moral orientation: A meta-analysis. *Psychological Bulletin, 126,* 703–726.

Jaggar, Alison M., & Rothenberg, Paula S. (1993). *Feminist frameworks: Alternative theoretical accounts of the relations between women and men* (3rd ed.). New York: McGraw-Hill.

Jakubowski, Patricia A. (1977). Assertive behavior and clinical problems of women. In E. I. Rawlings & D. K. Carter (Eds.), *Psychotherapy for women.* Springfield, IL: Charles C. Thomas.

Jakubowski-Spector, Patricia. (1973). Facilitating the growth of women through assertiveness training. *Counseling Psychologist, 4,* 75.

James, Stanlie M., & Busia, Abena. (Eds.). (1993). *Theorizing Black feminisms: The visionary pragmatism of Black women.* New York: Routledge.

Jamison, Kay R., Wellisch, D. K., & Pasnau, R. O. (1978). Psychosocial aspects of mastectomy: I. The woman's perspective. *American Journal of Psychiatry, 135,* 432–436.

Janowsky, Jeri S., Chavez, B., Zamboni, B., & Orwoll, E. (1998). The cognitive neuropsychology of sex hormones in men and women. *Developmental Neuropsychology, 14,* 421–440.

Janson-Smith, Deirdre. (1980). Sociobiology: So what? In Brighton Women & Science Group, *Alice through the microscope.* London: Virago.

Jay, Karla, & Young, Allen. (1979). *The gay report.* New York: Summit Books.

Jeanquart-Barone, Sandy. (1993). Trust differences between supervisors and subordinates: Examining the role of race and gender. *Sex Roles, 29,* 1–12.

Jenkins, Sharon R. (1987). Need for achievement and women's careers over 14 years: Evidence for occupational structure effects. *Journal of Personality and Social Psychology, 53,* 922–932.

Jennison, K. M., & Johnson, K. A. (2001). Parental alcoholism as a risk factor for DSM-IV-defined alcohol abuse and dependence in American women: The protective benefits of dyadic cohesion and marital communication. *American Journal of Drug and Alcohol Abuse, 27,* 349–374.

Johnson, Anne M., Wadsworth, Jane, Wellings, Kaye, & Field, Julia. (1994). *Sexual attitudes and lifestyles.* London: Blackwell.

Johnson, Cathryn. (1994). Gender, legitimate authority, and leader-subordinate conversations. *American Sociological Review, 59,* 122–135.

Joiner, Greg W., & Kashubeck, Susan. (1996). Acculturation, body image, self-esteem, and eating-disorder symptomatology in adolescent Mexican American women. *Psychology of Women Quarterly, 20,* 419–436.

Joiner, R. E., Heatherton, Todd F., Rudd, M. D., & Schmidt, N. (1997b). Perfectionism, perceived weight status, and bulimic symptoms: Two studies testing a diathesis-stress model. *Journal of Abnormal Psychology, 106,* 145–153.

Joiner, Thomas E., Heatherton, Todd F., & Keel, P. K. (1997a). Ten-year stability and predictive validity of five bulimia-related indicators. *American Journal of Psychiatry, 154,* 1133–1138.

Jones, James M. (1991). Psychological models of race: What have they been and what should they be? In J. D. Goodchilds (Ed.), *Psychological perspectives on human diversity in America.* Washington, DC: American Psychological Association.

Jourard, Sydney M. (1974). *Healthy personality: An approach from the viewpoint of humanistic psychology.* New York: Macmillan.

Kahn, Arnold S., Mathie, V. A., & Torgler, C. (1994). Rape scripts and rape acknowledgement. *Psychology of Women Quarterly, 18,* 53–66.

Kalil, Kathleen, Gruber, James, Conley, Joyce, & Sytniac, Michael. (1993). Social and family pressures on anxiety and stress during pregnancy. *Pre- and Perinatal Psychology Journal, 8,* 113–118.

Kamerman, Sheila B. (2000). Parental leave policies. *Social Policy Report of the Society for Research in Child Development, 14,* 1–15.

Kandall, Stephen R. (1996). *Substance and shadow: Women and addiction in the United States.* Cambridge, MA: Harvard University Press.

Kaplan, Helen S. (1995). *The sexual desire disorders: Dysfunctional regulation of sexual motivation.* New York: Brunner/Mazel.

Kaplan, Helen S., & Sager, Clifford J. (1971, June). Sexual patterns at different ages. *Medical Aspects of Human Sexuality, 10*–23.

Kaplan, Helen Singer. (1979). *Disorders of sexual desire.* New York: Simon & Schuster.

Katchadourian, H. A., & Lunde, D. D. (1972). *Fundamentals of human sexuality.* New York: Holt, Rinehart & Winston.

Katz, Jennifer, & Farrow, Sherry. (2000). Discrepant self-views and young women's sexual and emotional adjustment. *Sex Roles, 42,* 781–806.

Katz, Joseph. (1983). White faculty struggling with the effects of racism. In J. H. Cones, J. F. Noonan, & D. Janha (Eds.), *Teaching minority students.* San Francisco: Jossey-Bass.

Kaufman, Gayle. (1999). The portrayal of men's family roles in television commercials. *Sex Roles, 41,* 439–458.

Kegel, A. H. (1952). Sexual functions of the pubococcygeus muscle. *Western Journal of Surgery, 60,* 521–524.

Kelly, Janice R., & Hutson-Comeaux, Sarah L. (1999). Gender-emotion stereotypes are context specific. *Sex Roles, 40,* 107–120.

Kendall-Tackett, Kathleen, Williams, L., & Finkelhor, D. (1993). Impact of sexual abuse on children: A review and synthesis of recent empirical studies. *Psychological Bulletin, 113,* 164–180.

Kendler, Kenneth S., et al. (2000). Childhood sexual abuse and adult psychiatric and substance use disorders in women: An epidemiological and cotwin control analysis. *Archives of General Psychiatry, 57,* 953–959.

Kerpelman, Jennifer L., & Schvaneveldt, P. (1999). Young adults' anticipated identity importance of career, marital, and parental roles: Comparisons of men and women with different role balance orientations. *Sex Roles, 41,* 189–218.

Kessler, Ronald, McGonagle, K., Swartz, M., Blazer, D., & Nelson, C. (1993). Sex and depression in the National Comorbidity Survey, I: Lifetime prevalence, chronicity, and recurrence. *Journal of Affective Disorders, 29*, 85–96.

Kessler, Ronald, McGonagle, K., Zhao, S., et al. (1994). Lifetime and 12-month prevalence of DSM-III-R psychiatric disorders in the United States: Results from the National Comorbidity Survey. *Archives of General Psychiatry, 51*, 8–19.

Kessler, S. J., & McKenna, Wendy. (1985). *Gender: An ethnomethodological approach.* Chicago: University of Chicago Press.

Key, Mary Ritchie. (1975). *Male/female language.* Metuchen, NJ: Scarecrow Press.

Kibria, Nazli. (1990). Power, patriarchy, and gender conflict in the Vietnamese immigrant community. *Gender & Society, 4*, 9–24.

Kidwell, C. S. (1976, December). The status of American Indian women in higher education. In National Institute of Education, *Conference on the Educational and Occupational Needs of American Indian women* (pp. 83–123). Washington, DC: U.S. Department of Education.

Kiecolt-Glaser, Janice K., & Newton, Tamara L. (2001). Marriage and health: His and hers. *Psychological Bulletin, 127*, 472–503.

Kilbey, M. Marlyne, & Burgermeister, Diane. (2001). Substance abuse. In J. Worell (Ed.), *Encyclopedia of women and gender* (pp. 1113–1128). San Diego: Academic Press.

Kilbourne, Jean. (1994). Still killing us softly: Advertising and the obsession with thinness. In P. Fallon, M. Katzman, & S. Woolley (Eds.), *Feminist perspectives on eating disorders* (pp. 395–418). New York: Guilford.

Kilmartin, Christopher T. (2000). *The masculine self* (2nd ed.). New York: McGraw-Hill.

Kim, Bryan S. K., Yang, Peggy H., Atkinson, Donald R., Wolfe, Maren M., & Hong, Sehee. (2001). Cultural value similarities and differences among Asian American ethnic groups. *Cultural Diversity and Ethnic Minority Psychology, 7*, 343–361.

Kim, Elaine H. (1990, Winter). "Such opposite creatures": Men and women in Asian American literature. *Michigan Quarterly Review, 29*, 68–93.

Kimball, Meredith M. (1989). A new perspective on women's math achievement. *Psychological Bulletin, 105*, 198–214.

Kimmel, Ellen B., & Crawford, Mary. (2001). Methods for studying gender. In J. Worell (Ed.), *Encyclopedia of women and gender* (pp. 749–758). San Diego: Academic Press.

Kimmel, Michael. (2000). "White men are this nation": Right-wing militias and the restoration of rural American masculinity. *Rural Sociology, 65*, 582–604.

Kimmel, Michael. (2001, December). Lecture delivered at the University of Wisconsin, Madison.

Kimmel, Michael S., & Messner, Michael A. (2001). *Men's lives* (5th ed.). Boston: Allyn and Bacon.

Kimura, Doreen, & Hampson, E. (1994). Cognitive pattern in men and women is influenced by fluctuations in sex hormones. *Current Directions, 3*, 57–60.

King, John, Bond, T., & Blandford, S. (2002). An investigation of computer anxiety by gender and grade. *Computers in Human Behavior, 18*, 69–84.

Kinsey, Alfred C., Pomeroy, Wardell B., Martin, Clyde E., & Gebhard, Paul H. (1953). *Sexual behavior in the human female.* Philadelphia: Saunders.

Kirschstein, Ruth L. (1996). Women physicians— Good news and bad news. *New England Journal of Medicine, 334*, 982–983.

Kivnick, Helen Q. (1983). Dimensions of grandparenthood meaning: Deductive conceptualization and empirical derivation. *Journal of Personality and Social Psychology, 44*, 1056–1068.

Klatsky, A. L., Armstrong, M. A., & Friedman, G. D. (1992). Alcohol and mortality. *Annals of Internal Medicine, 117*, 646–654.

Klebanov, Pamela K., & Jemmott, John B. (1992). Effects of expectations and bodily sensations on self-reports of premenstrual symptoms. *Psychology of Women Quarterly, 16*, 289–310.

Kling, Kristen C., Hyde, J., Showers, C., & Buswell, B. (1999). Gender differences in self-esteem: A meta-analysis. *Psychological Bulletin, 125*, 470–500.

Klinkenberg, D., & Rose, S. (1994). Dating scripts of gay men and lesbians. *Journal of Homosexuality, 26*(4), 23–35.

Klonoff, Elizabeth A., Landrine, Hope, & Campbell, Robin. (2000). Sexist discrimination may account for well-known gender differences in psychiatric symptoms. *Psychology of Women Quarterly, 24*, 93–99.

Klonoff, Elizabeth A., Landrine, Hope, & Ullman, Jodie B. (1999). Racial discrimination and psychiatric symptoms among Blacks. *Cultural Diversity and Ethnic Minority Psychology, 5*, 329–339.

Knox, Sarah S., & Czajkowski, Susan. (1997). The influence of behavioral and psychosocial factors on cardiovascular health in women. In S. Gallant, G. Keita, & R. Royak-Schaler (Eds.), *Health care for women: Psychological, social, and behavioral influences* (pp. 257–272). Washington, DC: American Psychological Association.

Kohlberg, Lawrence. (1966). A cognitive-developmental analysis of children's sex-role concepts and attitudes. In E. E. Maccoby (Ed.), *The development of sex differences.* Stanford: Stanford University Press.

Kohlberg, Lawrence. (1969). Stage and sequence: The cognitive-developmental approach to socialization. In D. A. Goslin (Ed.), *Handbook of socialization theory and research.* Chicago: Rand McNally.

Kolbo, Jerome R., Blakely, Eleanor, & Engleman, D. (1996). Children who witness domestic violence: A review of empirical literature. *Journal of Interpersonal Violence, 11,* 281–293.

Koonin, L. M., et al. (1991, July). Abortion surveillance, United States, 1988. *Morbidity and Mortality Weekly Report, 40,* No. SS-1, 15–42.

Koss, Mary P. (1990). The Women's Mental Health Research Agenda: Violence against women. *American Psychologist, 45,* 374–380.

Koss, Mary P. (1993). Rape: Scope, impact, interventions, and public policy responses. *American Psychologist, 48,* 1062–1069.

Koss, Mary P., et al. (1987). The scope of rape: Incidence and prevalence in a national sample of higher education students. *Journal of Consulting and Clinical Psychology, 55,* 162–170.

Koss, Mary P., et al. (1988). Stranger and acquaintance rape: Are there differences in the victim's experience? *Psychology of Women Quarterly, 12,* 1–24.

Koss, Mary P., & Cook, Sarah L. (1994). Facing the facts: Date and acquaintance rape are widespread forms of violence. In M. Koss et al. (Eds.), *No safe haven.* Washington, DC: American Psychological Association.

Koss, Mary P., Goodman, Lisa A., Browne, Angela, Fitzgerald, Louise F., Russo, Nancy F., & Keita, Gwendolyn P. (1994). *No safe haven: Male violence against women at home, at work, and in the community.* Washington, DC: American Psychological Association.

Koss, Mary P., & Heslet, Lynette. (1992). Somatic consequences of violence against women. *Archives of Family Medicine, 1,* 53–59.

Koss, Mary P., Koss, Paul G., & Woodruff, W. Joy. (1991). Deleterious effects of criminal victimization on women's health and medical utilization. *Archives of Internal Medicine, 151,* 342–347.

Kowalski, Robin M., & Chapple, Tracy. (2000). The social stigma of menstruation: Fact or fiction? *Psychology of Women Quarterly, 24,* 74–80.

Kring, Ann M., & Gordon, Albert H. (1998). Sex differences in emotion: Expression, experience, and physiology. *Journal of Personality and Social Psychology, 74,* 686–703.

Kuhn, D. (1976). Short-term longitudinal evidence for the sequentiality of Kohlberg's early stage of moral development. *Developmental Psychology, 12,* 162–166.

Kuhn, Thomas S. (1970). *The structure of scientific revolutions.* Chicago: University of Chicago Press.

Kunkel, Adrianne W., & Burleson, Brant R. (1998). Social support and the emotional lives of men and women: An assessment of the different cultures perspective. In D. Canary & K. Dindia (Eds.), *Sex differences and similarities in communication* (pp. 101–126). Mahwah, NJ: Erlbaum.

Kushner, M. G., Sher, K. J., & Beitman, B. D. (1990). The relation between alcohol problems and the anxiety disorders. *American Journal of Psychiatry, 147,* 685–695.

Ladas, Alice K., Whipple, Beverly, & Perry, J. D. (1982). *The G-spot.* New York: Holt, Rinehart & Winston.

LaFrance, Marianne. (1981). Gender gestures: sex, sex-role, and nonverbal communication. In C. Mayo & N. Henley (Eds.), *Gender and nonverbal behavior.* New York: Springer-Verlag.

LaFromboise, Teresa D., Berman, Joan, S., & Sohi, Balvindar K. (1994). American Indian women. In L. Comas-Diaz & B. Greene (Eds.), *Women of color: Integrating ethnic and gender identities in psychotherapy* (pp. 30–71). New York: Guilford.

LaFromboise, Teresa, Choney, Sandra B., James, Amy, & Running Wolf, Paulette R. (1995). American Indian women and psychology. In H. Landrine (Ed.), *Bringing cultural diversity to feminist psychology: Theory, research, and practice* (pp. 197–240). Washington, DC: American Psychological Association.

LaFromboise, Teresa D., Heyle, Anneliese M., & Ozer, Emily J. (1990). Changing and diverse roles of women in American Indian culture. *Sex Roles, 22,* 455–476.

Lahn, B., & Page, D. (1997). Functional coherence of the human Y chromosome. *Science, 278,* 675–680.

Laird, Joan, & Green, Robert-Jay (Eds.). (1996). *Lesbians and gays in couples and families.* San Francisco: Jossey-Bass.

Lakoff, Robin. (1973). Language and woman's place. *Language and Society, 2,* 45–79. (Reprinted 1975 in paperback. New York: Harper & Row.)

Lal, Shafali. (2002). Giving children security: Mamie Phipps Clark and the racialization of child psychology. *American Psychologist, 57,* 20–28.

Lamb, C. Sue, Jackson, Lee A., Cassiday, Patricia B., & Priest, Doris J. (1993). Body figure preferences of men and women: A comparison of two generations. *Sex Roles, 28,* 345–358.

Lamb, Michael E. (1979). Paternal influences and the father's role. *American Psychologist, 34,* 938–943.

Lamb, Sharon. (2001). *The secret lives of girls.* New York: Free Press.

Lamberts, Steven, et al. (1997). The endocrinology of aging. *Science, 278,* 419–424.

Landrine, Hope. (1987). On the politics of madness: A preliminary analysis of the relationship between social roles and psychopathology. *Psychological Monographs, 113*(3), 341–406.

Landrine, Hope. (1988a). Depression and stereotypes of women: Preliminary empirical analyses of the gender-role hypothesis. *Sex Roles, 19,* 527–541.

Landrine, Hope. (1988b). Revising the framework of abnormal psychology. In P. Bronstein & K. Quina (Eds.), *Teaching a psychology of people.* Washington, DC: American Psychological Association.

Landrine, Hope. (1989). The politics of personality disorder. *Psychology of Women Quarterly, 13,* 325–339.

Landrine, Hope. (Ed.). (1995). *Bringing cultural diversity to feminist psychology.* Washington, DC: American Psychological Association.

Landrine, Hope, & Klonoff, Elizabeth A. (2001). Health and health care: How gender makes women sick. In J. Worell (Ed.), *Encyclopedia of women and gender* (pp. 577–592). San Diego: Academic Press.

Landrine, Hope, Klonoff, Elizabeth A., & Brown-Collins, Alice. (1992). Cultural diversity and methodology in feminist psychology. *Psychology of Women Quarterly, 16,* 145–163.

Landrine, Hope, Klonoff, Elizabeth A., & Brown-Collins, Alice. (1995). Cultural diversity and methodology in feminist psychology: Critique, proposal, empirical example. In H. Landrine (Ed.), *Bringing cultural diversity to feminist psychology* (pp. 55–76). Washington, DC: American Psychological Association.

Lanius, Cynthia. (2002). GirlTECH: Getting girls interested in computers. Available online at *www.math.rice.edu/~lanius/club/girls.html.*

LaRossa, Ralph, Jaret, Charles, Gadgil, Malati, & Wynn, G. (2001). Gender disparities in Mother's Day and Father's Day comic strips: A 54-year history. *Sex Roles, 44,* 693–718.

Larson, Reed W., Richards, Maryse H., & Perry-Jenkins, Maureen. (1994). Divergent worlds: The daily emotional experience of mothers and fathers in the domestic and public spheres. *Journal of Personality and Social Psychology, 67,* 1034–1046.

Laumann, Edward O., Gagnon, John H., Michael, Robert T., & Michaels, Stuart. (1994). *The social organization of sexuality: Sexual practices in the United States.* Chicago: University of Chicago Press.

Laumann, Edward O., Paik, Anthony, & Rosen, Raymond. (1999). Sexual dysfunction in the United States: Prevalence and predictors. *Journal of the American Medical Association, 281,* 537–544.

Lavine, Howard, Sweeney, D., & Wagner, S. (1999). Depicting women as sex objects in television advertising: Effects on body dissatisfaction. *Personality and Social Psychology Bulletin, 25,* 1049–1058.

Lawler, Andrew. (1999). Tenured women battle to make it less lonely at the top. *Science, 286,* 1272–1278.

Lazarus, A. (1985). Psychiatric sequelae of legalized elective first trimester abortion. *Journal of Psychosomatic Obstetrics and Gynecology, 4,* 141.

Lazarus, Arnold A. (1974). Women in behavior therapy. In V. Franks & V. Burtle (Eds.), *Women in therapy.* New York: Brunner/Mazel.

Leaper, Campbell, Anderson, K., & Sanders, P. (1998). Moderators of gender effects on parents' talk to their children: A meta-analysis. *Developmental Psychology, 34,* 3–27.

Lear, M. W. (1973, January 28). Is there a male menopause? *New York Times Magazine,* January 28.

LeDoux, Joseph E. (1994). Emotion-specific physiological activity: Don't forget about CNS physiology. In P. Ekman & R. J. Davidson (Eds.), *The nature of emotion: Fundamental questions* (pp. 248–251). New York: Oxford University Press.

Leiblum, Sandra R., & Rosen, Raymond C. (1989). *Principles and practice of sex therapy* (2nd ed.). New York: Guilford.

Leiblum, Sandra R., & Rosen, Raymond C. (Eds.). (1988). *Sexual desire disorders.* New York: Guilford.

Leifer, Myra. (1980). *Psychological effects of motherhood: A study of first pregnancy.* New York: Praeger.

Leinbach, M., & Fagot, Beverly. (1993). Categorical habituation to male and female faces: Gender schematic processing in infancy. *Infant Behavior and Development, 16,* 317–332.

Leinbach, Mary D. (1993). Which one is the daddy? Children's use of conventionally and metaphorically gendered attributes to assign gender to animal figures. Presented at the meeting of the Society for Research in Child Development, New Orleans.

Lenney, Ellen. (1977). Women's self-confidence in achievement settings. *Psychological Bulletin, 84,* 1–13.

Lenney, Ellen. (1981). What's fine for the gander isn't always good for the goose: Sex differences in self-confidence as a function of ability area and comparison with others. *Sex Roles, 7,* 905–924.

Leonard, D. K., & Jiang, J. (1999). Gender bias and the college prediction of the SATs: A cry of despair. *Research in Higher Education, 40,* 375–407.

Lepowsky, Maria A. (1993). *Fruit of the motherland: Gender in an egalitarian society.* New York: Columbia University Press.

Lerman, Hannah. (1986). From Freud to feminist personality theory. *Psychology of Women Quarterly, 10,* 1–18.

Lerner, Harriet G. (1985). *The dance of anger: A woman's guide to changing the patterns of intimate relationships.* New York: Harper & Row.

LeVay, Simon. (1991). A difference in hypothalamic structure between heterosexual and homosexual men. *Science, 253,* 1034–1037.

Levendosky, Alytia, Huth-Bocks, A., & Semel, M. (2002a). Adolescent peer relationships and mental health functioning in families with domestic violence. *Journal of Clinical Child and Adolescent Psychology, 31,* 206–218.

Levendosky, Alytia, Huth-Bocks, A., Semel, M., & Shapiro, D. (2002b). Trauma symptoms in preschool-age children exposed to domestic violence. *Journal of Interpersonal Violence, 17,* 150–164.

Levenson, Robert W., Carstensen, Laura L., & Gottman, John M. (1994). The influence of age and gender on affect, physiology, and their interrelations: A study of long-term marriages. *Journal of Personality and Social Psychology, 67,* 56–68.

Levine, James, et al. (2001). The work burden of women. *Science, 294,* 812.

Levine, Michael P., Smolak, Linda, Moodey, Anne F., Shuman, Melissa D., & Hessen, Laura D. (1994). Normative developmental challenges and dieting and eating disturbances in middle school girls. *International Journal of Eating Disorders, 15,* 11–20.

Levinson, Daniel J. (1978). *The seasons of a man's life.* New York: Ballantine.

Levy, Gary D. (1994). High and low gender schematic children's release from proactive interference. *Sex Roles, 30,* 93–108.

Levy, Gary D. (1999). Gender-typed and non-gender-typed category awareness in toddlers. *Sex Roles, 41,* 851–874.

Levy, Jere. (1976). Cerebral lateralization and spatial ability. *Behavior Genetics, 6,* 171–188.

Levy-Agresti, Jere, & Sperry, Roger W. (1968). Differential perceptual capacities in major and minor hemispheres. *Proceedings of the National Academy of Science, 61,* 1151.

Lewin, Miriam, & Wild, Cheryl L. (1991). The impact of the feminist critique on tests, assessments, and methodology. *Psychology of Women Quarterly, 15,* 581–596.

Lex, Barbara W. (2000). Gender and cultural influences on substance abuse. In R. Eisler & M. Hersen (Eds.), *Handbook of gender, culture, and health* (pp. 255–298). Mahwah, NJ: Erlbaum.

Liang, Belle, Tracy, A., Taylor, C., Williams, L., Jordan, J., & Miller, J. (2002). The Relational Health Indices: A study of women's relationships. *Psychology of Women Quarterly, 26,* 25–35.

Liben, Lynn S., et al. (2002). The effects of sex steroids on spatial performance: A review and an experimental clinical investigation. *Developmental Psychology, 38,* 236–253.

Lieber, Eli, Chin, Dorothy, Nihira, Kazuo, & Mink, Iris T. (2001). Holding on and letting go: Identity and acculturation among Chinese immigrants. *Cultural Diversity and Ethnic Minority Psychology, 7,* 247–261.

Liem, Ramsay, Lim, Benedict A., & Liem, Joan H. (2000). Acculturation and emotion among Asian Americans. *Cultural Diversity and Ethnic Minority Psychology, 6*, 13–31.

Lightdale, Jenifer R., & Prentice, Deborah A. (1994). Rethinking sex differences in aggression: Aggressive behavior in the absence of social roles. *Personality and Social Psychology Bulletin, 20*, 34–44.

Lindsey, Eric W., Mize, J., & Pettit, G. (1997). Differential play patterns of mothers and fathers of sons and daughters: Implications for children's gender role development. *Sex Roles, 37*, 643–662.

Lindsey, Eric W., & Mize, Jacquelyn. (2001). Contextual differences in parent-child play: Implications for children's gender role development. *Sex Roles, 44*, 155–176.

Lindsey, Robert. (1988, February 1). Circumcision under criticism as unnecessary to newborn. *New York Times*, A1.

Linn, Marcia C., & Hyde, Janet S. (1990). Gender, mathematics, and science. *Educational Researcher, 18*(8), 17–19, 22–27.

Linn, Marcia C., & Petersen, Anne C. (1985). Emergence and characterization of sex differences in spatial ability: A meta-analysis. *Child Development, 56*, 1479–1498.

Lippa, Richard A., Martin, L., & Friedman, H. (2000). Gender-related individual differences and mortality in the Terman longitudinal study: Is masculinity hazardous to your health? *Personality and Social Psychology Bulletin, 26*, 1560–1570.

Lips, Hilary M. (1989). Gender-role socialization: Lessons in femininity. In Jo Freeman (Ed.), *Women: A feminist perspective* (4th ed.). Mountain View, CA: Mayfield Publishing.

Liss, Miriam, Hoffner, Carolyn, & Crawford, Mary. (2000). What do feminists believe? *Psychology of Women Quarterly, 24*, 279–284.

Liu, Peter, & Chan, Connie S. (1996), Lesbian, gay, and bisexual Asian Americans and their families. In J. Laird & R. Green (Eds.), *Lesbians and gays in couples and families*. San Francisco: Jossey-Bass.

Loewenstein, Sophie F., et al. (1981). A study of satisfactions and stresses of single women in midlife. *Sex Roles, 7*, 1127–1141.

Loftus, Elizabeth F. (1993). The reality of repressed memories. *American Psychologist, 48*, 518–537.

Loftus, Elizabeth F., Polonsky, Sara, & Fullilove, Mindy T. (1994). Memories of childhood sexual abuse: Remembering and repressing. *Psychology of Women Quarterly, 18*, 67–84.

Longhurst, James G., & Weiss, Erica. (1998). Use of psychotropic medications during lactation. *American Journal of Psychiatry, 155*, 1643.

Lonsway, Kimberly A. (1996). Preventing acquaintance rape through education: What do we know? *Psychology of Women Quarterly, 20*, 229–266.

Lonsway, Kimberly A., & Kothari, Chevon. (2000). First year campus acquaintance rape education: Evaluating the impact of a mandatory intervention. *Psychology of Women Quarterly, 24*, 220–232.

Loo, Robert, & Thorpe, Karran. (1998). Attitudes toward women's roles in society: A replication after 20 years. *Sex Roles, 39*, 903–912.

LoPiccolo, Joseph, & Stock, Wendy E. (1986). Treatment of sexual dysfunction. *Journal of Consulting and Clinical Psychology, 54*, 158–167.

LoPiccolo, Leslie. (1980). Low sexual desire. In S. R. Leiblum & L. A. Pervin (Eds.), *Principles and practice of sex therapy*. New York: Guilford Press.

Lorber, Judith, et al. (1981). On *The Reproduction of Mothering*: A methodological debate. *Signs, 6*(3), 482–513.

Lorber, Judith, & Farrell, Susan A. (Eds.). (1991). *The social construction of gender*. Newbury Park, CA: Sage.

Lott, Bernice, & Maluso, D. (1993). The social learning of gender. In A. E. Beall & R. J. Sternberg (Eds.), *The psychology of gender* (pp. 99–126). New York: Guilford.

Lott, Juanita Tamayo. (1990). A portrait of Asian and Pacific American women. In S. Rix (Ed.), *The American woman 1990–91*. New York: Norton.

Lowenthal, M. F., et al. (1975). *Four stages of life: A comparative study of women and men facing transitions*. San Francisco: Jossey-Bass.

Lubinski, David, Benbow, C., Shea, D., Eftekhari-Sanjani, H., & Halvorson, M. (2001). Men and women at promise for scientific excellence: Similarity not dissimilarity. *Psychological Science, 12*, 309–317.

Luker, Kristin. (1975). *Taking chances: Abortion and the decision not to contracept*. Berkeley: University of California Press.

Lundberg, Ulf, & Patt, Deirdre. (2000). Neurohormonal factors, stress, health, and gender. In R. Eisler & M. Hersen (Eds.), *Handbook of gender, culture, and health* (pp. 21–42). Mahwah, NJ: Erlbaum.

Lynn, David B. (1974). *The father: His role in child development*. Monterey, CA: Brooks/Cole.

Lytle, L. Jean, Bakken, L., & Romig, C. (1997). Adolescent female identity development. *Sex Roles, 37,* 175–186.

Lytton, Hugh, & Romney, David M. (1991). Parents' differential socialization of boys and girls: A meta-analysis. *Psychological Bulletin, 109,* 267–296.

Macaulay, Monica, & Bruce, Colleen. (1997). Don't touch my projectile: Gender bias and stereotyping in syntactic examples. *Language: Journal of the Linguistic Society of America, 73,* 798–825.

Maccoby, Eleanor E. (1998). *The two sexes: Growing up apart, coming together.* Cambridge, MA: Harvard University Press.

Maccoby, Eleanor E. (2002). Gender and group process: A developmental perspective. *Current Directions in Psychological Science, 11,* 54–58.

Maccoby, Eleanor E., & Jacklin, Carol N. (1973). Stress, activity and proximity seeking: Sex differences in the year-old child. *Child Development, 44,* 34–42.

Maccoby, Eleanor E., & Jacklin, Carol N. (1974). *The psychology of sex differences.* Stanford: Stanford University Press.

Macdonald, Nancy E., & Hyde, Janet S. (1980). Fear of success, need achievement, and fear of failure: A factor-analytic study. *Sex Roles, 6,* 695–712.

Mackey, Wade, C. (2001). Support for the existence of an independent man-to-child affiliative bond: Fatherhood as a biocultural invention. *Psychology of Men and Masculinity, 2,* 51–66.

Mackie, Gerry. (1996). Ending footbinding and infibulation: A convention account. *American Sociological Review, 61,* 999–1017.

MacKinnon, Catharine A. (1979). *Sexual harassment of working women.* New Haven: Yale University Press.

MacKinnon, Catharine A. (1982). Feminism, Marxism, method, and the state: An agenda for theory. In N. O. Keohane et al. (Eds.), *Feminist theory.* Chicago: University of Chicago Press.

MacMillan, Harriet L., et al. (2001). Childhood abuse and lifetime psychopathology in a community sample. *American Journal of Psychiatry, 158,* 1878–1883.

Magaña, J. R., & Carrier, J. M. (1991). Mexican and Mexican American male sexual behavior and spread of AIDS in California. *Journal of Sex Research, 28,* 425–441.

Mahalik, James R., Locke, Benjamin D., Theodore, Harry, Cournoyer, Robert J., & Lloyd, Brendan F. (2001). A cross-national and cross-sectional comparison of men's gender role conflict and its

relationship to social intimacy and self-esteem. *Sex Roles, 45,* 1–14.

Maisch, H. (1972). *Incest.* New York: Stein and Day.

Major, Brenda. (1989). Gender differences in comparisons and entitlement: Implications for comparable worth. *Journal of Social Issues, 45*(4), 99–115.

Major, Brenda, Barr, Leslie, Zubek, Josephine, & Babey, Susan H. (1999). Gender and self-esteem: A meta-analysis. In W. Swann, J. Langlois, & L. Gilbert (Eds.), *Sexism and stereotypes in modern society: The gender science of Janet Taylor Spence* (pp. 223–254). Washington, DC: American Psychological Association.

Malamuth, Neil M. (1998). The confluence model as an organizing framework for research on sexually aggressive men: Risk, moderators, imagined aggression, and pornography consumption. In R. Geen & E. Donnerstein (Eds.), *Aggression: Theoretical and empirical reviews.* New York: Academic Press.

Malamuth, Neil M., Sockloskie, R., Koss, M., & Tanaka, J. (1991). Characteristics of aggressors against women: Testing a model using a national sample of college students. *Journal of Consulting and Clinical Psychology, 59,* 670–681.

Malatesta, C., Culver, C., Tesman, J., & Shepard, B. (1989). The development of emotion expression during the first two years of life. *Monographs of the Society for Research in Child Development, 50,* serial no. 219.

Malone, T. W., & Lepper, M. R. (1986). Making learning fun: A taxonomy of intrinsic motivation for learning. In R. Snow & M. Farr (Eds.), *Aptitude, learning, and instruction* (Vol. 3). Hillsdale, NJ: Erlbaum.

Manber, Rachel, & Bootzin, Richard. (1997). Sleep and the menstrual cycle. *Health Psychology, 16,* 209–214.

Mandel, William. (1975). *Soviet women.* Garden City, NY: Anchor.

Mansfield, Phyllis K., Koch, Patricia B., & Voda, Ann M. (1998). Qualities midlife women desire in their sexual relationships and their changing sexual response. *Psychology of Women Quarterly, 22,* 285–304.

Marchetti, Gina. (1993). *Romance and the "yellow peril": Race, sex, and discursive strategies in Hollywood fiction.* Berkeley: University of California Press.

Marcus, Dale E., & Overton, W. F. (1978). The development of cognitive gender constancy and sex preferences. *Child Development, 49,* 434–444.

Marshall, W. L. (1993). A revised approach to the treatment of men who sexually assault adult females. In G. Hall et al. (Eds.), *Sexual aggression* (pp. 142–165). Washington, DC: Taylor & Francis.

Marshall, W. L., & Pithers, W. D. (1994). A reconsideration of treatment outcome with sex offenders. *Criminal Justice and Behavior, 21,* 10–27.

Marsiglio, William, Amato, Paul, Day, Randal, & Lamb, Michael. (2000). Scholarship on fatherhood in the 1990s and beyond. *Journal of Marriage and the Family, 62,* 1173–1191.

Martin, Carol L. (1999). A developmental perspective on gender effects and gender concepts. In W. Swann, J. Langlois, & L. Gilbert (Eds.), *Sexism and stereotypes in modern society: The gender science of Janet Taylor Spence* (pp. 45–74). Washington, DC: American Psychological Association.

Martin, Carol L. (2000). Cognitive theories of gender development. T. Eckes & H. Trautner (Eds.), *The developmental social psychology of gender* (pp. 91–122). Mahwah, NJ: Erlbaum.

Martin, Carol L., & Dinella, Lisa M. (2001). Gender development: Gender schema theory. In J. Worell (Ed.), *Encyclopedia of women and gender* (pp. 507–522). San Diego: Academic Press.

Martin, Carol L., & Halverson, C. F. (1983). The effects of sex-typing schemas on young children's memory. *Child Development, 54,* 563–574.

Martin, Carol L., & Little, J. K. (1990). The relation of gender understanding to children's sex-typed preferences and gender stereotypes. *Child Development, 61,* 1427–1439.

Martin, Del. (1976). *Battered wives.* San Francisco: Glide Publications.

Martin, Del, & Lyon, Phyllis. (1972). *Lesbian/Woman.* San Francisco: Glide Publications.

Martin, Mary, & Gentry, J. (1997). Stuck in the model trap: The effects of beautiful models in ads on female pre-adolescents and adolescents. *Journal of Advertising, 26,* 19.

Martin, M. K., & Voorhies, B. (1975). *Female of the species.* New York: Columbia University Press.

Marván, Maria L., & Cortés-Iniestra, Sandra. (2001). Women's beliefs about the prevalence of premenstrual syndrome and biases in recall of premenstrual changes. *Health Psychology, 20,* 276–280.

Masters, William H., & Johnson, Virginia E. (1966). *Human sexual response.* Boston: Little Brown.

Masters, William H., & Johnson, Virginia E. (1970). *Human sexual inadequacy.* Boston: Little Brown.

Matthews, Alicia K., & Hughes, Tonda L. (2001). Mental health service use by African American women: Exploration of subpopulation differences. *Cultural Diversity and Ethnic Minority Psychology, 7,* 75–87.

Matthews, Karen A. (1982). Psychological perspectives on the Type A behavior pattern. *Psychological Bulletin, 91,* 293–323.

Matthews, Karen A., et al. (1997). Women's Health Initiative. *American Psychologist, 52,* 101–116.

Mays, Vickie M., & Cochran, Susan D. (1987). Acquired immunodeficiency syndrome and Black Americans: Social psychological issues. *Public Health Reports, 102,* 224–231.

McArthur, Leslie, & Eisen, S. (1976a). Achievement of male and female storybook characters as determinants of achievement behavior by boys and girls. *Journal of Personality and Social Psychology, 33,* 467–473.

McClelland, David C., Atkinson, J. W., Clark, R. A., & Lowell, F. L. (1953). *The achievement motive.* New York: Appleton-Century-Crofts.

McClintock, Martha K. (1971). Menstrual synchrony and suppression. *Nature, 229,* 244–245.

McConaghy, Nathaniel. (1987). A learning approach. In J. H. Geer & W. T. O'Donohue (Eds.), *Theories of human sexuality* (pp. 287–334). New York: Plenum.

McConnell, Allen R., & Fazio, Russell H. (1996). Women as men and people: Effects of gender-marked language. *Personality and Social Psychology Bulletin, 22,* 1004–1013.

McCormick, Cheryl M., & Teillon, Sarah M. (2001). Menstrual cycle variation in spatial ability: Relation to salivary cortisol levels. *Hormones and Behavior, 39,* 29–38.

McCormick, Naomi B. (1994). *Sexual salvation: Affirming women's sexual rights and pleasures.* New York: Praeger.

McCreary, Donald R., Newcomb, M., & Sadava, S. (1998). Dimensions of the male gender role: A confirmatory analysis in men and women. *Sex Roles, 39,* 81–96.

McCreary, Donald R., & Sadava, Stanley W. (2001). Gender differences in relationships among perceived attractiveness, life satisfaction, and health in adults as a function of body mass index and perceived weight. *Psychology of Men and Masculinity, 2,* 108–116.

McDonald, Justin D. (2000). A model for conducting research with American Indian participants. In *Guidelines for research in ethnic minority communities* (pp. 12–15). Washington, DC: American Psychological Association.

McEwen, Bruce S. (2001). Estrogen effects on the brain: Multiple sites and molecular mechanisms. *Journal of Applied Physiology, 91,* 2785–2801.

McFarlane, Jessica, Martin, Carol L., & Williams, Tannis M. (1988). Mood fluctuations: Women versus men and menstrual versus other cycles. *Psychology of Women Quarterly, 12,* 201–224.

McFarlane, Jessica M., & Williams, Tannis M. (1994). Placing premenstrual syndrome in perspective. *Psychology of Women Quarterly, 18,* 339–374.

McGraw-Hill Book Company. (1974). *Guidelines for equal treatment of the sexes in McGraw-Hill Book Company publications.* New York: McGraw-Hill.

McGue, Mark, & Slutske, W. (1996). The inheritance of alcoholism in women. In J. M. Howard et al. (Eds.), *Women and alcohol: Issues for prevention research.* National Institute on Alcohol Abuse and Alcoholism Research Monograph No. 32, NIH Publication No. 96–3817 (pp. 65–91).

McHugh, Maureen C., Frieze, Irene H., & Hanusa, Barbara H. (1982). Attributions and sex differences in achievement: Problems and new perspectives. *Sex Roles, 8,* 467–479.

McHugh, Maureen C., Koeske, Randi D., & Frieze, Irene H. (1986). Issues to consider in conducting nonsexist psychological research: A guide for researchers. *American Psychologist, 41,* 879–890.

McKay, R. (1978). One child families and atypical sex ratios in an elite black community. In R. Staples (Ed.), *The black family.* Belmont, CA: Wadsworth.

McKelvey, Mary W., & McKenry, Patrick C. (2000). The psychosocial well-being of Black and White mothers following marital dissolution. *Psychology of Women Quarterly, 24,* 4–14.

McKenna, Wendy, & Denmark, Florence L. (1978, March). *Gender and nonverbal behavior as cues to status and power.* Paper presented at the New York Academy of Sciences.

McKenna, Wendy, & Kessler, Suzanne J. (1977). Experimental design as a source of sex bias in social psychology. *Sex Roles, 3,* 117–128.

McKinlay, John B., McKinlay, Sonja M., & Brambilla, Donald J. (1987). Health status and utilization behavior associated with menopause. *American Journal of Epidemiology, 125,* 110–121.

McKinlay, Sonja M., Brambilla, D. J., & Posner, J. G. (1992). The normal menopause transition. *American Journal of Human Biology, 4,* 37–46.

McKinlay, Sonja M., & Jeffreys, Margot. (1974). The menopausal syndrome. *British Journal of Preventive and Social Medicine, 28*(2), 108.

McKinley, Nita M. (1998). Gender differences in undergraduates' body esteem: The mediating effect of objectified body consciousness and actual/ideal weight discrepancy. *Sex Roles, 39,* 113–124.

McKinley, Nita M., & Hyde, Janet S. (1996). The Objectified Body Consciousness Scale: Development and validation. *Psychology of Women Quarterly, 20,* 181–215.

McKinnon, Jesse, & Humes, Karen. (1999). *The Black population in the United States.* U.S. Census Bureau. Available online at *www.census.gov.*

McLanahan, Sara, & Adams, Julia. (1987). Parenthood and psychological well-being. *Annual Review of Sociology, 5,* 237–257.

McMahan, Ian D. (1971, April). *Sex differences in causal attributions following success and failure.* Paper presented at Eastern Psychological Association Meetings.

McMahan, Ian D. (1972, April). *Sex differences in expectancy of success as a function of task.* Paper presented at Eastern Psychological Association Meetings.

McMillan, Julie R., et al. (1977). Women's language: Uncertainty or interpersonal sensitivity and emotionality? *Sex Roles, 3,* 545–560.

McMillen, Curtis, Zuravin, Susan, & Rideout, Gregory. (1995). Perceived benefit from child sexual abuse. *Journal of Consulting and Clinical Psychology, 63,* 1037–1043.

McNair, Shannon, Korva-Petrova, A., & Bhargava, A. (2001). Computers and young children in the classroom: Strategies for minimizing gender bias. *Early Childhood Education Journal, 29,* 51–55.

McNally, Richard J., Clancy, S., Schacter, D., & Pitman, R. (2000). Personality profiles, dissociation, and absorption in women reporting repressed, recovered, or continuous memories of childhood sexual abuse. *Journal of Consulting and Clinical Psychology, 68,* 1033–1037.

McNally, Richard J., Clancy, Susan, & Schacter, Daniel. (2001). Directed forgetting of trauma cues in adults reporting repressed or recovered memories of childhood sexual abuse. *Journal of Abnormal Psychology, 110,* 151–156.

Mead, Margaret. (1935). *Sex and temperament in three primitive societies.* New York: William Morrow.

Mead, Margaret. (1949). *Male and female.* New York: William Morrow.

Mead, Margaret, & Kaplan, Frances B. (Eds.) (1965). *American women: The report of the President's Commission on the Status of Women.* New York: Charles Scribner's.

Meana, Marta, & Binik, Yitzchak. (1994). Painful coitus: A review of female dyspareunia. *Journal of Nervous and Mental Disease, 182,* 264–272.

Medicine, B. (1982). Native American women look at mental health. *Plainswoman, 6,* 7.

Mednick, Martha T. (1989). On the politics of psychological constructs: Stop the bandwagon, I want to get off. *American Psychologist, 44,* 1118–1123.

Mednick, Martha T., & Thomas, Veronica G. (1993). Women and the psychology of achievement: A view from the eighties. In F. L. Denmark & M. A. Paludi (Eds.), *Psychology of women: A handbook of issues and theories.* Westport, CT: Greenwood.

Meece, Judith L., Eccles Parsons, Jacquelynne, et al. (1982). Sex differences in math achievement: Toward a model of academic choice. *Psychological Bulletin, 91,* 324–448.

Meeker, B. F., & Weitzel-O'Neill, P. A. (1977). Sex roles and interpersonal behavior in task-oriented groups. *American Sociological Review, 42,* 91–104.

Meinert, Curtis L. (1995). The inclusion of women in clinical trials. *Science, 269,* 795–796.

Mendelson, B., Mendelson, M., & White, D. (2001). Body-esteem scale for adolescents and adults. *Journal of Personality Assessment, 76,* 90–106.

Merrill, Lex L., Thomsen, C., Sinclair, B., Gold, S., & Milner, J. (2001). Predicting the impact of child sexual abuse on women: The role of abuse severity, parental support, and coping strategies. *Journal of Consulting and Clinical Psychology, 69,* 992–1006.

Merskin, Debra. (1999). Adolescence, advertising, and the ideology of menstruation. *Sex Roles, 40,* 941–958.

Messner, Michael. (1990). Boyhood, organized sports, and the construction of masculinities. *Journal of Contemporary Ethnography, 18,* 416–444.

Messner, Michael A. (1998). The limits of "the male sex role": An analysis of the men's liberation and men's rights movements' discourse. *Gender and Society, 12,* 255–276.

Meyerowitz, Beth E. (1980). Psychosocial correlates of breast cancer and its treatments. *Psychological Bulletin, 87,* 108–131.

Meyerowitz, Beth E., Bull, Andrea A., & Perez, Martin A. (2000). Cancers common in women. In R. Eisler & M. Hersen (Eds.), *Handbook of gender, culture, and health* (pp. 197–226). Mahwah, NJ: Erlbaum.

Meyers, Diana T. (2001). The rush to motherhood—Pronatalist discourse and women's autonomy. *Signs: Journal of Women in Culture and Society, 26,* 735–773.

Michaud, Shari L., & Warner, R. (1997). Gender differences in self-reported response to troubles talk. *Sex Roles, 37,* 527–540.

Milburn, Michael A., Mather, Ro, & Conrad, S. (2000). The effects of viewing R-rated movie scenes that objectify women on perceptions of date rape. *Sex Roles, 43,* 645–664.

Milburn, Norweeta, & D'Ercole, Ann. (1991). Homeless women: Moving toward a comprehensive model. *American Psychologist, 46,* 1161–1169.

Milburn, Sharon S., Carney, Dana R., & Ramirez, Aaron M. (2001). Even in modern media, the picture is still the same: A content analysis of Clipart images. *Sex Roles, 44,* 277–294.

Milgram, Stanley. (1965). Some conditions of obedience and disobedience to authority. *Human Relations, 18,* 57–76.

Milgram, Stanley. (1974). *Obedience to authority.* New York: Harper & Row.

Mill, John Stuart. (1869). The subjection of women. (Reprinted in *Three essays by J. S. Mill.* London: Oxford University Press, 1966.)

Miller, B. A., et al. (1993). *SEER cancer statistics review: 1973–1990* (NIH Publication No. 93–2789). Bethesda, MD: National Cancer Institute.

Miller, C. L. (1983). Developmental changes in male/female voice classification by infants. *Infant Behavior and Development, 6,* 313–330.

Miller, Casey, & Swift, Kate. (1991). *Words and women* (2nd ed.). New York: Harper Collins.

Miller, Casey, & Swift, Kate. (1995). *The handbook of nonsexist writing for writers, editors, and speakers.* London: The Women's Press.

Miller, Jean B. (1983). The construction of anger in women and men. *Work in progress,* No. 83-01. Wellesley, MA: Stone Center.

Miller, Kathleen, Sabo, D., Farrell, M., Barnes, G., & Melnick, M. (1998). Athletic participation and sexual behavior in adolescents: The different worlds of boys and girls. *Journal of Health and Social Behavior, 39,* 108–123.

Millett, Kate. (1969). *Sexual politics.* Garden City, NY: Doubleday.

Millhausen, Robin R., & Herold, Edward S. (1999). Does the sexual double standard still exist? Perceptions of university women. *Journal of Sex Research, 36,* 361–368.

Mingo, Clo, Herman, Carla J., & Jasperse, Marla. (2000). Women's stories: Ethnic variations in women's attitudes and experiences of menopause, hysterectomy, and hormone replacement therapy. *Journal of Women's Health and Gender-Based Medicine, 9,* S–27–S–38.

Minuchin, Salvador, Rosman, Bernice L., & Baker, L. (1978). *Psychosomatic families: Anorexia nervosa in context.* Cambridge, MA: Harvard University Press.

Mischel, Walter. (1966). A social-learning view of sex differences in behavior. In E. E. Maccoby (Ed.), *The development of sex differences.* Stanford: Stanford University Press.

Mitchell, Ellen S., & Woods, Nancy F. (2001). Midlife women's attributions about perceived memory changes: Observations from the Seattle Midlife Women's Health Study. *Journal of Women's Health and Gender-Based Medicine, 10,* 351–362.

Mitchell, James E. Raymond, Nancy, & Specker, Sheila. (1993). A review of the controlled trials of pharmacotherapy and psychotherapy in the treatment of bulimia nervosa. *International Journal of Eating Disorders, 14,* 229–247.

Mitchell, Valory, & Helson, Ravenna. (1990). Women's prime of life: Is it the 50s? *Psychology of Women Quarterly, 14,* 451–470.

Monahan, Lynn, Kuhn, Deanna, & Shaver, Philip. (1974). Intrapsychic versus cultural explanations of the "fear of success" motive. *Journal of Personality and Social Psychology, 29,* 60–64.

Moorman, Jeanne E. (1987). The history and the future of the relationship between education and marriage. *Population Index, 53,* 386–387.

Moradi, Bonnie, Fischer, Ann R., Hill, Melanie S., Jome, LaRae M., & Blum, Sasha A. (2000). Does "feminist" plus "therapist" equal "feminist therapist"? *Psychology of Women Quarterly, 24,* 285–296.

Moradi, Bonnie, Tokar, D., Schaub, M., Jome, L., & Serna, G. (2000). Revisiting the structural validity of the Gender Role Conflict Scale. *Psychology of Men and Masculinity, 1,* 62–69.

Morawski, Jill G. (1994). *Practicing feminisms, reconstructing psychology.* Ann Arbor: University of Michigan Press.

Morawski, Jill G., & Bayer, Betty M. (1995). Stirring trouble and making theory. In H. Landrine (Ed.), *Bringing cultural diversity to feminist psychology: Theory, research, and practice* (pp. 113–138). Washington, DC: American Psychological Association.

Morell, Virginia. (1995). Zeroing in on how hormones affect the immune system. *Science, 269,* 773–775.

Morgan, Betsy L. (1998). A three-generational study of tomboy behavior. *Sex Roles, 39,* 787–800.

Morley, J. E., et al. (1997). Testosterone and frailty. *Clinics in Geriatric Medicine, 13,* 685–695.

Morokoff, Patricia J., Mays, Vickie M., & Coons, Helen L. (1997). HIV infection and AIDS. In S. Gallant, G. Keita, & R. Royak-Schaler (Eds.), *Health care for women Psychological, social, and behavioral influences* (pp. 273–294). Washington, DC: American Psychological Association.

Morrison, Ann M., et al. (1992). *Breaking the glass ceiling: Can women reach the top of America's largest corporations?* (Updated ed.). Reading, MA: Addison-Wesley.

Moses, Stephen, et al. (1990). Geographical patterns of male circumcision practices in Africa: Association with HIV seroprevalence. *International Journal of Epidemiology, 19,* 693–697.

Moses, Yolanda T. (1989). *Black women in academe.* Washington, DC: Association of American Colleges.

Moulds, Michelle L., & Bryant, Richard A. (2002). Directed forgetting in acute stress disorder. *Journal of Abnormal Psychology, 111,* 175–179.

Moulton, Janice R., Robinson, G. M., & Elias, Cherin. (1978). Psychology in action: Sex bias in language use: "Neutral" pronouns that aren't. *American Psychologist, 33,* 1032–1036.

Moulton, R. (1970). A survey and re-evaluation of the concept of penis envy. *Contemporary Psychoanalysis, 7,* 84–104.

Mowbray, Carol T., & Herman, Sandra E. (1992). Gender and serious mental illness: A feminist perspective. *Psychology of Women Quarterly, 16,* 107–126.

Moya, Paula M. L. (2001). Chicana feminism and postmodernist theory. *Signs: Journal of Women in Culture and Society, 26,* 441–484.

Moyer, A. (1997). Psychosocial outcomes of breast conserving surgery versus mastectomy: A meta-analytic review. *Health Psychology, 16,* 284–298.

Muehlenhard, Charlene, Friedman, D. E., & Thomas, C. M. (1985). Is date rape justifiable? The effects of dating activity, who paid, and men's attitudes toward women. *Psychology of Women Quarterly, 9,* 297–310.

Muehlenhard, Charlene L., & Kimes, Leigh A. (1999). The social construction of violence: The case of sexual and domestic violence. *Personality and Social Psychology Review, 3,* 234–245.

Muehlenhard, Charlene L., & McCoy, Marcia L. (1991). Double standard/double bind: The sexual double standard and women's communication about sex. *Psychology of Women Quarterly, 15,* 447–462.

Mulac, Anthony. (1998). The gender-linked language effect: Do language differences really make a difference? In D. Canary & K. Dindia (Eds.), *Sex differences and similarities in communication* (pp. 127–154). Mahwah, NJ: Erlbaum.

Mumenthaler, Martin S., O'Hara, Ruth, Taylor, J., Friedman, L., & Yesavage, J. (2001). Relationship between variations in estradiol and progesterone levels across the menstrual cycle and human performance. *Psychopharmacology, 155,* 198–203.

Murnen, Sarah K. (2000). Gender and the use of sexually degrading language. *Psychology of Women Quarterly, 24,* 319–327.

Murnen, Sarah K., & Smolak, Linda. (2000). The experience of sexual harassment among grade-school students: Early socialization of female subordination? *Sex Roles, 43,* 1–18.

Murnen, Sarah K., & Stockton, Mary. (1997). Gender and self-reported sexual arousal in response to sexual stimuli: A meta-analytic review. *Sex Roles, 37,* 135–154.

Murrell, Audrey. (2001). Career achievement: Opportunities and barriers. In J. Worell (Ed.), *Encyclopedia of women and gender* (pp. 211–218). San Diego: Academic Press.

Myers, Linda J., Abdullah, S., & Leary, G. (2000). Conducting research with persons of African descent. In *Guidelines for research in ethnic minority communities* (pp. 5–8). Washington, DC: American Psychological Association.

Nadel, Lynn, & Jacobs, W. Jake. (1998). Traumatic memory is special. *Current Directions in Psychological Science, 7,* 154–157.

Nash, Heather C., & Chrisler, Joan C. (1997). Is a little (psychiatric) knowledge a dangerous thing? The impact of premenstrual dysphoric disorder on perceptions of premenstrual women. *Psychology of Women Quarterly, 21,* 315–322.

National Center for Health Statistics. (2001). *National vital statistics report, 48*(18). Available online at *www.cdc.gov/nchs/.*

Neal-Barnett, Angela M., & Crowther, Janis H. (2000). To be female, middle class, anxious, and Black. *Psychology of Women Quarterly, 24,* 129–136.

Neergaard, Lauran. (1999). Prescribe drugs by gender, studies suggest. *Associated Press.*

Nelson, Lori J., & Cooper, Joel. (1997). Gender differences in children's reactions to success and failure with computers. *Computers in Human Behavior, 13,* 247–267.

Neville, Brian, & Parke, Ross D. (1997). Waiting for paternity: Interpersonal and contextual implications of the timing of fatherhood. *Sex Roles, 37,* 45–60.

Newcombe, Nora S., Mathason, Lisa, & Terlecki, Melissa. (2002). Maximization of spatial competence: More important than finding the cause of sex differences. In A. McGillicuddy–De Lisi & R. De Lisi (Eds.), *Biology, society, and behavior: The development of sex differences in cognition* (pp. 183–206). Westport, CT: Ablex.

Newman, Leonard S., Cooper, J., & Ruble, D. (1995). Gender and computers: II. Interactive effects of knowledge and constancy on gender-stereotyped attitudes. *Sex Roles, 33,* 325–351.

Niemann, Yolanda F., Jennings, Leilani, Rozelle, Richard M., Baxter, James C., & Sullivan, Elroy. (1994). Use of free responses and cluster analysis to determine stereotypes of eight groups. *Personality and Social Psychology Bulletin, 20,* 379–390.

Nieva, Veronica F., & Gutek, Barbara A. (1981). *Women and work: A psychological perspective.* New York: Praeger.

Nindl, B. C., et al. (2001). Testosterone responses after resistance exercise in women: Influence of regional fat distribution. *International Journal of Sport Nutrition and Exercise Metabolism, 11,* 451–465.

Nishith, Pallavi, Mechanic, Mindy B., & Resick, Patricia A. (2000). Prior interpersonal trauma: The contribution to current PTSD symptoms in female rape victims. *Journal of Abnormal Psychology, 109,* 20–25.

No sexism please, we're Webster's. (1991, June 24). *Newsweek*, p. 59.

Nolen-Hoeksema, Susan. (1987). Sex differences in unipolar depression: Evidence and theory. *Psychological Bulletin, 101,* 259–282.

Nolen-Hoeksema, Susan. (1991a). *Sex differences in depression.* Stanford, CA: Stanford University Press.

Nolen-Hoeksema, Susan. (1991b). Responses to depression and their effects on the duration of depressive episodes. *Journal of Abnormal Psychology, 100,* 569–582.

Nolen-Hoeksema, Susan. (2001). Gender differences in depression. *Current Directions in Psychological Science, 10,* 173–176.

Nolen-Hoeksema, Susan, & Girgus, Joan S. (1994). The emergence of gender differences in depression during adolescence. *Psychological Bulletin, 115,* 424–443.

Noll, Stephanie M., & Fredrickson, Barbara L. (1998). A mediational model linking self-objectification, body shame, and disordered eating. *Psychology of Women Quarterly, 22,* 623–636.

Norris, Jeanette, Nurius, Paula S., & Dimeff, Linda A. (1996). Through her eyes: Factors affecting women's perception of and resistance to acquaintance sexual aggression threat. *Psychology of Women Quarterly, 20,* 123–146.

Norton, Arthur J., & Moorman, Jeanne E. (1987). Current trends in marriage and divorce among American women. *Journal of Marriage and the Family, 49,* 3–14.

Nowell, Amy, & Hedges, Larry V. (1998). Trends in gender differences in academic achievement from 1960 to 1994: An analysis of differences in mean, variance, and extreme scores. *Sex Roles, 39,* 21–44.

Oakley, Anne. (1974). *The sociology of housework.* Bath, England: Pitman.

O'Brien, Marion, et al. (2000). Gender-role cognition in three-year-old boys and girls. *Sex Roles, 42,* 1007–1026.

O'Connor, Pat. (1992). *Friendships between women.* New York: Guilford.

Offir, Carole W. (1982). *Human sexuality.* New York: Harcourt, Brace, Jovanovich.

Ogletree, Shirley M., & Ginsburg, H. (2000). Kept under the hood: Neglect of the clitoris in common vernacular. *Sex Roles, 43,* 917–926.

Ogunwole, Stella. (2002). *The American Indian and Alaska Native Population: 2000.* Current Population Reports, U.S. Census Bureau. Available online at *www.census.gov.*

Oinonen, Kirsten A., & Mazmanian, Dwight. (2001). Effects of oral contraceptives on daily self-ratings of positive and negative affect. *Journal of Psychosomatic Research, 51,* 647–658.

Okazaki, Sumie. (1998). Teaching gender issues in Asian American psychology: A pedagogical framework. *Psychology of Women Quarterly, 22,* 33–52.

O'Keefe, Eileen S. C., & Hyde, Janet S. (1983). The development of occupational sex-role stereotypes: The effects of gender stability and age. *Sex Roles, 9,* 481–492.

O'Leary, Ann, & Jemmott, Loretta S. (Eds.). (1996). *Women and AIDS: Coping and care.* New York: Plenum.

O'Leary, Virginia E., & Flanagan, Elizabeth H. (2001). Leadership. In J. Worell (Ed.), *Encyclopedia of women and gender* (pp. 645–656). San Diego: Academic Press.

Oliver, Mary Beth, & Hyde, Janet S. (1993). Gender differences in sexuality: A meta-analysis. *Psychological Bulletin, 114,* 29–51.

O'Neil, James, Helms, B., Gable, R., David, L., & Wrightsman, L. (1986). Gender Role Conflict Scale: College men's fear of femininity. *Sex Roles, 4,* 335–350.

Orbuch, Terri L., & Custer, Lindsay. (1995). The social context of married women's work and its impact on Black husbands and White husbands. *Journal of Marriage and the Family, 57,* 333–345.

Orloff, Kossia. (1978). The trap of androgyny. *Regionalism and the Female Imagination, 4*(ii), 1–3.

O'Sullivan, Lucia, Graber, J., & Brooks-Gunn, J. (2001). Adolescent gender development. In J. Worell (Ed.), *Encyclopedia of gender* (pp. 55–67). San Diego: Academic Press.

Otterbein, K. F. (1979). A cross-cultural study of rape. *Aggressive Behavior, 5,* 425–435.

Oudshoorn, N. E. J. (1997). Menopause, only for women? The social construction of menopause as an exclusively female condition. *Journal of Psychosomatic Obstetrics and Gynecology, 18,* 137–144.

Oyewumi, Oyeronke. (1997). *The invention of women: Making an African sense of Western gender discourses.* Minneapolis: University of Minnesota Press.

Oyewumi, Oyeronke. (2000). Family bonds/conceptual binds: African notes on feminist epistemologies. *Signs: Journal of Women in Culture and Society, 25,* 1093–1098.

Paige, Karen E. (1971). Effects of oral contraceptives on affective fluctuations associated with the menstrual cycle. *Psychosomatic Medicine, 33,* 515–537.

Parke, Ross D. (1979). Perspectives in father-infant interaction. In J. D. Osofsky (Ed.), *Handbook of infant development.* New York: Wiley.

Parke, Ross D., & O'Leary, S. E. (1976). Father-mother-infant interaction in the newborn period. In K. Riegel & J. Meacham (Eds.), *The developing individual in a changing world* (Vol. 2). The Hague: Mouton.

Parlee, Mary B. (1973). The premenstrual syndrome. *Psychological Bulletin, 80,* 454–465.

Parlee, Mary B. (1978). The rhythms in men's lives. *Psychology Today,* 82–91.

Parlee, Mary B. (1981). Appropriate control groups in feminist research. *Psychology of Women Quarterly, 5,* 637–644.

Parlee, Mary B. (1983). Menstrual rhythms in sensory processes: A review of fluctuations in vision, olfaction, audition, taste, and touch. *Psychological Bulletin, 93,* 539–548.

Patterson, Charlotte. (1992). Children of lesbian and gay parents. *Child Development, 63,* 1025–1042.

Patterson, Charlotte J. (2000). Family relationships of lesbians and gay men. *Journal of Marriage and the Family, 62,* 1052–1069.

Pauwels, Anne. (1998). *Women changing language.* London: Longman.

Pearlin, Leonard, & Johnson, J. S. (1977). Marital status, life-strains and depression. *American Sociological Review, 42,* 704–715.

Pearson, Jane L., Hunter, Andrea G., Ensminger, Margaret E., & Kellam, Sheppard G. (1990). Black grandmothers in multigenerational households. *Child Development, 61,* 434–442.

Peplau, L. Anne. (1993). Lesbian and gay relationships. In L. D. Garnets & D. C. Kimmel (Eds.), *Psychological perspectives on lesbian and gay male experience* (pp. 395–419). New York: Columbia University Press.

Peplau, L. Anne, & Conrad, Eva. (1989). Beyond nonsexist research: The perils of feminist methods in psychology. *Psychology of Women Quarterly, 13,* 381–402.

Peplau, L. Anne, et al. (1982). Being old and living alone. In L. A. Peplau & D. Perlman (Eds.), *Loneliness.* New York: Wiley.

Peplau, L. Anne, & Garnets, Linda D. (2000). A new paradigm for understanding women's sexuality and sexual orientation. *Journal of Social Issues, 56,* 329–350.

Peplau, L. Anne, Veniegas, Rosemary C., & Campbell, Susan M. (1996). Gay and lesbian relationships. In R. C. Savin-Williams & K. M. Cohen (Eds.), *The lives of lesbians, gays, and bisexuals* (pp. 250–273). Fort Worth, TX: Harcourt Brace.

Peplau, Letitia Anne. (1982). Research on homosexual couples: An overview. *Journal of Homosexuality, 8*(2), 3–8.

Peplau, Letitia Anne, Cochran, Susan, Rook, Karen, & Padesky, Christine. (1978). Loving women: Attachment and autonomy in lesbian relationships. *Journal of Social Issues, 34*(3), 7–27.

Pequegnat, Willo, & Stover, Ellen. (1999). Considering women's contextual and cultural issues in HIV/STD prevention research. *Cultural Diversity and Ethnic Minority Psychology, 5,* 287–291.

Percec, Ivona, Plenge, R., Nadeau, J., Bartolomei, M., & Willard, H. (2002). Autosomal dominant mutations affecting X inactivation choice in the mouse. *Science, 296,* 1136–1139.

Perry, Elissa L., Schmidtke, J., & Kulik, C. (1998). Propensity to sexually harass: An exploration of gender differences. *Sex Roles, 38,* 443–460.

Perry, J. D., & Whipple, Beverly. (1981). Pelvic muscle strength of female ejaculators: Evidence in support of a new theory of orgasm. *Journal of Sex Research, 17,* 22–39.

Perry-Jenkins, Maureen, Repetti, Rena L., & Crouter, Ann C. (2000). Work and family in the 1990s. *Journal of Marriage and the Family, 62,* 981–998.

Petersen, Anne, Sarigiani, P., & Kennedy, R. (1991). Adolescent depression: Why more girls? *Journal of Youth and Adolescence, 20,* 247–271.

Peterson, John, & Bakeman, Roger. (1988). The epidemiology of adult minority AIDS. *Multicultural Inquiry and Research on AIDS, 2*(1), 1–2.

Peterson, Rolf A. (1983). Attitudes toward the childless spouse. *Sex Roles, 9,* 321–332.

Pettigrew, Thomas. (1964). *A profile of the Negro American.* Princeton, NJ: Van Nostrand.

Phares, Vicky, & Compas, Bruce E. (1992). The role of fathers in child and adolescent psychopathology: Make room for daddy. *Psychological Bulletin, 111,* 387–412.

Pheterson, G. I., Kiesler, S. B., & Goldberg, P. A. (1971). Evaluation of the performance of women as a function of their sex, achievement, and personal history. *Journal of Personality and Social Psychology, 19,* 114–118.

Phillips, Leslie. (1977, September 9). For women, sexual harassment is an occupational hazard. *Boston Globe.*

Phinney, Jean S., & Rotheram, Mary Jane. (Eds.). (1987). *Children's ethnic socialization.* Newbury Park, CA: Sage.

Phoenix, C. H., Goy, R. W., Gerall, A. A., & Young, W. C. (1959). Organizing action of prenatally administered testosterone propionate on the tissues mediating mating behavior in the female guinea pig. *Endocrinology, 65,* 369–382.

Piaget, J. (1954). *The construction of reality in the child.* New York: Basic Books.

Pilkington, N. W., & D'Augelli, A. R. (1995). Victimization of lesbian, gay, and bisexual youth in community settings. *Developmental Psychology, 23,* 33–56.

Pinzone-Glover, Holly A., Gidycz, Christine A., & Jacobs, Cecilia D. (1998). An acquaintance rape prevention program: Effects on attitudes toward women, rape-related attitudes, and perceptions of rape scenarios. *Psychology of Women Quarterly, 22,* 605–622.

Pipher, Mary. (1994). *Reviving Ophelia: Saving the selves of adolescent girls.* New York: Putnam.

Piran, Niva. (2001). Eating disorders and disordered eating. In J. Worell (Ed.), *Encyclopedia of women and gender* (pp. 369–376). San Diego: Academic Press.

Pithers, W. D. (1993). Treatment of rapists. In G. Hall et al. (Eds.), *Sexual aggression* (pp. 167–196). Washington, DC: Taylor & Francis.

Pizzey, Erin. (1974). *Scream quietly or the neighbors will hear.* London: If Books.

Plant, E. Ashby, Hyde, Janet S., Keltner, Dacher, & Devine, Patricia G. (2000). The gender stereotyping of emotions. *Psychology of Women Quarterly, 24,* 81–92.

Pleck, Joseph H. (1975). Masculinity-femininity: Current and alternate paradigms. *Sex Roles, 1,* 161–178.

Pleck, Joseph H. (1981). *The myth of masculinity.* Cambridge, MA: MIT Press.

Polce-Lynch, M., Myers, B., Kliewer, W., & Kilmartin, C. (2001). Adolescent self-esteem and gender: Exploring relations to sexual harassment, body image, media influence, and emotional expression. *Journal of Youth and Adolescence, 30,* 225–244.

Polce-Lynch, Mary, et al. (1998). Gender and age patterns in emotional expression, body image, and self-esteem: A qualitative analysis. *Sex Roles, 38,* 1025–1048.

Pope, Ken. (2001). Sex between therapists and clients. In J. Worell (Ed.), *Encyclopedia of women and gender* (pp. 955–962). New York: Academic Press.

Pope, Kenneth S., Levenson, H., & Schover, L. R. (1979). Sexual intimacy in psychology training: Results and implications of a national survey. *American Psychologist, 34,* 682–689.

Porter, Natalie P., Geis, Florence L., & Walstedt, Joyce J. (1978). *Are women invisible as leaders?* Paper presented at American Psychological Association Meetings, Toronto, August.

Posavac, Heidi D., Posavac, S., & Posavac, E. (1998). Exposure to media images of female attractiveness and concern with body weight among young women. *Sex Roles, 38,* 187–202.

Powell, Barbara. (1977). The empty nest, employment, and psychiatric symptoms in college-educated women. *Psychology of Women Quarterly, 2,* 35–43.

Prange, A. J., & Vitols, M. M. (1962). Cultural aspects of the relatively low incidence of depression in southern Negroes. *International Journal of Social Psychiatry, 8,* 104–112.

Prentky, Robert A. (1997). Arousal reduction in sexual offenders: A review of antiandrogen interventions. *Sexual Abuse: A Journal of Research and Treatment, 9,* 335–347.

Pridal, Cathryn G., & LoPiccolo, Joseph. (2000). Multielement treatment of desire disorders: Integration of cognitive, behavioral, and systemic therapy. In S. Leiblum & R. Rosen (Eds.), *Principles and practice of sex therapy* (3rd ed., pp. 57–84). New York: Guilford.

Profet, Margie. (1993). Menstruation as a defense against pathogens transported by sperm. *Quarterly Review of Biology, 68,* 335–381.

Pryor, John B., Giedd, Janet L., & Williams, Karen B. (1995). A social psychological model for predicting sexual harassment. *Journal of Social Issues, 51*(1), 69–84.

Pryor, John B., & Stoller, Lynnette M. (1994). Sexual cognition processes in men high in the likelihood to sexually harass. *Personality and Social Psychology Bulletin, 20,* 163–169.

Pryor, John B., & Whalen, Nora J. (1997). A typology of sexual harassment: Characteristics of harassers and the social circumstances under which sexual harassment occurs. In W. O'Donohue (Ed.), *Sexual harassment: Theory, research, and treatment.* Needham Heights, MA: Allyn and Bacon.

Pugliesi, Karen. (1992). *The social construction of premenstrual syndrome: Explaining problematic emotion.* Paper presented at the American Sociological Association meetings, Pittsburgh.

Quina, Kathryn, et al. (1999). Focusing on participants: Feminist process model for survey modification. *Psychology of Women Quarterly, 23*, 459–484.

Quinn, Diane M., & Spencer, Steven J. (2001). The interference of stereotype threat with women's generation of mathematical problem-solving strategies. *Journal of Social Issues, 57*, 55–72.

Raag, Tarja, & Rackliff, C. L. (1998). Preschoolers' awareness of social expectations of gender: Relationships to toy choices. *Sex Roles, 38*, 685–700.

Rabinowitz, Vita C., & Sechzer, Jeri A. (1993). Feminist perspectives on research methods. In F. L. Denmark & M. A. Paludi (Eds.), *Psychology of women: Handbook of issues and theories.* Westport, CT: Greenwood.

Ragan, Janet H. (1982). Gender displays in photographs. *Sex Roles, 8*, 33–44.

Raley, R. Kelly. (1996). A shortage of marriageable men? A note on the role of cohabitation in Black-White differences in marriage rates. *American Sociological Review, 61*, 973–983.

Ramey, Estelle. (1972). Men's cycles. *Ms.*, Spring, 8–14.

Ransby, Barbara. (2000). Black feminism at twenty-one: Reflections on the evolution of a national community. *Signs: Journal of Women in Culture and Society, 25*, 1215–1222.

Ransdell, Lynda B. (2001). A chronology of the study of older women's health: Data, discoveries, and future directions. *Journal of Women and Aging, 13*, 39–55.

Rawlings, Edna I., & Carter, Dianne K. (1977). Feminist and nonsexist psychotherapy. In E. I. Rawlings & D. Carter (Eds.), *Psychotherapy for women.* Springfield, IL: Charles C. Thomas

Rebelsky, Freda, & Hanks, C. (1971). Fathers' verbal interaction with infants in the first three months of life. *Child Development, 42*, 63–68.

Reid, Pamela T. (1993). Poor women in psychological research: Shut up and shut out. *Psychology of Women Quarterly, 17*, 133–150.

Reid, Pamela T., & Bing, Vanessa M. (2000). Sexual roles of girls and women: An ethnocultural lifespan perspective. In C. B. Travis & J. W. White (Eds.), *Sexuality, society, and feminism* (pp. 141–166). Washington, DC: American Psychological Association.

Reid, Pamela T., Haritos, Calliope, Kelly, Elizabeth, & Holland, Nicole E. (1995). Socialization of girls: Issues of ethnicity in gender development. In H. Landrine (Ed.), *Bringing cultural diversity to feminist psychology: Theory, research, and practice* (pp. 93–112). Washington, DC: American Psychological Association.

Reinharz, Shulamit. (1992). *Feminist methods in social research.* New York: Oxford University Press.

Reitz, Ronda R. (1999). Batterers' experiences of being violent: A phenomenological study. *Psychology of Women Quarterly, 23*, 143–166.

Reskin, Barbara F. (1988). Occupational resegregation. In S. Rix (Ed.), *The American woman 1988–89.* New York: Norton.

Reyna, V., & Brainerd, C. (1998). Fuzzy-trace theory and false memory: New frontiers. *Journal of Experimental Child Psychology, 71*, 194–209.

Rice, Joy. (2001). Family roles and patterns: Contemporary trends. In J. Worell (Ed.), *Encyclopedia of gender* (pp. 411–424). San Diego: Academic Press.

Rich, Adrienne. (1980). Compulsory heterosexuality and lesbian existence. *Signs, 5*, 631–660.

Richman, Erin L., & Shaffer, David R. (2000). "If you let me play sports": How might sport participation influence the self-esteem of adolescent females? *Psychology of Women Quarterly, 24*, 189–199.

Riggs, Janet M. (1997). Mandates for mothers and fathers: Perceptions of breadwinners and care givers. *Sex Roles, 37*, 565–580.

Riley, J. L., et al. (1998). Sex differences in the perception of noxious experimental stimuli: A meta-analysis. *Pain, 74*, 181–187.

Riley, Joseph L., Robinson, M., Wise, E., & Price, D. (1999). A meta-analytic review of pain perception across the menstrual cycle. *Pain, 81*, 225–235.

Rind, Bruce, Tromovitch, Philip, & Bauserman, Robert. (1998). A meta-analytic examination of assumed properties of child sexual abuse using college samples. *Psychological Bulletin, 124*, 22–53.

Rix, Sara E. (Ed.). (1988). *The American woman 1988–89.* New York: Norton.

Rix, Sara E. (Ed.). (1990). *The American woman, 1990–91.* New York: Norton.

Roberts, L. J., & Leonard, K. E. (1997). Gender differences and similarities in the alcohol and marriage relationship. In R. W. Wilsnack & S. C. Wilsnack (Eds.), *Gender and alcohol* (pp. 417–444). New Brunswick NJ: Rutgers University Center of Alcohol Studies.

Roberts, Shauna S. (1990, Jan.–Feb.). Koop's aborted report. *Journal of NIH Research, 2*, 28.

Robey, Elizabeth B., Canary, Daniel J., & Burggraf, Cynthia S. (1998). Conversational maintenance behaviors of husbands and wives: An observational analysis. In D. Canary & K. Dindia (Eds.), *Sex differences and similarities in communication* (pp. 373–392). Mahwah, NJ: Erlbaum.

Robins, Lee N., et al. (1984). Lifetime prevalence of specific psychiatric disorders in three sites. *Archives of General Psychiatry, 41,* 949–958.

Robinson, Ira, Ziss, Ken, Ganza, Bill, Katz, Stuart, & Robinson, Edward. (1991). Twenty years of the Sexual Revolution, 1965–1985. *Journal of Marriage and the Family, 53,* 216–220.

Rodin, Judith, Silberstein, L. R., & Striegel-Moore, R. H. (1985). Women and weight: A normative discontent. In T. B. Sonderegger (Ed.), *Psychology and gender: Nebraska Symposium on Motivation* (pp. 267–307). Lincoln: University of Nebraska Press.

Rodin, Mari. (1992). The social construction of premenstrual syndrome. *Social Science and Medicine, 35,* 49–56.

Rodriguez, Ned, Ryan, Susan W., Vande Kemp, Hendrika, & Foy, David W. (1997). Posttraumatic stress disorder in adult female survivors of childhood sexual abuse: A comparison study. *Journal of Consulting and Clinical Psychology, 65,* 53–59.

Rogers, Michelle L., & Bird, Chloe. (1999). Do gender differences in the effects of equity in paid work and household labor on depression hold across ethnic and racial groups? Working Paper, Population Studies and Training Center, Brown University.

Rohner, Ronald P., & Veneziano, Robert A. (2001). The importance of father love: History and contemporary evidence. *Review of General Psychology, 5,* 382–405.

Root, Maria P. P. (1990). Disordered eating in women of color. *Sex Roles, 22,* 525–536.

Root, Maria P. P. (1994). Mixed-race women. In L. Comas-Diaz & B. Greene (Eds.), *Women of color: Integrating ethnic and gender identities in psychotherapy* (pp. 455–478). New York: Guilford.

Root, Maria P. P. (1995). The psychology of Asian American women. In H. Landrine (Ed.), *Bringing cultural diversity to feminist psychology: Theory, research, and practice* (pp. 265–302). Washington, DC: American Psychological Association.

Rosaldo, Michelle Z. (1974). Women, culture, and society: A theoretical overview. In M. Z. Rosaldo & L. Lamphere (Eds.), *Woman, culture, and society.* Stanford: Stanford University Press.

Rosen, D. H. (1974). *Lesbianism: A study of female homosexuality.* Springfield, IL: Charles C. Thomas.

Rosen, Raymond C., & Leiblum, Sandra R. (1987). Current approaches to the evaluation of sexual desire disorders. *Journal of Sex Research, 23,* 141–162.

Rosen, Raymond C., & Leiblum, Sandra R. (1995a). Hypoactive sexual desire. *Psychiatric Clinics of North America, 18,* 107–121.

Rosen, Raymond C., & Leiblum, Sandra R. (1995b). Treatment of sexual disorders in the 1990s: An integrated approach. *Journal of Consulting and Clinical Psychology, 63,* 877–890.

Rosenberg, Lynn. (1993). Hormone replacement therapy: The need for reconsideration. *American Journal of Public Health, 83,* 1670–1673,

Rosenberg, Morris. (1965). *Society and the adolescent self-image.* Princeton, NJ: Princeton University Press.

Rosenkrantz, P. S., et al. (1968). Sex-role stereotypes and self-concepts in college students. *Journal of Consulting and Clinical Psychology, 32,* 287–295.

Rosenthal, Robert. (1966). *Experimenter effects in behavioral research.* New York: Appleton-Century-Crofts.

Ross, C. W., & Mirowsky, J. (1988). Child care and emotional adjustment to wives' employment. *Journal of Health and Social Behavior, 29,* 127–138.

Ross, Catherine E., Mirowsky, J., & Goldsteen, K. (1990). The impact of the family on health: Decade in review. *Journal of Marriage and the Family, 52,* 1059–1078.

Ross, David, & Stevenson, John. (1993, Nov.–Dec.). HRT and cardiovascular disease. *British Journal of Sexual Medicine,* 10–13.

Rostosky, Sharon S., & Travis, Cheryl B. (1996). Menopause research and the dominance of the biomedical model 1984–1994. *Psychology of Women Quarterly, 20,* 285–312.

Roter, Debra L., & Hall, Judith A. (1997). Gender differences in patient-physician communication. In S. Gallant, G. Keita, & R. Royak-Schaler (Eds.), *Health care for women: Psychological, social, and behavioral influences* (pp. 57–72). Washington, DC: American Psychological Association.

Rothbaum, B. O., Foa, E. D., Riggs, D. S., Murdock, T., & Walsh, W. (1992). A prospective examination of post-traumatic stress disorder in rape victims. *Journal of Traumatic Stress, 5,* 455–475.

Rothblum, Esther D. (1993). Personal communication.

Rothblum, Esther D., & Brehony, Kathleen A. (1993). *Boston marriages.* Amherst: University of Massachusetts Press.

Rothblum, Esther D., & Factor, Rhonda. (2001). Lesbians and their sisters as a control group: Demographic and mental health factors. *Psychological Science, 12,* 63–69.

Rotundo, E. Anthony. (1993). *American manhood: Transformations in masculinity from the Revolution to the modern era.* New York: Basic Books.

Royak-Schaler, Renee, Stanton, Annette L., & Danoff-Burg, Sharon. (1997). Breast cancer: Psychosocial factors influencing risk perception, screening, diagnosis, and treatment. In S. Gallant, G. Keita, & R. Royak-Schaler (Eds.), *Health care for women: Psychological, social, and behavioral influences* (pp. 295–314). Washington, DC: American Psychological Association.

Rozée, Patricia D., & Koss, Mary P. (2001). Rape: A century of resistance. *Psychology of Women Quarterly, 25,* 295–311.

Ruan, Fang Fu, & Bullough, Vern L. (1992). Lesbianism in China. *Archives of Sexual Behavior, 21,* 217–226.

Rubin, Lillian. (1979). *Women of a certain age.* New York: Harper & Row.

Rubin, Robert T., Reinisch, June M., & Haskett, R. F. (1981). Postnatal gonadal steroid effects on human behavior. *Science, 211,* 1318–1324.

Ruble, Diane, & Martins, Carol. (1998). Gender development. *Handbook of child psychology: Socialization, personality, and social development* (Vol. 5, pp. 933–1016). New York: Wiley.

Ruble, Diane N. (1977). Premenstrual symptoms: A reinterpretation. *Science, 197,* 291–292.

Rumenick, Donna K., Capasso, Deborah R., & Hendrick, C. (1977). Experimenter sex effects in behavioral research. *Psychological Bulletin, 84,* 852–887.

Rushton, J. Philippe. (1992). Cranial capacity related to sex, rank, and race in a stratified random sample of 6,325 U.S. military personnel. *Intelligence, 16,* 401–413.

Russell, Diana. (1982). *Rape in marriage.* New York: Macmillan.

Russo, Nancy F. (1979). Overview: Sex roles, fertility, and the motherhood mandate. *Psychology of Women Quarterly, 4,* 7–15.

Russo, Nancy F. (1990). Overview: Forging research priorities for women's mental health. *American Psychologist, 45,* 368–373.

Russo, Nancy F., Amaro, Hortensia, & Winter, M. (1987). The use of inpatient mental health services by Hispanic women. *Psychology of Women Quarterly, 11,* 427–442.

Russo, Nancy F., & Green, Beth L. (1993). Women and mental health. In F. L. Denmark & M. A. Paludi (Eds.), *Psychology of women: Handbook of issues and theories.* Westport, CT; Greenwood.

Russo, Nancy F., Horn, Jody D., & Schwartz, Robert. (1992). U.S. abortion in context: Selected characteristics and motivations of women seeking abortions. *Journal of Social Issues, 48*(3), 183–202.

Russo, Nancy F., & Vaz, Kim. (2001). Addressing diversity in the Decade of Behavior: Focus on women of color. *Psychology of Women Quarterly, 25,* 280–294.

Russo, Nancy Felipe, & O'Connell, Agnes N. (1980). Models from our past: Psychology's foremothers. *Psychology of Women Quarterly, 5,* 11–54.

Rust, Paula C. R. (2000). Bisexuality: A contemporary paradox for women. *Journal of Social Issues, 56,* 205–222.

Ruth, Sheila. (Ed.). (1990). *Issues in feminism: An introduction to women's studies* (2nd ed.). Mountain View, CA: Mayfield.

Sabo, Don. (1992). Pigskin, patriarchy, and pain. In M. S. Kimmel & M. A. Messner (Eds.), *Men's lives.* New York: Macmillan.

Sabogal, F., Marin, G., Otero-Sabogal, R., Marin, B., & Perez-Stable, E. (1987). Hispanic familism and acculturation: What changes and what doesn't? *Hispanic Journal of Behavioral Sciences, 9,* 397–412.

Sachs-Ericsson, Natalie, & Ciarlo, J. (2000). Gender, social roles, and mental health: An epidemiological perspective. *Sex Roles, 43,* 605–628.

Sadker, Myra, & Sadker, David. (1985, March). Sexism in the schoolroom of the '80s. *Psychology Today, 19,* 54–57.

Salgado de Snyder, V. Nelly, Acevedo, Andrea, Diaz-Perez, Maria, & Saldivar-Garduno, Alicia. (2000). Understanding the sexuality of Mexican-born women and their risk for HIV/AIDS. *Psychology of Women Quarterly, 24,* 100–109.

Salgado de Snyder, V. Nelly, Cervantes, Richard C., & Padilla, Amado M. (1990). Gender and ethnic differences in psychosocial stress and generalized distress among Hispanics. *Sex Roles, 22,* 441–454.

Salmon, Peter, & Marchant-Haycox, Susan. (2000). Surgery in the absence of pathology: The relationship of patients' presentation to gynecologists' decisions for hysterectomy. *Journal of Psychosomatic Research, 49*, 119–124.

SAMSHA (Substance Abuse and Mental Health Services Administration). (1999). *National Household Survey on Drug Abuse: Population Estimates 1998*. No. (SMA) 99-3327, Rockville, MD.

Sanday, Peggy R. (1981). The socio-cultural context of rape: A cross-cultural study. *Journal of Social Issues, 37*, 5–27.

Sanday, Peggy R. (1988). The reproduction of patriarchy in feminist anthropology. In M. M. Gergen (Ed.), *Feminist thought and the structure of knowledge*. New York: New York University Press.

Sanday, Peggy R. (1990). *Fraternity gang rape*. New York: New York University Press.

Sandberg, John F., & Hofferth, Sandra L. (2001). *Changes in children's time with parents, U.S. 1981–1997*. Report No. 01-475. Ann Arbor: Population Studies Center, University of Michigan.

Sanders, Cheryl J. (1988). Ethics and the educational achievements of Black women. *Religion and Intellectual Life, 5*(4), 7–16.

Sankis, Lizabeth M., Corbitt, Elizabeth M., & Widiger, Thomas A. (1999). Gender bias in the English language? *Journal of Personality and Social Psychology, 77*, 1289–1295.

Sannibale, C., & Hall, W. (2001). Gender-related symptoms and correlates of alcohol dependence among men and women with a lifetime diagnosis of alcohol use disorder. *Drug and Alcohol Review, 20*, 369–383.

Santos de Barona, Maryann, & Barona, A. (2000). A model for conducting research with Hispanics. In *Guidelines for research in ethnic minority communities* (pp. 9–11). Washington, DC: American Psychological Association.

Satterfield, Arthur T., & Muehlenhard, Charlene L. (1997). Shaken confidence: The effects of an authority figure's flirtatiousness on women's and men's self-rated creativity. *Psychology of Women Quarterly, 21*, 395–416.

Savin-Williams, Ritch C. (1998). The disclosure to families of same-sex attractions by lesbian, gay, and bisexual youths. *Journal of Research on Adolescence, 8*, 49–68.

Savin-Williams, Ritch. (2001). Suicide attempts among sexual-minority youths. *Journal of Consulting and Clinical Psychology, 69*, 983–991.

Sax, Leonard. (2001). Reclaiming kindergarten: Making kindergarten less harmful to boys. *Psychology of Men and Masculinity, 2*, 3–12.

Sayers, Dorothy. (1946). *Unpopular opinions*. London: Victor Gollancz.

Sayers, Janet. (1991). *Mothers of psychoanalysis*. New York: Norton.

Sayre, Anne. (1978). *Rosalind Franklin and DNA*. New York: Norton.

Schiebinger, Londa. (2000). Has feminism changed science? *Signs: Journal of Women in Culture and Society, 25*, 1171–1176.

Schlenker, Jennifer, A., Caron, S., & Halterman, W. (1998). A feminist analysis of *Seventeen* magazine: Content analysis from 1945 to 1995. *Sex Roles, 38*, 135–150.

Schneider, Tamera R., et al. (2001). The effects of message framing and ethnic targeting on mammography use among low-income women. *Health Psychology, 20*, 256–266.

Schow, Douglas A., Redmon, B., & Pryor, J. (1997). Male menopause: How to define it, how to treat it. *Postgraduate Medicine, 101*, 62–79.

Schreurs, Karlein M. G., & Buunk Bram P. (1996). Closeness, autonomy, equity, and relationship satisfaction in lesbian couples. *Psychology of Women Quarterly, 20*, 577–592.

Schuetz, E., Furuya, K., & Schuetz, J. (1995). Interindividual variation in expression of P-glycoprotein in normal human liver and secondary hepatic neoplasms. *Journal of Pharmacology and Experimental Therapeutics, 275*, 1011–1018.

Schulman, K. A., et al. (1999). The effect of race and sex on physicians' recommendations for cardiac catheterization. *New England Journal of Medicine, 340*, 618–626.

Schulz, Muriel R. (1975). The semantic derogation of woman. In B. Thorne & N. Henley (Eds.), *Language and sex: Difference and dominance*. Rowley, MA: Newbury-House.

Seavy, Carol A., Katz, Phyllis A. & Zalk, Sue R. (1975). Baby X: The effects of gender labels on adult responses to infants. *Sex Roles, 1*, 103–110.

Segnan, N. (1997). Socioeconomic status and cancer screening. In M. Kogevinas et al. (Eds.), *Social inequalities and cancer* (IARC Scientific Publication No. 138, pp. 369–376). Lyon, France: International Agency for Research on Cancer.

Segura, Denise A., & Pierce, Jennifer L. (1993). Chicana/o family structure and gender personality: Chodorow, familism, and psychoanalytic sociology revisited. *Signs, 19*, 62–91.

Seidlitz, Larry, & Diener, Ed. (1998). Sex differences in the recall of affective experiences. *Journal of Personality and Social Psychology, 74,* 262–271.

Seligman, Martin E. P. (1975). *Helplessness: On depression, development and death.* San Francisco: Freeman.

Sellers, Robert M., Smith, M., Shelton, J., Rowley, S., & Chavous, T. (1998). Multidimensional model of racial identity: A reconceptualization of African American racial identity. *Personality and Social Psychology Review, 2,* 18–39.

Serbin, Lisa A., Connor, Jane M., & Iler, Iris. (1979). Sex-stereotyped and nonstereotyped introductions of new toys in the preschool classroom: An observational study of teacher behavior and its effects. *Psychology of Women Quarterly, 4,* 261–265.

Serbin, Lisa A., et al. (1973). A comparison of teacher response to the preacademic and problem behavior of boys and girls. *Child Development, 44,* 796–804.

Serbin, Lisa A., Powlishta, Kimberly K., & Gulko, Judith. (1993). The development of sex typing in middle childhood. *Monographs of the Society for Research in Child Development, 58*(2), 1–93.

Shachar, Sandra A., & Gilbert, Lucia A. (1983). Working lesbians: Role conflicts and coping strategies. *Psychology of Women Quarterly, 7,* 244–256.

Shainess, Natalie. (1977). The equitable therapy of women in psychoanalysis. In E. I. Rawlings & D. K. Carter (Eds.), *Psychotherapy for women.* Springfield, IL: Charles C. Thomas.

Shanor, Karen. (1978). *The sexual sensitivity of the American male.* New York: Ballantine.

Shaver, Phillip. (1976). Questions concerning fear of success and its conceptual relatives. *Sex Roles, 2,* 305–320.

Shaw, L. B. (1984). Retirement plans of middle-aged married women. *Gerontologist, 24,* 154–159.

Shelton, Beth A., & John, Daphne. (1993). Ethnicity, race, and difference: A comparison of white, Black, and Hispanic men's household labor time. In J. C. Hood (Ed.), *Men, work, and family* (pp. 131–150). Newbury Park, CA: Sage.

Shepard, David S. (2002). A negative state of mind: Patterns of depressive symptoms among men with high gender role conflict. *Psychology of Men and Masculinity, 3,* 3–8.

Shepela, Sharon T., & Levesque, L. (1998). Poisoned waters: Sexual harassment and the college climate. *Sex Roles, 38,* 589–612.

Sherman, Julia A. (1971). *On the psychology of women: A survey of empirical studies.* Springfield, IL: Charles C. Thomas.

Sherman, Julia A. (1978). *Sex-related cognitive differences.* Springfield, IL: Charles C. Thomas.

Sherman, Julia A. (1982). Mathematics, the critical filter: A look at some residues. *Psychology of Women Quarterly, 6,* 428–444.

Sherman, Linda A., Temple, R., & Merkatz, Ruth B. (1995). Women in clinical trials: An FDA perspective. *Science, 269,* 793–795.

Sherwin, Barbara B. (1991). The psychoendocrinology of aging and female sexuality. *Annual Review of Sex Research, 2,* 181–198.

Shields, Stephanie A. (1975). Functionalism, Darwinism, and the psychology of women: A study in social myth. *American Psychologist, 30,* 739–754.

Shields, Stephanie A. (2000). Thinking about gender, thinking about theory: Gender and emotional experience. In A. Fischer (Ed.), *Gender and emotion: Social psychological perspectives* (pp. 3–23). Cambridge, UK: Cambridge University Press.

Shields, Stephanie A., & Cooper, Pamela E. (1983). Stereotypes of traditional and nontraditional childbearing roles. *Sex Roles, 9,* 363–376.

Shih, Margaret, Pittinsky, T., & Ambady, N. (1999). Stereotype susceptibility: Identity salience and shifts in quantitative performance. *Psychological Science, 10,* 80–83.

Shilts, Randy. (1993). *Conduct unbecoming: Lesbians and gays in the U.S. military, Vietnam to the Persian Gulf.* New York: St. Martin's Press.

Siegel, J. S. (1978). *Prospective trends in the size and structure of the elderly population, impact of mortality trends, and some implications.* U.S. Bureau of the Census, Current Population Reports (Special Studies Series P-23, no. 59, 2nd printing, rev.). Washington, DC: U.S. Government Printing Office.

Sigmon, Sandra, et al. (2000). Menstrual reactivity: The role of gender specificity, anxiety sensitivity, and somatic concerns in self-reported menstrual distress. *Sex Roles, 43,* 143–162.

Sigmon, Sandra T., et al. (2000). The impact of anxiety sensitivity, bodily expectations, and cultural beliefs on menstrual symptom reporting: A test of the menstrual reactivity hypothesis. *Journal of Anxiety Disorders, 14,* 615–633.

Signorielli, Nancy, & Bacue, Aaron. (1999). Recognition and respect: A content analysis of prime-time television characters across three decades. *Sex Roles, 40,* 527–544.

Signorielli, Nancy, McLeod, D., & Healy, E. (1994). Gender stereotypes in MTV commercials: The beat goes on. *Journal of Broadcasting and Electronic Media,* 91–101.

Silverstein, Louise B. (1996). Fathering is a feminist issue. *Psychology of Women Quarterly, 20,* 3–38.

Simes, M. R., & Berg, D. H. (2001). Surreptitious learning: Menarche and menstrual product advertisements. *Health Care for Women International, 22,* 455–469.

Simon, J. G., & Feather, N. T. (1973). Causal attributions for success and failure at university examinations. *Journal of Educational Psychology, 64,* 45–56.

Simon, R., & Fleiss, J. (1973). Depression and schizophrenia in hospitalized patients. *Archives of General Psychiatry, 28,* 509–512.

Simoni-Wastila, Linda. (1998). Gender and psychotropic drug use. *Medical Care, 36,* 88–94.

Simoni-Wastila, Linda. (2000). The use of abusable prescription drugs: The role of gender. *Journal of Women's Health and Gender-Based Medicine, 9,* 289–297.

Sincharoen, Sirinda, & Crosby, Faye. (2001). Affirmative action. In J. Worell (Ed.), *Encyclopedia of women and gender* (pp. 69–80). San Diego: Academic Press.

Smith, D. Randall, DiTomaso, Nancy, Farris, George F., & Cordero, Rene. (2001). Favoritism, bias, and error in performance ratings of scientists and engineers: The effects of power, status, and numbers. *Sex Roles, 45,* 337–358.

Smith, David M., & Gates, Gary J. (2001). *Gay and lesbian families in the United States: Same-sex unmarried partner households.* Washington, DC: Human Rights Campaign

Smith, Howard L., & Grenier, Mary. (1982). Sources of organizational power for women: Overcoming structural obstacles. *Sex Roles, 8,* 733–746.

Smith, Kristin, Downs, Barbara, & O'Connell, Martin. (2001). Maternity leave and employment patterns: 1961–1995. *Current Population Reports.* U.S. Census Bureau.

Smolak, Linda, & Striegel-Moore, Ruth. (2001). Body image concerns. In J. Worell (Ed.), *Encyclopedia of gender* (pp. 201–210). San Diego: Academic Press.

Snyder, Rita, & Hasbrouck, Lynn. (1996). Feminist identity, gender traits, and symptoms of disturbed eating among college women. *Psychology of Women Quarterly, 20,* 593–598.

Snyder, T. D., & Hoffman, C. M. (2000). U.S. Department of Education, National Center for Education Statistics. *Digest of Education Statistics, 1999,* NCES 2000–031. Washington, DC: U.S. Department of Education.

Sohn, David. (1982). Sex differences in achievement self-attributions: An effect-size analysis. *Sex Roles, 8,* 345–357.

Spelman, Elizabeth V. (1988). *Inessential woman: Problems of exclusion in feminist thought.* Boston: Beacon Press.

Spence, Janet T., & Buckner, Camille E. (2000). Instrumental and expressive traits, trait stereotypes, and sexist attitudes: What do they signify? *Psychology of Women Quarterly, 24,* 44–62.

Spence, Janet T., & Helmreich, Robert L. (1978). *Masculinity and femininity.* Austin: University of Texas Press.

Spence, Janet T., & Helmreich, Robert L. (1980). Masculine instrumentality and feminine expressiveness: Their relationships with sex-role attitudes and behaviors. *Psychology of Women Quarterly, 5,* 147–163.

Spence, Janet T., Helmreich, Robert L., & Stapp, Joy. (1975). Ratings of self and peers on sex-role attributes and their relation to self-esteem and conceptions of masculinity and femininity. *Journal of Personality and Social Psychology, 32,* 29–39.

Spencer, Steven J., Steele, Claude M., & Quinn, Diane M. (1999). Stereotype threat and women's math performance. *Journal of Experimental Social Psychology, 35,* 4–28.

Spitzer, Brenda L., Henderson, K., & Zivian, M. (1999). Gender differences in population versus media body sizes: A comparison over four decades. *Sex Roles, 40,* 545–566.

Sprecher, Susan, Barbee, A., & Schwartz, P. (1995). "Was it good for you, too?": Gender differences in first sexual intercourse experiences. *Journal of Sex Research, 32,* 3–15.

Sprecher, Susan, & Hatfield, Elaine. (1996). Premarital sexual standards among U.S. college students: Comparison with Russian and Japanese students. *Archives of Sexual Behavior, 25,* 261–288.

Sprecher, Susan, McKinney, Kathleen, & Orbuch, Terri L. (1987). Has the double standard disappeared? An experimental test. *Social Psychology Quarterly, 50,* 24–31.

Srebnik, Debra S., & Saltzberg, Elayne A. (1994). Feminist cognitive-behavioral therapy for negative body image. *Women & Therapy, 15,* 117–133.

Stanton, Annette L., et al. (1998). Treatment decision making and adjustment to breast cancer: A longitudinal study. *Journal of Consulting and Clinical psychology, 66,* 313–322.

Stanton, Annette L., Lobel, M., Sears, S., & DeLuca, R. (2002). Psychosocial aspects of selected issues in women's reproductive health: Current status and future directions. *Journal of Consulting and Clinical Psychology, 70,* 751–770.

Staples, Robert. (1978). Masculinity and race: The dual dilemma of black men. *Journal of Social Issues, 34*(1), 169–183.

Steele, Claude M. (1997). A threat in the air: How stereotypes shape intellectual identity and performance. *American Psychologist, 52,* 613–629.

Steele, Claude M., & Aronson, J. (1995). Stereotype threat and the intellectual test performance of African Americans. *Journal of Personality and Social Psychology, 69,* 797–811.

Steele, Jennifer, James, Jacquelyn, & Barnett, Rosalind. (2002). Learning in a man's world: Examining the perceptions of undergraduate women in male-dominated academic areas. *Psychology of Women Quarterly, 26,* 46–50.

Steiger, John C. (1981). The influence of the feminist subculture in changing sex-role attitudes. *Sex Roles, 7,* 627–634.

Steil, Janice. (2001a). Marriage: Still "his" and "hers"? In J. Worell (Ed.), *Encyclopedia of gender* (pp. 677–686). San Diego: Academic Press.

Steil, Janice M. (2001b). Family forms and member well-being: A research agenda for the Decade of Behavior. *Psychology of Women Quarterly, 25,* 344–363.

Steil, Janice M., & Hay, Jennifer L. (1997). Social comparison in the workplace: A study of 60 dual-career couples. *Personality and Social Psychology Bulletin, 23,* 427–438.

Steil, Janice, McGann, Vanessa L., & Kahn, Anne S. (2001). Entitlement. In J. Worell (Ed.), *Encyclopedia of women and gender* (pp. 403–410). San Diego: Academic Press.

Stein, Aletha H., & Bailey, Margaret M. (1973). The socialization of achievement orientation in females. *Psychological Bulletin, 80,* 345–366.

Stein, P. J., & Hoffman, Steven. (1978). Sports and male role strain. *Journal of Social Issues, 34*(1), 136–150.

Steinberg, Karen K., et al. (1991). A meta-analysis of the effect of estrogen replacement therapy on the risk of breast cancer. *Journal of the American Medical Association, 265,* 1985–1990.

Steiner, Meir. (1998). Perinatal mood disorders. *Psychopharmacology Bulletin, 34,* 301–306.

Steinmetz, Suzanne K. (1977). Wifebeating, husband beating—A comparison of the use of physical violence between spouses to resolve marital rights. In M. Roy (Ed.), *Battered Women.* New York: Van Nostrand.

Steinpreis, Rhea E., Anders, K., & Ritzke, D. (1999). The impact of gender on the review of the curricula vitae of job applicants and tenure candidates: A national empirical study. *Sex Roles, 41,* 509–528.

Stephens, W. N. (1961). A cross-cultural study of menstrual taboos. *Genetic Psychology Monographs, 64,* 385–416.

Stern, Marilyn, & Karraker, Katherine H. (1989). Sex stereotyping of infants: A review of gender labeling studies. *Sex Roles, 20,* 501–522.

Stevenson, Michael R., & Black, Kathryn N. (1988). Paternal absence and sex-role development: A meta-analysis. *Child Development, 59,* 793–814.

Stewart, Abigail J., & Chester, N. L. (1982). The exploration of sex differences in human social motives: Achievement, affiliation, and power. In A. J. Stewart (Ed.), *Motivation and society* (pp. 172–218). San Francisco: Jossey-Bass.

Stice, Eric. (2001). A prospective test of the dual-pathway model of bulimic pathology: Mediating effects of dieting and negative affect. *Journal of Abnormal Psychology, 110,* 124–135.

Stice, Eric, & Bearman, S. (2001). Body-image and eating disturbances prospectively predict increases in depressive symptoms in adolescent girls: A growth curve analysis. *Developmental Psychology, 37,* 597–607.

Stockdale, Margaret S. (1998). The direct and moderating influences of sexual-harassment pervasiveness, coping strategies, and gender on work-related outcomes. *Psychology of Women Quarterly, 22,* 521–536.

Storms, Michael D. (1981). A theory of erotic orientation development. *Psychological Review, 88,* 340–353.

Storms, Michael D., et al. (1981). Sexual scripts for women. *Sex Roles, 7,* 699–708.

Story, Mary, French, S., Resnick, M., & Blum, R. (1995). Ethnic/racial and socioeconomic differences in dieting behaviors and body image perceptions in adolescents. *International Journal of Eating Disorders, 18,* 173–179.

Straus, Murray A. (1980). Wife beating: How common and why? In M. A. Straus and G. T. Hotaling (Eds.), *The social causes of husband-wife violence.* Minneapolis: University of Minnesota Press.

Straus, Murray A., & Gelles, Richard J. (1990). *Physical violence in American families.* New Brunswick NJ: Transaction.

Strickland, Bonnie R. (1988). Sex-related differences in health and illness. *Psychology of Women Quarterly, 12,* 381–399.

Striegel-Moore, Ruth H., Goldman, Susan L., Garvin, Vicki, & Rodin, Judith. (1996). A prospective study of somatic and emotional symptoms of pregnancy. *Psychology of Women Quarterly, 20,* 393–408.

Striegel-Moore, Ruth H., & Smolak, Linda. (2000). The influence of ethnicity on eating disorders in women. In R. Eisler & M. Hersen (Eds.), *Handbook of gender, culture, and health* (pp. 227–254). Mahwah, NJ: Erlbaum.

Stroebe, Margaret, Stroebe, W., & Schut, H. (2001). Gender differences in adjustment to bereavement: An empirical and theoretical review. *Review of General Psychology, 5,* 62–83.

Sue, David. (2000). Health risk factors in diverse cultural groups. In R. Eisler & M. Hersen (Eds.), *Handbook of gender, culture, and health* (pp. 85–104). Mahwah, NJ: Erlbaum.

Sue, Stanley. (1977). Community mental health services to minority groups: Some optimism some pessimism. *American Psychologist, 32,* 616–624.

Sue, Stanley, & Morishima, J. (1982). *The mental health of Asian Americans: Contemporary issues in identifying and treating mental problems.* San Francisco: Jossey-Bass.

Sue, Stanley, & Sue, Derald W. (2000). Conducting psychological research with the Asian American/Pacific Islander population. In *Guidelines for research in ethnic minority communities* (pp. 2–4). Washington, DC: American Psychological Association.

Sullins, Carolyn D. (1998). Suspected repressed childhood sexual abuse: Gender effects on diagnosis and treatment. *Psychology of Women Quarterly, 22,* 403–418.

Sutherland, H., & Stewart, I. (1965). A critical analysis of the premenstrual syndrome. *Lancet, 1,* 1180–1183.

Sutton-Smith, B., & Rosenberg, B. G. (1970). *The sibling.* New York: Holt, Rinehart & Winston.

Svarstad, Bonnie L., et al. (1987). Gender differences in the acquisition of prescribed drugs: An epidemiological study. *Medical Care, 25,* 1089–1098.

Swendsen, Joel D., & Mazure, Carolyn M. (2000). Life stress as a risk factor for postpartum depression: Current research and methodological issues. *Clinical Psychology: Science and Practice, 7,* 17–31.

Swim, Janet, Borgida, E., Maruyama, G., & Myers, D. G. (1989). Joan McKay versus John McKay: Do gender stereotypes bias evaluations? *Psychological Bulletin, 105,* 409–429.

Swim, Janet K. (1994). Perceived versus meta-analytic effect sizes: An assessment of the accuracy of gender stereotypes. *Journal of Personality and Social Psychology, 66,* 21–36.

Swim, Janet K., Hyers, Lauri L., Cohen, Laurie L., & Ferguson, Melissa J. (2001). Everyday sexism: Evidence for its incidence, nature, and psychological impact from three daily diary studies. *Journal of Social Issues, 57,* 31–54.

Tamir, Lois M. (1982). *Men in their forties: The transition to middle age.* New York: Springer.

Tannen, Deborah. (1991). *You just don't understand: Women and men in conversation.* New York: Ballantine.

Tannen, Deborah. (1994). *Talking from 9 to 5: How women's and men's conversational styles affect who gets ahead, who gets credit, and what gets done at work.* New York: Morrow.

Task Force on the Glass Ceiling Initiative. (1993). *Report of the Governor's Task Force on the Glass Ceiling Initiative.* Madison, WI: State of Wisconsin.

Tavris, Carol. (1992). *The mismeasure of woman.* New York: Simon & Schuster.

Taylor, Marylee C., & Hall, Judith A. (1982). Psychological androgyny: Theories, methods, and conclusions. *Psychological Bulletin, 92,* 347–366.

Taylor, Pamela L., Tucker, M. Belinda, & Mitchell-Kernan, Claudia. (1999). Ethnic variations in perceptions of men's provider role. *Psychology of Women Quarterly, 23,* 741–762.

Taylor, R. (1976). Psychosocial development of black youth. *Journal of Black Studies, 6,* 353–372.

Taylor, Shelley E. (2002). *The tending instinct: Women, men, and the biology of nurturing.* New York: Times Books.

Taylor, Shelley E., et al. (2000). Biobehavioral responses to stress in females: Tend-and-befriend, not fight-or-flight. *Psychological Review, 107,* 411–429.

Tedeschi, Richard G., Park, Crystal, & Calhoun, Lawrence. (Eds.). (1998). *Posttraumatic growth: Positive change in the aftermath of crisis.* Hillsdale, NJ: Erlbaum.

Tenenbaum, Harriet R., & Leaper, Campbell. (2002). Are parents' gender schemas related to their children's gender-related cognitions? A meta-analysis. *Developmental Psychology, 38*, 615–630.

Terman, Lewis, & Miles, C. (1936). *Sex and personality.* New York: McGraw-Hill.

Terman, Lewis M., & Oden, Melita H. (1947). *The gifted child grows up.* Stanford, CA: Stanford University Press.

Terry, Jennifer, & Calvert, Melodie (Eds.). (1997). *Processed lives: Gender and technology in everyday life.* London: Routledge.

Testa, Maria, & Livingston, Jennifer A. (1999). Qualitative analysis of women's experiences of sexual aggression: Focus on the role of alcohol. *Psychology of Women Quarterly, 23*, 573–590.

Theodore, H., & Lloyd, B. (2000). Age and gender role conflict: A cross-sectional study of Australian men. *Sex Roles, 42*, 1027–1042.

Theorell, Töres, & Härenstam, Annika. (2000). Influence of gender on cardiovascular disease. In R. Eisler & M. Hersen (Eds.), *Handbook of gender, culture, and health* (pp. 161–177). Mahwah, NJ: Erlbaum.

Therrien, Melissa, & Ramirez, Roberto. (2000). *The Hispanic population in the United States: March 2000*, Current Population Reports, P20-535. Washington, DC: U.S. Census Bureau.

Thomas, A., & Sillen, S. (1972). *Racism and Psychiatry.* Secaucus, NJ: Citadel.

Thomas, Jerry K., & French, Karen E. (1985). Gender differences across age in motor performance: A meta-analysis. *Psychological Bulletin, 98*, 260–282.

Thomas, Veronica G., & Miles, Shari E. (1995). Psychology of Black women: Past, present, and future. In H. Landrine (Ed.), *Bringing cultural diversity to feminist psychology: Theory, research, and practice* (pp. 303–330). Washington, DC: American Psychological Association.

Thompson, J. Kevin, & Heinberg, Leslie J. (1999). The media's influence on body image disturbance and eating disorders: We've reviled them, now can we rehabilitate them? *Journal of Social Issues, 55*, 339–353.

Thompson, Janice L. (1991). Exploring gender and culture with Khmer refugee women: Reflections on participatory feminist research. *Advances in Nursing Science, 13*, 30–48.

Thompson, K. L., Bundy, K. A., & Wolfe, W. R. (1996). Social skills training for young adolescents: Cognitive and performance components. *Adolescence, 31*, 505–521.

Thompson, Sharon H., Corwin, S. J., & Sargent R. G. (1997). Ideal body size beliefs and weight concerns of fourth-grade children. *International Journal of Eating Disorders, 21*, 297–284.

Thompson, Teresa L., & Zerbinos, Eugenis. (1997). Television cartoons: Do children notice it's a boy's world? *Sex Roles, 37*, 415–432.

Thomson, Rob, & Murachver, Tamar. (2001). Predicting gender from electronic discourse. *British Journal of Social Psychology, 40*, 193–208.

Thomson, Rob, Murachver, Tamar, & Green, James. (2001). Where is the gender in gendered language? *Psychological Science, 12*, 171–175.

Tiefer, Leonore. (1991). Historical, scientific, clinical, and feminist criticisms of "The Human Sexual Response Cycle" model. *Annual Review of Sex Research, 2*, 1–24.

Tiefer, Leonore. (1995). *Sex is not a natural act, and other essays.* Boulder, CO: Westview.

Tiefer, Leonore. (1996). Towards a feminist sex therapy. *Women and Therapy, 19*, 53–64.

Tiefer, Leonore. (2000). The social construction and social effects of sex research: The sexological model of sexuality. In C. B. Travis & J. W. White (Eds.), *Sexuality, society, and feminism* (pp. 79–108). Washington, DC: American Psychological Association.

Tiefer, Leonore. (2001). A new view of women's sexual problems: Why new? Why now? *Journal of Sex Research, 38*, 89–96.

Tien, Liang. (1994). Southeast Asian American refugee women. In L. Comas-Diaz & B. Greene (Eds.), *Women of color: Integrating ethnic and gender identities in psychotherapy* (pp. 479–504). New York: Guilford.

Tjaden, P. & Thoennes, N. (1998, November). Prevalence, incidence, and consequences of violence against women: Findings from the National Violence Against Women Survey. *National Institute of Justice, Centers for Disease Control and Prevent Research Brief.*

Todd, Janet L., & Worell, Judith. (2000). Resilience in low-income, employed, African American women. *Psychology of Women Quarterly, 24*, 119–128.

Tolman, Deborah L., & Szalacha, Laura A. (1999). Dimensions of desire: Bridging qualitative and quantitative methods in a study of female adolescent sexuality. *Psychology of Women Quarterly, 23*, 7–40.

Tong, Rosemarie P. (1998). *Feminist thought* (2nd ed.). Boulder, CO: Westview Press.

Tooby, J., & Cosmides, L. (1992). The psychological foundations of culture. In J. Barkow, L. Cosmides, & J. Tooby (Eds.), *The adapted mind: Evolutionary psychology and the generation of culture* (pp. 19–136). New York: Oxford University Press.

Touchette, Nancy. (1991, July). HIV-1 link prompts circumspection on circumcision. *Journal of NIH Research, 3,* 44–46.

Travis, Cheryl B. (1988a). *Women and health psychology: Biomedical issues.* Hillsdale, NJ: Lawrence Erlbaum.

Travis, Cheryl B. (1988b). *Women and health psychology: Mental health issues.* Hillsdale, NJ: Lawrence Erlbaum.

Travis, Cheryl B. (1993). Women and health. In F. L. Denmark & M. A. Paludi (Eds.), *Psychology of women: Handbook of issues and theories.* Westport, CT: Greenwood.

Travis, Cheryl B., & Compton, Jill D. (2001). Feminism and health in the Decade of Behavior. *Psychology of Women Quarterly, 25,* 312–323.

Trentham, Susan, & Larwood Laurie. (1998). Gender discrimination and the workplace: An examination of rational bias theory. *Sex Roles, 38,* 1–28.

Tresemer, David. (1974). Fear of success: Popular, but unproven. *Psychology Today, 7*(10), 82.

Tripp, Margaret M., & Petrie, Trent A. (2001). Sexual abuse and eating disorders: A test of a conceptual model. *Sex Roles, 44,* 17–32.

Trivers, R. L. (1972). Parental investment and sexual selection. In B. Campbell (Ed.), *Sexual selection and the descent of man.* Chicago: Aldine.

True, Reiko Homma. (1990). Psychotherapeutic issues with Asian American women. *Sex Roles, 22,* 477–486.

Tsai, Mavis, & Uemura, Anne. (1988). Asian Americans: The struggles, the conflicts, and the successes. In P. Bronstein & K. Quina (Eds.), *Teaching a psychology of people* (pp. 125–133). Washington, DC: American Psychological Association.

Tserotas, K., & Merino, G. (1998). Andropause and the aging male. *Archives of Andrology, 40,* 87–93.

Tsui, Lisa. (1998). The effects of gender, education, and personal skills self-confidence on income in business management. *Sex Roles, 38,* 363–374.

Turner, Barbara F. (1982). Sex-related differences in aging. In B. B. Wolman (Ed.), *Handbook of developmental psychology.* Englewood Cliffs, NJ: Prentice-Hall.

Twenge, Jean M. (1997). Attitudes toward women, 1970–1995: A meta-analysis. *Psychology of Women Quarterly, 21,* 35–52.

Twenge, Jean M. (1999). Mapping gender: The multifactorial approach and the organization of gender-related attributes. *Psychology of Women Quarterly, 23,* 485–502.

Twenge, Jean M. (2001). Changes in women's assertiveness in response to status and roles: A cross-temporal meta-analysis, 1931–1993. *Journal of Personality and Social Psychology, 81,* 133–145.

Tyler, F. B., Sussewell, D. R., & Williams-McCoy, J. (1985). Ethnic validity in psychotherapy. *Psychotherapy, 22,* 311–320.

Tyler, Leona E. (1965). *The psychology of human differences.* New York: Appleton-Century-Crofts.

Ullman, Sarah E. (1996). Social reactions, coping strategies, and self-blame attributions in adjustment to sexual assault. *Psychology of Women Quarterly, 20,* 505–526.

Ullman, Sarah E., Karabatsos, George, & Koss, Mary P. (1999). Alcohol and sexual aggression in a national sample of college men. *Psychology of Women Quarterly, 23,* 673–690.

Unger, Rhoda. (1979). Toward a redefinition of sex and gender. *American Psychologist, 34,* 1085–1094.

U.S. Bureau of Labor Statistics. (1976, January). *Employment and earnings* (Table 2). Washington, DC: U.S. Government Printing Office.

U.S. Bureau of Labor Statistics. (1990, January). *Employment and earnings* (Table 22). Washington, DC: U.S. Government Printing Office.

U.S. Bureau of the Census. (2000). Available online at *www.census.gov.*

U.S. Department of Education/National Center for Education Statistics. (2000). *Trends in educational equity for girls and women,* NCES 2000-030, compiled by Y. Bae, S. Choy, C. Geddes, J. Sable, & T. Snyder. Washington, DC: Author.

U.S. Department of Justice. (1998). *Violence by intimates.* Washington, DC: Author. Available online at *www.usdoj.gov.*

U.S. Department of Labor. (1992). *Pipelines of progress: A status report on the glass ceiling.* Washington, DC: U.S. Government Printing Office.

U.S. Department of Labor. (2002). *Median annual earnings in current and 1999 dollars for year-round full-time workers by sex, 1951–99.*

Available online at *www.dol.gov/dol/wb/public/wb_pubs/achart.htm.*

Ussher, Jane M. (1996). Premenstrual syndrome: Reconciling disciplinary divides through the adoption of a material-discursive epistemological standpoint. *Annual Review of Sex Research, 7,* 218–251.

Valanis, Barbara G., et al. (2000). Sexual orientation and health: Comparisons in the Women's Health Initiative sample. *Archives of Family Medicine, 9,* 843–853.

Valentine, Sean R. (2001). Men and women supervisors' job responsibility, job satisfaction, and employee monitoring. *Sex Roles, 45,* 179–198.

Van Goozen, Stephanie, Cohen-Kettenis, P., Gooren, L., Frijda, N., & Van de Poll, N. (1995). Gender differences in behaviour: Activating effects of cross-sex hormones. *Psychoneuroendocrinology, 20,* 343–363.

Van Lankveld, Jacques. (1998). Bibliotherapy in the treatment of sexual dysfunctions: A meta-analysis. *Journal of Consulting and Clinical Psychology, 66,* 702–708.

Vandewater, Elizabeth A., & Stewart, Abigail J. (1998). Making commitments, creating lives: Linking women's roles and personality at midlife. *Psychology of Women Quarterly, 22,* 717–738.

Vasquez, Melba J. T. (1994). Latinas. In L. Comas-Diaz & B. Greene (Eds.), *Women of color: Integrating ethnic and gender identities in psychotherapy* (pp. 114–138). New York: Guilford.

Vasquez, Melba J. T., & Baron, Augustine. (1988). The psychology of the Chicano experience: A sample course structure. In P. Bronstein & K. Quina (Eds.), *Teaching a psychology of people.* Washington, DC: American Psychological Association.

Vasta, Ross, Knott, Jill A., & Gaze, Christine E. (1996). Can spatial training erase the gender differences on the water-level task? *Psychology of Women Quarterly, 20,* 549–568.

Vazquez-Nuttall, Ena, Romero-Garcia, I., & DeLeon, B. (1987). Sex roles and perceptions of femininity and masculinity of Hispanic women: A review of the literature. *Psychology of Women Quarterly, 11,* 409–426.

Veniegas, Rosemary C., & Conley, Terri D. (2000). Biological research on women's sexual orientations: Evaluating the scientific evidence. *Journal of Social Issues, 56,* 267–282.

Veroff, Joseph, Depner, C., Kukla, R., & Douvan, E. (1980). Comparison of American motives: 1957 versus 1976. *Journal of Personality and Social Psychology, 39,* 1004–1013.

Veroff, Joseph, Douvan, Elizabeth, & Kukla, R. (1981). *The inner American: A self-portrait from 1957 to 1976.* New York: Basic Books.

Veronesi, Umberto, et al. (1981). Comparing radical mastectomy with quadrantectomy, axillary dissection, and radiotherapy in patients with small cancers of the breast. *New England Journal of Medicine, 305,* 6–11.

Vivero, Veronica N., & Jenkins, Sharon R. (1999). Existential hazards of the multicultural individual: Defining and understanding "cultural homelessness." *Cultural Diversity and Ethnic Minority Psychology, 5,* 6–26.

Vogeltanz, Nancy D., & Wilsnack, Sharon C. (1997). Alcohol problems in women: Risk factors, consequences, and treatment strategies. In S. Gallant, G. Keita, & R. Royak-Schaler (Eds.), *Health care for women: Psychological, social, and behavioral influences* (pp. 75–96). Washington, DC: American Psychological Association.

Voyer, Daniel. (1996). On the magnitude of laterality effects and sex differences in functional lateralities. *Laterality, 1,* 51–83.

Voyer, Daniel, Nolan, C., & Voyer, S. (2000). The relation between experience and spatial performance in men and women. *Sex Roles, 43,* 891–916.

Voyer, Daniel., Voyer, S., & Bryden, M. P. (1995). Magnitude of sex differences in spatial abilities: A meta-analysis and consideration of critical variables. *Psychological Bulletin, 117,* 250–270.

Waite, Linda J., & Gallagher, Maggie. (2000). *The case for marriage: Why married people are happier, healthier, and better off financially.* New York: Doubleday.

Waldron, J. (1976). Why do women live longer than men? *Social Science and Medicine, 10,* 349–362.

Waldron, J., & Johnston, S. (1976). Why do women live longer than men? *Journal of Human Stress, 2,* 19–29.

Waldron, Vincent R., & Di Mare, Lesley. (1998). Gender as a culturally determined construct: Communication styles in Japan and the United States. In D. Canary & K. Dindia (Eds.), *Sex differences and similarities in communication* (pp. 179–202). Mahwah, NJ: Erlbaum.

Walfish, S., & Myerson, Marilyn. (1980). Sex role identity and attitudes toward sexuality. *Archives of Sexual Behavior, 9,* 199–204.

Walker, Lawrence J. (1984). Sex differences in the development of moral reasoning: A critical review. *Child Development, 55,* 677–691.

Walker, Lenore E. (1980). Battered women. In A. Brodsky & R. Hare-Mustin (Eds.), *Women and psychotherapy.* New York: Guilford.

Walker, Lenore E. (1989). *Terrifying love: Why battered women kill and how society responds.* New York: Harper & Row.

Walker, Lenore E. (1991). Post-traumatic stress disorder in women: Diagnosis and treatment of battered women syndrome. *Psychotherapy, 28,* 1–9.

Walker, Lenore E. A. (2001). Battering in adult relations. In J. Worell (Ed.), *Encyclopedia of women and gender* (pp. 169–188). San Diego: Academic Press.

Wallston, Barbara S. (1981). What are the questions in psychology of women? A feminist approach to research. *Psychology of Women Quarterly, 5,* 597–617.

Walsh, Margaret, Hickey, C., & Duffy, J. (1999). Influence of item content and stereotype situation on gender differences in mathematical problem solving. *Sex Roles, 41,* 219–240.

Walsh, Mary R. (1977). *Doctors wanted: No women need apply.* New Haven: Yale University Press.

Walters, Ellen E., & Kendler, Kenneth S. (1995). Anorexia nervosa and anorexic-like syndromes in a population-based female twin sample. *American Journal of Psychiatry, 152,* 64–71.

Wang, Nancy. (1995). Born Chinese and a woman in America. In J. Adleman & G. Enguidanos (Eds.), *Racism in the lives of women* (pp. 97–110). New York: Haworth.

Ward, L. Monique, & Caruthers, Allison. (2001). Media influences. In J. Worell (Ed.), *Encyclopedia of gender* (pp. 687–702). San Diego: Academic Press.

Ward, Russell A., & Spitze, Glenna. (1998). Sandwiched marriages: The implications of child and parent relations for marital quality in midlife. *Social Forces, 77,* 647–666.

Warr, M. (1985). Fear of rape among urban women. *Social Problems, 32,* 239–250.

Watkins, Patti L., & Whaley, Diane. (2000). Gender role stressors and women's health. In R. Eisler & M. Hersen (Eds.), *Handbook of gender, culture, and health* (pp. 43–62). Mahwah, NJ: Erlbaum.

Watzlawick, P. (Ed.). (1984). *The invented reality: Contributions to constructivism.* New York: Norton.

Wayment, Heidi A., & Peplau, L. Anne. (1995). Social support and well-being among lesbian and heterosexual women: A structural modeling approach. *Personality and Social Psychology Bulletin, 21,* 1189–1199.

Weatherall, Ann. (1998). Women and men in language: An analysis of seminaturalistic person descriptions. *Human Communication Research, 25,* 275–292.

Weinberg, S. K. (1955). *Incest behavior.* New York: Citadel Press.

Weissman, Myrna M., Bland, Roger, Joyce, Peter R., Newman, Stephen, Wells, J. Elisabeth, & Wittchen, Hans-Ulrich. (1993). Sex differences in rates of depression: Cross-national perspectives. *Journal of Affective Disorders, 29,* 77–84.

Weissman, Myrna M., & Klerman, G. L. (1987). Gender and depression. In R. Formanek & A. Gurian (Eds.), *Women and depression: A lifespan perspective* (pp. 3–18). New York: Springer.

Weisstein, Naomi. (1971). Psychology constructs the male, or the fantasy life of the male psychologist. In M. H. Garskof (Ed.), *Roles women play: Readings toward women's liberation.* Belmont, CA: Brooks/Cole.

Weisstein, Naomi. (1982, November). Tired of arguing about biological inferiority? *Ms.,* 41–46.

Weitlauf, Julie C., Cervone, D., Smith, R., & Wright, P. (2001). Assessing generalization in perceived self-efficacy: Multidomain and global assessments of the effects of self-defense training for women. *Personality and Social Psychology Bulletin, 27,* 1683–1691.

Weitzman, Lenore J. (1986). *The divorce revolution.* New York: Free Press.

Weitzman, Lenore J., Eifles, D., Hodaka, E., & Ross, C. (1972). Sex role socialization in picture books for preschool children. *American Journal of Sociology, 72,* 1125–1150.

Weller, Leonard, Weller, A., & Avinir, O. (1995). Menstrual synchrony: Only in roommates who are close friends? *Physiology and Behavior, 58,* 883–889.

Wellington, Sheila, & Giscombe, Katherine. (2001). Women and leadership in corporate America. In C. Costello & A. Stone (Eds.), *The American Woman, 2001–02* (pp. 87–106). New York: Norton.

Welsh, Deborah P., Rostosky, Sharon S., & Kawaguchi, Myra C. (2000). A normative perspective of adolescent girls' developing sexuality. In C. B. Travis & J. W. White (Eds.), *Sexuality, society, and feminism* (pp. 111–140). Washington, DC: American Psychological Association.

Welsh, Sandy. (1999). Gender and sexual harassment. *Annual Review of Sociology, 25,* 169–190.

West, Candace, & Zimmerman, D. H. (1983). Small insults: A study of interruptions in cross-sex conversations between unacquainted persons. In B. Thorne, C. Kramarae, & N. Henley (Eds.), *Language, gender, and society* (pp. 102–117). Rowley, MA: Newbury House.

Wester, Stephen R., Crown, Cynthia L., Quatman, Gerald L., & Heesacker, Martin. (1997). The influence of sexually violent rap music on attitudes of men with little prior exposure. *Psychology of Women Quarterly, 21,* 497–508.

Whatley, Mark A. (1993). For better or worse: The case of marital rape. *Violence and Victims, 8,* 29–39.

White, Aaronette M., Strube, Michael J., & Fisher, Sherri. (1998). A Black feminist model of rape myth acceptance: Implications for research and antirape advocacy in Black communities. *Psychology of Women Quarterly, 22,* 157–176.

White, Evelyn C. (Ed.). (1994). *The Black women's health book.* Seattle: Seal Press.

Whitley, Bernard E. (1997). Gender differences in computer-related attitudes and behavior: A meta-analysis. *Computers in Human Behavior, 13,* 1–22.

Whitley, Bernard E., McHugh, Maureen C., & Frieze, Irene H. (1986). Assessing the theoretical models for sex differences in causal attributions of success and failure. In J. S. Hyde & M. C. Linn (Ed.), *The psychology of gender: Advances through meta-analysis.* Baltimore: Johns Hopkins University Press.

Whorf, B. L. (1956). *Language, thought, and reality.* Cambridge, MA: MIT Press.

Wichstrom, Lars. (1999). The emergence of gender difference in depressed mood during adolescence: The role of intensified gender socialization. *Developmental Psychology, 35,* 232–245.

Widom, C. S., Ireland, T., & Glynn, P. J. (1995). Alcohol abuse in abused and neglected children followed up: Are they at increased risk? *Journal of Studies on Alcohol, 56,* 207–217.

Wigfield, Allan, Battle, Ann, Keller, Lisa B., & Eccles, Jacquelynne S. (2002). Sex differences in motivation, self-concept, career aspiration, and career choice: Implications for cognitive development. In A. McGillicuddy-De Lisi & R. De Lisi (Eds.), *Biology, society, and behavior: The development of sex differences in cognition* (pp. 93–126). Westport, CT: Ablex.

Wilkinson, Sue. (1999). Focus groups: A feminist method. *Psychology of Women Quarterly, 23,* 221–244.

Williams, Christine, Giuffre, P., & Dellinger, K. (1999). Sexuality in the workplace: Organizational control, sexual harassment, and the pursuit of pleasure. *Annual Review of Sociology, 25,* 73–168.

Williams, John E., Satterwhite, R., & Best, D. (1999). Pancultural gender stereotypes revisited: The five-factor model. *Sex Roles, 40,* 513–526.

Williams, Juanita H. (1983). *Psychology of women* (2nd ed.). New York: Norton.

Williams, Linda M. (1992). Adult memories of childhood abuse: Preliminary findings from a longitudinal study. *The APSAC Advisor, 5,* 19–20.

Williams, Linda M. (1994). Recall of childhood trauma: A prospective study of women's memories of child sexual abuse. *Journal of Consulting and Clinical Psychology, 62,* 1167–1176.

Williams, Martin H. (1992). Exploitation and inference: Mapping the damage from therapist-patient sexual involvement. *American Psychologist, 47,* 412–421.

Williams, Norma. (1988). Role making among married Mexican American women: Issues of class and ethnicity. *Journal of Applied Behavioral Science, 24,* 203–217.

Willingham, W., & Cole, N. (1997). *Gender and fair assessment.* Mahwah, NJ: Erlbaum.

Wilsnack, Sharon, Vogeltanz, N. D., Klassen, A. D., & Harris, T. R. (1997). Childhood sexual abuse and women's substance abuse: National survey findings. *Journal of Studies on Alcohol, 58,* 264–271.

Wilson, Edward O. (1975). *Sociobiology: The new synthesis.* Cambridge, MA: Harvard University Press.

Wilson, Edward O. (1978). *On human nature.* Cambridge, MA: Harvard University Press.

Wilson, G. Terence, Vitousek, Kelly M., & Loeb, Katharine L. (2000). Stepped care treatment for eating disorders. *Journal of Consulting and Clinical Psychology, 68,* 564–572.

Wilson, J. D., et al. (1984). Recent studies on the endocrine control of male phenotypic development. In M. Serio et al. (Eds.), *Sexual differentiation: Basic and clinical aspects.* New York: Raven.

Wilson, William Julius. (1996). *When work disappears: The world of the new urban poor.* New York: Knopf.

Winer, Gerald A., Makowski, D., Alpert, H., & Collins, J. (1988). An analysis of experimenter effects on responses to a sex questionnaire. *Archives of Sexual Behavior, 17*, 257–263.

Winstead, Barbara, & Griffin, Jessica. (2001). Friendship styles. In J. Worell (Ed.), *Encyclopedia of gender* (pp. 481–492). San Diego: Academic Press.

Wise, P. M., et al. (2001). Estradiol is a protective factor in the adult and aging brain. *Brain Research Review, 37*, 313–319.

Wisocki, Patricia A., & Skowron, Jeffrey. (2000). The effects of gender and culture on adjustment to widowhood. In R. Eisler & M. Hersen (Eds.), *Handbook of gender, culture, and health* (pp. 429–448). Mahwah, NJ: Erlbaum.

Wiswell, Thomas, et al. (1987). Declining frequency of circumcision: Implications for changes in the absolute incidence and male to female sex ratio of urinary tract infections in early infancy. *Pediatrics, 79*, 338–342.

Wittig, Michele A. (1979). Genetic influences on sex-related differences in intellectual performance: Theoretical and methodological issues. In M. A. Wittig & A. C. Peterson (Eds.), *Sex-related differences in cognitive functioning: Developmental issues.* New York: Academic Press.

Wittig, Michele A. (1985). Metatheoretical dilemmas in the psychology of gender. *American Psychologist, 40*, 800–811.

Wittig, Michele A., & Skolnick, Paul. (1978). Status versus warmth as determinants of sex differences in personal space. *Sex Roles, 4*, 493–503.

Wizemann, Theresa M., & Pardue, Mary-Lou. (Eds.). (2001). *Exploring the biological contributions to human health: Does sex matter?* Washington, DC: National Academy Press.

Wolf, Naomi. (1991). *The beauty myth.* New York: William Morrow.

Wolpe, Joseph, & Lazarus, A. A. (1966). *Behavior therapy techniques: A guide to the treatment of neuroses.* New York: Pergamon Press.

Women's Bureau, U.S. Department of Labor. (2000). *20 facts on women workers.* Washington, DC: U.S. Department of Labor. Available online at *www.dol.gov/dol/wb.*

Wood, Julia T. (1994). *Gendered lives: Communication, gender, and culture.* Belmont, CA: Wadsworth.

Wood, Wendy, & Eagly, Alice H. (2002). A cross-cultural analysis of the behavior of women and men: Implications for the origins of sex differences. *Psychological Bulletin, 128*, 699–727.

Woods, Nancy F. (2000). The U.S. women's health research agenda for the twenty-first century. *Signs: Journal of Women in Culture and Society, 25*, 1269–1274.

Woods, Nancy F., et al. (1998). Perceived stress, physiologic stress arousal, and premenstrual symptoms: Group differences and intra-individual patterns. *Research in Nursing and Health, 21*, 511–523.

Woods, Nancy F., Mitchell, E., & Lentz, M. (1995). Social pathways to premenstrual symptoms. *Research in Nursing and Health, 18*, 225–237.

Woods, Nancy F., Mitchell, E., & Lentz, M. (1999). Premenstrual symptoms: Delineating symptom clusters. *Journal of Women's Health and Gender-Based Medicine, 8*, 1053–1062.

Woodside, D. Blake, & Garfinkel, Paul E. (1992). Age of onset of eating disorders. *International Journal of Eating Disorders, 12*, 33–36.

Worell, Judith, & Johnson, Dawn M. (2001). Feminist approaches to psychotherapy. In J. Worell (Ed.), *Encyclopedia of women and gender* (pp. 425–437). New York: Academic Press.

Worell, Judith, & Remer, Pam. (1992). *Feminist perspectives in therapy: An empowerment model for women.* New York: Wiley.

Worell, Judith, & Remer, Pam. (2002). *Feminist perspectives in therapy: An empowerment model for women.* New York.

Wright, L. J., Kalantaridou, S. N., & Calis, K. A. (2002). Update on the benefits and risks of hormone replacement therapy. *Formulary, 27*(2), 78.

Wright, Logan, Schaefer, Arlene B., & Solomons, G. (1979). *Encyclopedia of pediatric psychology.* Baltimore: University Park Press.

Wyatt, Gail E. (1997). *Stolen women: Reclaiming our sexuality, taking back our lives.* New York: Wiley.

Wyche, Karen F., & Rice, Joy K. (1997). Feminist therapy: From dialogue to tenets. In J. Worell & N. Johnson (Eds.), *Shaping the future of feminist psychology: Education, research, and practice* (pp. 57–71). Washington, DC: American Psychological Association.

Ying, Yu-Wen, Coombs, Mary, & Lee, Peter A. (1999). Family intergenerational relationship of Asian American adolescents. *Cultural Diversity and Ethnic Minority Psychology, 5*, 350–363.

Yoder, Janice D., & Kahn, Arnold S. (1992). Toward a feminist understanding of women and power. *Psychology of Women Quarterly, 16*, 381–388.

Yoder, Janice D., & Kahn, Arnold S. (1993). Working toward an inclusive psychology of women. *American Psychologist, 48,* 846–850.

Yoder, Janice D., Schleicher, Thomas L., & McDonald, Theodore W. (1998). Empowering token women leaders: The importance of organizationally legitimated credibility. *Psychology of Women Quarterly, 22,* 209–222.

York, J. L., & Welte, J. W. (1994). Gender comparison of alcohol consumption in alcoholic and nonalcoholic populations. *Journal of Studies on Alcohol, 55,* 743–750.

Young, W. C., Goy, R., & Phoenix, C. (1964). Hormones and sexual behavior. *Science, 143,* 212–218.

Zabin, Laurie S., Hirsch, Marilyn B., & Emerson, Mark R. (1989). When urban adolescents choose abortion: Effects on education, psychological status, and subsequent pregnancy. *Family Planning Perspectives, 21*(6), 248–255.

Zambrana, Ruth. (1988). A research agenda on issues affecting poor and minority women: A model for understanding their health needs. *Women & Health, 12,* 137–160.

Zea, Maria C., Reisen, Carol A., & Poppen, Paul J. (1999). Psychological well-being among Latino lesbians and gay men. *Cultural Diversity and Ethnic Minority Psychology, 5,* 371–379.

Zeman, J., & Garber, J. (1996). Display rules for anger, sadness, and pain: It depends on who is watching. *Child Development, 67,* 957–973.

Zigler, Edward F., & Frank, Meryl. (Eds.). (1988). *The parental leave crisis.* New Haven: Yale University Press.

Zilbergeld, Bernie. (1978). *Male sexuality.* Boston: Little, Brown.

Zilbergeld, Bernie. (1992). *The new male sexuality.* New York: Bantam Books.

Zilbergeld, Bernie. (1999). *The new male sexuality.* (Rev. ed.). New York: Bantam Books.

Zilbergeld, Bernie, & Ellison, Carol R. (1980). Desire discrepancies and arousal problems in sex therapy. In S. R. Leiblum & L. A. Pervin (Eds.), *Principles and practice of sex therapy.* New York: Guilford Press.

Zilbergeld, Bernie, & Evans, M. (1980, August). The inadequacy of Masters and Johnson. *Psychology Today, 14* (3), 28–43.

Zillman, Dolf, Weaver, J., Mundorf, N., & Aust, C. (1986). Effects of an opposite-gender companion's affect to horror on distress, delight, and attraction. *Journal of Personality and Social Psychology, 51,* 586–594.

Zimmerman, Don H., & West, Candace. (1975). Sex roles, interruptions and silences in conversation. In B. Thorne & N. Henley (Eds.), *Language and sex: Difference and dominance.* Rowley, MA: Newbury House.

Zuckerman, M., & Wheeler, L. (1975). To dispel fantasies about the fantasy-based measure of fear of success. *Psychological Bulletin, 82,* 932–946.

Photo Credits

CHAPTER 1
p. 3, Elizabeth Crews/The Image Works; p. 5, *Cathy* by Cathy Guisewite © Universal Press Synidate; p. 18 (left), Justin Sullivan/Getty Images; p. 18 (right), David Young-Wolff/Photo Edit; p. 21, Staatliche Museen Pressischer Kulturbesitz; p. 26, Courtesy Dr. Kenneth B. Clark

CHAPTER 2
p. 38 (left), The Schlesinger Library, Radcliffe College; p. 38 (center), Corbis-Bettmann; p. 38 (right), Corbis-Bettmann; p. 40, Jerry Howard/Positive Images; p. 46, Miriam Austerman/Animals, Animals; p. 52, Gale Zucker/Stock Boston; p. 65, Reprinted with special permission of King Features Syndicate; p. 68, *Calvin and Hobbes* by Bill Watterson © Universal Press Syndicate; p. 74, Johnny Crawford/The Image Works

CHAPTER 3
p. 87, Chip Henderson/Stone/Getty Images; p. 94, Catherine Ursillo/Photo Researchers

CHAPTER 4
p. 123, Matthew Naythons/Stock Boston; p. 125, Barbara Alper/Stock Boston; p. 127, Eastcott-Momatiuk/The Image Works; p. 133, John Sohm/Chromosohm/Stock Market/Corbis; p. 137, Cleve Bryant/Photo Edit

CHAPTER 5
p. 144, Bob Daemmrich/The Image Works; p. 150 (top), Stone/Getty Images; p. 150 (bottom), Stone/Getty Images; p. 151, Jose Jimenez/La Primera Hora/Getty Images

CHAPTER 6
p. 168, Courtesy the author; p. 175, Lawrence Migdale

CHAPTER 7
p. 185, *Cathy* by Cathy Guisewite © Universal Press Syndicate; p. 189 (top left), Bob Daemmrich/The Image Works; p. 189 (top right), Anton Albert/The Image Works; p. 189 (bottom), Cindy Charles/Photo Edit; p. 193, Bob Daemmrich/The Image Works; p. 198, Michelle Stocker/*The Capital Times*, Madison, WI; p. 201, Stone/Getty Images; p. 207, Barbara Alper/Stock Boston

CHAPTER 8

p. 225, Illustration 1994 by Nicole Hollander; p. 231, Russula nigricans, August 28, 1893, from *The Art of Beatrix Potter*, copyright © Frederick Warne & Co., 1955. Courtesy of the Armit Trust

CHAPTER 9

p. 242 (top), Fred Pedrick/The Image Works; p. 242 (bottom), Shiong/Rothco; p. 249, © The New Yorker Collection 1987 Leo Cullum from cartoonbank.com. All rights reserved; p. 253, Blair Seitz/Photo Researchers; p. 258 (top), Michael Hayman/Stock Boston; p. 258 (bottom), Michael Newman/Photo Edit; p. 263, Stone/Getty Images

CHAPTER 10

p. 269, Source: Kimble Mead; p. 276, Stone/Getty Images; p. 277, A Delta Book published by Dell Publishing, a division of Bantam Doubleday, Dell Publishing Group, Inc.; p. 279, Spencer Grant/Photo Edit

CHAPTER 11

p. 301, Amy Etra/Photo Edit; p. 307, Spencer Platt/Newsmakers/Getty Images; p. 312, Courtesy American Cancer Society

CHAPTER 12

p. 340, Jonathan Nourok/Photo Edit

CHAPTER 13

p. 354, Stefan Zaklin/Getty Images; p. 360, Photo Researchers; p. 363, AP/Wide World; p. 368, Mark Richards/Photo Edit

CHAPTER 14

p. 376, Cartoonists and Writers Syndicate; p. 378, David Friedman/Getty Images; p. 382, Marian Henley. Reprinted by permission of the artist; p. 388, National Coalition Against Domestic Violence; p. 390, Michael Newman/Photo Edit; p. 398, Bob Daemmrich/The Image Works; p. 401, National Center for Victims of Crime

CHAPTER 15

p. 410, Stone/Getty Images; p. 416, Susan Rosenberg/Photo Researchers; p. 423, Bill Bachmann/Photo Edit; p. 436, Michael Newman/Photo Edit

CHAPTER 16

p. 441, Adam@Home by Brian Bassett © Universal Press Syndicate; p. 446, Michael Newman/Photo Edit; p. 450, Michael Newman/Photo Edit; p. 461 (left), David Silverman/Getty Images; p. 461 (right), AP/Wide World

CHAPTER 17

p. 475 (left), Robert Brenner/Photo Edit; p. 475 (right), Tony Freeman/Photo Edit; p. 479, Engleman/Rothco

Index